THE ADAPTIVE BRAIN I
Cognition, Learning, Reinforcement, and Rhythm

THE ADAPTIVE BRAIN I

Cognition, Learning, Reinforcement, and Rhythm

Edited by

Stephen GROSSBERG

Center for Adaptive Systems
Boston University
Boston, Massachusetts
U.S.A.

1988

NORTH-HOLLAND
AMSTERDAM · NEW YORK · OXFORD · TOKYO

ISBN　　: 0 444 70413 2
ISBN Set: 0 444 70415 9

The other volume in this set is:
The Adaptive Brain II: Vision, Speech, Language, and Motor Control, S. Grossberg, Ed., (1987).

Publishers:
ELSEVIER SCIENCE PUBLISHERS B.V.
P.O. Box 1991
1000 BZ Amsterdam
The Netherlands

Sole distributors for the U.S.A. and Canada:
ELSEVIER SCIENCE PUBLISHING COMPANY, INC.
52 Vanderbilt Avenue
New York, N.Y. 10017
U.S.A.

This volume was originally published as volume 42 of the series Advances in Psychology

PRINTED IN THE NETHERLANDS

Dedicated to

William Estes

and

John Staddon

With Admiration

EDITORIAL PREFACE

The mind and brain sciences are experiencing a period of explosive development. In addition to experimental contributions which probe the widest possible range of phenomena with stunning virtuosity, a true theoretical synthesis is taking place. The remarkable multiplicity of behaviors, of levels of behavioral and neural organization, and of experimental paradigms and methods for probing this complexity present a formidable challenge to all serious theorists of mind. The challenge is, quite simply, to discover unity behind this diversity by characterizing a small set of theoretical principles and mechanisms capable of unifying and predicting large and diverse data bases as manifestations of fundamental processes. Another part of the challenge is to explain how mind differs from better understood physical systems, and to identify what is new in the theoretical methods that are best suited for a scientific analysis of mind.

These volumes collect together recent articles which provide a unified theoretical analysis and predictions of a wide range of important psychological and neurological data. These articles illustrate the development of a true theory of mind and brain, rather than just a set of disconnected models with no predictive generality. In this theory, a small number of fundamental dynamical laws, organizational principles, and network modules help to compress a large data base. The theory accomplishes this synthesis by showing how these fundamental building blocks can be used to design specialized circuits in different neural systems and across species. Such a specialization is analogous to using a single Schrödinger equation in quantum mechanics to analyse a large number of different atoms and molecules.

The articles collected herein represent a unification in yet another sense. They were all written by scientists within a single research institute, the Center for Adaptive Systems at Boston University. The fact that a single small group of scientists can theoretically analyse such a broad range of data illustrates both the power of the theoretical methods that they employ and the crucial role of interdisciplinary thinking in achieving such a synthesis. It also argues for the benefits that can be derived from supporting more theoretical training and research programs within the traditional departments charged with an understanding of mind and brain phenomena.

My colleagues and I at the Center for Adaptive Systems have repeatedly found that fundamental processes governing mind and brain can best be discovered by analysing how the behavior of individuals successfully adapts in real-time to constraints imposed by the environment. In other words, principles and laws of behavioral self-organization are rate-limiting in determining the design of neural processes, and problems of self-organization are the core issues that distinguish mind and brain studies from the more traditional sciences.

An analysis of real-time behavioral adaptation requires that one identify the functional level on which an individual's behavioral success is defined. This is not the level of individual nerve cells. Rather it is the level of neural systems. Many examples can now be given to illustrate the fact that one cannot, in principle, determine the properties which govern behavioral success from an analysis of individual cells alone. An analysis of individual cells is insufficient because behavioral properties are often emergent properties due to interactions among cells. Different types of specialized neural circuits govern different combinations of emergent behavioral properties.

On the other hand, it is equally incorrect to assume that the properties of individual cells are unimportant, as many proponents of artificial intelligence have frequently done to promote the untenable claim that human intelligence can be understood through an analysis of Von Neumann computer architectures. Carefully designed single cell properties are joined to equally carefully designed neural circuits to generate the subtle relationships among emergent behavioral properties that are characteristic of living organisms.

In order to adequately define these circuits and to analyse their emergent behavioral properties, mathematical analysis and computer simulation play a central role. This is inevitable because self-organizing behavioral systems obey nonlinear laws and often contain very large numbers of interacting units. The mathematical theory that has emerged from this analysis embodies a biologically relevant artificial intelligence, as well as contributing new ideas to nonlinear dynamical systems, adaptive control theory, geometry, statistical mechanics, information theory, decision theory, and measurement theory. This mathematical work thus illustrates that new mathematical ideas are needed to describe and analyse the new principles and mechanisms which characterize behavioral self-organization.

We trace the oceans of hyperbole, controversy, and rediscovery which still flood our science to the inability of some investigators to fully let go of unappropriate technological metaphors and nineteenth century mathematical concepts. Although initially attractive because of their simplicity and accessibility, these approaches have regularly shown their impotence when they are confronted by a nontrivial set of the phenomena that they have set out to explain. A unified theoretical understanding cannot be achieved without an appropriate mathematical language in our science any more than in any other science.

A scientist who comes for the first time to such a new theoretical enterprise, embedded in such a confusing sociological milieu, may initially become disoriented. The very fact that behavioral, neural, mathematical, and computer analyses seem to permeate every issue defies all the traditional departmental boundaries and intellectual prejudices that have separated investigators in the past. After this initial period of disorientation passes, however, such a scientist can begin to reap handsome intellectual rewards. New postdoctoral fellows at the Center for Adaptive Systems have, for example, arrived with a strong training in experimental psychology augmented by modest mathematical and computer coursework, yet have found themselves within a year performing advanced analyses and predictions of previously unfamiliar neural data through computer simulations of real-time neural networks. The theoretical method itself and the foundation of knowledge to which it has already led can catapult a young investigator to the forefront of research in an area which would previously have required a lifetime of study. We have found often that problems which seemed impossible without the theory became difficult but tractable with it.

In summary, the articles in these volumes illustrate a theoretical approach which analyses how brain systems are designed to form an adaptive relationship with their environment. Instead of limiting our consideration to a few performance characteristics of a behaving organism, we consider the developmental and learning problems that a system as a whole must solve before accurate performance can be achieved. We do not take accurate performance for granted, but rather analyse the organizational principles and dynamical mechanisms whereby it is achieved and maintained. Such an analysis is necessary if only because an analysis of performance *per se* does not impose sufficiently many constraints to determine underlying control mechanisms. The unifying power of such theoretical work is due, we believe, to the fact that principles of adaptation—such as the laws governing development and learning—are fundamental in determining the design of behavioral mechanisms.

A preface precedes each article in these volumes. These commentaries link the articles together, highlight some of their major contributions, and comment upon future directions of research. The work reported within these articles has been supported by the Air Force Office of Scientific Research, the Army Research Office, the National Science Foundation, and the Office of Naval Research. We are grateful to these agencies for making this work possible.

We are also grateful to Cynthia Suchta for doing a marvelously competent job of typing and formatting the text, and to Jonathan Marshall for expertly preparing the index and proofreading the text. Beth Sanfield and Carol Yanakakis also provided valuable assistance.

Stephen Grossberg
Boston, Massachusetts
March, 1986

TABLE OF CONTENTS

Chapter 1

A PSYCHOPHYSIOLOGICAL THEORY OF REINFORCEMENT, DRIVE, MOTIVATION, AND ATTENTION

Preface

The first three chapters of the volume form a triptych of self-contained but mutually supportive articles. Together these articles describe a neural theory of cognitive-emotional interactions which identifies and joins together mechanisms of short term memory, conditioning, long term memory, reinforcement, drive, attention, and arousal.

The entire theory can be derived from a few gedanken experiments. The gedanken experiments in Chapter 1 suggest solutions to the *synchronization problem* and the *persistence problem* of classical conditioning. The synchronization problem asks how associations due to pairing of a conditioned stimulus (CS) with an unconditioned stimulus (UCS) can be learned in real-time when the time lags separating the CS and UCS can vary across learning trials, as they typically do in a natural environment. Although this problem seems innocuous enough, the answer requires an analysis of how a learning system knows the difference between motivationally relevant and irrelevant environmental stimuli.

The persistence problem asks how an organism can process many stimuli in parallel, as typically occurs *in vivo*, without extinguishing all of its previous learning about these stimuli. In particular, if many stimuli are processed simultaneously and if some of these stimuli are already conditioned to responses which are mutually incompatible, then what prevents all the stimuli from rapidly becoming conditioned to all the conditioned responses? If this did occur, rapid counterconditioning, and hence extinction, would be caused between the original stimulus–response associations. This problem also seems quite innocuous, but it leads to an analysis of how attentional mechanisms can buffer predictive associations against rapid degradation by the relentless flux of irrelevant stimuli.

Neither the synchronization problem nor the persistence problem is a salient property of a single conditioning experiment. The problems are too obvious to be thought about when one is worrying only about a paradoxical datum. Instead, these problems are *design* problems whose fundamental importance on the level of adaptive mechanism became apparent through an analysis of thousands of conditioning experiments. The solution of these problems leads to a neural network architecture in which mechanisms of classical conditioning, instrumental conditioning, and cognitive modulation of conditioning are unified. These neural network architectures may be interpreted in terms of interactions between thalamo-cortical and hypothalamo-hippocampal systems.

These architectures embody the first *adaptive resonance theory* (ART) circuit and the first *gated dipole* opponent process to be discovered. Later chapters suggest a critical role for ART circuits in the normal and abnormal learning of cognitive recognition codes (Chapters 2 and 4), including codes for speech processing, word recognition, and motor planning (Volume II). Later chapters use a gated dipole opponent process to quantitatively analyse data about mammalian circadian rhythms (Chapters 6–8), photoreceptor transduction (Volume II), and perceptual grouping or segmentation (Volume II). These results collectively illustrate how the identification of a fundamental neural network module through an analysis of one type of real-time adaptation enables one to use a variant on the module to solve different problems of real-time adaptation. On the level of lay language, functional relationships between appetitive circuits, circadian rhythms, photoreceptor transduction, and perceptual segmentation are not evident. On the level of a mathematical analysis of the emergent behavioral properties controlled by a gated dipole opponent process, they become transparent.

In summary, fundamental network modules such as an ART circuit and a gated dipole circuit were discovered through a conceptual analysis of real-time adaptation, and the relevance of these circuits to a broad range of functionally related data was discovered through a systematic mathematical and numerical analysis of these circuits in a wide variety of environmental and anatomical variations. These properties illustrate key elements of our method for analysing behavioral self-organization. The success of these circuits in organizing large interdisciplinary data bases suggests that they will remain building blocks in any future theory that supplants the present stage of understanding. The role of the gedanken experiments in disclosing these building blocks suggests that they, too, will find a place in any future theory. The fact that a theory of behavioral self-organization must itself self-organize to cope with ever more subtle behavioral issues suggests that the present theory will indeed be supplanted, but we believe this will happen in an evolutionary way rather than a revolutionary way.

Another theme that permeates this chapter concerns the functional units of short term memory (STM) and of long term memory (LTM). The mathematical theory of associative learning on which this chapter is based proved that the functional unit of associative learning is a spatial pattern of LTM traces which encodes a spatial pattern of STM traces. In order for LTM traces to encode spatial patterns of STM traces, each LTM trace must be able to increase or to decrease due to learning, so that it can match its target STM trace. Such an associative law violates the Hebb Postulate which has been used in many conditioning models. The Hebb Postulate asserts that associative pairing of two events always causes an increase in their LTM trace. The Hebb Postulate seems plausible when one assumes that the functional unit of associative learning is an individual LTM strength which grows due to pairing of its presynaptic and postsynaptic cells. As soon as one acknowledges that neural networks process *spatial patterns* of STM and LTM traces, a non-Hebbian associative law is required. Thus to understand the results in the chapter, one needs to consider how its microscopic processing laws and macroscopic network architectures fit together in a harmonious way to generate the emergent behavioral properties that the chapter seeks to explain. The same type of multilevel analysis is needed to unify all the data which are considered within these volumes.

Journal of Theoretical Neurobiology **1**, 286 369 (1982)
©1982 Australian Scientific Press
Reprinted by permission of the publisher

A PSYCHOPHYSIOLOGICAL THEORY OF REINFORCEMENT, DRIVE, MOTIVATION, AND ATTENTION

Stephen Grossberg†

Abstract

This article derives a real-time theory of motivated behavior and presents some of its physiological and pharmacological correlates. The theory mechanistically explicates instrumental concepts such as reinforcement, drive, incentive motivation, and habit, and describes their relationship to cognitive concepts such as expectancy, competition, and resonance. The theory shows how a real-time analysis of an animal's adaptive behavior in prescribed environments can disclose network principles and mechanisms which imply a restructuring and unification of data in terms of design principles and mechanisms rather than the vicissitudes of experimental methodology or historical accident. A comparative analysis and unification of other theories is then possible, such as the classical theories of Hull, Spence, Neal Miller, Estes, Logan, Livingston, and John. The data which are discussed include overshadowing and unblocking; suppression by punishment; reinforcement contrast effects; hypothalamic self-stimulation; differential effects of drive, reinforcement, incentive motivation, expectancies, and short-term memory competition on learning rate, behavioral choice, and performance speed; the role of polyvalent cortical cells, multiple sensory representations, recurrent on-center off-surround neocortical and paleocortical interactions, hippocampal-hypothalamic, medial forebrain bundle, and thalamocortical interactions on motivated behavior; effects of drugs like chlorpromazine, reserpine, monoamine oxidase inhibitors and amphetamine on instrumental behavior. Of special interest are network "hippocampal" computations that are suggested to accomplish several distinct roles: influence transfer of short-term to long-term memory both directly and indirectly, directly by triggering conditioning of conditioned reinforcers, indirectly by generating positive attentional feedback to neocortical polyvalent cells; and influence the organization of a motor map which controls approach and avoidance behavior by eliciting motivationally biased signals to this motor mapping system.

---

† Supported in part by the National Science Foundation (NSF IST-80-00257) and the Air Force Office of Scientific Research (AFOSR 82-0148).

1. Introduction

The phenomena of classical and instrumental conditioning are wonderfully varied, interesting, and confusing (Bolles, 1967; Brush, 1971; Campbell and Church, 1969; Estes, 1969; Gilbert and Sutherland, 1969; Honig, 1966; Mackintosh, 1974; Pearce and Hall, 1980; Rescorla and Wagner, 1972; Tapp, 1969; Wagner, 1978). It has often seemed nigh impossible to state a law, or generalization, in this area that does not admit important exceptions. For example, are classical conditioning and instrumental conditioning mechanistically independent? If not, exactly how are they related? Do specific drives really exist, such as a hunger drive? Do generalized drives exist, such as an exploratory drive? If so, why do both types of drives exist? Are drives independent, such as hunger and thirst, or hunger and exploratory drive? What is the difference between a drive and an incentive? What is the difference between a drive and a habit? Do drives have some properties of habits? In particular, can drives act as stimuli that can be associatively joined to responses, or do they act simply as sources of energy? Is reinforcement due to drive reduction? If so, what drive is reduced to reinforce language behavior? If not, why does reinforcement often seem to be related to drive reduction? The list of questions goes on and on. After a while, one can become exhausted by the sheer variety of concepts, and by the seemingly endless introduction of exceptional rules or subtle distinctions to handle difficult special cases.

Because these difficulties are so formidable on the level of consensual language, we need to find a formal language which is powerful enough to describe instrumental concepts and mechanisms without ambiguity. A method must be found whereby this formal language can be constructed. Such a method has been gradually developed over the past two decades. The method starts by identifying environmental pressures to which an organism must adapt in order to survive. In other words, the theory is derived from real-time constraints on the self-organization (learning, development) of individual behavior. The method shows how each environmental problem is solved by a principle of behavioral organization. These principles are realized by mathematical laws which embody the principles in the most parsimonious, or minimal, way. Once a minimal solution is found, one can more readily classify individual and species differences as variations on the minimal theme. In every case studied to the present, these mathematical realizations can be interpreted as neural networks.

The derivation of these principles and laws can be achieved using thought experiments which show us, in simple stages, how prescribed environmental pressures force adaptive designs on the behaving brain. I contend that various other psychologial theories have failed to derive significant conclusions about brain design because they have ignored real-time constraints on the self-organization of individual behavior. The concepts that arise from this procedure are, not surprisingly, related to traditional ideas, but they diverge from traditional ideas in crucial ways that allow us to penetrate into areas where the traditional notions are misleading or too vague to follow.

This procedure eventually leads to a principled reorganization of the data. For example, our first thought experiment is about a dilemma concerning classical conditioning (Grossberg, 1971a). Namely, how does a network learn associatively despite the fact that the time intervals between successive CS and UCS presentations can vary across learning trials? This seemingly innocent question forces us into explicit mechanisms of instrumental conditioning, into a role for cognitive processing in the direct evaluation of reinforcement, and to the threshold of studies about short term memory, attention, and the development of cognitive codes. Herein I follow the path by which these mechanisms were historically derived, since it provides a convenient route through the data along a gradually rising conceptual pathway. Each constraint along this pathway provides us with a necessary constraint on network design, which we then translate into a minimal realization before classifying related possibilities. Similar mechanistic conclusions can be derived from a thought experiment about cognitive development (Grossberg, 1980a, 1984). This multiplicity of derivations, always leading to conclusions that support and sharpen previous results, endows the theory with an aura of conceptual coherence and robustness.

The historical procedure is not without its expository difficulties. Each stage of the derivation sheds new light on a variety of nontrivial data. However, in a living organism, often mechanisms other than the ones that have just been derived are also at work. My choice is whether to defer all interpretations until the whole theory is derived, or to provide data markers along the way using experiments that emphasize the mechanisms then being discussed. I have chosen the latter procedure and along the way will try to direct the reader to the related mechanisms too.

For example, I was led to mechanisms for reinforcement and incentive motivation before being driven by the theory to consider expectation mechanisms. In the theory, these two classes of mechanisms often closely interact, but are distinct. In the data, it is often hard to tease them apart. Thus Mackintosh (1974, p.233), after a sophisticated data analysis, wrote that

> Stimuli associated with reinforcement do not motivate instrumental responses; they may become established as goals for instrumental responses. Their effect on instrumental behavior therefore may be similar to that of unconditional reinforcers; they may, in other words, serve as conditional reinforcers.

I will also argue that stimuli which are associated with reinforcements can serve as conditioned reinforcers. However, I will argue, contrary to Mackintosh, that such stimuli can motivate instrumental responses and that, although they may become established as goals, this goal property is, strictly speaking, related to expectancy mechanisms and not to reinforcer properties *per se*.

To understand the distinction between Mackintosh's claim that reinforcers do not motivate instrumental responses, and my claim that they do, one must understand what position Mackintosh is arguing against: namely, the classical idea that motivation acts in a nonspecific fashion. The theoretical development in this paper argues against the classical position, but also leads to a mechanism of motivation that is important in reinforced behavior. The theory also shows how the reinforcing properties of stimuli can easily be confused with their motivating properties. It hereby suggests how Mackintosh could be led by considerations of parsimony to eliminate motivation from his discussion. I will argue that the two concepts are really fundamentally distinct, and will attach them to distinct psychophysiological parameters.

Once we embrace the evolutionary method, we must be prepared to organize our mechanistic understanding into a succession of conceptual stages. The article is structured as such a succession. This procedure is inherent in the evolutionary method, and is the price we pay for understanding very well, sometimes painfully well, just what each stage's organizational principles do and do not imply.

2. Buffer the Learning Cells

Before beginning the thought experiment, let us put it into perspective with some introductory remarks. It is obvious that cells which are capable of learning should be buffered against being activated except by appropriate inputs. In particular, during adult human behavior, cells near the sensory and motor periphery should not be capable of substantial learning. If adult retinas could learn, we would see a superposition of all the visual scenes that occurred for hours past. If adult motor neurons could learn, our next motion would be an inaccurate weighted average of all our recent motor commands. To prevent this, the cells that are most capable of learning will, in the adult, be found away from the sensory or motor periphery, where they are carefully surrounded by protective networks. This is one reason why learning cells have either been hard to isolate by blind electrode penetrations, or where cells have been reliably isolated,

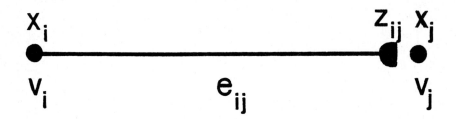

Figure 1. Short-term memory traces (or potentials) x_i at cell populations v_i emit signals along the directed pathways (or axons) e_{ij} which are gated by long-term memory traces z_{ij} before they can perturb their target cells v_j.

they often have disappointing learning capabilities (Hoyle, 1977; Kandel, 1976; Morrell, 1961).

3. A Digression on Classical Conditioning

The thought experiment demonstrates that classical and instrumental conditioning share certain mechanisms in common. These mechanisms embed, or buffer, the cells capable of learning in a network that prevents the cells' activation except under appropriate circumstances. The thought experiment builds upon prior work which derives the laws of associative learning from the simplest concepts of classical conditioning; see Grossberg (1974, 1982a) for a review. In this work, laws for neural networks are derived from a real-time analysis of how pairing a conditioned stimulus (CS) with an unconditioned stimulus (UCS) on learning trials enables the CS to elicit a conditioned response (CR), or UCR-like event, on performance trials. The network dynamics are described by interactions between the *short-term memory* (STM) *traces* $x_i(t)$ of cell body populations v_i and the *long-term memory* (LTM) *traces* $z_{jk}(t)$ of the axonal pathways e_{jk} from v_j to v_k, as in Figure 1. For present purposes, the exact form of these interactive STM–LTM laws is not important. What is important are two properties of these laws.

A. The unit of LTM is a *spatial pattern*.

B. There exists a *stimulus sampling operation*.

By (A) I mean the following. Consider the network in Figure 2a. This network depicts the minimal anatomy that is capable of learning by classical conditioning. The population v_o receives a CS-activated input. Population v_o can thereupon emit signals along its axons e_{oi} whose terminals, or synaptic knobs, S_{oi} $(i = 1, 2, \ldots, n)$ abut on the UCS-activated populations v_1, v_2, $\ldots$, v_n. The LTM traces z_{oi} are computed at the synaptic knob terminals. Each z_{oi} computes a time average of the signal along e_{oi} multiplied by the STM trace x_i of v_i. In particular, z_{oi} cannot discern the value of x_i unless the axonal signal is positive. *Stimulus sampling* means that z_{oi} can only detect the effect of the UCS pattern on x_i at times when signals from v_o reach the synaptic knob S_{oi}.

The network of Figure 2a is called an *outstar* because it can be symmetrically redrawn as in Figure 2b. Property (A) means that an outstar can learn an arbitrary spatial pattern. A *spatial pattern* is a UCS to the cells $v_1, v_2, \ldots, v_n$ whose intensities have a fixed relative size throughout time; that is, the input $I_i(t)$ to v_i satisfies $I_i(t) = \theta_i I(t)$, $i = 1, 2, \ldots, n$. The constants, or "reflectances," θ_i are nonnegative and are normalized such that $\sum_{k=1}^{n} \theta_k = 1$ to achieve the convention that $I(t)$ is the total

UCS input; viz., $I(t) = \sum_{k=1}^{n} I_k(t)$. The outstar can learn the pattern weights $\theta = (\theta_1, \theta_2, \ldots, \theta_n)$ at a rate that depends upon the size of the CS input $I_0(t)$ and the total UCS input $I(t)$ (Grossberg, 1970a).

The *stimulus sampling probabilities* of an outstar are the relative LTM traces

$$Z_{oi} = z_{oi} \left(\sum_{k=1}^{n} z_{ok} \right)^{-1}. \tag{1}$$

As CS–UCS pairing takes place, the functions Z_{oi} approach the values θ_i, respectively. During later performance trials, a CS input to v_0 creates equal signals in the e_{oi} axons. These signals are gated, or multiplied, by the LTM traces z_{oi}. Since each z_{oi} is proportional to θ_i, the gated signal to v_i is also proportional to θ_i. The CS hereby elicits responses in the STM traces x_i that are proportional to θ_i. In short, after CS–UCS pairing, the CS can reproduce the pattern θ_i.

Stimulus sampling can be described as follows. The stimulus sampling probabilities z_{oi} can change *only* when signals from v_0 reach the synaptic knobs S_{oi}. Unless the CS perturbs these knobs, their LTM traces cannot "see" what UCS patterns are received at the cells $v_1, v_2, \ldots, v_n$.

These simple ideas about classical conditioning can be generalized to prove a universal theorem about associative learning. The universal theorem guarantees unbiased spatial patterning by arbitrarily many, simultaneously active sampling populations that are activated by arbitrary continuous data preprocessing in an essentially arbitrary anatomy (Grossberg, 1969a, 1971b, 1972a). The same laws also, for example, imply many properties and predictions of serial learning, paired associate, and free recall data (Grossberg, 1969b, 1978a; Grossberg and Pepe, 1971). In the present article, I will develop implications of these laws that are based on properties (A) and (B) above.

4. Motor Synergies as Evolutionary Invariants

Although I will not dwell on these applications and generalizations of the associative learning laws, the reader should realize that the outstar is a general purpose pattern learning device. To illustrate this fact, suppose that the pattern weights θ describe the relative activities of motor control cells, and that these constant relative activities are transmuted into fixed relative rates of muscle contraction across their controlled muscle groups. Then the fact that an outstar can learn and later perform a spatial pattern without destroying the memory of the pattern means that a motor synergy can be learned and stably performed by a single command population v_0. The fact that the same pattern θ can be performed by different CS sampling signals means that performance of the motor synergy is effected by synchronous contraction of all the muscles. Distinct synchronous performance signals can alter the absolute muscle contraction rates through time, but preserve the relative contraction rates. Since the muscle positions before outstar read-out do not equal the terminal motor pattern encoded by θ, these invariant ratios will be easier to measure nearer to the end than the beginning of the synergetic motion. Analogous properties have recently been reported during motor performance (Kelso *et al.*, 1979; Soechting and Lacquaniti, 1981). From the perspective of the present theory, these properties reflect an invariant of the learning or evolutionary process; namely, that outstars encode pattern ratios which are left invariant by synchronous performance signals.

5. A Thought Experiment: The Synchronization Problem of Classical Conditioning

Our thought experiment will be based on obvious real-time constraints which classical conditioning imposes upon a behaving individual. The fact that the constraints

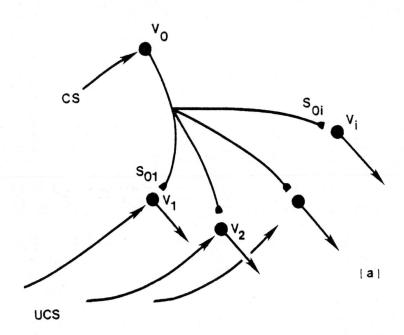

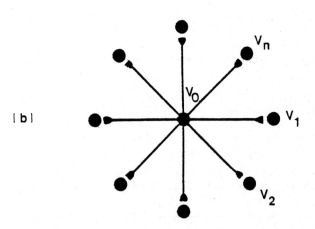

Figure 2. (a) The conditioned stimulus (CS) activates population v_0 which thereupon sends sampling signals to the unconditioned stimulus (UCS) activated populations $v_1, v_2, \ldots, v_n$. (b) The *outstar* is the minimal network capable of classical conditioning.

are obvious does not mean that they are trivial. In the present case, it means they are so ubiquitous and we have adapted so well to them that they seem obvious. The very obviousness of these constraints gives force to our argument.

The two main constraints are the following (Grossberg, 1971a):

C. The time intervals between CS and UCS presentation on successive learning trials can differ; and

D. The CS alone can elicit a CR on performance trials.

Postulate (C) describes the fact that successive stimulus presentations under natural conditions in real-time are not always perfectly synchronized; postulate (D) describes the outcome of classical conditioning, and simply asserts that this simplest example of associative learning is possible. We now show that to satisfy these postulates in a world wherein events continually buffet our senses, and wherein our long-term memories are spatially, albeit nonlocally, coded requires additional network structure.

To see this, we observe a continual stream of patterns from the viewpoint of an outstar. We ask, how can an outstar learn anything at all if unsynchronized patterns continually flow by? In particular, suppose that the outstar O_i attempts to learn a prescribed pattern $\theta^{(1)}$ in a sequence $\theta^{(1)}$, $\theta^{(2)}$, ... of spatial patterns by practicing as the sequence is presented on successive learning trials. Denote O_i's sampling population, or source, by $v_1^{(2)}$ and O_i's sampled populations, or border, by the field $F^{(1)} = \{v_1^{(1)}, v_2^{(1)}, \ldots, v_n^{(1)}\}$. If postulate (C) holds, then the time lag between the CS that excites $v_1^{(2)}$ and the onset of the UCS sequence $\theta^{(1)}, \theta^{(2)}, \theta^{(3)}, \ldots$ that perturbs $F^{(1)}$ can be different on successive learning trials. If $v_1^{(2)}$ fires whenever the CS occurs, then O_i can sample a different pattern $\theta^{(k)}$ on every learning trial. O_i will consequently learn an average pattern that is derived from all the sampled patterns; i.e., "noise." To avoid this catastrophe, O_i must know when to sample the "important" pattern $\theta^{(1)}$. Somehow the onset of sampling by $v_i^{(2)}$ and the arrival of the UCS at the field $F^{(1)}$ of sampled cells must be synchronized so that O_i can sample $\theta^{(1)}$, and only $\theta^{(1)}$, on successive trials.

How can the onset of $v_1^{(2)}$ sampling be synchronized to occur a fixed time before the UCS arrives at $F^{(1)}$ if the CS and UCS onset times are themselves unsynchronized? This can only happen, in principle, if several properties are imposed.

First, the CS itself must be insufficient to elicit a sampling signal from $v_1^{(2)}$. Second, the UCS must let $v_1^{(2)}$ know when it will arrive at $F^{(1)}$ by sending a signal to $v_1^{(2)}$. Third, $v_1^{(2)}$ must be prevented from eliciting a sampling signal unless large CS *and* UCS signals converge simultaneously at $v_1^{(2)}$. In other words, $v_1^{(2)}$ should not fire at all unless it represents the CS and should not fire until the correct time before the UCS arrives at $F^{(1)}$. In particular, if the CS input arrives so long before the UCS that its signal to $v_1^{(2)}$ decays before the UCS signal reaches $v_1^{(2)}$, then $v_1^{(2)}$ cannot fire. Fourth, the UCS signal must arrive at $v_1^{(2)}$ before the UCS pattern activates $F^{(1)}$, since $v_1^{(2)}$ must be able to send a signal to $F^{(1)}$ in time to sample $\theta^{(1)}$. In other words, the UCS activates a bifurcating pathway. One branch in the pathway *arouses* $v_1^{(2)}$; that is, it gets $v_1^{(2)}$ ready to sample the UCS that will soon perturb $F^{(1)}$. The other branch delivers the UCS pattern to $F^{(1)}$ a little while later (Figure 3). Fifth, the UCS does not know to which CS it will be paired in a given experiment. It could be paired with any CS. The above argument holds for every CS with which the UCS can possibly be associated. Thus the UCS must be able to arouse all of the sampling cells that these CS's activate; namely, the whole field $F^{(1)} = \{v_1^{(2)}, v_2^{(2)}, \ldots, v_n^{(2)}\}$ of CS-activated sampling cells. Thus the

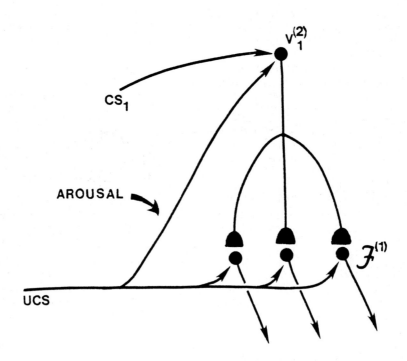

Figure 3. Population $v_1^{(2)}$ can fire only if CS and UCS arousal signals simultaneously converge upon it. The UCS input bifurcates to deliver a UCS pattern at $F^{(1)}$ and arousal to sampling cells like $v_1^{(2)}$.

UCS *nonspecifically* arouses the entire field $F^{(2)}$ just before it delivers its pattern to $F^{(1)}$ (Figure 4).

In summary, simultaneous convergence of the CS input and the UCS nonspecific arousal at a sampling cell are needed to fire this cell. This mechanism synchronizes the onset of CS-activated sampling signals from $F^{(2)}$ and the arrival of UCS patterns at $F^{(1)}$ on successive learning trials. Synchronization is a necessary condition in order for practice on successive trials to avoid massive associative confusions among spatially encoded patterns that stream into the network through time.

6. Some Experimental Connections

Before continuing with the thought experiment and the consequent derivation of increasingly precise neural structure, let us realize that some basic psychophysiological facts are already coming into view.

(i) *Nonspecific arousal*

The thought experiment teaches us that sampling cells cannot fire unless they are nonspecifically aroused, even if they receive specific CS inputs. At least since the work of Moruzzi and Magoun (1949), it has been known that inactivity of nonspecific subcortical projection systems to the cerebral cortex can prevent the cortex from supporting conscious behavior. The field $F^{(2)}$ of sampling cells become a rudimentary analog of the cortex in our thought experiment.

(ii) *Events have cue and arousal functions*

To organize the flood of data that followed Moruzzi and Magoun's study, Hebb (1955) suggested that every sensory event has two quite different effects: its *cue* function and its *arousal* or *vigilance* function. The cue function represents the information in the event that selectively guides behavior. The arousal function energizes the behavior. Hebb suggested that learning without arousal is not possible. Hull (1943) had earlier dichotomized information and energetic variables by distinguishing habit strength $(_SH_R)$ from drive (D). Hull suggested that drives energize habits via the multiplicative law $_SE_R =_S H_R < D$ for reaction potential $_SE_R$. Actually, the distinction between information, or reason, and energy, or passion, is a very old one that was already embraced by the rationalists (Bolles, 1967) in their efforts to construct a comprehensive philosophical framework by which to understand human behavior. The distinction has even been a force guiding social policy as in Vienna during the time of Wittgenstein (Janik and Toulmin, 1973), where men were supposed to embody the principle of reason, and woman the principle of passion that was considered to be destructive of reason. This belief was used to justify various unpleasant social policies. By contrast with the Viennese notion, the thought experiment requires both principles to compute the simplest memories, reasonable or not.

In Figure 4, the UCS has both a cue and an arousal function due to its bifurcating pathway, but the CS has only a cue function. Does this distinction say something basic about the difference between CS and UCS? The next section will suggest an answer.

(iii) *Polyvalent cells*

The thought experiment implies that the sampling cells can be polyvalent cells, or cells that are influenced by more than one modality. For example, if the CS is a tone and the UCS is a visual cue of food, then both auditory and visual cues will be needed to fire the corresponding sampling cells. In other words, the sampling cells only fire in response to the sum of CS and UCS inputs, and their firing patterns influence the occurrence or nonoccurrence of network learning. John (1966, 1967) has discovered neocortical cells that satisfy all of these properties.

(iv) *D.C. potential shifts*

Such workers as Rusinov (1953) and Morrell (1961) have shown that electrodes that induce anodal d. c. potential shifts of cortical tissue can augment conditioning within the cortex, whereas cathodal d. c. shifts tend to inhibit conditioning. These results suggest that the anodal d. c. shifts have effects on cortical activity that are analogous to nonspecific arousal.

7. Conditioned Arousal

To continue the thought experiment, we now consider postulate (D). This postulate is that classical conditioning is possible, or that the CS alone can elicit a CR after conditioning occurs. In particular, after conditioning occurs, a CS input to $F^{(2)}$ can elicit a sampling signal that reads out the learned pattern across $F^{(1)}$. Postulate (D) forces us to consider the following paradox. If a cell in $F^{(2)}$ can only be fired when a specific CS signal and a nonspecific UCS signal converge on the cell, then how does the CS alone fire the cell after learning occurs?

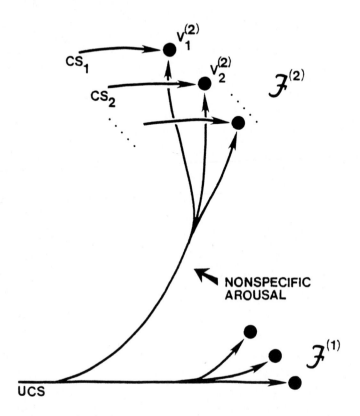

Figure 4. A UCS-activated arousal is nonspecifically delivered to all the sampling cells $F^{(2)}$ because it cannot be known *a priori* which CS–UCS association will be imposed by the environment.

In order for a cell $v_i^{(2)}$ to fire, it must receive simultaneous specific and nonspecific signals. However, only the CS is present on recall trials to activate both of these signals, since during recall trials, no UCS is presented to activate the nonspecific pathway. Thus the CS itself must activate both pathways. Before learning occurs, the CS does not have this capability. Somehow, as a result of pairing the CS and the UCS on learning trials, the CS gains control over the nonspecific pathway that is activated by the UCS. In other words, the nonspecific arousal pathway can be conditioned, and the CS can sample this conditionable pathway (Figure 5).

In summary, two conditioning processes occur in parallel during classical conditioning: (1) the CS, via $F^{(2)}$, samples the cells in $F^{(1)}$ that control the CR; and (2) the CS also samples the cells that control nonspecific arousal. Once the CS accomplishes both tasks, it can, by itself, fire cells in $F^{(1)}$ that read out the learned CR pattern from $F^{(1)}$.

An important implication of this argument is that there must exist cells, other than sampling cells $F^{(2)}$ and sampled cells $F^{(1)}$, that participate in classical conditioning.

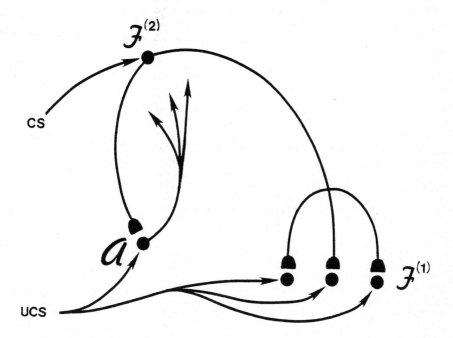

Figure 5. On learning trials, the CS samples both the UCS pattern at $F^{(1)}$ and the nonspecific arousal source A.

These are the arousal cells, denoted by A in Figure 5, at which the CS and UCS signals gain control of nonspecific arousal signals to the sampling cells.

8. Secondary Reinforcers

The network in Figure 5 begins to explain how secondary reinforcers operate. The UCS in a given learning experiment might have been only the CS in a previous learning experiment. How is this possible? For example, consider an animal L at two successive stages, E_1 and E_2, of its development. At stage E_1, L salivates in response to the smell of food but not to visual presentation of food. After classical conditioning with CS = visual presentation of food and UCS = smell of food, the animal salivates when it sees the food. This ability characterizes stage E_2.

Now a second conditioning experiment is performed in which CS = ringing bell and UCS = visual presentation of food. Ultimately, L salivates when it hears the ringing bell. How does the visual presentation of food in the first experiment enable this event to become a UCS in the second experiment?

The network in Figure 5 suggests an answer. The UCS of the first experiment is a UCS because it controls both the nonspecific arousal pathway and a specific pathway. The CS of this experiment becomes a UCS by gaining control over the nonspecific arousal pathway as well as its specific pathway. We can now begin to see that activation of the nonspecific arousal pathway is closely related to the motivational properties of the UCS, and that any cue that can activate such a pathway acquires motivational properties. The synchronization property of classical conditioning has hereby begun to force us into basic mechanisms of instrumental conditioning.

9. Minimal Network Realization of Conditioned Nonspecific Arousal

We now have enough information available to construct the minimal network capable of conditioning nonspecific arousal and using it to elicit overt behavior. We know that the CS, via cells in $F^{(2)}$, can learn to activate nonspecific arousal from A. The arousal, in turn, is needed to elicit sampling signals to $F^{(1)}$. We now show that the CS-activated cells that sample A and that receive feedback from A cannot be the same cells.

Figure 6 depicts the four general ways in which the CS can act. Figure 6a is impossible for the following reason. The CS-activated cells $F^{(2)}$ cannot fire on recall trials unless they are aroused by A. Cells in A cannot fire, however, unless they are activated by $F^{(2)}$. Hence the cells that sample A cannot be the same as the cells that are aroused by A.

Figure 6b tries to remedy this difficulty by expanding the cells $v_i^{(2)}$ of $F^{(2)}$ into two successive stages $v_{i1}^{(2)}$ and $v_{i2}^{(2)}$ of processing, in which the first stage $v_{i1}^{(2)}$ excites the second stage $v_{i2}^{(2)}$, and in which one stage samples A and the other stage is aroused by A. In Figure 6b, however, the connections to A are in the wrong order. Stage $v_{i1}^{(2)}$ can only fire if it is aroused by A, but A can only fire on recall trials if it is sampled by $v_{i2}^{(2)}$, which in turn can only fire if it is activated by $v_{i1}^{(2)}$. This is again an impossible arrangement. Consequently, two processing stages only help if they are connected in the correct fashion.

Both the networks in Figure 6c and 6d are possible, but Figure 6d enjoys an important advantage. In Figure 6c, the CS activates both stages $v_{i1}^{(2)}$ and $v_{i2}^{(2)}$. Stage $v_{i1}^{(2)}$ samples the arousal cells A, and stage $v_{i2}^{(2)}$ can fire if it receives the CS input plus feedback from A. Thereupon $v_{i2}^{(2)}$ samples the pattern at $F^{(1)}$. The major disadvantage of this network is that sampling of $F^{(1)}$ becomes impossible as soon as the CS shuts off. In Figure 6d, the CS activates stage $v_{i1}^{(2)}$, which thereupon sends a signal to stage $v_{i2}^{(2)}$ and samples A. Stage $v_{i2}^{(2)}$ can fire when it receives the signal from $v_{i1}^{(1)}$ plus a feedback signal from A. Thereupon $v_{i2}^{(2)}$ samples the pattern across $F^{(1)}$. This network can be modified so that learning is still possible after the CS terminates.

To show what I have in mind, let me anticipate the argument a little by making the following observation. In instrumental conditioning experiments, the learning subject scans stimuli and emits behaviors before a reward or punishment occurs. What keeps the internal representations of the stimuli and behavior active after they terminate so that the later reinforcements can influence their interrelationships? In other words, at what stage of network processing does storage in short term memory (STM) occur?

There is a simple answer in Figure 6d: let the stage $v_{i1}^{(2)}$ reverberate in response to a CS signal (Figure 7). Then $v_{i1}^{(2)}$ can send persistent signals to stage $v_{i2}^{(2)}$. Both stages "code" their CS in the sense that they are selectively activated by it. However, stage $v_{i2}^{(2)}$ can only sample $F^{(1)}$ if it also receives arousal from A. Stage $v_{i1}^{(2)}$ persistently samples A, but cannot learn to activate A until a UCS occurs. Thus STM reverberation can occur at $v_{i1}^{(2)}$ without erroneously eliciting sampling signals from $v_{i2}^{(2)}$.

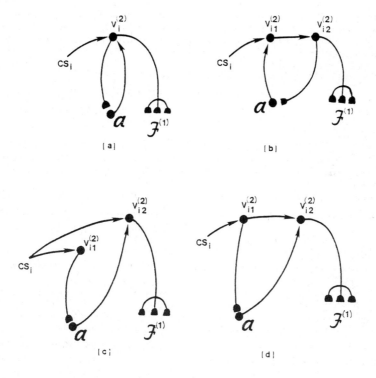

Figure 6. Networks (a) and (b) do not work because their polyvalent cells can never fire. Network (c) can fire but it is incapable of storing the CS in STM. Network (d) is the minimal network capable of realizing postulates (A)–(D) and storing the CS in STM.

This is not possible in the network of Figure 6c. If a reverberatory loop is added to $v_{i1}^{(2)}$, then nothing is accomplished, since $v_{i1}^{(2)}$ cannot activate $v_{i2}^{(2)}$ directly, and can only activate $v_{i2}^{(2)}$ indirectly after learning has already occurred, which prevents habit learning by $v_{i2}^{(2)}$ after its CS terminates. If a reverberatory loop is added to $v_{i2}^{(2)}$, and if $v_{i2}^{(2)}$ can fire this loop after the CS terminates and before learning occurs, then $v_{i2}^{(2)}$ can fire without arousal from A, which is impossible. Hence Figure 6d is the only minimal anatomy that can solve the synchronization problem and can also accomodate CS-activated STM. Consequently, this anatomy will be used in the following discussion.

10. Secondary Conditioning: A Principle of Equivalence for the Anatomy of CS and UCS

Given that a CS can acquire UCS properties due to practice, we can conclude that important features of the anatomical representations of CS and UCS are often the same. To see this, let L be exposed to a sequence E_1, E_2, ... of classical conditioning experiments. Denote the CS of E_i by CS_i and the UCS of E_i by UCS_i. Let the CS of E_i be the UCS of E_{i+1}; that is,

$$UCS_{i+1} = CS_i, \quad i \geq 1. \tag{2}$$

In other words every CS can become a future UCS and every UCS can have been a past CS except possibly UCS_1, on whose arousal properties the entire sequence of higher-order conditioning is built up.

The time scale of each conditioning experiment is short, on the order of minutes. I assume that new intercellular pathways cannot be wholly created or destroyed during the short time needed to go from any stage E_i to the next stage E_{i+1}. It follows that there exists a common anatomical representation for CS and UCS processing except possibly for UCS_1. By Section 9 every CS_i has a representation with at least two successive stages $(v_{i1}^{(2)}, v_{i2}^{(2)})$ of processing. Thus every UCS_i, $i > 1$, has the same representation. In other words, all CS and UCS inputs, except possibly UCS_1, are delivered to $F^{(2)}$. Figure 8 illustrates the equivalence of these representations.

I call the property of common representation for CS and UCS pathways CS-UCS *path equivalence*. Path equivalence is the anatomical substrate that makes secondary conditioning possible.

Let us now summarize how the network in Figure 8 works during a classical conditioning experiment. Let the CS activate $v_{11}^{(2)}$ and the UCS activate $v_{21}^{(2)}$. When the CS occurs, $v_{11}^{(2)}$ fires and sends signals to $v_{12}^{(2)}$ and to the arousal population A. Nothing else happens until the UCS arrives at $v_{21}^{(2)}$. This is because $v_{12}^{(2)}$ can only fire if it receives an input from $v_{11}^{(2)}$ *and* from A, but the signal from $v_{11}^{(2)}$ to A is initially too small to fire A. When the UCS perturbs $v_{21}^{(2)}$, $v_{21}^{(2)}$ sends a signal to $v_{22}^{(2)}$ and to A. The $v_{21}^{(2)}$ signals are large enough to fire A, *because* the cue firing $v_{21}^{(2)}$ is a UCS. When A fires, it releases nonspecific signals to all cells $v_{12}^{(2)}$, $v_{22}^{(2)}$, $v_{32}^{(2)}$, ... in $F^{(2)}$. Now three things happen. First, since $v_{11}^{(2)}$ and A are both active, the LTM traces in the synaptic knobs of $v_{11}^{(2)}$ axons get stronger. When these traces get strong enough, the CS alone will be able to fire $v_{12}^{(2)}$. Second, the arousal signal from A combines with the UCS derived signal from $v_{21}^{(2)}$ at $v_{22}^{(2)}$, thereby firing signals from $v_{22}^{(2)}$ to $F^{(1)}$. These signals elicit the UCS pattern in the populations of $F^{(1)}$. Third, because the arousal signal from A is nonspecific, it also combines with the CS-derived signal from $v_{11}^{(2)}$ at $v_{12}^{(2)}$, thereby firing signals from

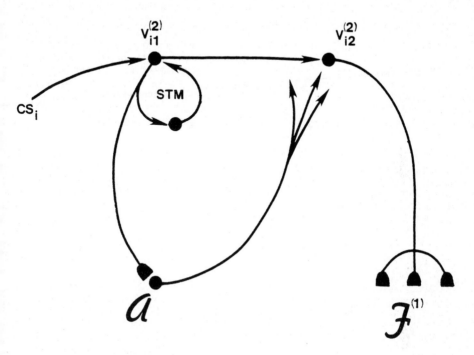

Figure 7. CS_1 can reverberate in STM at $v_{i1}^{(2)}$ as it emits sampling signals to A without being able to fire the polyvalent sampling cells $v_{i2}^{(2)}$.

$v_{12}^{(2)}$ to $F^{(1)}$. These signals sample the UCS-elicited pattern at $F^{(1)}$. Consequently, the CS begins to acquire UCS properties, both by learning to control the arousal pathway A, and by learning to elicit (a component of) the UCS-induced pattern at $F^{(1)}$.

Path equivalence also provides an elegant answer to the question: how does the UCS arouse the CS with just the right time lag to sample UCS onset at $F^{(1)}$? The same arousal which allows $v_{22}^{(2)}$ to read out the UCS pattern across $F^{(1)}$ also allows $v_{12}^{(2)}$ to emit sampling signals to read in this UCS pattern.

11. Are Drives Energizers or Sources of Information?

Path equivalence has an important intuitive meaning. Consider the stages E_1 and E_2 of Section 8 for definiteness. What intuitive fact has changed when the equation

$$CS_1 = \text{visual presentation of food} \tag{3}$$

is replaced by

$$UCS_2 = \text{visual presentation of food?} \tag{4}$$

Visual presentation of food has taken on the significance of food by being conditioned to the arousal cells A. The cue has acquired an internal meaning for L. Arousal prepares

L to be able to learn that the cue CS_1 signals forthcoming satisfaction of the internal demand for food. In particular, arousal is not merely an energizer, as Hull (1943) or Hebb (1955) suggested. It can have a cue function also, albeit a cue function concerning the internal state of L rather than the external state of the world.

Equations (3) and (4) describe cues that are related to hunger. Similar equations can also be written for cues that are related to thirst, sexual arousal, or fear, among other internal organismic states. Moreover, the same cue could have served as the CS for UCS's that are relevant to any of these states, just as a bell associated with shock can elicit autonomic signs of fear, whereas the same bell associated instead with food can elicit salivation. This observation is summarized in the postulate:

E. A given cue can be associated with any of several organismic states.

12. External Facts versus Internal Demands

Postulate (E) implies that the arousal cells A are broken into several functionally distinct, but not necessarily independent, populations. These populations will be denoted individually by D_1, D_2, ..., D_m, and collectively by D, because they play the role of drive representations in the network. To represent hunger and thirst by different drive representations does not imply that the two representations are built up from disjoint cells. If the two representations do share cells, then every input to one representation will also deliver an input to the other representation whose relative intensity depends on the overlap of cells between the two representations.

Given the existence of several drive representations D_1, D_2, ..., D_m, the previous discussion implies that each population $v_{i1}^{(2)}$ in $F^{(2)}$ can sample several drive representations D_j, and that each D_j sends signals to several populations $v_{i2}^{(2)}$. In just the same sense that signals from D to $F^{(2)}$ are nonspecific, also signals from $F^{(2)}$ to D are nonspecific (Figure 9). Nonetheless, there are quantitatively more cells in $F^{(2)}$ to which D projects than conversely. Since each $v_{i1}^{(2)}$ can now send signals to several D_j's, it is the source of an outstar. Consequently, each sensory representation can learn a spatial pattern of activity across the several drive representations as it is paired through time with UCS inputs. At each time, this spatial pattern summarizes the entire past history of drive state activations that occurred while its source cell was active.

An important issue concerns the *reciprocity* of connections between sensory and drive representations. If $v_{i1}^{(2)}$ projects to D_j, does D_j always project to $v_{i2}^{(2)}$? If not, then $v_{i1}^{(2)}$ can be conditioned to drive D_j without D_j being able to release sampling signals from $v_{i2}^{(2)}$. Henceforth we always assume reciprocity for definiteness, although obvious modifications of our argument extend to the nonreciprocal case. We do not, however, assume *equipotentiality* of connections; namely, it is not necessary to our argument that each sensory representation projects to all drive representations, or that it projects with the same path strength to any pair of drive representations. Such asymmetries can influence if and how long learning can take, or even whether or not a particular learned behavior will be masked by a competing and more salient behavior. However they do not influence the primary network structure that our postulates imply. They are rather species-specific variations on this primary structure (Bitterman and Mackintosh, 1969; Seligman and Hager, 1972).

13. Internal Facts versus External Demands: Existence of Homeostatic, or Drive, Inputs

Thus far if a sensory representation in $F^{(2)}$ becomes associated with a drive representation and a pattern across $F^{(1)}$, it will release the $F^{(1)}$ pattern whenever the sensory

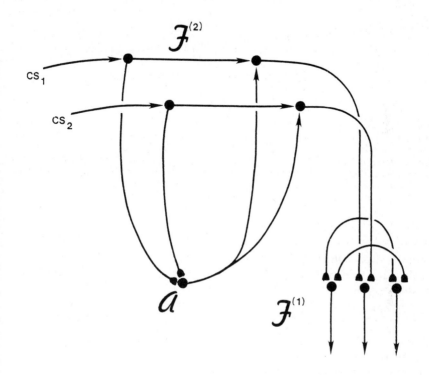

Figure 8. Since each CS can rapidly acquire UCS properties, both CS's and UCS's possess a common anatomical substrate, except perhaps the primal, or pre-wired, UCS's.

representation is activated. For example, a visual cue of food could always elicit eating behavior no matter how satiated the organism was. This property could, of course, have disastrous consequences. Speaking intuitively, the problem is clear: Some index of organismic need must exist to prevent unappropriate consummation. More generally, indices of the organism's internal states must be introduced to modulate its reactions to available external cues.

At this point in the theory, it could have happened that no plausible modification of the previously derived network dynamics could overcome this difficulty. Quite to the contrary, however, there exists a discernible symmetry in the networks, but a missing mechanism mars this symmetry, and its introduction will overcome our difficulty.

This symmetry is based on the fact that the representations of external cues project

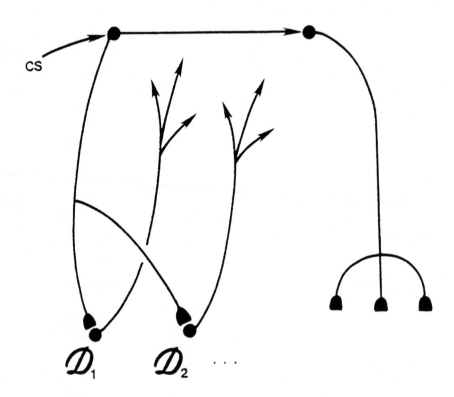

Figure 9. Each CS can sample the several drive representations $D_1, D_2, \ldots, D_m$. Each drive representation can, in turn, deliver nonspecific arousing signals to the CS's.

nonspecifically to the representations of internal drive states, *and conversely*. In a clear sense, the drive states are also representations of cues, albeit cues that are internal to the organism, rather than cues in the external world. The symmetry is marred by the fact that external cue representations can fire only if a specific external cue signal summates with a nonspecific internal drive signal. By contrast, the internal drive representations can fire whenever they receive a nonspecific external cue signal (Figure 10). To remove this asymmetry, a specific internal drive signal should also be necessary to fire the internal drive representation. If an external cue representation could fire without an external cue being present, we would say that a type of hallucinatory event had occurred. Letting drive representations fire in the absence of specific internal drive signals is like permitting drive hallucinations to occur. Introducing specific drive inputs eliminates this network asymmetry and begins to overcome the satiety problem.

The above discussion can be organized around the following postulate:

F. Observable behavior is influenced by an organism's drives.

If this postulate were imposed in a theoretical vacuum, it would be just a vaguely stated triviality. Given the mechanisms that we have already derived, its minimal

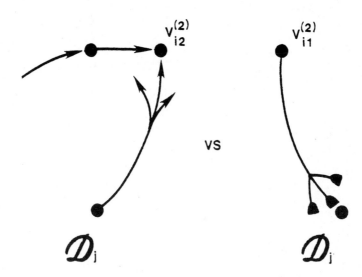

Figure 10. A sensory representation $v_{i2}^{(2)}$ can fire only if it receives a specific external cue input plus a nonspecific internal drive input. By contrast, a drive representation D_i can fire whenever it receives a nonspecific external cue input. This asymmetry has unpleasant behavioral implications.

realization is to suppose, first, that there exist specific internal drive inputs to the drive representations whose sizes provide a measure of internal organismic needs; and second, that the drive representations can fire only if a sufficiently large specific internal drive signal occurs simultaneously with a sufficiently large nonspecific external cue signal (Figure 11). The drive representations are therefore also constructed from polyvalent cells.

The network's symmetry suggests the following question. Are both types of polyvalent cells anatomically homologous *in vivo*? I suggest that both cell types be identified with pyramidal cells. In particular, the $F^{(2)}$ polyvalent cells are suggested to play the role of cortical pyramidal cells, whereas the D polyvalent cells are associated with hippocampal pyramidal cells (Shepherd, 1974). The feedback loop between $F^{(2)}$ and D thus becomes a rudimentary analog of the feedback exchange that takes place between cortex and hippocampus to regulate motivated behavior (Gabriel *et al.*, 1980; Grossberg, 1975).

14. Conditioned Reinforcers, Drives, Incentive Motivation, and Habits

At this point, I can begin to psychologically interpret network mechanisms, use the interpretation to sharpen and modify classical psychological theories, and explain various data as manifestations of the adaptive designs that organisms have evolved to solve the synchronization problem.

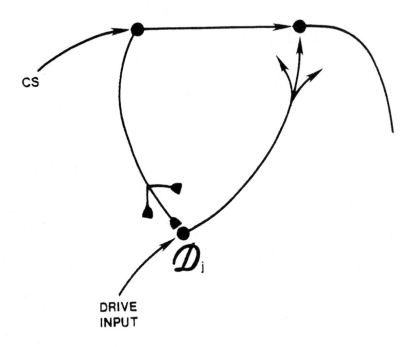

CS

DRIVE
INPUT

Figure 11. The drive representations are also constructed from polyvalent cells whose firing requires convergence of a specific internal drive input plus a nonspecific external cue input.

Consider Figure 12. This figure labels network mechanisms in suggestive psychological jargon. *Reinforcement* acts by changing the spatial pattern that is coded in LTM when an active external cue representation samples the pattern of activity playing across the internal drive representations. As an external cue representation builds up large LTM traces in some of its pathways to the drive representations, its cue acquires *conditioned reinforcer* properties. In particular, its cue can be used as a UCS in a classical conditioning experiment. An organism's *drive* state is represented by the spatial pattern of drive inputs across its drive representations at a given time. Conditioned reinforcer and drive inputs merge at the drive representations, so that the LTM patterns that are learned by the conditioned reinforcer pathways are mixtures of reinforcement and drive information, rather than solely of reinforcement information.

When conditioned reinforcer and drive inputs combine with sufficient vigor at a drive representation, nonspecific arousal can be released. Each drive representation is a distinct source of arousal. Its arousal level is called the *incentive motivation* associated with the drive. Thus drive, reinforcer, and incentive signals are conceptually distinct. This distinction sharpens the familiar observation that motivation can be absent even though drive is high if an appropriate cue is missing. Also motivation can be absent even though an appropriate cue is present if the drive is low.

Finally, the incentive motivation joins with an external cue input to learn or read out an LTM pattern that represents *habit strength*. Read-out of such an LTM pattern

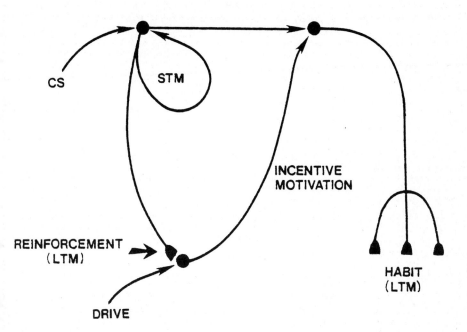

Figure 12. The processing stages forced by the synchronization problem admit psychological labels which enable us to sharpen and modify classical psychological theories.

can activate a command that controls a behavioral act. LTM changes thus occur at two loci in the network: they record the net pattern of reinforcer and drive data at the internal drive representations, and they record the pattern of behavioral commands at the habit representations.

15. Comparison with Hullian Concepts

In Hull's theory, a drive energizes any and all behavior. As Bolles (1967, p.183) clearly summarizes, according to Hull, "only that behavior occurs which has the strongest associative connections, and drive merely determines the strength of the dominant response." In the present theory, drive also has an energizing effect, since without it, nonspecific incentive signals cannot be released. However, drive also plays an informative and an associative role: informative because a drive input energizes only certain incentive pathways at the expense of others; associative because drive data can change the LTM patterns that are encoded by conditioned reinforcers.

Hull also suggests, at least formally, that drives and incentives play a symmetric role in their influence on habits. The Hullian law

$$_sE_R = {}_sH_R \times D \times V \times K \tag{5}$$

says that drive level D, stimulus intensity V, and incentive motivation K all multiply habit strength $_sH_R$ to determine reaction potential $_sE_R$. In some ways, our networks support the Hullian formation, since external cues, drives, and incentives all collaborate to read out the LTM patterns that encode network habits. However, in the network, external cues (akin to V) are gated by reinforced LTM patterns before they supply conditioned reinforcer inputs to the drive representations. Conditioned reinforcers and drive inputs (akin to D) determine incentive motivation (akin to K). Then incentive motivation and external cue inputs (akin to V) are gated by habits (akin to $_SH_R$). Let us adopt a Hullian type of notation $_SC_R$ for conditioned reinforcer LTM patterns that gate external cue signals on their way to drive representations. Then a Hullian analog of the network equations can be written as

$$K = {}_SC_R \times V \times D \tag{6}$$

and

$$_SE_R = {}_SH_R \times V \times K. \tag{7}$$

The most important features of (6) and (7) are that stimulus intensity V influences both K and $_SE_R$, that K is not independent of V and D, and that $_SC_R$ does not equal $_SH_R$. However, even this refinement of the Hullian formalism omits most of the network's spatiotemporal structure. It is meant to celebrate Hull's intuition and to mark a path that leads beyond his formalism.

In the next few sections, I will use network mechanisms to analyse classical data, concepts, and theories. These classical contributions need to be mechanistically classified before later contributions that build on their shoulders can be differentiated into variations on old themes versus really new insights.

16. Data on Conditioned Reinforcers and Drives

In the network, external stimuli become conditioned reinforcers when their pathways to drive representations are classically conditioned. Kelleher (1966, pp. 179–81) reviews experimental evidence that "stimuli become conditioned reinforcers through respondent conditioning."

In the network, a larger drive input can facilitate both performance and learning, albeit on different time scales. Performance is rapidly facilitated because a larger drive input can more vigorously activate its drive representation, which elicits incentive motivational signals, which energizes the performance of motivationally compatible habits. Learning is more slowly affected along both direct and indirect pathways. A large drive input can more vigorously activate its drive representation, which can then be directly sampled by the conditioned reinforcer LTM traces of active external cue representations. An indirect effect on learning occurs when the large incentive motivational signals elicited by the drive representation change the habits that can be sampled by active external cue representations. In various animals, weight loss is a good indicator of their motivation to learn a task leading to food reward (Stolurow, 1951; Bolles, 1967, Chapter 7). These data suggest that decrements in weight may cause proportional increments in the size of the drive input to the hunger drive representation. Such a drive input increment can energize both learning and performance in the manner suggested above.

Due to the interaction between performance and learning processes, the energizing effects of a drive input are not sufficient to explain network dynamics. Associative factors modulate a drive's efficacy, since the cues of an unfamiliar situation must become conditioned reinforcers and conditioned habit strength sources before they can efficiently control a learned behavior. In fact, when a hungry animal is introduced into an unfamiliar situation, its initial feeding behavior is often less vigorous than its feeding behavior later on, after it has already eaten enough to partially reduce its hunger. Such data, controlled for various alternative interpretations, have led to the conclusion that an animal's familiarity with the eating situation is a significant associative factor that influences the vigor of its feeding behavior (**Bolles, 1967**, Chapter 8; Moll, 1964).

17. Data on Reinforcement

In the network, reinforcing effects occur when a large conditioned reinforcer input interacts with a large drive input to fire a drive representation, which is then sampled by an active cue representation. Bindra (1968) provides experimental evidence that confirms this view of reinforcement. Bindra argues that there must exist a common neural locus where sensory inputs arising from incentive objects interact with the neural changes due to drive manipulation. These neural loci are the drive representations in the network. Scott and Pfaffman (1967) come to a similar conclusion from their studies of the hypothalamus, and Valenstein (1969) reviews more data of this type. Valenstein *et al.* (1970) report data in which "hypothalamic stimulation ... seems to create conditions which excite the neural substrate underlying well-established response patterns....Discharging this sensitized or excited substrate is reinforcing and it can provide the motivation to engage in instrumental behavior....Rats which display stimulus-bound eating prefer the combination of food and brain stimulation to brain stimulation....The brain stimulation does not fully activate all the neural circuits underlying reinforcement...." These data are explicable if we assume that network drive representations include, or are activated by, these hypothalamic sites, and that brain stimulation acts like a drive input, albeit an artificial one. Then the network interpretation of the Valenstein *et al.* data is that conditioned reinforcer inputs must be bolstered by drive inputs in order to activate the drive representations, which thereupon simultaneously release incentive signals and cause learned changes in the conditioned reinforcer LTM patterns.

18. Data on Self-Stimulation

Does electrode current in the hypothalamus act like a drive input as the Valenstein *et al.* data suggest? Olds (1955, 1958, 1977) reviews data on self-stimulation behavior that supports this view. Olds showed that a rat will learn to push a lever at high rates if it activates an electrode placed at suitable sites in its lateral hypothalamus. Often the rat will turn away from food or a mate to press the lever with great vigor until it becomes exhausted. Sites which elicit such consummatory self-stimulation behavior have been generally called the pleasure center. More detailed studies of self-stimulation suggest that the electrode input acts like a specific drive input. An electrode placed in an area associated with hunger loses its reinforcing effect when the animal is satiated, and the rate of lever pressing for self-stimulation increases when the animal is hungry. These data suggest that the usual hunger drive input summates with the artificial electrode input. In a similar fashion, an electrode placed at certain other hypothalamic sites will elicit faster lever pressing after androgen is injected. Androgen normally has the effect of motivating sexual behavior. At such loci, self-stimulation disappears almost completely after castration, which presumably eliminates the usual drive input to these loci. Similarly, higher current levels are needed to achieve self-stimulation as the androgen level subsides, indicating once again the energizing effect of drive inputs. This latter effect can be reversed by injections of testosterone propionate in oil.

By contrast, if androgen is injected when the electrode is located at hunger-related sites, then the lever-pressing rate decreases. If the animal is deprived of food when the electrode is at sex-related sites, then the lever-pressing rate again decreases. Thus the various drive loci reciprocally inhibit, or compete with each other, whereas electrode input at a given drive locus works synergetically with the drive input at this locus. Section 28 discusses how drive competition is realized by network mechanisms.

In the network, self-stimulation can be explained as follows. At the moment when the exploring animal accidentally presses the lever, sensory cues of events immediately preceding this act are active in sensory STM, and the motor commands for pressing the lever are active in motor STM. The lever press releases a large artificial drive input to its drive representation, large enough in fact to fire the drive representation. The conditioned reinforcer pathways of the active cues which abut the drive representation are hereby conditioned. Also incentive motivation is released that enables the active cues to learn the motor commands controlling lever pressing behavior. As trials proceed, the sensory cues of the lever gradually gain control over lever-pressing behavior, because their conditioned reinforcer and conditioned habit pathways are progressively strengthened on each trial by the electrode current that reliably follows the lever press.

This description helps us to understand why self-stimulation behavior is labile. In particular, self-stimulation shows poor resistance to extinction, poor carry-over of performance between learning sessions, and is a poor source of secondary reinforcement (Bolles, 1967, Chapter 9; Mogenson *et al.*, 1965; Stein, 1958). A basic difficulty is that, without electrode current available to continually reinforce the drive and habit pathways, the shifting pattern of drive and conditioned reinforcer inputs can act to remove adequate input for firing the drive representation or to competitively inhibit the drive representation that had received electrode input. Other sources of lability are disconfirmation of expectancies after continuously rewarded trials and the lack of experimental contingencies between the animal's expectancies and the onset of current (Grossberg, 1982a, 1984).

19. Reinforcement Without Drive Reduction

Self-stimulation data were a major embarrassment for Hull's central thesis that an event is reinforcing if it reduces a drive. Hull's idea seems to be supported by commonsensical experiences such as: you will learn a task to eat, and thereby reduce your hunger drive; or you will learn a task to escape shock, and thereby reduce your pain and fear. However, what drive is reduced when an animal pushes a lever to pump as much electric current as it can into its lateral hypothalamus? In a clear intuitive sense, the animal is working to increase, not to decrease, electric current. Moreover, why does an animal self-stimulate more if its hunger drive is increased and the electrode is placed in a hunger-related locus?

One might argue that the self-stimulation paradigm is so abnormal that the animal's behavior is not really reinforced, but only seems to be reinforced. However, once the floodgates were opened, many other behaviors could be cited that seem to violate the drive reduction principle. As an early example, Sheffield (1951) found that sexually naive male rats will learn an instrumental response if they are rewarded by being allowed to copulate with receptive females, but not allowed to ejaculate. What drive is reduced in this situation?

We are now faced with an important dilemma. If drive reduction is not really the mechanism of reinforcement, then why does common sense so strongly suggest that it is? A deeper version of this dilemma is this. Is it correct to claim that shock reduction and hunger reduction are both examples of a common drive reduction mechanism? There is a clear sense in which shock is an aversive cue, so that reducing it might well be positively rewarding. In other words, reducing a negative cue can have a positively rewarding effect. But is hunger always aversive? Is sexual desire always aversive? What is aversive about anticipating a marvelous dinner and eating it with gusto? It would be aversive, to be sure, if the dinner were cancelled at the last minute. Is this aversive reaction due directly to hunger, or is it due to the frustration that is triggered when we learn that the expected feast has been called off?

If we agree that hunger or sexual desire can be positive drives, not negative drives like fear, then why should reducing them hereby be reinforcing? The commonsense basis for believing in drive reduction hereby collapses. But then why do hunger and sexual desire sometimes seem aversive? Here we must distinguish between very high levels of these drives and normal levels. At normal levels, one can easily confuse the frustration caused by delayed gratification of the drive with the drive itself.

In the network, a positive drive input must be high before reinforcement can occur, because otherwise its drive representation cannot fire and cause LTM changes in abutting conditioned reinforcer pathways. The drive reduction that follows consummatory behavior is not, however, reinforcing. Instead, it prevents consummation after satiety occurs. This type of drive reduction occurs slowly in time. The sudden reduction of a reinforcing cue or the sudden nonoccurrence of an expected reinforcer can also have reinforcing effects, but these rapid events do not reduce a drive input, although they do modify the activity of the drive representations (Grossberg, 1982a, 1984).

20. Go Mechanism, Amplifiers, Now Print

Several authors have proposed alternatives to the drive reduction hypothesis to explain data about reinforcement. Each author developed his own vocabulary to describe his concepts, but all of them seem to have been building towards similar mechanisms. I will provide a comparative analysis to clarify some advantages of a network theory.

Miller (1963) introduced "go" mechanisms that "act to intensify ongoing responses to cues" that "are subject to conditioning with contiguity being sufficient," such that "the strength of the CR is determined to a great degree by the strength of the UCS," and "when a chain of cues leads to a UCS for the 'go mechanism,' it is most strongly conditioned to those nearer to the UCS."

Miller's mechanism is analogous to an incentive motivational signal. Incentive motivation acts to "intensify ongoing response to cues" by controlling the size of signals in the habit strength pathways, and can be "conditioned with contiguity being sufficient" in the conditioned reinforcer pathways. Moreover, CS strength is "determined to a great degree by the strength of the UCS" due to two factors acting together. The UCS input at the drive representations directly enhances performance in response to the CS by eliciting incentive motivational signals that amplify the CS-activated signals in the habit strength patways. The UCS input also indirectly strengthens the CS by enhancing conditioning of the CS-activated conditioned reinforcer pathways, and thereby enabling the CS to activate stronger incentive motivational signals on later trials. These two effects can be experimentally distinguished because the direct effect acts quickly whereas the indirect effect builds up slowly.

Miller's pioneering concepts provide a useful intuitive description, but one that is weakened by lumping together several mechanisms that are invisible without a real-time theory.

Estes (1969) develops analogous concepts within his framework of stimulus sampling theory. He suggests that the occurrence of a response requires summation of input from external stimulus and internal drive sources. Drives and rewards serve as response amplifiers. On learning a trial, the organism S draws a sample of available discriminative cues and scans these cues until an element is processed which is connected with a permissible response. This response will be evoked only if an amplifier element appropriate to the response is simultaneously scanned. Stimuli can be conditioned to amplifier elements by contiguity, and the base rate of amplifier elements associated with a given drive increases as S's need increases.

The amplifier elements of Estes' theory play the role of incentive motivational signals in the network. Many of the intuitive distinctions described by Estes' theory are also found in the network theory. The two theories nonetheless differ in important ways that have limited further development of the Estes theory, but not of the network theory. The concepts of the Estes theory are expressed in the probabilistic language of stimulus sampling theory. External cues and amplifier elements are said to be scanned, presumably by some probabilistic serial mechanism, and conditioning of cues to amplifier elements changes the probability of a successful joint scan of cues and amplifiers. By contrast, in the network theory, the probabilities of scanning amplifier elements are replaced by activity patterns that exist across all the drive representations at each time. Thus a serial scan is replaced by a parallel pattern. The activities of drive representations are not probabilities, nor are they scanned. It is hard to overemphasize the importance of the distinction. A larger drive activity will, other things being equal, cause a higher probability of that drive influencing observable behavior. However, on each trial the drive activity influences the computations that determine observable behavior. It is not possible to fail to scan an active drive representation on a given trial.

Estes' theory omits other distinctions that are important in the network theory. For example, Estes suggests that internal drives set the base rate of amplifier elements, and that external cues modulate this rate. The network analog of amplifier elements is incentive motivational signals, or alternatively the activities at drive representations that induce these signals. However, internal drive inputs are conceptually distinct from incentive motivational signals in the network. It is just as inadmissible to let drive inputs fire incentive motivational signals—i.e., set the base rate of amplifier elements in the absence of conditioned reinforcer signals—as it is to let external cue signals sample habit strengths in the absence of incentive motivational signals.

In the network theory, patterned LTM traces vary slowly through time and gate rapidly fluctuating signals from the external cue representations to the drive representations. In the sampling model, these two distinct processes are lumped into the probability that a scanned cue will be associated with an amplifier element. A conditioned reinforcer LTM trace can, however, be very large even if, due to the momentary STM inactivity of the cue representation, there is a zero probability of "scanning an amplifier element" at that time. Thus, the network's way of representing the effects of prior reinforcement do not neatly correspond to the probabilistic concepts of the sampling theory.

More generally, the framework of stimulus sampling theory cannot easily represent the internal geometry of specific and nonspecific pathways, or the several time scales on which STM and LTM traces fluctuate. These deficiencies become especially evident when the network theory incorporates antagonistic rebound mechanisms (Grossberg, 1972c, 1981a, 1982a, 1984) and expectancy mechanisms (Grossberg, 1976b, 1980a, 1982a, 1984) to understand various conditioning and attentional phenomena. In a stimulus sampling context, these concepts are hard to motivate or to represent, but in a network framework they arise in a natural fashion. Thus despite its great heuristic value as a tool for classifying a variety of learning experiments, the stimulus sampling theory becomes increasingly unwieldy and inaccurate as it attempts to represent the intervening variables that govern complex learning behavior.

Logan (1969) claimed that rewards "excite" rather than "strengthen" habits by providing "incentive motivation" that favors their execution. Though the distinction between "exciting" and "strengthening" a habit might seem obscure, with the network theory as a guide, a possible mechanistic interpretation is suggested. The reward elicits incentive motivational signals that allow the habit to be released. This is the "exciting" effect of a reward. I claim, however, that the reward can also "strengthen" the habit in two distinct ways, albeit indirectly and on a slower time scale. One strengthening effect of a reward is due to the conditioned reinforcer learning that it can trigger. Such learning can strengthen the incentive motivational signal which a reinforcing cue can elicit to "energize" the habit on later performance trials. A second "strengthening" effect of reward is more direct. It is due to the fact that a larger incentive motivational signal can cause a larger sampling signal to be emitted from a cue's polyvalent cells to the habit representation. A larger sampling signal implies a faster rate of habit learning, which can "strengthen" the habit measured after a fixed number of learning trials.

Livingston (1967) also has a similar mechanism in mind in his discussion of a "Now Print" mechanism that can control the learning rate.

It is remarkable that so many languages have been used to describe the same mechanisms. The rigorous explication of these mechanisms will hopefully unify the languages used to discuss them.

21. Data on Incentive Motivation

A male animal left alone will busily do many things characteristic of his species, such as grooming, eating, exploring. He does not look sexually motivated. However, if a female animal is presented to him, his behavior can dramatically change (Beach, 1956; Bolles, 1967, Chapter 7). This example distinguishes between sex drive and observable motivated sexual behavior in the presence of appropriate external stimuli. Drive without external cues need not elicit motivated behavior. In the network theory, drive inputs cannot fire drive representations unless they are supplemented by an auxiliary input source such as reinforced signals from cue representations.

Furthermore, external stimuli without drive need not elicit motivated behavior. Seward and Proctor (1960) and Seward *et al.* (1958, 1960) found that if an animal is not hungry, then no amount of food will be adequate to reinforce its behavior. In the network theory, without drive inputs, no amount of conditioned reinforcer input can fire the drive representations. These experiments support the hypothesis that the polyvalent cells of drive representations need simultaneously converging reinforcing and drive inputs to vigorously fire.

An analogous type of experiment shows that cues can be trained to elicit appropriate behavior even if two or more drives are simultaneously active. Kendler (1946) trained rats who were simultaneously hungry and thirsty in a T maze. Food was on one side of the T maze and water was on the other side. The animals were forced alternately to the two sides, and rapidly learned the discrimination. When they were just hungry or just thirsty on a test trial, the rats went to the correct side with high probability. As Bolles (1967, Chapter 9) notes, this plausible result is embarrassing to a simple stimulus-response theory of conditioning, since on training trials, turning left and turning right should be associated to both the hunger and thirst cues, but then how is discrimination learned? In the network theory, the explanation is simple. The drive inputs of hunger and thirst cannot by themselves fire their drive representations. When food is eaten, its reinforced path to the hunger drive representation combines with the hunger drive input to selectively fire the hunger drive representation. The external cues associated with the food thereupon become conditioned reinforcers with respect to the hunger drive representation. A similar argument holds when water is drunk. Variations on the original Kendler experiment supported a role for incentive motivation (Kendler and Levine, 1951; Kendler *et al.*, 1952), but provided no mechanistic description of how incentive motivation differs from drive and reinforcement. Some recent theories of conditioning have fallen into difficulties analogous to those implied by the Kendler (1946) data, because they do not include the notions of a drive representation and incentive motivation (Hall and Pearce, 1980). Similar ideas to those described herein have been used to overcome these difficulties (Grossberg, 1982a).

In Hullian theory and its variations, incentive motivation is often denoted by r_G. Tracking the existence and properties of r_G has led to many beautiful experiments and ingenious, if sometimes tortured, conceptualizations. Bolles' (1967) book provides a stimulating account of many classical efforts. Often the mysterious r_G was invoked because some other concept, such as drive or reinforcment, was inadequate, as in the above experiments. One did not know what r_G itself was, but one could often say what the other concepts were not. For example, many experimentalists claimed that incentive motivation is mediated by an anticipatory goal reaction. As Bolles (1967, p.332) wrote: "Drives push and incentives pull." Drives are unlearned, whereas incentives are learned. Drives describe the organism's momentary state, whereas incentives summarize the organism's history. Incentives are thus used to explain many of the performance variations that are not directly due to momentary drives or to associative properties of habits. For example, Crespi (1942, 1944) emphasized the motivational properties of incentives by running different groups of rats in a straight alley to large or small quantities of food. Not surprisingly, large-amount animals performed better than small-amount animals. Then Crespi switched half of each group after twenty trials from high to low or from low to high. Performance changed rapidly to new levels commensurate with the new reward contingencies. The performance shifts were too fast to be explained by changes in drive level or changes in associative habits. In the network, changing the level of reinforcement rapidly changes the size of inputs due to the food itself, and thus the ambient level of polyvalent cell activation, even without a change in drive input level, or a change in conditioned reinforcer properties of external cues.

The classical r_G concept faces several fundamental difficulties. One difficulty is summarized by Bolles' (1967) phrase: "The anticipatory goal response is the only serious proposal that has been made for a mechanism to account for incentive motivation" (p.336). The Mackintosh (1974) view that was summarized in Section 1 is a more recent version of this idea. The problem is that this viewpoint lumps together several distinct processes under the r_G label. Truly anticipatory behavior often involves a behavioral plan whose unfolding is regulated by expectations that are matched against environmental feedback (Grossberg, 1978b, 1980a). By contrast, incentive motivation per se can seem to guide anticipatory behavior without either plans or expectancies being operative. For example, suppose that external cues excite a generalization gradient of related cue representations and that all of the excited cue representations sample the drive and habit representations with a strength that depends on how excited they get due to the external cue. To test whether the animal "anticipated" a certain cue or outcome, one might use related cues versus unrelated cues on test trials. Or one might use related versus unrelated response measures. A differential effect on performance might suggest the action of anticipatory goal responses, but really no cognitive type of expectancy or anticipation need be involved. There exist basic reasons for the operation of expectancies even in simple conditioning paradigms (Grossberg, 1981a, 1982a, 1984), but for now let us note that incentive motivation and expectancy matching are wholly distinct mechanisms that tend to get badly obscured in the r_G literature.

Some of the multiple roles ascribed to r_G are legitimate, as when Bolles (1967, p.354) asks if incentives "reinforce instrumental behavior, motivate it, or simply provide stimulus control for it?" In the network, the answer is: all of the above, but using different pathways than can operate on different time scales.

22. Secondary Reinforcement and Hull's Paradox

Hull's use of drive reduction together with r_G created a serious paradox (Bolles, 1967, p.355). Hull claimed that a stimulus associated with drive reduction acquires secondary reinforcing power. It can act the same way as drive reduction does in later learning experiments. Hull supposed that the mechanism for this is r_G. Thus the occurrence of r_G should act like drive reduction. However, the motivating effects of a secondary reinforcer were also ascribed to an increase in incentive motivation, or r_G. How can r_G both be drive reducing and drive increasing? Given Hull's formulation, it seemed hard to argue that r_G is both reinforcing and motivating.

This problem is overcome in the network theory. Drive reduction is abandoned, and path equivalence shows how a UCS can be reinforcing, via its effects on the LTM of other active conditioned reinforcer pathways, and motivating, via its effects on the firing of habit strength pathways.

23. Late Nonspecific Potential Shifts

Some seemingly paradoxical data have been collected by doing discrimination learning on animals with implanted electrodes. John and Morgades (1969) reported that, in trained animals, discriminative stimuli elicit characteristic responses that are distributed rather uniformly across extensive cellular regions, and that these uniform reactions manifest themselves as an increase in the later components of evoked brain potentials as training goes on. The paradox is as follows. Why should an increase in the animal's discriminative ability correspond to a more uniform distribution across space of cell potentials? Why don't the potentials get more discriminative also?

Several authors have interpreted this result by claiming that, as discrimination improves, the "information" about the discrimination is spread uniformly across the network, akin to an equipotentiality or hologram type of concept. This idea creates several problems when we ask how nerves can retrieve this uniformly scattered information, since all discriminations will become uniformly distributed across the same neural tissue. In a holographic theory, such decoding relies on the existence of precisely calibrated periodic sampling probes. Within the active neuropile, a much more chaotic temporal behavior prevails.

In the network theory, this interpretation seems to be unnecessary at best. As discrimination training proceeds, the external cues gain control over incentive motivational pathways as they become conditioned reinforcers. Since the incentive motivational pathways are nonspecific, the cues can deliver their signature quite uniformly to all the sites that receive the incentive motivational signals. These uniform signals are "late" because it takes longer for them to feed through the drive representations and then back via incentive motivational pathways than it does for the cues to directly activate sensory STM. However, the "information" in the network is not carried by these signals. The information is carried in the polyvalent properties that determine which cells will fire, and in the LTM patterns that will subsequently be read out.

It is somewhat surprising that John himself did not reach this conclusion, since John (1966, 1967) has also reported that neocortical polyvalent cells require both CS and UCS input in order to fire. Perhaps John's oversight was due to the theoretical property that after discrimination has taken place, this is no longer true; then the CS alone is a sufficient external cue to fire its pathway. John's data thus contained a gap, and because he took the data at face value, he was led to a paradoxical hypothesis.

The contingent negative variation (CNV) is a slowly varying cortical potential shift that is a likely neural substrate of incentive motivational signals. Walter (1964) hypothesized that the CNV shifts the average baseline of the cortex by depolarizing the apical dendritical potentials of cortical pyramidal cells and thereby priming the cortex for action. This is why the CNV has been associated with an animal's expectancy, decision (Walter, 1964), motivation (Irwin et al., 1966), preparatory set (Low et al., 1966), and arousal (McAdam, 1969). The CNV has also been described as a conditionable wave. Thus far in the network theory, the incentive motivational pathway can be conditioned only indirectly when a cue acquires conditioned reinforcer properties that are reflected by that cue's growing ability to elicit incentive motivational signals. We will return to the question of whether incentives can be directly conditioned in Section 25.

24. An Emergent Neocortical Analog

We have now amassed enough empirical evidence to suggest some anatomical analogs of the wiring diagram in Figure 13 (Grossberg, 1978b). These analogs are suggested tentatively for several reasons. Most importantly, when the synchronization postulates are supplemented by new postulates, more processing stages will be imposed on the evolving network. Consequently, although anatomical interpretations of some network processing stages can be identified with reasonable assurance, the stages just before and after these stages have a more ambiguous anatomical interpretation. Also species-specific variations on network themes must be anticipated. Anatomical markers are nonetheless useful to facilitate comparison with neural data, and also to indicate that the formal network stages have plausible neural interpretations. Below two possible interpretations of Figure 13 will be suggested. Each interpretation leads to definite questions about cortical dynamics.

Both interpretations depend on identifying the second stages $v_{i2}^{(2)}$ of sensory processing with cortical pyramidal cells, which are the output cells of cerebral neocortex

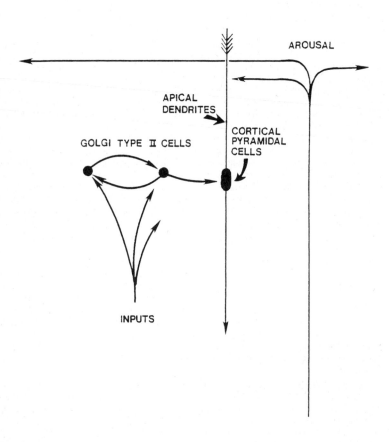

Figure 13. An interpretation of network dynamics in terms of nonspecific arousal afferents to the apical dendrites of cortical pyramidal cells, and CS-stimulated reverberation
of Golgi type-II interneurons whose output simulates the pyramidal cells.

(Shepherd, 1974; Sholl, 1956). The work of John (1966, 1967) on polyvalent cortical cells and of Walter (1964) on the CNV both suggest that we identify these polyvalent cells with cortical pyramidal cells. Given this interpretation, what are the cells subserving the other stages? The main difference between the two interpretations concerns the issue: Do the first sensory stages $v_{i1}^{(2)}$ occur in the cortex or not?

Suppose "yes." Then the cells which subserve STM storage at the first stage of the sensory representation are cortical interneurons. These interneurons are excited by cortical inputs, mutually excite each other, and send excitatory signals to pyramidal cells (Figure 14a). We identify these interneurons with Golgi Type II cells (Crosby et al., 1962; Peters et al., 1979). The pyramidal cells cannot fire unless they also receive arousal inputs that, following Walter (1964), are assumed to prime their apical dendrites (Figure 14b). The main source of ambiguity concerns another class of cortical output cells that would also have to exist. These are the output cells in the first stages of the sensory representations, which can fire to the drive representations even without incentive motivational support (Figure 14c). If all cortical output cells are pyramidal cells (Shepherd, 1974), then these pyramidal cells would differ both in their firing rules and their output targets from the pyramidal cells depicted in Figure 14a. Their output targets would be drive representations that are in, or associated with, the hypothalamic and hippocampal sites at which drive inputs are evaluated, as the results of Scott and Pfaffman (1967) and Valenstein et al. (1970), as well as numerous other investigators, suggest (Grossman, 1967; Haymaker et al., 1969; Olds, 1977; Swaab and Schadé, 1974). These outputs could be triggered by cortical inputs, supplemented perhaps by STM reverberation, but without the support of incentive motivational signals. Perhaps these output cells are small pyramidal cells whose dendrites abut the cortical input pathways and interneurons with close proximity. Since many pyramidal cells have apical dendrites that rise to the upper layers of the cortex, this anatomical interpretation will fail if all pyramidal cells can be shown to require nonspecific incentive motivational input to their apical dendrites before they can fire.

Two main points in this interpretation are useful even if it does not survive the test just described. First, the division of a sensory representation into two successive stages is not a mysterious anatomical notion. It can, for example, be realized as the distinction between interneurons and output cells. Second, the polyvalent rules for output cell firing suggest one reason why certain neural tissues, such as neocortex and hippocampus, receive inputs which are segregated into distinct lamina. By running the dendrites of output cells through these lamina, one can control which combination of inputs is needed to fire the cells. This is especially true if the output cells with larger cell bodies and axons also have larger dendritic trees. Then the output cells that can fire most directly to spinal centers will require convergence from more input sources, and thus a less ambiguous configuration of input data, to fire their larger cell bodies (Grossberg, 1978b).

The alternative anatomical interpretation is suggested by the possibility that cortical pyramids cannot be fired without incentive inputs to their apical dendrites. In species where this is true, the first stage of sensory representation would be represented at an anatomical level prior to the cortex, such as within a specific thalamic nucleus (Anderson and Eccles, 1953; Crosby et al., 1962; Gabriel et al., 1980; Grossman, 1967; Macchi and Rinvik, 1976; Tsumoto et al., 1978). Then the first sensory representation and its STM reverberation woud exist in the thalamus, from which ascending cortical projections and descending limbic projections (Figure 15a) would arise. The drive representations would again deliver input to apical dendrites of pyramidal cells, but now the problem of firing cortical outputs without simultaneous incentive motivational inputs is averted. Also, cortical interneurons could reverberate among themselves and feed their activity to pyramidal cells (Figure 15b), but these interneurons would no longer fire the first sensory representations, which no longer exist in the cortex.

These anatomical constraints can help students of thalamocortical dynamics to cor-

Chapter 1

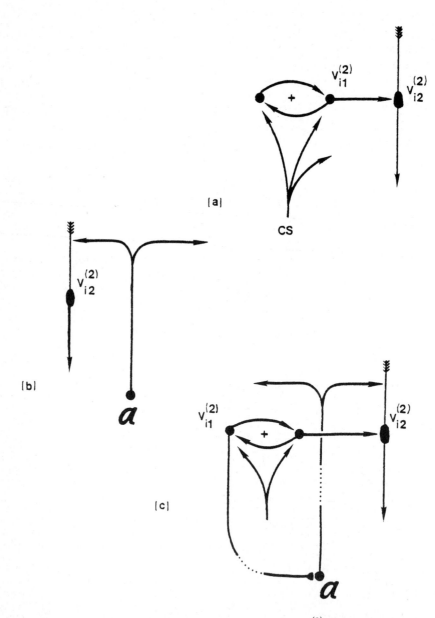

Figure 14. (a) CS inputs excite Golgi type-II interneurons at $v_{i1}^{(2)}$ which reverberate and excite the pyramidal cells $v_{i2}^{(2)}$. (b) The pyramidal cells also receive nonspecific arousal inputs from the drive representations. (c) If the STM-reverberation is intracortical, the nonpolyvalent cortical output cells exist which can sample the drive representations.

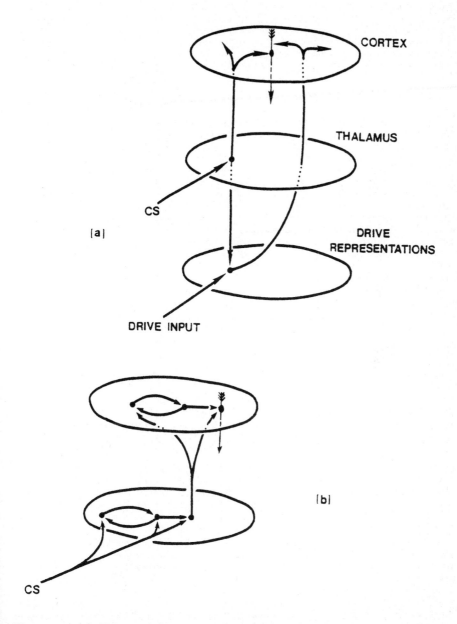

Figure 15. (a) CS input excites nonpolyvalent thalamic cells which send signals both to neocortex and drive representations. (b) Intrathalamic and/or cortical reverberatory interneurons are now distinct from the nonpolyvalent output cells $v_{i1}^{(2)}$.

relate a given species variation with the corresponding network variation without losing sight of the fact that the entire class of networks can compute qualitatively similar functional transformations. An experimental framework wherein these anatomical alternatives may be testable has been developed by Gabriel *et al.* (1980), who have studied stimulus-reinforcement contingencies that are controlled by hippocampal interactions with cingulate cortex and anteroventral nucleus of the thalamus.

25. Motivational Set: Is Incentive Motivation Conditionable?

Postulates (C) and (D) contain the main content of the synchronization problem and impose the basic network pathways with which we have been working. Once this formal framework is before us, it takes on a life of its own in two senses. First, it becomes clear that the network, as it stands, does not have certain important properties, but it is also easy to modify the network so that it does have these properties. Second, the overall structure of the network possesses a discernible symmetry. Improving this symmetry modifies the network so that it possesses new behavioral properties. The first and second procedures, moreover, both lead to the same modifications. Why are these modifications necessary? The answer is that there are other organizational principles than the synchronization problem at work *in vivo*. The synchronization problem fortunately implies enough network structure to force us into simple examples of these other principles, and in fact this was one route whereby the principles were discovered. This route is followed here because it is the most efficient way to derive mechanisms of reinforcement and attention. In Grossberg (1980a), these properties are derived from principles concerning the development of cognitive codes, which imply synchronization properties as a special case.

In Section 13, the symmetry properties of the network suggest that drive inputs exist. Postulate (F) gave this formal observation behavioral meaning by recognizing the need for a satiety mechanism. Now the symmetry properties suggest another network addition. The nonspecific conditioned reinforcer pathways from external cue representations to internal drive representations are conditionable. By contrast, the nonspecific incentive motivational pathways from internal drive representations to external cue representations are not. Should they be? Given the interpretation in Section 23 of the incentive motivational pathways as a CNV substrate, this question becomes: Can the CNV be directly conditioned? Are the apical dendrites of neocortical pyramidal cells the locus of this conditioning process?

If incentive motivation is conditionable, then we have at our disposal a mechanism for establishing a subliminal motivational set. After conditioning occurs, a CS could excite its drive representation via conditioned reinforcer signals. Then the internal drive representation could deliver incentive motivational signals preferentially to those external cue representations with which it was previously associated. In this way, activating a given external cue representation could sensitize an ensemble of motivationally related external cue representations via incentive motivational feedback. The sensitized representations form the subliminal motivational set.

The conditionability of incentive motivation is a necessary condition for avoiding some unpleasant behavioral properties. All of these properties are a result of the fact that incentive motivation is nonspecific. How can bad properties arise from this fact? We seemed to require that arousal be nonspecific to solve the synchronization problem in the first place (Section 5). I am not denying this basic insight. It implies, and I reaffirm, that nonspecific arousal inputs are all initially strong enough to fire polyvalent sensory cells when they converge with CS inputs. In other words, the LTM traces across the nonspecific arousal pathways are all strong enough to cause large gated signals in response to arousal inputs. Still otherwise expressed, the pattern of LTM traces across the nonspecific arousal pathways is initially quite uniform and each LTM pathway is viable. I now suggest that conditioning can change this uniform LTM pattern by differentially strengthening the LTM traces that abut these polyvalent representations at which CS signals and incentive signals simultaneously converge during learning trials.

The unpleasant properties include the following examples. Suppose that two conditioned reinforcers, CS_1 and CS_2, are turned on simultaneously. Let each reinforcer preferentially project to a different drive representation D_1 and D_2, respectively. Let the drive input to D_1 be zero but the drive input to D_2 be large. Also suppose that CS_2 has not been conditioned to a motor habit. Cue CS_1, by itself, could only activate the first stage of its sensory representation, since the drive input to D_1 is too small to release incentive motivation from D_1. Cue CS_2, by itself, could only elicit an internal emotional reaction compatible with its drive representation. By contrast, if both cues are presented and the incentive pathways are not conditionable, then CS_2 can motivate performance of CS_1's habit, because D_2 will deliver incentive signals nonspecifically to all polyvalent cells, including those which represent CS_1.

In another version of the same dilemma, CS_1 and CS_2 are both conditioned to motor habits, the drive input to D_1 is again zero whereas the drive input to D_2 is large, but the intensity of CS_1 is large whereas that of CS_2 is small. Since CS_2 delivers equal incentives to the polyvalent cells of CS_1 and CS_2, the habit corresponding to CS_1 is favored because of CS_1's larger intensity despite the occurrence of zero drive input to D_1.

Another unpleasant consequence of unconditionable incentive is this. When we consider language behavior, we will want to understand how an internal need, such as hunger, can initiate an external language communication like "I am hungry. What is there to eat?" This cannot be done in the present framework if the drive representations project uniformly to all cortical representations.

Consequently, I make the following postulate:

G. A given incentive can be associated with any of several external cue representations.

The minimal realization of postulate (G) is to suppose that incentive motivational signals are conditionable, and thus that subliminal motivational sets can be learned. This conclusion can be summarized in a fancier language that takes on important meaning when one studies the development of cognitive codes: conditioned reinforcer pathways and conditioned incentive motivational pathways are dual pathways in a network feedback module.

26. Distinct Cortical Recurrent Loops for STM and LTM

Each formal constraint on network design needs to be realized in a physically plausible way. In the present instance, we need to ask: How can incentives be conditioned in the cortical analogs of Figure 14? How can the arousal pathway to the apical dendrites of pyramidal cells be conditioned at times when the pyramidal cells fire? In particular, how do the synaptic contacts at the apical dendrites know when the pyramidal cell body is firing?

There exist two possible answers. One suggests that an intracellular conditioning pathway exists, and the other than an intercellular conditioning pathway exists. The intracellular answer posits that cell body firing activates antidromic action potentials, or other signals, that invade the dendritic tree and condition whatever apical dendrite synapses are active at the time (Figure 16a). The intercellular answer suggests that active pyramidal cell axons also excite recurrent axon collaterals. These collaterals activate interneurons that terminate at the arousal cell-apical dendrite synapses and cause a conditioned change via a shunting mechanism at those apical dendrite synapses which are active (Figure 16b).

Both of these mechanisms suggest that cortical conditioning is driven by the suprathreshold activity of the pyramidal cells. Subthreshold activity is insufficient. Moreover, both mechanisms include the pyramidal cell in excitatory recurrent interactions that

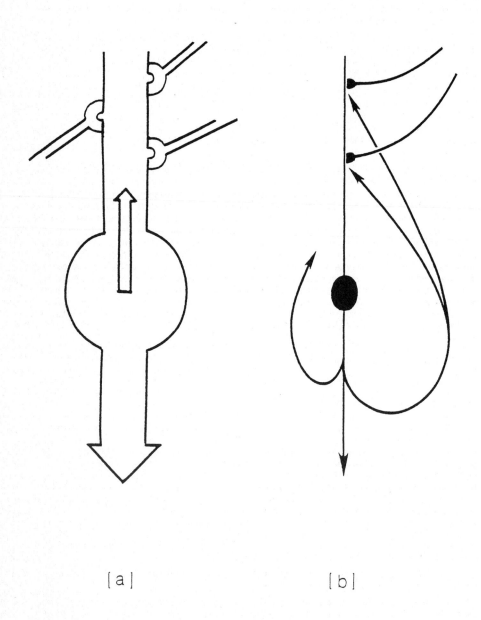

[a]   [b]

Figure 16. (a) Cell body spiking might trigger massive antidromic action potentials that drive post-synaptic conditioning effects of simultaneously active synapses. (b) Cell body spiking might activate feedback pathways which drive conditioning of simultaneously active synapses by a presynaptic gating action.

are prerequisites for LTM storage, and that are distinct from the excitatory recurrent interactions that subserve STM storage.

These observations lead to several experimental questions. Can the CNV be conditioned if the pyramidal cells are prevented from firing? Under what circumstances *in vivo* do antidromic action potentials invade apical dendrites? Do synapses of cortical interneurons terminate on the synaptic knobs or dendritic spines of extracortical afferents to the apical dendrites? Do these interneurons get activated by pyramidal cell axon collaterals?

27. Motivation-Dependent Responses to Sensory Cues: Multiple Sensory Representations or Developmental Competition for Synaptic Sites?

This section introduces a refinement of network design that satisfies another behavioral postulate in a minimal way.

In the network as it stands, once a sensory representation gains control over an incentive pathway and a habit, it cannot be used to learn another habit which is motivated by a different incentive pathway. For example, a visual cue at a choice point could elicit a left turn to get food, but it could not elicit a left turn to get food when hungry and a right turn to get food when thirsty. Of course, cues to the left or the right of the choice point could be preferentially associated with one or the other drive representation. Here we consider how a single cue could be differentially influenced by more than one drive. The issue of what cue combinations have internal representations will not be considered here. In Grossberg (1978b, Sections 25–47) I discuss how context-dependent internal representations, notably representations which are sensitive to particular sequences of events, can be generated. Herein I ask how any such representation can be differentially influenced by more than one drive. This property may not exist in all species.

The property in question can be achieved by allowing every sensory cue to be represented in several subregions each of which receives incentive pathways preferentially from a different drive representation. One way to do this is to let the sensory cues excite multiple sensory representations (Woolsey, 1958; Zeki, 1974) that are laid out in distinct network (e.g., cortical) regions. Another way is to suppose that, at the time when incentive pathways from the drive representations are developing, they compete with each other for synaptic space at each sensory representation, much as ocular dominance columns develop in the visual system (Hubel and Wiesel, 1977), or as corticostriatal terminals become fenestrated (Goldman-Rakic, 1981). As a result of this competition, the cells in each sensory representation will be parcelled out into cell groups which receive more incentive pathways from one drive representation than any other. Here multiple incentive sensory representations do not exist, but within each sensory representation the incentive pathways from different drive representations are clustered into distinguishable bundles. Looking over the entire cellular tissue, one would discern a patchwork quilt of overlapping sensory and drive sensitive areas. This configuration, should it exist, might be an evolutionary precursor of networks in which multiple sensory representations have been fully elaborated by a combination of synaptic competition abetted by a cell sorting process that segregates cells that become committed to particular drive representations into distinct sensory representations (Steinberg, 1970).

The behavioral constraint that yields this network refinement, where it exists, is summarized by the following postulate:

H. A discriminative cue can elicit distinct responses in different motivational contexts.

Multiple visual and auditory sensory representations are known to exist in vertebrate cerebral cortex (Woolsey, 1958; Zeki, 1974) but their relationship to drive-dependent response elaboration seems not to have been investigated. An effort should be made to study the patterns of axonal degeneration of drive representations in sensory areas and to correlate these patterns with that species' ability to discriminate cues in different motivational contexts. For example, what is the degeneration pattern of a drive region that supports enhanced self-stimulation when the animal is hungry? Sexually motivated?

28. Sensory-Drive Heterarchy: Competitive Decisions After Drives and Conditioned Reinforcers Interact

Typically, several external cues and drive representations are simultaneously active. How does the network decide which cues will be capable of eliciting observable behavior? What are the rules for parallel processing of cues? These general questions can be refined into a series of specialized issues which eventually force us to study new principles of network design. One of these principles leads to mechanisms whereby populations compete with each other (Grossberg, 1970b, 1973, 1980b). Sometimes the competition is organized in a feedforward anatomy (Figure 17a), but if the results of the competition are also stored in STM, a feedback anatomy is used (Figure 17b), whose feedback loops can store the pattern after its generating inputs terminate.

What keeps the network from simultaneously releasing two or more motivationally incompatible behaviors, such as eating and copulation? This question, phrased affirmatively, becomes our next postulate.

I. Motivationally incompatible behaviors compete.

Some form of competition between network channels is needed to sense the momentary balance of drives and available cues, and to decide which behavior is most appropriate at any time. Below a simple example of feedforward competition illustrates that this can be done. I will also indicate why feedforward competition is insufficient. It will then be shown that the anatomical stage at which competition acts must be carefully programmed in the network. If the competition occurs one synapse too soon, the network could not possibly survive.

To fix ideas, consider the following example of competition. Let n cell populations $v_1, v_2, \ldots, v_n$ be given and suppose that each population v_i is excited by a fluctuating input $I_i(t)$. Suppose that input $I_i(t)$ also inhibits all the populations v_k, $k \neq i$, with the same strength that it excites v_i. Let all the inputs, both excitatory and inhibitory, summate at each v_i, and let the activity $x_i(t)$ of v_i decay back to equilibrium at rate A when no inputs occur. Then

$$\frac{d}{dt} x_i = -Ax_i + J_i \qquad (8)$$

where J_i is the net input

$$J_i = I_i - \sum_{k \neq i} I_k \qquad (9)$$

to v_i. To see how the competition works, define the total input $I = \sum_{k=1}^{n} I_k$ and the relative input sizes $\theta_i = I_i I^{-1}$. Since each $I_i(t)$ can fluctuate wildly through time, so too can $I(t)$ and each $\theta_i(t)$. However, each J_i can be written as

$$J_i = 2I_i - I \qquad (10)$$

which is the same as

$$J_i = 2I(\theta_i - 1/2). \qquad (11)$$

Since the θ_i's sum up to 1, at most one θ_i can exceed $1/2$ at any time. By (11), at most one J_i can be positive at any time. By (8), the v_i corresponding to this J_i is excited, whereas all other v_j are inhibited. Thus no matter how wildly the inputs fluctuate, the competition uses a majority rule to choose a definite winner at any time. The mechanism in (8) and (9) is called an additive feedforward on-center (excite v_i) off-surround (inhibit all v_k, $k \neq i$) network.

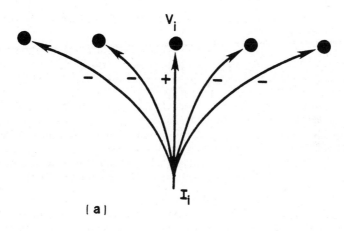

[a]

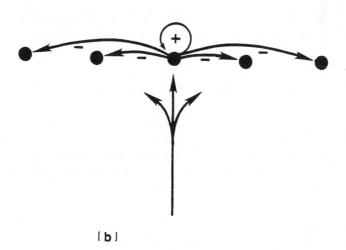

[b]

Figure 17. In (a), a feedforward on-center/off-surround network allows input to compete before generating outputs. In (b), a feedback competition allows the winning populations to have their activities stored in STM.

Not all networks of this type will perform a simple majority rule computation. For example, in the network

$$\frac{d}{dt}x_i = -Ax_i + I_i - \sum_{k=1}^{n} I_k B_{ki},\qquad(12)$$

the net inhibition of v_i by I_k is $I_k B_{ki}$, where B_{ki} measures the strength of the (k,i)th inhibitory pathway. The B_{ki} can easily be chosen so that more than one v_i can be excited at any time. Majority rule competition occurs if the inhibitory signals of the off-surround are broadly distributed across the field of populations.

These details are not our main concern now. The reader can, however, readily notice several basic deficiencies of majority rule competition, and more generally of feedforward competitive laws. For example, what happens if no θ_i exceeds $1/2$? Does the network simply do nothing? How can a network be designed that can retune its own sensitivity until a winning channel is found? What happens if the conditioned reinforcer inputs fluctuate very quickly? Does the motivational baseline also fluctuate because each J_i does? How can fluctuating cue and drive inputs be translated into a steady motivational baseline during the performance of each motivated act? What if inputs fluctuate so fast that J_i switches from positive to negative before its act can be performed? How can enough inertia be built into the competition to permit an act to be performed before motivation switches to another incentive channel? These are the types of crucial questions that can only be answered by mathematical analysis, because they all depend on surprising properties of competition to feedback networks (Grossberg, 1973, 1975, 1981b, 1982a, 1982b, 1984).

For now, we content ourselves with considering the following question. At what stage of network processing does the competition act? There are two main alternatives, and one of them leads to disaster.

The first alternative allows the drives to compete among themselves before they are acted upon by conditioned reinforcers (Figure 18a). The second alternative lets drive inputs interact with conditioned reinforcer inputs at the drive representations before the drive representations compete among themselves (Figure 18b). The first alternative is called a drive hierarchy and the second alternative is called a sensory-drive heterarchy for the following reason.

In a drive hierarchy, only the largest, or prepotent, drive can deliver a positive input to its drive representation. If no external cue is present that is compatible with this drive, then no incentive motivation can be released. The disaster is this. Even if external cues are available that are compatible with large, but nonprepotent, drive inputs, none of these cues can trigger observable behavior.

The sensory-drive heterarchy overcomes this dilemma. Here any drive representation can fire if it receives conditioned reinforcer and drive inputs. Then the active drive representations compete among themselves to decide which one will release incentive motivation. If no external cues compatible with the prepotent drive are available, then its drive representation does not fire, so it does not prevent a drive representation with a smaller drive input from winning the competition. Moreover, if two drive representations D_1 and D_2 both receive positive drive inputs D_1 and D_2, respectively, such that $D_1 > D_2$, nonetheless D_2 can win the competition if its conditioned reinforcers are more active than those of D_1. In all, the sensory-drive heterarchy computes which combination of available cues and drives is dominant at any moment, not just which drive is dominant at any moment.

To illustrate the heterarchical concept, I will describe some rules that simplify real-time computations which occur in competitive feedback networks. To start, let us suppose that drive inputs D_i and conditioned reinforcer inputs S_i combine multiplicatively at D_i. This rule can be interpreted in several ways. It formally says that both

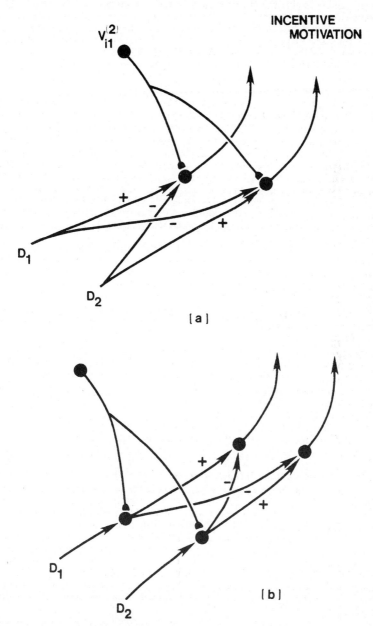

Figure 18. In (a), a drive hierarchy prevents incentive motivation from being released except by the prepotent drive. In (b), a non-prepotent drive input can elicit incentive motivation if it is augmented by sufficiently strong conditioned reinforcer inputs.

factors are needed to fire D_i. It can be physiologically interpreted by saying that drive inputs sensitize drive representations to conditioned reinforcer inputs, or that drive inputs gate conditioned reinforcer inputs. Although we formally write products like $S_i D_i$ below, in a finer physiological description, cues and drives do not play a symmetric role. A simple version of the heterarchical idea is the rule: D_i fires only if

$$S_i D_i > \max(\epsilon, S_k D_k : k \neq i) \tag{13}$$

where ϵ is a threshold that must be attained before any drive representation can fire. By (13), only one drive representation can fire at any time; namely, that D_i whose gated cue inputs $S_i D_i$ are maximal. This law builds some temporal stability into the delivery of incentive motivation, since inequality (13) can persevere throughout a time interval during which the individual cue signals S_j are fluctuating wildly. The simplest law whereby a stable baseline of motivation is also achieved follows readily from (13). Let $x_i(t)$ be the activity of D_i at time t. Suppose that all the drive representations remain inactive, or at best subliminally active, until (13) holds at some D_i. Then x_i is rapidly amplified by feedback competitive interactions until it attains the value $B > 0$, which is the suprathreshold motivational baseline. All other x_j are quickly driven to zero by the recurrent competition, and these motivational values are then stored in STM while (13) holds. In mathematical terms,

$$x_i = \begin{cases} B & \text{if } S_i D_i > \max(\epsilon, S_k D_k : k \neq i), \\ 0 & \text{otherwise.} \end{cases} \tag{14}$$

The rule (14) is the simplest law that builds some temporal stability and a motivational baseline into the heterarchical computation. This rule also overcomes a disadvantage of majority rule competition: Just so long as some $S_i D_i$ exceeds the threshold ϵ, which can be a small parameter or even zero, a motivational choice is made, and one drive representation achieves the baseline value B. Figure 19 schematizes an anatomy that can compute this competitive rule.

The performance of a competitive feedback network is more complex than equation (14). For example, such networks can maintain any of a finite, or infinite, set of operating levels even after their inputs are shut off (Grossberg, 1973, 1978c, 1980a, 1980b). The inputs can determine, by their own size, which operating level will be chosen. Moreover, inputs that are left on can modify the network's possible operating levels. These subtleties will not be needed to draw our main conclusions.

Even the rule (14) is deceptively simple, because S_i is the net effect of all conditioned reinforcers on D_i. If $I_m b_{mi}$ is the output from the mth sensory representation $v_{mi}^{(2)}$ to D_i, and z_{mi} is the LTM trace in the pathway from $v_{mi}^{(2)}$ to D_i, then

$$S_i = \sum_{m=1}^{n} I_m b_{mi} z_{mi}. \tag{15}$$

Substituting (15) into (14) yields

$$x_i = \begin{cases} B & \text{if } \sum_{m=1}^{n} I_m D_i b_{mi} z_{mi} > \max(\epsilon, \sum_{m=1}^{n} I_m D_k b_{mk} z_{mk} : k \neq i), \\ 0 & \text{otherwise.} \end{cases} \tag{16}$$

Moreover, z_{mi} summarizes the entire reinforcement history between the mth internal representation $v_{m1}^{(2)}$ and D_i by correlating all past occurrences of I_m and x_i. The simplest such law (Grossberg, 1964, 1968, 1971b, 1972a) says that z_{mi} computes a time-average,

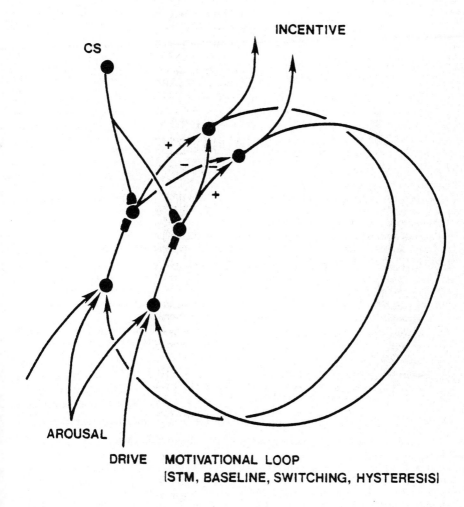

Figure 19. A feedback competitive network whose signals are modulated by slow transmitter gates can maintain a steady motivational baseline, and can switch between motivational channels in response to sufficiently large changes in conditioned reinforcer, drive, or arousal inputs.

with constant decay rate c, of the product of signal I_m and postsynaptic potential x_i. Then

$$\frac{d}{dt} z_{mi} = -c z_{mi} + d_{mi} I_m x_i \qquad (17)$$

which is the same as

$$z_{mi}(t) = z_{mi}(0) e^{-ct} + d_{mi} \int_0^t e^{-c(t-v)} I_m(v) x_i(v) dv. \qquad (18)$$

Equations (16) and (18) together summarize the simplest heterarchical computation. These equations illustrate how an animal's present decisions, as in (16), can reflect all of its past reinforcement, drive, and motivational history, as in (18). In particular, z_{mi} in (18) correlates I_m with x_i, where I_m connotes the momentary strength of a CS or UCS input, and x_i connotes the momentary strength of a motivational variable that is determined by all the present drives and cues, as well as all the prior drives and cues that ever influenced the network. Thus the conditioned reinforcer LTM traces feed upon themselves: They guide the present motivational decision, which is thereupon sampled and alters their LTM values. Perhaps the most important thing to keep in mind about (16) and (18) is not all the subtleties of these feedback effects, but rather that the formalism summarizes so much subtlety in just two equations.

The heterarchical concept elegantly explains how an animal's observable behavior can seem to be unrelated to a specific drive until an appropriate releasing cue is presented (Bolles, 1967): A high drive D_i can occur while $x_i = 0$ if another drive representation D_j wins the heterarchical competition. The heterarchical concept also clarifies some differential effects of parametric changes in drive and reinforcement on learning rate versus performance speed in the following way.

29. Differential Effects of Drive and Reinforcement on Learning Rate versus Performance Speed

An increase in drive level can affect the probability that a rat will run down an alley to be rewarded, its reaction time to run, and the vigor of the running response (Estes, 1958; Mackintosh, 1974). In particular, increasing drive decreases the likelihood that the rat will indulge in competing behaviors (Cotton, 1953). This fact can induce a complex interaction between drives and learning, since an animal who runs only a little before competing responses interfere can learn a different response series than an animal who continues running down the alley (Bolles, 1967; Campbell and Kraeling, 1953). If these momentary effects of drive on performance are synthesized into a behavioral plan, then different running responses can be engendered on later trials, even if the drive level is changed.

To see how drive can alter probability and reaction time of running, consider (16). In (16), an increase of D_i increases the probability that, and decreases the reaction time with which, D_i will win the heterarchical competition. Once D_i wins, $x_i = B$ no matter how large D_i is. In other words, increasing D_i can reduce the reaction time and increase the probability of running, but not necessarily alter the motivational baseline that supports the running response. To understand how the motivational level and the induced running speed can depend on drive input and conditioned reinforcer input size, one needs to study the operating levels B of competitive feedback networks in some detail. This study will not be given here. Instead, I will indicate how the simplest heterarchical rules help to explain various other data to lend further support to the heterarchical concept.

The following paradoxical finding can, for example, be explained. Animals that are trained on high drive can maintain their high drive performance characteristics when they are switched to low drive (Capaldi, 1971; Mackintosh, 1974; Zaretsky, 1966), but not conversely (Bolles, 1967; Desse and Carpenter, 1951). The perseverative effect of high drive performance during low drive suggests that high drive influences performance through a learned effect. Analogously, a large value of D_i in (16) on learning trials increases the probability that x_i wins the competition. By (18), those LTM traces z_{mi} with active cues I_m will attain large values. These cues thereupon enjoy powerful conditioned reinforcer properties which can motivate the animal to run. On low drive trials, these cues are still available, their inputs I_m are still large, and they are still gated by large z_{mi} values that were learned under high drive. Consequently the gated inputs $I_m z_{mi}$ remain large after the switch to low drive trials. Suppose that D_i is decreased, but is large enough for D_i, with the help of large terms $I_m z_{mi}$, to still reliably win the heterarchical competition. Then the high drive performance level will persist into the low drive situation because it is bolstered by conditioned reinforcer inputs. If D_i can regularly win the competition in this way, then the LTM traces z_{mi} continue to be boosted on low drive trials if they follow high drive trials. The converse transition, from low drive to high drive, does not show persistence. For example, given low drive levels at the outset, D_i cannot reliably win the competition, so little learning occurs. An increase of drive then rapidly causes a higher performance level to occur because it directly changes the competitive balance.

Amount of reinforcement can influence rate of learning as well as asymptotic learning speed (Mackintosh, 1974). Moreover, a change in reinforcement level from high to low, or conversely, can quickly change the animal's response rate (Crespi, 1942; Mackintosh, 1974; Zeaman, 1949) by contrast with the effects of changing drive level.

Why do parametric changes in drive and reinforcement level have different effects on performance? Several factors can work together to produce these properties. One such factor is the following. A large reinforcement on each trial creates a large cue input I_m. The cue input directly excites the polyvalent sensory cells, unlike drive inputs, as well as indirectly exciting the polyvalent sensory cells via incentive feedback to these cells. The larger reinforcer's cue properties hereby increase the readout of its habit on a moment-by-moment basis. Consequently, a sudden change in reinforcer level can cause rapid performance changes, even if the motivational feedback itself has only one suprathreshold level. Ths explanation of reinforcer effects depends on the existence of variable I_m values. Changes in reinforcement that do not change I_m do not have these properties. For example, an increased concentration of sucrose or saccharin in a liquid reward reliably has these effects.

Reinforcer effects can also be influenced by the action of disconfirmed expectancies. To illustrate this possibility, I will use properties that are discussed in Sections 32–34, below. These remarks can be skipped on a first reading.

An animal who expects a high probability of reinforcement can experience a negative incentive motivational rebound on a trial during which an expected reward does not occur because the reinforcement probability has been reduced (Grossberg, 1972c, 1975). The rebound has the same effect as an increase in negative drive input even though no change in internal drive has occurred. The rebound can hereby rapidly reduce the net motivational support for the behavior and reduce the animal's response rate. In a similar fashion, when a low probability of reinforcement is expected, a positive incentive motivational rebound can supplement direct consummatory inputs on a trial when the animal is unexpectedly rewarded due to an increase in reinforcement probability. A rapid increase in motivational support is hereby achieved. Transient overshoots in incentive motivational outputs can hereby occur due to unexpected changes in reinforcing events. These transients can reflect themselves in transient behavioral contrast effects (Mackintosh, 1974). Sustained behavioral contrast effects can be produced after the transient effects are encoded in LTM by the conditioned reinforcer and incentive motivational pathways. This analysis differs from the one that Hull (1952) and Spence (1956) gave to explain these effects. These authors assumed that reinforcement decrement directly influences incentive level. I claim that the direct effects are specific cue effects, including a lower probability of winning the heterarchical competition if the reinforcement decrement is sufficiently large. Indirect effects include rebound effects that are triggered by rapid changes in cue level or by unexpected events.

30. Drives and Reinforcers: Multiplicative, Additive, or Neither?

Hull (1952) claimed that reinforcement and drive interact multiplicatively, whereas Spence (1956) claimed that they are independent, or interact additively. Experiments to test this distinction have tended to yield mixed results. Some experiments suggest additivity (Reynolds and Pavlik, 1960; Pavlik and Reynolds, 1963). If either the drive level or the reinforcement level is assigned a very low value, however, a significant multiplicative interaction is found (Seward et $al.$, 1958; Seward et $al.$, 1960).

The rule (16) sheds some light on this controversy. In (16), drives D_i and cues S_i do interact multiplicatively. However, the competitive law also contains additive elements. For example, given a fixed S_i level, the competition computes whether $D_i \leq \epsilon S_i^{-1}$, which is an additive effect. Similarly given a fixed level D_i, the competition computes whether $S_i \geq \epsilon D_i^{-1}$, which is again an additive effect. Moreover, given fixed levels S_i and S_j, the competition computes the sign of $S_i D_i - S_j D_j$, which is a linear combination of D_i and D_j, again an additive effect. The same is true if D_i and D_j are fixed while S_i and S_j vary. Both additive and multiplicative elements enter the heterarchical computation. The multiplicative effects are rate-limiting at very small values of S_i and/or D_i, since no matter how large S_i is, if $D_i \simeq 0$ it follows that $S_i D_i \simeq 0 < \epsilon$, and no matter how large D_i is, if $S_i \simeq 0$ it follows that $S_i D_i \simeq 0 < \epsilon$.

A final comment on the motivational baseline is in order. The existence of such a baseline illustrates how a recurrent network can store an activity level in STM despite the existence of sufficiently small temporal perturbations in its inputs. This is not, however, all the recurrent networks can do. Their overall operating levels can be influenced by the size of specific inputs as well as by nonspecific shunting interactions, so that in $vivo$ the motivational level need not be constant through time. Our main point has been that these operating levels can defend themselves against momentary fluctuations in cues or drives until a hysteresis boundary is reached, after which a switch to a new level can be rapidly effected.

31. Suppression by Punishment

The discussion thus far has focused on how an animal can learn consummatory behavior. It has not considered how an animal can rapidly modify or terminate consummatory behavior when changing environmental contingencies render the behavior maladaptive. In particular, we have not considered how an aversive cue can suppress behavior. Nor have we considered how the nonoccurrence of an expected consummatory goal object can suppress behavior. Now the minimal mechanisms of aversive conditioning, whether by punishment or frustration, will be reviewed. I will conclude that the mechanism whereby a punishing event suppresses behavior, via classical conditioning, automatically possesses properties which enable the unexpected nonoccurrence of a desired goal object to extinguish behavior, via instrumental conditioning. This important fact, which sets my theory apart from other efforts to model reinforced behavior, follows from the gating properties of chemical transmitters in competitive anatomies (Grossberg, 1972c, 1981a, 1982a, 1982b, 1984).

Many experiments about punishment and avoidance are thoroughly reviewed elsewhere (Bolles, 1969; Dunham, 1971; Estes, 1969; Grossberg, 1972b, 1975; Mackintosh, 1974; Pearce and Hall, 1980). A basic theme running through this literature elaborates the fact that punishment can suppress goal-oriented behavior without extinguishing knowledge of the goal. Here, I will only be interested in showing how a punishment and avoidance mechanism easily flows from the ideas which are already at our disposal.

Various subtle conditioning properties—such as self-punitive behavior, overshadowing, superconditioning, learned helplessness, peak shift and behavioral contrast, partial reinforcement acquisition effect and novelty as a reinforcer—have elsewhere been derived as properties of the mechanisms in prescribed input environments (Grossberg, 1972b, 1972c, 1975, 1981a, 1982a, 1984).

Our point of departure is the fact that CS-activated sampling cells are polyvalent (Section 5). This fact is a double-edged sword. It prevents the sampling cells from firing unless they simultaneously receive specific cue input and nonspecific arousal inputs. But it also forces the sampling cells to fire when these input conditions are achieved. Without additional network structure, these polyvalent cells must fire at disastrously unappropriate times as environmental contingencies change.

In particular, suppose that a cue CS_1 has been conditioned to a positive incentive motivational source and to a prescribed motor habit. Then whenever the drive subserving the motivational source is high, presentation of the cue will elicit the behavior because the polyvalent cells in its representation receive convergent specific and nonspecific inputs. This behavior will continue to occur no matter how unappropriate its consequences have become; e.g., if pressing a lever in response to the cue lever now elicits shock instead of food.

Some mechanism is needed to stop behavior that prior contingencies have started. In a theoretical vacuum, this factual triviality is not very constraining on possible theories. It becomes highly constraining, however, when it is recast as a formal design within the networks that have already been derived. We therefore ask: How can the polyvalent cells be prevented from firing? Can this be done such that the mechanisms for starting versus stopping behavior are symmetric?

A dual side of this issue exists. It is the following issue: Suppose that a mechanism for stopping unappropriate behavior can be found. What prevents this mechanism from stopping all future behavior? How can more appropriate behavior be selected despite the suppressive effects of this mechanism? For example, while an aversive cue is on, such as an intense shock, an animal might emit many erroneous escape behaviors before a random act succeeds in terminating the aversive cue. How can the correct escape act be learned despite the fact that the prior errors are not learned?

This observation can be rephrased as a postulate.

J^-. Onset of an aversive event can suppress new reinforced learning.

J^+. Offset of an aversive event can trigger new reinforced learning.

We ask for the minimal change in network design that can realize postulate (J^-). First we note that a change of LTM habit strengths in the pathways from sensory to motor representations cannot suffice for the following reasons:

(1) *Passive extinction*. If cell firing is prevented in these pathways for a long time, then the LTM traces might slowly decay. However, this process takes too long to prevent postulate (J^-) from being violated. Also there exist variations of the LTM law (17) in which no passive extinction occurs; for example, laws such as

$$\frac{d}{dt}z_{mi} = I_m d_{mi}(-z_{mi} + x_i) \qquad (19)$$

wherein offset of the sampling signal $I_m d_{mi}$ from population v_m to v_i shuts off the rate of change dz_{mi}/dt of the LTM trace z_{mi}. Even where passive decay is possible, it can be retarded or reversed if recall trials intermittently occur while the animal is hungry. Then positive incentive motivational feedback can fire the sampling cells and thereby refresh, or restore, suprathreshold LTM levels via post-tetanic potentiation (Grossberg, 1969c).

(2) *Interfering habit*. Another possible way to disrupt the habit strength LTM traces is to suppose that the aversive event (e.g., shock) directly generates a motor command

at the motor representations which interferes with the command read-out via the habit strengths. As the cue representations sample this new command, their habit strengths can encode it in LTM, rather than the previous consummatory command.

This mechanism also suffers from severe flaws. First, the network cannot learn specific avoidance tasks, since the shock stimulus rather than a specific avoidance response maintains the new motor command. Second, the network remains conditioned to the old drive representation, say a hunger representation. It can thus indulge in autonomic preparations for eating without being able to eat. Finally, the network remains maladaptively fearless, since only positive consummatory drives are conditional to external cues. The fearful meaning of the aversive event is nowhere represented in the network.

A mechanism is needed which can rapidly react to an aversive cue; viz., an STM mechanism. Since fast changes in motor commands do not suffice, we must consider fast changes due to the cue and drive properties of aversive events. These STM changes must be capable of driving slower LTM changes in conditioned reinforcer and incentive motivational pathways that can encode adaptive behavioral modifications.

The minimal drive property of an aversive event will now be introduced (Grossberg, 1972b, 1972c). Let shock create an input at its own drive representation D_f. Let this input be a monotone increasing function of shock intensity. Suppose that D_f can elicit signals which inhibit the positive incentive motivational outputs of positive drive representations. Also suppose that cue representations send conditional pathways to D_f as well as to the other drive representations (Figure 20). Six important conclusions follow from this simple construction. (i) An intense shock can rapidly suppress consummatory behavior by inhibiting the motivating effects of positive reinforcers. The polyvalent sampling cells are hereby prevented from firing even when the first stages of their internal representations are firing. (ii) This suppression does not extinguish the LTM of the habits that are already encoded in the motor commands. It merely prevents these habits from being read out by polyvalent cell signals during unappropriate circumstances. (iii) This type of suppression can occur much faster than passive extinction of LTM traces. (iv) An intense shock can also prevent new habits from being learned by inhibiting release of sampling signals from polyvalent cells. (v) If an external cue is present only when the shock is on, its internal representation can learn a strong LTM connection to the A_f drive representation even though its polyvalent cells cannot fire. On later trials, onset of this cue can hereby elicit the suppressive (and emotional) effects of shock in the absence of shock. The cue hereby becomes a CS^+ that elicits a conditioned emotional response (Estes and Skinner, 1941). (vi) If a cue which has previously been conditioned to a positive motivational source remains on while shock is on, its LTM trace to the A_f drive representation can grow. Eventually, the cue's gated signals to the consummatory and A_f representations can become approximately equal, or the signal to A_f might even be larger. After the output from these drive representations compete, the cue's net motivational effect on polyvalent sampling cells approaches zero, or a negative value. The cue's ability to motivate consummatory behavior has hereby been extinguished by competing signals from the A_f representation even if it continues to elicit a large conditioned output from the consummatory drive representation.

32. Antagonistic Rebound and Learned Avoidance

To deal with postulate (J^+), we must again face the rigid law which governs polyvalent cell firing. When a shock input terminates, the input to A_f terminates. This event eliminates the direct source of suppression due to the shock. When this happens, the motor command (e.g., the lever press) which terminated the shock is active in STM, and the sensory feedback cues contingent upon this command (e.g., looking at the lever) have activated their internal representations. How can associative links between these active sensory and motor representations be learned? What motivational source enables the polyvalent cells of the sensory feedback cues to release sampling signals?

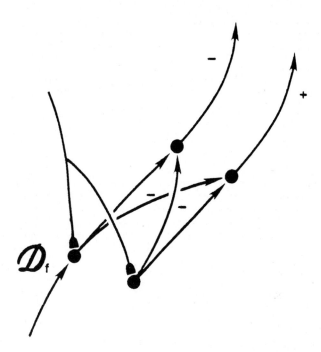

Figure 20. When a drive representation whose activation is associated with the emotion of fear is included in the network and given negative incentive motivational properties, it helps to explain many properties of conditioned emotional responses.

What motivational source is sampled by the sensory feedback cues to endow them with conditioned reinforcer properties?

Our main dilemma is that offset of shock removes a source of negative input from the polyvalent cells' motivation. We need more, however, to fire a polyvalent cell. We need a source of positive motivation that is triggered by the offset of shock. This positive motivational source must be on only transiently after shock turns off. If it were on permanently, it could be used to motivate behaviorally irrelevant sensory-motor associations.

We therefore conclude that another arousal source exists. Speaking heuristically, this new arousal source supplies the motivational support for learning an avoidance response. Its activity is correlated with the internally perceived relief that can occur after offset of a fearful cue under appropriate experimental conditions (Denny, 1971; Masterson, 1970; Reynierse and Rizley, 1970).

Let us introduce a symmetric notation to highlight the relationship between the fear and relief representations. Denote by D_f^- the arousal cells that are excited by termination of shock input at the cells D_f, which we henceforth denote by D_f^+. The D_f^+ cells are "on" cells. They are turned on by shock, and remain on until shock is turned off. The cells D_f^- are "off" cells. They are turned on temporarily by shock termination. On-cells and off-cells are familiar physiological components (Thompson, 1967, pp. 253, 349). Our theoretical task is to understand well enough how these components are designed to derive quantitative predictions about them.

The on-cells and off-cells are assumed to reciprocally inhibit each other to generate an incentive motivational output corresponding to fear, or to relief, but not both simultaneously.

The operation whereby offset of shock can elicit transient relief is called *antagonistic rebound*. The classical notion that instrumental reinforcement is due to drive reduction when shock terminates is replaced by rebound from negative-incentive motivational on-cells to positive-incentive motivational off-cells. Similarly, offset of a positive-incentive motivational on-cell can generates a negative-incentive motivational off-rebound, as when a food source is suddenly withdrawn, even if no reduction of hunger drive has occurred.

At this point, we are very close to understanding the *gated dipole* mechanism on which all the more advanced properties of reinforcement, motivation, and expectational processes of the theory depend. This and the next section will sketch a few qualitative properties of the rebound concept which need no mathematics to be understood, and will motivate the derivation of the gated dipole theory.

The network must be expanded once again to allow cues to become conditioned to the new arousal source (Figure 21). Thus each sensory representation now sends pathways (axons) to D_f^- as well as to D_f^+ and other arousal sources, such as the hunger representation D_h. At any time, the synaptic knobs of each cue representation encode in their LTM traces a spatial pattern which represents a weighted average through time of all the motivational activities that the representation sampled while it was active. The net motivational output to polyvalent cells is determined by the inputs from all drive and cue representations. Even if half the cues send large conditioned signals to D_f^-, no positive incentive will be generated if the other half of the cues send equally large conditioned cues to D_f^+. The competition between drive representations will annihilate these large inputs before an output can be elicited. Similarly, shock termination yields little relief via antagonistic rebound if it is accompanied by onset of a conditioned aversive cue, as in a two-way shuttle box. Even shock termination is not necessarily rewarding in all environmental contexts. For the purpose of deriving the rebound mechanism, the section considers the simple case wherein a single aversive cue is turned on and off through time.

33. Slowly Accumulating Transmitter Gates in Tonically Aroused Competing Channels Cause Antagonistic Rebound

The heuristic argument leading to the dipole theory can be divided into eight steps.

(1) *Existence of a tonic input.* When shock terminates, the relief center D_f^- can emit a transient output. What input energizes this output? Offset of a shock input merely removes input activity. Some other input source must energize the relief rebound.

Since shock offset is the only change in external input, the input that energizes relief must be internally generated. Terminating shock somehow unmasks the effects of this internal input. The internal input to D_f^- is therefore not turned on or off by shock offset. It is also not turned off by shock onset, since then it would always be off. The internal input is therefore on throughout the learning experiment. It is a *tonic input*.

(2) *Existence of accumulation-depletion.* Output from the relief center is always transient. How is this accomplished? No externally driven input is available to accomplish this. The relief output is somehow depleted by its own activity. In other words, when shock is on, an accumulation process occurs in the relief center. After shock is

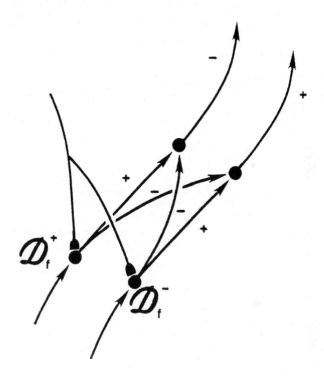

Figure 21. A gated dipole in which fear and relief drive representations compete helps to explain various data about the balance between positive and negative reinforcement and extinction.

turned off, the relief output is an increasing function of the amount accumulated at each time. This amount is gradually depleted until the relief output shuts off.

(3) *Competition between fear and relief.* We suppose that at most one of the outputs from D_f^+ to D_f^- is nonzero at any time. In other words, either fear or relief, but not both, can be experienced by the network at any given time. Thus the final state of processing in D_f^+ and D_f^-, before incentive motivational outputs are generated, is due to competition, or mutual inhibition, of the D_f^+ and D_f^- signals.

(4) *Existence of nonspecific accumulation-depletion in both channels.* When shock is off for a long time, outputs from both D_f^+ and D_f^- are zero. Thus the accumulation process at D_f^-, driven by its tonic input, is balanced by a process going on at D_f^+. The simplest idea is that a parallel process of accumulation-depletion, driven by its own tonic input that equals that D_f^- tonic input, takes place in the fear channel. In particular, the tonic input is delivered nonspecifically to both channels. It is therefore called a *nonspecific arousal* input. When shock is turned on, the shock input summates with the tonic input in the fear channel.

(5) *The rebound is slow.* It lasts at least seconds rather than milliseconds. It is a slow process compared to the fluctuation rates of cell potentials in response to input changes. After shock terminates, neither the fear nor the relief channel receives an externally driven input. Without an additional mechanism at work, their outputs would rapidly equalize, but they do not. Thus there exists a process slower than potential fluctuations that can bias output from D_f^+ and D_f^- in favor of D_f^- after shock terminates.

(6) *Both fear and relief are increasing functions of shock duration and intensity.* Both increasing duration (Annau and Kamin, 1961; Boe, 1966; Borozci *et al.*, 1964; Church *et al.*, 1967; Keehn, 1963; Strouthes, 1965) and intensity (Annau and Kamin, 1961; Boren *et al.*, 1959; D'Amato *et al.*, 1967; Huff *et al.*, 1967; Johnson and Church, 1965; Kamin *et al.*, 1963; Martin and Reiss, 1969; Reiss, 1970) can influence the strength of conditioned emotional responses and conditioned avoidance responses. These results suggest that both channels contain slowly varying processes which parametrically depend on shock intensity and duration when shock is on, and which counterbalance each other when shock is off for long intervals.

(7) *The relative balance of accumulation is changed by shock.* What causes the relief rebound to shut itself off? Is complete depletion of the accumulated product at D_f^- responsible for this property? Were this the case, then the tonic input alone could deplete D_f^-, since it is the only input to D_f^-. By symmetry, during shock, the shock input plus the tonic input could surely deplete D_f^-. This does not occur, however, since the fear reaction is maintained by a long shock. A weaker conclusion is therefore necessary. Shock shifts the relative balance of accumulation in the two channels by depleting the fear channel more than the relief channel.

(8) *Signal size is a joint function of input size and amount accumulated.* This observation is crucial. During a relief rebound, both D_f^+ and D_f^- receive equal arousal inputs which ultimately balance the amounts accumulated by D_f^+ and D_f^-, and thereby shut off incentive outputs. Before this can happen, D_f^- output exceeds D_f^+ output because D_f^- accumulation exceeds D_f^+ accumulation. In other words, given a fixed input size (the equal arousal inputs to D_f^+ and D_f^-), output is an *increasing* function of amount accumulated. This is true in each of the two channels.

When shock is on, increasing shock intensity increases D_f^+ output, since it causes an increase in fear. Increasing shock intensity also *decreases* the amount accumulated at D_f^+; this is the basis of rebound at D_f^- when shock is turned off. Thus output is not a function of accumulation level alone, since then increasing shock intensity would have decreased D_f^+ output by decreasing the amount accumulated at D_f^+. Output size is a joint function of input size (a fast variable) and accumulation level (a slow variable).

These arguments are sufficiently constraining to be capable of reducing our theory to rubble. When they were first made in Grossberg (1972c), however, it was already apparent that the theory could quantitatively realize their demands with no difficulty. This was because the necessary laws had already been derived from associative learning postulates in Grossberg (1968, 1969c). For completeness, I review the simplest version of the transmitter gating rules that are needed to understand gated dipole dynamics. More detailed derivations and analyses of these laws are found in Grossberg (1980a, 1981a, 1982a).

The simplest law whereby a chemical transmitter z gates an input signal S to yield an output signal T is

$$T = Sz, \tag{20}$$

where $z(t)$ obeys an accumulation-depletion law of the form

$$\frac{dz}{dt} = A(B - z) - T.$$ (21)

That this law satisfies the basic requirement (8) is easily seen. Simply solve for the steady-state output T_∞ in response to a constant input $S = S_0$ by setting $dz/dt = 0$ in (21). The steady-state transmitter level z_∞ is

$$z_\infty = \frac{AB}{A + S_0}$$ (22)

and the output is

$$T_\infty = S_0 z_\infty = \frac{ABS_0}{A + S_0}.$$ (23)

As desired, z is a slow accumulation-depletion variable which, by (22), *decreases* as S_0 increases; yet the output T *increases* as S_0 increases because T is a joint function of the input S and the accumulation-depletion variable z. When slowly accumulating transmitter gates that possess these properties are embedded in a tonically aroused competitive anatomy (Figure 22), properties that rationalize a large body of data can be derived. When LTM rules such as (17) are clearly distinguished from accumulation-depletion rules such as (21), the theory is led to a pharmacological interpretation of conditioned reinforcer and motivational properties in terms of two distinct transmitter systems, whose most probable interpretation in the light of available data seemed in 1972, and still seems now in the light of a vastly expanded data base, to describe cholinergic-catecholaminergic interactions (Butcher, 1978; Friedhoff, 1975a, 1975b).

Perhaps the single most surprising dipole property is the fact that a nonspecific arousal increment which occurs while the on-channel of a gated dipole is active can cause an antagonistic rebound. This fact was soon realized to mean that a surprising event, by triggering an arousal increment, can disconfirm and thereby rapidly extinguish the motivational support of a conditioned reinforcer. The same action of a surprising event can also enhance the rewarding effect of a reward which occurs on a trial when nonreward is expected. Then the rebound due to the reward's unexpectedness can summate with the unconditional action of the reward, as in partial reward paradigms. In other words, the gated dipole machinery which produces a rebound in reaction to offset of a specific cue in classical conditioning can also produce a rebound in response to nonoccurrence of an expected event in instrumental conditioning. This property necessitates a major break with drive reduction theory, since positive and negative rewards can hereby be manipulated by changing expectancies and environmental contingencies, even if no change in drive occurs.

34. Dipole Fields in Motivational Processing by the Hippocampal-Hypothalamic Axis

Our derivation has led us from the synchronization problem of classical conditioning to the notion of a gated dipole that regulates the balance between on-cell and off-cell activation in each drive representation. With these facts in hand, we can achieve a deeper understanding of how to marry the concept of a sensory-drive heterarchy between several motivational channels (Section 28) with the concept of a gated dipole within each motivational channel (Section 32). This marriage leads to the concept of a *dipole field*, a concept which is also basic in the design of cortical sensory processing areas (Grossberg, 1976b, 1980a). To reach this concept, I state postulate (J^+) in somewhat more general terms as a distinct postulate.

K. Offset of a conditioned reinforcer can have reinforcing properties of opposite sign.

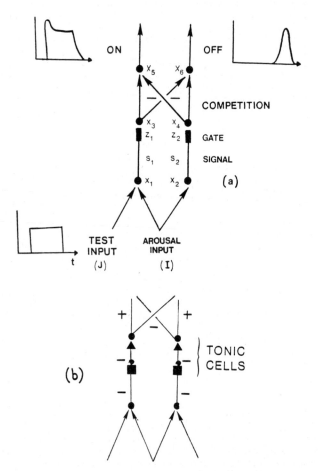

Figure 22. Two examples of gated dipoles. In (a), the phasic input J and the arousal input I add in the on-channel, thereby activating the STM trace x_1. The arousal input I also perturbs the STM trace x_2 in the off-channel. Consequently, $x_1 > x_2$. Then x_1 and x_2 elicit signals $f(x_1)$ and $f(x_2)$ in their respective pathways. Since $x_1 > x_2$, also $f(x_1) > f(x_2)$. Each signal is gated (multiplied) by an excitatory transmitter z_1 or z_2 (in the square synapses) before the gated signals $f(x_1)z_1$ and $f(x_2)z_2$ activate their target cells. The STM traces x_5 and x_6 then satisfy $x_5 > x_6$. Each STM trace elicits an excitatory signal down its own pathway and an inhibitory signal to the other pathway. The net effect after competition takes place is an output from the on-channel. The text describes how a rapid offset of J triggers an antagonistic rebound that transiently excites the off-channel. In (b), another version of a gated dipole is depicted. Here each excitatory gating pathway is replaced by a two-stage disinhibitory pathway that is constructed from two successive inhibitory links. The cells which receive these transmitter signals are assumed to be tonic (internally and persistently activated). The net effect of an input to the two-stage disinhibitory pathway is to release its output cell from tonic inhibition and to thereby excite it.

This postulate implies that the dipole geometry is recurrent, or a feedback geometry. This is because the conditionable LTM pathways of conditioned reinforcing cues end *after* each dipole's transmitter gating stage, so they can learn both the on-reactions and the off-reactions of the dipole. These LTM pathways also end *before* each dipole's transmitter gating stage, so their offset can elicit an antagonistic rebound, as postulate (K) requires. In order for these pathways to end both before and after the transmitter gating stage, the dipole pathways must close upon themselves in positive feedback loops. Moreover, since the on-cells and off-cells in each dipole compete, these feedback loops are part of a recurrent on-center off-surround network. Otherwise expressed, this feedback construction endows offset of conditioned reinforcing cues with secondary conditioning properties.

The competitive feedback anatomy also enjoys several other important properties, such as its ability to defend its operating level against small input fluctuations, thereby guaranteeing a stable motivational baseline, and to control sharp motivational switching between incompatible motivational alternatives. From a general information-processing point of view, these properties are at least as basic as the secondary conditioning property of postulate (K). What is important for our present purposes is to realize that a connection exists between secondary conditioning and these other properties. Also postulate (K) was the concept which originally forced my realization that feedback competitive networks play an important role in motivational processing (Grossberg, 1972c), and it is an accessible property whereby to instruct students who are familiar with reinforcement but unfamiliar with cognitive processing or psychophysiology.

Several general properties of competitive feedback networks are so basic for our present needs that I will review them here (Grossberg, 1973, 1975, 1980a). The feedback channels excite themselves and inhibit each other. Due to the positive feedback loops, there exists the danger that the network will amplify small noise levels into large activities and thereby flood itself with noise. Noise amplification is prevented if the feedback signals are sigmoid, or S-shaped, functions of cell activity; in particular, if spiking frequency is a sigmoid function of cell potential. The faster-than-linear growth of the sigmoid signal at small activity levels guarantees noise suppression; for example, a signal function $f(w)$ that behaves like a power $aw^n (a > 0, n > 1)$ at small values of the activity w is faster-than-linear at these activities.

The sigmoid signal also guarantees that the network behaves like a tunable filter. In other words, there exists a *quenching threshold* (QT) that must be exceeded by a cell's activity before the positive feedback signals can effectively maintain activity in its loop. If some combination of drive, arousal, and conditioned reinforcer input exceeds the QT and wins the motivational competition, then feedback signaling can amplify the activity in the winning drive representation as it competitively suppresses other drive representations until a prescribed operating level is attained and maintained through time. I identify this maintenance property with short-term memory (STM) storage in the motivational processor. Mechanisms which maintain a proper balance between the size of the QT and of arousal inputs, drive inputs, and incentive inputs are clearly of the greatest importance for achieving proper operating characteristics within a dipole field.

Figure 23 depicts a network that marries together these several processing constraints. This is not the only possibility *in vivo*, but my discussion will attempt to be sufficiently principled to abet recognition of thematic variation across species. Figure 23 builds up a dipole field in which a sensory-drive heterarchy exists between motivational channels, gated dipoles exist within motivational channels, LTM conditioning of a conditioned reinforcer pathway is driven by positive feedback within its motivational channel, and the polyvalent cells are activated by a two-stage disinhibitory reaction to drive and arousal inputs (Figure 22b). In Figure 23, pathways 1 and 2 correspond to specific, but complementary, drive inputs within a single dipole. Pathways labeled 3 carry the arousal signals to this dipole. Cells 4 and 5 receive these inputs and thereupon inhibit the tonically active cells 6 and 7. All tonically active cells have open symbols; phasically active cells have closed symbols. The pathways 4 → 6 and 5 → 7 are assumed to contain slow transmitter gates (square synapses; catecholaminergic?). If input 1 exceeds input 2, then the transmitter in pathway 4 → 6 is depleted more than the transmitter in pathway 5 → 7, thereby calibrating the dipole for a possible antagonistic rebound later on.

The tonic cells 6 and 7 equally inhibit each other until input 1 exceeds input 2. Then cell 6 is inhibited more than cell 7. This has the net effect of disinhibiting polyvalent cell 8 and further inhibiting polyvalent cell 9. Due to the polyvalent nature of cells 8 and 9, these events are insufficient to fire cell 8, but if the inhibition from cell 7 to cell 9 is sufficiently large, then it can prevent cell 9 from firing at all. We therefore restrict our next comments to cell 8 and its competitors. Apart from the feedback between cells 6 and 7, all of our remarks to this point discuss feedforward mechanisms. The competition between 6 and 7 could also be made feedforward by adding some more interneurons to the network. Our next remarks are concerned with feedback properties of the network.

Cells 8 and 10 are the polyvalent cells of two different motivational channels whose drive inputs constitute on-signals, or consummatory signals. These cells receive input not only from their respective dipoles but also from conditioned reinforcing cues along LTM pathways such as 11 and 12 (cholinergic?). These conditioned reinforcer inputs combine with drive inputs at their respective polyvalent cells, which thereupon begin to generate outputs if their thresholds are exceeded. At this stage, the several polyvalent cells compete among themselves via the "intrinsic" feedback inhibitory pathways 13 (GABA? see Siegel *et al.*, 1976), as they simultaneously try to excite themselves via positive feedback pathways. For example, cell 8 excites itself along the positive feedback pathway 8 → 4 → 6 → 8. The winner of this sensory-drive heterarchical competition has its activity stored in STM. Suppose for definiteness that the winner is cell 8. Now several things happen.

First, the positive feedback pathway 8 → 4 → 6 → 8 substantially depletes the transmitter gate in pathway 4 → 6. Hence *after* a motivational decision has been made, a fixed increment in arousal can cause a much larger rebound within a dipole than *before* a motivational decision has been made. This formal property can be used to experimentally test whether a transmitter gate occurs within a particular network's positive feedback loop. Second, the positive feedback amplifies the activity of cell 8 to the point where active LTM pathways (e.g., 11) abutting on cell 8 can be conditioned. This amplification of cell 8's activity might manifest itself *in vivo* as sustained bursting behavior of this polyvalent cell. Within this network, only the outcome of sensory-drive heterarchical competition can drive LTM changes. Subliminal shifts in the pattern of dipole inputs can have, at best, a small effect on LTM.

35. Some Pharmacological and Physiological Correlates of Motivational Dipole Fields

Some of the circuitry of Figure 23 can be used to explain the following psychopharmacological data, which are admirably reviewed by Olds (1977, pp. 59–75). Chlorpromazine and reserpine deplete amine stores. This is analogous to depleting the transmitter in the gating synapses of pathways 4 → 6 and 5 → 7. *In vivo* this manipulation depresses behavior. In Figure 23, it disinhibits the tonic inhibition of the polyvalent cells, and makes it harder for the polyvalent cells to fire. When these drugs are combined with monoamine oxidase inhibitors (MAOI), then the amines are released but they remain undegraded. This produces a lot of extra free amines. This operation would inhibit the tonic inhibitory interneurons in Figure 23. *In vivo* this manipulation abets self-stimulation, as it also would in Figure 23 by making it easier for the polyvalent cells to fire and thus for conditioned reinforcer pathways of lever press cues to get conditioned.

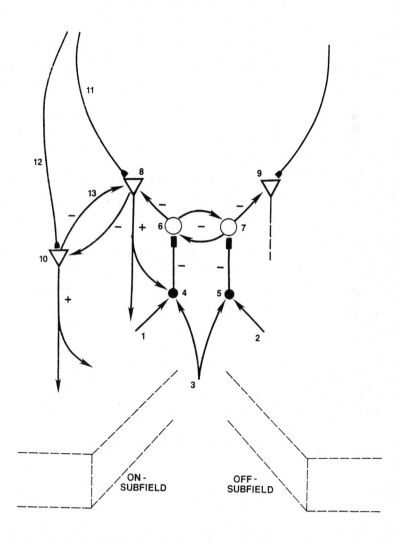

Figure 23. A dipole field of drive representations whose conditioning, motivational, and anatomical implications are summarized in the text.

Amphetamines release amines and prevent their reuptake, so they act like releasers and MAOI taken together. Amphetamine can also abet self-stimulation behavior. More interestingly, amphetamines can augment slow behavior and depress fast behavior. In small doses, amphetamine can facilitate eating, but in larger doses it can suppress eating. Such effects can be explained as an inverted U in gated dipole responsiveness when its net arousal level is parametrically increased (Grossberg, 1972c, 1981a, 1982b— Appendix A).

Even the highly schematic dipole field in Figure 23 requires a considerable amount of neural circuitry to carry out the competitive interactions within each dipole and between subsets of dipoles, and to deliver positive feedback signals back to the appropriate channels. A nice feature of these circuits is that simple growth rules can be suggested whereby such circuits might develop. For example, conditioned reinforcer pathways grow to polyvalent cells, dipole inhibitory interneurons grow among tonic cells, drive and arousal pathways grow to gating cells, and feedback inhibitory interneurons grow among polyvalent cells. In other words, simple chemical labels and a certain degree of symmetry in the initial network geometry can go a long way towards explaining the developmental feasibility of these circuits.

Various data suggest that these formal circuits are analogous to the neural circuits joining the hypothalamus, septum, amygdala, and hippocampus (Bridge and Hatton, 1973; DeFrance, 1976; Haymaker et al., 1969; MacLean, 1970; Olds, 1977). I have elsewhere suggested that the dipole computations are related to reciprocal hypothalamic interactions, notably between lateral and ventromedial hypothalamus; that the polyvalent cells are analogous to hippocampal pyramidal cells; and that the feedback pathways are analogous to the medial forebrain bundle (Grossberg, 1972c, 1975). This interpretation implies that certain hippocampal pyramidal cells are influenced by both the conditioned reinforcing properties of signals of cortical origin and the drive properties of signals of hypothalamic origin; that these pyramidal cells compete via recurrent inhibitory interneurons; that the bursting behavior of these pyramidal cells can drive conditioned changes; and that the output of these pyramidal cells is important for the transfer of STM into LTM not only directly by driving conditioned reinforcer changes but also indirectly via the effects of incentive motivational signals on the firing of cortical polyvalent cells. One might particularly note that self-stimulation is suppressed by either upstream or downstream blockade of the medial forebrain bundle (Stein, 1958). Of course the formal circuits do not presume to include all the cells that are needed to conduct business between hypothalamus and hippocampus in vivo. Nonetheless, the circuits help to explain a surprisingly large body of data, they illustrate how simple environmental pressures can lead to circuits of the type found in vivo, and they embody principles of network design which are robust enough to illuminate significantly more complex circuits.

36. Competition, Normalization, and STM Among Sensory Representations

In fact, these same principles can be used to explain a variety of perceptual, cognitive, and neocortical properties that are presently inexplicable without them. To quickly show why this is true, I ask the reader to consider the following dilemma. Vigorous firing of polyvalent cells in Figure 23 should occur only if sufficiently large conditioned reinforcer and drive inputs combine to exceed the polyvalent thresholds. However, different sensory events can excite very different numbers of cortical feature detectors. If conditioned reinforcer inputs from a simple tone are enough to fire the polyvalent cell given a simultaneous drive input, what prevents conditioned reinforcer inputs from billions more cells from firing the cell without a simultaneous drive input? Even worse, if the latter input isn't too big, then won't the tone input be too small? Clearly the total input from these internal representations must be insensitive to the total number of active cells. Otherwise expressed, the total suprathreshold activity of the sensory field must be normalized, or conserved. A constraint on the decision rules whereby the sensory-drive heterarchy maintains its sensitivity to drive and reinforcer inputs hereby leads to the following postulate about the limited capacity of STM across cue representations.

L. The total activity across the internal representatoins of sensory cues is regulated.

Postulate (L), just like postulate (K), can be derived from more basic considerations, in this case considerations about how a sensory field can accurately register patterned data at all (Grossberg, 1980a, Appendices C and D). Postulate (L) has the virtues of relating a property of sensory fields to a property of motivational decisions, and of being immediately accessible.

The sensory inputs to the motivational polyvalent cells come from the first stages $v_{i1}^{(2)}$ at which STM reverberation takes place. Postulate (L) requires that interactions occur among these representations to prevent their outputs from increasing linearly with the number of excited sensory cells. These interactions must be inhibitory to keep the total output from growing without bound. These negative interactions must be feedback interactions to balance the positive feedback that maintains sensory STM. In all, the populations $v_{i1}^{(2)}$ are joined together by recurrent on-center off-surround interactions. We are now faced with a question on whose answer the life of the theory depends: Can competitive feedback interactions regulate the total activity of their network?

It is most gratifying that the answer is "yes" if the interactions are of shunting type (which is the type that the membrane equations of neurophysiology obey) and if the feedback inhibition is of sufficiently long range across the field of populations (Grossberg, 1973, 1980a—Appendix D). This is, moreover, the same formal property that maintains a steady motivational operating level in the feedback competitive networks of the sensory-drive heterarchy. I call this formal property *normalization*. The need for a normalization property of one sort or another has long been recognized in psychology. Even Freud writes: "The nervous system endeavors to keep constant something in its functional condition that may be described as the 'sum of excitation' " (Freud and Breuer, 1959, p.30). Maintaining this sum in a competitive network whose shunting interactions approximate multiplicative rules helps to explain the partial successes of probabilistic models in studies of coding and memory. However, the probabilistic axioms do not well match the functional transformations of feedback competitive networks (Grossberg, 1978a). As often occurs in the history of science, an intuitively plausible property must go through several stages of mathematical explication before it can be cast in a mechanistic framework that reveals all of its implications.

One of these implications occurs in the competition among the network's external cue representations no less than in the network's sensory-drive heterarchy. A quenching threshold exists if the competitive feedback signals are chosen to be sigmoid functions of their activity levels. This QT will shortly be seen to be of major importance in attentional processing, since it helps to regulate which cues are attended and which are suppressed.

The cells $v_{i1}^{(2)}$ can now also be seen to be the on-cells of a dipole field. Just as offset of a conditioned reinforcer input to a drive representation can trigger an antagonistic rebound in the complementary drive representation of its gated dipole, offset of sensory cues must be able to transiently excite off-cells whose output signals can be used to learn conditioned reactions to the offset events; for example, to learn to push a lever in response to the offset of a light. Thus the sensory processor is envisaged to be not merely a shunting competitive feedback network, but rather a pair of such networks organized as a dipole field. To drive antagonistic rebounds between the on-cells and off-cells of this field, there must exist a nonspecific arousal system gated by a slowly varying transmitter (catecholaminergic?), as well as specific sensory on-inputs and off-inputs that play the role in sensory representations which specific drive inputs play in drive representations.

The symmetry of the total network is hereby extended once again to include dipole fields in both sensory and drive representations. I view the existence of such dipole fields as a basic principle of cortical architecture, whether it be neocortical architecture of sensory representations or the paleocortical architecture of the hippocampus and its attendant structures.

37. Attention and the Persistence Paradox of Parallel Processing

Because of this increased symmetry in the overall network geometry, another asymmetry now becomes apparent. At the drive representations, both specific internal inputs (drive inputs) and nonspecific external inputs (conditioned reinforcer inputs) combine to control which representations will be stored in STM by the feedback competition. At the sensory representations, this is not yet true. Only the specific external inputs (external cue inputs) regulate the competitive feedback at the first stages $v_{i1}^{(2)}$. The nonspecific internal inputs (incentive motivational inputs) control only the polyvalent second stages $v_{i2}^{(2)}$, which thus far have been excluded from the STM competition. Are there pressing psychological reasons, apart from symmetry considerations, which require us to include the polyvalent cells in the STM competition? Can the polyvalent cells be included in the STM feedback exchange without destroying the functional requirements that led us to distinguish the stages $v_{i1}^{(2)}$ from $v_{i2}^{(2)}$ in the first place?

The answer to these questions is "yes." The physiological requirements are illustrated by the following thought experiment, which shows how disastrous our associative links could become if classical conditioning were controlled by a feedforward network (Grossberg, 1975, 1980a). In Figure 24a two classical conditioning experiments are depicted, one in which stimulus S_2 is the UCS for response R_2 and S_1 is its CS, and one in which S_1 is the UCS for R_1 and S_2 is its CS. What would happen if each cue S_1 and S_2 is conditioned to its own response R_1 or R_2, respectively, before a classical conditioning experiment occurs in which S_1 and S_2 are alternately scanned? This is the typical situation in real life, where we scan many cues in parallel, or intermittently, and many of these cues already have their own associations. If classical conditioning were a passive feedforward process, then cross-conditioning from S_1 to R_2 and from S_2 to R_1 would rapidly occur, as in Figure 24b. By contrast, we know from daily experience that the persistence of learned meanings can endure despite the fact that cues that are processed in parallel often control incompatible responses. What feedback mechanisms of our attentional processor prevent rapid associative short-circuits from occurring?

Stated in a theoretical vacuum, this dilemma does not imply a particular mechanism, which is one reason why, despite its accessibility to all of us, it is not often even mentioned as a dilemma. At the present juncture of our theoretical construction, by contrast, the dilemma leads us to include the polyvalent cells $v_{i2}^{(2)}$ in the STM competition. Before showing why this is so, I summarize this constraint as postulate (P^4), where (P^4) reminds us both of the alliterative aspects of the section title and of the pathetic consequences of not imposing it.

P^4. Persistence of learned meanings during parallel processing of motivationally incompatible cues is possible.

Our mechanistic task is to prevent S_1 from becoming a conditioned reinforcer of R_2 and S_2 from becoming a conditioned reinforcer of R_1. Even if S_1 and S_2 are simultaneously scanned, we must prevent their first stages $v_{11}^{(2)}$ and $v_{21}^{(2)}$, respectively, from sending sustained sampling signals to the wrong drive representation. To achieve this in the present theory, at least three stages of processing are needed, two of which already exist in the network as it stands:

(1) When S_1 and S_2 are scanned, $v_{11}^{(2)}$ and $v_{21}^{(2)}$ send conditioned reinforcer signals to

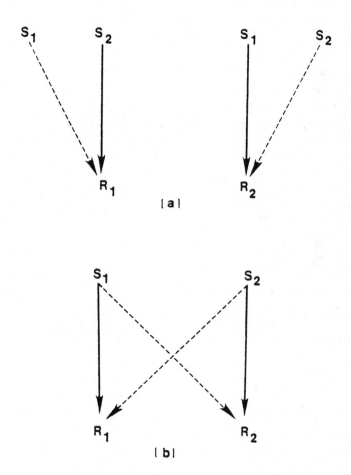

Figure 24. Classical conditioning cannot be a passive feedforward process during real behavior. In (a), S_1 acts as a CS for S_2, whereas S_2 acts as a CS for S_1. In (b), parallel processing of S_1 and S_2, each previously conditioned to responses R_1 and R_2, would yield cross-conditioning (dotted lines).

the drive representations in order to test which drive channels they control. This step answers the question: Do S_1 and S_2 control incompatible drives?

(2) The sensory-drive heterarchy determines which drive representation is stronger at each moment.

(3) Somehow $v_{i1}^{(2)} \to D$ sampling signals are shut off in the weaker channel.

If property (3) can be achieved, then incentive motivational sampling will be restricted to motivationally compatible cues at each time, and attentional switching can change the class of sampling cues. How do the first stages $v_{i1}^{(2)}$ know which drive representation is stronger at any time? Feedback from drive representations to sensory representations is necessary to achieve this property. By Section 25 the incentive motivational feedback from the drive representations D to the second stages $v_{i2}^{(2)}$ is conditionable. Hence only these second stages which are compatible with the winning drive representation will receive strong feedback. Postulate (P^4) now suggests that when these polyvalent cells $v_{i2}^{(2)}$ fire, they send positive feedback to their respective first stages $v_{i1}^{(2)}$. In all, the incentive motivational feedback from D_i will excite only $v_{i1}^{(2)}$ ($i = 1, 2$). If D_1 is the winner, the STM activity of $v_{11}^{(2)}$ will hereby be amplified. How does this amplification rapidly inhibit $v_{21}^{(2)}$ to prevent it from sampling D_1 in a sustained fashion?

The answer is obvious due to the fact that the total activity of the first stages is normalized by the competition for STM activity which takes place among the external cue representations (Section 36). Increasing the STM activity of $v_{11}^{(2)}$ automatically decreases the STM activity of $v_{21}^{(2)}$ via the competitive feedback between these representations. This competitive feedback can, moreover, totally suppress $v_{21}^{(2)}$ if it drives its activity below the quenching threshold.

The minimal solution to the dilemma imposed by postulate (P^4) is depicted in Figure 25. In Figure 25, the polyvalent cells are part of the STM competition, but they do not fire unless they receive incentive motivational signals, so that we have not destroyed the functional constraint that forced us to distinguish the cells $v_{i1}^{(2)}$ from $v_{i2}^{(2)}$ in the first place. This construction was used in Grossberg (1975) to explain a variety of data about attention and discrimination learning. A more recent body of data are discussed using these mechanisms in Grossberg (1982a).

38. Sensory Incentive versus Motor Incentive: The Hippocampus as a Cognitive Map

To abet a fuller understanding of Figure 25, I should review a distinction from the Grossberg (1975) article which has recently been partially confirmed by data suggesting that the hippocampus is a cognitive map (O'Keefe and Nadel, 1978). In its strongest form, the O'Keefe and Nadel hypothesis claims an absolute spatial map of an animal's world in which place unit cells code where an animal is located within this map at any time. This view contrasts with data which describe the occurrence of classical conditioning at hippocampal pyramidal cells using the rabbit nictitating membrane paradigm (Berger and Thompson, 1978). These latter data can be interpreted as LTM changes within conditioned reinforcer pathways at the polyvalent cells of the sensory-drive heterarchy. Various data summarized by O'Keefe and Nadel (1978) can also be interpreted using the sensory-drive heterarchy. These data probe the effects which unexpected events have on consummatory activity. Within the sensory-drive heterarchy, an unexpected event can rapidly terminate consummatory activity and release a complementary mode of orienting activity by causing antagonistic rebound of the consummatory activity's motivational source. For example, hippocampectomized rats do not orient to

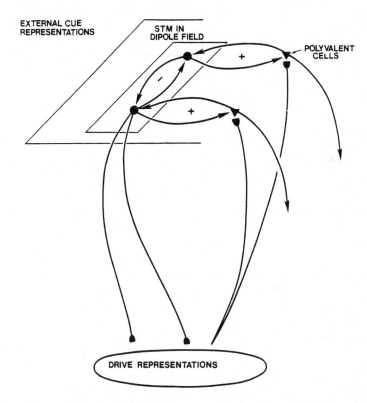

Figure 25. Suppose that a set of nodes, or cells, in the dipole field is activated by an external scene. A pattern of STM activity across the nodes represents the scene. Each such node sends an excitatory signal to its polyvalent node, or cell. Signal size is an increasing function of STM activity. These specific signals are insufficient to fire the polyvalent cells. Sufficiently large incentive motivational signals from a drive representation must simultaneously converge upon the polyvalent cells to fire them. The incentive motivational pathways are conditionable. A drive representation will therefore preferentially activate those polyvalent cells whose cues were paired with this drive representation in the past. The drive representation can hereby fire a subset of the polyvalent cells which are activated by the external scene. The relative rate of firing of each polyvalent cell will depend jointly on the STM activity of its trigger cues in the scene and on the relative size of its LTM trace in the conditioned reinforcer pathway. When a polyvalent cell fires, it delivers positive feedback signals to the cue-activated cells which supply it with specific STM signals. This positive feedback from polyvalent cells selectively augments the STM activities of certain cue-activated cells, which thereupon more strongly inhibit the STM of other representations in the dipole field using the STM normalization property. The incentive motivational properties of certain cues hereby alter the set of cues to which the network pays attention. The polyvalent cells which can maintain their firing can also read out the learned patterns (e.g., motor commands) to other parts of the network.

a novel stimulus while they are indulging in a consummatory activity, such as running towards a reward. They cannot "shift attention during the presentation of a novel stimulus or in a mismatch situation" (O'Keefe and Nadel, 1978, p.250). This type of effect can be qualitatively understood in the theory as it stands.

Various data concerning the manner in which animals explore an environment until they learn its spatial relationships cannot be understood unless we advance the theory further. This deficiency holds even though the notion of an absolute spatial map can be severely criticized on philosophical, no less than scientific, grounds. A weaker notion cannot, however, be so easily criticized; namely, that of a bilaterally organized motor map of approach and avoidance gradients which are built up from signal patterns that are biased by motivationally excitatory and inhibitory conditioned pathways. I shall now indicate how such a view is suggested by postulate (P^4).

The mechanism which solves postulate (P^4) works if the feedback from drive representations to sensory representations is positive. The case of drives, such as fear and frustration, which have a negative motivational sign requires further argument. In other words, we have not yet exploited the dipole structure of the sensory-drive heterarchy.

The problem is this. If the conditioned feedback from a negative drive representation to sensory representations were negative, then it would differentially suppress activity in the corresponding sensory representations, rather than enhance their activity, in violation of postulate (P^4). Increasing the learned fearfulness of a given cue, in a fixed context of other cues, would hereby decrease the attention paid to it. This would be a most maladaptive property. Moreover, fearful cues could not overshadow or block learning in response to other cues, which is false (Kamin, 1968, 1969).

Hence a distinction must be made between channels which regulate learned persistence of negative meanings and channels which carry negative incentive motivation (Figure 26). The former channels help to focus attention on meaningful cues. Whether these cues have a positive or a negative meaning, the feedback which they control is positive. As a consequence, sensory attention can be differentially focused on these cues as they become more meaningful. The latter channels have a motor significance. They help to control approach of positive cues and avoidance of negative cues.

This distinction suggests that the output from the sensory-drive heterarchy bifurcates. One pathway carries conditionable feedback signals to sensory cortical representations. These feedback signals are analogous to the contingent negative variation (Section 25). The other pathway carries motivational signs to a field of sensory representations which lies further downstream in the network. The motivational signs differentially weight the activities of their respective cue representations, with positive signs having an excitatory effect and negative signs an inhibitory effect. These differentially weighted cue representations then project to a bilaterally organized motor map, wherein the bilateral asymmetry of the map's activity pattern at any time controls the network's approach and avoidance tendencies at this time. I suggest that the O'Keefe and Nadel (1978) data on place learning are probing properties of this latter pathway.

39. Expectancy Matching and Attentional Reset: Unblocking and Dishabituation

The introduction of dipole field structure into the sensory representations propels our motivational theory deeper into the realm of perceptual and cognitive theory, and indeed no mature motivational theory can entirely avoid discussion of cognitive influences. For the sake of completeness, I will briefly review how the mismatch of feedback expectancies with feedforward data patterns can reset a dipole field by triggering an increment in its nonspecific arousal level. I will also indicate how the same arousal increment which causes antagonistic rebounds in dipoles that have previously been very active can simultaneously enhance the on-reactions of dipoles that have previously been only weakly active and of the novel cues that caused the arousal increment. In other

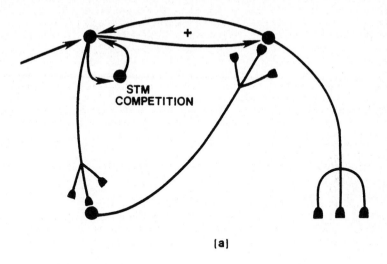

(a)

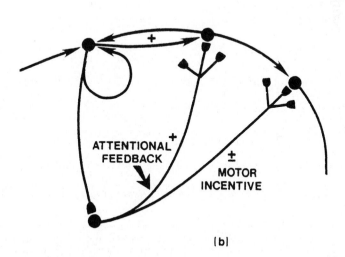

(b)

Figure 26. In (a), positive feedback from $v_{i2}^{(2)}$ to $v_{i1}^{(2)}$ can be used to selectively enhance sensory representations which are compatible with a given incentive, and thereby to indirectly overshadow other sensory representations via the STM competition. In (b), the positive attentional feedback pathway is distinguished from the positive or negative pathway which assigns emotional signs to a cue-modulated motor map.

words, expectancy mismatch due to an unexpected event can disconfirm previously active representations as it enhances previously suppressed and newly activated representations. I will not discuss how the internal representations which release the feedback expectancies are encoded, and how once encoded they can learn the proper feedback expectancy. For these discussions, the reader might consult Grossberg (1972a, 1976a, 1976b, 1978b, 1980a).

The expectancy-matching mechanism is an automatic property of certain feedback competitive networks. When such a network is designed to suppress uniform patterns (Figure 27a), a sum of two mismatched input patterns will also be suppressed, since the peaks and troughs of one pattern will tend to correspond to the troughs and peaks of the other pattern, respectively (Figure 27b). By contrast, such a network reacts to two matched patterns by amplifying its activities (Figure 27c). These properties are due to automatic gain control by the inhibitory feedback signals. They are reviewed in Grossberg (1980a, Appendix C). In the present theory, these feedback competitive networks are in the on-cell subfield and off-cell subfield of each dipole field.

The expectancy mismatch mechanism is illustrated in Figure 28. In Figure 28, an afferent data pattern elicits activity across a competitive network $F^{(1)}$ as it also activates a nonspecific arousal source A. The activity within $F^{(1)}$ rapidly inhibits the arousal source. The pattern across $F^{(1)}$ then elicits signals to the next stage $F^{(2)}$ of network processing. These signals act like an adaptive filter. The patterned output of this filter is contrast enhanced and normalized as it is read into STM at $F^{(2)}$. This STM pattern, in turn, reads out a learned feedback template or expectancy to $F^{(1)}$. If the expectancy mismatches the afferent data pattern at $F^{(1)}$, then activity across $F^{(1)}$ is inhibited, whereupon the arousal source A is disinhibited. A pulse of arousal is hereby released and rapidly resets the filtered chunks which were active in STM across $F^{(2)}$. The two successive stages $F^{(1)}$ and $F^{(2)}$ of pattern processing are part of the network's *attentional* subsystem. The arousal channel is part of the network's *orienting* subsystem. The inhibitory link between the two subsystems illustrates the complementary relationship between attentional and orienting reactions (Grossberg, 1975, 1982a, 1984).

Why the arousal pulse can rebound very active dipoles and enhance the on-reactions of weakly active dipoles can only be understood by mathematically analysing gated dipole dynamics, as in Grossberg (1984, Appendix A). Such an analysis indicates how a suitably chosen sigmoid signal function can determine the minimal arousal increment $g(I, J)$ which can rebound a dipole whose net arousal level is I and whose specific input in its on-channel exceeds I by J. One finds that

$$g(I, J) = \frac{A - I(I + J) + (A + I^2)^{1/2}[A + (I + J)^2]^{1/2}}{2I + J}. \tag{24}$$

Function $g(I, J)$ is a decreasing function of J. In other words, a fixed arousal increment ΔI can more easily rebound dipoles which have large prior on-reactions J than dipoles with smaller prior on-reactions J. If $\Delta I > g(I, J)$, a rebound occurs. If $\Delta I < g(I, J)$, an enhanced on-reaction occurs. By (24),

$$g(I, 0) = AI^{-1} \tag{25}$$

whereas

$$g(I, \infty) = (A + I^2)^{1/2} - I. \tag{26}$$

Consequently $g(I, \infty)$ can equal any fraction $1/n < 1/2$ of $g(I, 0)$; viz.,

$$g(I, \infty) = \frac{1}{n} g(I, 0), \tag{27}$$

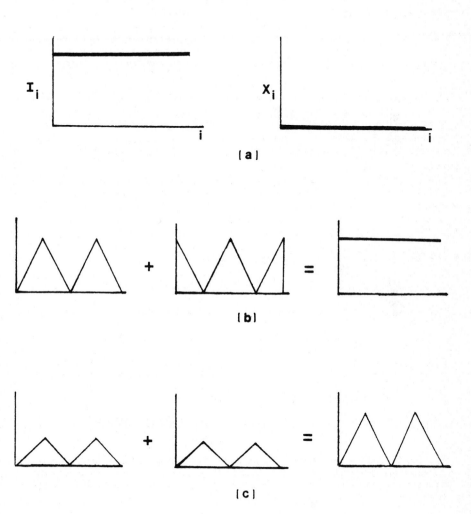

Figure 27. In (a), a uniform pattern of inputs I_i is transformed into a zero pattern of activities X_i. In (b), two mismatched patterns add to generate an approximately uniform total input pattern, which will be suppressed by the mechanism of (a). In (c), two matched patterns add to yield a total input pattern that can elicit more vigorous activation than either input pattern taken separately.

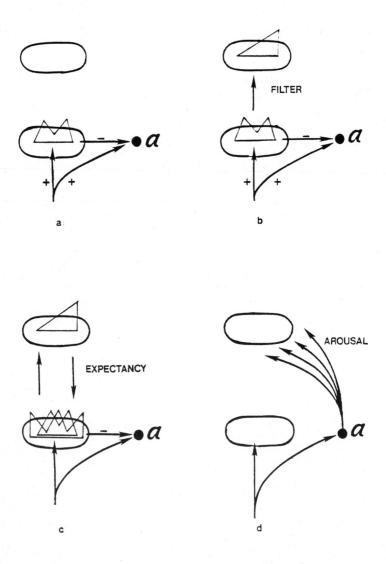

Figure 28. In (a), afferent data elicit activity across $F^{(1)}$ and an input to the arousal source A that is inhibited by $F^{(1)}$. In (b), the pattern $F^{(1)}$ maintains inhibition of A as it is filtered and activates $F^{(2)}$. In (c), the feedback expectancy from $F^{(2)}$ is matched against the pattern at $F^{(1)}$. In (d), the mismatch attenuates activity across $F^{(1)}$ and thereby disinhibits A, which releases a nonspecific arousal signal to $F^{(2)}$.

if

$$I = \sqrt{\frac{A}{n(n-2)}}.$$ (28)

In other words, $g(I, J)$ can decrease to an arbitrarily small fraction of its maximal value $g(I, 0)$ as J increases. This means that the mechanism whereby a fixed ΔI can differentially trigger an antagonistic rebound or an enhanced on-reaction is robust. Interestingly, the size of I determines how big this effect can be, since (28) shows that the relative effect increases as I decreases. One can also readily check that the on-reaction of a dipole is also enhanced if a specific input J accompanies an increment ΔI in arousal just so long as the total input remains in the faster-than-linear part of the signal function $f(w)$. This property helps to explain the enhanced STM storage of a novel event.

The remainder of this section indicates that the attentional and orienting mechanisms depicted in Figure 28 need not be housed in physically disjoint networks. They can be diffusely interspersed among one another, much as the visual cortical projections of retinal X-cells and Y-cells mutually interpenetrate (Breitmeyer, 1980; Robson, 1975). I offer this example not to exhaust the possibilities, but to stimulate further study of this question.

Figure 29 depicts one possible network realization of this type. The dotted lines 1 describe a nonspecific arousal pathway which terminates at the specific on-cell and off-cell of the depicted dipole. Pathway 2 is the specific on-cell input to the on-cell 3. The remainder of this figure through cell 6 depicts a standard dipole geometry. I have made the transmitter gate 4 excitatory to avoid making the figure unnecessarily complicated. Stage 6 sends inputs into the feedback anatomy of the network. The positive feedback loop 6 $\leftrightarrow$ 7 is the recurrent on-center corresponding to the dipole's on-cell axis. Looking along the axis of the on-subfield, one sees negative feedback pathways, such as 8, to the on-channels of other dipoles, such as cell 9. This competitive feedback network will compute pattern matches.

The new additions to the network are the arousal cells, such as 10, which are interspersed among the feedback interneurons. All of the interneurons such as 7, 9, and 10 would be considered part of "intrinsic" feedback circuits if they were observed in cortical tissue. Cell 10 receives a positive input from cell 6 just as cell 7 does. What is different is that cell 7 inhibits cell 10, as do all the contiguous dipole-related cells. The inhibitory link 7 $\to$ 10 prevents cell 10 from firing when cell 7 is on, just as in Figure 23.

A pattern of feedback expectancy signals is also delivered to cells such as 7 and 9. If this feedback pattern matches the feedforward data pattern across the dipole on-cells, then inhibition of cell 10 is maintained as the network resonates the feedback template pattern. If a mismatch occurs, then cell 7 is inhibited, but cell 6 is not. In other words, interneurons such as 7 and 9 form a matching interface. Cell 10 is hereby disinhibited and elicits an arousal burst to the next processing stage. An interesting feature of this construction is that the arousal can be distributed among local groups of cells. One need not reset the whole tissue due to a mismatch in just one of its spatial channels. Local readjustments of templates with data can occur until the entire tissue can achieve resonance. Otherwise expressed, these local arousal sources can cause readjustments in system coding and tuning on a channel-by-channel basis, and can thereby bias the processing in contiguous channels until the entire tissue achieves resonance.

40. Concluding Remarks

This article illustrates how a real-time analysis of an individual's adaptive moment-by-moment behavior in prescribed environments can disclose network principles and mechanisms that admit a physiological and pharmacological interpretation. Each of

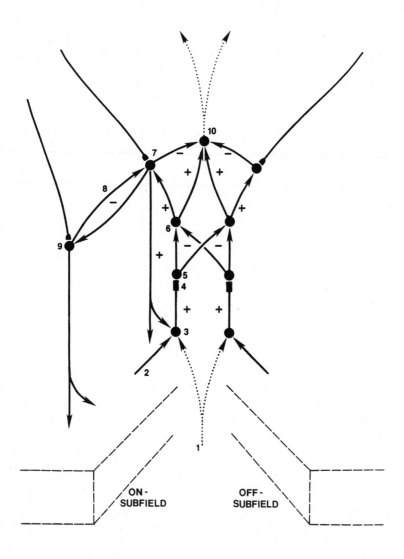

Figure 29. This figure depicts an anatomy in which selective reset of local groups of cells can be achieved until the entire tissue can achieve resonance. The text describes the network's operation step by step.

these principles leads to a class of mathematical design problems, each of these problems can be solved, and in the light of the solutions, an interdisciplinary restructuring and unification of the data is implied in terms of design principles and mechanisms rather than the vicissitudes of experimental methodology or historical accident. This article has focused on the designs which are forced by the synchronization problem and the persistence paradox, and has used these designs to explicate the ideas contained in various classical theories and data. Related articles in this series (Grossberg, 1981a, 1982a, 1984) have used similar ideas to explain a wide variety of recent interdisciplinary data and have suggested interdisciplinary experiments to independently cross-check these ideas.

REFERENCES

Anderson, P. and Eccles, J.C., Inhibitory phasing of neuronal discharge. *Nature*, 1962, **196**, 645–647.

Annau, Z. and Kamin, L.J., The conditioned emotional response as a function of intensity of the US. *Journal of Comparative and Physiological Psychology*, 1961, **54**, 428–432.

Beach, F.A., Characteristics of masculine "sex drive". In M.R. Jones (Ed.), **Nebraska symposium on motivation**. Lincoln: University of Nebraska Press, 1956.

Berger, T.W. and Thompson, R.F., Neuronal plasticity in the limbic system during classical conditioning of the rabbit nictitating membrane response, I: The hippocampus. *Brain Research*, 1978, **145**, 323–346.

Bindra, D., Neurophysiological interpretation of the effects of drive and incentive-motivation on general activity and instrumental behavior. *Psychological Review*, 1968, **75**, 1–22.

Bitterman, M.E. and Mackintosh, N.J., Habit-reversal and probability learning: Rats, birds, and fish. In R.M. Gilbert and N.S. Sutherland (Eds.), **Animal discrimination learning**. New York: Academic Press, 1969.

Boe, E.E., Effect of punishment duration and intensity on the extinction of an instrumental response. *Journal of Experimental Psychology*, 1966, **72**, 125–131.

Bolles, R.C., **Theory of motivation**. New York: Harper and Row, 1967.

Boren, J.J., Sidman, M., and Herrnstein, R.J., Avoidance, escape and extinction as functions of shock intensity. *Journal of Comparative and Physiological Psychology*, 1959, **52**, 420–425.

Borozci, G., Storms, L.H., and Broen, W.E., Response suppression and recovery of responding at different deprivation levels as functions of intensity and duration of punishment. *Journal of Comparative and Physiological Psychology*, 1964, **58**, 456–459.

Breitmeyer, B.G., Unmasking visual masking: A look at the "why" behind the veil of the "how". *Psychological Review*, 1980, **87**, 52–69.

Bridge, J.G. and Hatton, G.I., Septal unit activity in response to alterations in bleed volume and osmotic pressure. *Physiological Behavior*, 1973, **10**, 769–774.

Brush, F.R., **Aversive conditioning and learning**. New York: Academic Press, 1971.

Butcher, L.L. (Ed.), **Cholinergic-monoaminergic interactions in the brain**. New York: Academic Press, 1978.

Campbell, B.A. and Kraeling, D., Response strength as a function of drive level and amount of drive reduction. *Journal of Experimental Psychology*, 1953, **45**, 97–101.

Campbell, B.A. and Church, R.M., **Punishment and aversive behavior**. New York: Appleton-Century-Crofts, 1969.

Capaldi, E.J., Memory and learning: A sequential viewpoint. In W.K. Honig and P.H.R. James (Eds.), **Amimal memory**. New York: Academic Press, 1971.

Church, R.M., Raymond, G.A., and Beauchamp, R.D., Response suppression as a function of intensity and duration of punishment. *Journal of Comparative and Physiological Psychology*, 1967, **63**, 39–44.

Cotton, J.W., Running time as a function of amount of food deprivation. *Journal of Experimental Psychology*, 1953, **46**, 188–198.

Crespi, L.P., Quantitative variation of incentive and performance in the white rat. *American Journal of Psychology*, 1942, **55**, 467–517.

Crespi, L.P., Amount of reinforcement and level of performance. *Psychological Review*, 1944, **51**, 341–357.

Crosby, E.C., Humphrey, T., and Lauer, E.W., **Correlative anatomy of the nervous system**. New York: Macmillan, 1962.

D'Amato, M.R., Fazzaro, J., and Etkin, M., Discriminated bar-press avoidance maintenance and extinction in rats as a function of shock intensity. *Journal of Comparative and Physiological Psychology*, 1967, **63**, 351–354.

Deese, J. and Carpenter, J.A., Drive level and reinforcement. *Journal of Experimental Psychology*, 1951, **42**, 236–238.

DeFrance, J.F., **The septal nuclei**. New York: Plenum Press, 1976.

Denny, M.R., Relaxation theory and experiments. In F.R. Brush (Ed.), **Aversive conditioning and learning**. New York: Academic Press, 1971.

Dickinson, A., Hall, G., and Mackintosh, N.J., Surprise and the attenuation of blocking. *Journal of Experimental Psychology: Animal Behavior Processes*, 1976, **2**, 213–222.

Dunham, P.J., Punishment: Method and theory. *Psychological Review*, 1971, **78**, 58–70.

Estes, W.K., Stimulus-response theory of drive. In M.R. Jones (Ed.), **Nebraska symposium on motivation**. Lincoln: University of Nebraska Press, 1958.

Estes, W.K., Outline of a theory of punishment. In B.A. Campbell and R.M. Church (Eds.), **Punishment and aversive behavior**. New York: Appleton-Century-Crofts, 1969.

Estes, W.K. and Skinner, B.F., Some quantitative properties of anxiety. *Journal of Experimental Psychology*, 1941, **29**, 390–400.

Freud, S. and Breuer, J., On the theory of hysterical attacks. In **Collected papers**, Volume 5. New York: Basic Books, 1959.

Friedhoff, A.J. (Ed.), **Catecholamines and behavior, Vol. I: Basic neurobiology**. New York: Plenum Press, 1975 (a).

Friedhoff, A.J. (Ed.), **Catecholamines and behavior, Vol. II: Neuropsychopharmacology**. New York: Plenum Press, 1975 (b).

Gabriel, M., Foster, K., Orona, E., Saltwick, S.E., and Stanton, M., Neuronal activity of cingulate cortex, anteroventral thalamus and hippocampal formation in discrimination conditioning: Encoding and extraction of the significance of conditional stimuli. *Progress in Psychobiological and Physiological Psychology*, 1980, **9**, 125–231.

Gilbert, R.M. and Sutherland, N.S., **Animal discrimination learning**. New York: Academic Press, 1969.

Goldman-Rakic, P.S., Prenatal formation of cortical input and development of cytoarchitectonic compartments in the neostriatum of the rhesus monkey. *Journal of Neuroscience*, 1981, **1**, 721–735.

Grossberg, S., **The theory of embedding fields with applications to psychology and neurophysiology**. New York: Rockefeller Institute for Medical Research, 1964.

Grossberg, S., Some physiological and biochemical consequences of psychological postulates. *Proceedings of the National Academy of Sciences*, 1968, **60**, 758–765.

Grossberg, S., On learning and energy-entropy dependence in recurrent and non-recurrent signed networks. *Journal of Statistical Physics*, 1969, **1**, 319–350 (a).

Grossberg, S., On the serial learning of lists. *Mathematical Biosciences*, 1969, **4**, 201–253 (b).

Grossberg, S., On the production and release of chemical transmitters and related topics in cellular control. *Journal of Theoretical Biology*, 1969, **22**, 325–364 (c).

Grossberg, S., Some networks that can learn, remember, and reproduce any number of complicated space-time patterns, II. *Studies in Applied Mathematics*, 1970, **49**, 135-166 (a).

Grossberg, S., Neural pattern discrimination. *Journal of Theoretical Biology*, 1970, **27**, 291-337 (b).

Grossberg, S., On the dynamics of operant conditioning. *Journal of Theoretical Biology*, 1971, **33**, 225-255 (a).

Grossberg, S., Pavlovian pattern learning by nonlinear neural networks. *Proceedings of the National Academy of Sciences*, 1971, **68**, 828-831 (b).

Grossberg, S., Pattern learning by functional-differential neural networks with arbitrary path weights. In K. Schmitt (Ed.), **Delay and funtional-differential equations and their applications**. New York: Academic Press, 1972 (a).

Grossberg, S., A neural theory of punishment and avoidance, I: Qualitative theory. *Mathematical Biosciences*, 1972, **15**, 39-67 (b).

Grossberg, S., A neural theory of punishment and avoidance, II: Quantitative theory. *Mathematical Biosciences*, 1972, **15**, 253-285 (c).

Grossberg, S., Contour enhancement, short-term memory, and constancies in reverberating neural networks. *Studies in Applied Mathematics*, 1973, **52**, 217-257.

Grossberg, S., Classical and instrumental learning by neural networks. In R. Rosen and F. Snell (Eds.), **Progress in theoretical biology**, Volume 3. New York: Academic Press, 1974.

Grossberg, S., A neural model of attention, reinforcement, and discrimination learning. *International Review of Neurobiology*, 1975, **18**, 263-327.

Grossberg, S., Adaptive pattern classification and universal recoding, I: Parallel development and coding of neural feature detectors. *Biological Cybernetics*, 1976, **23**, 121-134 (a).

Grossberg, S., Adaptive pattern classification and universal recoding, II: Feedback, expectation, olfaction, and illusions. *Biological Cybernetics*, 1976, **23**, 187-202 (b).

Grossberg, S., Behavioral contrast in short-term memory: Serial binary memory models or parallel continuous memory models? *Journal of Mathematical Psychology*, 1978, **17**, 199-219 (a).

Grossberg, S., A theory of human memory: Self-organization and performance of sensory-motor codes, maps, and plans. In R. Rosen and F. Snell (Eds.), **Progress in theoretical biology**, Vol. 5. New York: Academic Press, 1978 (b).

Grossberg, S., Competition, decision, and consensus. *Journal of Mathematical Analysis and Applications*, 1978, **66**, 470-493 (c).

Grossberg, S., How does a brain build a cognitive code? *Psychological Review*, 1980, **87**, 1-51 (a).

Grossberg, S., Biological competition: Decision rules, pattern formation, and oscillations. *Proceedings of the National Academy of Sciences*, 1980, **77**, 2338-2342 (b).

Grossberg, S., Psychophysiological substrates of schedule interactions and behavioral contrast. In S. Grossberg (Ed.), **Mathematical psychology and psychophysiology**. Providence, RI: American Mathematical Society, 1981 (a).

Grossberg, S., Adaptive resonance in development, perception, and cognition. In S. Grossberg (Ed.), **Mathematical psychology and psychophysiology**. Providence, RI: American Mathematical Society, 1981 (b).

Grossberg, S., The processing of expected and unexpected events during conditioning and attention: A psychophysiological theory. *Psychologcal Review*, 1982, **89**, 529-572 (a).

Grossberg, S., **Studies of mind and brain: Neural principles of learning, perception, development, cognition, and motor control.** Boston: Reidel Press, 1982 (b).

Grossberg, S., Some psychophysiological and pharmacological correlates of a developmental, cognitive, and motivational theory. In R. Karrer, J. Cohen, and P. Tueting (Eds.), **Brain and information: Event related potentials.** New York: New York Academy of Sciences, 1984.

Grossberg, S. and Pepe, J., Spiking threshold and overarousal effects on serial learning. *Journal of Statistical Physics*, 1971, **3**, 95–125.

Grossman, S.P., **A textbook of physiological psychology.** New York: Wiley and Sons, 1967.

Hall, G. and Pearce, J.M., Latent inhibition of a CS during CS-UCS pairings. *Journal of Experimental Psychology: Animal Behavior Processes*, 1979, **5**, 31–42.

Haymaker, W., Anderson, E., and Nauta, W.J.H., **The hypothalamus.** Springfield, IL: C.C. Thomas, 1969.

Hebb, D.O., Drives and the CNS (conceptual nervous system). *Psychological Review*, 1955, **62**, 243–254.

Hinson, J.M. and Staddon, J.E.R., Behavioral competition: A mechanism for schedule interactions. *Science*, 1978, **202**, 432–434.

Honig, W.K., **Operant behavior: Areas of research and application.** New York: Appleton-Century-Crofts, 1966.

Hoyle, G., **Identified neurons and behavior of arthropods.** New York: Plenum Press, 1977.

Hubel, D.H. and Wiesel, T.N., Functional architecture of macaque monkey visual cortex. *Proceedings of the Royal Society of London (B)*, 1977, **198**, 1–59.

Huff, F.W., Piantanida, T.P., and Morris, G.L., Free operant avoidance responding as a function of serially presented variations in UCS intensity. *Psychonomic Science*, 1967, **8**, 111–112.

Hull, C.L., **Principles of behavior.** New York: Appleton-Century-Crofts, 1943.

Hull, C.L., **A behavior system.** New Haven: Yale University Press, 1952.

Irwin, D.A., Rebert, C.S., McAdam, D.W., and Knott, J.R., Slow potential change (CNV) in the human EEG as a function of motivational variables. *Electroencephalography and Clinical Neurophysiology*, 1966, **21**, 412–413.

Janik, A. and Toulmin, S., **Wittgenstein's Vienna.** New York: Simon and Schuster, 1973.

John, E.R., Neural processes during learning. In R.W. Russell (Ed.), **Frontiers in physiological psychology.** New York: Academic Press, 1966.

John, E.R., **Mechanisms of memory.** New York: Academic Press, 1967.

John, E.R. and Morgades, P.P., Neural correlates of conditioned responses studied with multiple chronically implanted moving electrodes. *Experimental Neurology*, 1969, **23**, 412–425.

Johnson, J.L. and Church, R.M., Effects of shock intensity on nondiscriminative avoidance learning of rats in a shuttlebox. *Psychonomic Science*, 1965, **3**, 497–498.

Kamin, L.J., "Attention-like" processes in classical conditioning. In M.R. Jones (Ed.), **Miami symposium on the prediction of behavior: Aversive stimulation.** Miami: University of Miami Press, 1968.

Kamin, L.J., Predictability, surprise, attention and conditioning. In B.A. Campbell and R.M. Church (Eds.), **Punishment and aversive behavior.** New York: Appleton-Century-Crofts, 1969.

Kamin, L.J., Brimer, C.J., and Black, A.H., Conditioned suppression as a monitor of fear in the course of avoidance training. *Journal of Comparative and Physiological Psychology*, 1963, **56**, 497-501.

Kandel, E.R., **Cellular basis of behavior: An introduction to behavioral neurobiology**. San Francisco: W.H. Freeman, 1976.

Keehn, J.D., Effect of shock duration on Sidman avoidance response rates. *Psychological Reports*, 1963, **13**, 852.

Kelleher, R.J., Chaining and conditioned reinforcement. In W.K. Honig (Ed.), **Operant behavior: Areas of research and application**. New York: Appleton-Century-Crofts, 1966.

Kelso, J.A.S., Southard, D.L., and Goodman, D., On the nature of human interlimb coordination. *Science*, 1979, **203**, 1029-1031.

Kendler, H.H., The influence of simultaneous hunger and thirst drives upon the learning of two opposed spatial responses of the white rat. *Journal of Experimental Psychology*, 1946, **36**, 212-220.

Kendler, H.H. and Levine, S., Studies of the effect of change of drive, I: From hunger to thirst in a T-maze. *Journal of Experimental Psychology*, 1951, **41**, 429-436.

Kendler, H.H., Levine, S., Altchek, E., and Peters, H., Studies of the effect of change of drive, II: From hunger to different intensities of thirst drive in a T-maze. *Journal of Experimental Psychology*, 1952, **44**, 1-4.

Livingston, R.B., Brain mechanisms in conditioning and learning. In F.O. Schmitt, T. Melnechuk, G.C. Quartan, and G. Adelman (Eds.), **Neurosciences research symposium summaries**, Vol. 2. Cambridge, MA: MIT Press, 1967.

Logan, F.A., The negative incentive value of punishment. In B.A. Campbell and R.M. Church (Eds.), **Punishment and aversive behavior**. New York: Appleton-Century-Crofts, 1969.

Low, M.D., Borda, R.P., Frost, J.D., and Kellaway, P., Surface negative slow potential shift associated with conditioning in man. *Neurology*, 1966, **16**, 711-782.

Macchi, G. and Rinvik, E., Thalamo-telencephalic circuits: A neuroanatomical survey. In A. Remond (Ed.), **Handbook of electroencephalography and clinical neurophysiology**, Vol. 2, Pt. 1. Amsterdam: Elsevier, 1976.

Mackintosh, N.J., An analysis of overshadowing and blocking. *Quarterly Journal of Experimental Psychology*, 1971, **23**, 118-125.

Mackintosh, N.J., **The psychology of animal learning**. New York: Academic Press, 1974.

Mackintosh, N.J., A theory of attention: Variations in the associability of stimuli with reinforcement. *Psychological Review*, 1975, **82**, 276-298.

Mackintosh, N.J., Overshadowing and stimulus intensity. *Animal Learning and Behavior*, 1976, **4**, 186-192.

Mackintosh, N.J., Bygrave, D.J., and Picton, B.M.B., Locus of the effect of a surprising reinforcer in the attenuation of blocking. *Quarterly Journal of Experimental Psychology*, 1977, **29**, 327-336.

Mackintosh, N.J. and Reese, B., One-trial overshadowing. *Quarterly Journal of Experimental Psychology*, 1979, **31**, 519-526.

MacLean, P.D., The limbic brain in relation to the psychoses. In P. Black (Ed.), **Physiological correlates of emotion**. New York: Academic Press, 1970.

Martin, L.K. and Reiss, D., Effects of US intensity during previous discrete delay conditioning on conditioned acceleration during avoidance conditioning. *Journal of Comparative and Physiological Psychology*, 1969, **69**, 196-200.

Masterson, F.A., Is termination of a warning signal an effective reward for the rat? *Journal of Comparative and Physiological Psychology*, 1970, **72**, 471–475.

McAdam, D.W., Increases in CNS excitability during negative cortical slow potentials in man. *Electroencephalography and Clinical Neurophysiology*, 1969, **26**, 216–219.

Miller, N.E., Some reflections on the law of effect produce a new alternative to drive reduction. In M.R. Jones (Ed.), **Nebraska symposium on motivation**. Lincoln: University of Nebraska Press, 1963.

Mogenson, G.J., Mullin, A.D., and Clark, E.A., Effects of delayed secondary reinforcement and response requirements on avoidance learning. *Canadian Journal of Psychology*, 1965, **19**, 61–73.

Moll, R.P., Drive and maturation effects in the development of consummatory behavior. *Psychological Reports*, 1964, **15**, 295–302.

Morrell, F., Electrophysiological contributions to the neural basis of learning. *Physiological Review*, 1961, **41**, 443–494.

Moruzzi, G. and Magoun, H.W., Brain stem reticular formation and activation of the EEG. *Electroencephalography and Clinical Neurophysiology*, 1949, **1**, 455–473.

O'Keefe, J.O. and Nadel, L., **The hippocampus as a cognitive map**. Oxford: Clarendon Press, 1978.

Olds, J., Physiological mechanisms of reward. In M.R. Jones (Ed.), **Nebraska symposium on motivation**. Lincoln: University of Nebraska Press, 1955.

Olds, J., Effects of hunger and sex hormone on self-stimulation of the brain. *Journal of Comparative Physiological Psychology*, 1958, **51**, 320–324.

Olds, J., **Drives and reinforcements: Behavioral studies of hypothalamic functions**. New York: Raven Press, 1977.

Pavlik, W.B. and Reynolds, W.F., Effects of deprivation schedule and reward magnitude on acquisition and extinction performance. *Journal of Comparative and Physiological Psychology*, 1963, **56**, 452–455.

Pearce, J.M. and Hall, G., A model for Pavlovian learning: Variations in the effectiveness of conditioned but not of unconditioned stimuli. *Psychological Review*, 1980, **87**, 532–552.

Peters, A., Proskauer, C.C., Feldman, M.L., and Kimerer, L., The projection of the lateral geniculate nucleus to area 17 of the rat cerebral cortex, V: Degenerating axon terminals synapsing with Golgi impregnated neurons. *Journal of Neurocytology*, 1979, **8**, 331–357.

Reiss, D., Sidman avoidance in rats as a function of shock intensity and duration. *Journal of Comparative and Physiological Psychology*, 1970, **73**, 481–485.

Rescorla, R.A., Variations in the effectiveness of reinforcement and nonreinforcement following prior inhibitory conditioning. *Learning and Motivation*, 1971, **2**, 113–123.

Rescorla, R.A. and Wagner, A.R., A theory of Pavlovian conditioning: Variations in the effectiveness of reinforcement and nonreinforcement. In A.H. Black and W.F. Prokasy (Eds.), **Classical conditioning II: Current research and theory**. New York: Appleton-Century-Crofts, 1972.

Reynierse, J.H. and Rizley, R.C., Relaxation and fear as determinants of maintained avoidance in rats. *Journal of Comparative and Physiological Psychology*, 1970, **72**, 223–232.

Reynolds, W.F. and Pavlik, W.B., Running speed as a function of deprivation period and reward magnitude. *Journal of Comparative and Physiological Psychology*, 1960, **53**, 615–618.

Robson, J.G., Receptive fields: Neural representation of the spatial and intensive attributes of the visual image. In E.C. Carterette and M.P. Friedman (Eds.), **Handbook of perception**, Volume 5. New York: Academic Press, 1975.

Rusinov, V.S., An electrophysiological analysis of the connecting function in the cerebral cortex in the presence of a dominant area. **Communications at the XIX international physiological congress, Montreal,** 1953.

Scott, J.W. and Pfaffmann, C., Olfactory input to the hypothalamus: Electrophysiological evidence. *Science,* 1967, **158,** 1592–1594.

Seligman, M.E.P. and Hager, J.L. (Eds.), **Biological boundaries of learning.** New York: Appleton-Century-Crofts, 1972.

Seward, J.P., Shea, R.A., and Davenport, R.H., Further evidence for the interaction of drive and reward. *American Journal of Psychology,* 1960, **73,** 370–379.

Seward, J.P., Shea, R.A., and Elkind, D., Evidence for the interaction of drive and reward. *American Journal of Psychology,* 1958, **71,** 404–407.

Seward, J.P. and Proctor, D.M., Performance as a function of drive, reward, and habit strength. *American Journal of Psychology,* 1960, **73,** 448–453.

Sheffield, F.D., The contiguity principle in learning theory. *Psychological Review,* 1951, **58,** 362–367.

Shepherd, G.M., **The synaptic organization of the brain.** New York: Oxford University Press, 1974.

Sholl, D., **The organization of the cerebral cortex.** London: Methuen, 1956.

Siegel, G.J., Albers, R.W., Katzman, R., and Agranoff, B.W., **Basic neurochemistry,** Second Edition. Boston: Little, Brown, and Co., 1976.

Soechting, J.F. and Lacquaniti, F., Invariant characteristics of a pointing movement in man. *Journal of Neuroscience,* 1981, **1,** 710–720.

Spence, K.W., **Behavior theory and conditioning.** New Haven: Yale University Press, 1956.

Squires, N.K., Donchin, E., Squires, K.C., and Grossberg, S., Redundant information in auditory and visual modalities: Inferring decision-related processes from the P300 component. *Journal of Experimental Psychology,* 1977, **3,** 299–315.

Stein, L., Secondary reinforcement established with subcortical stimulation. *Science,* 1958, **127,** 466–467.

Steinberg, M.S., Does differential adhesion govern self-assembly processes in histogenesis? Equilibrium configurations and the emergence of a hierarchy among populations of embryonic cells. *Journal of Experimental Zoology,* 1970, **173,** 395–434.

Stolurow, L.M., Rodent behavior in the presence of barriers, II: The metabolic maintenance method: a technique for caloric drive control and manipulation. *Journal of Genetic Psychology,* 1951, **79,** 289–355.

Strouthes, A., Effect of CS-onset UCS-termination delay, UCS duration, CS-onset UCS-onset interval, and number of CS-UCS pairings on conditioned fear response. *Journal of Experimental Psychology,* 1965, **69,** 287–291.

Swaab, D.F. and Schadé, J.P. (Eds.), **Integrative hypothalamic activity: Progress in brain research,** Volume 41. Amsterdam: Elsevier, 1974.

Tapp, J.T., **Reinforcement and behavior.** New York: Academic Press, 1969.

Thompson, R.F., **Foundations of physiological psychology.** New York: Harper and Row, 1967.

Tsumoto, T., Creutzfeldt, O.D., and Legéndy, C.R., Functional organization of the corticofugal system from visual cortex to lateral geniculate nucleus in the cat. *Experimental Brain Research,* 1978, **32,** 345–364.

Valenstein, E.S., Biology of drives. In F.O. Schmitt, T. Melnechuk, G.C. Quarton, and G. Adleman (Eds.), **Neurosciences research symposium summaries,** Volume 3. Cambridge: MIT Press, 1969.

Valenstein, E.S., Cox, V.C., and Kakolewski, J.W., Reexamination of the role of the hypothalamus in motivation. *Psychological Review*, 1970, **77**, 16–31.

Wagner, A.R., Expectancies and the priming of STM. In S.H. Hulse, H. Fowler, and W.K. Honig (Eds.), **Cognitive processes in animal behavior**. Hillsdale, NJ: Erlbaum, 1978.

Walter, W.G., Slow potential waves in the human brain associated with expectancy, attention, and decision. *Arch. Psychiat. Nervenkr.*, 1964, **206**, 309–322.

Woolsey, C.N., Organization of somatic sensory and motor areas of the cerebral cortex. In H.F. Harlow and C.N. Woolsey (Eds.), **Biological and biochemical bases of behavior**. Madison: University of Wisconsin Press, 1958.

Zaretsky, H.H., Learning and performance in the runway as a function of the shift in drive and incentive. *Journal of Comparative and Physiological Psychology*, 1966, **62**, 218–221.

Zeaman, D., Response latency as a function of the amount of reinforcement. *Journal of Experimental Psychology*, 1949, **39**, 446–483.

Zeki, S.M., Functional organization of a visual area in the posterior bank of the superior temporal sulcus of the rhesus monkey. *Journal of Physiology*, 1974, **242**, 827–841.

Chapter 2

SOME PSYCHOPHYSIOLOGICAL AND PHARMACOLOGICAL CORRELATES OF A DEVELOPMENTAL, COGNITIVE, AND MOTIVATIONAL THEORY

Preface

Part I of this Chapter contains the gedanken experiment from which the adaptive resonance theory (ART) was derived. ART circuits contain an attentional subsystem and an orienting subsystem whose interactions enable the circuit to self-stabilize its learning, in response to an arbitrary input environment, as the emergent cognitive code becomes globally self-consistent. One of the fundamental contributions of the theory is to show how top-down attentional mechanisms are used to stabilize the learning of a cognitive recognition code. This analysis also treats many issues concerning how signal and noise should be defined in a self-organizing cognitive system; in particular, how the definition of signal and noise depend upon the context-sensitive patterning of all activations across the network, as well as upon its entire learning history.

The article compares the operations and properties of an ART circuit with interdisciplinary data, notably data about evoked potentials and neural substrates of learning and memory. The original derivation of the ART circuit anticipated the publication of many of these data properties. This comparison thus illustrates the theory's predictive competence.

Part II of the article shows how mechanisms of an ART circuit can be specialized to build circuits capable of mimmicking data about conditioning, reinforcement, drive, incentive motivation, normal and abnormal appetitive rhythms, and certain mental disorders. Part II thus links with the mechanisms derived in Chapter 1, and illustrates how multiple derivations lead to the same set of mechanisms.

Part II also notes that a number of mental disorders exhibit behavioral properties which mirror formal inverted U properties of gated dipole opponent processes. These disorders include juvenile hyperactivity, Parkinsonism, simple schizophrenia, and hyperphagic eating. The example of hyperphagic eating illustrates how a circuit's emergent properties can control a complex behavior. In a functionally underaroused gated dipole appetitive circuit, the circuit does not interpret its satiety signals in a normal fashion. This does not, however, imply that satiety inputs are the only signals which can control termination of eating. The momentary *balance* of ultradian hunger inputs, ultradian satiety inputs, rapidly fluctuating conditioned reinforcer inputs, and circadian arousal inputs determines the ability of each gated dipole appetitive circuit to compete with all other gated dipole appetitive circuits to decide which circuit will release the motivational signals that energize its appetitive behavior.

In particular, a decrease in hunger input can both alter the dipole's sensitivity and prevent its release of motivational signals, even if the dipole's satiety input is defective. An increase in conditioned reinforcer input due to appetitively salient sensory cues can also help to release or inhibit motivational signals. Thus the manner in which homeostatic and nonhomeostatic input *patterns* influence gated dipole output is the focus of our study. We suggest that an analysis of hyperphagic eating which focuses only upon whether the satiety *pathway* is viable or not cannot lead to a sufficient understanding of eating behavior, or for that matter any other behavior that is partly controlled by gated dipole processing.

Brain and Information: Event Related Potentials 425: 58–151 (1984)
R. Karrer, J. Cohen, and P. Tueting (Eds.)
©1984 New York Academy of Sciences
Reprinted by permission of the publisher

SOME PSYCHOPHYSIOLOGICAL AND PHARMACOLOGICAL CORRELATES OF A DEVELOPMENTAL, COGNITIVE, AND MOTIVATIONAL THEORY

Stephen Grossberg†

PART I

1. Introduction: Self-Organizing Internal Representations

Studies of event-related potentials (ERPs) can probe a level of neural organization that has behavioral meaning. ERP experiments thereby encourage us to formulate precisely the design problems that are solved by the behaving brain and to translate these design statements into a formal language that is powerful enough to explain how behavioral, physiological, and pharmacological processes are related.

I suggest that these design problems have eluded traditional physical and mathematical thinking because they address a fundamentally new physical situation. These problems concern the design of self-organizing systems, or systems that can generate new internal representations in response to changing environmental rules. This article sketches a psychophysiological theory of how new internal representations are generated. The theory suggests how some ERP-creating mechanisms help to control the self-organization process and how to test these assertions empirically.

In particular, I will suggest that a P300 can be elicited whenever short term memory (STM) is reset by a massive antagonistic rebound within the catecholamine arousal system (Grossberg, 1972b, 1976b, 1978a, 1980a). This suggestion illustrates a sense in which P300s with different anatomical generators can be functionally similar. It also shows why task relevance is important in eliciting P300s, since STM cannot be reset unless it is already active. I will also indicate, however, how a neocortical rebound might elicit a hippocampal rebound by rapidly inhibiting reinforcing signals from cortex to hippocampus. Since the cortical rebound resets a cognitive process and the hippocampal rebound resets a motivational process in the theory (Grossberg, 1975), P300s with different anatomical generators can be functionally dissimilar. Due to the importance of interactions between cognitive and motivational processes for the understanding of both types of processes, I will discuss both cognitive and motivational processes herein and will suggest new explanations and predictions in both domains using the same mechanisms, albeit in different anatomical configurations. I will also suggest that functional

† Supported in part by the Air Force Office of Scientific Research (AFOSR 82-0148) and the National Science Foundation (NSF IST-80-00257).

homologs of many normal and abnormal motivational properties exist in cognitive properties due to the control of both classes of properties by common mechanisms, notably mechanisms mediated by cholinergic-catecholaminergic interactions. Using these homologs, known motivational phenomena can be used to suggest designs for new types of cognitive experiments and vice versa.

The theory also suggests how a mismatch detector, which regulates mismatch negativity in the theory, can sometimes elicit a P300 by triggering a burst of nonspecific arousal to the catecholamine system. An unexpected event can thereby elicit a formal N200 followed by a P300.

Antagonistic rebounds can be caused in the absence of a mismatch-contingent arousal burst, as in the hippocampal example above or in a variety of other situations. I suggest that such rebounds occur during perceptual switches between alternative interpretations of an ambiguous figure (Grossberg, 1978a, 1980a) and that each switch elicits a P300 as STM is reset, despite the absence of prior mismatch negativity. The P300s, in turn, elicit negative components, other than mismatch negativity, that play the role of processing negativity in the theory. This processing negativity is assumed to occur as each newly activated STM representation matches the input data compatible with its perceptual interpretation. In this situation, positive activity can elicit negative activity, rather than conversely.

I will also suggest situations, notably overshadowing experiments, in which a monotonic decrease of P300 can predict either a contingent negative variation (CNV) increase or decrease, depending on whether the eliciting cue is predictively relevant or irrelevant in the situation. Also, situations can be contemplated in which processing negativity may either be insensitive or sensitive to stimulus probability, depending on whether the negativity corresponds to the completion of the internal representation of a given item or matching of a predicted item in a probabilistically controlled sequence of items. In this latter connection, the theory suggests how the same anatomical region can emit P300s of different latencies and sizes due to the way in which different sequences of items activate cell populations with different reset parameters. P300 properties in the theory can, moreover, change as long-term memory (LTM) encoding of sequence properties masks individual item codes as a result of sequence repetition (Grossberg, 1978a).

All these interpretations associate formal physiological mechanisms of the theory with a measurement on the scalp. The theory might, of course, be physiologically correct without its scalp interpretation being correct. The same problem is routinely faced in the ERP experimental literature whenever scalp measurements are used to infer brain processes, since we do not yet have a complete theory relating the two levels of description.

ERP interpretations such as those above emerge in the theory as manifestations of how short-term memory and long-term memory mechanisms influence the processing of expected and unexpected events during the self-organization process. To adequately probe these processing interactions, ERP measures might profitably be appended to a greater variety of experimental paradigms wherein STM and LTM properties are highly structured and controllable on the behavioral level. In this regard, I note that STM can be reset by mechanisms other than antagonistic rebound, notably by renormalization of a limited capacity STM system during attentional shifts (Grossberg, 1973, 1975). This multiplicity of possible STM transactions in a neural network requires a finer processing description than is afforded by consensual language or computer analogies and a richer experimental repertoire to probe this description than has traditionally been used in the ERP literature.

Because the theory relates pharmacological systems to STM and LTM properties, it also suggests some pharmacological manipulations that should cause significant ERP measurements. ERPs used as a psychophysiological interface between behavioral and pharmacological paradigms can become a powerful tool for testing psychological, physiological, and pharmacological theories.

2. The Stability-Plasticity Dilemma in Adult Perception

The design problem on which I will base my article is called the stability-plasticity dilemma. This design problem is easy to state because it is so basic. I will state it in several ways to that everyone can resonate with at least one way.

How can a system's adaptive mechanisms be stable enough to resist environmental fluctuations that do not alter its behavioral success, but plastic enough to change rapidly in response to environmental demands that do alter its behavioral success? How are stability without rigidity and adaptability without chaos achieved?

For example, visuomotor maps for reaching towards seen objects seem to be stable in adults until inverting prisms are used to disrupt them, as in the work of Richard Held and his colleagues (Held, 1961, 1967; Held and Hein, 1963). Then a rapid adaptation can occur. Depth percepts seem to be stable in adults until a telestereoscope is used to alter the expected relationships between cues for the kinetic depth effect and cues for retinal disparity, as in the work of Hans Wallach and his colleagues (Wallach and Karsh, 1963a, 1963b; Wallach *et al.*, 1963). Again a rapid adaptation occurs.

If adaptive memory elements can change quickly in response to behaviorally important environmental events, then what prevents them from changing quickly in response to *all* signals that they process, whether meaningful or not—in particular to fluctuations that do not reflect system success or failure? This issue shows that many neural potentials and signals are invisible to the adaptation process and, from a functional viewpoint, are noise rather than signal. To define behavioral relevance, we need to choose a level of discourse that focuses on the interactions within the system as a whole, rather than on local computations at each cell, which cannot distinguish functional signal from noise. It is because this choice is made in my theory that formal analogs of ERPs like N200, P300, and CNV rapidly arise therein.

3. Critical Period Termination and Cholinergic-Catecholaminergic Interactions

The stability-plasticity issue arises in the infant, no less than in the adult, when we consider how certain environmentally sensitive perceptual critical periods are terminated. Pettigrew and Kasamatsu's recent experiments on kittens probe this issue on a physiological and pharmacological level. Kasamatsu and Pettigrew (1976) show that 6-hydroxydopamine poisoning of the catecholaminergic arousal system to the visual cortex during the visual critical period can prevent normal plasticity from occurring. Pettigrew and Kasamatsu (1978) also show that selective addition of noradrenaline after the critical period has terminated can restore plasticity. This latter experiment raises the question: Why should adding a little more noradrenaline restore plasticity when the noradrenaline in the cortical arousal system was perfectly functional all along?

My explanation of this puzzle is based on a model of cholinergic-catecholaminergic interactions that appeared before the Pettigrew and Kasamatsu work was carried out (Grossberg, 1972b, 1976a, 1976b). This model also has implications, to be discussed below, for understanding normal and abnormal cholinergic-catecholaminergic interactions, as in Parkinsonism, hyperphagia, juvenile hyperactivity, drug withdrawal, categorical boundary shifts, intragastric drinking, schedule-induced polydipsia, self-stimulation, kindling, and simple schizophrenia. The Pettigrew paradigm suggests another way to test this model using ERPs, notably P300. The local P300 should be abolished by the 6-hydroxydopamine manipulation. See Part II for these applications.

4. Hypothesis Testing and Error Correction in a Fluctuating Environment

The stability-plasticity dilemma can also be stated in terms of a system's hypothesis testing or error correction capabilities. How are coding errors corrected, or adaptations to a changing environment effected, if individual cells cannot even detect that these errors or changes have occurred?

The importance of learned hypotheses in perception and cognition was apparent to Helmholtz over a century ago when he formulated his concept of unconscious inference (Boring, 1950). The inadequacy of traditional physical and mathematical ideas for the purpose of explicating such self-organizing psychological processes has had momentous historical effects since Helmholtz's time. For one, the great interdisciplinary successes of Helmholtz, Maxwell, and Mach in physics and psychology during the last half of the nineteenth century did not inspire interdisciplinary disciples. Instead, the next generation of scientists split physics and psychology into separate scientific streams and psychology entered a century of "turmoil and revolution" (Hilgard and Bower, 1975, p.2).

During the last decade, experiments on Pavlovian conditioning, notably on the factors that control attentional shifts, have actively probed the unconscious inference issue in a more modern setting. I have in mind the ingenious experiments of, among others, Dickinson *et al.* (1976), Hall and Pearce (1979), Kamin (1969), Mackintosh *et al.* (1977), Mackintosh and Reese (1979), Pearce and Hall (1980), Rescorla (1971), and Rescorla and Wagner (1972). Unfortunately, the theories that these workers have suggested to explain their experiments are filled with paradoxes (Grossberg, 1982a). Various popular information processing theories, such as those of Schneider and Shiffrin (1976), also contain serious internal paradoxes because they do not understand the stability-plasticity dilemma (Grossberg, 1978a, 1978b).

I will now summarize some of the Pavlovian experiments because they raise issues about the stability-plasticity dilemma. A thought experiment will consider these issues again from a deeper information processing viewpoint.

5. Attention Shifts in Pavlovian Experiments

First I will summarize some main points about attention shifts by discussing a series of four idealized experiments. Then I will review a striking recent experiment of Mackintosh *et al.* (1977) to illustrate some finer points, as well as the paradoxes into which several scientists have been driven by the pressure of recent data.

Figure 1 summarizes the four idealized experiments. Experiment 1 reminds us that an indifferent cue or conditioned stimulus (CS), such as a flashing light, when properly paired with an unconditioned stimulus (US), such as a shock, can be trained to elicit some of the consequences of the US in the form of a conditioned response (CR), such as various indices of fear. Experiment 2 points out that if two equally salient cues, such as a flashing light (CS_1) and a tone (CS_2), appear simultaneously during conditioning trials before the shock (US) occurs, then each of the cues can separately elicit a fearful reaction (CR) on recall trials. The individual cues in a cue complex are thus separately conditionable in some experiments.

Experiments 3 and 4 show that this conclusion is not always true, illustrating the importance of this paradigm for attentional studies. Experiment 3 is a hybrid constructed by performing Experiment 1 before Experiment 2. In other words, the subject is trained to fear the light before a long series of compound light-tone training trials is undertaken. When the tone is presented on recall trials, it does not elicit a fear reaction, in contrast to Experiment 2. Somehow, prior conditioning of the light has "blocked" later conditioning of the tone.

Experiment 4 clarifies the meaning of Experiment 3 by altering the US on the compound trials. For example, suppose that US_1, which follows the light, is a prescribed shock level and that US_2, which follows the tone on compound light-tone trials, is a different shock level. If US_2 is sufficiently different from US_1, then the tone does elicit a conditioned reaction on recall trials. Moreover, if $US_2 > US_1$, then the tone elicits fear, whereas if $US_2 < US_1$, then the tone elicits relief.

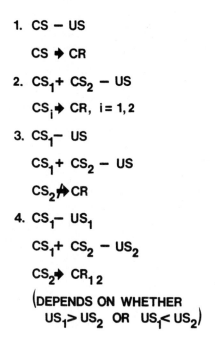

1. $CS - US$

   $CS \rightarrow CR$

2. $CS_1 + CS_2 - US$

   $CS_i \rightarrow CR, \ i = 1, 2$

3. $CS_1 - US$

   $CS_1 + CS_2 - US$

   $CS_2 \not\rightarrow CR$

4. $CS_1 - US_1$

   $CS_1 + CS_2 - US_2$

   $CS_2 \rightarrow CR_{1 \, 2}$

   $\left(\text{DEPENDS ON WHETHER} \atop US_1 > US_2 \ \text{OR} \ US_1 < US_2 \right)$

Figure 1. Four experiments to illustrate overshadowing. See text.

The meaning of these experiments can be summarized in five statements (Grossberg, 1975, 1980a):

1. Many learning subjects are minimal adaptive predictors who only learn about relevant cues. If a subject uses a set of cues, perhaps idiosyncratic to each subject, to generate behavior that elicits expected consequences, then all other cues will be treated as irrelevant. This is why CS_2 in Experiment 3 does not condition well; CS_1 already perfectly predicts the US. By contrast, CS_2 in Experiment 4 predicts a change in the expected consequence; namely, US_2 rather than US_1.

2. Unexpected consequences somehow redefine the set of relevant cues to which we will pay attention. In Experiment 3, US in response to CS_1 is expected, whereas in Experiment 4, US_2 in response to CS_1 is not. That is why CS_2 conditions well in Experiment 4 but not in Experiment 3.

3. Unexpected consequences often occur after the cues to which we attend have terminated. Somehow these consequences work "backwards in time" on the internal representations of attended and unattended cues to abet the influence of erroneously unattended cues. The conditioned stimuli must therefore be stored in some fashion so that they can be influenced by later unexpected consequences.

4. By its very nature, an unexpected event occurs at a moment when the subject does not know which of the myriad of unattended cues should have been attended. Whatever the effects of the unexpected consequence on cue storage, they must affect all the stored representations, since the subject cannot distinguish those which are correct

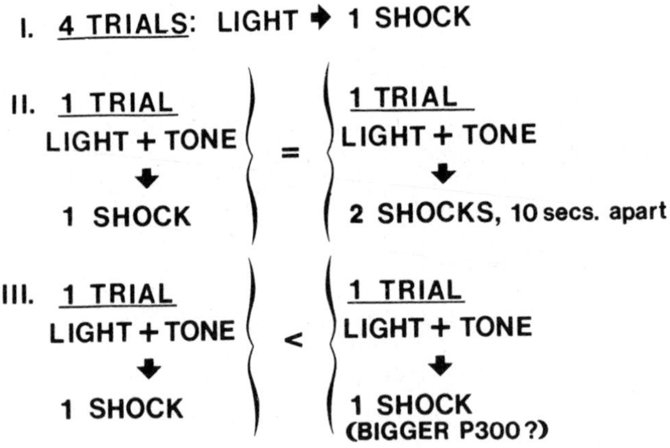

I. <u>**4 TRIALS**</u>: **LIGHT** ➜ **1 SHOCK**

II. <u>**1 TRIAL**</u>
    LIGHT + TONE
    ➜
    1 SHOCK
=
<u>**1 TRIAL**</u>
LIGHT + TONE
➜
2 SHOCKS, 10 secs. apart

III. <u>**1 TRIAL**</u>
    LIGHT + TONE
    ➜
    1 SHOCK
<
<u>**1 TRIAL**</u>
LIGHT + TONE
➜
1 SHOCK
(BIGGER P300?)

Figure 2. Three stages of the 1977 Mackintosh *et al.* experiment. See text.

from those which are incorrect. In other words, the novel event influences cue storage by a nonspecific mechanism that somehow differentially influences, or resets, attended cues and unattended cues.

    5. Novelty *per se* must be distinguished from what is learned about the experimental situation. Otherwise expressed, STM reset must be distinguished from what is encoded in LTM. For example, both the events $US_2 > US_1$ and $US_2 < US_1$ in Experiment 4 are novel. However, CS_2 can become a source of fear if $US_2 > US_1$ and a source of relief if $US_2 < US_1$.

6. Transient Effects: Causality, STM Reset, and P300

    The remarkable experiment of Mackintosh *et al.* (1977) shows that the conditioning situation is still more subtle by focusing on transient conditioning changes. Figure 2 summarizes part of this experiment.

    In part 1 of the experiment, all rats experience four trials on which a light (CS) is followed by a shock (US). In part 2 of the experiment, two groups of rats receive an additional single compound light-tone trial. In one group (group I) the light-tone compound is followed by a single shock. In the other group (group II), the light-tone compound is followed by two successive shocks that are presented ten seconds apart. A recall trial using the tone alone shows essentially identical fear conditioning to the tone in both groups. In other words, the second shock seems not to have affected tone conditioning.

The remarkable feature of the experiment becomes apparent when two other groups of rats are tested in part 3 of the experiment. One of these groups (group III) receives the same training as group I plus a single compound light-tone trial followed by a single shock before a recall trial using a tone CS is preformed. The other group (group IV) receives the same training as group II plus a single compound light-tone trial followed by a single shock before a recall trial using a tone CS is performed. In other words, part 3 of the experiment simply adds an identical learning manipulation onto the group I and II learning paradigms, which by themselves elicited the same reaction to the tone. Remarkably, group IV exhibits better fear conditioning to the tone than group III.

This is a fascinating experimental finding. How can a test after identical second compound trials have different effects if a test after different first compound trials had identical effects? This experiment seems to violate causality on the behaviorally observable level and forces us to conceptualize the behaviorally unobservable mechanisms that underlie attentional shifts.

My explanation of this experiment suggests that the tone on the second compound trial in group IV is more surprising than the tone on the second compound trial in group III and therefore elicits a larger P300 (Grossberg, 1982a).

Mackintosh suggested an explanation of the experiment that led him into a paradox. I shall quote Pearce and Hall's (1980) summary of Mackintosh's position before indicating that their explanation also leads to a paradox. I mention these paradoxes because ERPs can be used to study more directly the attentional processes whose opaqueness on the behavioral level has led to these paradoxes.

Pearce and Hall (1980, p.537) state: "According to Mackintosh, the tone conditions normally on the first compound trial in all groups but loses associability when a single shock occurs on this trial, since it predicts this outcome less well than the light." It seems to me that this explanation is either circular or fails to explain the data. Mackintosh says that the tone loses associability because it predicts the single shock less well than the light. However, on the first compound trial, the tone is an even worse predictor of shock than it is on the second trial. Why does the tone condition normally on the first trial if on this trial it is the worst possible predictor of shock, having never before been correlated with shock? The transient conditioning to the tone when it first appears shows that its very unexpectedness can abet its initial conditioning. I suggest below how it does so by resetting STM in a way that elicits a P300.

Pearce and Hall (1980) realize Mackintosh's error. Unfortunately, they build their concepts using the Rescorla-Wagner (1972) learning equation, which does not distinguish STM from LTM effects. Their conclusion (p.538) is therefore equally paradoxical: "stimuli that fully predict their consequences will be denied access to the processor ... a stimulus is likely to be processed to the extent that it is not an accurate predictor of its consequences." One implication of this position is that a US that is an excellent predictor of food will be ignored. Thus, Mackintosh emphasizes the expected at the expense of the unexpected, whereas Pearce and Hall make the opposite mistake. What is needed is a theory that shows how STM and LTM mechanisms work together to balance between the processing of expected and unexpected events.

Distinguished ERP scholars are not immune to the error of lumping STM and LTM properties together. Donchin makes the following interesting hypothesis in the EPIC VI panel reports, which must, I believe, be sharpened to distinguish STM and LTM effects before it is freed from paradoxical implications: "P300 amplitude will predict the degree to which the eliciting items will be remembered." I suggest, by contrast, that, when the eliciting item is irrelevant, P300 can predict the degree to which the eliciting item will be extinguished (Section 60). If one reads "remembered as irrelevant" instead of "extinguished," Donchin's assertion can perhaps be salvaged, but this interpretation twists language too much to make the assertion informative. At bottom, this difficulty arises because a large P300 can reflect an STM reset that does not predict what the representations newly stored in STM will encode in LTM. The experimental paradigm as a whole will determine the data that are available for LTM encoding.

7. A Thought Experiment About Self-Organization of SP Codes

The following thought experiment indicates that certain constellations of formal properties should appear together in the data and that certain sequences of cognitive operations should occur that can be tested by searching for a corresponding temporal ordering of these constellations.

Several constellations of properties arise in the thought experiment because it concludes that several design principles work together to correct errors and test hypotheses about codes that satisfy the stability-plasticity (SP) criterion. The thought experiment requires only some general properties from these constellations for its completion. The mechanisms that subserve these general properties can be specialized in many ways to accomplish specific tasks without destroying the general properties. In this sense, the thought experiment suggests the minimal general purpose machinery needed to generate SP codes. To adapt this general machinery to special task requirements also requires hard work, but work that is greatly abetted by using the general processing mechanisms as a conceptual framework.

The thought experiment has appeared either implicitly or explicitly in several other articles (Grossberg, 1976b, 1978a, 1980a, 1981a). I repeat it here for two main reasons. First, seveal of the formal mechanisms that it suggests reflect recent data about ERPs, or describe the relationships of ERPs to other experimental measures that have not previously been discussed. Second, several important points which were only briefly discussed in previous expositions are more fully explained here to clarify relationships between cognitive and motivational processes.

8. The Problem of Stimulus Equivalence

The thought experiment is a story that begins in the middle, rather than the beginning, to avoid an infinite regress. We suppose that certain events have already been "coded," and ask how the system can correct an error that occurs when other events erroneously elicit the same "code." Telling any story requires the choice of an appropriate level of discourse. I consider the processing of *patterns* that are *continuously* fluctuating across space and time within *cellular* tissues. If any one of these italicized words were eliminated, I would have found it impossible, or at best unintuitive, to even state what the design problems are, let alone to solve them. In particular, considering feature detectors instead of patterns, binary rather than continuous data, or linear systems rather than cells would cause a serious reduction of mechanistic insight, and has indeed caused serious internal problems in theories that embrace alternative languages as fundamental. I analyse some of these problems in Grossberg (1978a, 1978b, 1978c, 1980a, 1980b, 1980c, 1981b, 1982a, 1982b).

Having chosen a level of discourse and a point of departure, we can begin our story. In Figure 3, two successive stages of processing are depicted. The reader can fix ideas by thinking of the first stage, $F^{(1)}$, as a specific thalamic nucleus and the second stage, $F^{(2)}$, as cortical, or of $F^{(1)}$ and $F^{(2)}$ as two successive cortical stages of processing. Suppose that, due to prior developmental trials, the pattern of activity, or potential, $x^{(1)}$, across the cells of $F^{(1)}$ elicits signals to $F^{(2)}$ that generate a characteristic pattern, or internal representation, $x^{(2)}$, of $x^{(1)}$ across $F^{(2)}$. Think of $x^{(2)}$ as representing $x^{(1)}$ across $F^{(2)}$.

For definiteness, suppose that $F^{(1)} \rightarrow F^{(2)}$ signals are elicited in the simplest possible way; in fact, a way that corresponds to what we know from elementary physiology. Let each activity at a cell (population) of $F^{(1)}$ be capable of generating an excitatory signal to all the cells in $F^{(2)}$ to which it is connected, and let each cell in $F^{(2)}$ add all the signals that it receives in this way. This simple rule implies that the signals from $F^{(1)}$ to $F^{(2)}$ act like a linear filter of the pattern, $x^{(1)}$, across $F^{(1)}$. Moreover, if the $F^{(1)} \rightarrow F^{(2)}$ pathways significantly diverge from each cell at $F^{(1)}$ and converge at each cell of $F^{(2)}$, then infinitely many patterns, $x^{(1)}$, can be represented by the same pattern, $x^{(2)}$. This simple fact raises the following fundamental problem.

Problem of Stimulus Equivalence. How does the system decide which pattern across $F^{(1)}$ should be allowed to have equivalent effects, notably the same observable behavior, due to equivalent processing at higher network levels?

9. Categorical Perception, Bayesian Statistics, and Temporally Unstable Feedforward Coding

This section considers the simplest version of the stimulus equivalence problem to clarify some issues. This section can be skipped on a first reading.

First we need some notation. Let the activity of the ith cell (population) $v_i^{(1)}$ of $F^{(1)}$ be denoted by $x_i^{(1)}$. Let the interaction strength of the pathway (axons) from $v_i^{(1)}$ in $F^{(1)}$ to $v_j^{(2)}$ in $F^{(2)}$ be denoted by z_{ij}. The simplest rule for generating a signal from $v_i^{(1)}$ to $v_j^{(2)}$ is to let the signal strength be $x_i^{(1)} z_{ij}$. Then the *total* input from $F^{(1)}$ to $v_j^{(2)}$ is

$$T_j = \sum_{i=1}^{n} x_i^{(1)} z_{ij}. \tag{1}$$

Suppose, for definiteness, that $F^{(2)}$ chooses the maximal input which it receives for STM storage and suppresses all other activities across $F^{(2)}$; that is,

$$x_j^{(2)} = \begin{cases} 1 & \text{if } T_j > \max_{k \neq j} T_k \\ 0 & \text{if } T_j < \max_{k \neq j} T_k. \end{cases} \tag{2}$$

It is then easily shown that a convex set P_j of patterns $x^{(1)}$ across $F^{(1)}$ will activate the same population $v_j^{(2)}$ of $F^{(2)}$. In other words, a filter followed by a choice implies categorical perception of patterns. The generality of this result argues against categorical perception as a phenomenon peculiar to speech (Studdert-Kennedy, 1980; Studdert-Kennedy et al., 1970). The category that codes a pattern across $F^{(1)}$ switches when the pattern is deformed so much that it crosses the boundary of some set P_j.

Equation (2) has various pleasant properties. It is a Bayesian rule for minimizing risk in the presence of uncertain data (Duda and Hart, 1973). Two successive filtering stages followed by a choice can encode significant global invariants of spatially distributed data (Grossberg, 1978a, Section 19), notably recognitions that are independent of the pattern's position in space (Fukushima, 1980). Given these pleasant properties in even the simplest examples, why do we need to go any further than a classification of the properties of a few feedforward STM storage rules like (2)?

The answer emerges only when we consider the stability-plasticity dilemma. Then we must study how the interaction strength vectors $z_j = (z_{1j}, z_{2j}, \ldots, z_{nj})$ change due

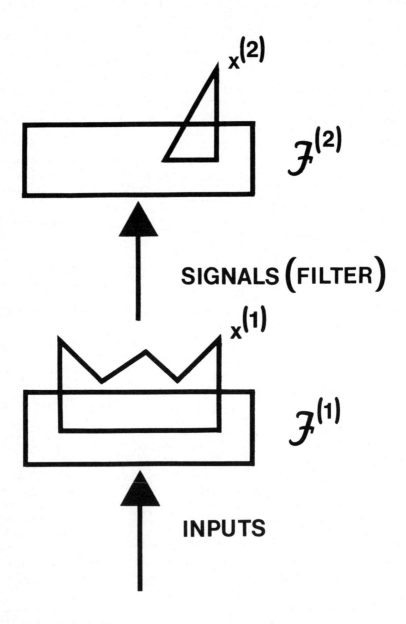

Figure 3. The activity pattern $x^{(1)}$ across $F^{(1)}$ is filtered to elicit a pattern $x^{(2)}$ across $F^{(2)}$.

to learning as a sequence of input patterns perturbs the network. Otherwise expressed, we must study the learning of new categorical boundaries. Various workers (Anderson *et al.*, 1977; Fukushima, 1980; Malsburg, 1973; Pérez *et al.*, 1975) have studied this problem on computers, using small numbers of input patterns, small numbers of cells in $F^{(2)}$, and some version of the associative learning law which I introduced in Grossberg (1964, 1967, 1968). What the computer studies do not reveal is that this learning rule is temporally unstable if the class of input patterns is significantly larger than the number of cells in $F^{(2)}$ (Grossberg, 1976a). Given such inputs, the coded meaning of a given pattern $x^{(1)}$ can continually change at $F^{(2)}$; its pattern class P_j can change through time. This property makes it impossible to build up a temporally stable hierarchy of codes without further structure; the coding pyramid would be build on perceptual quicksand.

After this theorem was proved, I could see that the feedback mechanism needed to stabilize a code developing response to an arbitrary input environment was just like adult Pavlovian experiments (Grossberg, 1975). The need for the same type of feedback mechanism in infant development and cognitive coding as well as in attentional examples encouraged me to strip away unnecessary details to derive the mechanism in general information processing terms. The thought experiment is the result.

I noted above that categorical boundaries can shift due to changes in the LTM traces, z_{ij}. This is not the only way to alter categorical boundaries. Section 37 will indicate how the boundaries can shift due to an interaction between habituation of transmitter gates and STM competition. Categorical shift mechanisms are often summarized under the single rubic of "adaptation." This terminology is insufficient because the shift due to habituation is functionally distinct from the shift due to new LTM encoding.

10. Unconscious Inferences: Why Do Learned Feedback Expectancies Exist?

After pattern $x^{(1)}$ has been trained to elicit pattern $x^{(2)}$ across $F^{(2)}$, suppose that a new pattern erroneously elicits a pattern (equivalent to) $x^{(2)}$ across $F^{(2)}$. How is this coding error corrected? To discuss this situation, I introduce a clearer notation. Denote $x^{(1)}$ by $x_1^{(1)}$, $x^{(2)}$ by $x_1^{(2)}$, the new pattern by $x_2^{(1)}$, and its representations across $F^{(2)}$ by $x_2^{(2)}$. I write $x_1^{(2)} = x_2^{(2)}$ to summarize that the representations of $x_1^{(1)}$ and $x_2^{(1)}$ are equivalent at $F^{(2)}$.

Defining the concept of "error" in all its ramifications is itself a formidable task. I will approach this definition by imposing only the simplest processing requirement: Rapidly shut off $x_1^{(2)}$ if it is in error to prevent further processing, notably observable behavior, from being erroneously elicited by $F^{(2)}$ output. This processing requirement focuses upon the internal consistency of the code across both stages $F^{(1)}$ and $F^{(2)}$, notably on the proper choice of stimulus equivalence classes at $F^{(1)}$ for patterns at $F^{(2)}$.

Reinforcement contingencies bear upon this issue only indirectly, although they will be seen in Section 30 to activate analogous mechanisms, albeit in distinct anatomies. To realize that internal consistency and reinforcement are distinct issues, let us contrast two situations: one in which the patterns $(x_1^{(1)}$ and $x_1^{(2)})$ are rewarded on early trials before being punished on later trials; the other in which the patterns $(x_1^{(1)}$ and $x_1^{(2)})$ are consistently rewarded on early trials, after which the patterns $(x_2^{(1)}$ and $x_1^{(2)})$ are consistently punished. In the former case, the world switches from reward to punishment of $x_1^{(1)}$. In the latter case, $x_1^{(1)}$ is consistently rewarded and $x_2^{(1)}$ is consistently punished. Changing the $F^{(2)}$ representation of $x_1^{(1)}$ when punishment occurs is not adaptive in the first case, since the representation of $x_1^{(2)}$ should be associated with punishment. Changing the $F^{(2)}$ representation of $x_2^{(1)}$ when punishment occurs is adaptive in the second case, reflecting the fact that $x_1^{(1)}$ is consistently rewarded, whereas $x_2^{(1)}$ is consistently punished.

How does the system know this difference, despite the fact that, in both cases, the same pattern $x_1^{(2)}$ across $F^{(2)}$ and the same temporal ordering of reward and punishment occur? How can the system as a whole detect when to recode $x_2^{(1)}$ at $F^{(2)}$ by a new pattern $x_2^{(2)}$ ($\neq x_1^{(2)}$) despite its earlier predilection to erroneously choose pattern $x_1^{(2)}$?

With these remarks as background, our first robust conclusion becomes clear. The error cannot be corrected using only $F^{(2)}$ as a source of data. So far as $F^{(2)}$ knows, when $x_1^{(2)}$ is active, the correct pattern, $x_1^{(1)}$, is active across $F^{(1)}$ and no error has occurred. In other words, the knowledge that an error has occurred resides in $F^{(1)}$; in particular, in the fact that $x_2^{(1)}$, not $x_1^{(1)}$, is active across $F^{(1)}$ when $x_1^{(2)}$ is active across $F^{(2)}$.

How does the system know this? On an error trial when $x_1^{(2)}$ occurs in $F^{(2)}$, $x_1^{(1)}$ is not presented to $F^{(1)}$. To compute an error, the system must somehow readout $x_1^{(1)}$ across $F^{(1)}$ to compare $x_1^{(1)}$ with $x_2^{(1)}$. Pattern $x_1^{(2)}$ is the only possible source of this readout in the present framework.

To understand how a readout can occur, we need to reconsider the developmental trials on which $x_1^{(1)}$ was presented to the system. On these trials, the system adjusted its adaptive filter to code $x_1^{(1)}$ by $x_1^{(2)}$. Now we conclude that, as adaptive filtering proceeded, pattern $x_1^{(2)}$ emitted signals from $F^{(2)}$ to $F^{(1)}$ whose pathways encoded the pattern $x_1^{(1)}$ in LTM (Figure 4). In this way, $x_1^{(2)}$ learns the pattern that it expects to find across $F^{(1)}$ due to developmental experience. This learned feedback expectancy, or template, plays the role of an unconscious inference in the theory. In the context of the stability-plasticity dilemma, the mysterious notion of expectancy becomes a processing constraint on testing whether an error has occurred.

Tolman's claim that subjects learn expectations or plans rather than habits (Tolman, 1932) also gains a more concrete meaning in this setting. Expectancy learning is, however, only part of a larger story, which clarifies both the genius and the limitations of classical theories that correctly isolated important processing fragments, but often at the price of being unable to wed them to the fragments that were prized by competing theoretical positions.

11. Processing Negativity and Match Detection

Figure 5 depicts the rapid sequence of events to which we have been led. In Figure 5a, feedforward inputs are encoded by pattern $x_2^{(1)}$ across $F^{(1)}$. This pattern is filtered by the $F^{(1)} \rightarrow F^{(2)}$ pathways and elicits pattern $x_1^{(2)}$ across $F^{(2)}$ (Figure 5b). Pattern $x_1^{(2)}$ thereupon reads out its learned feedback expectancy across $F^{(1)}$ (Figure 5c). To fully understand how this happens, we need to study adaptive filtering (Malsburg, 1973; Grossberg, 1976a; Pérez *et al.*, 1975) and associative pattern learning by parallel sampling sources (Grossberg, 1969a, 1970, 1972c, 1974). For present purposes, we are more interested in an intuitive constellation of properties than in their generative mathematical mechanism.

The expectancy should manifest itself in a constellation of four properties. (1) It is carried by a *specific* pathway; that is, a pathway which reads out differentiated patterns. (2) It is carried by a *conditionable* pathway. This will only be apparent when new items

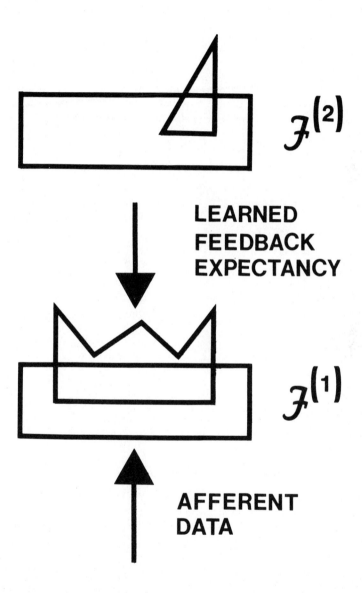

Figure 4. The pattern $x_1^{(2)}$ across $F^{(2)}$ elicits a feedback pattern $x_1^{(1)}$ to $F^{(1)}$, which is the pattern that is sampled across $F^{(1)}$ during previous developmental trials. The field $F^{(1)}$ is an interface where feedforward data and learned feedback expectancies are compared.

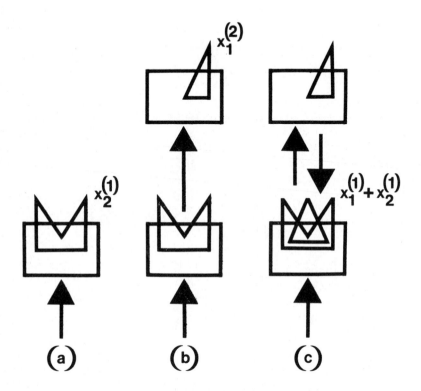

Figure 5. Stages (a), (b), and (c) schematize the rapid sequence of events whereby feedforward data is filtered and activates a feedback expectancy that is matched against itself.

are being encoded. I think that such a conditionable pathway would probably carry a cholinergic transmitter (Section 30). (3) It is carried by a *feedback* pathway. (4) It is activated when a *match* occurs between actual and expected data.

I associate this formal event with its processing negativity or match detector or selection negativity component that is discussed by Ritter *et al.* (1983). Testing the conditionability of this component might be possible using a variant of the following experiment. Present the same configuration of n lights to the left visual field on each trial. Use enough lights to make learning the configuration possible but nontrivial. Present n lights to the right visual field but in a different configuration on each trial. Choose a task that requires intermittent attention to each visual field. If processing negativity is independent of stimulus probability, then varying the lights in the right visual field should cause no change in this component. If processing negativity is conditionable, a progressive enhancement of this component should occur as the light configuration to the left visual field is learned.

12. Novel Events Trigger Nonspecific Arousal

Given that $F^{(2)}$ can read out a learned expectancy to $F^{(1)}$, both $x_1^{(1)}$ and $x_2^{(1)}$ can be simultaneously activated across $F^{(1)}$, despite the fact that only $x_2^{(1)}$ is presented by external means.

We can now ask the next design question: How does mismatch of $x_1^{(1)}$ and $x_2^{(1)}$ at $F^{(1)}$ shut off the incorrect code $x_1^{(2)}$ at $F^{(2)}$? At this point, we need to realize that, just as the information available at $F^{(2)}$ is limited, so also the information available at $F^{(1)}$ is limited, and that the two types of limitations, being complementary, can be overcome when $F^{(1)}$ and $F^{(2)}$ work together. At $F^{(2)}$, we cannot detect that an error has occurred. At $F^{(1)}$, we can detect that an error has occurred by computing the mismatch between $x_1^{(1)}$ and $x_2^{(1)}$. However, we do not know which cells across $F^{(2)}$ caused the error. Any pattern whatsoever across $F^{(2)}$ could have read out the erroneous template $x_1^{(1)}$. Whatever cells at $F^{(2)}$ are active across $F^{(2)}$ when mismatch occurs at $F^{(1)}$ should be inhibited. Since $F^{(1)}$ cannot know which cells in $F^{(2)}$ are active, mismatch across $F^{(1)}$ must elicit a nonspecific event (viz., the same signal) to every cell in $F^{(2)}$. Somehow, the internal organization of $F^{(2)}$ will respond to this nonspecific event by selectively inhibiting its active cells. I will call the nonspecific event nonspecific arousal to make contact with classical physiological vocabulary.

I conclude that an unexpected or novel event triggers a burst of nonspecific arousal that is calibrated by a mismatch between a feedback expectancy and feedforward data. This conclusion reminds us that unexpected consequences in the Pavlovian experiments of Section 5 trigger a nonspecific event that resets the balance between overshadowed and attended cues.

13. Mismatch Negativity (N200)

I will interpret activation of the nonspecific arousal source as a formal analog of the mismatch negativity component of the N200 that is discussed by Ritter *et al.* (1983). This type of mismatch negativity satisfies the following constellation of four formal properties that are orthogonal to the formal properties of processing negativity. (1) It is carried by a *nonspecific* pathway; namely, one that reads out the same signal to every recipient cell. By "nonspecific," I do not necessarily imply "intermodal," only "equal." I think that such a pathway would probably carry a catecholaminergic transmitter (Section 26). (2) It is carried by an *unconditionable* pathway. (3) It is carried by a *feedforward* pathway. (4) It is activated when a *mismatch* occurs between actual and expected data.

The possible relationship of mismatch negativity to the orienting reaction will become clearer in Section 16.

14. The Noise-Saturation Dilemma: Noise Suppression and Pattern Matching in Shunting On-Center Off-Surround Networks

We have concluded that mismatch at $F^{(1)}$ triggers a burst of nonspecific arousal to $F^{(2)}$. We must now ask: How does this happen? Our first step is to ask: How does mismatch at $F^{(1)}$ transform the activity across $F^{(1)}$? Our next step is to ask: How does the matching transformation at $F^{(1)}$ trigger arousal to $F^{(2)}$?

We can now assert that pattern mismatch at $F^{(1)}$ shuts off activity across $F^{(1)}$. Suppose not. Since both $x_1^{(1)}$ and $x_2^{(1)}$ elicit $x_1^{(2)}$ across $F^{(2)}$, leaving these patterns on across $F^{(1)}$ would lock the system into an uncorrectable error and allow $x_2^{(1)}$ to train its $F^{(1)} \rightarrow F^{(2)}$ filter to better elicit the error $x_1^{(2)}$, using the same LTM mechanism that $x_1^{(1)}$ used to train the filter to elicit $x_1^{(2)}$ on its developmental trials. Rapidly shutting off $F^{(1)}$ prevents this erroneous adaptive filtering from occurring and will provide a basis for triggering nonspecific arousal to $F^{(1)}$.

One might legitimately worry at this stage that designing a mismatch detector is too sophisticated an evolutionary task. In reply, I will point out that mismatch detection is part of a constellation of properties whose mechanism solves a fundamental design problem. This design problem, which I call the noise-saturation dilemma (Grossberg, 1973, 1978d, 1980a), confronts all cellular tissues and must be solved before continuously fluctuating patterns can be registered at all. Once the problem is frontally attacked, one realizes that a host of properties, such as matching, masking, normative drifts, tuning, spatial frequency detection, filling-in, lightness computation, STM temporal order information, STM resonance, traveling or standing waves, all emerge in a coherent way as special processing capabilities of this general purpose mechanism. See Grossberg (1981a, Sections 10–27) for a recent review. All too many recent models, notably in artificial intelligence, have failed to realize this basic fact, which is one reason why every property in these models is based on a separate computational trick. Throughout this article, I will insist on principled solutions to our design problems rather than *ad hoc* tricks.

The noise-saturation dilemma is easy to state because it is so basic. Consider Figure 6. In Figure 6a, a differentiated pattern of inputs, I, is poorly registered in the cell activities, x_i, because the overall input intensity level is too small to override internal cellular noise. In Figure 6b, all the inputs are proportionally amplified to escape the cells' noisy range without destroying relative input importance (as when the reflectances of a picture remain constant despite its illumination at successively higher light intensities). Since cells have finitely many excitable sites, the smallest inputs are now large enough to turn on all the sites of their receptive cells; hence, the larger inputs might not be able to differentially excite their receptive cells, since there might be no more sites to turn on in these cells. The input differences are thereby lost because the activities saturate as all the cell sites are activated. Thus, in a cellular tissue, sensitivity loss can occur at both low and high input intensities. As the inputs fluctuate between these extremes, the possibility of accurately registering input patterns is imperiled.

I have elsewhere proved that mass action competitive networks can automatically retune their sensitivity as inputs fluctuate to register input differences without noise or saturation contaminants. In a neural context, these systems are called on-center off-surround networks. Otherwise expressed, a network whose cells obey membrane equations (not additive equations) and interact via an anatomy with a narrow excitatory focus and broadly distributed inhibition can automatically retune its sensitivity due to automatic gain control by the inhibitory signals. In this processing context, one proves that all the variegated properties mentioned above hold.

For the present purposes, we need only notice that a noise suppression mechanism implies a pattern matching mechanism. Figure 7a depicts a network that responds to a uniform pattern by suppressing it. This is easily accomplished in a mass action competitive network. Intuitively, noise suppression means that zero spatial frequency patterns are inhibited or that inputs that do not discriminate one feature detector from another are inhibited.

Given the property of noise suppression, mismatched input patterns are inhibited (Figure 7b) because their peaks and troughs add to create an approximately uniform total input pattern, and is hence inhibited as noise. No sustained processing negativity

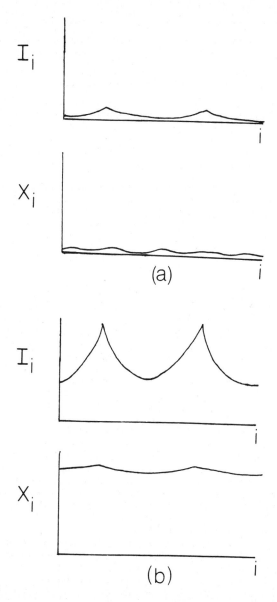

Figure 6. The noise-saturation dilemma: (a) At low input intensities, the input pattern $(I_1, I_2, \ldots, I_n)$ is poorly registered in the activity pattern $(x_1, x_2, \ldots, x_n)$ because of noise. (b) At high input intensities, the input pattern is poorly registered in the activity pattern because of saturation.

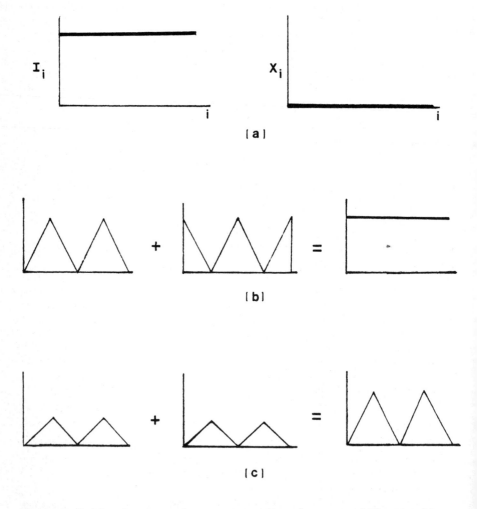

Figure 7. In (a), noise suppression converts a uniform (or zero spatial frequency) input pattern into a zero activity pattern. In (b), two mismatched patterns add to generate an approximately uniform total input pattern, which is suppressed by the mechanism of (a). In (c), two matched input patterns add to yield a total input pattern that is more active than either pattern taken separately.

occurs in this case. By contrast, it can be proved that the sum of matched patterns is amplified (Figure 7c) by an interaction between reflectance processing and Weber law modulation. Processing negativity is thereby elicited.

At this point, the reader might rightly wonder: How mismatched must the patterns be before they are significantly inhibited? How "uniform" is uniform in these mass action competitive systems? This is not an idle question because the whole point about these systems is that they can be retuned. A signal to this system that nonspecifically modulates the gain, or sensitivity, of the inhibitory interneurons within $F^{(1)}$ can shift the size of the criterion, or quenching threshold (QT), that determines how uniform the pattern must be before being quenched (Grossberg, 1973, 1981a). Even if reinforcement affected only the QT of $F^{(1)}$, it could cause recoding of $x_2^{(1)}$ across $F^{(2)}$. Controlling the QT of $F^{(1)}$ and $F^{(2)}$ via nonspecific inhibitory gain control is one way to refine categorical boundaries at one extreme, or to shut off $F^{(1)}$ and $F^{(2)}$ entirely during intermodality attention shifts and sleep at the other extreme.

15. Disinhibition of Mismatch Negativity by Unexpected Events

Having shut off activity across $F^{(1)}$ due to pattern mismatch, we now ask how this event can trigger nonspecific arousal to $F^{(2)}$. What is the source of the activity that energizes the arousal pulse? Is it endogenous (internally driven and tonic) or exogenous (externally driven and phasic)? If it were endogenous, arousal would flood $F^{(2)}$ whenever $F^{(1)}$ was inactive, whether due to active pattern mismatch or passive inactivity. This conclusion is unacceptable. Somehow the system must know the difference between inactivity due to active mismatch, which should trigger arousal, and passive inactivity, which should not.

If the arousal is delivered exogenously, or with the input, this problem is averted and leads to a classical physiological conclusion (Hebb, 1955). In Figure 8, the input pathway bifurcates before reaching $F^{(1)}$. One branch, as before, delivers specific information to $F^{(1)}$ that is progressively evaluated in the hierarchy $F^{(2)}$, $F^{(3)}$,....The other branch activates the arousal source A. Given that A is activated whenever an input is processed, why doesn't A release arousal to $F^{(2)}$ unless mismatch occurs at $F^{(1)}$? In light of Section 14, we can rephrase this question as follows: How does activity across $F^{(1)}$ suppress output from A, and inhibition of activity across $F^{(1)}$ release output from A? Clearly, the cells across $F^{(1)}$ send inhibitory pathways to A that attenuate activity when $F^{(1)}$ is active. The system can differentiate between active mismatch and passive inactivity because activity across $F^{(1)}$ inhibits A, whereas mismatch at $F^{(1)}$ disinhibits A.

We have been led to postulate the following rapid sequence of events (Figure 9). The input activates pattern $x_2^{(1)}$ at $F^{(1)}$ and the arousal source A (Figure 9a). Pattern $x_2^{(1)}$ inhibits A and is filtered by the specific pathway $F^{(1)} \to F^{(2)}$, thereby activating $x_1^{(2)}$ across $F^{(2)}$ (Figure 9b). Pattern $x_1^{(2)}$ reads out its learned feedback expectancy $x_1^{(1)}$ across $F^{(1)}$, whence pattern matching is initiated (Figure 9c). Mismatch causes inhibition of $F^{(1)}$, which disinhibits A and unleashes a burst of nonspecific arousal (mismatch negativity) upon $F^{(2)}$.

This interpretation of the generator of mismatch negativity adds another verifiable property to the constellation. The source of arousal should be a feedforward pathway that bifurcates off the specific thalamocortical pathway that processes the input. Which feedforward pathway should be transected to selectively abolish mismatch negativity?

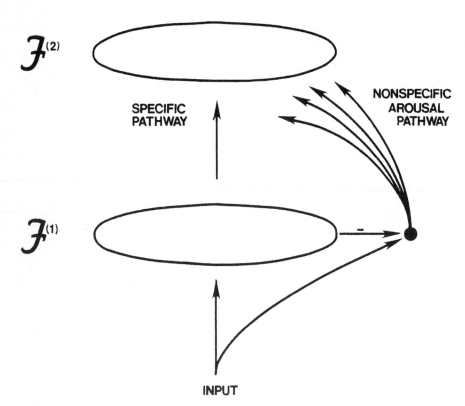

Figure 8. The input data bifurcates into a specific pathway that carries the data's cue or feature information and a nonspecific pathway that activates a source of arousal.

16. Attentional versus Orienting Subsystems: Error Perseveration, P300, and the Hippocampus

The bifurcation of input pathways into specific and nonspecific branches is a special case of a general network design (Grossberg, 1975, 1978a). The specific branch $F^{(1)}, F^{(2)}, \ldots$ is part of the network's attentional subsystem for refining the processing of expected events. The nonspecific branch A is part of the network's orienting subsystem for reorganizing the network in response to unexpected events.

The reader might legitimately protest: Why do you need two distinct subsystems? Why not just let mismatch at $F^{(1)}$ directly shut off the pattern at $F^{(2)}$? The answer to this question contains one of the most important processing insights of this article. If this suggestion were implemented, shutting off the pattern at $F^{(2)}$ would deactivate the feedback expectancy $x_1^{(1)}$ from $F^{(2)}$ to $F^{(1)}$, thereby reinstating $x_2^{(1)}$ across $F^{(1)}$. The cycle of erroneous $x_1^{(2)}$ coding of $x_1^{(1)}$ would begin again, and the network would perseverate in an uncorrectable error. The orienting subsystem overcomes the error

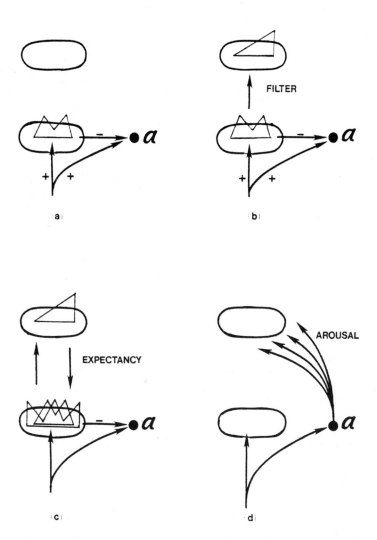

Figure 9. In (a), feedforward data elicit activity across $F^{(1)}$ and an input to the arousal source A, which is rapidly inhibited by $F^{(1)}$. In (b), the pattern at $F^{(1)}$ maintains inhibition of A as it is filtered and activates $F^{(2)}$. In (c), the feedback expectancy from $F^{(2)}$ is matched against the pattern at $F^{(1)}$. In (d), mismatch attenuates activity across $F^{(1)}$ and thereby disinhibits A, which releases a nonspecific arousal signal to $F^{(2)}$.

perseveration problem that would occur using direct reset of $F^{(2)}$.

From this perspective, it is of interest that hippocampectomized rats do not orient to a novel stimulus while they are indulging in a consummatory activity, such as running towards a reward. The cannot "shift attention during the presentation of a novel stimulus or in a mismatch situation" (O'Keefe and Nadel, 1978, p.250).

Another interesting connection can be mentioned at this time at the risk of leaping ahead too fast. I will conclude in Section 21 that the burst of mismatch negativity can reset STM and thereby elicit a P300. This fact raises the question: Given that the arousal burst that elicits a formal P300 is part of the orienting subsystem, what is the relationship between the P300 and the orienting response (OR)? This issue is discussed in the chapter on Orienting and P300 by Donchin *et al.* (1984). In light of Figure 8, the question can be mechanistically translated as: What is the relationship between an arousal burst from A and the OR? A partial answer is suggested in Grossberg (1978a) using the concept of a QT mentioned in Section 14.

I suggest that activation of A can trigger an arousal burst that is funneled (directly or indirectly) into several pathways: One pathway resets $F^{(2)}$, as in Figure 9. For definiteness, suppose that another pathway nonspecifically sensitizes those networks at which the terminal motor maps that control spatial orientation are subliminally fluctuating through time. This nonspecific gain control change lowers the QT of these networks. Their terminal motor maps are bootstrapped from a subliminal status to supraliminal reverberation in motor STM. The supraliminal motor patterns can thereupon read out motor commands that drive the spatial orientation process.

The theory suggests that a strong functional link may exist between P300 and at least one aspect of the OR. This link anatomically takes the form of the generator of mismatch negativity and physiologically is expressed as a nonspecific activity that drives sensory STM reset in the attentional subsystem and gain changes such as those which regulate the storage of commands in motor STM in the orienting subsystem.

17. Parallel Hypothesis Testing in Real Time: STM Reset and Renormalization

Our next design problem is: How does the increment in nonspecific arousal selectively shut off active cells across $F^{(2)}$? This mechanism must possess three properties.

(1) Selective inhibition of active cells: Only the active cells read out the expectancy to $F^{(1)}$ that may mismatch afferent data there. A mismatch implies that an erroneous category at $F^{(2)}$ is active; hence, it must be suppressed. Inactive cells at $F^{(2)}$ should not be suppressed both because they did not read out the expectancy and because they must be available for possible coding of $x_2^{(1)}$ during the next time interval. Otherwise the error correction process would grind to a halt.

(2) Enduring inhibition of active cells: The arousal-initiated inhibition of cells across $F^{(2)}$ must be enduring as well as selective to prevent error perseveration. Otherwise, as soon as $x_1^{(2)}$ is inhibited, the feedback expectancy $x_1^{(1)}$ would be shut off, $x_2^{(1)}$ would be unmasked across $F^{(1)}$ and would reinstate $x_2^{(2)}$ across $F^{(2)}$ once again. To prevent error perseveration, the inhibited cells must stay inhibited long enough for $x_2^{(1)}$ to activate a distinct pattern $F^{(2)}$ during the next time interval. The inhibition is, therefore, slowly varying compared to the time scale of filtering, feedback expectancy, and mismatch.

Once a selective and enduring inhibition is achieved, the network is almost capable of rapid hypothesis testing. The inhibition "renormalizes" or "conditionalizes" the field $F^{(2)}$ to respond differently to pattern $x_2^{(1)}$ during the next time interval. If the next pattern elicited by $x_2^{(1)}$ across $F^{(2)}$ also creates a mismatch at $F^{(1)}$, then it will be suppressed and $F^{(2)}$ will be normalized again. In this fashion, a sequence of rapid pattern reverberations between $F^{(1)}$ and $F^{(2)}$ can successively conditionalize $F^{(2)}$ until either a match occurs or a set of uncommitted cells is activated with which $x_2^{(1)}$ can build a learned filter from $F^{(1)}$ to $F^{(2)}$ and a learned expectancy from $F^{(2)}$ to $F^{(1)}$.

The third property will be discussed separately, since it is one of the surprising, but basic, mathematical consequences of a mechanism that I have already mentioned.

18. Contrast Enhancement and STM Normalization in Competitive Feedback Networks

The third property is needed to prevent the system from inhibiting too much and thereby terminating the error correction process.

(3) Contrast enhancement and normalization of STM activity: If $x_1^{(2)}$ is the pattern that $x_2^{(1)}$ originally excites and $x_1^{(2)}$ is inhibited by the arousal burst, then how does $x_2^{(1)}$ activate any pattern whatsoever across $F^{(2)}$ during the next time interval?

Otherwise expressed, if $x_2^{(1)}$ can elicit a pattern in the next time interval, why couldn't it elicit this pattern during the first time interval, when the pattern would be inhibited by the arousal burst? How can we escape from this deadly circular argument? How do we do so in a principled fashion?

We already know that the noise-saturation dilemma confronts all pattern-processing cellular tissues. Hence, we expect $F^{(2)}$ to be a mass action competitive network. If the competitive interactions were distributed in a feedforward fashion, with input pathways sending off inhibitory input branches from their excitatory on-centers, then the problem just posed could not be surmounted. However, if the competitive interactions are distributed in a feedback fashion, such that the cells themselves send off positive and negative feedback signals to other cells (Figure 10), then the required properties occur as mathematical consequences of this design. These facts were proved in Grossberg (1973) and are reviewed in Grossberg (1980a, 1981a). The positive feedback pathways endow $F^{(2)}$ with a capability for storing patterns in STM. I conclude that a network that can solve the noise-saturation dilemma and that is capable of STM storage can overcome a serious obstacle to cognitive hypothesis testing.

The two crucial properties of this mechanism that we need are contrast enhancement of input patterns and normalization (conservation, adaptation) of the total suprathreshold STM activity across the network. A network that fails to possess these properties is a bad design from the viewpoint of hypothesis testing.

To see how these properties overcome our difficulty, consider Figure 11. Figure 11a depicts the input pattern that $x_2^{(1)}$ generates at $F^{(2)}$ due to filtering by the $F^{(1)} \to F^{(2)}$ pathway. This input pattern is rapidly contrast enhanced before generating the activity pattern $x_1^{(2)}$ across $F^{(2)}$. (The choice of maximal input leading to categorical perception, which was discussed in Section 3, is an extreme case of contrast enhancement.) The contrast enhancement process prevents small inputs from being represented in STM by $x_1^{(2)}$ (Figure 11b).

After $x_1^{(2)}$ is inhibited, that part of the input pattern which activated the inhibited cells is no longer effective. Only the cells that receive small inputs are free to be excited. In a feedforward competitive network, these small inputs would elicit small activities that might be insufficiently large to drive subsequent network events. In a feedback competitive network, by contrast, the total suprathreshold STM activity tends to be conserved. Thus, the uninhibited cells inherit the STM activity that used to energize

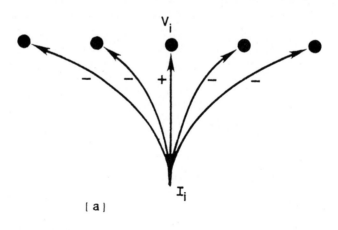

[a]

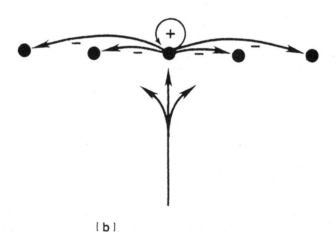

[b]

Figure 10. (a) A feedforward competitive network. (b) A feedback competitive network.

the inhibited cells. The small inputs generate a large pattern in STM (Figure 11c) and, moreover, a pattern that is distinct from the inhibited pattern $x_i^{(2)}$.

19. Limited Capacity STM System: Automatic versus Controlled Processing

Many remarks can (and have!) been made about this STM mechanism. Its prop-

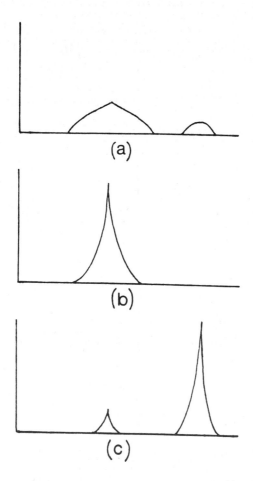

Figure 11. The input pattern in (a) elicits activity pattern $x_1^{(2)}$ in (b) by suppressing small inputs and contrast enhancing large inputs. After $x_1^{(2)}$ is suppressed, the small input activities inherit normalized activity from the suppressed populations to elicit the distinct activity pattern in (c).

erties are reflected in a vast body of data, but many scientists seem not to realize this because they are as yet unaware of how much is known about competitive systems. Perhaps the most obvious conclusion is that the STM normalization property dynamically explains why STM is a limited capacity system, a fact postulated in essentially all cognitive models that distinguish STM from LTM. It is not usually realized, however, that special versions of this same property can be used to explain aspects of behavioral contrast during discrimination learning (Grossberg, 1975, 1981b), of free recall and reaction time data without assuming that a serial buffer exists (Grossberg, 1978b), of LTM encoding by sequence-sensitive cognitive or motor chunks that are capable of rapidly competing in STM to select the most informative and best predictive chunks in a given temporal context (Grossberg, 1978a), and so on.

These STM concepts also show how to escape the serious internal paradoxes of information processing theories, like that of Schneider and Shiffrin (1976), which arise from associating a serial process with the serial properties of controlled search and a parallel process with the parallel properties of automatic search. The untenability of this assumption is suggested when we consider the learning of any new list of familiar items. Each familiar item is assumed to be processed by a parallel process, while each unfamiliar inter-item contingency is processed by a serial process. Does anyone seriously believe that the brain rapidly alternates between parallel and serial processing in this situation? Moreover, how does the brain know how to switch from a hybrid of serial and parallel processing to exclusively parallel processing as the whole list becomes unitized? When we view a picture whose left half contains a familiar face and whose right half contains a collection of unfamiliar features, how does the visual field split itself into a parallel half and a serial half? How does the field get reintegrated as a parallel processor as the unfamiliar features are unitized? The conceptually paradoxical nature of this hypothesis is also reflected in unexplained data. Why is it so that the "time for automatic search is at least as long as that for a very easy controlled search" (Schneider and Shiffrin, 1976)? Do not these data violate our intuitive understanding of the concept "automatic"? No more so than the Schneider and Shiffrin hypothesis, which shows that the accepted intuitive understanding of the concepts "serial" and "parallel" is wanting.

I have elsewhere explained such data without assuming that serial properties imply a serial process, indeed by explicating what kind of parallel process can generate both automatic and controlled properties in different experimental paradigms given different degress of learning (Grossberg, 1978a, Section 61). I mention this fact here because one might be tempted to say off-hand that the hypothesis testing scheme described herein is a serial process. This is false! Its operations unfold sequentially in time, but its mechanisms are parallel. This distinction cannot be overemphasized. In my papers cited above, such distinctions lead to different predictions of the two types of theory as well as to philosophically less paradoxical concepts.

Excellent theorists are spawning these paradoxes because they are confronting mechanisms that cannot easily be inferred using a black-box approach. As another example, STM normalization is an operation akin to summing all the probabilities of possible events to 1 and multiplicative shunting laws are suggestive of multiplying the probabilities of statistically independent events to compute their joint probability. The hypothesis testing by rapid parallel STM reset and normalization might then, to a black-box theorist, be analogized to a serial estimation procedure whereby conditional expectations are updated based on prior information. This analogy leads to an incorrect understanding of how the mechanism works and of what it is doing with the hypotheses.

I hope that ERP workers will not passively accept paradoxical information processing theories. Rather, I hope that ERP methods will be used to help test these theories. Such an approach can both enhance the importance of ERP methods and dampen the depressing dogma that any instantiation of an information processing concept is as good as any other.

20. Sigmoid Signal Functions and Noise Suppression

I will mention one more seemingly innocuous property of feedback competitive networks before continuing my story. This property will be seen to imply unsuspected inverted U and overshadowing effects in Part II of this article.

The positive feedback signaling in competitive feedback networks can be a mixed blessing if it is not properly designed. Positive feedback can subserve such desirable properties as STM storage, contrast enhancement, and normalization. It can also, if improperly designed, flood the network with noise generated by its own activity. This noise amplification property will have disastrous effects on network processing whenever it occurs, and it can occur in formal network "seizures" and "hallucinations" (Ellias and Grossberg, 1975; Ermentrout and Cowan, 1979; Grossberg, 1973; Kaczmarek and Babloyantz, 1977; Schwartz, 1980).

A proper choice of signal function prevents noise amplification (Grossberg, 1973); namely, a sigmoid, or S-shaped, signal function. The use of a sigmoid signal function implies the existence of a QT in a competitive feedback network. The QT property, in turn, controls a feedback network's ability to be tuned and to achieve contrast enhancement. The sigmoid signal inhibits noise as another manifestation of the QT property. Freeman (1979) provides data and a careful model of sigmoid signaling in the olfactory system.

21. P300 and STM Reset: Updating of the Schema

Only the third property that is needed for rapid hypothesis testing, namely STM normalization, has thus far been given a mechanistic interpretation. The two properties of selective and enduring STM reset will next be mechanistically explicated. Before doing this, let us pause to review our main conclusion about error correction in intuitive terms.

Unexpected events can trigger a burst of nonspecific arousal (N200) that resets STM by rapidly inhibiting active representations and allowing less active representations to achieve STM storage by inheriting normalized STM activity. In somewhat less mechanistic terms, the formal N200 can cause "updating of the schema" within the network. I use this phrase from the Orienting and P300 chapter (Donchin *et al.*, 1984) because the process of STM reset is hypothesized to elicit a P300 in my theory.

The Donchin *et al.* suggestion and my own conception will be seen to diverge in several basic ways. For one, I will commit myself to an explicit physiological and pharmacological mechanism subserving the P300. I will also show that this mechanism suggests several operations other than mismatch detection that can trigger a formal P300, and that go beyond alternative theories. Finally, I will show that there are other ways to reset STM (viz., "update the schema") than to trigger a P300. The P300 mechanism that I will describe was first used in both a motivational and cognitive context in Grossberg (1972b).

22. Gated Dipoles: Antagonistic Rebound Due to Slow Transmitter Gating in Competing Channels

The next design problem is quite subtle: How can a nonspecific event, such as arousal, have specific consequences of any kind, let alone generate an exquisitely graded, enduring, and selective inhibition of active cells? How can a one-dimensional command selectively reorganize an information processing scheme of very high dimensions? My solution will make an essential use of chemical transmitters and competition. Arousal, transmitters, and competition are all ubiquitous in the nervous system. The network *interactions* between these ingredients will be shown to literally create information processing properties. These interactions are invisible to microelectrodes and chemical assays, and are only dimly reflected in most behavioral experiments. Mathematics is the tool that most easily probes this interactive level at the present time.

The design problem can be restated in a suggestive way: What cells selectively shut off the active cells in $F^{(2)}$ and keep them off while $x_2^{(1)}$ is being recoded by a renormalized STM pattern across $F^{(2)}$? This reinterpretation faces the fact that a *deus ex machina* cannot be invoked to carry out the reset operation. There are only cells and more cells to do so. We therefore conclude that, associated with each of the cells (or cell populations) that need to be turned off, there exist other cells, specifically related to them, whose activation can maintain selective inhibition. Let us call the cells that are turned on by $F^{(1)} \rightarrow F^{(2)}$ signal on-cells, and the cells that selectively inhibit them off-cells.

Having come this far, we can now recognize that these (on-cell, off-cell) pairs, or dipoles, need to exist in the nervous system for an even more primitive reason. What I will show is that the mechanism that achieves the more primitive demand automatically has the property of dipole reset. Because there exists more than one way to cause a dipole reset, there is also more than one way to cause a P300 in my theory.

The more primitive property answers the question: How does offset of an event act as a cue for a learned response? For example, suppose that I wish to press a lever in response to the offset of a light. If light offset simply turned off the cells that code for light being on, then there would exist no cells whose activity could selectively elicit the lever press response after the light was turned off. Offset of the light cannot only turn off the cells that are turned on by the light. Light offset must also selectively turn on cells that will transiently be active after the light is shut off. The activity of these off-cells (the cells that are turned on by light offset) can then activate the motor commands leading to the lever press. Let us call the transient activation of the off-cell by cue offset antagonistic rebound (Figure 12).

In a reinforcement context, I claim that such an antagonistic rebound is the basis for a relief reaction (Denny, 1971) upon offset of a sustained fear-eliciting cue (Estes and Skinner, 1941). In a perceptual context, I claim that such an antagonistic rebound is the basis for a negative aftereffect upon offset of a sustained image (Brown, 1965, p.483; Helmholtz, 1866, 1962).

I will now describe a minimal model capable of elicitng a sustained on-response to onset of a cue and a transient antagonistic rebound to offset of the cue. The intuitive postulates that led to the model's original derivation are given in Grossberg (1972b). An alternative derivation is given in the Appendix. The Appendix also derives a variety of gated dipole properties that are helpful in understanding aspects of normal and abnormal motivated behavior and ERPs.

Consider Figure 13. In Figure 13a, a nonspecific arousal input, I, is delivered equally to both the on-channel and the off-channel, whereas a test input, J (e.g., light or shock) is delivered only to the on-cell channel. These inputs activate the potentials x_1 and x_2, which create signals S_1 and S_2 in the on-channel and off-channel, respectively. Since $I + J > I$, $S_1 > S_2$. What happens next is crucial. The Appendix proves the following assertions rigorously.

The square synapses in Figure 13 contain chemical transmitters z_1 and z_2. Each transmitter slowly accumulates to a target level. The slow accumulation rate is essential to the model's properties. The target level is achieved by a constant transmitter production rate that is reduced by feedback inhibition proportional to the transmitter concentration. When a signal S_1 reaches the synaptic knobs containing z_1, transmitter is released at a rate proportional to $T_1 = S_1 z_1$. The multiplicative effect of z_1 on S_1 to yield T_1 is called a transmitter gating of the signal S_1. The gating law just says that S_1 and z_1 interact via mass action to elicit T_1. In particular, if either $S_1 = 0$ or $z_1 = 0$, then $T_1 = 0$.

One proves that, if $S_1 > S_2$, then $T_1 > T_2$. That is, transmitter is released at a faster rate by larger signals. Consequently, potential x_3 exceeds potential x_4. These potentials then emit competing signals. Potential x_5 wins the competition over x_6 and emits output signals that are the on-reaction of the network.

So far everything seems quite elementary. Only now do we exploit the slow accumulation rate and the transmitter gating law to show how a transient antagonistic rebound is generated by rapid offset of J.

Because both transmitter stores had accumulated almost equal amounts of transmitter before J turned on, the faster transmitter depletion rate in the on-channel than the off-channel when J is on implies that $z_1 < z_2$, despite the fact that $S_1 z_1 > S_2 z_2$.

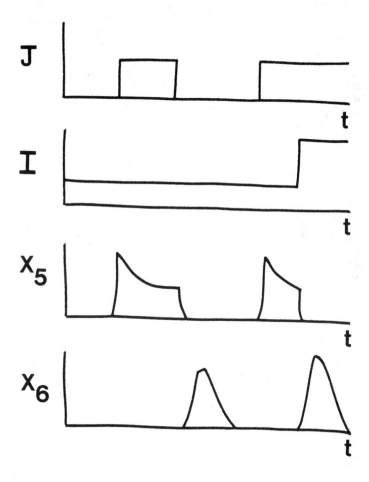

Figure 12. An on-response, x_5, occurs to rapid onset of a specific on-input, J. Either rapid offset of J or onset of nonspecific arousal I causes an off-reaction x_6, or antagonistic rebound. The notation is explained in Section 22 and Figure 13.

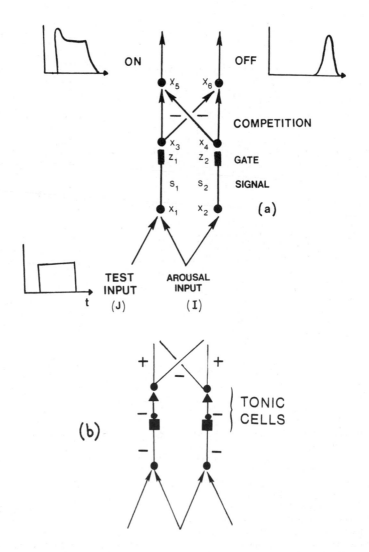

Figure 13. Two examples of gated dipoles. In (a), the phasic input, J, and the arousal input, I, add in the on-channel. The arousal input also perturbs the off-channel. Each input is gated by a slowly varying excitatory transmitter (square synapses). Then the channels compete before eliciting a net on-response or off-response. In (b), the slowly varying transmitters are inhibitory and the net effect of two successive inhibitory transmitters (e.g., DA and GABA) is a net disinhibitory effect.

When J is shut off, both channels receive the equal arousal input I. The potentials x_1 and x_2 rapidly equalize, as do the signals S_1 and S_2. By contrast, the inequality $z_1 < z_2$ persists because transmitter accumulates slowly! Thus, right after J shuts off, $S_1 z_1 < S_2 z_2$, $x_3 < x_4$, and the off-channel wins the signal competition. An antagonistic rebound is thereby initiated.

The rebound is transient because the transmitters gradually repond to the equal signals I by reaching a common level $z_1 = z_2$. Then $S_1 z_1 = S_2 z_2$, and the competition shuts off the rebound.

There exist many variations on the gated dipole theme. Figure 13b points out that the slow transmitters can be inhibitory stages of a disinhibitory pathway. I interpret dopamine and noradrenaline to be the slow inhibitory transmitters in motivational and/or cognitive dipoles. The disinhibitory concept rationalizes many effects of drugs such as amphetamine, chlorpromazine, 6-OHDA, and MAO inhibitors on behavior. The Appendix shows that a single cell, rather than an intercellular network, as in Figure 13, can act like a gated dipole. Such a dipole exists, I contend, in vertebrate photoreceptors (Carpenter and Grossberg, 1981). A full understanding of the gated dipole concept requires that we be able to distinguish the varied anatomical substrates of gated dipoles from their commonly shared functional properties.

23. Tolerance Implies Withdrawal: Rebound Insomnia and a Way Out

The above account depends upon the property that the phasic input, J, gradually depletes z_1 more than z_2 until z_1 equilibrates to the total tonic plus phasic input level, $I + J$, rather than the tonic input level, I. This gradual adaptation is a type of transmitter habituation. It is the type of habituation due to progressive depletion of a slowly varying chemical gate, not the type of habituation that occurs when nonspecific gain control gradually raises the QT of a network and thereby decreases its sensitivity.

Within the gated dipole context, habituation is a prerequisite for antagonistic rebound in response to input offset. If the net production rate could be increased fast enough to offset the increase in depletion due to the gating action, then no habituation and no rebound would occur.

This type of habituation-rebound interaction goes by different names in different experimental contexts. I believe that an important class of examples, whose biochemical substrates seem to be as yet unclear, occurs in situations where the sustained action of a drug causes tolerance to the drug. If the drug acts like a signal whose effect is modulated by a depletable chemical gate, then tolerance can be interpreted as habituation of the gate. More drug S is needed to generate the same net effect $T = Sz$ as z decreases due to habituation. Rapid removal of the drug, or signal, S before the gate z can re-equilibrate to its resting level will cause an antagonistic rebound, or withdrawal reaction. If this hypothesis is correct, one way to prevent withdrawal is to prescribe the therapeutic drug with parallel doses of another drug that speeds up the production rate of the gating chemical to offset its more rapid rate of depletion.

Richard Solomon (personal communication) has collected data on imprinting that exhibit temporal properties analogous to those of drug addiction. In my theory, the formal bridge between these two types of phenomena is the gated dipole concept. Another important phenomenon that should be further analysed from this perspective is rebound insomnia (Ostwald, 1971), which exhibits both habituation and rebound. This example is particularly desirable from a theoretical perspective because Carpenter and I have suggested that suitably connected gated dipoles can generate oscillations whose formal properties resemble circadian rhythms (Carpenter and Grossberg, 1983a, 1983b).

24. A Nonspecific Arousal Burst Triggers an Antagonistic Rebound: Mismatch Triggers a P300

The main property that is needed to understand how an N200 can trigger a P300 (Figure 12) is not intuitively obvious, although it can be proved using simple algebra (Appendix). We need to understand how a nonspecific event, such as a mismatch-contingent arousal burst, can selectively suppress the active on-cells, yet spare the inactive on-cells, across a field of gated dipoles. The Appendix proves that the following remarkable property holds in the gated dipole of Figure 13a if the signals S_1 and S_2 are linear functions of their respective inputs.

The off-rebound size in response to a sustained input J and a sudden arousal increment of size ΔI is

$$\text{OFF} = \frac{ABJ(\Delta I - A)}{(A + I + J)(A + I)}, \tag{3}$$

where A and B are positive constants. Note that a positive off-reaction occurs only if $\Delta I > A$. This criterion is independent of J, which means that an arousal increment ΔI that is sufficiently large to rebound any dipole will be large enough to rebound all dipoles in a field. In other words, if the mismatch is "wrong" enough to trigger a large arousal increment, then all erroneously active cells will simultaneously be rebounded. By contrast, the size of the rebound is an increasing function of the on-input J and equals 0 if $J = 0$. Rebound size is, thus, selective, despite the fact that all active dipoles can be rebounded at once.

Some readers might at this point complain: These formal properties are quite delightful to be sure, but you have proved them using a linear signal function. We thought that a sigmoid signal function is needed to avoid noise suppression in a competitive feedback network; these gated dipoles occur at $F^{(2)}$, which is such a network. Do these properties also obtain when a sigmoid signal function is used?

This is the type of question that only a confrontation between two physical principles can engender. The answer will be given shortly in terms of inverted U effects, analgesic effects, overshadowing effects, and a host of other physical insights that dropped out of the mathematical skies when I asked the same question. Before addressing this matter, let us face some of the implications of the results that we already have before us.

25. An Arousal Test of the Gating Transmitter

The fact that a nonspecific arousal burst can selectively reset a gated dipole suggests one way to test which transmitter(s) are used in the dipole (Figure 14). For example, suppose that one has behavioral control of the phasic on-input (J) (e.g., a conditioned reinforcer such as food, or a localized electrode signal). Suppose that one has also localized a putative off-channel (e.g., a satiety channel) and can micropipette various transmitter antagonists into this location. Finally, suppose that an arousal source (I) modulates this system (e.g., electrical stimulation of the reticular formation). Figure 14a depicts the responses one should find to a sustained phasic on-input when an arousal burst occurs. Figure 14b depicts the responses one should find to the same inputs if one has successfully poisoned the transmitter in the off-channel.

At the present time, this experiment serves more as a thought experiment to sharpen conceptual understanding than an experiment one would run breathlessly to the lab to do. The experiment does suggest, however, that being able to correlate on-reactions and off-reactions at nearby electrode positions is a serious goal for those who wish to study behavioral effects of transmitter dynamics, say by using a microelectrode with multiple recording sites (Kuperstein and Whittington, 1981).

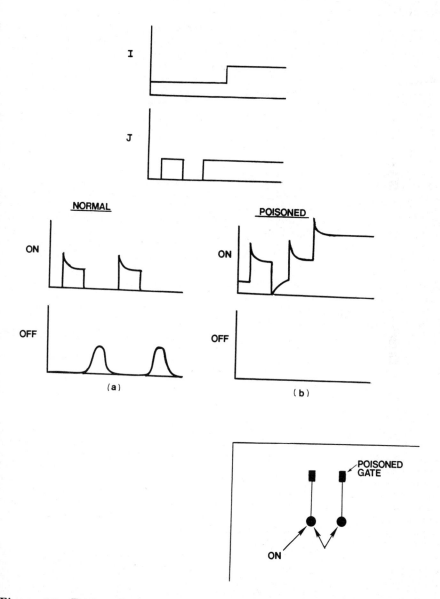

Figure 14. Testing whether a network is a gated dipole and what its off-channel transmitter is. The effect of an arousal burst is depicted (a) before and (b) after the off-channel transmitter is poisoned. Note that an off-rebound occurs in response to phasic cue offset in the on-channel of the poisoned dipole. A sustained on-response follows an arousal increment in a poisoned dipole, instead of a transient off-response.

26. P300, Catecholamine Rebound, CNV Rebound, Critical Period Termination

In all the physical examples where gated dipoles have heretofore been used, the transmitter gate has either been identified as a catecholaminergic transmitter, such as DA or NA (Grossberg, 1972b, 1975, 1976b, 1980a), or as an ion acting like a second messenger, such as Ca^{++} (Carpenter and Grossberg, 1981; Grossberg, 1968). To discuss the cortical P300, I suggest that the transmitter is a catecholamine, probably NA (Pettigrew and Kasamatsu, 1978). This interpretation leads us to several important conclusions.

(1) The P300 occurs whenever STM is reset by a massive antagonistic rebound within the cortical catecholaminergic arousal system.

(2) STM reset by antagonistic rebound is not the same operation as STM reset by renormalization. Although a rebound often precedes a renormalization, a renormalization can occur due to an attention shift in the absence of a rebound. Whereas a rebound is a transient effect due to the action of a slow transmitter gate, a renormalization is a sustained effect of a limited capacity STM field that does not depend on transmitter gating. In this regard, Tecce (1979) has elegantly studied a possible CNV rebound effect, but this effect may really be due to renormalization. A test of time scale is needed to discriminate the two possibilities.

(3) The distinction between rebound and renormalization shows that Donchin's phrase "updating of the schema" is insufficient to capture the role of P300. The fact that an antagonistic rebound can be due either to offset of a phasic cue or to onset of an arousal burst suggests that no single phrase about P300 can capture its processing implications.

The distinction between phasic cue offset and arousal burst onset is, I believe, important for understanding how a cortical P300 might precede a hippocampal P300 if a surprising event rebounds cortical STM while positive conditioned reinforcers are being attended. I suggest that the cortical rebound will register a cortical P300. Inhibiting the conditioned reinforcer withdraws phasic reinforcing input from the hippocampus, whose dipole structure responds with a hippocampal P300. Part II discusses these issues in greater detail.

(4) The above mechanisms indicate how environmentally sensitive critical periods might be terminated and dynamically maintained by the action of learned feedback expectancies. These expectancies modulate an arousal mechanism that buffers already coded populations by shutting them off so rapidly in response to erroneous STM coding that LTM recoding is impossible. In other words, the mechanism helps to stabilize the LTM code against continual erosion by environmental fluctuations as it drives the search for new codes.

If this conclusion is correct, then all the machinery we have postulated should develop before the end of the critical period that it is controlling. These mechanisms include: (a) gated cortical dipoles (P300), (b) catecholaminergic arousal (N200), (c) lateral inhibition across $F^{(1)}$ and $F^{(2)}$, and (d) corticothalamic or corticocortical conditionable feedback pathways (cholinergic?).

Two cautionary comments should be made. First, the timing and even the form of the ERPs in (a) and (b) in the infant can differ from those in the adult, as discussed by Kurtzberg *et al.* (1984) and Otto *et al.* (1984), without denying their role in critical period termination. Second, I wish to carefully emphasize the words *environmentally sensitive* critical periods. Prewired developmental unfolding is not included in this discussion, although all the mechanisms would work in a prewired setting if endogenously driven input patterns replaced exogenously driven input patterns, and if the QTs of the system were kept low enough to allow pattern processing to unfold.

27. A P300 Test of the Critical Period Buffer Mechanism

A variant of the oddball paradigm can be used to test whether the buffering mechanism I have suggested helps to terminate the visual critical period. A pair of visual stimuli should be constructed from complementary feature configurations, such as a white bar (bars) on a black field and a black bar (bars) on a white field. These stimuli should be presented sequentially in such a way that the complementary features excite the same retinal positions.

Two experimental groups would be needed: a group that receives the two stimuli in a regular alternating sequence and a group that receives each stimulus 50% of the time in a random order. Although both groups receive the stimuli the same number of times, the random group should experience larger P300s and a faster rate of feature encoding.

These advantages would be explained by the antagonistic rebounds that occur when a stimulus different from the one expected occurs. If complementary cortical feature detectors are organized into dipole pairs, the rebound cue to the nonoccurrence of the expected stimulus should add on to the direct effect of the actual stimulus, since it is complementary to the expected stimulus, thereby enhancing the cortical reaction to the actual stimulus and driving faster LTM encoding in its adaptive filter.

If this prediction turns out to be true, it will support my contention that functional homologs exist between cortical and motivational rebound mechanisms, since a similar mechanism can be used to explain the partial reinforcement acquisition effect (Grossberg, 1975).

28. Adaptive Resonance: A Solution to the Stability Plasticity Dilemma

My previous discussions have worried about how to protect already encoded populations from adventitious recoding by erroneous events. Now I will summarize what happens when a correct encoding occurs. A pattern across $F^{(1)}$ elicits a representation across $F^{(2)}$ that reads out a template that matches the pattern. As I mentioned in Section 14, a pattern match amplifies the reaction that occurs to the pattern alone. Due to pattern matching, the interfield signals $F^{(1)} \rightarrow F^{(2)}$ and $F^{(2)} \rightarrow F^{(1)}$ mutually reinforce each other and activities at both levels are amplified and locked into STM. In short, an STM resonance is established. Because the STM activities persist much longer in time during the resonant state than the passive decay rates of individual cells would allow, or than the durations between rapid reset operations in the mismatch situation would allow, the slowly varying LTM traces in the adaptive filter and expectancy pathways now have sufficient time to sample the STM patterns and to store them in LTM. I therefore call this dynamic state an adaptive resonance (Grossberg, 1976b, 1978a, 1980a).

I should emphasize a subtle point about the adaptive resonance idea. Before resonance occurs, the LTM traces in the filtering and expectancy pathways do a perfectly good job of controlling the readout of activities across $F^{(2)}$ and $F^{(1)}$, respectively. However, the LTM traces cannot change in response to these STM activities unless the STM activities resonate long enough for the slowly varying LTM traces to sample them. The LTM traces are adaptively blind to the STM activities that they direct until resonance occurs. My solution to the stability-plasticity dilemma freely admits that the LTM traces are potential victims of all the local signals that they process, but saves the LTM traces from chaotic recoding by ensuring that only resonant signals can drive significant LTM changes. The resonant signals, in turn, can only occur when the system as a whole determines that the local signals are worthy of LTM encoding.

The resonant state provides a context-sensitive interpretation of the data that explicates in neural terms the idea that the network is paying attention to the data. The fact that LTM encoding is driven by STM resonance provides a mechanistic explanation of the psychological fact that a relationship exists between paying attention to an event and coding it in LTM (Craik and Lockhart, 1972; Craik and Tulving, 1975).

Freeman (1975, 1980) has provided the most beautiful data I know of that measure a perceptually driven resonance on the physiological level. It might be instructive to perform ERP experiments in parallel with Freeman's physiological experiments to determine which ERPs reflect the resonant state. Presumably, some type of slow negative wave will be measured.

At this point, I can summarize simply and precisely what I mean by the "code" of a network. The code is the set of dynamically stable resonances that the network can support in response to a prescribed input environment. I believe that a major task of cognitive psychology is to classify how prescribed initial choices of the filtering, competition, expectancy, and dipole parameters bias the network to learn different invariants of the data, or categorical boundaries, in response to prescribed sequences of input patterns. This assertion celebrates James Gibson's wonderful experimental intuition, which led him, despite an almost total ignorance of processing substrates, to realize that the perceptual system "resonates to the invariant structure or is attuned to it" (Gibson, 1979, p.249).

The remaining sections will apply the ideas that are physically or mathematically latent in the previous paragraphs towards the explanation and prediction of interdisciplinary data. Various of these data have not been explained before to the best of my knowledge.

PART II

29. The Dipole Field

Part II of this article will use the foundation built up in Part I to derive networks that model cognitive and motivational interactions. An understanding of such interactions is indispensable to the student of abnormal behavior, since a breakdown within either type of network can upset the interactive balance within the system as a whole. Such an understanding is also useful to persons who are interested in normal cognitive or attentional behavior to clarify how changes in motivational parameters (e.g., hunger, thirst, fear, relief) can alter cognitive processing, how cognitive processes can feed back upon themselves via pathways that run through motivational mechanisms, and how data and paradigms about motivational phenomena can suggest homologous studies of cognitive phenomena.

A paradigm wherein motivational influences on cognitive processing occur has, for example, recently been developed by Bower and his colleagues (Bower, 1981; Bower *et al.*, 1981). These investigators have studied how subjects' moods during learning can influence their recall when the same or incongruent moods are active during recall. Their results are compatible with my hypothesis (Grossberg, 1972a, 1972b, 1975), reviewed below, that incentive motivational feedback from positive or negative drive representations to cognitive representations is positive, nonspecific, conditionable, and modulates LTM encoding and readout of the cognitive representations. To test whether this mood effect on memory is due to the type of hippocampal-to-cortical feedback that I envisage, a CNV measure might be added to the Bower *et al.* paradigm. If so, learned associations between mood and memory should elicit larger CNVs during recall of mood-congruent lists than during other manipulations.

An example wherein cognitive processing may interact with motivational processing is suggested by the discovery of a hippocampal P300 by Halgren *et al.* (1980). If cortical P300s are ever going to be functionally disentangled from hippocampal P300s, a paradigm is needed wherein the two types of P300s can be differentially manipulated by the experimenter. I suggest the use of a conditioning-attentional paradigm below. To understand my prediction in this paradigm, one needs to study the motivational networks on their own terms, notably how a cortical P300 may elicit a hippocampal

P300 and how changes in conditioned reinforcer or drive input strength may alter the size of the hippocampal P300. A hippocampal P300 was predicted in Grossberg (1980a).

Studies of abnormal syndromes, such as juvenile hyperactivity or simple schizophrenia, need to distinguish whether motivational, cognitive, or both types of processes are faulty. For example, I will compare hyperactive behavior with predictions of a formal syndrome that occurs whenever a gated dipole is underaroused. The same formal syndrome occurs whether the gated dipole occurs in a motivational or a cognitive network, but its behavioral manifestations will be different in the two cases. Whatever the interpretation, an underaroused gated dipole exhibits an elevated response threshold, a hypersensitive reaction to a suprathreshold increment in its on-input, and a hyposensitive antagonistic rebound to a phasic decrement that halves its on-input. In a motivational context, these properties might yield hypersensitivity to increments in cues like ice cream or shock, but hyposensitive antagonistic reactions to a partial withdrawal of these cues. In a cognitive context, by contrast, one might expect elevated sensory thresholds and weaker negative aftereffects to decrements in color or orientation cues (Grossberg, 1980a).

The ubiquitous occurrence of gated dipoles also suggests tests of habituation and dishabituation in both motivational and cognitive processors. Due to the slow habituation rate of a gated dipole's transmitters, slow onset of a shock can be less negatively reinforcing than rapid onset to the same shock asymptote. For the same formal reason, slow onset of a sensory cue may lead to weaker initial STM storage of the cue and thus to a smaller P300 when STM is reset. I suggest also that the slow reaction rate of a gating chemical may explain why slow shutting off of a shock may be less positively reinforcing, or why slow removal of an addicting drug can lessen withdrawal symptoms, which I view as a type of antagonistic rebound phenomenon. On the cognitive level, slow removal of a phasic cue may cause a smaller P300 for the same mechanistic reason.

To complement these habituation-related effects of slow chemical gates, I also suggest that certain dishabituation phenomena may occur in motivational and cognitive processes due to gated dipole mediation, that these phenomena should vary in characteristic ways with the arousal level, and that some of these variations may be testable using ERPs. For example, I suggest that, when environmental contingencies unexpectedly change, STM reset in response to the novel event has properties that endow both previously overshadowed cues and the novel cues with an advantage in STM storage that may be testable using a P300 measure. The enhancement of the STM activity at previously overshadowed representations is interpreted as a dishabituation reaction in my theory. The theory indicates how behavioral manipulations of unexpected events may elicit physiological dishabituation reactions caused by pharmacologically identified gating reactions that are related to psychophysiological P300 measures. If a network's arousal level is lowered into the underaroused range, the same STM reset mechanism can enhance, or dishabituate, STM activities that would ordinarily be reset, or rebounded. This property can both reduce the P300 and cause attentional reset problems. I also suggest that, when this underaroused dishabituation reaction occurs in suitable motivational or motor command networks, it can cause a paradoxical enhancement of a reinforcer's potency or a motor reaction akin to Parkinsonian bracing and should influence the ERPs that subserve these events in a manner homologous to the influence on P300 in cognitive examples. Due to the existence of such pervasive interrelationships between cognitive and motivational phenomena, I will move freely between both types of examples below to present the theory in a way that I feel most efficiently presents the formal ideas and their connections. The reader who is primarily interested in just one type of example is invited to skip sections of lesser interest on a first reading.

One of the most important implications of the thought experiment of Part I has not yet been systematically explored. How can we marry the gated dipole structure to the mass action competitive feedback structure? Consider, in particular, those structures wherein a nonspecific arousal burst can rebound activities that are reverberating

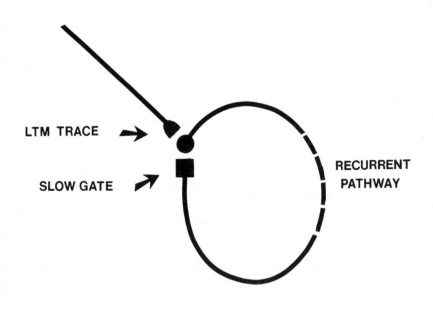

LTM TRACE →

SLOW GATE ↗

RECURRENT
PATHWAY

◀ = CHOLINERGIC

■ = CATECHOLAMINERGIC

Figure 15. A conditionable cue pathway feeds into a gated feedback loop. The LTM trace in the conditionable pathway is assumed to be cholinergic, whereas the gate is assumed to be catecholaminergic.

in STM after the cues that initiated STM storage have terminated. In order for this to happen, the STM feedback loops must contain the transmitter gates, so that STM activity can differentially deplete the active STM loops and thereby prepare them for rebound. Figure 15 summarizes this structural arrangement by depicting a conditionable input pathway abutting a gated feedback pathway. I will henceforth assume that the transmitter in a conditionable input pathway is cholinergic and that the transmitter in a gated STM feedback loop is catecholaminergic (Grossberg, 1972b), since a large body of data is compatible with this suggestion. Some of these data will be reviewed below.

There exists another way to derive Figure 15, even when no arousal-initiated rebound exists. This alternative derivation holds when the off-cells represent features or behavioral categories that are complementary to those represented by the on-cells; e.g., fear vs. relief, hunger vs. satiety, vertical red bar on green field vs. vertical green bar on red field, etc. The derivation proceeds in three steps (Grossberg, 1972b).

(1) Sudden offset of a conditioned cue input can cause a rebound, much as offset of a conditioned source of fear can elicit relief (Denny, 1971; Masterson, 1970; McAllister and McAllister, 1970). To accomplish this rebound, the cue input is delivered to the network at a stage before the transmitter gate. Only in this way can the cue deplete the gate so that its offset can drive a rebound.

(2) Onset of a cue input can elicit sampling signals capable of encoding a rebound in LTM, much as a tone that turns on contingent upon shock offset can become a source of conditioned relief (Dunham, 1971; Dunham *et al.*, 1969; Hammond, 1968; Rescorla, 1969; Rescorla and LoLordo, 1965; Weisman and Litner, 1969). Thus, the cue input is delivered to the network at a stage after the transmitter gate, where the rebound can be sampled.

(3) Properties (1) and (2) are true for all cues that can be conditioned to these categories, since whether a given cue will be conditioned to onset or to offset of any particular category is not known *a priori*. Thus, every cue input is delivered both before and after the transmitter gating stage. The transmitter gate thus occurs in a feedback pathway, as in Figure 15.

The existence of two distinct derivations leading to a similar network design is important, since not every recurrent network that can be reset by offset of a cue need possess a mismatch-contingent arousal source, even though an arousal source *per se* is required. These derivations suggest that the anatomical design in Figure 15 is basic and that the input mechanisms that control rebound in this common design can be adapted to satisfy specialized processing constraints.

One further constraint can readily be satisfied by this design. The cue inputs arrive before the stage of dipole competition so that at most one of the complementary outputs (on-cell vs. off-cell) can be positive at any time. The next section depicts the minimal anatomy that joins together gated dipole feedback pathways and conditionable cue input pathways that terminate before the dipole competition stage.

30. Drives, Conditioned Reinforcers, Incentive Motivation, and CNV

Figure 16 depicts such a minimal anatomy and assigns to its pathways a motivational interpretation. In Figure 16, the specific inputs to the gated dipole are of two kinds: internal drive inputs and external cue inputs. For definiteness, let the positive drive input increase with hunger and let the negative drive input increase with satiety, either due to gastric distention or slower metabolic factors (Anand and Pillai, 1967; Janowitz *et al.*, 1949; LeMagnen, 1972; Sharma *et al.*, 1961). Let the drive inputs and the nonspecific arousal input be gated by a catecholaminergic transmitter in both the on-channel and the off-channel to calibrate the proper relative sizes of on and off dipole responses.

Let each external cue input send a conditionable pathway to both the on-channel and the off-channel of the dipole, so that each cue can become a conditioned reinforcer of either positive or negative sign, depending on whether the LTM trace is larger in its on-channel or in its off-channel. To calibrate the relative sizes of these LTM traces in an unbiased fashion, I assume that the transmitter system that subserves LTM encoding in both branches is the same and is cholinergic. These chemical interpretations may eventually have to be changed, but the processing requirements of accurately calibrating relative rebound or conditioned reinforcer strength across competing channels are robust.

The cells at which external cue, drive, and arousal inputs converge are assumed to be polyvalent: These cells cannot fire vigorously unless both their external cue and their internal drive inputs are sufficiently large. The outputs from these polyvalent

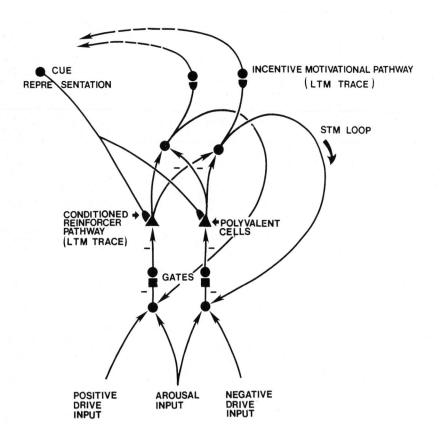

Figure 16. Drive inputs and (conditioned) reinforcer inputs are the specific inputs to a gated dipole whose outputs deliver (conditioned) incentive motivational signals back to internal representations of external cues. These outputs also feed back to a stage before the slow gates, so that offset of a reinforcing signal can drive a rebound, whereas onset of a conditioned reinforcer pathway can initiate encoding by its LTM traces of the gated activity pattern. This STM feedback loop can store a motivational decision against small input perturbations (hysteresis), maintain a steady motivational baseline (normalization), and regulate sharp motivational switching (contrast enhancement).

cells compete before generating a net dipole output in either the on-cell or the off-cell channel, but not both. These dipole outputs play the role of incentive motivation in the theory.

Drives, reinforcers, and incentives are conceptually distinct in Figure 16, by contrast with several other motivational theories (Bolles, 1967; Estes, 1969; Mackintosh, 1974; Miller, 1963). For example, Mackintosh (1974, p.233) writes: "Stimuli associated with reinforcers do not motivate instrumental responses" and advocates "discarding the idea of incentive as motivation and replacing it with the idea of incentive as the anticipation of a goal." Part of the difference between our two positions is semantic, since Mackintosh is arguing against the classical view of Hull and Spence that incentive motivation is a type of nonspecific motivation that activates all response tendencies indifferently. The present theory also argues against this position since, within it, incentive motivation is carried by a conditionable pathway that can differentially amplify certain STM representations above others due to prior conditioning. I also suggest that this conditionable incentive pathway subserves a motivational component of the CNV (Cant and Bickford, 1967; Grossberg, 1975; Irwin et al., 1966). However, the present theory recognizes and distinguishes both the motivational and the expectancy properties of cues and views Mackintosh's reaction against Hull and Spence as an instance of throwing out the baby with the bathwater.

The existence of polyvalent cells is compatible with the intuition that incentive motivation need not be released even when drive is high if compatible cues are unavailable. For example, a male animal left alone will busily do the many things characteristic of his species, such as grooming, eating, and exploring. He does not look sexually motivated. However, if a female animal is presented to him, his behavior can change dramatically (Beach, 1956; Bolles, 1967, Chapter 7). Incentive motivation need not be released even when compatible cues are available if drive is low. Seward and Proctor (1960) and Seward et al. (1958, 1960) found that, if an animal is not hungry, then no amount of food will be adequate to reinforce its behavior.

31. Extinction, Conditioned Emotional Responses, Conditioned Avoidance Responses, and Secondary Conditioning

This section reviews how LTM sampling by each cue of both the on-channel and the off-channel contributes to the explanation of some basic motivational processes (Grossberg, 1972a, 1972b) and thereby indirectly supports the claim that both LTM pathways need to be built up from similarly calibrated transmitter mechanisms.

A similar design will be used in Section 57 to explain how incentive motivational feedback regulates attentional processing. The simplest LTM law says that LTM encoding occurs only when a cue pathway and a contiguous polyvalent cell are simultaneously active.

Suppose that, during early learning trials, a cue occurs just before a large unconditioned signal, such as a shock, which turns on the on-channel. This unconditional signal elicits the incentive output of the on-channel, which triggers a fear reaction, even before learning occurs. By associating the cue with shock on learning trials, its LTM trace abutting the on-channel grows much larger than its LTM trace abutting the off-channel. If the cue is then presented by itself, the LTM-gated signal to the on-channel is much larger than the LTM-gated signal to the off-channel. The on-channel wins the dipole competition, so the cue elicits fear. The cue has thus become a conditioned reinforcer that can elicit a conditioned emotional response (CER) (Estes and Skinner, 1941).

Now suppose that environmental contingencies change after the cue has become a CER. Suppose that the cue no longer reliably predicts future events and that an unexpected event occurs while the cue is on.

Suppose that the unexpected event triggers an antagonistic rebound in the off-channel. Since the cue is on, its LTM trace abutting the off-channel will grow. If this occurs sufficiently often, the off-LTM trace will grow as large as the on-LTM trace. After this happens, presenting the cue will generate comparable LTM-gated signals to both the on-channel and the off-channel. After these signals compete, the net incentive motivational output will be very small. The cue is no longer a CER. It has been rapidly extinguished by expected events.

This cue is extinguished because it remains on both before and after the unexpected event. It is an irrelevant cue with respect to the contingency that triggered the unexpected event. By contrast, a cue that turns on right after the unexpected event occurs will sample only the off-reaction of the dipole. Only its LTM trace abutting the off-channel will grow. Later presentations of the cue will elicit a large off-reaction. If the off-reaction corresponds to a relief reaction, then the cue has become a source of conditioned relief by being paired with offset of a source of fear. Although the cue has never been paired with a positive reward, it can thereafter be used as a positive reinforcer or source of consummatory motivation. This mechanism helps us to understand how avoidance behavior can be persistently maintained long after an animal no longer experiences the fear that originally motivated avoidance learning (Grossberg, 1972a, 1972b, 1975; Maier *et al.*, 1969; Seligman and Johnston, 1973; Solomon *et al.*, 1953).

A similar argument shows how secondary conditioning can occur. For example, offset of a positive (or negative) conditioned reinforcer can drive an antagonistic rebound that conditions a cue whose onset is contingent upon the offset event to be a negative (or positive) conditioned reinforcer. This mechanism uses the feedback in the gated dipole in a major way. Offset of the reinforcer can elicit a rebound because it occurs at a stage before the gate, whereas sampling of the rebound can occur because the new cue delivers its signals at a stage after the gate.

32. Cholinergic-Catecholaminergic Interactions in Drinking versus the Brain as a Chemical Bath

Various data about drinking are clarified by the conceptualization of drives, reinforcers, and incentives and by the labeling of cholinergic and catecholaminergic interactions in Figure 16. The main difference between feeding and drinking from the viewpoint of Figure 16 is the use of thirst and satiety drive inputs instead of hunger and satiety drive inputs, and the existence of different prewired US inputs and possibly different feature fields of CS inputs to the two types of gated dipoles. The theory suggests that similar formal properties hold in cognitive networks. Since the motivational data base seems to be a more developed source of examples at the present time, it will be used in the next few sections to support some of the theory's implications.

Theories about drinking have often grown from the hope that there exist unitary behavioral correlates of pharmacological manipulations, as if the brain were a homogeneous chemical bath that reacts linearly to its chemical environment. This attitude was encouraged by early results in which injection of norepinephrine elicited feeding, whereas injection of cholinergic drugs elicited drinking at the same hypothalamic site (Fisher and Coury, 1962; Grossman, 1962). These results did not long survive further experimentation.

The reader can interpret all the following data in terms of the cholinergic-catecholaminergic interactions that are hypothesized to occur at gated dipoles. Degeneration of monoamine neurons due to injection of 6-hydroxydopamine (6-OHDA) can cause both adipsia and aphagia (Smith, 1973; Ungerstedt, 1968). Anticholinergic drugs such as scopolamine can inhibit cholinergic drinking but not angiotensin or isoproterenol drinking, although anticholinergic drugs only partially block natural deprivation thirst at drug levels that totally abolish cholinergic drinking. Haloperidol, a selective dopamine blocker at low dosages, can suppress angiotensin drinking but spare cholinergic drinking. The combined effects of scopolamine and haloperidol can be additive, leading to total suppression of drinking (Fisher, 1973). Such experiments led Fisher to conclude that "It appears highly unlikely that *any* of the major components of thirst utilize or are entirely dependent upon a single transmitter substance" (p.260). Fisher (1973) found this conclusion "discouraging...what is perhaps surprising is the lack of evidence for a single final common path that would be dependent on the availability of a particular transmitter" (p.260).

My theory was capable of explaining these data when Fisher expressed this opinion (Grossberg, 1972a, 1972b), but possibly because the theory was derived from behavioral postulates concerning an animal's adaptability to a fluctuating environment, its relevance has not yet been noticed by experimentalists on hunger and thirst. This is true, I believe, because a gap exists between known experimental data and the functional properties whereby the theory unifies these data. This gap is partly due to the difficulty of undertaking interactive experiments, but even more so to the lingering view that the brain can be treated like a chemical bath.

This view is illustrated by recent writing of even so distinguished a contributor as Olds (1977), who discusses how monoamine transmitters might influence the rewarding effects of brain stimulation in the following terms:

... if the amines packaged and ready in vesicles inside of nerve terminals were required to make brain stimulation rewarding, then getting them out of the vesicles should have damaged rather than improved this effect. If the amines were already released, and if this was all there was to reward, then why was the animal still stimulating its brain? (p.60)

Because the brain's functional heterogeneity is not well approximated by a chemical bath analogy, questions concerning whether transmitter is packaged or released at isolated synapses provide little functional insight.

A distinction that is often missed in the drinking literature is between expectancy mechanisms and drive or reinforcement mechanisms. This confusion can possibly be cleared up by adding an ERP manipulation that can more directly measure expectancy changes. An instance of this confusion is summarized in the next section.

33. Intragastric versus Normal Drinking

Kissileff (1973) compares a rat's lever-pressing behavior for water that it can drink with its lever-pressing behavior for water that is intragastrically self-injected. On the first day that an animal is switched from drinking to intragastric self-injection, it self-injects far more fluid than it would normally drink, and its first bout of drinking is usually prolonged. After several days of self-injection, lever pressing occurs with reduced frequency. Kissileff attributes the initial overinjection of fluid to an oropharyngeal expectancy of fluid that is not fulfilled. Kissileff compares these data to data of Miller *et al.* (1957), who show that less water is drunk following fifteen minutes of drinking than following fifteen minutes of intragastric injection of the same amount of water. Kissileff suggests that, in the latter case, an oropharyngeal expectancy has not been met.

Without further analysis, these data do not unambiguously implicate an expectancy in the mechanistic sense. I shall indicate how the data might be explained in terms of drive and conditioned reinforcer concepts. I do not deny the possible influence of expectancies in this situation. In fact, I will suggest that, if the expectancy mechanism were rate-limiting, it might lead to the opposite conclusion, which can be tested using a P300 measure.

First let us realize that a lever-press command and a taste pathway might control different levels of net positive incentive if only because of differences in their times of activation during a meal. An elegant LeMagnen (1972) experiment illustrates this distinction. LeMagnen associated a different taste, A, B, C, or D, with the onset of quartiles of a single meal and noted that food intake was amplified almost four-fold. An experiment should be done in which the distinct tastes, A, B, C, or D, are associated with the same stage of each meal, but the stage would be varied across animals from meal onset to satiety. One would then test how presenting the distinct tastes during quartiles of a single test meal alters total food intake as a function of how satiated the animal was when the taste was presented during learning trials. Let us suppose, for the sake of argument, that the total food intake decreases as the association is made closer to satiety.

Now consider an experiment in which a lever press precedes a large food or water reward. The lever press occurs while the net appetitive drive is high; it is, therefore, associated with a maximally positive reaction at the drive representations. Taste and other oropharyngeal pathways that remain active throughout the ingestional interval are, by contrast, associated with incentive motivational patterns that become progressively less positive as fast satiety reactions start to occur. Thus a lever press cue might, by virtue of the instrumental contingency, control a more positive incentive reaction than oropharyngeal cues. Consequently, in the absence of oropharyngeal cues, the larger positive incentive reaction controlled by the lever press cues might cause more eating or drinking to occur, even if no expectancies are operative. This is the first alternative to the expectancy explanation that must be ruled out. If the animal is willing to work harder for larger rewards in a given situation, then conditioned reinforcer factors can play an important role. They can arise due to an interaction between a cue's developing conditioned reinforcer properties and the cue's times of occurrence within the time intervals between high drive and satiety.

A second alternative that must be ruled out is that oropharyngeal receptors, such as those sensitive to mouth dryness or temperature, might generate drive inputs when the mouth is too dry, or hot, and that such drive inputs could activate their drive representations until consummatory behavior rapidly reduces the drive inputs by moistening or cooling the mouth. This oropharyngeal mechanism is related to an expectancy mechanism, but is not itself an expectancy mechanism. It is related to an expectancy mechanism because when the drive inputs are matched by appropriate conditioned reinforcer inputs at the drive representations, then the system can go into a resonance that triggers consummatory behavior. Can a characteristic negative wave be associated with this resonance? The main fact to be explained is not, however, that the resonance occurs, but why it lasts longer if water is not drunk. This can be explained by the drive properties of the system, not its expectancy properties: The oropharyngeal drive is reduced when the water is drunk. Where the expectancy properties of the system are dominant over its drive properties, the opposite result might well occur, since disconfirming the expectancy of water might extinguish the lever press, rather than prolong it. P300 experiments to more directly test this assertion would greatly clarify the meaning of these data. Such an expectancy effect might well be in these data, but it often acts on a slower time scale than a single bout of drinking.

An example of another slowly developing oropharyngeal conditioned reinforcer change seems to be prandial drinking, which is significantly controlled by oropharyngeal factors related to eating dry food. Prandial drinking develops gradually in rats who are recovering from lateral hypothalamic lesions, in desalivate rats, and in rat pups (Kissileff, 1969, 1971; Teitelbaum and Epstein, 1962).

Another way of pointing out the problem in assigning expectancy properties a rate-limiting role in these data is the following. Bellows (1939) has demonstrated the persistence of drinking in dogs after esophagostomy. As Kissileff (1973) himself notes, these data demonstrate "facilitation by oropharyngeal stimuli associated with drinking in water lack and the necessity of postingestive stimuli for relatively sustained inhibition of drinking" (p.173). If oropharyngeal stimuli facilitate drinking, then why do animals drink less when oropharyngeal cues are activated than when drinking is intragastric? These data again implicate either differential conditioned reinforcer properties of lever-press versus oropharyngeal cues or the drive-reducing effects of water on oropharyngeal receptors, rather than expectancy signals *per se*.

Various other properties of eating or drinking need to be mechanistically distinguished. For example, the eating rate can be transiently accelerated at the onset of an eating bout (Booth *et al.*, 1976) and is a joint function of food palatability and prior food deprivation. Is the rate reduction due to intracellular habituation of transmitters in the active incentive motivational feedback loops or to the action of fast satiety reactions? By explicating motivational concepts clearly enough, experiments can be designed to test such differences.

34. Schedule-Induced Polydipsia, Frustration, and Expectancy Matching

A motivational phenomenon wherein expectancies do seem to play a dominant role is schedule-induced polydipsia (Falk, 1961a, 1961b), which has not previously been mechanistically explained. This phenomenon vividly demonstrates how far an animal's drinking behavior can deviate from homeostatic control. Very hungry animals drink much more water than they need if food is intermittently available on a spaced reward schedule and water is freely available (Hudson and Singer, 1979; Kissileff, 1973; Rossellini, 1979; Wallace and Singer, 1976). The degree of polydipsia can be decreased by decreasing an animal's hunger, increasing the amount of food reinforcement, or increasing the palatability of food. Kissileff (1973) summarizes evidence, such as that above, which suggests that frustration plays a role in regulating schedule-induced polydipsia, notably frustration reduction when water is drunk to reduce the frustrating effects of the nonoccurrence of expected food (Grossberg, 1975). He goes on to say about the frustrative hypothesis that "it classifies a mystery as an enigma" (p.167). In Figure 16, the sudden decrease of a positive reinforcer can elicit a frustrative rebound to drive basic processes of secondary conditioning and extinction. To the extent that frustration is an enigma, the basic processes themselves are enigmas, which is unfortunately true within the traditional motivational literature. Why these frustrative effects have seemed to be enigmatic in the experimental literature is clarified by the following theoretical considerations.

After the organism builds up an expectancy that a cue will occur, the unexpected nonoccurrence of that cue can cause widespread antagonistic rebounds, some of them frustrative rebounds. The offset of an expected cue can, however, elicit an antagonistic rebound by two distinct mechanisms, which develop at different rates through time: offset of the cue as a conditioned reinforcer, the effect of which is to withdraw activity along specific pathways, and offset of the cue as an expected event, the effect of which is to increase activity along nonspecific pathways. My discussion of overshadowing in Section 57 will, in fact, suggest that a rebound driven by the latter mechanism can sometimes elicit a rebound driven by the former mechanism. Both of these events are presently hypothesized to cause P300s, but P300s with different scalp distributions due to their hypothesized generators in neocortex and hippocampus, respectively. A successful addition of a P300 manipulation to such experiments would provide important information, especially since schedule-induced polydipsia is not the only interim, or adjunctive, behavior that can occur if food is scheduled to be intermittently available to very hungry animals. For example, aggression can occur if a target animal is available (Azrin *et al.*, 1966) even if drinking occurs when water is available (Falk, 1971). The particular interim responses that will occur depend both on the organism being studied and on the environmental possibilities to which the organism is exposed (Staddon and Ayres, 1975). In addition to understanding how certain interim responses can reduce frustration, we must therefore also study how the several motivational sources in a dipole field compete among themselves to determine which one will control overt behavior.

35. Self-Stimulation and Kindling

The distinctions among drive, reinforcement, and incentive motivation are also basic in explaining effects such as self-stimulation, wherein the stimulating electrode can act like an artificial drive input whose behavioral effects, via an incentive motivational output, can be augmented or diminished by the concurrent action of natural drive and conditioned reinforcer inputs (Grossberg, 1971; Olds, 1977). For example, rats work harder to receive a burst of electrical impulses than a single pulse (Olds, 1977). This fact is explicable because the polyvalent cells must integrate their afferents over time before they are sufficiently stimulated to overcome their polyvalent thresholds. Also, a signal that predicts brain reward greatly augments the number of pedal presses that a rat will make for the reward (Cantor, 1971). This fact is explicable if a signal becomes a conditioned reinforcer: Signals (e.g., tones) associated with brain reward can become rewarding (Knott and Clayton, 1966; Stein, 1958; Trowill and Hynek, 1970) in the theory because, when activity in the cholinergic pathway is correlated with active reverberation in the recurrent catecholaminergic pathway, LTM traces at the jointly active synaptic interfaces are enhanced. Consequently, if a signal comes just before brain reward, it can greatly augment the number of pedal presses that a rat will make for that reward, since the strengthened cholinergic pathway activated by the signal abets firing of its polyvalent target cells. From this perspective, the anatomical overlap between self-stimulation sites and reward sites (Hoebel and Teitelbaum, 1962; Margules and Olds, 1962; Caggiula and Hoebel, 1966; Mogensen and Stevenson, 1966) exists because the sensory cues that eventually elicit self-stimulation do so by becoming conditioned reinforcers via the cholinergic pathways whose LTM traces are altered by the stimulating effects of the electrode on polyvalent cell firing.

The status of electrode inputs as an artificial drive input whose signals converge on polyvalent target cells is supported by data showing that, at electrode currents below the rewarding threshold, electrodes in the hypothalamic drinking center will elicit self-stimulation only if water (acting like a reinforcer) is available (Mendelson, 1967; Mogensen and Morgan, 1967). Similar data have been collected with electrodes placed in a feeding center in the presence of food reward (Coons and Cruce, 1968; Poschel, 1968). The ability of electrode inputs to summate with natural drive inputs, as well as the specificity of drive representations, is illustrated by data in which rats were shown to press one lever when hungry and another lever when thirsty (Gallistel and Beagley, 1971), female rats lever pressed at a rate that varied with their estrous cycles (Prescott, 1966), and male rats lever pressed at a rate that varied with experimentally manipulated androgen concentrations (Olds, 1958).

A subtle feature of self-stimulation studies is that a rewarding train of impulses can be made aversive either by increasing the duration of the impulse train or by preventing the animal from controlling the onset times of stimulating pulses (Olds, 1977). The latter effect is understandable if uncontrolled electrode inputs are occuring at a time when an unexpected event triggers an antagonistic rebound that, in this case, activates a negative incentive motivational pathway. I do not argue this too forcefully, however, because arguments about an animal's expectations are routinely confused in the experimental literature with arguments about nonexpectational habituation processes. Adding a P300 measure to these studies can play an important role in overcoming these confusions.

Let me focus instead on the paradox inherent in the fact that elongating rewarding pulse trains can make them less, rather than more, rewarding. I suggest that two effects going on at once, in opposite directions, at different rates, and within distinct anatomical pathways, can explain this effect. Moreover, these two effects are inherent in our discussion of cholinergic-catecholaminergic interactions. Consider Figure 17. Figure 17 depicts an electrode in a positive incentive pathway. The electrode can also, possibly, produce a smaller input in a nearby negative pathway by electrical currents. The electrode must be turned on long enough to overcome the polyvalent cell threshold in its pathway and to win the competition between pathways for storage in short term memory. Other things being equal, these effects of electrode input will strengthen the active cholinergic synapses that converge on the active feedback pathway. Past a certain electrode input duration and intensity, however, the catecholaminergic transmitter is depleted, or habituates, to such a low level that the net signal due to electrode input plus drive input plus arousal input, all gated by the depleted transmitter in the positive pathway, is smaller than the net signal due to (possible) electrode input plus drive input

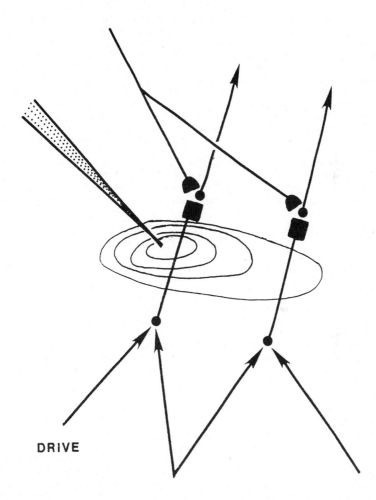

DRIVE

Figure 17. An electrode input acts like an artificial drive input to a contiguous drive representation. It thereby abets firing of this representation but can also depress the feedback loop's sensitivity by depleting its transmitter gate.

plus arousal input, all gated by a less depleted transmitter in the negative pathway. Then the net gated signals, after the competition takes place, favor the negative pathway. The negative effect of long electrode bursts is suggested to be an interactive effect due to depletable transmitter gates in competing pathways.

This explanation suggests why kindling is more efficacious in response to a series of brief electrode bursts than in response to a single burst of the same total duration (Goddard, 1967). The single burst maximizes the depletion of the transmitter, whereas the shorter bursts are long enough to open the feedback loop but short enough to prevent the transmitter from being unduly depleted during each burst. In particular, the interburst duration must be sufficiently long to offset intraburst habituation effects. Consequently, each shorter burst can drive the learning process which, in turn, can enhance the reaction on successive learning trials. One further fact is needed to qualitatively understand kindling; namely, that the conditionable pathway is also part of a feedback loop whose activation is easier on successive learning trials for the same reason that conditioned reinforcers abet the firing of polyvalent cells. That conditionable pathways are part of feedback loops is a basic fact about adaptive resonances. But is the feedback pathway that augments the kindling reaction via conditioning the same feedback pathway that reduces the kindling reaction via transmitter habituation? In general, I suggest that the answer is "no." For example, the gates that habituate during an STM resonance are not the same pathways as the LTM traces that encode new filtering and expectancy patterns. Kindling experiments that can differentiate these predicted opposite effects along conditioning-reset and cholinergic-catecholaminergic dichotomies will greatly enhance our understanding of the kindling phenomenon by relating it more closely to the large literature on psychopharmacological substrates of motivated behavior.

36. Critical Period Reversal, P300 Suppression, and a Test of LTM Encoding by Cholinergic Pathways

A major design feature in Figure 16 has not yet been exploited. Since a similar design is suggested to hold in cognitive as well as motivational dipole fields, I will use this feature to suggest an explanation of the Pettigrew and Kasamatsu data on critical period termination and reversal. I will also relate this explanation to a P300 prediction. Then I will suggest an experiment to decide between two alternative hypotheses about how cholinergic-catecholaminergic interactions control LTM changes.

In Figure 16, the incentive motivational output bifurcates. One branch sends signals to perceptual and cognitive thalamocortical representations. The other branch feeds back to excite its own pathway at a stage before its transmitter gate. After a polyvalent cell fires, it competes with other polyvalent cell channels to test which channels can return positive feedback to themselves. A winning channel can resonate in STM via its feedback pathway. Such a resonance can sustain prolonged polyvalent cell firing which can, in turn, drive LTM changes at active conditioned reinforcer synapses that abut the resonating polyvalent cell.

What would happen to such a circuit if 6-OHDA poisoned the transmitter gate? By destroying the gate, the possibility of STM resonance is also eliminated, and, with it, LTM plasticity. What would happen if catecholamine were poured over a cortical dipole field? Such a manipulation would have two major effects. It would bypass the buffering mechanism that depends on antagonistic rebound to maintain code stability. It does this by upsetting the relative balance of transmitter between on-cell and off-cell channels. It would also override polyvalent constraints by directly activating the synapses postsynaptic to the transmitter gates. The combined effects of these actions would be to allow various combinations of inputs that could not previously overcome buffering and polyvalent constraints to elicit STM resonance and subsequent LTM encoding.

If a P300 measure is added to a 6-OHDA manipulation in the Pettigrew situation, then the P300 should be attenuated or obliterated, since antagonistic rebound cannot occur in the absence of the gates. If an experiment is chosen that elicits mismatch negativity both before and after the 6-OHDA manipulation, then the hypothesis that the generator of mismatch negativity is fedforward to the P300 generator would be supported (Section 21).

The 6-OHDA experiment focuses on the catecholaminergic contribution to LTM encoding. Part of the subtlety involved in teasing apart cholinergic from monoaminergic influences on learning is clarified by the theoretical conclusion that the target cells where these influences converge are polyvalent cells. For example, conditioned reinforcer, drive, and arousal influences must all be sufficiently active before the target cell can fire vigorously enough to win the competition among drive representations and thereby amplify and maintain its activity via positive feedback. Learning can be prevented in a given cholinergic pathway if the catecholaminergic input to that pathway is too weak for the combined effects of its inputs to overcome the competition from other pathways. This learning deficit does not imply that the catecholaminergic transmitter directly regulates the chemistry of laying down an LTM trace via positive feedback. It only says that the catecholaminergic transmitter modulates a given pathway's ability to win the competition. The amplified activity due to positive feedback within the winning pathway might be the prerequisite postsynaptic condition for learning at the cholinergic synapse.

Catecholamines can influence LTM in either of two ways, neither of which contradicts the hypothesis that the LTM trace is part of a cholinergic system. The weak hypothesis is that catecholamine input is a necessary condition for winning the competition among drive representations, but that the postsynaptic learning signals elicited by a winning pathway are not catecholaminergic; e.g., they might be Ca^{++} or cAMP. The strong hypothesis is that catecholaminergic input directly drives the postsynaptic protein synthesis process, as well as postsynaptic-to-presynaptic learning signals, and that winning the competition merely amplifies this direct catecholaminergic effect. Even the strong hypothesis requires an extra chemical influence (cholinergic?) to select only active synapses to be the ones at which learning will occur.

One way to test this alternative is to insert electrodes in lateral hypothalamic sites at which an animal can learn to self-stimulate. Sites should be chosen (say) at which the animal presses the bar more for stimulation as it becomes thirstier (Olds, 1977). Then deplete catecholamines with 6-OHDA. Finally, seek a level of electrode stimulation that again supports self-stimulation. If sites at which new learning can be achieved in the absence of catecholaminergic involvement can be found, then the weak hypothesis is favored. Not all self-stimulation sites are theoretically plausible candidates for this manipulation. Only sites where iontophoretically applied acetylcholine elicits a rapid enhancement of self-stimulation should be considered. If the electrode is placed along the catecholaminergic feedback loop in Figure 16, but at a stage before the catecholaminergic gate, then 6-OHDA will obliterate the effect of electrode input at the polyvalent cells.

These distinctions between direct effects on LTM and modulatory effects due to drive and arousal manipulations enable us to interpret the following data implicating cholinergic influences on memory.

The large suppressant effect of atropine on psychogenic polydipsia (Burks and Fisher, 1970) compared with its much smaller effect on regulatory drinking (Blass and Chapman, 1971) led Kissileff (1973) to conclude that "acetylcholine may play a greater role in emotionally driven drinking than in drinking driven by thirst" (p.168). Otherwise expressed, atropine might act by weakening conditioned influences on drinking without weakening drive influences on drinking. Kissileff (1973) also reviews evidence that, when homeostatic mechanisms are eliminated by lateral hypothalamic damage, drinking can recover but under oropharyngeal controls. Routtenberg and Kim (1978) review evidence that neostriatal cholinergic interneurons play an important role in the long term memory consolidation process, including the fact that scopolamine, a cholinergic blocking agent, has a potent effect on human memory (Drachman and Leavitt, 1974). Mabry and Campbell (1978) claim that scopolamine affects adult but not immature rats, even though amphetamine can produce hyperactivity in immature rats. Is the differential effect of scopolamine at later ages due to the fact that learned representations have not been incorporated into the cholinergic system until these ages?

Marsh et al. (1971) have reported an impairment in intermediate, but not immediate, memory of Parkinsonian patients' performance on a paired associate task. L-dopa therapy is reported to improve the patients' performance on this task. At the present time, this memory impairment has not been unambiguously explained as a weak or strong involvement of the dopamine system in long term memory formation. An improvement in immediate memory of Parkinsonian patients after L-dopa therapy has also been reported (Barbeau et al., 1971; Cotzias et al., 1969). These data are also compatible with both the weak and strong hypotheses, since, in both cases, a catecholaminergic transmitter gates the feedback pathways that store the neural activity in STM.

37. Gestalt Switching Due to Ambiguous Figures and Habituation Induced Shifts of Categorical Boundaries

My explanation of the Pettigrew and Kasamatsu data shows how P300 and negative ERP components might be pharmacologically dissociated. Such a dissociation should also be possible without pharmacological intervention. A P300 that is elicited without prior mismatch negativity and that precedes rather than follows processing negativity should occur during perceptual switches between alternative interpretations of an ambiguous figure, such as the Necker cube or monocularly viewed rivalrous patterns (Brown, 1965; Rauschecker et al., 1973). The tendency to alternate can be explained by the fact that persistent reverberation within an active STM representation tends to deplete its transmitter gates, thereby weakening the reverberation and providing a growing advantage to the inhibited, and therefore undepleted, alternative STM representation. When the active STM representation reaches a critical level of depletion, the alternative representation is sufficiently disinhibited to let the competitive feedback dynamics contrast enhance its activity into a state of STM resonance. This STM switch can be driven thalamocortically, without intervention of a mismatch-initiated arousal burst, by the interaction of competitive feedback and STM-induced habituation of transmitter gates. If the perceptual switches are associated with massive off-rebounds, then they should elicit a sequence of P300s. After a switch occurs, a newly activated STM representation can read out a feedback expectancy whose match with the ambiguous data can elicit processing negativity. Papakostopoulos (1976) suggests a similar processing concept when he writes that P300 acts "to arrest planned behavior or to generate the bases for alternation from one behavioral act to another."

It might be difficult to measure these P300s because they occur spontaneously rather than under experimental control. A helpful fact is that the alternation rate in monocular rivalry is up to three times faster with gratings constructed from complementary colors than with black and white gratings. I suggest an explanation of this fact in Grossberg (1980a).

A similar combination of gate habituation and STM competition can help to explain shifts in categorical boundaries that are not due to new LTM encoding (Sawusch and Nusbaum, 1979). Situations in which Gestalt switches occur should also elicit categorical boundary shifts, but experimentalists have often been more interested in the switches per se than in testing this hypothesis.

38. Motivational Switching and Hysteresis Without a Mythical Cusp Catastrophe

Some fundamental mathematical properties of gated dipoles will now be summarized. Proofs of the inverted U properties are given in the Appendix.

The positive feedback loops in the gated dipole of Figure 16 turn this network into a feedback competitive network. The slowly varying transmitter gates do not alter the fact that a feedback gated dipole shares many properties with other feedback competitive networks. For example, the dipole now has an STM storage capability which means that it can defend a motivational decision against sufficiently small momentary fluctuations in cue or arousal inputs. This hysteresis property helps to provide the inertia needed to carry out a sustained motivated act during irrelevant environmental perturbations. The STM normalization property refines this capability by maintaining a temporally stable baseline of incentive motivation. The contrast enhancement property helps to control sharp motivational switching between behavioral alternatives when the net balance of inputs succeeds in overcoming the hysteretic inertia of the previous motivational choice.

Frey and Sears (1978) have built sigmoid and hysteresis properties into a cusp catastrophe model of conditioning and attention. Although their model provides one way to visualize sudden switches, the catastrophe variables do not correspond to physical variables and the model provides no physical explanation of why sigmoid and hysteresis properties appear in the data. The gated dipole theory provides a physical explanation that does not correspond to a cusp catastrophe and implies a large body of data and predictions, such as those below, which are invisible to the cusp picture.

The STM hysteresis and normalization properties do not depend on the transmitter gates. Some deeper properties do. A sigmoid signal function is the simplest function that can overcome noise amplification in a feedback competitive network (see Section 20). When sigmoid feedback signals are used in a gated dipole, this network possesses inverted U properties that are reflected in a large body of data about normal and abnormal behavior. I will present these properties in constellations to help experimentalists decide when gated dipoles are generating the data. I will first state the formal properties using the motivational terminology in Figure 16 to fix ideas.

The main new fact is this: If the arousal level is chosen either too small or too large, both the on-reactions and the off-rebounds of the dipole are severely reduced. In motivational terms, either underarousal or overarousal can cause emotional depression. The underaroused depressive syndrome is, however, starkly different from the over-aroused depressive syndrome both in its etiology and in its constellation of properties (Grossberg, 1972b).

39. Formal Symptoms of Underaroused Depression

The following properties of an underaroused gated dipole are proved in the Appendix and will be used to discuss clinical syndromes and drug effects in the next few sections.

(1) High threshold: The threshold phasic input (e.g., intensity of conditioned reinforcer or perceptual event) that can elicit a supraliminal output is abnormally high.

(2) Suprathreshold hyperexcitability: The sensitivity of the dipole to suprathreshold phasic input increments is abnormally high. In other words, a fixed increment in phasic input within the suprathreshold range can elicit an abnormally large on-reaction output.

Thus, the underaroused syndrome is hyperexcitable despite an elevated threshold. The reader may find this result paradoxical, because a low threshold often implies high suprathreshold sensitivity.

(3) Paradoxical on-reaction to unexpected events: The threshold arousal increment that can elicit an antagonistic rebound is abnormally high. Smaller arousal increments elicit an enhanced on-reaction, despite the fact that they would have elicited off-rebounds in a normally aroused dipole.

(4) Paradoxical insensitivity to phasic decrements: A rapid reduction of phasic input from an intensity of J to half intensity $J/2$, may not elicit a rebound, even though reduction of $J/2$ to 0 does elicit a rebound. This property is a special case of a formula that determines when reduction of input intensity J_1 to intensity K_1 at arousal level I_1 will elicit a larger rebound than reduction of input J_2 to K_2 at arousal level I_2. The interesting feature of reducing J to $J/2$ as compared to reducing $J/2$ to 0 is that both manipulations cause a change of $J/2$ units in phasic input.

In Grossberg (1972b), I used this property to predict how rewarding arbitrary shock offset combinations will be, and to explain the known advantage of $J/2 \to 0$ over $J \to J/2$ offset. I also related the size of this advantage to an animal's ability to learn escape from a discrete fear cue and to the advantage of partial reward over continuous reward. All these factors should vary together as the animal's arousal level is parametrically increased. I hope that the current interest in arousal-related diseases at the present time, which is greater than that in 1972, will encourage testing of these indices to sharpen our understanding of the transition from normal to abnormal syndromes.

40. Formal Symptoms of Overaroused Depression

(1) Low threshold: The threshold phasic input that can elicit a suprathreshold output is abnormally low. However, this does not influence observable behavior because of (2) suprathreshold hypoexcitability: The sensitivity of the dipole to suprathreshold phasic input increments is abnormally low. In other words, a fixed increment in the phasic input within the suprathreshold range can elicit an abnormally small on-reaction output.

Thus, the overaroused depressive syndrome is a low-threshold, suprathreshold hyposensitive syndrome—again, a paradoxical combination.

In a feedback gated dipole, insufficient production of the gating transmitter can reduce the amount of feedback within the dipole and thereby depress its operating level. This type of depression can reduce the total nonspecific input to the dipole, but it should not be confused with a reduction in the size of the externally applied nonspecific arousal input.

41. The Inverted U is Not a Unitary Concept

Inverted U effects are familiar both in psychophysiology (Hebb, 1955) and in discrimination learning (Berlyne, 1969). Lest the reader therefore casually dismiss the importance of the gated dipole syndrome, I should emphasize that there exists more than one type of inverted U. For example, Grossberg and Pepe (1970, 1971) showed that a different inverted U can occur during the processing of serial events, such as a list or a sentence. In a network capable of processing serial events—which is not a gated dipole!—the overaroused syndrome leads to contextual collapse, a reduction of associative span, and fuzzy response categories. We predicted that the approach to overarousal would manifest itself during serial learning by a reversal of the relative learning rate at the beginning versus the end of the list and by a shift of the list position of maximal learning difficulty (the bow in the serial position curve) from its skewed position nearer to the end of the list towards a symmetric position at the list's middle. Despite the importance of these predictions for understanding normal serial learing and simple schizophrenia (Maher, 1977) and overarousal disorders, they have not been tested or widely understood during the decade since their appearance.

42. Inverted U in P300 and CNV

Inverted Us have been found in ERPs. Tecce and Cole (1974) reported an inverted U in the CNV, which will be attributed to the dynamics of a gated dipole field in Sections 51–53. The P300 is reduced both in hyperactive children and schizophrenics, as the reviews (this volume) on aberrant development and psychopathology have shown. I do not, however, share the opinion that a low amplitude of P300 must reflect a deficit common to these diagnostic entities. I will instead argue that hyperactive children are underaroused and simple schizophrenics are overaroused in the gated dipole sense. The two types of P300 should therefore be reduced because they occur at opposite ends of the inverted U.

The next few sections summarize some facts about abnormal syndromes that are clarified by formal properties of the gated dipole inverted U.

43. Parkinson Bracing, Starting, and Stopping

In Parkinson's disease, dopamine-rich cells of the substantia nigra show marked degeneration (Weiner and Klawans, 1978). This structural correlate of the disease helps to rationalize the symptomatic improvement L-dopa therapy can effect, since L-dopa is a pharmacological "up." I suggest that its use lifts the underaroused gated dipoles that control the affected motor skills to a more normal range of dipole arousal and sensitivity. Animal models of Parkinson's disease support the underarousal hypothesis. Intraventicular application of 6-OHDA severely depletes brain catecholamines and thereby produces symptoms such as catalepsy, akinesia, and Parkinson bracing (Levitt and Teitelbaum, 1975; Schallert et al., 1978a, 1978b, 1979).

I suggest that the following Parkinsonian symptoms are manifestations of the underaroused depressive syndrome. The higher threshold for activating a dipole manifests itself in the difficulties Parkinsonian patients have in initiating movements. The suprathreshold excitability manifests itself in the difficulties these patients have in terminating movements after they begin; that is, after a large enough phasic input is applied to generate hyperexcitable suprathreshold cyclic behavior in the gated feedback loops of the underaroused motor command oscillators.

The reader might wonder at this point how oscillators have crept into the gated dipole story. G.A. Carpenter and I show in Carpenter and Grossberg (1983) that the activities of feedback dipoles with slowly varying gates can endogenously oscillate, even though feedforward gated dipoles and feedback dipoles with rapidly varing gates cannot oscillate. That story lies beyond the scope of this article, however.

A particularly interesting Parkinsonian symptom is bracing; namely, "if suddenly pushed forward or backward while standing, many people with Parkinson's brace rigidly without stepping, or with short shuffling steps which are unable to counteract their fall" (Schallert et al., 1979). Why don't these patients right themselves as normal people do, or just fall over? I associate this property with the paradoxical enhanced on-reaction that occurs in response to unexpected events in the underaroused depressive syndrome. An enhanced on-reaction would strengthen the current motor pattern, rather than rebounding it to an antagonistic pattern that would abet a righting reaction. At a somewhat higher arousal level (or transmitter concentration), small rebounds can occur in the gated dipole. I associate these small rebounds with the short shuffling steps that occur in 6-OHDA treated rats who have recovered a limited degree of spontaneous locomotion. To test this bracing hypothesis, one might try to measure the negative ERP component corresponding to the motor analog of a mismatch-contingent arousal burst, and to show that a brace, as opposed to passive inaction, correlates with the size of this ERP in response to an unexpected push.

In the articles cited above, Teitelbaum and his colleagues have claimed that, in Parkinson's disease, the subsystem that maintains postural configurations, or static stable equilibria, is working properly, but that the subsystem that regulates dynamic transactions such as walking, orienting, and exploring is deficient. I agree with this claim to the extent that a dynamic deficiency exists because the rebound, or reset, capabilities of gated dipoles are depressed.

44. Juvenile Hyperactivity

I suggest that juvenile hyperactivity is another instance of the underaroused depressive syndrome. Certain hyperactive children suffer from catecholamine deficiencies (Shaywitz et al., 1977; Shekim et al., 1977). These data clarify why pharmacological "ups" like amphetamine can be helpful in treating these children (Swanson and Kinsbourne, 1976; Weiss and Hechtmann, 1979). Nonetheless, were it not for the theoretical analysis of dipole dynamics, why hyperexcitability should follow from underarousal would still be a mystery.

The dipole model also suggests an experimental question that still seems to be insufficiently studied: Are the behavioral thresholds of hyperactive behaviors higher than normal thresholds for these behaviors? At the EPIC VI meeting, Roy Halliday called my attention to the work of Weber and Sulzbacher (1975), who showed that thresholds during an electroencephalic audiometry test performed on hyperactive children were reduced by medication. If the paradoxical properties (3) and (4) of the underaroused syndrome also hold when threshold elevation is recorded, say in a study of reward and motivation, then a much stronger test would be achieved.

Before considering other underaroused syndromes, it will be useful to briefly mention two important overaroused examples.

45. Schizophrenic Overarousal

Some types of schizophrenia have been ascribed to dopamine hyperactivity of cells in the ventromedial tegmental area, medial to the substantia nigra, that terminate in the limbic forebrain or cortex (Lloyd, 1978), thereby providing the basis for an overaroused syndrome. Dopaminergic agonists, such as L-dopa and amphetamine, can produce a behavioral syndrome, including repetitive activity or perseveration (read: breakdown of the reset system) that has been compared to schizophrenia (Riklan, 1973; Wallach, 1974). Various antipsychotic drugs block dopamine receptors (Kuhar *et al.*, 1978) and, in sufficient quantities, can produce a catalepsy that is reminiscent of Parkinson's disease (Hornykiewicz, 1975). The fact that an underaroused syndrome can be transmuted into an overaroused syndrome using a given drug and that the reverse transformation can be effected by an oppositely acting drug suggests that the two syndromes are external points on an inverted U of a common mechanistic substrate.

46. Analgesia: Endorphins versus Loud Noise

Overarousal is not always a bad thing. A high net arousal level can cause good as well as bad effects. Where such a high level is due to a nonspecific input, say due to loud noise (Gardner *et al.*, 1961), it can reduce the aversiveness (incentive output) of an unpleasant input; e.g., shock. Such a nonspecific input might be caused by a baseline shift in reticular formation output in response to the noise. An effect akin to overarousal can be caused by a potent specific input to the competing dipole channel, say an increment due to increased production or release of endorphins (Gintzler, 1980; Guillemin, 1978).

Although both manipulations will depress the negative incentive output, they should nonetheless be experimentally distinguishable. The nonspecific input desensitizes the dipole's reaction to the aversive phasic input, but does not change the level of this input. The competing specific input, by contrast, has an effect equivalent to both increasing the arousal level and decreasing the aversive phasic input size.

This equivalence is based on a simple trick that greatly aids the understanding of gated dipoles. Many inputs can perturb a dipole through time. Conditioned reinforcer signals from a large number of internal representations, arousal and drive inputs, and internal feedback signals are all operative. The dipole cannot determine what the input sources are, but only their net efect. I therefore consider the total input size that is felt in the on-channel (L_1) and in the off-channel (L_2) at the stage just before the gate. I call the smaller input the net arousal level I; that is, $I = \min(L_1, L_2)$, and I call the difference between the two inputs the net phasic input J; that is, $J = \mid L_1 - L_2 \mid$. A nonspecific arousal increment increases I but leaves J alone. A specific competing input increases I and decreases J in such a way that $I + J$ remains approximately constant until the competing input wins (Appendix).

This distinction can be tested by doing studies in which the crossover point from negative to positive net incentive is studied as both the negative and positive inputs are parametrically varied. No such crossover can exist in response to parametric increments in nonspecific arousal.

The next few sections use the inverted U in gated dipole dynamics to suggest how some normal and abnormal motivational cycles work. I present these results not only to explain some paradoxical phenomena for their own sake but also for two other reasons: to sharpen conceptions of how motivational cycles can modulate cognitive processing by altering the incentive motivational signals to sensory and cognitive representations through time and to illustrate how gated dipoles with no endogenous oscillatory properties can be made to persistently oscillate when their outputs generate suitable feedback inputs. The frequency of these rhythms can be made as fast or as slow as we please by changing network parameters. The motivational cycles, operating on a slow time scale, are better studied at the present time, so they will be cited for illustrative purposes. These motivational examples may shed light on faster cognitive rhythms that are functionaly homologous. The reader who wishes to focus primarily on cognitive processes can proceed directly to Section 51.

47. The Hyperphagic Syndrome and the Mythical Set-Point

I will now explain hypothalamic hyperphagia as an instance of underaroused depression and will argue that the notion of set-point has confused more than clarified the explanation of this syndrome. Since animals with lesions in the ventromedial hypothalamus (VMH) eat voraciously until they become obese, it has been claimed that VMH lesions increase the animals' set-point for body weight (Woods *et al.*, 1974). Since animals with lesions in the lateral hypothalamus (LH) become aphagic, it has been claimed that LH lesions decrease the animals' set-point for body weight (Keesey *et al.*, 1976). Both sets of authors also suggest that, once a weight set-point is determined, the animals eats so as to reduce the error signal that compares its present weight with the weight set-point. Both sets of authors identify an observable behavioral property with an unobservable neural mechanism.

I will argue that, if anything, VMH lesions decrease the animals' set-point, a viewpoint that is closer in spirit to the Hirsch (1972) model for feeding behavior. I will go further by arguing that the very notion of set-point is inappropriate because it does not illuminate the adaptive design that is disrupted by VMH lesions. Instead, I will indicate how suitable VMH lesions cause the animal to become motivationally underaroused, which is the sense in which the animals' set-point is reduced.

The behavioral properties to be explained include the following ones. VMH lesioned animals (e.g., rats) eat voraciously (hyperphagia) until they become obese. Initially, they seem to have a higher hunger drive (Kent and Peters, 1973; Singh, 1973; Wampler, 1973), which manifests itself in an extended bout of eating followed by discrete meals at a reduced intermeal interval (Balagura, 1972). After the animals become obese, they maintain their higher weight against environmental perturbations (Hoebel and Teitelbaum, 1966; Olds, 1977; Teitelbaum, 1955), a fact which can sorely tempt one to assume that the brain contains a set-point that is increased by VMH lesions.

The behavior of lesioned animals before they become obese can differ notably from their behavior after they become obese. Both dynamic (nonobese) hyperphagics and normal animals eat appreciable amounts of a diet that has been adulterated by kaolin, cellulose, or quinine sulphate (Kennedy, 1953; Stominger, Brobeck, and Cort, 1953; Teitelbaum, 1955). Obese hyperphagics reject diets at concentrations of adulterants that are insufficient to disturb feeding by normal animals. By contrast, obese hyperphagics markedly increase their intake of food to which 50% dextrose has been added, whereas normal animals decrease their intake of this diet, since sugar is a more concentrated source of calories than the standard diet (Teitelbaum, 1955).

These data are paradoxical because of the following considerations. Let us start with the classical idea that the overeating that results from VMH lesions is a release phenomenon. The simplest version of this idea suggests that animals eat until they reach a new weight, one at which their hunger motivation is again low. By this argument, the exaggerated sensitivity of the obese animals to negative stimulus qualities of adulterated food might be interpreted as a consequence of low hunger motivation due to prior overeating. This viewpoint suggests that the animal is insufficiently interested in unpleasant food to bother eating it. Such an argument fails to explain why the obese animal overeats in response to positive stimulus qualities of food, as when dextrose is added to its diet. Why doesn't the hypothetical reduction in hunger motivation reduce the animal's interest in all foods? Instead, the obese animal is hypersensitive to both the positive and the negative stimulus qualities of food. Teitelbaum (1955, p.160) noted these "changes in the reactivity of hyperphagic rats to the stimulus aspects of the diet" and realized that "some change in the internal environment operates in combination with the change in reactivity to the stimulus provided by food." How these changes occur in the animals' sensitivity to external stimuli has not been adequately explained in the past twenty-five years. One reason for this gap is that the phenomena involve "nonhomeostatic" mechanisms that are generally not well understood. A related reason is that not all VMH lesions produce finickiness to stimulus qualities, even if they do produce obesity (Graff and Stellar, 1962; Hoebel, 1976). Thus, to understand the VMH syndrome, one needs a sufficiently precise theory about the interaction between internal and external environmental factors to distinguish how different lesions can differentially induce obesity or finickiness.

My explanation of the hyperphagic syndrome will agree with the classical idea that the hyperphagia is a release phenomenon and will also agree that the obese animal has low hunger motivation, but in a sense that must be carefully defined. I will suggest that certain lesions cause the animal to become motivationally underaroused and that, whenever an animal becomes underaroused in this fashion, it automatically becomes hypersensitive to the conditioned reinforcer properties of relevant stimuli. Indeed, VMH-lesioned animals can become generally irritable and excessively reactive to all stimuli (Paxinos and Bindra, 1973; Wheatley, 1944).

48. Hypothalamic Stimulation and Rebound Eating

Before using a gated dipole model to explain hyperphagic data, I will mention some classical data about eating that illustrate how behavioral tests can lead to significant pharmacological inferences if we possess a good conceptual bridge between the two levels. These data support the hypothesis that a gated dipole helps control eating behavior.

The existence of slow transmitter gates between competitive pathways involving lateral hypothalamic and ventromedial hypothalamic sites is suggested by behavioral antagonistic rebound effects. Such effects can occur after hypothalamic stimulation terminates (Grastyan, 1968; Olds et al., 1971; Wyrwicka and Dobrzecka, 1960). For example, during stimulation of the anterior part of the ventromedial hypothalamus and the adjacent posterior part of the anterior nucleus, hungry animals stop eating, yet, following offset of such stimulation, satiated animals start eating. Is the onset of eating accompanied by a hippocampal P300?

49. A Normal versus Hyperphagic Feeding Cycle

To see how a dipole can explain the obesity and finickiness that occur after certain VMH lesions, I will suppose that the lesion partially eliminates the cells or pathways along which the net arousal input and the satiety drive input are delivered to the off channel. I will also suppose that the hunger dipole competes with other motivational dipoles (thirst, sex) to decide which dipole will win the motivational competition. Suppose that, on the average, positive incentive motivational output at least T in size is needed to win this competition to induce eating.

Figure 18 summarizes the idealized changes through time in hunger and satiety inputs in a normal dipole. In Figure 18a, the nonspecific arousal level, L, plus a small satiety input, K_2, equal the net arousal level, I, just before a meal. The net arousal level, I, then falls in the range of normal dipole sensitivity. The net phasic input, J, is large because it is the difference of a large hunger input, K_1, and a small satiety input, K_2. Since I is of normal size, then, as J increases, the incentive motivational output in the on-channel eventually exceeds the level, T, that is needed to win the motivational competition. Eating then begins. As eating proceeds, a fast satiety signal due to gastric distention causes an increase in K_2 before K_1 can significantly change. The input, K_1, will change later as the food is digested. As a result of the change in K_2, I increases while J decreases to keep $I + J$ approximately constant. At this point, one might wonder whether eating will cease as soon as T is no longer exceeded. This is not generally true, because the feedback loops in the motivational dipole possess hysteresis properties that can keep eating active until J becomes quite small, as in Figure 18b. All we need to know now is that K_2 increases quickly before K_1 can decrease, so that I becomes large and J becomes small.

How large and how small? This depends on the value of T that is needed to elicit eating and, thus, on the amount of competition from other motivated behaviors that can be elicited by the behavioral situation. If T is very large (high competition), then eating can cause the dipole to approach an overaroused condition (high I due to high K_2). When this happens, the dipole becomes insensitive to further increments in K_2 due to the inverted U property. By contrast, if T is smaller, then I will not grow as much, so that the dipole remains more sensitive to novel appetitive or aversive food cues. All in all, I increases and J decreases until eating stops. As digestion proceeds, both K_1 (hunger) and K_2 (satiety) signals decrease (Figure 18c). As a result, I decreases and J remains small. The dipole's sensitivity increases, but it cannot win the motivational competition because J remains small. Finally, the hunger input, K_1, begins to grow again until eating is once more elicited. Note that, in this analysis, the total duration of a meal depends both on the I value and the J value that obtains when the meal begins.

Figure 19 idealizes the drive input changes that can occur when the K_2 pathway is partially destroyed. The main change is a reduction in the K_2 input and the arousal input that perturb the off-channel. Consequently, the net arousal level, I, is reduced and the dipole is underaroused. The K_1 hunger input that is needed to achieve an on-output that exceeds T is thus smaller than the K_1 level needed to exceed T in the normal dipole (Figures 18 and 19a). Two properties are thus achieved. The dipole is hyperactive because it is underaroused and the hunger level that elicits eating can be less than normal, although it will be of normal or greater than normal size right after the operation that causes the lesion. The reduction in the threshold K_1 size needed to elicit eating helps to explain why hyperphagic animals can seem poorly motivated.

Once eating begins, it can be rapidly stopped only if the K_2 input can grow enough to increase I and decrease J until the dipole shuts off. However, if the K_2 pathway is seriously damaged, then the K_2 input cannot grow significantly in response to rapid gastric reactions to food. When this is true, eating can persist until the K_1 input decreases as a result of slower digestive effects (Figure 19b). This is not the same mechanism that terminates a meal in the normal dipole. An animal controlled by an underaroused dipole will thus become obese by eating persistently right after its lesion in the off-channel.

After the animal becomes obese, the situation changes. The input, K_1, never gets a chance to grow to large values because of the hypersensitivity of the underaroused dipole to K_1 increments. These smaller K_1 increments trigger eating; eating persists until the K_1 increments are withdrawn. In this way, the animal can defend its new weight against environmental fluctuations even though there exists no "set-point" in the dipole. Note also that the intermeal interval can be reduced because a smaller-than-normal increment in K_1 is needed to initiate the next meal.

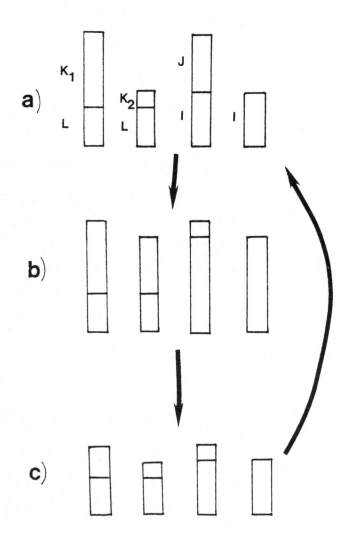

Figure 18. A normal gated dipole feeding cycle. (a) A large hunger input, K_1, and a small satiety input, K_2, trigger eating by keeping I moderate and J large. (b) Fast growth of the satiety input shuts off eating by increasing I and decreasing J. (c) Digestion decreases I while keeping J small. Then K_1 increases and the cycle begins again.

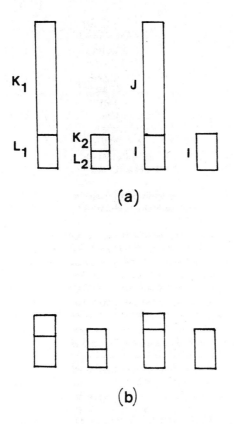

(a)

(b)

Figure 19. A hyperphagic gated dipole feeding cycle. (a) Damage to the off-channel can make K_2 and L small, thereby decreasing I and increasing J. Voracious eating is thereby triggered. (b) Eating is terminated by a reduction in K_1, not in K_2. Thereafter, smaller than normal increments in K_1 can trigger eating since L, hence I, remains small.

How can one achieve a syndrome wherein obesity occurs without finickiness? This is formally easy to do. The similarity of the lesion that produces obesity-without-finickiness to the lesion that produces obesity-with-finickiness helps to explain why this syndrome has caused so much confusion. Figure 20b illustrates this formal lesion. It destroys cells and/or pathways in the off-channel after the stage at which the signals are gated, by contrast with the previous lesion, which destroyed cells and/or pathways in the off-channel before the stage at which signals are gated.

Because the lesion occurs after the gating stage, the specific and nonspecific inputs are of normal size. The dipole is not underaroused; hence, it is not hyperactive. However, the competition from the off-channel to the on-channel is eliminated, as are the negative incentive motivational outputs from the off-channel. Even though K_2 increases rapidly as eating occurs, the competitive signal due to K_2 is not felt by the on-channel. Once again, the on-channel is shut off by the slow decrease of K_1 due to digestive factors

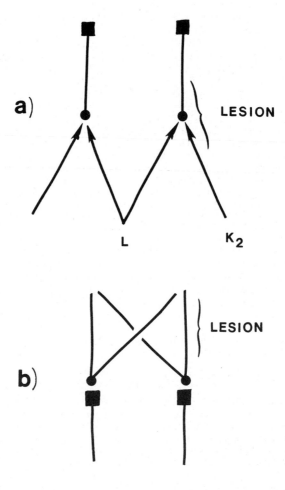

Figure 20. Lesions that influence a network's obesity and finickiness. The lesion in (a) occurs before the transmitter gating stage. It thereby lowers the network's net arousal level and causes a full-blown underaroused syndrome. The lesion in (b), by contrast, does not alter the net arousal level. Rather, it merely weakens the inhibitory effects of satiety inputs that occur after the transmitter gating stage.

rather than by the rapid increase of K_2 due to gastric distention. Consequently, the animal eats abnormally large meals and becomes obese.

50. Some Other Drug-Induced Inverted U's and Hypothalamic-Hippocampal Interactions

The underaroused depressive syndrome helps to explain how dopamine damage can yield sensitivity to weak sensory stimuli but intolerance of intense sensory stimuli (Stricker and Zigmond, 1976).

The fact the D-amphetamine sulfate activates feeding in an anorectic cat at the same dose (2 mg kg^{-1}) that totally inhibits feeding in a normal cat can be viewed as an inverted U effect (Wolgin *et al.*, 1976), as can the fact that amphetamine augments slow behavior and depresses fast behavior (Dews, 1958). Also in normal cats, smaller amounts of norepinephrine can have effects opposite to those of larger amounts (Leibowitz, 1974).

A more speculative inverted U effect concerns the modulatory effect of septal input on the firing rate of hypothalamic cells (Mogensen, 1976). If a hypothalamic neuron is firing slowly, then septal input speeds up its firing rate (ascending end of inverted U), whereas if the hypothalamic neuron is firing rapidly, then septal input slows down its firing rate (descending end of inverted U). The possible existence of competing pathways in septal-hypothalamic interactions is supported by the observation that, in unanesthetized rats, some cells increase firing rates and other cells decrease firing rates during drinking (Bridge, 1976). Also, the mediodorsal septum tends to excite hypothalamic neurons via the fornix, whereas the bed nucleus of the stria terminalis tends to inhibit hypothalamic neurons and wide regions of septum contribute both to the fornix and to the stria terminalis (Mogensen, 1976). Edinger and Siegel (1976) report competitive interactions between the medial and lateral septum and relate this competitive geometry to the effects of afferents from the forsal and ventral hippocampus.

The hippocampus is interpreted as the final common path of the model's drive and reinforcer interactions in Sections 51–53. I postulate that it emits several types of output after a winning drive representation is chosen. The medial forebrain bundle (Haymaker *et al.*, 1969; MacLean, 1970) is suggested to be the anatomical analog of the formal feedback loops that run through the model's circuits (Grossberg, 1972b, 1975).

We are now ready to begin our study of how cognitive and motivational networks reciprocally interact to control the shifting focus of attention through time.

51. Adaptive Resonance Between Dipole Fields

Figure 21 depicts the minimal network that I need to mechanistically explain attentional data. Figure 21 describes a feedback module wherein sensory and drive representations send signals to each other via nonspecific excitatory conditionable pathways. These representations are organized into dipole fields. Each dipole field is capable of STM contrast enhancement, normalization, hysteresis, and rebound. The interfield conditionable pathways send branches to both the on-cells and the off-cells of the dipole fields.

The conditionable pathways from sensory-to-drive representations encode the conditioned reinforcer properties of external cues. The conditionable pathways from drive-to-sensory representations encode the incentive motivational properties of internal drives. Adaptive resonance occurs within this network when the reinforcing properties of active external cues sufficiently match the motivational properties of active internal drives to lock STM into a global interpretation of the data.

In the theory I developed in Grossberg (1971, 1972a, 1972b, 1975), the final processing stage in the external cue representations is assumed to be cortical and the final processing stage in the drive representations is assumed to be hippocampal. Gabriel

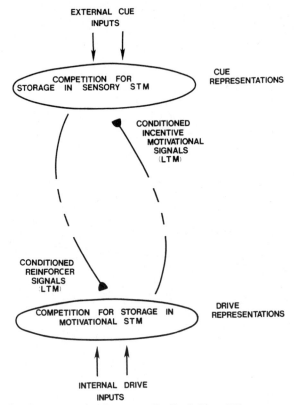

Figure 21. Adaptive resonance between dipole fields. When external cues excite the STM traces of their internal representations, these internal representations elicit signals that are distributed nonspecifically across their drive representations. During conditioning, the pattern of reinforcing and drive inputs to the drive representations can alter the LTM traces within certain of these signal pathways, as in Figure 16. The corresponding external cues thus acquire conditioned reinforcer properties.

On recall trials, the conditioned reinforcer signals from external cues combine with internal drive inputs at the drive representations to determine which drive representations will fire. Ouptut from the drive representations plays the role of incentive motivation in the theory. Incentive motivation is released from a given drive representation only if the momentary balance of conditioned reinforcer signals plus internal drive inputs competes favorably against these factors within the other drive representations.

The incentive motivational pathways are also nonspecific and conditionable. Each drive representation can become conditioned to the class of cues to which it has been associated in the past. Activating a drive representation creates an STM bias that favors the STM storage of motivationally compatible cues. Those external cue representations which receive the most vigorous combination of incentive motivational signals plus external cue inputs can compete most favorably for the limited capacity (normalized) STM activity and thereby be best attended. Figure 23 describes this process in greater detail.

et al. (1980) summarized recent data that support a qualitatively similar conclusion. They write "the hippocampal formation is a region critical for encoding, or 'modeling' of stimulus-reinforcement contingencies" (p.189). They note that the hippocampus is reciprocally connected with cingulate cortex and with the anteroventral nucleus of the thalamus and summarize data suggesting that cortical "codes inappropriate to the stimulus item being presented would create mismatch with the hippocampal model, thereby eliciting code-suppression in cortex and thalamus. Thus, no response would occur" (p.216).

52. A Motivational Dipole Field: Drive-Reinforcer Matching and Motivational Competition

Figure 22 depicts an anatomy that possesses the minimal drive representation properties that I will need. In this anatomy, each motivational channel possesses a positive feedback loop that runs through a gated dipole. These positive feedback loops are the on-centers of the competitive feedback network that joins together the motivational channels. The competitive feedback network provides a matching interface (Section 14) that runs across the motivational channels. At this particular matching interface, spatial patterns of (conditioned) reinforcer signals are matched with spatial patterns of drive signals. Only a sufficiently good match can trigger sustained polyvalent cell firing. If this network's QT is tuned so high that only a single winning channel can reverberate in STM, then sharp motivational switching will occur. Such a setting of the QT defines the channels as motivationally incompatible. A lower setting of the QT permits compatible combinations of drive representations to be synergistically activated. Possible QT settings depend on the choice of numerical network parameters and can vary across species and individuals without changing the underlying design principle.

53. Theta, CNV, and Motor Potential Correlates of a Hippocampal Model

Figure 22 summarizes some of the main ideas in the theory of hypothalamic-hippocampal interactions developed in Grossberg (1972, 1972a, 1972b, 1975). The conditioned reinforcer learning at polyvalent cells helps to explain the conditioning at hippocampal pyramidal cells that Berger and Thompson (1978) report in their studies of the rabbit nictitating membrane response. The STM resonance within gated dipole feedback loops that accompanies conditioned reinforcer learning helps rationalize the theta rhythm that accompanies hippocampal conditioning.

The theory postulates that incentive motivational output from polyvalent cells branches into at least two functionally distinct pathways. One branch controls attentional processing by returning conditionable feedback to external cue representations (Section 29). All these feedback pathways are excitatory to abet STM storage of those representations which are postsynaptic to pathways whose LTM traces have grown due to favorable conditioning contingencies. My theory accepts the idea that it is adaptive to carefully attend to fearful cues, if only to better escape from them.

I believe that this positive conditionable incentive motivational pathway is probed by the Bower (1981) experiments on the effects of mood on memory. In particular, Bower does not find that sad-congruent lists are learned any worse than happy-congruent lists. He also finds that incongruent moods can interfere with recall, which can be explained by the competitive interactions between drive representations and cue representations. I believe that this incentive motivational branch is a formal analog of the pathways *in vivo* that activate a motivational component of the CNV. If this is so, then learning of mood-to-memory associations in Bower's paradigm may yield larger CNVs during mood-congruent recall than in Bower's other recall conditions.

The outputs from the other incentive motivational branch are not all excitatory. These outputs are assumed to preserve their motivational sign, whether positive or negative, and to be used as inputs to a spatial map. It is hypothesized that the spatial

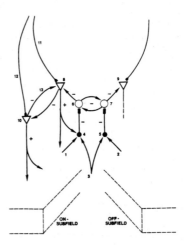

Figure 22. A motivational dipole field. Pathways 1 and 2 carry specific, but complementary, drive inputs (e.g., hunger vs. satiety) to a single dipole. Pathways labeled
3 carry nonspecific arousal to this dipole. Cells 4 and 5 add these inputs and thereupon inhibit the tonically active cells 6 and 7. (Tonic cells have open symbols; phasic
cells have closed symbols.) Pathways 4 → 6 and 5 → 7 contain slow transmitter gates
(square synapses) assumed to be catecholaminergic. If input 1 exceeds input 2, then
the transmitter in pathway 4 → 6 is depleted more than the transmitter in pathway
5 → 7, thereupon calibrating the dipole for a possible antagonistic rebound later on.

The tonic cells 6 and 7 inhibit each other equally until input 1 exceeds input 2.
Then cell 6 is inhibited more than cell 7. This imbalance disinhibits tonic cell 8 and
further inhibits tonic cell 9. Both cells 8 and 9 are polyvalent, meaning that all their
excitatory inputs must be active for these cells to vigorously fire. (Triangles denote
polyvalence.) The polyvalent cells are assumed to be pyramidal cells. Because cells
8 and 9 are polyvalent, a larger input to cell 1 than to cell 2 cannot fire these cells.
However, such an imbalance can prevent cell 9 from firing.

To see how cell 8 can fire, we consider the polyvalent cells 8 and 10 of two different motivational channels. Cells 8 and 10 compete via the inhibitory (interneuronal)
pathways 13. Polyvalent cells 8 and 10 also receive inputs from external cue representations via conditionable pathways 11 and 12, respectively, whose LTM traces (within the
filled hemicircles abutting 8 and 10) encode conditioned reinforcer properties of their
respective external cues. These LTM traces are assumed to be cholinergic.

The conditioned reinforcer inputs combine with drive and arousal inputs at their
respective polyvalent cells, which begin to fire if their thresholds are exceeded. The
polyvalent cells thereupon compete among themselves via the "intrinsic" feedback inhibitory pathways, 13, as they simultaneously try to excite themselves via positive
feedback pathways such as 8 → 4 → 6 → 8.

If, for example, cell 8 wins the competition, then the transmitter gate in 4 → 6
is depleted as the suprathreshold reverberation bursting through cell 8 via pathway
8 → 4 → 6 → 8 drives LTM changes in pathway 11. The reverberation thus induces
conditioned reinforcer changes even as it prepares the network for motivational reset by
rapid offset of 11 or a rapid increment in 13.

distribution of active motivational signs determines the momentary approach or avoidance direction read out from the spatial map. O'Keefe and Nadel (1978) clarify this aspect of the hippocampal functioning. Although the O'Keefe and Nadel concept of an absolute map of an animal's position in space can be criticized on philosophical no less than on scientific grounds, a weaker notion should, I believe, receive further study. This is the concept of a bilaterally organized spatial map in which the asymmetry of excitatory and inhibitory incentive signals with respect to the map's body axis controls the net approach versus avoidance direction of motion.

The existence of hippocampal place and misplace cells (O'Keefe and Nadel, 1978) suggests the possibility that a gated dipole structure exists within this hippocampal spatial map; in particular, that the spatial map is a specialized dipole field whose dipoles may be organized symmetrically with respect to the map body's axis. If such an organization exists, then an unexpected event can reset the direction of motion to one complementary to the direction pursued before the unexpected event occurred. If, by contrast, the dipoles just rebound the agonist-antagonist patterns of active muscle commands, then the unexpected event will cause coordinated motor braking without a change in direction.

The hypothesized existence of both a CNV branch and a spatial mapping branch of the incentive motivational computation helps rationalize why CNV and motor ERPs are often so closely related (Tecce, 1972). A theory capable of sharply distinguishing CNV from motor ERPs would need to incorporate better how bilaterally organized signed spatial maps are organized and how their commands are read out as motor behavior. The final sections of this article will consider how the hypothesized CNV branch of the incentive motivational output helps explain conditioning and attentional data. To show how I think this CNV branch influences attentional processing, I shall first need to describe the processing at cue representations in greater detail.

54. A Sensory Dipole Field: The Synchronization Problem and DC Potential Shifts

Figure 23 depicts the minimal anatomy that I will need to join together external cue representations. This dipole field has more structure than that in Figure 22 because it solves a specialized design problem, which I call the synchronization problem of classical conditioning. The synchronization problem recognizes that, without specialized network buffers, Pavlovian associations could rapidly extinguish whenever a CS and US were presented with different interstimulus delays on successive learning trials. The synchronization problem was solved in Grossberg (1971) and provided the impetus for my later work on reinforcement and motivation.

I hope that the reader wants to ask, What does a lack of synchronization between CS and US delays across Pavlovian trials have to do with reinforcement and motivation? The answer is found in the minimal network that solves the synchronization problem. In this network, drives and conditioned reinforcers interact to control incentive motivational feedback that is necessary to fire polyvalent cortical cells. This solution to the synchronization problem clarifies how Pavlovian and instrumental paradigms can engage common network mechanisms, a fact that has inspired various two-factor learning theories (Dunham, 1971) and complicated efforts to dissociate instrumental from Pavlovian effects in biofeedback paradigms.

For my present purposes, I need to emphasize one difference between Figures 22 and 23. The anatomy in Figure 23 separates the firing of polyvalent cells from the STM reverberation through gated dipoles. Due to this property, a sensory representation can reverberate in STM and thereby deliver signals to a polyvalent cell, or cells, without firing those cells. A polyvalent cell in Figure 23 can fire only if it simultaneously receives STM signals from an external cue representation and incentive motivational signals from a drive representation. This property is analogous to John's (1966, 1967) reports that certain polyvalent cortical cells involved in cortical conditioning can fire only in response

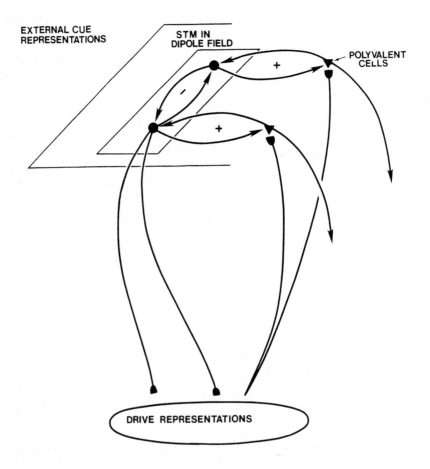

Figure 23. Specific STM signals to the polyvalent cells are insufficient to fire these cells. Sufficiently large incentive motivational signals must simultaneously converge upon the polyvalent cells to fire them. When a polyvalent cell fires, it delivers positive feedback signals to the cells that supply it with specific STM signals. This positive feedback selectively augments the STM activities of these cells, which thereupon more strongly inhibit their competitors for normalized total STM activity.

to a sum of CS and US signals. The property is also analogous to the effects of anodal dc potential shifts on cortical conditioning (Morrell, 1961; Rusinov, 1953). In my theory, the anodal dc shift replaces the requirement of an incentive motivational signal to fire polyvalent cortical output cells.

55. Secondary Conditioning

The functional separation of STM reverberation and polyvalent cell firing implies the following description of how a CS acquires US properties to control observable behavior. Let a CS activate the population v_{11}, which thereupon begins to reverberate in STM. Then v_{11} sends specific signals to the polyvalent cell population v_{12} (among others) and nonspecific signals to the drive representations. Nothing else happens until a US arrives at population v_{21}. This is because v_{12} can fire only if its receives an input from v_{11} and an incentive motivational input from a drive representation, but the signal from v_{11} to the drive representations is initially too small to fire them. When the US perturbs v_{21}, v_{21} sends signals to the polyvalent cells v_{22} and to the drive representations. These latter signals can fire a certain drive representation, if its drive input is large enough, because the cue firing v_{21} is a US for that drive representation, which I will henceforth denote by D_2. When D_2 fires, it releases nonspecific incentive motivational signals to all the external cue representations. Now five things happen.

First, since v_{11} and D_2 are both active, the LTM traces in the pathway from v_{11} to D_2 are strengthened. When these LTM traces get strong enough, the CS alone will be able to fire D_2. Second, the nonspecific incentive motivational signal from D_2 combines with the US-derived signal from v_{21} at v_{22}, thereby firing polyvalent cell signals from v_{22} that read out a UR pattern. Third, because the incentive motivational signal is nonspecific, it also combines with the CS-derived signal from v_{11} at v_{12}, thereby firing the polyvalent cells v_{12}. Fourth, since D_2 and v_{12} are both active, the LTM traces in the pathway from D_2 and v_{12} are strengthened. Fifth, the polyvalent cells v_{12} fire sampling signals to the cells at which the UR pattern is being read out. These signals encode (a fractional component of) the UR in the LTM traces of this pathway. The encoded pattern will henceforth be read out as a CR pattern. The CS thus acquires US properties by learning to control conditioned reinforcer, incentive motivational, and habit strength LTM traces.

This network provides a simple answer to the synchronization question: How does the US turn on the CS with just the right time lag to sample read out of the UR pattern? The same incentive motivational burst that allows v_{22} to read out the UR also allows v_{12} to emit sampling signals that read in the CR.

In Grossberg (1982c), I suggest two interpretations of the cue representation anatomy in Figure 23, one in terms of intracortical interactions and the other in terms of thalamocortical interactions. In both interpretations, the pyramidal cells are assumed to be cortical, but the differences between the two interpretations lead to testable predictions.

56. Valenstein Effect: Nonspecific Drive Representations or Nonspecific Conditioned Reinforcers and Conditioned Incentives?

A controversy that bears on the existence of nonspecific conditionable projection systems between cognitive and motivational processors is the Valenstein effect (Valenstein *et al.*, 1969, 1970). The Valenstein effect is often cited as evidence against the existence of anatomically separate motivational systems in the hypothalamus, since the behavior elicited in response to hypothalamic stimulation can gradually change without any alteration in the stimulation parameters. For example, if the food which a rat originally ate in response to stimulation is removed from its cage, then alternative behaviors such as drinking or gnawing can gradually emerge. The specificity controversy has been intelligently debated by marshalling a wide variety of experimental results (Teitelbaum, 1973; Valenstein, 1973), but I believe that the controversy is a misplaced one because the Valenstein effect can occur whether or not hypothalamic motivational sites are anatomically disjoint. The controversy has focused on the wrong issue. Whether or not the motivational sites are disjoint, external cue representations send pathways nonspecifically across several motivational systems. Conditioning of these pathways is one step whereby cues acquire conditioned reinforcer properties. Morever, feedback pathways from each motivational system reach nonspecifically across many external cue representations. Conditioning of these feedback pathways is one step whereby cues acquire incentive motivational properties. These nonspecific conditionable interactions of external cue representations with motivational representations can give rise to the Valenstein effect even if the motivational representations are entirely disjoint (Grossberg, 1971, 1972a, 1972b). In other words, the controversy has been elaborated within the homeostatic viewpoint, although the phenomenon can be explained by nonhomeostatic mechanisms.

Both Teitelbaum (1973) and Valenstein (1973) recognize that there must exist mechanisms that decide which motivated behavior will appear at any time. Teitelbaum argues by analogy with von Bekesy's model of cochlear "funneling," and Valenstein calls a similar process "channeling." Unfortunately, these personal languages are inadequate as tools to dissect the functional components in the data.

With the above results as background, we can now analyse some interactions between cognitive and motivational networks during conditioning and attention shifts, as well as some of their predicted ERP substrates.

57. Discrimination and Overshadowing Due to Conditioned Incentive Motivational Feedback: CNV Correlates

In his book **Conditioned Reflexes**, Pavlov (1927) gave a brilliant account of how individual cues could be extinguished while the same cues presented as a composite could elicit conditioned responses, and how more intense or more salient cues in a composite could progressively overshadow the other cues in the composite as conditioning proceeded. The four experiments reviewed in Figure 1 are a version of these classical experiments. The following overshadowing and discrimination learning experiments will be used to illustrate both how conditioned incentive motivation helps determine which cues will be overshadowed and how CNV and P300 measures might correlate with these conditioned changes.

Newman and Baron (1965) reinforced pigeons who pecked a vertical white line on a green key (the S^+) but not a green key alone (the S^-). They tested cue discrimination by tilting the line at various orientations during recall trials. A generalization gradient of pecking was found, indicating that the vertical line was discriminated. By contrast, no generalization gradient was found if the S^- on learning trials was a red key or if the S^- was a vertical white line on a red key.

Newman and Benefeld (Honig, 1970) also used a vertical white line on a green key as S^+ and a green key as S^-, but tested and found generalization of the line orientation on a black key. They also tested generalization on a black key following training without a green S^- and again found a generalization gradient, in contrast to the case where testing used a green key. They interpreted this effect as "cue utilization during testing rather than cue selection during learning." This interpretation does not explain how the orientation cue could be learned on training trials if it was not discriminated using a green background on test trials, yet how the orientation cue could be discriminated using a black background on test trials if it was not learned on training trials. The reader might already sense that STM normalization will somehow come to the rescue.

My explanation of these data begins by noting that color cues are prepotent over orientation cues in the pigeon, other things being equal. Consequently, when a vertical white line on a green background is first presented, the green representations will partially overshadow the orientation representations. (I will talk about "green" and "orientation" representations as a shorthand for more sophisticated coding notions that we do not need here.) Grossberg (1978a, Sections 39–40; 1983, Sections 33–44) describes some factors that control how prepotent representations can mask the STM activities of other representations due to competitive feedback interactions.

When the line-on-green cues are first presented, they will enjoy an additional advantage in their STM storage. Their unexpectedness in the context of the experiment's situational cues will strengthen the STM activities of the line-on-green cues as the STM activities of the situational cue representations are rebounded. These rebounds should elicit a P300.

After the line-on-green representations are initially stored in STM, the green cues can increase their relative STM advantage as they acquire conditioned reinforcer and conditioned incentive motivational properties. Figure 23 shows that, when an external cue representation can activate its polyvalent cells using conditioned reinforcer-incentive feedback, polyvalent cells can, in turn, feed back to the cue representations to further enhance their own STM activity. Due to STM normalization among the cue representations, the differential enhancement of some representations acts to the detriment of other representations.

The orientation representations can also acquire conditioned reinforcer and incentive motivational properties as long as their STM activities exceed the network's QT. Their learning rates will be slower than those of the green representations, since their sampling signals in the conditionable pathways are smaller, due to their smaller STM activities. Hence, their conditioned pathways will remain weaker than those of the green representations. As conditioning continues, the orientation representations might be entirely quenched if the conditioned advantage of the color cues becomes sufficiently great to drive orientational STM activities below the QT by competitive feedback across the cue representations.

The unexpected nonoccurrence of reward in response to the green key causes an antagonistic rebound that differentially excites the off-cells of the previously most active STM representations. The active incentive motivational pathways thereupon sample a large off-response in the green representational dipoles. As this experimental contingency recurs on several trials, the net incentive motivational feedback to the green dipoles becomes progressively smaller due to dipole competition between the conditioned on-cell and off-cell pathways to these dipoles.

Even zero net incentive feedback may not be small enough to extinguish the green representation, however, because of the innate advantage of color over orientation. Negative net incentive feedback may be needed to overcome green's innate competitive advantage. Net negative feedback is needed if net positive conditioned reinforcer-incentive feedback to the orientation representation is not sufficient to offset the innate competitive advantage of the color representation when the latter receives zero net conditioned feedback.

This discussion suggests that, although the CNV is always a negative potential in the large, it may cause off-reactions in the cortical dipoles corresponding to predictively irrelevant but prepotent cues even as it strengthens the on-reactions of cortical dipoles corresponding to predictive but nonprepotent cues. I am not sure how this effect can be measured by ERPs, but it should be greatest when the initial advantage of the nonprepotent cue relative to the prepotent cue is as large as possible.

This mechanism easily explains why the white vertical line is discriminated on a black background during test trials even if it is not discriminated on a green background during test trials in an experiment without a green S⁻ on learning trials. Removing green on test trials eliminates competitive feedback from the color representations to the orientation representations. The STM field is thus renormalized. In the renormalized field, even small conditioned reinforcer-incentive feedback signals can provide the white-vertical-orientation representation with a significant competitive advantage for STM storage.

58. The Problem of Perseverating Prepotent Cues

The above mechanism shows how conditionable reinforcer-incentive feedback enables representations to overcome innate competitive STM disadvantages. Some further remarks might clarify why the incentive pathway needs to send branches both to the on-cells and to the off-cells of cortical dipoles. The main benefit is that some cues can lose net positive feedback as other cues gain net positive feedback while both sets of cues are conditioned to the same drive representation. This property avoids the following dilemma.

Suppose the rebound that conditions zero net feedback to the green representation occurs among the drive representations rather than among the cue representations. Then rebound activates a negative drive representation and the net conditioned reinforcer feedback (rather than the net incentive feedback) controlled by the green representation becomes small. This mechanism is unstable for the following reason. As soon as the orientation representation takes over in STM, its positive conditioned reinforcer signals activate the positive drive representation. When this drive representation sends conditioned incentive feedback to the cortex, the green representation receives conditioned positive feedback too, since the negative drive representation is momentarily inhibited. Then the green representation can quickly overshadow the orientation representation using its innate competitive advantage. As soon as the green representation is reinstated in STM, its conditioned reinforcer signals lead to read-out of net negative incentive from the competing drive representations. The green representation is consequently shut off, the orientation representation is disinhibited, and the cycle repeats itself.

Any viable alternative to the present network description must also avoid this problem of perseverating prepotent representations. In particular, a more sophisticated coding analysis would replace "green" and "orientation" representations with heterarchical network encodings wherein one representation's prepotence for masking other representations would depend on its heterarchical position as well as peripheral factors (Grossberg, 1978a, 1983).

59. Cortical Reset Triggers Hippocampal Reset: Two Distinct P300s

At this point, the reader might rightly worry, Haven't you thrown away one good property to salvage another one? Shouldn't there also be a rebound in the drive representation due to the nonoccurrence of expected reward after the green key is presented? After all, this is a frustrating situation in the motivational sense, no less than a situation that needs counterconditioning in the cognitive sense.

I fully agree. First, the rebound among the cortical dipoles is sampled by the LTM traces of the active incentive motivational pathway. Next, offset of the green representations in the cortex shuts off their positive conditioned reinforcer signals to the positive drive representation. Finally, the sudden reduction in conditioned reinforcer input is felt by this drive representation. If the reduction is large enough, STM hysteresis within the positive drive representation is overcome and an antagonistic drive rebound occurs that activates the negative drive representation in its dipole. Any cue that is initially stored in STM at this time can acquire negative conditioned reinforcer properties by sampling this negative drive rebound (Section 31).

The above discussion predicts that the nonoccurrence of expected reward can trigger a cortical P300 by mismatching a learned expectancy. The reset of cortical STM can thereupon trigger a hippocampal rebound by rapidly withdrawing conditioned reinforcer input. If these P300 predictions hold up, they will clarify that a P300 can be elicited by different operations in different brain regions. They will also refine our understanding of the information processing substrates of overshadowng and discrimination learning by distinguishing rebounds that motivationally extinguish cues due to their cognitive irrelevance, without extinguishing their conditioned reinforcer pathways, from rebounds that directly elicit new conditioned reinforcer learning.

60. P300 Size Predicts Nothing About What is Encoded in LTM

I can now illustrate my contention of Section 6 that a large P300 predicts nothing general about LTM. All it tells us is that an STM reset has occurred. The STM reset event will enable advantageously stored cues to elicit large sampling signals, but what these signals encode in LTM will depend on the entire experimental context.

For example, the unexpected occurrence of a reward in response to the line-on-green cue will elicit a P300. As this P300 shrinks on successive rewarded trials, the line-on-green cue should elicit a growing motivational CNV. By contrast, the unexpected nonoccurrence of a reward in response to green alone will elicit a P300. As the P300 shrinks on successive unrewarded trials, the green cue should elicit a shrinking motivational CNV. A conditioned response is learned in the former case, whereas a conditioned response is extinguished in the latter case. P300 size does not differentiate these opposite outcomes in LTM.

61. The Mackintosh, Bygrave, and Picton Experiment: A P300 Prediction

Since a more complete analysis of the moment-by-moment network processing of the Mackintosh *et al.* (1977) experiment (Section 6) has appeared elsewhere (Grossberg, 1982a), I will only briefly summarize my main hypothesis here and make a P300 prediction. I suggest that the main effect of the second shock on the first compound trial is to make the occurrence of the tone on the second compound trial more unexpected within the context of the experiment's situational cues. This greater unexpectedness elicits a larger P300 and gives the tone greater initial STM activity. The larger STM activity elicits larger sampling signals in the conditioned reinforcer pathways of the tone representations. The larger sampling signal supports faster conditioning of the conditioned reinforcer LTM traces that abut the negative drive representation that is activated by the shock. The tone thus becomes motivationally more fear-inducing due to the cognitive effects of a prior shock.

62. Concluding Remarks

This article has attempted to show how a properly posed thought experiment about hypothesis testing in a changing environment can suggest new information processing concepts and mechanisms. The physiological realizations of these concepts reveal new cognitive and motivational neural designs that can be tested by a combination of psychological, physiological, pharmacological, and evoked potential techniques.

I have also indicated that surprising mathematical properties of these designs shed new light on important behavioral syndromes. The explanation of these syndromes does not lie in an ever finer dissection of brain components. Rather, one must study the interactions within neural tissues because these interactions literally create the behavioral properties. In particular, no amount of saying that too little catecholamine correlates with Parkinsonism and juvenile hyperactivity or too much catecholamine correlates with schizophrenia can explain the behavioral properties of underaroused or overaroused depression.

Evoked potential experiments can probe this interactive neural level. They are, therefore, a powerful tool for studying neural designs that purport to clarify the development and stability of cognitive and motivational processes.

APPENDIX

GATED DIPOLES

63. Transmitters as Gates

The transmitter model presented here was derived from associative learning postulates in Grossberg (1968, 1969b). The gated dipole model was derived from conditioning postulates in Grossberg (1972b). The transmitter derivation below shows that our transmitter law is the minimal dynamic law for unbiased transmission using a depletable signal (Grossberg, 1980a).

We start by asking the following question: What is the simplest law whereby one nerve cell can send unbiased signals to another nerve cell? The simplest law says that if a signal S passes through a given nerve cell v_1, the signal has a proportional effect

$$T = SB, \qquad (4)$$

where $B > 0$, on the next nerve cell v_2. Such a law permits unbiased transmission of signals from one cell to another.

A difficulty occurs, however, if the signal from v_1 to v_2 is due to the release of a chemical $z(t)$ from v_1 that activates v_2. If such a chemical transmitter is persistently released when S is large, what keeps the net signal, T, from getting smaller and smaller as v_1 runs out of transmitter? Some means of replenishing or accumulating the transmitter must exist to counterbalance its depletion due to release from v_1.

Based on this discussion, we can rewrite (4) in the form

$$T = Sz \qquad (5)$$

and ask, How can the system keep z replenished so that

$$z(t) \cong B \qquad (6)$$

at all times t? This is a question about the sensitivity of v_2 to signals from v_1, since if z could decrease to very small values, even large signals S would have only a small effect on T.

Equation (5) has the following interpretation. The signal, S, causes the transmitter, z, to be released at a rate $T = Sz$. Whenever two processes, such as S and z, are multiplied, we say that they interact by mass action, or that z gates S. Thus, (5) says that z gates S to release a net signals T, and (6) says that the cell tries to replenish z to maintain the system's sensitivity to S.

What is the simplest law that joins together both (5) and (6)? It is the following differential equation for the net rate of change, dz/dt, of z:

$$\frac{dz}{dt} = A(B - z) - Sz. \qquad (7)$$

Equation (7) describes the following four processes going on simultaneously.

Accumulation or Production and Feedback Inhibition

The term $A(B - z)$ enjoys two possible interpretations, depending on whether it represents a passive accumulation process or an active production process.

In the former interpretation, there exist B sites to which transmitter can be bound, z sites are bound at time t, and $B - z$ sites are unbound. Then the term $A(B - z)$ says simply that transmitter is bound at a rate proportional to the number of unbound sites.

In the latter interpretation, two processes go on simultaneously. The term AB on the right-hand side of (7) says that z is produced at a rate AB. The term $-Az$ says that once z is produced, it inhibits the production rate by an amount proportional to the concentration of z. In biochemistry, such an inhibitory effect is called feedback inhibition by the end product of a reaction. Without feedback inhibition, the constant rate of production, AB, would eventually cause the cell to burst. With feedback inhibition, the net production rate is $A(B - z)$, which causes $z(t)$ to approach the finite amount, B, as we desire by (6). The term $A(B - z)$ thus enables the cell to accumulate a target level B of transmitter.

Gating and Release

The term $-Sz$ in (7) says that z is released at a rate Sz, as we desire by (5). As in (5), release of z is due to mass action activation of z by S or to gating of S by z.

The two equations (5) and (7) describe the simplest dynamic law that corresponds to the constraints (5) and (6). Equations (5) and (7) begin to reconcile the two constraints of unbiased signal transmission and maintenance of sensitivity when the signals are due to release of transmitter.

64. Intracellular Adaptation and Habituation

First let us determine how the net signal, $T = Sz$, reacts to a sudden change in S. We will suppose that $z(t)$ reacts slowly compared to the rate with which S can change. For definiteness, suppose that $S(t) = S_0$ for all times $t \leq t_0$ and that, at time $t = t_0$, $S(t)$ suddenly increases to S_1. By (7), $z(t)$ reacts to the constant value $S(t) = S_0$ by approaching an equilibrium value $z(t_0)$. This equilibrium value is found by setting $dz/dt = 0$ in (7) and solving for

$$z(t_0) = \frac{AB}{A + S_0}. \tag{8}$$

By (8), a larger value of S_0 causes more transmitter to be released. In other words, $z(t_0)$ is a decreasing function of S_0. By contrast, (5) implies that the net signal to v_2 at time t_0 is

$$S_0 z(t_0) = \frac{ABS_0}{A + S_0}. \tag{9}$$

By (9), the rate of transmitter release is an increasing function of S_0. Now let $S(t)$ switch to the value $S_1 > S_0$. Because $z(t)$ is slowly varying, $z(t)$ approximately equals $z(t_0)$ for a while after $t = t_0$. Thus, the net signal to v_2 during these times is approximately equal to

$$S_1 z(t_0) = \frac{ABS_1}{A + S_0}. \tag{10}$$

Equation (10) has the same form as a Weber law, $J(A + I)^{-1}$. The signal S_1 is evaluated relative to the baseline, S_0, just as J is evaluated relative to I. This Weber law is due to slow intracellular adaptation of the transmitter gate to the input level through time. It is not due to fast intercellular lateral inhibition across space, as reviewed in Grossberg (1980a, Appendix C and D).

As $z(t)$ in (7) begins to respond to the new transmitter level, $S = S_1$, $z(t)$ gradually approaches the new equilibrium point that is determined by $S = S_1$; namely

$$z(\infty) = \frac{AB}{A + S_1}. \tag{11}$$

The net signal consequently decays to the asymptote,

$$S_1 z(\infty) = \frac{ABS_1}{A + S_1}. \tag{12}$$

Thus, after $S(t)$ switches from S_0 to S_1, the net signal S_z jumps from (9) to (10) and then gradually decays to (12). The exact course of this decay is described by the equation

$$S_1 z(t) = \frac{ABS_1}{A + S_0} e^{-(A+S_1)(t-t_0)} + \frac{ABS_1}{A + S_1} \left(1 - e^{(A+S_1)(t-t_0)}\right) \tag{13}$$

for $t \geq t_0$, which shows that the rate, or gain, $A + S_1$ of the response increases with the signal S_1, just as in the case of shunting lateral inhibition (Grossberg, 1980a). The sudden increment followed by slow decay can be intuitively described as an overshoot followed by habituation to the new sustained signal level, S_1. Both intracellular adaptation and habituation occur whenever a transmitter fluctuates more slowly than the signals that it gates. The size of the overshoot can be found by subtracting (12) from (10). For definiteness, let $S_0 = f(I)$ and $S_1 = f(I + J)$, where $f(w)$ is a function that transmutes the inputs I and $I + J$ that exist before and after the increment J into net signals S_0 and S_1, respectively. Then the overshoot size is approximately

$$S_1 z(t_1) - S_1 z(\infty) = \frac{ABf(I + J)[f(I + J) - f(I)]}{[A + f(I)][A + f(I + J)]}. \tag{14}$$

In Section A4 below, I will show that the rebound size in response to specific cue offset is related to (14) in a way that allows us to estimate both $f(w)$ and the arousal level, I.

Much confusion can be avoided by realizing that more than one type of habituation can occur in the nervous system. Intracellular habituation due to a slow transmitter gate is not the only type of habituation. An intercellular variety of habituation can also occur. After a feedback expectancy is learned, a mismatch of the feedback expectancy with feedforward data can trigger an orienting reaction, or a dishabituation of the network's orienting subsystem. Feedback expectancies and slow gates are both needed to regulate perceptual and motivational events, but they are quite distinct. For example, I suggested in Section 37 that bistable perception of ambiguous figures is caused, even when the eye does not move, by a temporally cyclic habituation of transmitter gates, which shifts the pattern of STM activity and thereby cyclically activates alternative feedback expectancies. The expectancy that is active at any time organizes the ambiguous visual data into an unambiguous global percept (Grossberg, 1978a, 1980a).

65. A Gated Dipole

I will now indicate how, if transmitters gate signals before the gated signals compete, antagonistic rebound can be elicited by offset of a specific cue, as in light-on versus light-off, or fear versus relief. I will also show how unexpected events can cause an antagonistic rebound. They do this by triggering an increase in the level of nonspecific arousal that is gated by all the transmitter pathways.

Figure 24 depicts the simplest network in which two channels receive inputs that are gated by slowly varying transmitters before the channels compete to elicit a net output response. Such a network is called a feedforward gated dipole. Two types of inputs will be introduced. Specific inputs are turned on and off by internal or external cues and nonspecific arousal inputs are on all the time, even though their size can vary through time. Each channel can have its own sum of specific inputs, K_1 or K_2, such as a hunger or satiety drive input, respectively, added to conditioned positive or negative reinforcing signals, and both channels receive the same arousal input, L. The total signals to the two channels are, therefore, $S_1 = f(K_1 + L)$, where the signal function, $f(w)$, is monotone increasing. We will see that the relative sizes of S_1 and S_2 and their rates of change through time relative to the transmitter fluctuation rate determine whether an antagonistic rebound will occur. To emphasize this fact, I define

$$I = \min(K_1 + L, K_2 + L) \tag{15}$$

and

$$J =| K_1 - K_2 | . \tag{16}$$

The quantity I determines the network's net arousal level and J determines how asymmetric the inputs are to the two channels. Suppose, for definiteness, that $K_1 > K_2$. Then $S_1 = f(I + J)$ and $S_2 = f(I)$.

The notational shift from $S_1 = f(K_1 + L)$ and $S_2 = f(K_2 + L)$ to $S_1 = f(I + J)$ and $S_2 = f(I)$ in (15) and (16) is motivated by more than formal convenience. The notation I and J emphasizes that the dipole doesn't know how many input sources are perturbing it through time. All it can compute is the net arousal level, I, and the degree of asymmetry, J, above I, whether one or a million input sources are active. If a million cues equally perturb the on-channel (positive reinforcers) and another million cues equally perturb the off-channel (negative reinforcers), the net effect of all the cues will be to increase I, not J. Thus, after dipole competition takes place, all these cues need not generate any incentive motivation. On the other hand, by increasing I, these cues can alter the sensitivity of the dipole to other asymmetrically distributed inputs due to the dipole's inverted U properties. This is the kind of simple but subtle distinction that the I and J notation emphasizes.

66. Rebound Due to Phasic Cue Offset

A rebound can be caused if, after the network equilibrates to the input J, the input is suddenly shut off. This effect is analogous to the reaction that occurs when a light is shut off or an aversive cue is shut off. To see how this rebound is generated, suppose that the arousal level is I and that the cue input is J. Let the total signal in the on-channel be $S_1 = f(I + J)$ and that in the off-channel be $S_2 = f(I)$. Let the transmitter in the on-channel, z_1, satisfy the equation

$$\frac{d}{dt}z_1 = A(B - z_1) - S_1 z_1 \tag{17}$$

and the transmitter in the off-channel, z_2, satisfy the equation

$$\frac{d}{dt}z_2 = A(B - z_2) - S_2 z_2. \tag{18}$$

After z_1 and z_2 equilibrate to S_1 and S_2, $(d/dt)z_1 = (d/dt)z_2 = 0$. Thus, by (17) and (18),

$$z_1 = \frac{AB}{A + S_1} \tag{19}$$

and

$$z_2 = \frac{AB}{A + S_2}. \tag{20}$$

Since $S_1 > S_2$, it follows that $z_1 > z_2$; that is, z_1 is depleted more than z_2. However, the gated signal in the on-channel is $S_1 z_1$ and the gated signal in the off-channel is $S_2 z_2$. Since

$$S_1 z_1 = \frac{ABS_1}{A + S_1} \tag{21}$$

and

$$S_2 z_2 = \frac{ABS_2}{A + S_2}, \tag{22}$$

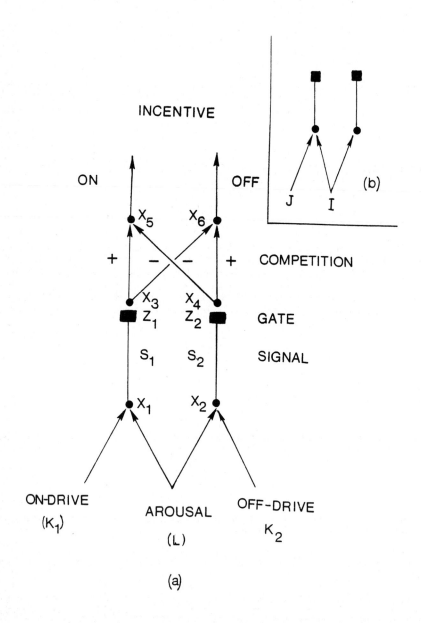

INCENTIVE

ON   OFF   (b)

X_5 X_6

+   −   −   +   COMPETITION

X_3 X_4
Z_1 Z_2 GATE

S_1 S_2 SIGNAL

X_1 X_2

ON-DRIVE   OFF-DRIVE
(K_1) AROUSAL K_2
                        (L)

(a)

Figure 24. (a) Specific inputs (K_1 and K_2) and a nonspecific input (L) have the same effect as (b) a specific input J and a net arousal level I if $K_1 > K_2$.

it follows from the inequality $S_1 > S_2$ that $S_1 z_1 > S_2 z_2$, despite the fact that $z_1 < z_2$. Thus, the on-channel gets a bigger signal that the off-channel. After the two channels compete, the input J produces a sustained on-input whose size is proportional to

$$S_1 z_1 - S_2 z_2 = \frac{A^2 B[f(I + J) - f(I)]}{[A + f(I)][A + f(I + J)]}. \tag{23}$$

Division of (14) by (23) yields an interesting relationship between the size of the overshoot in the on-channel and the size of the steady-state on-input; namely,

$$\frac{on - overshoot}{steady\ on - input} = \frac{f(I + J)}{A}, \tag{24}$$

which provides an estimate of $f(w)$ if J is parametrically varied. In particular, if $f(w)$ is a linear signal, $f(w) = w$, then (23) becomes

$$S_1 z_1 - S_2 z_2 = \frac{A^2 B J}{(A + I)(A + I + J)}, \tag{25}$$

which is an increasing function of J (more fear given more shock) but a decreasing function of I (linear analgesic effect).

Now shut J off to see how an antagonistic rebound (relief) is generated. The cell potentials rapidly adjust until new signal values, $S_1^* = f(I)$ and $S_2^* = f(I)$, obtain. However, the transmitters z_1 and z_2 change much more slowly, so that (19) and (20) are approximately valid in a time interval that follows J offset. Thus, the gated signals in this time interval approximately equal

$$S_1^* z_1 \cong \frac{AB f(I)}{A + f(I + J)} \tag{26}$$

and

$$S_2^* z_2 \cong \frac{AB f(I)}{A + f(I)}. \tag{27}$$

Thus, $S_1^* z_1 < S_2^* z_2$. The off-channel now gets the bigger signal, so an antagonistic rebound occurs, the size of which is approximately

$$S_2^* z_2 - S_1^* z_1 = \frac{AB f(I)[f(I + J) - f(I)]}{[A + f(I)][A + f(I + J)]}. \tag{28}$$

Division of (28) by (23) yields an interesting relationship between the maximal off-output and the steady on-output; namely,

$$\frac{off - output}{on - output} = \frac{f(I)}{A}, \tag{29}$$

which provides an estimate of $f(w)$ as I is parametrically varied. A comparison of (24) with (29) shows that, as I is parametrically varied, (24) should have the same graph as (29), shifted by J. This comparison provides an estimate of J (that is, of how the behavioral input is transformed into neural units) and also a strong test of the model. Once $f(w)$ is estimated, (23) and (28) can be verified.

If $f(w) = w$ in (28), then

$$S_2^* z_2 = S_1^* z_1 = \frac{ABIJ}{(A+I)(A+I+J)}. \tag{30}$$

The rebound is then an increasing function of J (offset of larger shock elicits more relief) and an inverted U function of I (an optimal arousal level exists).

The rebound is transient because the equal signals, $S_1 = S_2 = f(I)$, gradually equalize the z_1 and z_2 levels until they both approach $AB(A+f(I))^{-1}$. Then $S_1 z_1 - S_2 z_2$ approaches zero, so the competition between channels shuts off both of their outputs.

67. Rebound Due to Arousal Onset

A surprising property of these dipoles of on-cell and off-cell pairs is their reaction to sudden increments in the arousal level, I. Such increments are, for example, thought to occur in response to unexpected events.

Suppose that the on-channel and the off-channel have equilibrated to the input levels I and J. Now suddenly increase I to I^*, thereby changing the signals to $S_1^* = f(I^* + J)$ and $S_2^* = f(I^*)$. The transmitters z_1 and z_2 continue to obey (19) and (20) for a while, with $S_1 = f(I + J)$ and $S_2 = f(I)$. A rebound occurs if $S_2^* z_2 > S_1^* z_1$. In general,

$$S_2^* z_2 - S_2^* z_1 = \frac{AB[f(I^*) - f(I^* + J)] + B[f(I^*)f(I + J) - f(I)f(I^* + J)]}{[A + f(I)][A + f(I + J)]}. \tag{31}$$

In particular, if $f(w) = w$, a rebound occurs whenever

$$I^* > I + A, \tag{32}$$

since then

$$S_2^* z_2 - S_1^* z_1 = \frac{ABJ(I^* - I - A)}{(A + I + J)(A + I)}. \tag{33}$$

Thus, given a linear signal function, a rebound will occur if I^* exceeds $I + A$ no matter how J is chosen. If the event is so unexpected that it increments the arousal level by more than amount A, then all on-cell off-cell dipoles in the network will simultaneously rebound. Moreover, the size of the off-cell rebound increases as a function of the size of the on-cell input, J, as (33) shows. In particular, no rebound occurs if the on-cell was inactive before the unexpected event occurs. Thus, the rebound mechanism is selective. It rebounds most vigorously those cells which are most active $(J \gg 0)$ and spares the inactive cells $(J \cong 0)$.

68. Inverted U in Dipole Output

The inverted U effect holds if $f(w)$ is a sigmoid function; that is, if $f(0) = df/dw(0) = 0$, $df/dw(w) > 0$ if $w > 0$, $f(\infty) < \infty$, and $d^2f/dw^2(w)$ changes sign once from positive to negative as w increases. In particular, if $f(w)$ is sigmoid, an inverted U occurs in the sustained on-output (23) as I is parametrically increased, despite the fact that an inverted U does not obtain in (25) when $f(w)$ is linear. To simplify the results, I use the signum function

$$\text{sgn}\{w\} = \begin{cases} +1 & \text{if } w > 0 \\ 0 & \text{if } w = 0 \\ -1 & \text{if } w < 0 \end{cases}. \tag{34}$$

I first consider the on-reaction in (23), which I denote by x_5 (Figure 24). I write the derivative of a function $g(I)$ as $g'(I)$. Then, by (23), for each fixed J,

$$
\begin{aligned}
\operatorname{sgn}\{x_5'(I)\} = \operatorname{sgn}\{ &A^2[f'(I+J) - f'(I)] + 2A[f(I)f'(I+J) \\
&- f(I+J)f'(I)] + [f^2(I)f'(I+J) - f^2(I+J)f'(I)]\}.
\end{aligned}
\tag{35}
$$

Since $f(w)$ is sigmoid,

$$
f(0) = f'(0) = 0.
\tag{36}
$$

Thus, by (35) and (36),

$$
\operatorname{sgn}\{x_5'(0)\} = \operatorname{sgn}\{A^2 f'(J)\} > 0.
\tag{37}
$$

At large values of I,

$$
f(I+J) > f(I),
\tag{38}
$$

whereas

$$
f'(I+J) < f'(I).
\tag{39}
$$

Consequently, each term in brackets on the right-hand size of (35) is negative. Thus, at large I values,

$$
\operatorname{sgn}\{x_5'(I)\} < 0.
\tag{40}
$$

The inequalities (37) and (40) show that, for fixed J, $x_5(I)$ increases and then decreases as a function of I. This is the inverted U for the on-reaction. In fact, since $f(\infty) < \infty$, (23) implies that $\lim_{I \to \infty} x_5(I) = 0$. A similar proof holds for the off-reaction.

69. Hypersensitive Underaroused Reaction to Phasic Increments

To illustrate why the underaroused syndrome is hypersensitive to phasic increments, suppose that I is chosen abnormally small and, consequently, that $f(I)$ is very small because of f's S-shaped graph. Let J represent the intensity of a fearful cue (e.g., a shock level) and let the dipole on-output (23) be correlated with the amount of fear. Since I is so small, the "fear threshold is raised" in the sense that a large value of J is needed to create a large net on-output than when J is chosen in the "normal" range. Although the fear threshold is high, once J is chosen sufficiently large to elicit a detectable net on-reaction, additional increments in J create larger than normal increments in fear. This is because the terms $f(I)$ in the numerator and denominator of (23) are abnormally small. More precisely, differentiating (23) with respect to J, we find the rate at which the on-output increases to unit increases in J. This rate is

$$
\frac{\partial}{\partial J}(S_1 z_1 - S_2 z_2) = \frac{A^2 B f'(I+J)}{[A + f(I+J)]^2}.
\tag{41}
$$

If $I + J$ is chosen so that $f(I + J)$ is small but growing rapidly, then $f'(I + J)$ is relatively large when the denominator, $[A + f(I + J)]^2$, is relatively small. In other words, underaroused depression is hyperexcitable despite its high threshold.

70. Paradoxical On-Reaction to Unexpected Events and Differential Enhancement of Overshadowed Cues

Two other properties of underaroused dipoles are related to Parkinsonian bracing. These properties, like underaroused hyperexcitability, are due to the faster-than-linear, or threshold, behavior of the S-shaped signal function, $f(w)$, at small activity values, w. Neither property holds if the signal function is linear, say $f(w) = w$. In particular, by (33), when $f(w) = w$, an arousal increment ΔI in response to an unexpected event causes a rebound whenever $\Delta I > A$. The minimal ΔI capable of causing a rebound is independent of the ambient arousal level, I. This property does not hold when $f(w)$ grows faster than linearly, say $f(w) = w^2$, which approximates the sigmoid shape of $f(w)$ at low arousal levels. By (31), a rebound occurs when $f(w) = w^2$ only if

$$\Delta I > g(I, J), \tag{42}$$

where the function

$$g(I, J) = \frac{A - I(I + J) + (A + I^2)^{1/2}[A + (I + J)^2]^{1/2}}{2I + J} \tag{43}$$

is a decreasing function of I. In fact, $g(I, J)$ approaches 0 as I is chosen arbitrarily large. Thus, a much larger ΔI is needed to rebound an underaroused dipole than a normally aroused dipole. Moreover, if $\Delta I < AJ^{-1}$, then when $I \cong 0$,

$$\frac{\partial}{\partial(\Delta I)} \left[\frac{(I + \Delta I + J)^2}{A + (I + J)^2} - \frac{(I + \Delta I)^2}{A + I^2} \right] > 0. \tag{44}$$

In other words, an arousal increment can actually enhance the on-output of an underaroused dipole instead of rebounding the dipole.

Use of a sigmoid function also helps explain how overshadowed cues can be enhanced even though very active cues are inhibited when an arousal burst occurs. This is because the function $g(I, J)$ is a decreasing function of J, as well as of I. This means that it is easier to rebound a more active STM representation than a less active STM representation.

71. Paradoxical Lack of Rebound to Phasic Decrement: Ordering of Reinforcement Magnitude

This section illustrates how several behavioral indices should all covary as arousal level is parametrically increased. The first index says that reducing J units of shock to $J/2$ units is less rewarding than reducing $J/2$ units of shock to 0 units, despite the fact that both operations reduce shock by $J/2$ units. This result is based on the fact that (23) and (28) include ratios of I and J effects as well as differences of I and J effects. In fact, this result can be generalized to a formula that predicts when reducing J_1 units of shock to K_1 units at arousal level I_1 is more reinforcing than reducing J_2 units of shock to K_2 units at arousal level I_2 (Grossberg, 1972b). To make these assertions, I assume that the size of the relief rebound caused by reducing the shock level is proportional to the rewarding effect of the manipulation, other things being equal (which is usually false!).

To derive these effects, it is convenient to use a signal function

$$f(w) = \max(w - C, 0). \tag{45}$$

Such a signal function has a threshold C, below which it equals 0 and above which it grows linearly. This threshold function approximates a sigmoid function in the activity range before saturation occurs. I will also use the following notation. I denote the steady-state on-reaction that occurs after a specific input of intensity J is kept on for S time units by $x_5(S, J \rightarrow K)$ and the off-rebound that occurs when intensity J is switched to K at time $t = S$ by $x_6(S^+, J + K)$. To compute $x_6(S^+, J \rightarrow K)$, I approximate the transmitters by the steady-state values at $t = S$ and the potentials by their new steady-state values in response to input K.

Let us choose an arousal level I that exceeds the threshold, C. Then, proceeding as in our previous computations, we find that

$$x_6\left(S^+, J \to \frac{J}{2}\right) = \frac{AB\frac{J}{2}(I - A - C)}{(D + I)(D + I + J)},\tag{46}$$

where $D = A - C$. By comparison, (23) and (28) imply that

$$x_5(S, J \to 0) = \frac{A^2 BJ}{(D + I)(D + I + J)}\tag{47}$$

and

$$x_6(S^+, J \to 0) = \frac{ABJ(I - C)}{(D + I)(D + I + J)},\tag{48}$$

from which it also follows that

$$x_6\left(S^+, \frac{J}{2} \to 0\right) = \frac{AB\frac{J}{2}(I - C)}{(D + I)(D + I + \frac{J}{2})}\tag{49}$$

and

$$\frac{x_6(S^+, K \to 0)}{x_5(S, K \to 0)} = A^{-1}(I - C)\tag{50}$$

for any $K > 0$. Comparing (46) and (49), we find that

$$x_6\left(S^+, \frac{J}{2} \to 0\right) > x_6\left(S^+, J \to \frac{J}{2}\right),\tag{51}$$

or that cutting J units in half is less rewarding that shutting off $J/2$ units. We also confirm that the ratio (50) increases with I, as in the more general equation (29). We can now substitute (50) into (46) to find that

$$x_6\left(S^+, J \to \frac{J}{2}\right) = \frac{A^2 B\frac{J}{2}[x_5^{-1}(S, K \to 0)x_6(S^+, K \to 0) - 1]}{(D + I)(D + I + J)}.\tag{52}$$

By (52), an arousal level that favors the possibility of learned avoidance in the presence of fearful cues also favors a large rewarding effect when the shock level is halved. If I is chosen to be small (underarousal), then x_6 in (46) can be negative (no rebound occurs) even if x_6 in (49) is positive (a rebound occurs).

72. Inhibiting Excitatory Resistance versus Exciting Inhibitory Conductance in Disinhibitory Incentive Motivational Pathways

Thus far, our discussion of gating effects has ignored the fact that the post-synaptic target cells possess only a finite number of excitable sites that can be turned on and off. This fact is, however, an important constraint on the design of cellular mechanisms, since, after all the sites are turned on, the target cell is insensitive to later input fluctuations; in other words, the target cell saturates. As I noted in Section 14, this noise-saturation dilemma is overcome by competitive interactions among cells that undergo mass action, or shunting, dynamics. Shunting dynamics occur, for example, in the membrane equation that is a cornerstone of experimental neurophysiology. Such an equation takes the form

$$C\frac{dV}{dt} = (V^+ - V)g^+ + (V^- - V)g^- + (V^p - V)g^p \tag{53}$$

for the time rate of change, dV/dt of a cell potential $V(t)$. The constant C is capacitance; the constants V^+, V^-, and V^p are saturation points for the excitatory, inhibitory, and passive channels, respectively; and the terms g^+, g^-, and g^p are conductances for the excitatory, inhibitory, and passive channels, respectively. I will assume by convention that $V^+ > V^p = 0 \geq V^-$. Then $V^+ \geq V(t) \geq V^-$ at all times t. Our previous discussion tacitly assumed that inputs that change g^+ or g^- are sufficiently small to prevent $V(t)$ from saturating at V^+ or V^-. Thus, the $V(t)$ terms in the excitatory and inhibitory channels of (53) have a negligible effect and we have until now ignored them. In general, however, this is false. Let us now study how including the saturation terms can sharpen our concepts.

To fix ideas, let $g^p = A$ (a positive constant), let $g^- = 0$, and let $g^+ = Sz$, where z is a slow transmitter that gates the input S. Also choose $C = 1$ for simplicity and write $V^+ = B$. Then

$$\frac{dV}{dt} = -AV + (B - V)Sz. \tag{54}$$

The equilibrium potential of (54) is found by setting $dV/dt = 0$. It is

$$V_\infty = \frac{BSz}{A + Sz}. \tag{55}$$

Had we ignored the excitatory term $-VSz$ of (54) to study

$$\frac{dV}{dt} = -AV + BSz \tag{56}$$

instead, we would have found the equilibrium potential $BA^{-1}Sz$. This is what we tacitly did to derive x_3 and x_4 in Figure 24. The steady-state on-potential V_∞ resembles Sz in that both increase as a function of Sz so both will habituate if either one does. However, (54) differs from (56) in two crucial ways. (1) Automatic Gain Control: The gain, or averaging rate, of $V(t)$ in (54) is $-(A + Sz)$, which increases as Sz increases. In (56), the gain is the constant A. (2) Saturation: V_∞ saturates at B as Sz becomes large.

Often it is desirable to prolong cell response, rather than speed it up, as input size increases. One way to accomplish this is to increase the resistance of the excitatory channel rather than its conductance. This operation hyperpolarizes (inhibits) rather than depolarizes (excites) the cell potential (Baylor and Hodgkin, 1974; Baylor *et al.*, 1974a, 1974b), but this reversal in sign is unimportant if the inhibited cell is part of a two-state disinhibitory pathway.

To slow down cell response in this way, let

$$\frac{dV}{dt} = -AV + (B - V)G, \tag{57}$$

as in (54), where $G(t)$ is the number of open membrane "gates" at time t. Also let

$$\frac{dG}{dt} = \alpha(\beta - G) - SzG. \tag{58}$$

Equation (58) says that G obeys an accumulation-depletion equation just like (7) with signal Sz. The term $\alpha(\beta - G)$ says that the system strives to keep β gates open. The term SzG says that open gates, which number G, are closed by the signal Sz. Suppose that gates open and close much more rapidly that V reacts to these changes. Then we can treat G as if it is always in equilibrium with respect to Sz and, by (58),

$$G \cong \frac{\gamma}{\alpha + Sz}, \tag{59}$$

where $\gamma = \alpha\beta$. By (59), when $S = 0$, the number of open gates, G, approaches $G_0 = \beta$ and the potential, V, approaches $V_0 = BG_0(A+G_0)^{-1}$. We are interested in the quantity $x = V_0 - V$, where V is the equilibrium potential induced by a prescribed input, S. The function x measures how much V is hyperpolarized by the gated signal Sz.

We find that

$$x = \frac{USz}{V + Sz} \tag{60}$$

where $U = \beta B(1 + \beta A^{-1})^{-1}$ and $V = \alpha + \gamma A^{-1}$. Note that V_∞ in (55) exhibits the same steady-state dependence on Sz as does x in (60). Nonetheless, the gain of (57) is $A + (\gamma/(\alpha + Sz))$, which is a decreasing function of Sz rather than an increasing function of Sz. All in all, (57) and (58) describe a tonically active cell ($V_0 > 0$) whose rate of inhibition by gated inputs Sz decreases as Sz increases.

To elicit a prolonged response to inputs in a disinhibitory pathway, suppse that the output $f(V)$ of (57) inhibits the conductance of the potential $W(t)$, as in the equation

$$\frac{dW}{dt} = -AW + (B - W)C - f(V)W. \tag{61}$$

The term $(B - W)C$ says that the cell maintains a tonic excitatory conductance. The term $-f(V)W$ says that the excitatory tonic activity is counteracted by inhibitory tonic activity. As V decreases due to an increase in Sz, $f(V)$ also decreases. The gain $A + f(V)$ of W is thus decreased as the asymptote of W is increased. All in all, a two-stage disinhibition in which the first stage increases excitatory resistance and the second stage decreases inhibitory conductance significantly prolongs the effect of an input pulse. Moreover, if $f(V) = kV$, then the steady-state depolarization, $W - W_0$, again has the form $USz(V + Sz)^{-1}$.

The design of this disinhibitory pathway raises the experimental equation: Do (for example) the DA-GABA feedback loops between the neostriatum and the substantia nigra (Groves *et al.*, 1978) contain cells whose increase in excitatory resistance causes a decrease in the inhibitory conductance of their target cells?

73. Intracellular Dipoles

Part of understanding a design principle is being able to recognize how different anatomies can compute the same functional properties. For example, if both excitatory and inhibitory conductances are nonzero in a cell membrane, and if at least one of these conductances is altered by a gated signal, then the cell potential can generate both on-overshoot and off-rebound effects. This system acts like an intracellular gated dipole. In particular, suppose that

$$\frac{dV}{dt} = -AV + (B - V)\frac{\gamma}{\alpha + Sz} - (V + C)D \tag{62}$$

and

$$\frac{dz}{dt} = E(F - z) - Sz. \tag{63}$$

The term $(B - V)(\gamma/(\alpha + Sz))$ in (62) acts like the on-channel of the dipole and the term $-(V + C)D$ acts like the off-channel. In response to a sustained increment in S, the on-channel overshoots, then habituates, as $z(t)$ in (63) is slowly depleted by the larger value of S. A sudden decrement in S causes the potential to rapidly decrease and then to slowly increase as $z(t)$ accumulates in response to the smaller value of S. Thus, a dipole can be realized by a single cell, rather than by two parallel competing pathways, as occurs in *Gekko gekko* rods (Carpenter and Grossberg, 1981; Kleinschmidt and Dowling, 1975).

74. Presynaptic Normalization by Transmitter Diffusion and Feedback Inhibition

When diffusion and reuptake of released transmitter can occur between synapses, the total amount of transmitter can be controlled by the extra feedback inhibition that is due to reuptake. Without reuptake, the simplest transmitter law at the ith synapse is

$$\frac{dz_i}{dt} = A(B - z_i) - S_i z_i \tag{64}$$

where S_i is the input and z_i is the transmitter at the synapse. With reuptake, and ignoring time-delay effects, the simplest transmitter law becomes

$$\frac{dz_i}{dt} = A(B - z_i - \sum_{k=1}^{n} S_k z_k C_{ki}) - S_i z_i, \tag{65}$$

where the term $-A S_k z_k C_{ki}$ describes the extra feedback inhibition due to uptake of released transmitter $S_k z_k$ from the kth synapse. To understand the normalizing effect of intercellular diffusion, consider the steady-state rate $T = \sum_{k=1}^{n} S_k z_k$ of total transmitter release in two extreme cases: (1) where no diffusion occurs (all $C_{ki} = 0$) and (2) where long-range diffusion occurs (all $C_{ki} = C > 0$). Suppose for definiteness that all inputs are equal, say $S_i = S$. By (65), in case (1),

$$T = \frac{nABS}{A + S} \leq ABn, \tag{66}$$

which increases linearly with the number of cell, n. In case (2),

$$T = \frac{nABS}{A + S + nCS} \leq ABC^{-1}, \tag{67}$$

whose maximum is independent of n. This result helps to explain the experiments of Stricker and Zigmond (1976) on recovery from damage to the dopaminergic synapses of the nigrostriatal bundle, since reducing the feedback inhibition from damaged cells allows undamaged cells to produce more transmitter in a compensatory fashion.

75. Paradoxical Inhibitory Action of Excitatory Transmitter on Tonically Aroused Cells

A tonically active cell that uptakes extracellular transmitter can generate paradoxical responses when the transmitter is extracellularly applied by an experimenter. In particular, extracellular release of an excitatory transmitter can have a net inhibitory effect on a postsynaptic cell that is normally excited by the transmitter. If the presynaptic cell uptakes extracellular transmitter at a rate proportional to transmitter concentration, then the net effect of applying extracellular transmitter will be inhibitory at all concentrations if it is inhibitory at any concentration. The critical level of tonic activity needed to cause net inhibition decreases as a function of the uptake rate. This possibility can create difficulties in interpreting central actions of those transmitters such as catecholamines, which can be tonically activated by an animal's state of deprivation and arousal.

To prove these properties, denote the habituated, or steady-state, rate of transmitter release in response to the tonic signal S in (7) by

$$T_\infty = S z_\infty = \frac{ABS}{A + S}. \tag{68}$$

Let a quantity J of transmitter be injected into a region near this synapse. Let the transmitter uptake rate by the synaptic knob equal the fraction θJ, and let the rate with which transmitter directly excites the postsynaptic cell equal the fraction ϕJ. By (7) the uptake of transmitter inhibits the rate of transmitter production via feedback inhibition. Then (7) becomes

$$\frac{dz}{dt} = A(B - \theta J - Z) - Sz, \tag{69}$$

whose habituated transmitter level is

$$z_\infty^* = \frac{A(B - \theta J)}{A + S}. \tag{70}$$

The habituated rate of transmitter release is therefore

$$T_\infty^* = S z_\infty^* = \frac{A(B - \theta J)S}{A + S} \tag{71}$$

and the total postsynaptic signal is

$$T_\infty^* + \phi J. \tag{72}$$

The transmitter J will have a net inhibitory effect on the postsynaptic cell if

$$T_\infty > T_\infty^* + \phi J, \tag{73}$$

which is true if

$$\frac{AS}{A + S} > \phi \theta^{-1}. \tag{74}$$

The most important property of (74) is that it does not depend on the transmitter concentration, J. It depends only on the tonic level, S, and on the uptake fraction, θ. If θ is close to 1, then a small tonic level, S, suffices to convert any concentration of excitatory transmitter into a net inhibitory response. This inhibitory effect can be eliminated either by pharmacologically blocking presynaptic transmitter uptake or by transecting the source of tonic input. The critical uptake fraction at which reversal of the inhibitory effect occurs depends on the size of the tonic postsynaptic signal $T_\infty(S)$ in (68), according to an equation of the form

$$\theta_{\text{crit}} = \frac{C}{1 + BT_\infty(S)}, \tag{75}$$

where B and C are positive constants. These results indicate that paradoxical transmitter sign reversals might seem to occur in the tonic cells of networks whose arousal level cannot be independently calibrated.

REFERENCES

Anand, B.K. and Pillai, R.V., Activation of single neurones in the hypothalamic feeding centres: Effect of gastric distension. *Journal of Physiology*, 1967, **192**, 63–77.

Anderson, J.A., Silverstein, J.W., Ritz, S.A., and Jones, R.S., Distinctive features, categorical perception, and probability learning: Some applications of a neural model. *Psychological Review*, 1977, **84**, 413–451.

Atkinson, R.C. and Shiffrin, R.M., Human memory: A proposed system and its control processes. In K.W. Spence and J.T. Spence (Eds.), **Advances in the psychology of learning and motivation research and theory**, Vol. 2. New York: Academic Press, 1968.

Azrin, N.H., Hutchinson, R.R., and Hake, D.F., Extinction-induced aggression. *Journal of Experimental Analysis of Behavior*, 1966, **9**, 191–204.

Balagura, S., Neurophysiologic aspects: Hypothalamic factors in the control of eating behavior. In F. Reichsman (Ed.), **Hunger and satiety in health and disease**. Basel, Switzerland: S. Karger, 1972.

Barbeau, A., Marsh, H., and Gillo-Joffroy, L., Adverse clinical side effects of L-dopa therapy. In F.A. McDowell and C.H. Markham (Eds.), **Recent advances in Parkinson's disease**. Philadelphia: F.A. Davis, 1971.

Baylor, D.A. and Hodgkin, A.L., Changes in time scale and sensitivity in turtle photoreceptors. *Journal of Physiology*, 1974, **242**, 729–758.

Baylor, D.A., Hodgkin, A.L., and Lamb, T.D., The electrical response of turtle cones to flashes and steps of light. *Journal of Physiology*, 1974, **242**, 685–727 (a).

Baylor, D.A., Hodgkin, A.L., and Lamb, T.D., Reconstruction of the electrical responses of turtle cones to flashes and steps of light. *Journal of Physiology*, 1974, **242**, 759–791 (b).

Beach, F.A., Characteristics of masculine "sex drive." In M.R. Jones (Ed.), **Nebraska symposium on motivation** (Vol. 4). Lincoln: University of Nebraska Press, 1956.

Bellows, R.T., Time factors in water drinking in dogs. *American Journal of Physiology*, 1939, **125**, 87–97.

Berger, T.W. and Thompson, R.F., Neuronal plasticity in the limbic system during classical conditioning of the rabbit nictitating membrane response, I: The hippocampus. *Brain Research*, 1978, **145**, 323–346.

Berlyne, D.E., The reward-value of indifferent stimulation. In J.T. Tapp (Ed.), **Reinforcement and behavior**. New York: Academic Press, 1969.

Blass, E.M. and Chapman, H.W., An evaluation of the contribution of cholinergic mechanisms to thirst. *Physiological Behavior*, 1971, **7**, 679–686.

Bolles, R.C., **Theory of motivation**. New York: Harper and Row, 1967.

Booth, D.A., Toates, F.M., and Platt, S.V., Control system for hunger and its implications in animals and man. In D. Novin, W. Wyrwicka, and G. Bray (Eds.), **Hunger: Basic mechanisms and clinical implications**. New York: Raven Press, 1976.

Boring, E.G., **A history of experimental psychology**, 2nd edition. New York: Appleton-Century-Crofts, 1950.

Bower, G.H., Mood and memory. *American Psychologist*, 1981, **36**, 129–148.

Bower, G.H., Gilligan, S.G., and Monteiro, K.P., Selectivity of learning caused by adaptive states. *Journal of Experimental Psychology: General*, 1981, **110**, 451–473.

Bridge, J.G., Unit activity in septal nuclei during water deprivation, drinking, and rehydration. In J.F. DeFrance (Ed.), **The septal nuclei**. New York: Plenum Press, 1976.

Brown, J.L., Afterimages. In C.H. Graham (Ed.), **Vision and visual perception.** New York: Wiley, 1965.

Burks, C.D. and Fisher, A.E., Anticholinergic blockade of schedule induced polydipsia. *Physiological Behavior*, 1970, **5**, 635–640.

Caggiula, A.R. and Hoebel, B.C., "Copulation-reward site" in the posterior hypothalamus. *Science*, 1966, **153**, 1284–1285.

Cant, B.R. and Bickford, R.G., The effect of motivation on the contingent negative variation (CNV). *Electroencephalography and Clinical Neurophysiology*, 1967, **23**, 594.

Cantor, M.B., Signaled reinforcing brain stimulation establishes and maintains reliable schedule control. *Science*, 1971, **174**, 610–613.

Carpenter, G.A. and Grossberg, S., Adaptation and transmitter gating in vertebrate photoreceptors. *Journal of Theoretical Neurobiology*, 1981, **1**, 1–42.

Carpenter, G.A. and Grossberg, S., Dynamic models of neural systems: Propagated signals, photoreceptor transduction, and circadian rhythms. In J.P.E. Hodgson (Ed.), **Oscillations in mathematical biology.** New York: Springer-Verlag, 1983 (a).

Carpenter, G.A. and Grossberg, S., A neural theory of circadian rhythms: The gated pacemaker. *Biological Cybernetics*, 1983, **48**, 35–59 (b).

Coons, E.E. and Cruce, J.A.F., Lateral hypothalamus: Food and current intensity in maintaining self-stimulation of hunger. *Science*, 1968, **159**, 1117–1119.

Cotzias, G.C., Papavasiliou, P.S., and Gellene, R., Modification of Parkinsonism—chronic treatment with L-dopa. *New England Journal of Medicine*, 1969, **280**, 337–345.

Craik, F.I.M. and Lockhart, R.S., Levels of processing: A framework for memory research. *Journal of Verbal Learning and Verbal Behavior*, 1972, **11**, 671–684.

Craik, F.I.M. and Tulving, E., Depth of processing and the retention of words in episodic memory. *Journal of Experimental Psychology: General*, 1975, **104**, 268–294.

Denny, M.R., Relaxation theory and experiments. In F.R. Brush (Ed.), **Aversive conditioning and learning.** New York: Academic Press, 1971.

Dews, P.B., Studies on behavior, IV: Stimulant actions of methamphetamine. *Journal of Pharmacological and Experimental Therapy*, 1958, **122**, 137–147.

Dickinson, A., Hall, G., and Mackintosh, N.J., Surprise and the attenuation of blocking. *Journal of Experimental Psychology: Animal Behavior Processes*, 1976, **2**, 213–222.

Donchin, E., Heffley, E., Hillyard, S.A., Loveless, N., Maltzman, I., Ohman, A., Rosler, F., Ruchkin, D., and Siddle, D., Cognition and event-related potentials, II: The relation of P300 to the orienting reflex. In R. Karrer, J. Cohen, and P. Tueting (Eds.), **Brain and information: Event related potentials.** New York: New York Academy of Sciences, 1984.

Drachman, D.A. and Leavitt, J., Human memory and the cholinergic system. *Archives of Neurology*, 1975, **30**, 113–121.

Duda, R.O. and Hart, P.E., **Pattern classification and scene analysis.** New York: Wiley and Sons, 1973.

Dunham, P.J., Punishment: Method and theory. *Psychological Review*, 1971, **78**, 58–70.

Dunham, P.J., Mariner, A., and Adams, H., Enhancement of off-key pecking by on-key punishment. *Journal of Experimental Analysis and Behavior*, 1969, **1**, 156–166.

Edinger, H. and Siegel, A., Functional aspects of the hippocampal-septal axis. In J.F. DeFrance (Ed.), **The septal nuclei.** New York: Plenum Press, 1976.

Ellias, S.A. and Grossberg, S., Pattern formation, contrast control, and oscillations in the short term memory of shunting on-center off-surround networks. *Biological Cybernetics*, 1975, **20**, 69–98.

Ermentrout, G.B. and Cowan, J.D., A mathematical theory of visual hallucination patterns. *Biological Cybernetics*, 1979, **34**, 137–150.

Ermentrout, G.B. and Cowan, J.D., Large scale spatially organized activity in neural nets. *SIAM Journal of Applied Mathematics*, 1980, **38**, 1–21.

Estes, W.K., Outline of a theory of punishment. In B.A. Campbell and R.M. Church (Eds.), **Punishment and aversive behavior**. New York: Appleton-Century-Crofts, 1969.

Estes, W.K. and Skinner, B.F., Some quantitative properties of anxiety. *Journal of Experimental Psychology*, 1941, **29**, 390–400.

Falk, J.L., The behavioral regulation of water and electrolyte balance. In **Nebraska symposium on motivation**, 1961, 9, 1–33 (a).

Falk, J.L., Production of polydipsia in normal rats by an intermittent food schedule. *Science*, 1961, **133**, 195–196 (b).

Falk, J.L., The nature and determinants of adjunctive behavior. *Physiological Behavior*, 1971, **6**, 577–588.

Fisher, A.E., Relations between cholinergic and other dispogens in the central mediation of thirst. In A.N. Epstein, H.R. Kissileff, and E. Stellar (Eds.), **The neuropsychology of thirst: New findings and advances in concepts**. Washington, DC: V.H. Winston, 1973.

Fisher, A.E. and Coury, J.N., Cholinergic tracing of a central neural circuit underlying the thirst drive. *Science*, 1962, **138**, 691–693.

Freeman, W.J., **Mass action in the nervous system**. New York: Academic Press, 1975.

Freeman, W.J., Nonlinear dynamics of paleocortex manifested in the olfactory EEG. *Biological Cybernetics*, 1979, **35**, 21–37.

Freeman, W.J., EEG analysis gives model of neuronal template-matching mechanism for sensory search with olfactory bulb. *Biological Cybernetics*, 1980, **35**, 221–234.

Frey, P.W. and Sears, R.J., Model of conditioning incorporating the Rescorla-Wagner associative axiom, a dynamic attention rule, and a catastrophe rule. *Psychological Review*, 1978, **85**, 321–340.

Fukushima, K., Neocognition: A self-organizing neural network model for a mechanism of pattern recognition unaffected by shift in position. *Biological Cybernetics*, 1980, **36**, 193–202.

Gabriel, M., Foster, K., Orona, E., Saltwick, S.E., and Stanton, M., Neuronal activity of cingulate cortex, anteroventral thalamus and hippocampal formation in discriminative conditioning: Encoding and extraction of the significance of conditional stimuli. *Progress in Psychobiological and Physiological Psychology*, 1980, **9**, 125–231.

Gallistel, C.R. and Beagley, G., Specificity of brain-stimulation reward in the rat. *Journal of Comparative and Physiological Psychology*, 1971, **76**, 199–205.

Gardner, W.J., Licklider, J.C.R., and Weisz, A.Z., Suppression of pain by sound. *Science*, 1961, **132**, 32–33.

Gibson, J.J., **The ecological approach to visual perception**. Boston: Houghton Mifflin, 1979.

Gintzler, A.R., Endorphin-mediated increases in pain threshold during pregnancy. *Science*, 1980, **210**, 193–195.

Goddard, G.V., Development of epileptic seizures through brain stimulation at low intensity. *Nature*, 1967, **214**, 1020–1021.

Graff, H. and Stellar, E., Hyperphagia, obesity, and finickiness. *Journal of Comparative and Physiological Psychology*, 1962, **55**, 418–424.

Grastyan, E., Commentary. In E. Gellhorn (Ed.), **Biological foundations of emotion**. Glenview, IL: Scott Foresman, 1968.

Grossberg, S., **The theory of embedding fields with applications to psychology and neurophysiology**. New York: Rockefeller Institute for Medical Research, 1964.

Grossberg, S., Nonlinear difference-differential equations in prediction and learning theory. *Proceedings of the National Academy of Sciences*, 1967, **58**, 1329–1334.

Grossberg, S., Some physiological and biochemical consequences of psychological postulates. *Proceedings of the National Academy of Sciences*, 1968, **60**, 758–765.

Grossberg, S., On learning and energy-entropy dependence in recurrent and nonrecurrent signed networks. *Journal of Statistical Physics*, 1969, **1**, 319–350 (a).

Grossberg, S., On the production and release of chemical transmitters and related topics in cellular control. *Journal of Theoretical Biology*, 1969, **22**, 325–364 (b).

Grossberg, S., Some networks that can learn, remember, and reproduce any number of complicated space-time patterns, II. *Studies in Applied Mathematics*, 1970, **49**, 135–166.

Grossberg, S., On the dynamics of operant conditioning. *Journal of Theoretical Biology*, 1971, **33**, 225–255.

Grossberg, S., A neural theory of punishment and avoidance, I: Qualitative theory. *Mathematical Biosciences*, 1972, **15**, 39–67 (a).

Grossberg, S., A neural theory of punishment and avoidance, II: Quantitative theory. *Mathematical Biosciences*, 1972, **15**, 253–285 (b).

Grossberg, S., Pattern learning by functional-differential neural networks with arbitrary path weights. In K. Schmitt (Ed.), **Delay and functional-differential equations and their applications**. New York: Academic Press, 1972 (c).

Grossberg, S., Contour enhancement, short-term memory, and constancies in reverberating neural networks. *Studies in Applied Mathematics*, 1973, **52**, 217–257.

Grossberg, S., Classical and instrumental learning by neural networks. In R. Rosen and F. Snell (Eds.), **Progress in theoretical biology** (Vol. 3). New York: Academic Press, 1974.

Grossberg, S., A neural model of attention, reinforcement, and discrimination learning. *International Review of Neurobiology*, 1975, **18**, 263–327.

Grossberg, S., Adaptive pattern classification and universal recoding, I: Parallel development and coding of neural feature detectors. *Biological Cybernetics*, 1976, **23**, 121–134 (a).

Grossberg, S., Adaptive pattern classification and universal recoding, II: Feedback, expectation, olfaction, and illusions. *Biological Cybernetics*, 1976, **23**, 187–202 (b).

Grossberg, S., A theory of human memory: Self-organization and performance of sensory-motor codes, maps, and plans. In R. Rosen and F. Snell (Eds.), **Progress in theoretical biology** (Vol. 5). New York: Academic Press, 1978 (a).

Grossberg, S., Behavioral contrast in short-term memory: Serial binary memory models or parallel continuous memory models? *Journal of Mathematical Psychology*, 1978, **17**, 199–219 (b).

Grossberg, S., Do all neural networks really look alike? A comment on Anderson, Silverstein, Ritz, and Jones. *Psychological Review*, 1978, **85**, 592–596 (c).

Grossberg, S., Communication, memory, and development. In R. Rosen and F. Snell (Eds.), **Progress in theoretical biology**, Vol. 5. New York: Academic Press, 1978 (d).

Grossberg, S., How does a brain build a cognitive code? *Psychological Review*, 1980, **87**, 1–51 (a).

Grossberg, S., Human and computer rules and representations are not equivalent. **Behavioral and Brain Sciences**, 1980, **3**, 136–138 (b).

Grossberg, S., Direct perception or adaptive resonance? *Behavioral and Brain Sciences*, 1980, **3**, 385 (c).

Grossberg, S., Adaptive resonance in development, perception, and cognition. In S. Grossberg (Ed.), **Mathematical psychology and psychophysiology**. Providence, RI: American Mathematical Society, 1981 (a).

Grossberg, S., Psychophysiological substrates of schedule interactions and behavioral contrast. In S. Grossberg (Ed.), **Mathematical psychology and psychophysiology**. Providence, RI: American Mathematical Society, 1981 (b).

Grossberg, S., Processing of expected and unexpected events during conditioning and attention: A psychophysiological theory. *Psychological Review*, 1982, **89**, 529–572 (a).

Grossberg, S., **Studies of mind and brain: Neural principles of learning, perception, development, cognition, and motor control**. Boston: Reidel Press, 1982 (b).

Grossberg, S., A psychophysiological theory of reinforcement, drive, motivation, and attention. *Journal of Theoretical Neurobiology*, 1982, **1**, 286–369 (c).

Grossberg, S., The adaptive self-organization of serial order in behavior: Speech, language, and motor control. In E.C. Schwab and H.C. Nusbaum (Eds.), **Pattern recognition by humans and machines**. New York: Academic Press, 1985.

Grossberg, S. and Pepe, J., Schizophrenia: Possible dependence of associational span, bowing, and primacy vs. recency on spiking threshold. *Behavioral Science*, 1970, **15**, 359–362.

Grossberg, S. and Pepe, J., Spiking threshold and overarousal effects in serial learning. *Journal of Statistical Physics*, 1971, **3**, 95–125.

Grossman, S.P., Direct adrenergic and cholinergic stimulation of hypothalamic mechanisms. *American Journal of Physiology*, 1962, **202**, 872–882.

Groves, P.M., Young, S.J., and Wilson, C.J., Nigrostriatal relations and the mechanisms of action of amphetamine. In L.L. Butcher (Ed.), **Cholinergic-monoaminergic interactions in the brain**. New York: Academic Press, 1978.

Guillemin, R., Peptides in the brain: The new endocrinology of the neuron. *Science*, 1978, **202**, 390–401.

Halgren, E., Squires, N.K., Wilson, C.L., Rohrbaugh, J.W., Babb, T.L., and Crandall, P.H., Endogenous potentials generated in the human hippocampal formation and amygdala by infrequent events. *Science*, 1980, **210**, 803–805.

Hall, G. and Pearce, J.M., Latent inhibition of a CS during CS-US pairings. *Journal of Experimental Psychology: Animal Behavior Processes*, 1979, 5, 31–42.

Hammond, L.J., Retardation of fear acquisition by a previously inhibitory CS. *Journal of Comparative and Physiological Psychology*, 1968, **66**, 756–758.

Haymaker, W., Anderson, E., and Nauta, W.J.H., **The hypothalamus**. Springfield, IL: C.C. Thomas, 1969.

Hebb, D.O., Drives and the CNS (conceptual nervous system). *Psychological Review*, 1955, **62**, 243–254.

Held, R., Exposure-history as a factor in maintaining stability of perception and coordination. *Journal of Nervous Mental Diseases*, 1961, **132**, 26–32.

Held, R., Dissociation of visual functions by deprivation and rearrangement. *Psychologische Forschung*, 1967, **31**, 338–348.

Held, R. and Hein, A., Movement-produced stimulation in the development of visually guided behavior. *Journal of Comparative and Physiological Psychology*, 1963, **56**, 872–876.

Helmholtz, H. von, **Handbuch der Physiologischen Optik** (1st ed.). Leipzig: Voss, 1866.

Helmholtz, H. von, **Physiological optics** (Vol. 2) (J.P. Southall, Ed.). New York: Dover, 1962 (originally published 1866).

Hilgard, E.R. and Bower, G.H., **Theories of learning**, 4th edition. Englewood Cliffs, NJ: Prentice-Hall, 1975.

Hirsch, J., Discussion. In F. Reichsman (Ed.), **Hunger and satiety in health and disease**. Basel, Switzerland: S. Karger, 1972.

Hoebel, B.G., Satiety: Hypothalamic stimulation, anorectic drugs, and neurochemical substrates. In D. Novin, W. Wyrwicka, and G. Bray (Eds.), **Hunger: Basic mechanisms and clinical implications**. New York: Raven Press, 1976.

Hoebel, B.G. and Teitelbaum, P., Hypothalamic control of feeding and self-stimulation. *Science*, 1962, **135**, 357–377.

Hoebel, B.G. and Teitelbaum, P., Weight regulation in normal and hypothalamic hyperphagic rats. *Journal of Comparative and Physiological Psychology*, 1966, **61**, 189–193.

Honig, W.K., Attention and the modulation of stimulus control. In D.I. Mostofsky (Ed.), **Attention: Contemporary theory and analysis**. New York: Appleton-Century-Crofts, 1970.

Hornykiewicz, O., Parkinsonism induced by dopaminergic antagonists. In D.B. Calne and A. Barbeau (Eds.), **Advances in neurology**. New York: Raven Press, 1975.

Hudson, R. and Singer, G., Polydipsia in the monkey generated by visual display schedules. *Physiological Behavior*, 1979, **22**, 379–381.

Irwin, D.A., Rebert, C.S., McAdam, D.W., and Knott, J.R., Slow potential change (CNV) in the human EEG as a function of motivational variables. *Electroencephalography and Clinical Neurophysiology*, 1966, **21**, 412–413.

Janowitz, H.D., Hanson, M.E., and Grossman, M.I., Effect of intravenously administered glucose on food intake in the dog. *American Journal of Physiology*, 1949, **156**, 87–91.

John, E.R., Neural processes during learning. In R.W. Russell (Ed.), **Frontiers in physiological psychology**. New York: Academic Press, 1966.

John, E.R., **Mechanisms of memory**. New York: Academic Press, 1967.

John, E.R. and Morgades, P.P., Neural correlates of conditioned responses studied with multiple chronically implanted moving electrodes. *Experimental Neurology*, 1969, **23**, 412–425.

Kaczmarek, L.K. and Babloyantz, A., Spatiotemporal patterns in epileptic seizures. *Biological Cybernetics*, 1977, **26**, 199–208.

Kamin, L.J., Predictability, surprise, attention, and conditioning. In B.A. Campbell and R.M. Church (Eds.), **Punishment and aversive behavior**. New York: Appleton-Century-Crofts, 1969.

Kasamatsu, T. and Pettigrew, J.D., Depletion of brain catecholamines: Failure of ocular dominance shift after monocular occlusion in kittens. *Science*, 1976, **194**, 206–209.

Keesey, R.E., Boyle, P.C., Kemnitz, J.W., and Mitchel, J.S., The role of the lateral hypothalamus in determining the body weight set point. In D. Novin, W. Wyrwicka, and G. Bray (Eds.), **Hunger: Basic mechanisms and clinical implications**. New York: Raven Press, 1976.

Kennedy, G.C., The role of depot fat in the hypothalamic control of food intake in the rat. *Proceedings of the Royal Society*, 1953, **140B**, 578–592.

Kent, M.A. and Peters, R.H., Effects of ventromedial hypothalamic lesions on hunger-motivated behavior in rats. *Journal of Comparative and Physiological Psychology*, 1973, **83**, 92–97.

Kissileff, H.R., Food-associated drinking in the rat. *Journal of Comparative and Physiological Psychology*, 1969, **67**, 284–300.

Kissileff, H.R., Acquisition of prandial drinking in weanling rats and in rats recovering from lateral hypothalamic lesions. *Journal of Comparative and Physiological Psychology*, 1971, **77**, 97–109.

Kissileff, H.R., Nonhomeostatic controls of drinking. In A.N. Epstein, H.R. Kissileff, and E. Stellar (Eds.), **The neuropsychology of thirst: New findings and advances in concepts**. Washington, DC: V.N. Winston, 1973.

Kleinschmidt, J. and Dowling, J.E., Intracellular recordings from Gekko photoreceptors during light and dark adaptation. *Journal of General Physiology*, 1975, **66**, 617–648.

Knott, P.D. and Clayton, K.N., Durable secondary reinforcement using brain stimulation as the primary reinforcer. *Journal of Comparative and Physiological Psychology*, 1966, **61**, 151–153.

Kuhar, M.J., Atweh, S.F., and Bird, S.J., Studies of cholinergic-monoaminergic interactions in rat brain. In L.L. Butcher (Ed.), **Cholinergic-monoaminergic interactions in brain**. New York: Academic Press, 1978.

Kuperstein, M. and Whittington, D.A., A practical 24-channel microelectrode for neural recording *in vivo*. *IEEE Transactions in Biomedical Engineering*, 1981, **28**, 288–293.

Kurtzburg, D., Vaughan, H.G. Jr., Courchesne, E., Friedman, D., Harter, M.R., and Putman, L., Developmental aspects of event-related potentials. In R. Karrer, J. Cohen, and P. Tueting (Eds.), **Brain and information: Event related potentials**. New York: New York Academy of Sciences, 1984.

Leibowitz, S.F., Adrenergic receptor mechanisms in eating and drinking. In F.O. Schmitt and F.G. Worden (Eds.), **The neurosciences third study program**. Cambridge, MA: MIT Press, 1974.

LeMagnen, J., Regulation of food intake. In F. Reichsman (Ed.), **Hunger and satiety in health and disease**. Basel, Switzerland: S. Karger, 1972.

Levitt, D.R. and Teitelbaum, P., Somnolence, akinesia, and sensory activation of motivated behavior in the lateral hypothalamic syndrome. *Proceedings of the National Academy of Sciences*, 1975, **72**, 2819–2823.

Lloyd, K.G., Observations concerning neurotransmitter interaction in schizophrenia. In L.L. Butcher (Ed.), **Cholinergic-monoaminergic interactions in the brain**. New York: Academic Press, 1978.

Mabry, P.D. and Campbell, B.A., Cholinergic-monoaminergic interactions during ontogenesis. In L.L. Butcher (Ed.), **Cholinergic-monoaminergic interactions in the brain**. New York: Academic Press, 1978.

Mackintosh, N.J., **The psychology of animal learning**. New York: Academic Press, 1974.

Mackintosh, N.J., Bygrave, D.J., and Picton, B.M.B., Locus of the effect of a surprising reinforcer in the attenuation of blocking. *Quarterly Journal of Experimental Psychology*, 1977, **29**, 327–336.

Mackintosh, N.J. and Reese, B., One-trial overshadowing. *Quarterly Journal of Experimental Psychology*, 1979, **31**, 519–526.

MacLean, P.D., The limbic brain in relation to the psychoses. In P. Black (Ed.), **Physiological correlates of emotion**. New York: Academic Press, 1970.

Maher, B.A., **Contributions to the psychopathology of schizophrenia.** New York: Academic Press, 1977.

Maier, S.F., Seligman, M.E.P., and Solomon, R.L., Pavlovian fear conditioning and learned helplessness effects on escape and avoidance behavior of (a) the CS-US contingency and (b) the independence of the US and voluntary responding. In B.A. Campbell and R.M. Church (Eds.), **Punishment and aversive behavior.** New York: Appleton-Century-Crofts, 1969.

Malsburg, C. von der, Self-organization of orientation sensitive cells in the striate cortex. *Kybernetik*, 1973, **14**, 85–100.

Margules, D.L. and Olds, J., Identical "feeding" and "rewarding" systems in the lateral hypothalamus of rats. *Science*, 1962, **135**, 374–375.

Marsh, G.C., Markham, C.M., and Ansel, R., Levodopa's awakening effect on patients with Parkinsonism. *Journal of Neurological and Neurosurgical Psychiatry*, 1971, **34**, 209–218.

Masterson, F.A., Is termination of a warning signal an effective reward for the rat? *Journal of Comparative and Physiological Psychology*, 1970, **72**, 471–475.

McAllister, W.R. and McAllister, D.E., Behavioral measurement of conditioned fear. In F.R. Brush (Ed.), **Aversive conditioning and learning.** New York: Academic Press, 1971.

Mendelson, J., Lateral hypothalamic stimulation in satiated rats: The rewarding effects of self-induced drinking. *Science*, 1967, **157**, 1077–1079.

Miller, N.E., Some reflections on the law of effect produce a new alternative to drive reduction. In M.R. Jones (Ed.), **Nebraska symposium on motivation.** Lincoln: University of Nebraska Press, 1963.

Miller, N.E., Sampliner, R.I., and Woodrow, P., Thirst reducing effects of water by stomach fistula vs. water by mouth measured by both a consummatory and an instrumental response. *Journal of Comparative and Physiological Psychology*, 1957, **50**, 1–5.

Mogensen, G.J., Septal-hypothalamic relationships. In J.F. DeFrance (Ed.), **The septal nucleus.** New York: Plenum Press, 1976.

Mogensen, G.J. and Morgan, C.W., Effects of induced drinking on self-stimulation of the lateral hypothalamus. *Experimental Brain Research*, 1967, **3**, 111–116.

Mogensen, G.J. and Stevenson, J.A.F., Drinking and self-stimulation with electrical stimulation of the lateral hypothalamus. *Physiological Behavior*, 1966, **1**, 251–259.

Morrell, F., Electrophysiological contributions to the neural basis of learning. *Physiological Review*, 1961, **41**, 443–494.

Newman, F.L. and Baron, M.R., Stimulus generalization along the dimension of angularity: A comparison of training procedures. *Journal of Comparative and Physiological Psychology*, 1965, **60**, 59–63.

O'Keefe, J.O. and Nadel, L., **The hippocampus as a cognitive map.** Oxford: Clarendon Press, 1978.

Olds, J., Effects of hunger and sex hormone on self-stimulation of the brain. *Journal of Comparative and Physiological Psychology*, 1958, **51**, 320–324.

Olds, J., **Drives and reinforcements: Behavioral studies of hypothalamic functions.** New York: Raven Press, 1977.

Olds, J., Allan, W.S., and Briese, E., Differentiation of hypothalamic drive and reward centers. *American Journal of Physiology*, 1971, **221**, 368–375.

Ostwald, I., Psychoactive drugs and sleep: Withdrawal rebound phenomena. *Triangle*, 1971, **10**, 99–104.

Otto, D., Karrer, R., Halliday, R., Horst, R., Klorman, R., Squires, N., Thatcher, R., Fenelon, B., and LeLord, G., Developmental aspects of event-related potentials: Aberrant development. In R. Karrer, J. Cohen, and P. Tueting (Eds.), **Brain and information: Event related potentials**. New York: New York Academy of Sciences, 1984.

Papakostopoulos, D., Appendix: The relationship between P300 and the CNV. In W.C. McCallum and J.R. Knott (Eds.), **The responsive brain**. Bristol: John Wright and Sons, 1976.

Pavlov, I.P., **Conditioned reflexes**. Oxford: Oxford University Press, 1927 (reprinted 1960 by Dover Press, New York).

Paxinos, G. and Bindra, D., Hypothalamic and midbrain neural pathways involved in eating, drinking, irritability, aggression, and copulation in rats. *Journal of Comparative and Physiological Psychology*, 1973, **82**, 1–14.

Pearce, J.M. and Hall, G., A model for Pavlovian learning: Variations in the effectiveness of conditioned but not of unconditioned stimuli. *Psychological Review*, 1980, **87**, 532–552.

Pérez, R., Glass, L., and Shlaer, R., Development of specificity in the cat's visual cortex. *Journal of Mathematical Biology*, 1975, **1**, 275–288.

Pettigrew, J.D. and Kasamatsu, T., Local perfusion of noradrenaline maintains visual cortical plasticity. *Nature*, 1978, **271**, 761–763.

Poschel, B.P.H., Do biological reinforcers act via the self-stimulation areas of the brain? *Physiological Behavior*, 1968, **3**, 53–60.

Prescott, R.G.W., Estrous cycle in the rat: Effects on self-stimulation behavior. *Science*, 1966, **152**, 796–797.

Rauschecker, J.P.J., Campbell, F.W., and Atkinson, J., Colour opponent neurones in the human visual system. *Nature*, 1973, **245**, 42–45.

Rescorla, R.A., Establishment of a positive reinforcer through contrast with shock. *Journal of Comparative and Physiological Psychology*, 1969, **67**, 260–263.

Rescorla, R.A., Variations in the effectiveness of reinforcement and nonreinforcement following prior inhibitory conditioning. *Learning and Motivation*, 1971, **2**, 113–123.

Rescorla, R.A. and LoLordo, V.M., Inhibition of avoidance behavior. *Journal of Comparative and Physiological Psychology*, 1965, **59**, 406–412.

Rescorla, R.A. and Wagner, A.R., A theory of Pavlovian conditioning: Variations in the effectiveness of reinforcement and nonreinforcement. In A.H. Black and W.F. Prokasy (Eds.), **Classical conditioning II: Current research and theory**. New York: Appleton-Century-Crofts, 1972.

Riklan, M., **L-dopa and Parkinsonism: A psychological assessment**. Springfield, IL: C.C. Thomas, 1973.

Ritter, W., Näätänen, R., Ford, J., Polich, J., Gaillard, A.W.K., Renault, B., Harter, M.R., Rohrbaugh, J., and Kutas, M., Cognition and event related potentials, I: The relation of negative potentials and cognitive processes. In R. Karrer, J. Cohen, and P. Tueting (Eds.), **Brain and information: Event related potentials**. New York: New York Academy of Sciences, 1984.

Rosellini, R.A., Schedule-induced polydipsia under conditions of restricted access to water. *Physiological Behavior*, 1979, **22**, 405–407.

Routtenberg, A. and Kim, H.-J., The substantia nigra and neostriatum: Substrate for memory consolidation. In L.L. Butcher (Ed.), **Cholinergic-monoaminergic interactions in the brain**. New York: Academic Press, 1978.

Rusinov, V.S., An electrophysiological analysis of the connecting function in the cerebral cortex in the presence of a dominant area. Communications at the XIX International Physiological Congress, Montreal, 1953.

Sawusch, J.R. and Nusbaum, H.C., Contextual effects in vowel perception, I: Anchor-induced contrast effects. *Perception and Psychophysics*, 1979, **25**, 292–302.

Schallert, T., DeRyck, M., Whishaw, I.Q., and Ramirez, V.D., Excessive bracing reactions and their control by atropine and L-dopa in an animal analogy of Parkinsonism. *Experimental Neurology*, 1979, **64**, 33–43.

Schallert, T., Whishaw, I.Q., DeRyck, M., and Teitelbaum, P., The postures of catecholamine-depletion catalepsy: Their possible adaptive value in thermoregulation. *Physiology and Behavior*, 1978, **21**, 817–820 (a).

Schallert, T., Whishaw, I.Q., DeRyck, M., and Teitelbaum, P., Compulsive, abnormal walking caused by anticholinergics in akinetic, 6-hydroxydopamine-treated rats. *Science*, 1978, **199**, 1461–1463 (b).

Schneider, W. and Shiffrin, R.M., Automatic and controlled information processing in vision. In D. LaBarge and S.J. Samuels (Eds.), **Basic processes in reading: Perception and comprehension**. Hillsdale, NJ: Erlbaum, 1976.

Schwartz, E.L., Computational anatomy and functional architecture of striate cortex: A spatial mapping approach to perceptual coding. *Vision Research*, 1980, **20**, 645–669.

Seligman, M.E.P. and Johnston, J.C., A cognitive theory of avoidance learning. In F.J. McGuigan and D.B. Lumsden (Eds.), **Contemporary approaches to conditioning and learning**. Washington, DC: V.H. Winston, 1973.

Seward, J.P. and Proctor, D.M., Performance as a function of drive, reward, and habit strength. *American Journal of Psychology*, 1960, **73**, 448–453.

Seward, J.P., Shea, R.A., and Davenport, R.H., Further evidence for the interaction of drive and reward. *American Journal of Psychology*, 1960, **73**, 370–379.

Seward, J.P., Shea, R.A., and Elkind, D., Evidence for the interaction of drive and reward. *American Journal of Psychology*, 1958, **71**, 404–407.

Sharma, K.N., Anand, B.K., Dua, S., and Singh, B., Role of stomach in regulation of activities of hypothalamic feeding centers. *American Journal of Physiology*, 1961, **201**, 593–598.

Shaywitz, B.A., Cohen, D.J., and Bowers, M.B., CSF monoamine metabolites in children with minimal brain dysfunction: Evidence for alteration of brain dopamine. *Journal of Pediatrics*, 1977, **90**, 67–71.

Shekim, W.O., Dekirmenjian, H., and Chapel, J.L., Urinary catecholamine metabolites in hyperkinetic boys treated with d-amphetamine. *American Journal of Psychiatry*, 1977, **134**, 1276–1279.

Singh, D., Effects of preoperative training on food-motivated behavior of hypothalamic, hyperphagic rats. *Journal of Comparative and Physiological Psychology*, 1973, **84**, 38–46.

Smith, G.P., Introduction: Pharmacology of thirst. In A.N. Epstein, H.R. Kissileff, and E. Stellar (Eds.), **The neuropsychology of thirst: New findings and advances in concepts**. Washington, DC: V.H. Winston, 1973.

Solomon, R.L., Kamin, L.J., and Wynne, L.C., Traumatic avoidance learning: The outcomes of several extinction procedures with dogs. *Journal of Abnormal and Social Psychology*, 1953, **48**, 291–302.

Staddon, J.E.R. and Ayres, S.L., Sequential and temporal properties of behavior induced by a schedule of periodic food delivery. *Behavior*, 1975, **54**, 26–49.

Stein, L., Secondary reinforcement established with subcortical stimulation. *Science*, 1958, **127**, 466–467.

Stominger, J.L., Brobeck, J.R., and Cort, B.L., Regulation of food intake in normal rats and in rats with hypothalamic hyperphagia. *Yale Journal of Biological Medicine*, 1953, **26**, 55–74.

Stricker, E.M. and Zigmond, M.J., Brain catecholamines and the lateral hypothalamic syndrome. In D. Novin, W. Wyrwicka, and G. Bray (Eds.), **Hunger: Basic
mechanisms and clinical implications**. New York: Raven Press, 1976.

Studdert-Kennedy, M., Speech perception. *Language and Speech*, 1980, **23**, 45–66.

Studdert-Kennedy, M., Liberman, A.M., Harris, K.S., and Cooper, F.S., Motor theory
of speech perception: A reply to Lane's critical review. *Psychological Review*, 1970,
77, 234–249.

Swanson, J.M. and Kinsbourne, M., Stimulant-related state-dependent learning in hyperactive children. *Science*, 1976, **192**, 1354–1356.

Tecce, J., Contingent negative variation (CNV) and psychological processes in man.
Psychological Review, 1972, **77**, 73–108.

Tecce, J., A CNV rebound effect. *Electroencephalography and Clinical Neurophysiology*, 1979, **46**, 546–551.

Tecce, J. and Cole, J.O., Amphetamine effects in man: Paradoxical drowsiness and
lowered electrical brain activity (CNV). *Science*, 1974, **185**, 451–453.

Teitelbaum, P., Sensory control of hypothalamic hyperphagia. *Journal of Comparative
and Physiological Psychology*, 1955, **48**, 156–166.

Teitelbaum, P., Discussion: On the use of electrical stimulation to study hypothala-
mic structure and function. In A.N. Epstein, H.R. Kissileff, and E. Stellar (Eds.),
The neuropsychology of thirst: New findings and advances in concepts.
Washington, DC: V.H. Winston, 1973.

Teitelbaum, P. and Epstein, A.N., The lateral hypothalamic syndrome: Recovery of
feeding and drinking after lateral hypothalamic lesions. *Psychological Review*, 1962,
69, 74–90.

Tolman, E.C., **Purposive behavior in animals and men**. New York: Century
Press, 1932.

Trowill, J.A. and Hynek, K., Secondary reinforcement based on primary brain stimulation reward. *Psychological Reports*, 1970, **27**, 715–718.

Understedt, U., 6-hydroxydopamine induced degeneration of central monoamine neurons. *European Journal of Pharmacology*, 1968, **5**, 107–110.

Valenstein, E.S., Invited comment: Electrical stimulation and hypothalamic function:
Historical perspective. In A.N. Epstein, H.R. Kissileff, and E. Stellar (Eds.), **The
neuropsychology of thirst: New findings and advances in concepts**. Washington, DC: V.H. Winston, 1973.

Valenstein, E.S., Cox, V.C., and Kakolewski, J.W., The hypothalamus and motivated
behavior. In J.T. Tapp (Ed.), **Reinforcement and behavior**. New York: Academic
Press, 1969.

Valenstein, E.S., Cox, V.C., and Kakolewski, J.W., Reexamination of the role of the
hypothalamus in motivation. *Psychological Review*, 1970,. **77**, 16–31.

Wallace, M. and Singer, G., Schedule induced behavior: A review of its general determinants, and pharmacological data. *Pharmacological and Biochemical Behavior*,
1976, **5**, 483–490.

Wallach, H. and Karsh, E.B., The modification of stereoscopic depth-perception and
the kinetic depth-effect. *American Journal of Psychology*, 1963, **76**, 429–435 (a).

Wallach, H. and Karsh, E.B., Why the modification of stereoscopic depth-perception
is so rapid. *American Journal of Psychology*, 1963, **76**, 413–420 (b).

Wallach, H., Moore, M.E., and Davidson, L., Modification of stereoscopic depth-perception. *American Journal of Psychology*, 1963, **76**, 191–204.

Wallach, M.B., Drug-induced stereotyped behavior: Similarities and differences. In E. Usdin (Ed.), **Neuropsychopharmacology of monoamines and their regulatory enzymes.** New York: Raven Press, 1974.

Wampler, R.S., Increased motivation in rats with ventromedial hypothalamic lesions. *Journal of Comparative and Physiological Psychology*, 1973, **84**, 268–274.

Weber, B.A. and Sulzbacher, S.I., Use of CNS stimulant medication in averaged electroencephalic audiometry with children with MBD. *Journal of Learning Disabilities*, 1975, **8**, 300–303.

Weiner, W.J. and Klawans, H.L., Cholinergic-monoaminergic interactions within the striatum: Implications for choreiform disorders. In L.L. Butcher (Ed.), **Cholinergic-monoaminergic interactions in the brain.** New York: Academic Press, 1978.

Weisman, R.G. and Litner, J.S., The course of Pavlovian extinction and inhibition of fear in rats. *Journal of Comparative and Physiological Psychology*, 1969, **69**, 667–672.

Weiss, G. and Hechtman, L., The hyperactive child syndrome. *Science*, 1979, **205**, 1348–1354.

Wheatley, M.D., The hypothalamus and affective behavior in cats: A study of the effects of experimental lesions with anatomical correlations. *Archives of Neurological Psychiatry*, 1944, **52**, 296–316.

Wolgin, D.L., Cytawa, J., and Teitelbaum, P., The role of activation in the regulation of food intake. In D. Novin, W. Wyrwicka, and G. Bray (Eds.), **Hunger: Basic mechanisms and clinical implications.** New York: Raven Press, 1976.

Woods, S.C., Decke, E., and Vasselli, J.R., Metabolic hormones and regulation of body weight. *Psychological Review*, 1974, **81**, 26–43.

Wyrwicka, W. and Dobrzecka, C., Relationship between feeding and satiation centers of the hypothalamus. *Science*, 1960, **132**, 941–949.

Chapter 3

PROCESSING OF EXPECTED AND UNEXPECTED EVENTS DURING CONDITIONING AND ATTENTION: A PSYCHOPHYSIOLOGICAL THEORY

Preface

This Chapter applies the theory of cognitive-emotional interactions that was developed in Chapters 1 and 2 to the analysis of other conditioning models and of a variety of conditioning data that these models have found difficult to explain. Many alternative models attempt to use a single equation, even a single equation obeyed by a single cell, to explain conditioning data. Such approaches have the advantage of simplicity, but they exclude most of the organizational principles and mechanisms that we would argue are reflected in conditioning data.

Some alternative models place their emphasis upon how expected events are processed, but then experience fatal paradoxes when confronted with properties of unexpected events. Some models do better with unexpected events, but then cannot deal with expected events. Many models are merely formal. They have no natural realization whatever as a real-time process. Other models do not adequately distinguish between sensory and cognitive processing of a stimulus and its processing as a reinforcing and motivationally salient event.

In order to deal with such basic issues, a more complex theory is needed than is customarily found in the literature on one-equation models. As Chapters 1 and 2 have indicated, this additional complexity can be traced to the need to solve basic environmentally imposed adaptive problems. Once circuits capable of parsimoniously solving these basic problems are identified, *no further mechanisms* are needed to analyse and predict a large data base.

These mechanisms include an attentional subsystem and an orienting subsystem, as well as the further division of the attentional subsystem into sensory representations, drive representations, and motor representations. Most alternative models do not include concepts to express the functions of the orienting subsystem or of the drive representations. They content themselves with stimulus–stimulus associations and stimulus–response associations. The present article argues that the orienting subsystem and the drive representations are key elements in the explanation of difficult conditioning data.

Particularly noteworthy is the manner in which the present theory explains attentional unblocking and dishabituation phenomena. In the present theory, dishabituation can occur when an expectancy mismatch within the attentional subsystem activates the orienting subsystem. The orienting subsystem, in turn, resets the sensory and cognitive codes that are stored in short term memory within the attentional subsystem. The reset mechanism utilizes emergent properties of a gated dipole opponent process.

A change in the arousal level of these cortical gated dipoles can alter the set of cues which are unblocked, or dishabituated, and the set of cues which are disconfirmed, or inhibited, by an unexpected event. An underaroused gated dipole can spuriously "unblock" events which, under normal arousal conditions, would have been disconfirmed. The same gated dipole properties can be used in motivational or motor circuits to analyse abnormal properties of affect or of motor control in an unexpected situation (Chapter 2). This type of comparison among cognitive, affective, and motor syndromes is impossible in a one-equation model, if only because a gated dipole cannot be defined by any one equation.

Psychological Review **89**, 529-572 (1982)
©1982 American Psychological Association, Inc.
Reprinted by permission of the publisher

PROCESSING OF EXPECTED AND UNEXPECTED EVENTS DURING CONDITIONING AND ATTENTION: A PSYCHOPHYSIOLOGICAL THEORY

Stephen Grossberg†

Abstract

Some recent formal models of Pavlovian and instrumental conditioning contain internal paradoxes that restrict their predictive power. These paradoxes can be traced to an inadequate formulation of how mechanisms of short-term memory and long-term memory work together to control the shifting balance between the processing of expected and unexpected events. Once this formulation is strengthened, a unified processing framework is suggested wherein attentional and orienting subsystems coexist in a complementary relationship that controls the adaptive self-organization of internal representations in response to expected and unexpected events. In this framework, conditioning and attentional constructs can be more directly validated by interdisciplinary paradigms in which seemingly disparate phenomena can be shown to share similar physiological and pharmacological mechanisms. A model of cholinergic-catecholaminergic interactions suggests how drive, reinforcer, and arousal inputs regulate motivational baseline, hysteresis, and rebound, with the hippocampus as a final common path. Extinction, conditioned emotional responses, conditioned avoidance responses, secondary conditioning, and inverted U effects also occur. A similar design in sensory and cognitive representations suggests how short-term memory reset and attentional resonance occur and are related to evoked potentials such as N200, P300, and contingent negative variation (CNV). Competitive feedback properties such as pattern matching, contrast enhancement, and normalization of short-term memory patterns make possible the hypothesis testing procedures that search for and define new internal representations in response to unexpected events. Long-term memory traces regulate adaptive filtering, expectancy learning, conditioned reinforcer learning, incentive motivational learning, and habit learning. When these mechanisms act together, conditioning phenomena such as overshadowing, unblocking, latent inhibition, overexpectation, and behavioral contrast emerge.

† Supported in part by the Air Force Office of Scientific Reseach (AFOSR 82-0148) and the National Science Foundation (NSF IST-80-00257).

INTERNAL PROBLEMS OF SOME CONDITIONING MODELS

1. Merging Parallel Streams of Theory on Conditioning and Attention

This article compares and contrasts two parallel streams of theoretical progress in the conditioning and attention literature since 1968, using the article of Pearce and Hall (1980) as a basis for discussion. One stream was energized by such seminal articles as those of Estes (1969), Kamin (1968, 1969), Mackintosh (1971), Rescorla and Wagner (1972), and Wagner and Rescorla (1972). The great heuristic value of these articles stimulated new developments in such articles as those of Dickinson, Hall, and Mackintosh (1976), Frey and Sears (1978), Hall and Pearce (1979), Mackintosh (1976), Mackintosh, Bygrave, and Picton (1977), Mackintosh and Reese (1979), Sutton and Barto (1981), and Wagner (1976, 1978). The other stream is found in a series of my own articles.

This is a good time to make this comparison because ideas from the two streams have gradually converged over the years. Once their remaining differences are resolved, both streams may be merged into a theoretical framework wherein conditioning, cognitive, motivational, psychophysiological, and pharmacological data can be discussed in a unified fashion. In this framework, theoretical alternatives and predictions can be studied using interdisciplinary paradigms that can probe interactions that are opaque to more conventional experiments. Some experiments of this type will be summarized below.

2. The Processing of Expected and Unexpected Events in Short-Term Memory and Long-Term Memory

I suggest that various difficulties faced by the first stream are due to the fact that it does not adequately probe how mechanisms of short-term memory (STM) and long-term memory (LTM) influence the shifting balance between the processing of expected and unexpected events. These difficulties take several related forms: (a) Internal paradoxes exist within the theories. (b) No one theory can explain all the relevant data. In fact, no one theory can explain all the data explicable by any of the other theories. (c) The theories provide formal, as opposed to physical, models of the data. These models have no verifiable properties outside of the conditioning experiments they are constructed to explain. When some of these formal properties are interpreted as physical mechanisms, they are found to be either paradoxical or to have no external experimental support.

To clarify these assertions I will review concepts from Pearce and Hall (1980) as a source for this first stream. To illustrate how my approach overcomes these difficulties, I will review concepts from Grossberg (1980) as a source for the second stream, although the main concepts and mechanisms that I will need appeared in Grossberg (1971, 1972a, 1972b, 1975).

3. Some Internal Paradoxes

First I will review an internal paradox that lies at the heart of the Pearce and Hall (1980) theory. Pearce and Hall assert that "stimuli that fully predict their consequences will be denied access to the processor....A stimulus is likely to be processed to the extent that it is not an accurate predictor of its consequences" (p.538). Or, "a stimulus will gain access to the processor only when it ... has been followed by a surprising event" (p.540). One consequence of this position is that an unconditioned stimulus (US) that is an excellent predictor of food will not be processed even if no conditioned stimulus (CS) is present. Despite this implication, Pearce and Hall state that "stimuli such as the USs used in typical conditioning procedures are always likely to gain access to the processor" (p.538). Pearce and Hall need this assumption because "conjoint processing of the CS and US representations results ... in an increase in the ability of the CS to excite what we may call a 'US memory' " (p.542). This is the main conditioning event of their theory.

In an effort to embed their hypothetical processor into a broader theoretical perspective, Pearce and Hall analogize the processor to the limited-capacity STM system of human information-processing models. Given this processing interpretation, the Pearce and Hall model simultaneously implies that an expected US will not be stored in STM because it is expected and will be stored in STM because it is a US. One might try to escape this contradiction by claiming that the processor somehow knows the difference between a CS and a US. Even if one could overcome the problem of showing how the processor knows this difference, one would then be faced by the harder problem of showing how the processor changes its mind about a cue when the cue switches from CS to US status as a result of prior conditioning, and is thereupon used as a US in a secondary conditioning paradigm.

One can summarize this internal contradiction within the Pearce and Hall theory by saying that these authors have emphasized the processing of events that have unexpected consequences at the cost of implying paradoxes about the processing of events that have expected consequences.

Mackintosh (1975) developed a theory that emphasizes the processing of events that have expected consequences at the cost of falling into difficulties when explaining the processing of unexpected events. Pearce and Hall (1980) summarized Mackintosh's position as follows: "He suggested that the associability (α) of a stimulus will increase if it predicts reinforcement more accurately than other stimuli present in the situation but will decrease if it predicts reinforcement less accurately" (p.536). This hypothesis was made to explain how conditioning of a Cue X is blocked if X is presented on compound trials AX after prior conditioning of Cue A has occurred. Mackintosh's hyothesis explains blocking by claiming that X does not condition well because A is a better predictor of the US due to its prior conditioning trials.

Mackintosh's hypothesis is, however, incompatible with the fact that the Cue X conditions normally on the first compound trial (Kamin, 1968; Mackintosh *et al.*, 1977; Rescorla and Wagner, 1972). This experimental result contradicts the hypothesis because on the first compound trial, Cue X is a worse predictor of the US than it is on the second compound trial. Why does the Cue X condition normally on the first trial if on this trial it is the worst possible predictor of the US, having never before been correlated with the US?

To escape this contradiction Mackintosh simply assumes that only the intensity of X, not its predictability, influences its associability on the first compound trial. Whether one considers this an internal paradox of his theory or an ad hoc restatement of the data is a matter of taste.

Despite this difficulty, Pearce and Hall (1980) write that "the success of Mackintosh's model ... convinces us that the principle it embodies—the modification of CS associability as a result of the consequences of one trial influencing conditioning on the next—must be a part of any successful theory" (p.537).

Wagner (1976, 1978) has attempted to give Mackintosh's ad hoc assumption a physical basis by assuming "that the associability of a CS is inversely related to the strength of an association between the CS and the context" (Pearce and Hall, 1980, p.549). Pearce and Hall (1980) criticize Wagner's concept by noting that "it is very difficult to see how a surprising shock omission ... or shock increase ... after a CS can reduce the strength of the association between the CS and the context and thus restore associability" (p.549). Their criticism does not distinguish between the processing of an event that is unexpected within a given context and the processing of an event that is followed by an unexpected US. I will suggest below how such distinctions tend to be blurred within these formal models and how they can be clarified using a physically based model.

4. The Need for Behaviorally Unobservable Mechanisms

The seriousness of the dilemma into which conditioning data have driven the formal models can be appreciated from the following considerations. Mackintosh (1975) says that events that have expected consequences are processed, whereas Pearce and Hall (1980) say that events that have unexpected consequences are processed. Both viewpoints are, moreover, supported by unimpeachable data. If the data support the idea that both expected and unexpected events are processed, then why have the formal theories avoided this conclusion?

The statement that both expected and unexpected events are processed can easily become predictively vacuous in a formal model, because such a model cannot easily distinguish the sense in which expected and unexpected events are processed in different ways. The alternative conclusion—that expected and unexpected events are processed in the same way—is dangerously close to saying that all events are processed in the same way, which is patently false.

Conditioning data need a theory that can avoid these fatal pitfalls. Such a theory must explain the sense in which expected and unexpected events are processed by different mechanisms. It must carefully delineate the properties of these mechanisms to avoid becoming vacuous or patently false. It must show how these properties can be empirically tested. Because expected and unexpected events are all just events on the behaviorally observable level, such a theory needs to establish a link with the behaviorally unobservable structures within which these processing distinctions can be physically interpreted and validated.

5. Causality Violation on the Behaviorally Observable Level

The step toward theories that invoke behaviorally unobservable processes in a substantive way runs against the grain for many psychologists today. This is true despite the fact that as a body of psychological data becomes more mature and quantitative, it bears more sharply on the behaviorally unobservable mechanisms that generate these data.

An important experiment which further demonstrates that conditioning data have reached this level of maturity was conducted by Mackintosh et al. (1977) and is reviewed by Pearce and Hall (1980). I will indicate below that an interpretation of these data using only behaviorally observable variables violates the causality of the conditioning process. To reject causality is tantamount to denying the very existence of a predictive conditioning theory. For my purposes, I will summarize only one aspect of this experiment.

In Part 1 of the experiment, all rats experienced four trials on which a light (CS) was followed by a shock (US). In Part 2 of the experiment, two groups of rats received an additional single compound light-tone trial. In one group (Group 1) the light-tone compound was followed by a single shock. In the other group (Group 2) the light-tone compound was followed by two successive shocks that were presented 10 sec. apart. A recall trial with the tone alone showed essentially identical fear conditioning to the tone in both groups. In other words, the second shock seems not to have affected tone conditioning.

The remarkable feature of the experiment becomes apparent when one considers two other groups of rats tested in Part 3 of the experiment. One of these groups (Group 3) received the same training as Group 1 did plus an additional compound light-tone trial followed by a single shock before a recall trial with the tone CS. The other group (Group 4) received the same training as did Group 2 plus an additional compound light-tone trial followed by a single shock before a recall trial with the tone CS. In other words, Part 3 of the experiment simply added an identical learning manipulation onto the Group 1 and 2 learning paradigms, which by themselves elicited the same reaction to the tone. Remarkably, the tone exhibited better fear conditioning for Group 4 than for Group 3.

This is a fascinating experimental finding. How can a test after identical second compound trials have different effects if tests after different first compound trials had identical effects? This experiment seems to violate causality on the behaviorally observable level and forces us to turn to behaviorally unobservable mechanisms for an explanation.

6. Some Unpredicted Data

The internal contradictions within the formal models are associated with predictive limitations. Pearce and Hall (1980) note that they cannot explain the following phenomena: (a) If two CSs differ markedly in their intensity or salience, the more salient cue can overshadow the less salient cue, but not conversely (p.541; Mackintosh, 1976). (b) Overshadowing effects can sometimes occur when only a single trial of compound conditioning is given (p.541; Mackintosh, 1971; Mackintosh and Reese, 1979). (c) The associability of a stimulus followed by surprising food remains high for future conditioning involving food but not for future conditioning involving shock (p.550; Dickinson and Mackintosh, 1979). (d) Low associability of a stimulus can be restored by presenting it in a novel context (p.550; Dexter and Merrill, 1969; Lantz, 1973; Lubow, Rifkin, and Alek, 1976). (e) The occurrence of a surprising event soon after a conditioning trial can influence learning on that trial (p.550; Kremer, 1979; Wagner, Rudy, and Whitlow, 1973). All of these phenomena can be explained by my theory. See Sections 33–45.

7. Formal versus Physical Concepts: A Second Type of LTM?

Formal models have an advantage over heuristic data analysis in that they commit one's thinking to a more precise, and therefore disconfirmable, set of concepts. Formal models also need to be compared with other related concepts in the theoretical literature to check their tenability as physical constructs. The main conditioning equations of the Pearce and Hall (1980) theory lead to a major qualitative conclusion when this comparison is made, namely, that "associability" is controlled by a form of LTM distinct from the LTM that is encoded by associative strength.

This conclusion follows from the Pearce and Hall associative equations:

$$\Delta V_A^{(n)} = S_A^{(n)} \alpha_A^{(n)} \lambda^{(n)} \tag{1}$$

and

$$\alpha_A^{(n)} = | \lambda^{(n-1)} - V_T^{(n-1)} | \tag{2}$$

or equation (1) and

$$\alpha_A^{(n)} = \frac{1}{c} \sum_{k=n-c}^{n-1} | \lambda^{(k)} - V_T^{(k)} | . \tag{3}$$

Equation (1) says that the change $\Delta V_A^{(n)}$ in the associative strength $V_A^{(n)}$ of Event A on trial n depends on the product of CS intensity $S_A^{(n)}$, associability $\alpha_A^{(n)}$, and US intensity $\lambda^{(n)}$ on trial n. Equation (2) says that the associability on trial n depends on—and *a fortiori* remembers—the difference between the US intensity and the aggregate associative strength $V_T^{(n-1)}$ on trial $n-1$. Equation (3) extends this notion to the idea that associability has a memory that extends $c(> 1)$ trials into the past.

All of the formal theories make some assumption concerning how events on a given trial influence associability on later trials. If these formal theories have physical validity, we must therefore determine whether two distinct types of LTM exist. If so, how does associability compute the difference between the US intensity and the aggregate associative strength of all experimental events despite the fact that these quantities are distributed across time and representational space? What sort of intervening processes can gather, add, or subtract all these data at each CS representation? Is there any physical evidence that such processes exist? If these formulations have no physical support as they stand, is it because the formal theories have lumped too many processes into a single equation?

8. Overexpectation, STM Signaling, LTM Gating, and Drive Representations

The scope of this article does not permit a derivation of my theory from first principles. I can, nonetheless, indicate how a bridge can be constructed from the Rescorla-Wagner framework, on which Pearce and Hall have built, toward my own framework. I do this by analysing an internal contradiction in the way Wagner and Rescorla (1972) use their associative equation to explain the phenomenon of "overexpectation." This contradiction arises because Wagner and Rescorla's intuitive explanation is incompatible with their formal associative equation. By explicating their intuitive explanation within their own formalism, I am led to a distinction between STM and LTM effects and to the concept of a drive representation.

The phenomenon of overexpectation was observed in an experiment wherein four groups of rats received cue combinations in a fear conditioning (CER) paradigm. On each conditioning trial a 2-min flashing light (A) and/or a 2-min tone (B) preceded a .5-sec .5-ma shock US. One group (A+B+) received 40 reinforced presentations of each cue, A and B, presented separately. Group A+B+/AB+ received, in addition, 40 more reinforced presentations of the AB compound. Two comparison groups received either 80 or 120 reinforced trials with only the compound stimulus. All groups then received 16 nonreinforced presentations of the AB compound while barpressing for food to test the degree of response suppression produced by the compound. Group A+B+ showed more conditioned suppression of barpressing for food during unreinforced test trials than any of the other groups.

Wagner and Rescorla (1972) discuss these results in terms of their associative equations

$$\Delta V_A = \alpha(\lambda - V_\Sigma) \tag{4}$$

and

$$\Delta V_B = \alpha(\lambda - V_\Sigma), \tag{5}$$

where V_A and V_B are the associative strengths of A and B, respectively, $V_\Sigma = V_A + V_B$, and λ is the US strength. They claim that when only Cue A is followed by shock, V_A will approach λ because then $V_\Sigma = V_A$. Similarly, when only Cue B is shocked, V_B will approach λ because then $V_\Sigma = V_B$. If, as in the experiment A+B+/AB+, the compound AB is thereupon shocked, then $V_\Sigma = V_A + V_B$. Consequently, both V_A and V_B will decrease when AB training begins because

$$\lambda - V_\Sigma \cong \lambda - 2\lambda < 0 \tag{6}$$

at the onset of compound training.

This explanation is inconsistent with equations (4) and (5) for the following reason: On the A+B+ trials, V_A and V_B are each assumed to approach λ even before compound AB trials begin. Because, by definition, $V_\Sigma = V_A + V_B$, this cannot happen because as soon as $V_\Sigma \geq \lambda$, $\Delta V_A \leq 0$ and $\Delta V_B \leq 0$. In other words, the Wagner and Rescorla (1972) model, when consistently applied, is inconsistent with the fact that more suppression can occur after A+B+ trials than after AB+ trials.

Rescorla and Wagner (1972) clearly intended that V_B should be irrelevant when only Cue A is presented and that V_A should be irrelevant when only Cue B is presented. Such a concept is needed to eliminate the effect of V_B on the V_A asymptote during A trials, and of V_A on the V_B asymptote during B trials. The switching on and off of an event's momentary relevance occurs rapidly on a trial-by-trial basis, whereas the growth of the associative strengths V_A and V_B is slowly varying across trials. Let us call the distinction between the rapid modulation of an event's activity and the slow changes in its associative strengths the difference between STM and LTM.

Had Wagner and Rescorla (1972) explicitly faced this processing implication of their own data, they might have redefined V_Σ as

$$V_\Sigma = S_A V_A + S_B V_B, \tag{7}$$

where S_A and S_B are the signals elicited by the active STM representations of Cues A and B, respectively. Then, if only A is presented, $S_B = 0$ and V_Σ depends only on V_A, whereas if only B is presented, $S_A = 0$ and V_Σ depends only on V_B.

Term $S_A V_A$ in equation (7) can be physically interpreted as follows: The STM-activated signal S_A reads out the LTM trace V_A via a *gating*, or multiplicative, action $S_A V_A$. Such an LTM gating action appears prominently in my work. It is, for example, crucial in my approach to serial and paired-associate verbal learning (Grossberg, 1969b; Grossberg and Pepe, 1971), free recall (Grossberg, 1978a, 1978b), and cognitive development (Grossberg, 1976a, 1976b, 1978b, 1980), as well as in my studies of conditioning and attention (Grossberg, 1968, 1969a, 1969b, 1969c, 1971, 1972a, 1972b, 1974, 1975, 1976a, 1976b, 1978a, 1978b, 1980, 1981b, 1982, 1984).

Once the modification in equation (7) is accepted, it becomes clear that the model must undergo a more major revision. This is true because the left-hand side and the right-hand side of equation (7) are not dimensionally the same. The right-hand side can fluctuate rapidly through time with S_A and S_B, whereas the left-hand side is a slowly varying associative strength. This observation could have already been made about the term $\lambda - V_\Sigma$ in equations (4) and (5), because US intensity λ is a rapidly varying (STM) quantity, whereas V_Σ is a slowly varying (LTM) quantity. Replacing V_Σ by $S_A V_A + S_B V_B$ in $\lambda - V_\Sigma$ avoids the problem of mixing apples with oranges if we interpret $\lambda - S_A V_A - S_B V_B$ as the amount by which a commonly shared STM representation is activated by the combined effects of λ and the LTM-gated signals $S_A V_A$ and $S_B V_B$.

This commonly shared STM representation cannot be the separate representations of either Cue A or Cue B. Moreover, activation of this new representation depends on the choice of reinforcer, because an associative strength learned with respect to a shock is not the same as an associative strength learned with respect to a food reinforcer. Even within the Rescorla-Wagner model, V_Σ feels the influence of a particular US's intensity λ. In my theory this new type of STM representation is called a *drive representation*.

An internal analysis of the Rescorla-Wagner equation has hereby distinguished sensory representations for cues such as A and B from drive representations corresponding to distinct reinforcing actions such as food, fear, and sex. Because each Cue A might be conditioned to any of several drive representations, we need to study how the *pattern* of LTM associative strengths V_{ij}, leading from the ith sensory representation to the jth drive representation, evolves through time. Once we accept the fact that the ith sensory representation can read out a pattern of LTM-gated signals $S_i V_{ij}$ across several drive representations (indexed by j), we need to discover an STM decision rule whereby incompatible drive representations can generate consistent observable behavior. We also need to discover a law for the selective change of V_{ij} due to the STM signal S_i of the ith CS and the intensity λ_j of the jth US.

9. Secondary Conditioning Implies That Cue and Drive Representations Are Distinct

Now that we have in mind sets not only of CSs but also of USs, we can use the fact that prior conditioning can transform a CS into the US of a later secondary conditioning experiment to constrain this law. In particular, the asymmetric role of US intensity λ_j and of CS intensity S_i in the modified Rescorla-Wagner equation,

$$\Delta V_{ij} = \alpha_{ij}(\lambda_j - \sum_k S_k V_{kj}) \tag{8}$$

shows that this equation cannot be strictly correct. I suggest that this problem of the Rescorla-Wagner framework is the reason why Pearce and Hall need to assume that two types of LTM exist (Section 33). Equation (8) also includes the Widrow-Hoff equation on which Sutton and Barto (1981) build.

The same argument shows that a secondary US representation is not a drive representation, because a CS representation is not a drive representation. Hence, conditioning from a CS to a drive representation is not the same process as conditioning from a CS to a US representation. This conclusion runs counter to the Pearce and Hall (1980) assertion "that the amount of learning is determined by the amount of simultaneous processing that the representations of the CS and US receive in the processor" (p.550).

In light of the above argument, it is not clear what "the processor" might physically represent, because CS representations and drive representations are qualitatively distinct concepts. In fact, Pearce and Hall (1980) note their model's inability to explain the Dickinson and Mackintosh (1979) data on selective effects of distinct reinforcers on associability and go on to say, "One way for our model to accommodate this result is to propose that there are separate processors for learning about different reinforcers such as food and shock" (p.550). A large body of data other than that of Dickinson and Mackintosh (1979) also suggests such a concept. My articles (Grossberg, 1971, 1972a, 1972b, 1975, 1982) review some of these data in light of the drive representation concept.

This type of internal analysis of the Rescorla-Wagner framework can be continued, but the breakdown of equation (8) indicates that some new theoretical principles are needed to go much further. The above theoretical exercise nonetheless clarifies my contention that the demand for explicit processing descriptions—within any theoretical framework—rapidly leads either to important new concepts or to unforseen contradictions.

SOME GENERAL PSYCHOPHYSIOLOGICAL CONCEPTS

10. An Alternative Processing Framework: Complementary Attentional and Orienting Subsystems

Having summarized some difficulties of one theoretical stream, I will compare the two streams—notably their explanations of expectancies, extinction, and STM priming—after my review of the second stream is complete. To start the review, I will sketch in broad strokes the general framework of my theory. Then I will review in more precise terms the several design principles and mechanisms that I need to quantify this framework.

In my theory an interaction between two functionally complementary subsystems is needed to process expected and unexpected events (Grossberg, 1975). A precursor of this concept is developed in the distinguished psychophysiological article of Routtenberg

(1968) on the "two-arousal hypothesis." My conception of these two subsystems will be seen to deviate from Routtenberg's view in several basic ways (Section 27).

Expected events are processed within a consummatory, or attentional, subsystem. This subsystem establishes ever more precise internal representations of and responses to expected cues. It also builds up the learned expectations that are used to characterize operationally the sense in which expected cues are expected. The attentional subsystem is, however, incapable of adapting to unexpected environmental changes. Left to its own devices, it would elicit ever more rigid, ever perseverative, reactions to the environment, much as hippocampectomized rats do not orient to a novel stimulus while they are indulging in consummatory activity, such as running toward a reward. Such rats cannot "shift attention during the presentation of a novel stimulus or in a mismatch situation" (O'Keefe and Nadel, 1978, p.250). The second subsystem is an orienting subsystem that overcomes the rigidity of the attentional subsystem when unexpected events occur and enables the attentional subsystem to adapt to new reinforcement and expectational contingencies.

Part of the difficulty in understanding conditioning and attentional data is due to the fact that these two subsystems interact in a subtle fashion. I will review in the following sections how both expected and unexpected events start to be processed by the attentional subsystem. When an unexpected event mismatches an active expectancy within this subsystem, the orienting subsystem is disinhibited. The orienting subsystem acts to rapidly reset STM within the attentional subsystem as it simultaneously energizes an orienting response.

By contrast, an expected event matches an active expectancy within the attentional subsystem. This matching process amplifies the STM activity patterns that are currently active within the attentional subsystem. These amplified, or resonant, STM activities inhibit the orienting subsystem as they simultaneously drive adaptive LTM changes, including the learning of new expectancies, internal representations (chunks), and habits.

11. The Stability-Plasticity Dilemma and Evoked Potential Correlates

The complementary attentional and orienting subsystems, indeed all the mechanisms that I will use, arise as the solution to a fundamental design problem concerning the self-organization (e.g., development, learning) of new internal representations (Grossberg, 1976a, 1976b, 1978b, 1980, 1982, 1984). I call this problem the *stability-plasticity dilemma*.

The stability-plasticity dilemma concerns how internal representations can maintain themselves in a stable fashion against the erosive effects of behaviorally irrelevant environmental fluctuations yet can nonetheless adapt rapidly in response to environmental fluctuations that are crucial to survival. How does a network as a whole know the difference between behaviorally irrelevant and relevant events even though its individual cells, or nodes, do not possess this knowledge? How does a network transmute this knowledge into the difference between slow and fast rates of adaptation, respectively? Classical examples of the stability-plasticity balance are found in the work of Held and his colleagues on rapid visual adaptation to discordant visuomotor data in adults (Held, 1961, 1967; Held and Hein, 1963) and in the work of Wallach and his colleagues on rapid visual adaptation to discordant cues for the kinetic depth effect and cues for retinal disparity (Wallach and Karsh, 1963a, 1963b; Wallach, Moore, and Davidson, 1963).

Because of the fundamental nature of the stability-plasticity dilemma, the mechanisms from which the two complementary subsystems are built have properties that imply psychophysiological, neurophysiological, and pharmacological predictions. For example, on the psychophysiological level, the disinhibition of the orienting subsystem due to an expectancy mismatch is suggested to correspond to the mismatch-negativity component of the N200 evoked potential complex. The STM reset in the attentional subsystem is suggested to correspond to a P300 evoked potential. The origin of the mismatch-negativity component in the orienting subsystem and its role in generating a P300 suggests a relationship between the P300 and the orienting reaction. The resonant STM activity that derives from an expectancy match in the attentional subsystem is suggested to correspond to the processing-negativity component of the N200 evoked potential complex.

This psychophysiological interpretation leads to a number of interdisciplinary predictions (Grossberg, 1984). For example, in Section 35, I suggest that the tone on the second compound trial in Group 4 of the Mackintosh, Bygrave, and Picton (1977) experiment is more unexpected than the tone on the second compound trial in Group 3, and should therefore elicit a larger P300 evoked potential.

Sections 12–25 review the concepts that I use to mechanize the attentional and orienting subsystems. Then Sections 26–51 use these concepts to explain conditioning and attentional data and to compare my theory with the formal models.

12. Gated Dipoles

The gated dipole design is needed to reset STM. In the present theory the term *STM* refers collectively to the suprathreshold activities of STM traces. An STM trace is computed at a network node where it equals the average potential of the cell, or cell population, that is represented by the node. An STM trace can passively decay at a node, but the important operations in the theory transform these traces in ways other than by passive decay. In particular, STM reset refers to a rapid change in STM, notably the rapid shutting off of activity at a subset of previously active nodes and the rapid turning on of activity at a subset of previously inactive nodes. The STM activities at different types of nodes represent different psychological processes. The gated dipoles to be discussed below are, for example, assumed to occur both in cognitive and in motivational networks. Activity of a gated dipole node in a cognitive network may represent the occurrence of a certain perceptual feature or a certain temporal ordering of events in an experiment. Activity of a gated dipole node in a motivational network may, by contrast, measure the level of perceived fear or relief. The theory suggests that similar formal properties obtain in gated dipoles wherever these dipoles are placed in a network. The theory also suggests how to place these mechanisms in different types of networks and how to interpret their formal properties in these different contexts.

The gated dipole design shows how slowly accumulating transmitter substances gate the signals in parallel network pathways before these pathways compete to elicit net on-cell or off-cell STM responses (Figure 1). These responses include a sustained on-response to cue onset and a transient antagonistic off-response, or rebound, to either cue offset or to arousal onset. The off-reactions drive the STM reset.

One way to motivate the antagonistic rebound concept is to ask: How does offset of an event act as a cue for a learned response? For example, suppose that I wish to press a lever in response to the offset of a light. If light offset simply turned off the cells that code for light being on, then there would be no cells whose activity could selectively elicit the lever-press response after the light was turned off. Light offset must also selectively turn on cells that will transiently be active after the light is shut off. The activity of these off-cells (the cells that are turned on by light offset) can then activate the motor commands leading to the lever press. Let us call the transient activation of the off-cell by cue offset antagonistic rebound.

In a reinforcement context I claim that such an antagonistic rebound is the basis for a relief reaction (Denny, 1971) upon offset of a sustained fear-eliciting cue. In a perceptual context I claim that such an antagonistic rebound is the basis for a negative aftereffect upon offset of a sustained image (Brown, 1965, p.483; Helmholtz, 1866, 1866/1962).

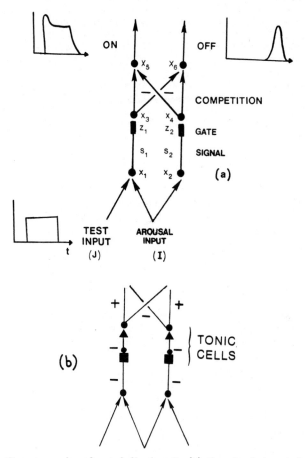

Figure 1. Two examples of gated dipoles. In (a) the phasic input J and the arousal input I add in the on-channel, thereby activating the short-term memory trace X_1. The arousal input I also perturbs the short-term memory trace X_2 in the off-channel. Consequently, $X_1 > X_2$. Then X_1 and X_2 elicit signals $f(X_1)$ and $f(X_2)$ in their respective pathways. Because $X_1 > X_2$, $f(X_1) > f(X_2)$ also. Each signal is gated (multiplied) by an excitatory transmitter Z_1 or Z_2 (in the square synapses) before the gated signals $f(X_1)Z_1$ and $f(X_2)Z_2$ activate their target cells. The short-term memory traces X_5 and X_6 then satisfy $X_5 > X_6$. Each short-term memory trace elicits an excitatory signal down its own pathway, and an inhibitory signal to the other pathway. The net effect after competition takes place is an output from the on-channel. The text describes how a rapid offset of J triggers an antagonistic rebound that transiently excites the off-channel. In (b) another version of a gated dipole is depicted. Here each excitatory gating pathway is replaced by a two-stage disinhibitory pathway that is constructed from two successive inhibitory links. The cells that receive these transmitter signals are assumed to be tonic (internally and persistently activated). The net effect of an input to the two-stage disinhibitory pathway is to release its output cell from tonic inhibition and thereby excite it.

13. Antagonistic Rebound to Cue Offset

I will now describe a minimal model capable of eliciting a sustained on-response to onset of a cue and a transient antagonistic rebound to offset of the cue. The intuitive postulates that led to the model's original derivation are given in Grossberg (1972b). An alternative derivation is given in Grossberg (1980, Appendix E). An extended discussion and mathematical analysis of the gated dipole is found in Grossberg (1981b, 1984). Herein I will merely provide an intuitive description of a gated dipole.

Consider Figure 1. In Figure 1a, a nonspecific arousal input I is delivered equally to both the on-channel and the off-channel, whereas a test input J (e.g., light or shock) is delivered only to the on-channel. These inputs activate the potentials X_1 and X_2, which create signals S_1 and S_2 in the on-channel and off-channnel, respectively. Because $I + J > I$, $X_1 > X_2$ and consequently, $S_1 > S_2$. What happens next is crucial.

The square synapses are assumed to contain chemical transmitters Z_1 and Z_2, respectively. Each transmitter slowly accumulates to a target level. The slow accumulation rate is essential to the model's properties. The target level is achieved by a constant transmitter production rate that is reduced by feedback inhibition proportional to the transmitter concentration. When a signal S_1 reaches the synaptic knobs containing Z_1, transmitter is released at a rate proportional to $T_1 = S_1 Z_1$. The multiplicative effect of Z_1 on S_1 to yield T_1 is called transmitter gating of the signal S_1. The gating law just says that S_1 and Z_1 interact via mass action to elicit T_1. In particular, if either $S_1 = 0$ or $Z_1 = 0$, then $T_1 = 0$.

One proves that if $S_1 > S_2$, then $T_1 > T_2$. That is, transmitter is released at a faster rate by larger signals. Consequently, potential X_3 exceeds potential X_4. These potentials then emit competing signals. Potential X_5 wins the competition over X_6 and emits output signals that are the on-reaction of the network.

So far everything seems quite elementary. Only now do we exploit the slow accumulation rate and the transmitter gating law to show how a transient antagonistic rebound is generated by rapid offset of J.

The faster transmitter depletion rate in the on-channel than in the off-channel when J is on implies that $Z_1 < Z_2$, despite the fact that $S_1 Z_1 > S_2 Z_2$. When J is shut off, both channels receive the equal arousal input I. The potentials X_1 and X_2 rapidly equalize, as do the signals S_1 and S_2. By contrast, the inequality $Z_1 < Z_2$ persists because transmitter accumulates slowly. Thus, right after J shuts off, $S_1 Z_1 < S_2 Z_2$, $X_3 < X_4$, and the off-channel wins the signal competition. An antagonistic rebound is thereby initiated.

The rebound is transient because the transmitters gradually respond to the equal signals I by reaching a common level $Z_1 = Z_2$. Then $S_1 Z_1 = S_2 Z_2$, and the competition shuts off the rebound.

There exist many variations on the gated dipole theme. Figure 1b points out that the slow transmitters can be inhibitory transmitters within a two-synapse disinhibitory pathway rather than excitatory transmitters within a one-synapse pathway. I interpret dopamine or noradrenaline to be the slow inhibitory transmitters in motivational and cognitive dipoles. The other inhibitory transmitter is often interpreted as gamma aminobutyric acid (Groves, Young, and Wilson, 1978). The disinhibitory concept rationalizes many effects of drugs such as amphetamine, chlorpromazine, 6-hydroxydopamine, and monoamine oxidase inhibitors on behavior (Grossberg, 1972b, 1984). A single cell, rather than an intercellular network as in Figure 1, can also act like a gated dipole. Such a dipole is suggested to exist in vertebrate photoreceptors (Carpenter and Grossberg, 1981) wherein calcium is suggested to act as the gating chemical. A full understanding of the gated dipole concept requires that we be able to distinguish the varied anatomical substrates of gated dipoles from their commonly shared functional properties.

14. Antagonistic Rebound to Arousal Onset

A surprising fact about gated dipoles is that a sudden arousal increment ΔI can trigger an antagonistic rebound despite the fact that both the on-channel and the off-channel receive equal arousal inputs (Figure 2). This mathematical property forced me to realize that an unexpected event, by triggering a burst of nonspecific arousal, could disconfirm an on-reaction by rapidly and selectively inhibiting it, thereby resetting STM.

I should be more precise about this property of arousal, because this precision has important implications for my explanation of overshadowing. The following remarkable property holds in the gated dipole of Figure 1a if the signals S_1 and S_2 are linear functions of their respective inputs. The off-rebound size in response to a sustained input J and a sudden arousal increment of size ΔI above the previous arousal level I is

$$\text{Off} = \frac{ABJ(\Delta I - A)}{(A + I + J)(A + I)}, \tag{9}$$

where A and B are positive constants. Note that a positive off-reaction occurs only if $\Delta I > A$. This criterion is independent of J, which means that an arousal increment ΔI that is sufficiently large to rebound any dipole will be large enough to rebound all dipoles in a field. More precisely, if the arousal increment is large enough, then all active dipoles will simultaneously be rebounded. This is because the size of the rebound is an increasing function of the on-input J and equals 0 if $J = 0$. Thus, rebound size is selective despite the fact that all active dipoles can be rebounded at once. I identify activation of the arousal source which resets the STM of a dipole field with the mismatch-negativity component of the N200 evoked potential complex. The STM reset event itself is identified with the P300 evoked potential.

Given that a sudden burst of nonspecific arousal can selectively reset a field of on-cells and off-cells, we need to consider how this arousal level is regulated. The theory explicates the idea that surprising events are arousing.

15. What Is An Expectation?

To discuss a surprising or unexpected event, we need to define what an expectation is and how it is computed. In my theory several levels of network processing interact to build up new internal representations. To fix ideas, consider two successive levels $F^{(1)}$ and $F^{(2)}$ in this network hierarchy. Each active node in $F^{(2)}$ is capable of sending feedback signals to a subset of nodes across $F^{(1)}$. Before these signals reach their target cells, they are gated by LTM traces that exist at the ends of the signal pathways (Figure 3). This gating action multiplies the signal and the LTM trace, just like the gating action of the transmitters in a gated dipole. In more precise terms, denote the feedback signal from the jth node $V_j^{(2)}$ in $F^{(2)}$ to the ith node in $V_i^{(1)}$ in $F^{(1)}$ by S_j. Denote the LTM trace in this feedback pathway by Z_{ji}. Then the net signal received by $V_i^{(1)}$ from $V_j^{(2)}$ is $S_j Z_{ji}$. All these signals add up to $V_i^{(1)}$ to generate a total signal

$$E_i = \sum_j S_j Z_{ji} \tag{10}$$

at $V_i^{(1)}$. The pattern

$$E = (E_1, E_2, \ldots, E_m) \tag{11}$$

of total feedback signals from $F^{(2)}$ to $F^{(1)}$ is identified with an expectation. An expectation is not an LTM trace or a family of LTM traces. It is not defined with respect

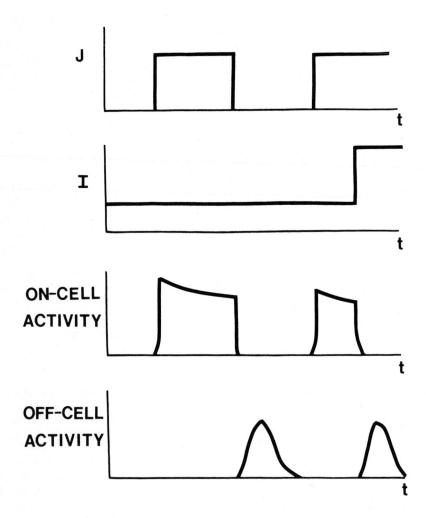

Figure 2. On and off responses of gated dipoles. After a gated dipole's transmitters equilibrate to an on-channel phasic input J, an antagonistic rebound or off-response can be generated by either rapidly shutting off the phasic input J or rapidly turning up the level of nonspecific arousal I. The latter type of rebound can reset short-term memory in response to an unexpected event that triggers a momentary arousal burst from the orienting subsystem.

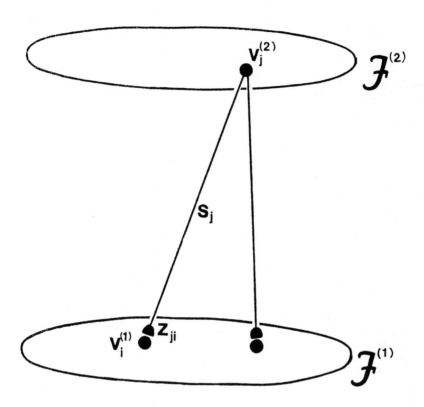

Figure 3. Short-term memory activity at a population $V_j^{(2)}$ in $F^{(2)}$ releases a signal S_j. This signal is gated by the long-term memory trace Z_{ji} on its way to a population $V_i^{(1)}$ in $F^{(1)}$. All these gated signals add at $V_i^{(1)}$ to generate a total input $E_i = \sum_j S_j Z_{ji}$. The pattern $E = (E_1, E_2, \ldots, E_m)$ of feedback signals is an expectation.

to a single cell. It is a feedback pattern derived from LTM-gated signaling across the entire network. Because the signals S_j depend on the momentary STM activities of the nodes in $F^{(2)}$, the expectation can quickly change even if there are no changes in the LTM traces. The signal S_j is an STM probe that reads out the LTM pattern $(Z_{j1}, Z_{j2}, \ldots, Z_{jm})$ as part of the expectation E.

The pattern E is called an expectation because the LTM trace Z_{ji} can change when the signal S_j from $V_j^{(2)}$ and the STM activity $X_i^{(1)}$ of $V_i^{(1)}$ are active long enough for the slowly varying LTM trace to respond to them. When this happens, the pattern $(Z_{j1}, Z_{j2}, \ldots, Z_{jm})$ of LTM traces can learn the pattern $(X_1^{(1)}, X_2^{(1)}, \ldots, X_m^{(1)})$ of STM activities (Grossberg, 1967, 1969c, 1972c, 1974). As the STM pattern across $F^{(1)}$ is encoded by $V_j^{(2)}$'s LTM traces, it becomes the pattern that $V_j^{(2)}$ expects to find at $F^{(1)}$ when it is active. Later STM activation of $V_j^{(2)}$ reads this LTM pattern into the expectation E via the gating action of the LTM traces Z_{ji} on the signal S_j. This gated signal pattern equals E only when $V_j^{(2)}$ is the only active node in $F^{(2)}$. When more than one node is active across $F^{(2)}$, E is a weighted average of the LTM patterns of all the active cells (Grossberg, 1968, 1976a, 1976b, 1980).

Neurophysiological evidence for the existence of such feedback expectancies, or templates, can be found in the distinguished work of Freeman (1975, 1980, 1981) on the olfactory system.

16. Unexpected Events Trigger a Mismatch-Modulated Arousal Burst

Having defined an expectation, I can now more easily describe how an unexpected event at $F^{(1)}$ triggers an arousal burst to $F^{(2)}$, which thereupon resets STM across $F^{(2)}$ via selective antagonistic rebounds.

At a moment when the feedback expectation E is active across $F^{(1)}$ (Figure 4a), suppose that an external event causes a feedforward input pattern U to be received by $F^{(1)}$ (Figure 4b). Suppose that U mismatches E (in a sense that is defined in Section 24). In my theory such a mismatch rapidly inhibits STM activity across $F^{(1)}$ (Figure 4c). Attenuating the STM activity in $F^{(1)}$ eliminates the inhibitory signal that $F^{(1)}$ delivers to the orienting, or arousal, subsystem $\mathcal{A}$ when $F^{(1)}$ is active. Because $\mathcal{A}$ also receives excitatory input due to the external event, the arousal subsystem $\mathcal{A}$ is disinhibited and releases a burst of nonspecific arousal across $F^{(2)}$ (Figure 4d).

The description of the disinhibition of $\mathcal{A}$ assumes that an external event excites both the attentional and the orienting subsystems but that the orienting subsystem can only release signals when a mismatch within the attentional subsystem occurs. An early precursor of this idea is the Hebb (1955) hypothesis that every event has a cue and a vigilance, or arousal, function. A more recent correlate is my interpretation of $\mathcal{A}$ as the generator of the mismatch-negativity evoked potential (Näätänen, Hukkanen, and Järvilechto, 1980). A subtle aspect of this interpretation is that the mismatch occurs in the attentional subsystem, whereas the disinhibited mismatch negativity is elicited in the orienting subsystem.

17. STM Reset versus STM Resonance

Before explaining how a pattern mismatch across $F^{(1)}$ can attenuate STM activity there, I need to discuss what happens if a pattern match occurs across $F^{(1)}$. By definition, such a match means that the external input that causes the feedforward pattern U is expected with respect to the feedback pattern E. The effect of this match is to amplify the STM activities of the matched pattern across $F^{(1)}$. Thus, a mismatch attenuates all activity across $F^{(1)}$, whereas a match amplifies patterned STM activity across $F^{(1)}$. I call the amplification of STM activity in a feedback module such as $F^{(1)}$ and $F^{(2)}$ an STM *resonance* (Grossberg, 1976b, 1978b, 1980).

Neurophysiological evidence for the existence of STM resonance has been described in the olfactory system by Freeman (1975, 1980, 1981) and in the visual system by Singer (1977, 1979). On a psychophysiological level, I identify this amplification of STM activity due to a pattern match with the *processing negativity* or *match detector* component of the N200 evoked potential complex (Grossberg, 1984).

We have hereby been led to distinguish two functionally distinct actions of expected and unexpected events. Expected events can generate an STM resonance, whereas unex-

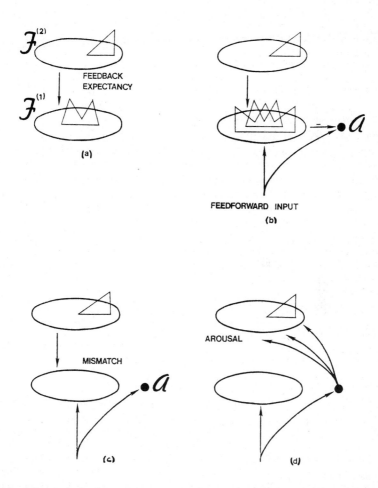

Figure 4. Mismatch-modulated arousal. In (a), a subliminal feedback expectancy E from $F^{(2)}$ to $F^{(1)}$ is maintained by short-term memory signaling from $F^{(2)}$. In (b), a feedforward input pattern U is also registered at $F^{(1)}$ as it simultaneously activates the arousal branch A. In (c), the mismatch between the two patterns across $F^{(1)}$ attenuates activity at this level. In (d), inhibition at $F^{(1)}$ removes inhibition from $F^{(1)}$ to A, thereby permitting A to unleash an arousal burst across $F^{(2)}$. Had the feedforward input matched the feedback expectancy, the amplified activity at $F^{(1)}$ would have inhibited the arousal source A.

pected events can trigger selective STM reset. A subtle aspect of these complementary STM transactions is that both of them occur within the attentional subsystem, although only one of them is mediated by the orienting subsystem. In other words, the organization of the brain into *structurally* complementary subsystems does not correspond in an obvious way to the *functional* complementarity in the processing of expected and unexpected events.

A deeper subtlety of this functional interaction is implicit in the previous discussion and will be rendered explicit in Section 26. There I will conclude that the very STM resonance that represents paying attention to an event activity prepares the attentional subsystem to be reset by the orienting subsystem. An STM resonance does this by selectively depleting, or habituating, the transmitter gates in the active channels of the gated dipoles from which $F^{(2)}$ is constructed. If an arousal burst perturbs these dipoles, then STM will be rapidly reset.

18. Chunking and Expectancy Learning

The concepts of STM reset and STM resonance become fully meaningful when they are used to describe how the stability-plasticity dilemma is solved, notably how new internal representations (chunks) and expectancies are learned and remembered.

To complete this description, I assume that $F^{(1)}$ can send feedforward signals to $F^{(2)}$. The feedback expectancy signals from $F^{(2)}$ to $F^{(1)}$ are thus part of a reciprocal exchange of signals between successive levels in the network hierarchy. Anatomical correlates of this reciprocal exchange are the reciprocal thalamocortical connections that seem to occur in all thalamoneocortical systems (Macchi and Rinvik, 1976; Tsumoto, Creutzfeldt, and Legéndy, 1976). Psychological correlates of this reciprocal exchange are the processes of recognition and recall that, when regulated by STM reset operations, lead to rapid hypothesis testing, or search, through associative memory (Grossberg, 1978a, 1978b).

The signals from $F^{(1)}$ to $F^{(2)}$ are gated by LTM traces before the signals reach their target cells. Then the gated signals are summed at each target cell, just as in equation (10). The reader with some engineering background will recognize that the transformation from an output signal pattern $S = (S_1, S_2, \ldots, S_m)$ to an input signal pattern $T = (T_1, T_2, \ldots, T_n)$, where $T_j = \sum_i S_i Z_{ij}$, defines a linear filter. Because the LTM traces Z_{ij} can change as a function of experience, this filter is called an *adaptive filter*. Both the adaptive filter due to $F^{(1)} \to F^{(2)}$ feedforward signaling and the learned expectation due to $F^{(2)} \to F^{(1)}$ feedback signaling obey the same gating laws and laws of associative learning. Their different intuitive interpretations are due to their different locations within the network as a whole.

When learning occurs in the LTM traces of the $F^{(1)} \to F^{(2)}$ pathways, the same input pattern U to $F^{(1)}$ will elicit a different STM pattern across $F^{(2)}$. Speaking intuitively, the internal representation of U across $F^{(2)}$ has changed. Just as an expectation is influenced by the $F^{(2)} \to F^{(1)}$ LTM traces, but is not identical with these traces, an internal representation is influenced by the $F^{(1)} \to F^{(2)}$ LTM traces, but is not identical with these traces.

19. The Code of Adaptive Resonances

With these comments in hand, I can now expand the notions of STM reset and STM resonance to include the self-organization process. If a feedback expectation E mismatches a feedforward input pattern U, then STM reset occurs before the LTM traces in the $F^{(1)} \to F^{(2)}$ pathways and the $F^{(2)} \to F^{(1)}$ pathways can change. Consequently, mismatched or erroneous interpretations of the environment cannot cause adaptive changes in LTM. The LTM traces can gate presently active signals prior to the reset event and can thereby alter network activity based on their past learning. However, the LTM traces are adaptively blind to the present network activity, including the signals that they gate, because the LTM traces are slowly varying relative to the rapid time scale of filtering, mismatch, and reset.

By contrast, if a feedback expectation E matches a feedforward input pattern U, then STM is amplified across $F^{(1)}$. The signals from $F^{(1)}$ to $F^{(2)}$ are thereby amplified so that STM activity across $F^{(2)}$ is also amplified. Then the signals from $F^{(2)}$ to $F^{(1)}$ are amplified, and the entire network locks into an STM resonance. This global STM event defines the perceptual or attentive moment.

Resonant STM activities can be encoded in LTM because they are large enough and last long enough for the LTM traces to respond to them. An STM resonance is thus a context-sensitive global interpretation of the input data that signifies that the network as a whole considers this interpretation worthy of being adaptively incorporated into the network's memory structure. I call the dynamic process whereby LTM adapts to resonant STM patterns an *adaptive resonance*.

Using the notion of adaptive resonance, it is now easy to state what the perceptual or cognitive code of a network is, although the simplicity of this statement hides numerous subtleties and the need for much future scientific work. The code of a network is the set of stable adaptive resonances that it can support in response to a prescribed input environment.

James Gibson's lifelong ingenuity as a student of perceptual phenomena led him to conclude that the perceptual system "resonates to the invariant structure or is attuned to it" (Gibson, 1979, p.249). Gibson has been criticized for emphasizing the phenomenal immediacy of perception at the cost of underemphasizing its processing substrates (Ullman, 1980). We can now understand that Gibson's emphasis was based on a correct intuition. The many processing steps, such as adaptive filtering, STM activation, readout of feedback expectancies, STM mismatch, disinhibition of orienting arousal, STM reset, and so forth, all involve perfectly good neural potentials, signals, and transmitters. However they are not accessible to consciousness. The conscious experience is, I suggest, the resonant or attentive moment, which seems to be immediate because it is a global event that energizes the system as a whole.

20. The Noise-Saturation Dilemma

Before turning to a consideration of conditioning data, we still need to understand how a pattern mismatch attenuates STM activity, how a pattern match amplifies STM activity, and how an STM resonance depletes the on-cell transmitter gate in a gated dipole. All of these properties follow from a study of competitive interactions between the cells at each of the several levels $F^{(1)}$, $F^{(2)}$, ..., $F^{(n)}$ of the network hierarchy.

The need for competitive interactions follows from a basic processing dilemma—*the noise-saturation dilemma*—that is faced by all cellular tissues, not only nerve cells, and must be solved before continuously fluctuating input patterns can be registered at all.

The noise-saturation dilemma is easy to state because it is so basic. Consider Figure 5. In Figure 5a, a differentiated pattern of inputs I_i is poorly registered in the activities, or STM traces, X_i because the overall input intensity is too small to override internal cellular noise. In Figure 5b, all the inputs are proportionally amplified to escape the cells' noisy range without destroying relative input importance (as when the reflectances of a picture remain constant despite its illumination at successively higher light intensities). Because all cells have only finitely many excitable sites, the smallest inputs are now large enough to turn on all the sites of their receptive cells; hence, the larger inputs might not be able to differentially excite their receptive cells, because there might be no more sites to turn on in these cells. The input differences are thereby lost because the activities saturate as all the cell sites are activated. Thus, in a cellular tissue, sensitivity loss can occur at both low and high input intensities. As the inputs fluctuate between these extremes, the possibility of accurately registering input patterns is imperiled.

I proved (Grossberg, 1973) that mass action competitive networks can automatically retune their sensitivity as inputs fluctuate to register input differences without noise or saturation contaminants. See Grossberg (1980, Appendices C and D) for a review. In a neural context these systems are called shunting on-center off-surround networks. Otherwise expressed, a network whose cells obey membrane equations (not additive equations) and that interact via an anatomy with a narrow excitatory focus and broadly distributed inhibition can automatically retune its sensitivity due to automatic gain control by the inhibitory signals.

21. STM Contrast Enhancement and Normalization: Hypothesis Testing and Overshadowing in a Limited-Capacity System

Because of the noise-saturation dilemma, competitive networks are ubiquitous wherever input patterns are accurately registered and transformed by cells. If these input patterns also need to be stored beyond the offset times of the inputs, as in STM representations that can remain active until later reinforcements can act upon them to influence LTM encoding, then the competitive networks must also be feedback networks (Figure 6) whose positive feedback loops can reverberate the STM activities after the inputs cease.

Competitive feedback networks also exist for a deeper processing reason that is related to the stability-plasticity dilemma. These networks need to possess the properties of *contrast enhancement* and *normalization* to carry out hypothesis testing operations leading to the self-organization of new internal representations after an unexpected event occurs. The property of contrast enhancement is the capability of the network to attenuate small inputs and amplify large inputs before storing the contrast enhanced input pattern in STM. The property of normalization is the tendency of the total suprathreshold STM activity across the network to be conserved through time.

These properties enable the network to solve a problem that could prevent it from adaptively reacting to an unexpected event. Mismatch across $F^{(1)}$ causes an STM reset across $F^{(2)}$. If the nodes that are activated by $F^{(1)} \rightarrow F^{(2)}$ signals are hereby inhibited, then how does $F^{(2)}$ get activated at all by these signals during the next time interval? Why does the entire network not shut down? How does an unexpected input to $F^{(1)}$ ever get encoded if a mismatch shuts down the whole system?

The contrast-enhancement property supplies part of the answer. Not all of the nodes in $F^{(2)}$ that receive inputs from $F^{(1)}$ have their activities stored in STM. Only the nodes that receive relatively large inputs have their activities stored in STM. Only those nodes whose activities get stored in STM are reset by the mismatch-modulated arousal burst. The nodes that receive smaller inputs are not reset because they did not reverberate in STM. These latter nodes can still respond to the signals from $F^{(1)}$ to $F^{(2)}$ in the next time interval.

The contrast-enhancement property thus shows how some input-activated nodes can be spared by the STM reset process. However, this property is not sufficient because these nodes, after all, receive such small inputs that they could not previously reverberate in STM. Why can they reverberate in STM after the nodes that received large inputs are inhibited by dipole rebounds?

The normalization property now comes to the rescue. The total suprathreshold STM activity tends to be conserved. Because the dipole-inhibited nodes can no longer compete for this conserved activity, the remaining input-excited nodes inherit it (Figure 7). Thus, the nodes that fared poorly in the competition for STM activity in the

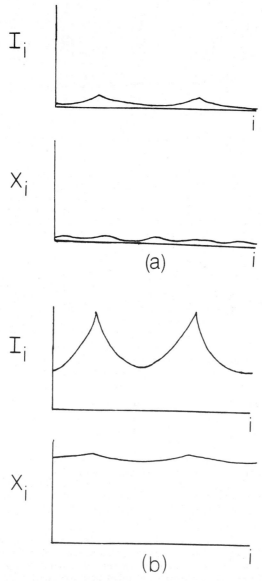

Figure 5. The noise-saturation dilemma. (a) At low input intensities, the input pattern $(I_1, I_2, \ldots, I_n)$ is poorly registered in the short-term memory activity pattern $(X_1, X_2, \ldots, X_n)$ because of internal noise in the cells. (b) At high input intensities, the input pattern is poorly registered in the short-term memory activity pattern because all of the cells' finitely many excitable sites get saturated.

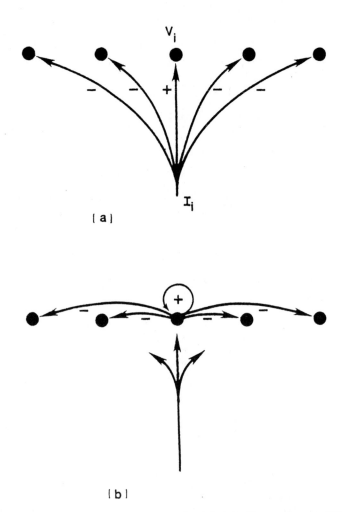

[a]

[b]

Figure 6. Two types of competitive networks. (a) A feedforward competitive network delivers both excitatory and inhibitory inputs to its receptive cells. This competitive input distribution allows the cells to respond to input patterns of widely varying background intensity without saturation. (b) A feedback competitive network generates excitatory and inhibitory feedback signals among its own cells. When these feedback signals are sigmoid, or S-shaped, functions of cell activity, the network can contrast-enhance the input pattern before storing it in short-term memory. This contrast-enhancement property follows from the sigmoid signal's ability to suppress, rather than amplify, noise through the network's excitatory feedback loops. The network also tends to conserve its total suprathreshold activity through time. This normalization property dynamically explains the limited capacity of short-term memory as a consequence of solving the noise-saturation dilemma.

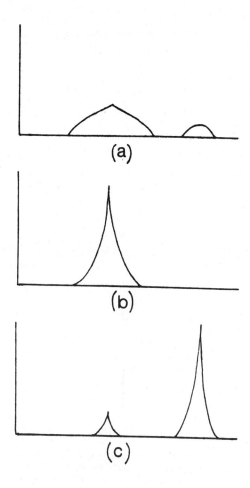

Figure 7. Renormalization. The input pattern in (a) elicits short-term memory activity pattern $X_i^{(2)}$ in (b) by suppressing small inputs and contrast-enhancing large inputs. After $X_i^{(2)}$ is suppressed by dipole rebounds, the small input activities inherit normalized activity from the suppressed populations to elicit the distinct short-term memory activity pattern in (c).

original field $F^{(2)}$ fare much better in the "renormalized" field wherein their strongest competitors have been inhibited by dipole rebounds. The successive renormalization of the field $F^{(2)}$ by rapid reset events can be viewed as a type of parallel hypothesis testing, or principal-component analysis, whereby the field zooms in on nodes capable of generating an STM resonance.

The way in which STM normalization influences the processing of unexpected events is relevant to my analysis of overshadowing. Because of STM normalization, increasing the STM activity of one representation forces a decrease in the STM activities of the representations with which the enhanced representation competes. Otherwise expressed, STM normalization provides a dynamical explanation of why STM is a limited capacity system.

It is important to realize that although competitive feedback networks possess the normalization property, competitive feedforward networks do not. An input is small in a feedforward network because it has already fared badly in the feedforward competitive interaction. The normalization property must occur after the stage of input delivery, not before or at this stage.

22. Overshadowing and Sigmoid Signal Functions

The discussion of contrast enhancement and normalization indicates some properties that are needed to accomplish hypothesis testing in response to an unexpected event. This discussion does not, however, show how these properties are obtained or whether other important properties coexist with them. We now need to review this issue in a more detailed fashion, because an important property that we need is still not available.

The need is clarified by considering a standard overshadowing experiment (Kamin, 1968, 1969). Suppose that an animal receives a series of CER conditioning trials wherein a Cue A (such as a light) is followed by a standard shock US. Let these trials be followed by a series of CER conditioning trials to the compound Cue AB (such as a light-tone combination) followed by the same shock US. A later test of Cue B's ability to suppress bar pressing for food shows that its fearfulness has been blocked by the prior conditioning of Cue A to the shock. By contrast, if the compound conditioning trials use a different level of shock as a US than was used during the conditioning of Cue A, then the conditionability of Cue B is restored.

In the light of the previous theoretical discussion, one might wish to say that the unexpected change of US at the onset of compound trials causes an STM reset that somehow amplifies Cue B's STM representation and thereby frees it from blocking. This wish is, however, incompatible with equation (9), which shows that all active representations are reset if any representation is reset. Is the present theory incompatible with basic facts of overshadowing?

At this point one must soberly face the fact that the theory would collapse without the benefit of mathematics. Indeed, it is quite impossible to understand the STM transformations during conditioning experiments without a suitable mathematical tool.

Equation (9) was derived under the hypothesis that a linear signal function transmutes the arousal signal I and the test signal J into signals S_1 and S_2 to the dipole gates. I will now say why a linear signal function can never be used in a competitive feedback network within a perceptual or cognitive processor. In fact, a linear signal function does not imply the contrast-enhancement property that is needed to reset STM in response to an unexpected event. The right kind of signal function gives all the properties that are needed, including the overshadowing property. This signal function is a sigmoid, or S-shaped, signal function. Such a signal function acts like a threshold at low cell activities and levels off at high cell activities.

23. Noise Suppression and Selective Enhancement, or Dishabituation, of Overshadowed Representations by Unexpected Events

A sigmoid signal function is needed for a basic processing reason. The positive feedback signaling in competitive feedback networks can be a mixed blessing if it is not properly designed. Positive feedback can subserve such desirable properties as STM storage and normalization. It can also, if improperly designed, flood the network with noise generated by its own activity. This noise amplification property will have disastrous effects on network processing whenever it occurs, and it can occur in formal network "seizures" and "hallucinations" (Ellias and Grossberg, 1975; Grossberg, 1973; Kaczmarek and Babloyantz, 1977; Schwartz, 1980).

A proper choice of signal function prevents noise amplification (Grossberg, 1973). The simplest physically plausible signal function that prevents noise amplification is the sigmoid signal function. The opposite of noise amplification is noise suppression. This noise suppression property attenuates small inputs to the network. By normalization, it thereby amplifies large inputs to the network. A competitive feedback network's contrast enhancement property is thus a variant of its noise suppression capability.

We can now re-analyse the response of a gated dipole to an arousal burst when a sigmoid signal, as opposed to a linear signal, is used. When this is done, one finds that the same arousal burst that rebounds the on-responses of very active dipoles will *enhance* the on-responses of weakly active dipoles. In other words, overshadowed representations in a dipole field can actually be enhanced by the same surprising event that inhibits more salient representations via antagonistic rebound. That all the properties that are needed occur automatically as a result of basic processing constraints like noise suppression is what I call a minor mathematical miracle. Minor mathematical miracles should not be taken lightly. They usually mean that the intuitive ideas that they reify contain a lot of truth.

To illustrate this new rebound property, let the sigmoid signal function be $f(w) = w^2(1 + w^2)^{-1}$. Because we are interested in the smallest, or threshold, increment ΔI that can cause a rebound, we can approximate $f(w)$ by w^2. Then, in the gated dipole of Figure 1, a rebound occurs to an arousal increment ΔI given a previous arousal level I and on-input J only if

$$\Delta I > g(I, J), \tag{12}$$

where the function $g(I, J)$ is defined by

$$g(I, J) = \frac{A - I(I + J) + (A + I^2)^{1/2}[A + (I + J)^2]^{1/2}}{2I + J}. \tag{13}$$

Because $g(I, J)$ is a decreasing function of J, it is easier to rebound an intensely activated dipole $(J \gg 0)$ than a weakly activated dipole $(J \cong 0)$.

If $\Delta I < g(I, J)$, then the arousal increment ΔI can cause an enhanced on-reaction rather than an off-rebound. These properties illustrate how the habituation of cell responses due to transmitter depletion can be dishabituated by an unexpected event. An electrode that is too coarse to distinguish between on-enhancements and off-rebounds near its recording site could record dishabituation of this type of response to an arousal increment at all electrode placements near previously active cells, whereas a more sensitive electrode could record both on-enhancements and off-rebounds as dishabituation reactions at some cell locations, as well as off-reactions at other cell locations.

24. Noise Suppression and Pattern Matching

A variant on the noise suppression theme implies a mechanism of pattern matching at $F^{(1)}$. A shunting competitive network can easily be designed to suppress uniform input patterns (Figure 8a). Such patterns represent noise in the sense that no node is differentiated from any other by the input. If a network can suppress a uniform input pattern, then it can suppress a sum of two mismatched input patterns (Figure 8b) because the mismatched peaks and troughs of the input patterns add to produce an almost uniform total pattern. By contrast, a sum of two matched input patterns yields an amplified network reaction (Figure 8c) because the network's shunting mechanism reacts to the sum of two patterns with a larger gain than to a single input pattern. See Grossberg (1980 or 1981a) for mathematical details.

25. Sigmoid Signals and Tuning: Multiple Effects of a US

One final consequence of sigmoidal signaling in a competitive feedback network can help us to understand conditioning experiments. Noise suppression due to sigmoid signaling also implies the following interesting property. A competitive feedback network undergoing sigmoidal feedback signaling possesses a parameter called a *quenching threshold* (QT). The QT defines the noise level of such a network, because the network inhibits activities that start out less than the QT and contrast-enhances activities that exceed the QT before storing them in STM. Any network with a QT can be tuned; by varying the QT the network's ability to store or suppress inputs can be altered through time.

For example, if an arousal source nonspecifically increases the level of shunting inhibition acting on a competitive network's feedback inhibitory interneurons, then the net disinhibitory action will cause the network's QT to decrease. The network's STM storage of input patterns will thereby be facilitated. This type of arousal event should not be confused with orienting arousal. It is the type of arousal that lowers and heightens the sensitivity of the attentional subsystem, as during sleep and wakefulness.

I will now briefly indicate how the concept of an attentional QT can be implicated during a conditioning experiment. To do this I will use some concepts intuitively that will be precisely defined in the next sections. Suppose that any cue that can activate a drive representation can also reduce the attentional QT. Then an unexpected US can have three distinct effects on attentional processing. As an unexpected event that mismatches active feedback expectancies, the US can remove some STM representations from overshadowing by differentially amplifying them. As a US *per se*, it can activate a drive representation and thereby further abet the STM storage of overshadowed cues by lowering the QT. This effect sensitizes the processing of all cues that survive STM reset and occurs later in time than STM reset. Finally, as a generator of conditioned incentive motivational feedback, the US can differentially strengthen STM activities of motivationally compatible cues. By contrast, an unexpected CS is only capable of eliciting differential STM reset because of mismatch with feedback expectancies.

All of the three effects itemized above depend on learning, but in different neural pathways and on different time scales. The first effect involves expectancy learning, the second effect involves conditioned reinforcer learning (which enables a cue to turn on a drive representation), and the third effect involves incentive motivational learning. If such a QT effect of a US exists, its generator will probably be turned on by signals that are elaborated within the hippocampus, which I identify as the final common pathway of the drive representations (Grossberg, 1971, 1975, 1980).

CONDITIONING AND ATTENTION

26. Gated Feedback Dipoles

We now have all the conceptual threads that we need to discuss conditioning and attention. Some loose threads still need to be tied, however. Then we will find that

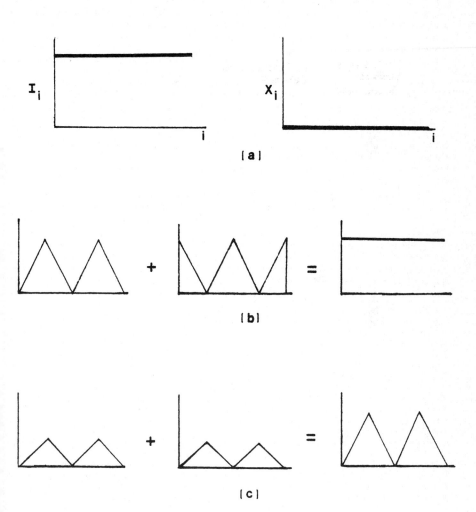

Figure 8. Pattern matching. In (a) the noise suppression property converts a uniform (or zero spatial frequency) input pattern (I_i) into a zero activity pattern (X_i). In (b), two mismatched input patterns add to generate an approximately uniform input pattern, which is suppressed by the mechanism of (a). In (c), two matched patterns add to yield a total input pattern that is more active than either pattern taken separately.

a large body of data falls into place with little difficulty. Because a deep theoretical understanding comes from knowing how particular mechanisms generate particular constellations of data properties, I will build up the mechanisms in stages and will supply data markers at each stage.

Two distinct design principles coexist at the same cells: gated dipoles and shunting competitive feedback networks. I will now show how to join these two principles into a single network. This can be done by making explicit a property that was mentioned in Section 22 without pursuing its implications. There I suggested that a nonspecific arousal burst could reset STM even after the cues that initiated STM storage had terminated. I used this property to begin an explanation of overshadowing. In order for this to happen, the STM feedback loops must contain the transmitter gates so that STM activity can differentially deplete the active STM loops and thereby prepare them for rebound. Figure 9 summarizes this structural arrangement by depicting a conditionable input pathway abutting a gated feedback pathway. I will henceforth assume that the transmitter in a conditionable input pathway is cholinergic and that the transmitter in a gated STM feedback loop is catecholaminergic (Grossberg, 1972b), because a large body of data is compatible with this suggestion (Butcher, 1978; Epstein, Kissileff, and Stellar, 1973; Friedhoff, 1975a, 1975b).

There is another way to derive Figure 9 even when no arousal-initiated rebound exists. This alternative derivation holds when the off-cells represent features or behavioral categories that are complementary to those represented by the on-cells: for example, fear versus relief, hunger versus satiety, vertical red bar on green field versus vertical green bar on red field, and so forth. The derivation proceeds in three steps (Grossberg, 1972b).

1. Sudden offset of a conditioned cue input can cause a rebound, much as offset of a conditioned source of fear can elicit relief (Denny, 1971; Masterson, 1970; McAllister and McAllister, 1971). To accomplish this rebound the cue input is delivered to the network at a stage *before* the transmitter gate. Only in this way can the cue deplete the gate so that its offset can drive a rebound.

2. Onset of a cue input can elicit sampling signals capable of encoding a rebound in LTM, much as a tone that is turned on contingent on shock offset can become a source of conditioned relief (Dunham, 1971; Dunham, Mariner, and Adams, 1969; Hammond, 1965; Rescorla, 1969; Rescorla and LoLordo, 1965; Weisman and Litner, 1969). Thus, the cue input is delivered to the network at a stage *after* the transmitter gate, where the rebound can be sampled.

3. Properties 1 and 2 are true for *all* cues that can be conditioned to these categories, because whether a given cue will be conditioned to the onset or to the offset of any particular category is not known *a priori*. Every cue input is delivered both before and after the transmitter gating stage. The transmitter gate thus occurs in a feedback pathway, as in Figure 9.

The existence of two distinct derivations leading to a similar network design is important, because not every recurrent network that can be reset by offset of a cue need possess a mismatch-contingent arousal source, even though an arousal source *per se* is required. These derivations suggest that the anatomical design in Figure 9 is basic and that the input mechanisms that control rebound in this common design can be adapted to satisfy specialized processing constraints.

One further constraint can readily be satisfied by this design. The cue inputs arrive before the stage of dipole competition so that at most one of the complementary cue outputs (on-cell versus off-cell) can be positive at any time. The next section depicts the minimal anatomy that joins together gated dipole feedback pathways that terminate before the dipole competition stage. This microcircuit is needed to build up both the sensory and the drive representation networks that are activated by conditioning and attentional manipulations.

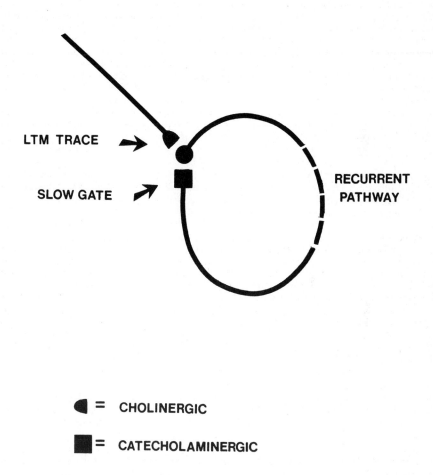

LTM TRACE →

SLOW GATE ↗

RECURRENT PATHWAY

◀ = CHOLINERGIC

■ = CATECHOLAMINERGIC

Figure 9. Slow gated feedback and long-term memory interaction. A conditionable pathway that is excited by a cue's internal representation feeds into a gated feedback loop. Because the gate occurs within a feedback loop, the conditionable pathway can achieve two distinct processing objectives. It can sample and store in its long-term memory (LTM) trace the gated output of the loop. It can also alter the short-term memory activity in the loop by changing its own signals through time. The LTM trace in the conditionable pathway is assumed to be part of a cholinergic interaction. The gate in the feedback loop is assumed to be part of a catecholaminergic interaction. The text and Figure 10 show how these components can be embedded into a gated feedback dipole.

27. Drives, Conditioned Reinforcers, Incentive Motivation, and CNV

Figure 10 depicts such a minimal anatomy and assigns to its pathways the motivational interpretation that turns the anatomy into a drive representation. In Figure 10 the specific inputs to the gated dipole are of two kinds: internal drive inputs and external cue inputs. In the case of eating, the positive drive input increases with hunger, and the negative drive input increases with satiety, owing either to gastric distension or to slower metabolic factors (Anand and Pillai, 1967; Janowitz, Hanson, and Grossman, 1949; LeMagnen, 1972; Sharma, Anand, Dua, and Singh, 1961). Let the drive inputs and the nonspecific arousal be gated by a catecholaminergic transmitter in both the on-channel and the off-channel to calibrate the proper relative sizes of dipole on-responses and off-responses.

Let each external cue input send a conditionable pathway to both the on-channel and the off-channel of the dipole. Each cue can become a conditioned reinforcer of either positive or negative sign, depending on which of its LTM traces in the on-channel or the off-channel is larger. To calibrate the relative sizes of these LTM traces in an unbiased fashion, I assume that the transmitter system that subserves LTM encoding in both branches is the same and is cholinergic. These chemical interpretations may eventually have to be changed, but the processing requirements of accurately calibrating relative rebound or conditioned reinforcer strength across competing channels are robust.

The cells at which external cue, drive, and arousal inputs converge are assumed to be *polyvalent*: These cells only fire vigorously when both their external cue and their internal drive inputs are sufficiently large. The outputs from these polyvalent cells compete before generating a net dipole output in either the on-cell or the off-cell channel, but not both. These dipole outputs play the role of *incentive motivation* in the theory. The existence of polyvalent cells is compatible with the intuition that incentive motivation need not be released even when drive is high if compatible cues are unavailable. For example, a male animal left alone will busily do the many things characteristic of his species, such as grooming, eating, exploring. He does not look sexually motivated. However, if a female animal is presented to him, his behavior can dramatically change (Beach, 1956; Bolles, 1967, Chapter 7). Incentive motivation need not be released even when compatible cues are available if drive is low. Seward and his colleagues (Seward and Proctor, 1960; Seward, Shea, and Elkind, 1958; Seward, Shea, and Davenport, 1960) found that if an animal is not hungry, then no amount of food will be adequate to reinforce its behavior.

Figure 10 suggests a different relationship between drive and incentive than is found in Routtenberg (1968). Routtenberg makes incentive and drive complementary concepts of his two-arousal hypothesis. In Figure 10 drive and incentive are both part of the attentional subsystem, which is complementary to the orienting subsystem. In my theory drive and arousal are not the same concept.

28. Extinction, Conditioned Emotional Responses, Conditioned Avoidance Responses, and Secondary Conditioning

To indicate how a gated feedback dipole works, the next two sections summarize some of its formal properties using reinforcement and motivation terminology. This section reviews how each cue's LTM sampling of both the on-channel and the off-channel contributes to the explanation of some basic conditioning processes (Grossberg, 1972a, 1972b) and thereby indirectly supports the claim that both LTM pathways need to be built up from similarly calibrated transmitter mechanisms. The simplest LTM law says that LTM encoding occurs only when a cue pathway and a contiguous polyvalent cell are simultaneously active (Grossberg, 1964, 1968; Hebb, 1949).

Suppose that during early learning trials, a cue occurs just before a large unconditional signal, such as a shock, turns on the on-channel. This unconditional signal elicits the incentive output of the on-channel, which triggers a fear reaction, even before

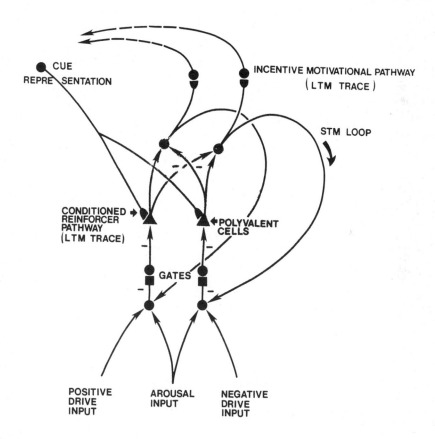

Figure 10. A motivational network: network with a gated feedback dipole hooked up to conditionable pathways from the internal representations of cues. The text describes how the feedback loops between external cue representations and internal drive representations, and between internal drive representations and themselves, join together mechanisms of reinforcement, drive, incentive motivation, competition, arousal, and short-term memory (STM). LTM = long-term memory.

learning occurs. By associating the cue with shock on learning trials, its LTM trace abutting the on-channel grows much larger than its LTM trace abutting the off-channel. If the cue is then presented by iteslf, the LTM-gated signal to the on-channel is much larger than the LTM-gated signal to the off-channel. The on-channel wins the dipole competition, so the cue elicits fear. The cue has to thereby become a conditioned reinforcer that can elicit a conditioned emotional response, or CER (Estes, 1969; Estes and Skinner, 1941).

Now suppose that after the cue has become an elicitor of a CER, environmental contingencies change. Suppose that the cue no longer reliably predicts future events and that an unexpected event occurs while the cue is on. Suppose that the unexpected event triggers an antagonistic rebound in the off-channel. Because the cue is on, its LTM trace abutting the off-channel will grow. If this occurs sufficiently often, the off-LTM trace will grow as large as the on-LTM trace. After this happens, presenting the cue will generate comparable LTM-gated signals to both the on-channel and the off-channel. After these signals compete, the net incentive motivation output will be very small. The cue no longer elicits a CER. It has been rapidly extinguished by unexpected events.

This cue is extinguished because it remains on both before and after the unexpected event. It is an irrelevant cue with respect to the contingency that triggered the unexpected event. By contrast, a cue that turns on right after the unexpected event occurs will sample only the off-reaction of the dipole. Only its LTM trace abutting the off-channel will grow. Later presentation of the cue will thereby elicit a large off-reaction. If the off-reaction corresponds to a relief reaction, then the cue has become a source of conditioned relief by being paired with offset of a source of fear. Although the cue has never been paired with a positive reward, it thereafter can be used as a positive reinforcer or source of consummatory motivation. This mechanism helps us to understand how avoidance behavior can be persistently maintained long after an animal no longer experiences the fear that originally motivated the avoidance learning (Grossberg, 1972a, 1972b, 1975; Maier, Seligman, and Solomon, 1969; Seligman and Johnston, 1973; Solomon, Kamin, and Wynne, 1953).

A similar argument shows how secondary conditioning can occur. For example, offset of a positive (or negative) conditioned reinforcer S_1 can drive an antagonistic rebound that conditions a cue S_2 whose onset is contingent upon the offset event to be a negative (or positive) conditioned reinforcer. This mechanism uses the feedback in the gated dipole in a major way. Offset of the reinforcer S_1 can elicit a rebound because it occurs at a stage prior to the gate, whereas sampling of the rebound can occur because cue S_2 delivers its signals at a stage subsequent to the gate.

29. Motivational Baseline, Switching, and Hysteresis

The positive feedback loops in the gated dipole of Figure 10 turn this network into a feedback competitive network. The slowly varying transmitter gates do not alter the fact that a feedback gated dipole shares many properties with other feedback competitive networks. For example, the dipole now has an STM storage capability, which means that it can defend a motivational decision against sufficiently small momentary fluctuations in cue or arousal inputs. This hysteresis property helps to provide the inertia needed to carry out a sustained, motivated act during irrelevant environmental perturbations. The STM normalization property refines this capability by maintaining a temporally stable baseline of incentive motivation. The contrast-enhancement property due to sigmoidal feedback signaling helps to control sharp motivational switching between behavioral alternatives when the net balance of inputs succeeds in overcoming the hysteretic inertia of the previous motivational choice.

Frey and Sears (1978) have suggested a formal model to explain some of these properties. Their model builds sigmoid and hysteresis properties into a cusp catastrophe model of conditioning and attention. Although their model provides one way to visualize sudden switches, the catastrophe variables do not correspond to physical variables, and the model provides no physical explanation of why sigmoid and hysteresis properties appear in the data. The gated dipole theory provides a physical explanation that does not correspond to a cusp catastrophe, and it implies a large body of data and predictions that are invisible to the cusp picture. For example, when sigmoid feedback signals are used in a gated dipole, this network also possesses inverted U properties that are reflected in a large body of data about normal and abnormal behavior (Grossberg, 1972b, 1984). These inverted U properties are part of the minor mathematical miracle.

Because of the importance of the gated dipole concept to my motivational theory, I will also discuss how the same mechanisms work in the case of hunger and satiety, rather than shock. In the case of hunger, a positive drive input increases with hunger, whereas a negative drive input increases with satiety. An increase in the positive drive input disinhibits the polyvalent cell that is two inhibitory synapses away. Suppose that this polyvalent cell also receives a large conditioned signal from a cue representation. In other words, the cue is a conditioned reinforcer with respect to this drive representation, and the cue is active in STM. Then the polyvalent cell can vigorously fire. Suppose at this moment that the negative drive input is small (e.g., the hunger level is high) and/or only weak conditioned signals reach the polyvalent cell of the negative drive representation. Then this polyvalent cell does not fire vigorously. Thus, after competition takes place, the positive drive channel wins. It can therefore emit incentive motivational signals to the cue representations. These conditionable signals help to regulate attention by modifying the total excitatory input pattern to the cue representations.

The positive drive channel can also deliver excitatory feedback to the cells that receive positive drive input. This excitatory feedback can sustain the activity of the positive drive representation. It can thereby store a motivational decision in STM against small input perturbations (hysteresis), maintain a steady motivational baseline (normalization), and regulate sharp motivational switching (contrast enhancement). All of these properties are STM properties. The sustained STM reverberation also allows contiguous LTM traces of active cue representations to encode the large activity of the positive drive representation at a rate that increases with the STM activity of the cue representation. These active cues can thereby become positive conditioned reinforcers.

If the incentive motivation from the positive drive representation supports sustained, motivated behavior (e.g., eating), then the negative drive input slowly grows (e.g., satiety increases). The increase in the negative drive input shuts off STM at the positive drive representation via the competitive interaction. The motivated behavior thereby loses its incentive motivation support (e.g., eating stops).

If positive conditioned reinforcer input is rapidly withdrawn before the negative drive input increases, then an antagonistic rebound can be elicited in the negative drive channel. This rebound rapidly terminates the motivated behavior. An antagonistic rebound can occur because a sudden reduction of positive conditioned reinforcer input reduces the signal within the feedback loop of the positive drive representation. The total signal to the transmitter gate in the positive drive channel is thereby reduced, and a rebound is elicited just as in Figures 1 and 2. A cue whose LTM traces sample the antagonistic rebound can become a negative conditioned reinforcer. A cue whose LTM traces sample both the positive drive representation and the negative drive representation is extinguished (irrelevant) with respect to this drive, because its positive and negative gated signals to the gated dipole inhibit each other at the competitive stage before any net incentive motivation can be released.

An issue of some importance concerns how strict the polyvalent constraint is on the firing of cells where external cue inputs and drive inputs converge. To illustrate this issue, suppose that a satiety input grows because of sustained eating. If the polyvalent constraint is strict, then the polyvalent cell that receives the large satiety input cannot fire at all unless it also receives a large cue input. If not, the satiety input cannot inhibit the positive incentive motivation that was supporting eating. If the polyvalent constraint is not strict, then small background cue inputs will suffice to permit polyvalent cell firing in response to sufficiently large satiety inputs. This problem is overcome by the network of Figure 12, because the drive inputs compete in that network before they influence the polyvalent cells. Once the concept of polyvalence is before us, we can begin to classify which networks best marry polyvalence to other important processing constraints.

30. Adaptive Resonance Between Dipole Fields

Now that we have a clearer view of how to design the microcircuitry of a gated feedback dipole, we need to build these microcircuits into a global processing scheme. The gated feedback dipoles are part of dipole fields wherein on-cells are joined by shunting competitive feedback networks, off-cells are joined by shunting competitive feedback networks, and on-cells are joined to off-cells via gated dipoles. The dipole fields themselves interact via adaptive filters, much as the fields $F^{(1)}$ and $F^{(2)}$ interact in Section 18.

Figure 11 depicts the macrocircuit that will be most prominent in my discussion of conditioning data. It describes a feedback module wherein sensory and drive representations send signals to each other via nonspecific excitatory conditionable pathways (adaptive filters). These representations are organized into dipole fields. Each dipole field is capable of STM contrast enhancement, normalization, hysteresis, and rebound. The interfield conditionable pathways send branches to both the on-cells and the off-cells of the dipole fields, just as they do to explain extinction and secondary conditioning in Section 28.

The conditionable pathways from sensory representations to drive representations encode the conditioned reinforcer properties of external cues. The conditionable pathways from drive representations to sensory representations encode the incentive motivation properties of internal drives. An adaptive resonance occurs within this network when the reinforcing properties of active external cues sufficiently match the motivational properties of active internal drives to lock STM into a global interpretation of the data.

In the theory that I developed in Grossberg (1971, 1972a, 1972b, 1975), the final processing stage in the external cue representations is assumed to be cortical, and the final processing stage in the drive representations is assumed to be hippocampal. Gabriel, Foster, Orona, Saltwick, and Stanton (1980) summarize recent data that support a qualitatively similar conclusion. They write: "the hippocampal formation is a region critical for encoding or 'modeling' of stimulus-reinforcement contingencies" (p. 189). They note that the hippocampus is reciprocally connected with cingulate cortex and with the anteroventral nucleus of the thalamus and summarize data suggesting that cortical "codes inappropriate to the stimulus item being presented would create mismatch with the hippocampal model, thereby eliciting code-suppression in cortex and thalamus" (p.189).

31. A Motivational Dipole Field: Drive-Reinforcer Matching and Motivational Competition

Now we need to fill in the microcircuitry of the dipole fields using Section 27 as a guide. Figure 12 depicts an anatomy that possesses the minimal drive representation properties that I will need. In this anatomy each motivational channel possesses a positive feedback loop that runs through a gated dipole. These positive feedback loops are the on-centers of a competitive feedback network that joins together motivational channels. The competitive feedback network provides a matching interface that runs across the motivational channels. At this interface, spatial patterns of (conditioned) reinforcer signals are matched with spatial patterns of drive signals. Only a sufficiently good match can trigger sustained polyvalent cell firing (Sections 17 and 27). If this network is tuned (Section 25) so that only a single winning channel can reverberate

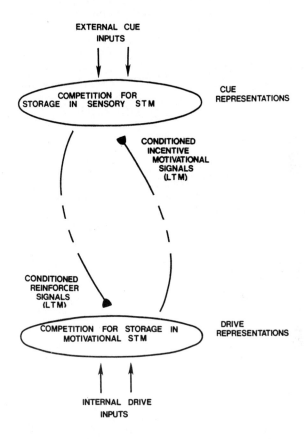

Figure 11. Adaptive resonance between dipole fields. When external cues excite the short-term memory (STM) traces of their internal representations, these internal representations elicit signals that are distributed nonspecifically across the various internal drive representations. During conditioning, the pattern of reinforcing and drive inputs to the drive representations can alter the long-term memory (LTM) traces within certain of these signal pathways, as Figure 10 has illustrated. The corresponding external cues thereby acquire conditioned reinforcer properties. On recall trials the conditioned reinforcer signals from external cues combine with internal drive inputs at the drive representations to determine which drive representations will fire. Output from the drive representations plays the role of incentive motivation in the network. Incentive motivation is released from a given drive representation only if the momentary balance of conditioned reinforcer signals plus drive inputs competes favorably against these factors within the other drive representations. The incentive motivational pathways are also nonspecific and conditionable. External cue representations that receive large incentive motivational feedback signals are favored in the competition for storage in sensory short-term memory, as Figure 13 describes in greater detail.

in STM, then sharp motivational switching will occur. Such a setting of the network defines the channels as being motivationally incompatible. A lower setting of the QT can permit compatible combinations of drive representations to be synergistically activated. Possible settings depend on the choice of numerical network parameters and can vary across species and individuals without changing the underlying design principle.

To understand in greater detail how a motivational dipole field works, I will summarize the processing stages in Figure 12 step by step. Pathways 1 and 2 carry specific, but complementary, drive inputs (e.g., hunger vs. satiety) to a single dipole. Pathways labeled 3 carry nonspecific arousal to this dipole. Cells 4 and 5 add these inputs and thereupon inhibit the tonically active cells 6 and 7. (Tonic cells have open symbols; phasic cells have closed symbols.) Pathways $4 \to 6$ and $5 \to 7$ contain slow transmitter gates (square synapses), assumed to be catecholaminergic. If Input 1 exceeds Input 2, then the transmitter in pathway $4 \to 6$ is depleted more than the transmitter in pathway $5 \to 7$, thereupon calibrating the dipole for a possible antagonistic rebound later on.

The tonic cells 6 and 7 equally inhibit each other until Input 1 exceeds Input 2. Then cell 6 is inhibited more than cell 7. This imbalance disinhibits tonic cell 8 and further inhibits tonic cell 9. Both cells 8 and 9 are polyvalent, meaning that all their excitatory inputs must be active for these cells to vigorously fire. (Triangles denote polyvalence.) The polyvalent cells are assumed to be pyramidal cells. Because cells 8 and 9 are polyvalent, a larger input to cell 1 than cell 2 cannot fire these cells. However, such an imbalance can prevent cell 9 from firing.

To see how cell 8 can fire, we consider the polyvalent cells 8 and 10 of two different motivational channels. Cells 8 and 10 compete via the inhibitory (interneuronal) pathways 13. The polyvalent cells 8 and 10 also receive inputs from external cue representations via the conditionable pathways 11 and 12, respectively, whose LTM traces (within the filled hemicircles abutting cells 8 and 10) encode conditioned reinforcer properties of their respective external cues. These LTM traces are assumed to be cholinergic.

The conditioned reinforcer inputs combine with drive and arousal inputs at their respective polyvalent cells, which begin to fire if their thresholds are exceeded. The polyvalent cells thereupon compete among themselves via the "intrinsic" feedback inhibitory pathways 13, as they simultaneously try to excite themselves via positive feedback pathways such as $8 \to 4 \to 6 \to 8$.

If, for example, cell 8 wins this competition, then the transmitter gate in pathway $4 \to 6$ is depleted as the suprathreshold reverberation bursting through cell 8 via pathway $8 \to 4 \to 6 \to 8$ drives LTM changes in pathway 11. The reverberation thus induces conditioned reinforcer changes even as it prepares the network for motivational reset by rapid offset of pathway 11 or a rapid increment in pathway 3.

32. A Sensory Dipole Field: The Synchronization Problem and DC Potential Shifts

Figure 13 depicts the minimal anatomy that I will need to join together external cue representations. This dipole field possesses additional structure compared to Figure 12 because it solves a specialized design problem, which I call the *synchronization problem* of classical conditioning. The synchronization problem recognizes that without specialized network buffers, Pavlovian associations could rapidly extinguish whenever a CS and US were presented with different inter-stimulus delays on successive learning trials. The synchronization problem was solved in Grossberg (1971) and provided the impetus for my later work on reinforcement and motivation.

For present purposes, I need to emphasize one difference between Figure 12 and Figure 13. The anatomy in Figure 13 separates the firing of polyvalent cells from the STM reverberation through gated dipoles. Owing to this property, a sensory representation can reverberate in STM and thereby deliver signals to a **polyvalent** cell, or cells, without

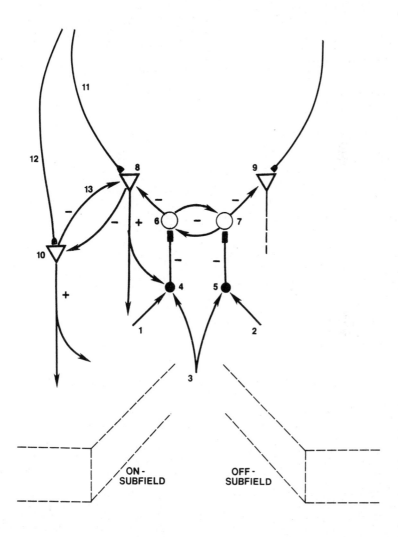

Figure 12. A motivational dipole field. The text describes how individual motivational dipoles are joined together by competitive feedback networks to regulate which dipole(s) will reverberate in STM and thereby release positive or negative incentive motivation in response to the changing balance of drive inputs, arousal inputs, and conditioned reinforcing signals.

Chapter 3

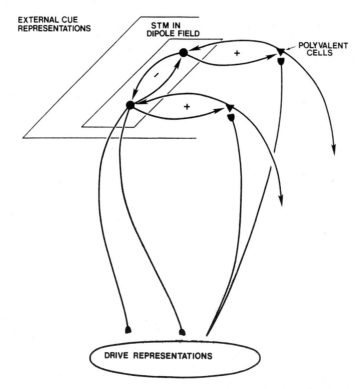

Figure 13. Interaction of external cue and incentive motivation signals at polyvalent cells. Let a set of nodes, or cells, in the dipole field be activated by an external scene. A pattern of short-term memory activity across the nodes represents the scene. Each such node sends an excitatory signal to its polyvalent node, or cell. Signal size is an increasing function of short-term memory activity. These specific signals are insufficient to fire the polyvalent cells. Sufficiently large incentive motivational signals from a drive representation must simultaneously converge on the polyvalent cells to fire them. The incentive motivational pathways are conditionable. A drive representation will therefore preferentially activate those polyvalent cells whose cues were paired with this drive representation in the past. The drive representation can thereby fire a subset of the polyvalent cells that are activated by the external scene. The relative rate of firing of each polyvalent cell will depend jointly on the short-term memory activity of its trigger cues in the scene and on the relative size of its long-term memory trace in the conditioned reinforcer pathway. When a polyvalent cell fires, it delivers positive feedback signals to the cue-activated cells that supply it with specific short-term memory signals. This positive feedback from polyvalent cells selectively augments the short-term memory activities of certain cue-activated cells, which thereupon can more strongly inhibit the short-term memory of other representations in the dipole field using the short-term memory normalization property. The incentive motivational properties of certain cues thereby alter the set of cues to which the network pays attention. The polyvalent cells that can maintain their firing can also read out learned patterns (e.g., motor commands) to other parts of the network.

firing these cells. A polyvalent cell in Figure 13 can fire only if it simultaneously receives STM signals from an external cue representation and incentive motivation signals from a drive representation. This property is analogous to John's (1966, 1967) reports that certain polyvalent cortical cells that are involved in cortical conditioning can fire only in response to a sum of CS and US signals. The property is also analogous to the effects of anodal DC potential shifts on cortical conditioning (Morrell, 1961; Rusinov, Note 1). In my theory, the anodal DC shift replaces the requirement of an incentive motivational signal to fire polyvalent cortical output cells.

33. The Multidimensional Nature of Secondary Conditioning

The functional separation of STM reverberation and polyvalent cell firing implies the following description of how a CS acquires US properties to control observable behavior (Grossberg, 1971). This description shows how to overcome the asymmetry between CS and US in the modified Rescorla-Wagner equation (8), explains the Dickinson and Mackintosh (1979) data on selective effects of distinct reinforcers on associability, and shows that drive representations are functionally separate "processors" from cue representations, in contrast with the Pearce and Hall (1980) theory.

Let a CS activate the population V_{11} (Figure 14), which thereupon begins to reverberate in STM. Then V_{11} sends specific signals to the polyvalent cell population V_{12} (among others) and nonspecific signals to the drive representations. Nothing else happens until a US arrives at population V_{21}. This is because V_{12} can fire only if it receives an input from V_{11} and an incentive motivation input from a drive representation, but the signal from V_{11} to the drive representations is initially too small to fire them. When the US perturbs V_{21}, V_{21} sends signals to the polyvalent cells V_{22} and to the drive representations. These latter signals can fire a certain drive representation, if its drive input is large enough, because the cue firing V_{21} is a US for that drive representation, which I will henceforth denote by D_2. When D_2 fires, it releases nonspecific incentive motivation signals to all the external cue representations. Now five things happen.

First, because V_{11} and D_2 are both active, the LTM traces in the pathway from V_{11} to D_2 are strengthened. When these LTM traces get strong enough, the CS alone will be able to fire D_2. Second, the nonspecific incentive motivational signal from D_2 combines with the US-derived signal from V_{21} at V_{22}, thereby firing polyvalent cell signals from V_{22}, which read out an unconditioned response (UR) pattern. Third, because the incentive motivation signal is nonspecific, it also combines with the CS-derived signal from V_{11} at V_{12}, thereby firing the polyvalent cells V_{12}. Fourth, because D_2 and V_{12} are both active, the LTM traces in the pathway from D_2 to V_{12} are strengthened. Fifth, the polyvalent cells V_{12} fire sampling signals to the cells at which the UR pattern is being read out. These signals encode (a fractional component of) the UR in the LTM traces of this pathway. The encoded pattern will henceforth be read out as a conditioned response (CR) pattern. The CS thereby acquires US properties owing to LTM encoding in conditioned reinforcer, incentive motivation, and habit strength pathways.

This network provides a simple answer to the synchronization question: How does the US turn on the CS with just the right time lag to sample read out of the UR pattern? The same incentive motivation burst that allows V_{22} to read out the UR also allows V_{12} to emit sampling signals that read in the CR.

In the remaining sections I will use the properties of adaptive resonance and reset in the cognitive circuits (Section 19) and in the cognitive-motivational circuits (Sections 30–33) to suggest explanations of conditioning and attentional data, including data that no single formal model can explain.

34. Unblocking, Context, and Habituation

Unblocking is produced by the surprising omission of a second shock (Dickinson, Hall, and Mackintosh, 1976). In my theory this is because the active internal repre-

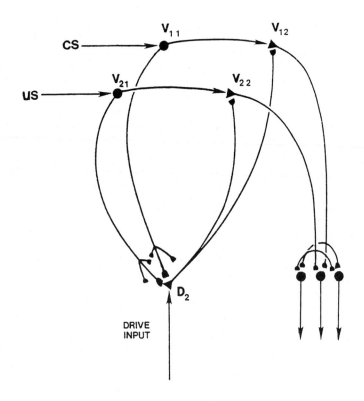

Figure 14. Path equivalence of CS and US representations. Both the conditioned stimulus (CS) and the unconditioned stimulus (US) activate similar network designs. This path equivalence property overcomes the asymmetry of CS and US contributions to the modified Rescorla-Wagner Equation 8. Firing of the polyvalent cells V_{12} and V_{22} is prevented except when sufficiently large specific signals from V_{11} and V_{21}, respectively, and nonspecific signals from D_2 simultaneously converge at the polyvalent cells. The network stages $\{V_{11}, V_{12}\}$ are part of the CS representation. The stages $\{V_{21}, V_{22}\}$ are part of the US representation. The CS and US activate similar network anatomies, but the LTM traces in these anatomies are not identically distributed. In particular, a US-activated signal from V_{21} to D_2 can fire D_2 if the drive input is sufficiently large. A CS-activated signal from V_{11} to D_2 cannot fire D_2. See the text for how CS–US pairing endows the CS with conditioned reinforcer, incentive motivation, and habit readout capabilities.

sentations of previously presented cues read out a learned expectancy whose mismatch by the unexpected event triggers dipole reset and consequent STM enhancement of previously overshadowed cues (Section 23).

Experiments might be designed to test how the amount of rebound or enhancement depends on the number of cues that have been stored in STM when the unexpected event occurs. Due to the limited-capacity restriction imposed by STM normalization, storing more cues can reduce the STM activity of each cue and thereby reduce the rate of transmitter depletion in each dipole gate. The rebound pattern in response to a fixed arousal burst will therefore change as a function of the number of active representations. The simplest version of this idea suggests that if more cues are simultaneously stored in STM for a given amount of time, then they will each be rebounded less by an unexpected event. Let us suppose that a less rebounded cue representation retains more STM activity than a more rebounded cue representation and that this residual activity can summate with the STM activity elicited by a later presentation of the same cue. Let two experimental groups differ according to how many cues are stored in STM and expose both groups to an unexpected stimulus array that includes one of the previously stored cues and a new cue. Suppose that the unexpected stimulus array resets STM by rebounding or enhancing the previously stored representations. Other things being equal, a less rebounded cue may preserve more residual STM activity for summation with its reoccurrence as part of the unexpected event. If this happens, the cue's total STM activity will be larger if it was part of a larger set of previously stored items than a smaller set of items. Hence, it will be better attended in the presence of the new cue.

However, other things are not usually equal. Storing more cues simultaneously may provide each cue with less STM activity due to the normalization property. Hence, the occurrence of a smaller reset per cue may provide no advantage to larger sets of cues. By contrast, storing more cues might cause more of their STM activities to be enhanced, rather than rebounded, by an unexpected event. When this occurs an advantage may indeed accrue to larger sets of cues. Both of these effects will be sensitive to the duration with which the cues are stored before they are reset. Large STM activities deplete their transmitter gates faster than small STM activities. Consequently, the relative disadvantage to smaller sets of stored cues may be greater if the storage duration is shorter. Finally, a switch from more stored cues to a new event that includes only one of these cues may cause a greater mismatch, and hence be more unexpected, than a switch from fewer stored cues to the same new event, although normalization tends to counter this effect also. The reset arousal burst that occurs after more cues are stored may thus be larger and may offset any advantage due to slower transmitter habituation. Parametric studies are needed in which the number of cues originally stored, the duration of storage, the number of new cues to be stored, and the amount of overlap between the two sets of cues are varied to disentangle the relative contributions of STM normalization, mismatch, and reset mechanisms on the reallocation of attention.

35. Double Shock Experiments: Initial STM Advantage of Surprising Events

To explain the interesting experiment of Mackintosh, Bygrave, and Picton (1977) (Section 5), I accept the fact that on the first compound trial, the tone is at its worst as a predictor of shock, having never before been paired with shock. I hereby avoid the internal problem within Mackintosh's theory (Section 3). Because the tone has never before been presented, it is most unexpected on the first compound trial. More precisely, on the first trial the tone possesses its maximal potency for mismatching the learned sensory expectancies that are operative in the situation, in particular, the expectancies that are controlled by situational cues. Consequently, tone onset triggers a relatively large STM reset that abets the STM storage of the tone's sensory representation. This is the first main point: The tone's very unexpectedness can enhance its initial STM storage without regard to what its STM representation samples later on. On successive tone presentations, this initial advantage will fade, other things being equal, as the tone is incorporated into the pattern of learned feedback expectancies.

After the tone's advantageous initial STM storage takes place, the tone's STM representation begins to emit several types of signals. Some of these signals initiate the process whereby the tone is incorporated into higher order chunks (Section 18). Others of these signals begin to sample the drive representations (Section 30). On the first compound trial, the light can also send negative conditioned reinforcer signals to the drive representation with which it was previously associated.

An important issue is: How much are the light's conditioned reinforcer signals reduced by the occurrence of the tone? For example, such a reduction can occur because of a direct STM competition between light and tone representations via the STM normalization effect. An indirect reduction can be due to antagonistic rebound of the active chunks that bind situational cues together into context-sensitive representations. Such a rebound can be triggered by the arousal burst that is contingent on the tone's unexpectedness in a given experimental context. Inhibiting these chunks can eliminate the subliminal feedback signaling to expected situational cues, including the light, and can therefore decrease the light's STM activity by removing a source of STM matching. This issue also arises on Trial 25 in Group Y of the Kamin (1969) experiment reviewed below (Section 45).

36. Conditioned Reinforcer Learning

After both the tone STM representation and the light STM representation send signals to the drive representations, the light representation can supraliminally activate the negative drive representation that was previously activated by shock on conditioning trials, because the light is now a conditioned reinforcer (Sections 27 and 33). Once this drive representation is supraliminally activated, the tone's sampling signals can acquire some negative conditioned reinforcer properties via LTM encoding during the first moments after tone-light onset. This LTM change can occur whenever the tone's sampling signals are contiguous with supraliminal activity at the drive representation. On the first compound trial, the tone representation emits unusually large sampling signals because it has acquired unusually large STM activity due to its unexpectedness. Large sampling signals cause their LTM traces to encode sampled STM patterns faster than do small sampling signals. The tone can therefore acquire negative incentive properties much more rapidly on a trial when it is unexpected than on a trial when it is expected. This fact explains why the tone can condition so well—as a conditioned reinforcer—on the trial when it is first presented.

37. Incentive Motivation Feedback Influences STM Competition

As the tone begins to acquire negative reinforcing properties by being conditioned to the negative drive representation, the firing of this drive representation also releases conditioned incentive motivation signals preferentially to the light representation (Figure 13). More precisely, the light representation activates its polyvalent cells directly and via the conditioned reinforcer-incentive motivation loop through the drive representations. Then these polyvalent cells thereupon feed excitatory signals back to the light representation to further enhance its STM activity. Because of STM normalization among the cue representations, the enhanced STM of the light representation competitively inhibits the STM of the tone representation. Whether this feedback inhibition can entirely shut off the tone representation depends on how many and how intense the prior light-shock trials were (and thus how large and selective the conditioned incentive feedback signals are) and on how surprising the tone was (and thus how big an advantage it acquired in its initial STM storage).

If the tone representation is entirely suppressed, it will have acquired negative conditioned reinforcer properties but no conditioned incentive-motivation feedback to its own sensory representation. Even this eventuality should not prevent the tone from eliciting fearful reactions when it is later presented alone. Because the light is not then present to suppress it, the STM normalization property allows the tone to be stored in STM, whereupon the tone's conditioned reinforcer signals can elicit a fear reaction.

38. Salience Influences Overshadowing

This explanation also shows why, when the two CSs differ markedly in their intensity or salience, the more salient cue can overshadow the less salient cue (Mackintosh, 1976). In my theory the greater cue saliency or intensity gives it an initially larger STM strength, larger LTM sampling signals between cue and drive representations, and thus a competitive advantage from the very start.

39. Overshadowing on a Single Trial

These concepts suggest how overshadowing effects can occur when only a single trial of compound conditioning is given (Mackintosh, 1971; Mackintosh and Reese, 1979). As seen above, the tone's best chance to avoid overshadowing is to achieve strong initial STM storage. Without an initial advantage the tone's conditioned reinforcer learning will be slow at best in the time interval before the light's incentive feedback enables it to suppress the tone's STM. I have also indicated above several ways to abet tone conditioning.

We are now ready to consider why a second shock 10 seconds after a first shock on the first compound trial need not make the tone more fearful. Also, we will see why two shocks on one trial followed by either one or two shocks on a second trial can lead to a more fearful tone than one shock on the first trial followed by either one or two shocks on a second trial.

40. The Tone Is More Unexpected After Two Shocks

If the tone is not on when the second shock occurs, then the tone's STM representation may not send sampling signals to the drive representation when it is activated by the second shock. Thus, the tone does not acquire more negative conditioned reinforcer strength because of the second shock on the first compound trial. Why then does the tone acquire significantly more negative conditioned reinforcer strength on the second compound trial? This can be explained by noting that the second shock on the first compound trial occurs after a series of trials during which only one shock occurs. Thus, the second shock is unexpected. Also, the second shock occurs after the tone has unexpectedly occurred. The tone's unexpected occurrence initiates the process whereby the tone representation is incorporated into the pattern of situational expectancies. The occurrence of the second shock then alters the pattern of learned situational expectancies beyond the alterations already triggered by the tone. Consequently, when a tone occurs on a second compound trial that follows two shocks, it is more unexpected than a tone that occurs on a second compound trial that follows one shock. Due to the tone's greater unexpectedness, the tone's initial STM storage on the second compound trial is greater, its sampling signals to the drive representations are larger, and its rate of conditioned reinforcer learning is accelerated. An independent test of the tone's greater unexpectedness would be achieved if the tone elicits a larger P300 evoked potential when it occurs after two shocks than after one shock.

This description of how a tone achieves its superior STM storage after two shocks than after one shock suggests that the light may also be better stored in STM after two shocks than after one shock, because both cues disconfirm the second shock component of the situational expectancies. A greater initial STM storage of the light does not prevent the tone from strengthening its negative reinforcer strength on the second compound trial for two reasons: (a) The relative advantage of the light is not greater than that of the tone, so the light will not competitively inhibit the tone via the normalization property during the phase of initial STM storage. (b) Once both the light and tone representations begin to send signals to the drive representations, the larger signals emitted by the light representation can speed up the tone's conditioned reinforcer learning by increasing the activity of the negative drive representation. One way to test the effect of the second shock on the initial STM storage of the light is to measure the P300 evoked potential that is triggered if the light alone, rather than a light-tone compound, is presented after one or two shocks.

41. Situational Cues

Having come this far, we are now ready to raise an issue that Pearce and Hall (1980) do not mention. When the second shock occurs on the first compound trial, it is a surprising event whose negative reinforcing properties will be conditioned to simultaneously active cue representations. These representations will include the representations of situational cues that are again present when the tone is presented on the test trial. Why does the tone-plus-situational cue read-out of negative conditioned reinforcer signals not create more negative incentive after the second shock than it does after the first shock? My answer is that the surprising occurrence of the tone on the test trials tends to suppress the STM of the situational cues via antagonistic rebounds. Then the tone's STM will tend to control the net conditioned reinforcer readout from attended sensory representations. To test this explanation, one might try covarying two experimental properties: the intensity of the second shock and how surprising the tone is on the next test trial.

42. Release From Overshadowing by an Unexpected US

In experiments wherein the tone is repeated during several compound trials, the tone's initial STM advantage due to its unexpectedness wears off as it is incorporated into the pattern of situational expectancies. The tone's conditionability thereby fades. If an unexpected US follows a light-tone combination, the tone's STM activity can be amplified owing to the differential enhancement of overshadowed representations by the STM reset event (Section 23). The US also activates a drive representation. Because of the simultaneity of enhanced STM activity in the tone representation and in the drive representation, the tone can acquire both conditioned reinforcer and incentive motivation properties. These LTM changes are not rapidly terminated by competitive signaling from the light representation because the STM of this representation has been attenuated by the reset event.

If the unexpected US reoccurs on several trials, its unexpectedness also fades. By the time this happens, however, the unexpected US has endowed the tone's representation with a conditioned positive feedback loop to itself via the drive representation. A shift gradually occurs as trials proceed from the tone's initial STM advantage due to the shock's unexpectedness—which is mediated by situational expectancies and the orienting subsystem—to a more lasting LTM advantage due to the tone's reinforcing and incentive motivation properties—which manifest themselves as an attentional resonance.

43. Modulation of US and Drive Input Effects by Expectancies, Conditioned Reinforcers, and Transmitter Habituation

A further remark needs to be made about which drive representation is activated by the shock US. This is a subtle matter because it depends on US intensity, the degree of US expectedness, and the conditioned reinforcing potency of the light representation due to prior learning.

Were a shock to suddenly turn on out of context, it would certainly activate a negative drive representation (Section 28). This need not happen if a shock turns on while the light representation is on. This is true because the light representation is already sending conditioned reinforcer signals to the negative drive representation when the shock occurs. The unexpectedness of the shock attenuates the STM activity of the light representation. A sudden reduction in conditioned reinforcing signals to the negative drive representation is thereby caused. The shock can offset this reduction in input by generating its own unconditional input to the negative drive representation. If the shock input is larger than the prior level of conditioned reinforcing signals, then the total input to the negative drive representation will increase and a fear reaction will be elicited. If, however, the shock-induced input is smaller than the conditioned reinforcer decrement, then the total input to the negative drive representation will suddenly decrease. The shock can thereby cause an antagonistic rebound that activates the positive drive representation that shares a gated dipole with the negative drive representation (Section 13). The onset of shock can thereby cause a transient relief reaction. This argument also indicates how an unexpected increase in a shock US can cause the tone to become a negative reinforcer, whereas an unexpected decrease in the shock US can cause the tone to become a positive reinforcer (Kamin, 1968, 1969; Rescorla, 1969; Wagner, 1969; Weisman and Litner, 1969), despite the fact that the shock US activates a negative drive representation in both cases. Given a fixed decrease in shock intensity, the rebound size should be an increasing function of shock unexpectedness (measured perhaps as a larger P300 evoked potential) and an increasing function of the conditioned reinforcer strength of the light (measured perhaps by the number of preceding light-shock trials). The emotional meaning of the shock is thus determined by an interaction of its unconditional input with the pattern of active expectancies and conditioned reinforcing signals at the moment of its occurrence. In Grossberg (1984) I propose that a similar argument, wherein hunger drive input replaces shock input, explains some paradoxical findings about eating and satiety. Oropharyngeal signals that are gated by conditioned reinforcer LTM traces are suggested to alter the effects of hunger drive input much as light-induced signals that are gated by conditioned reinforcer LTM traces are suggested to alter the effect of shock input.

Varying the suddenness with which a shock is turned on can alter these conclusions by influencing both the expectancy and the reinforcing properties of shock. One effect of shock onset rate on reinforcement is the following: Suppose that a shock slowly turns on from an initial intensity of 0 to a final intensity of J. Because the shock increase is gradual, the transmitter in the on-channel of the gated dipole is gradually depleted, or habituates, at a rate proportional to signal strength times the amount of available transmitter (Section 13). Because the transmitter level accumulates slowly, by the time the shock intensity J is reached, the amount of transmitter Z can be much smaller than its maximal amount B. Thus the effect of intensity J is proportional to $f(J + I)Z$, where I is the arousal level, and $f(w)$ is the sigmoid signal (Section 22). By contrast, a sudden shock creates the signal $f(J + I)B$, where $B > Z$, because transmitter is fully accumulated when the shock intensity suddenly switches from intensity 0 to intensity J. Sudden shocks can thereby be more negatively reinforcing than gradually increasing shocks (Church, 1969; Miller, 1960). In Grossberg (1984) I suggest a similar argument about transmitter habituation rates in gated dipoles to explain drug tolerance and withdrawal effects, including symptoms like rebound insomnia. Many of the expectancy, reinforcing, and transmitter habituation effects that occur during conditioning experiments have mechanistic analogs in other behavioral and clinical syndromes.

44. Latent Inhibition

Similar concepts can be used to explain the following interesting Hall and Pearce (1979) experiment. In Stage 1 of this experiment, a tone was paired with a weak shock in the experimental group. In the control group a light was paired with the same shock. In the next stage the tone preceded a stronger shock in both groups. In the experimental group, learning was slower. In my theory this occurs because the tone is more unexpected in the control group, thereby acquiring a greater initial advantage in STM, and therefore conditions faster, as in Section 43.

Rather than continue to explain other data that Pearce and Hall (1980) mention, I will suggest an explanation of some classical experiments that seem to go beyond the capabilities of all the formal theories. I will also suggest an interdisciplinary paradigm to test my explanations.

45. Interaction of STM Reset, STM Normalization, and LTM Gating in CER Experiments

The STM normalization property often holds only partially, due to the fact that feedback inhibitory interactions can decrease as a function of intercellular distances. These distance-dependent interactions help to define the generalization gradients that determine which cues mutually interact during conditioning experiments (Grossberg, 1975, 1981b). A possible instance of a partial STM normalization effect due to Pavlovian conditioning is the somewhat faster learning of a conditioned emotional response to a compound stimulus than to its component stimuli (Kamin, 1969). Parametric studies of compound training trials using approximately equal salient stimuli whose similarity is parametrically altered across experiments, followed by extinction of the compound, or of each component taken separately across groups in each experiment, would provide useful theoretical information about the interaction between the degree of STM normalization and the rate of CER learning.

Another piece of data reported in Kamin (1969) also suggests an STM normalization effect. His Group Y first learned a CER to a noise stimulus (N) on 16 trials, then received a nonreinforced compound light-noise (LN) stimulus for 8 trials, and finally received 4 more nonreinforced N trials. His Group Z also received 16 CER trials with stimulus N, but these trials were followed by 12 nonreinforced trials with N. Three main effects were found: The first LN trial in Group Y showed a larger suppression ratio than the first nonreinforced N trial in Group Z. The suppression ratio increased on successive nonreinforced trials of LN in Group Y and of N in Group Z. On the first nonreinforced N trial in Group Y (its 25th trial), the suppression ratio suddenly dropped to the value that it had on the first nonreinforced LN trial. This suppression ratio was, moreover, lower than the suppression ratio on Trial 25 in Group Z.

Kamin was impressed by the rapidity with which the suppression ratio changed on the first nonreinforced LN trial and on the first nonreinforced N trial for Group Y. He realized that the Y animals rapidly noticed L and that their processing of L somehow attenuated the suppression. In my theory the surprising occurrence of L abets its STM storage, weakens the STM storage of N via STM normalization, and thereby reduces the negative conditioned reinforcing signals from L to the drive representations.

That an STM rather than an LTM effect is primary on the transitional trials is further suggested by what happens on Trial 25 in Group Y. When N is then presented without L, its representation can acquire a larger STM activity. This representation can then read out—on that very trial—a larger negative conditioned reinforcing signal to the drive representations. The negative reinforcing LTM trace is there to be read out because the extinction of the N representation on LN trials was slowed owing to its small STM activity.

46. Overshadowing During Key Pecking

Newman and Baron (1965) reinforced pigeons who pecked a vertical white line on a green key (the $S+$) but not a green key alone (the $S-$). They tested cue discrimination by tilting the line at various orientations during recall trials. A generalization gradient of pecking was found, indicating that the vertical line was discriminated. By contrast, no generalization gradient was found if the $S-$ on learning trials was a red key or if the $S-$ was a vertical white line on a red key.

Newman and Benefeld (cited in Honig, 1970) used a vertical white line on a green key as $S+$ and a green key as $S-$ but tested and found generalization of the line orientation on a black key. They also tested generalization on a black key following training without a green $S-$ and again found a generalization gradient, by contrast with the case where testing used a green key. They interpreted this effect as "cue utilization during testing rather than cue selection during learning" (p.202). This interpretation does not explain how the orientation cue could be learned on training trials if it was not discriminated using a green background on test trials yet could be discriminated using a black background on test trials if it was not learned on training trials.

My explanation of these data begins by noting that color cues are prepotent over orientation cues in the pigeon, other things being equal. Consequently, when a vertical white line on a green background is first presented, the green representations will partially overshadow the orientation representations. (I will talk about "green" and "orientation" representations as a shorthand for more sophisticated coding notions that we do not need here.) Grossberg and Levine (1975) and Levine and Grossberg (1976) describe some factors that control how prepotent representations can mask the STM activities of other representations due to competitive feedback interactions.

When the line-on-green cues are first presented, they enjoy an additional advantage in their STM storage. Their unexpectedness in the context of the experiment's situational cues will strengthen the STM activities of the line-on-green cues as the STM activities of the situational cue representations are rebounded. These rebounds should elicit a P300 evoked potential.

After the line-on-green representations are initially stored in STM, the green cues can increase their relative STM advantage as they acquire conditioned reinforcer and conditioned incentive motivation properties. They do this by means of the conditioned-reinforcer-incentive-motivation loop, the polyvalent cell firing constraint, and the STM normalization property in the manner described within Section 37.

The orientation representations can also acquire conditioned reinforcer and incentive motivation properties just so long as their STM activities are not suppressed. Their learning rates will be slower than those of the green representations, because their sampling signals in the conditionable pathways are smaller due to their smaller STM activities. Hence, their conditioned pathways will remain weak compared to those of the green representations. As conditioning continues, the orientation representations may be entirely suppressed if the conditioned advantage of the color cues becomes sufficiently great to drive orientational STM activities to zero by competitive feedback across the cue representations.

The unexpected nonoccurrence of reward in response to pecking the green key causes an antagonistic rebound that excites the off-cells of the previously most active STM representations. The active incentive motivational pathways thereupon sample a large off-response in the green representational dipoles (Figure 11). As this experimental contingency reoccurs on several trials, the *net* incentive motivation feedback to the green dipoles becomes progressively smaller due to dipole competition between the conditioned on-cell and off-cell pathways to these dipoles. This is just the extinction mechanism of Section 28 acting at the sensory representations rather than at the drive representations.

Even zero net incentive feedback may not be small enough to extinguish the green representation, however, because of the innate advantage of color over orientation. Negative net incentive feedback may be needed to overcome green's innate competitive advantage. Net negative feedback is needed if net positive conditioned reinforcer-incentive feedback to the orientation representation is not sufficient to offset the innate competitive advantage of the color representation when the latter receives net zero conditioned feedback.

This framework explains why the white vertical line is discriminable on a background during test trials even if it is not discriminable on a green background during test trials in an experiment without a green $S-$ on learning trials. Removing green on test trials eliminates competitive feedback from the color representations to the orientation representations. The STM field is thereby renormalized. In the renormalized field, even small conditioned-reinforcer—incentive-motivation feedback signals can provide the white vertical line representation with a significant competitive advantage for STM storage.

47. The Problem of Perseverating Prepotent Cues

The above discussion shows how the conditioned-reinforcer—incentive-motivation feedback loop enables representations to overcome innate competitive STM disadvantages. Some further remarks might clarify why the incentive motivation pathway must send branches to both the on-cells and off-cells of cortical dipoles, just as the conditioned reinforcer pathway sends branches to both the on-cells and off-cells of the drive representation dipoles. The main benefit is that some cues can lose net positive feedback as other cues gain net positive feedback while both sets of cues are conditioned to the same drive representation. This property avoids the following dilemma.

Suppose that rebound that conditions zero net feedback to the green representation occurs among the drive representations rather than among the cue representations. Then rebound activates a negative drive representation, and the net conditioned reinforcer output controlled by the green representation becomes small, rather than the net incentive motivational output driven by a large conditioned reinforcer output becoming small, as in Section 46. This mechanism is unstable for the following reason: As soon as the orientation representation takes over in STM, its positive conditioned reinforcer signals activate the positive drive representation. When this drive representation sends incentive motivational feedback to the cortex, the green representation receives conditioned positive feedback because the negative drive representation is momentarily inhibited. Then the green representation can quickly overshadow the orientation representation because of its innate competitive advantage. As soon as the green representation is reinstated in STM, its conditioned reinforcer signals cause readout of net negative incentive from the competing drive representation. The green representation is consequently shut off, the orientation representation is disinhibited, and the cycle repeats itself.

Any viable alternative to the present network description must also avoid this problem of perseverating prepotent representations. In particular, a more sophisticated coding analysis would replace "green" representations and "orientation" representations with heterarchical network encodings wherein one representation's prepotence for masking other representations would depend on its heterarchical position with respect to all representations. In Grossberg (1978b, Sections 25–47) I suggest some rules whereby heterarchical masking can be designed to choose those chunks that provide the most informative prediction in a prescribed cue context during recognition and recall.

48. Two Distinct P300 Evoked Potentials in Cortex and Hippocampus

The previous discussion of overshadowing during key pecking suggests a striking psychophysiological prediction. I have argued that the unexpected nonoccurrence of reward in response to pecking the green key can gradually extinguish the net incentive motivation to the green representation. This occurs as the incentive motivation LTM traces sample the antagonistic rebound within the green representation on successive nonreinforced trials. The reset of the green representation also has an immediate effect on each trial. Offset of this representation rapidly shuts off conditioned reinforcer input to the positive drive representation. If the green representation has been conditioned to the drive representation on sufficiently many previous reinforcer trials, the reduction in conditioned reinforcer input will be large enough to overcome the STM hysteresis that defends the positive drive representation against reset. Then a rebound will occur within the drive dipole itself, thereby activating its negative drive representation. If a new cue is stored in STM at the time of this negative drive rebound, it will become a negative conditioned reinforcer by sampling the rebound.

Let us consider the minimal assumption that any massive antagonistic rebound in a catecholamine dipole system is registered as a P300 evoked potential—keeping in mind that rebounds in different brain regions may occur yet ultimately be associated with distinct evoked potentials. Then the above discussion predicts that the nonoccurrence of expected reward can trigger a cortical P300 by mismatching a learned expectancy. The reset of cortical STM can thereupon trigger a hippocampal P300 by rapidly withdrawing conditioned reinforcer input. The size of this second P300 should, moreover, depend on the strength of the conditioned reinforcer due to the number of preceding conditioning trials. If these P300 predictions hold up, they will clarify that a P300 can be elicited by different operations in different brain regions. They will also refine our understanding of the information processing substrates of overshadowing and discrimination learning by distinguishing rebounds that motivationally extinguish cues owing to their cognitive irrelevance from rebounds that directly elicit new conditioned reinforcer learning.

49. Nonmonotonic Relation Between P300 and CNV

The key pecking experiment also suggests a psychophysiological test that would argue for P300 as a measure of STM reset and against P300 as a measure of LTM learning. I suggest that the unexpected occurrence of a reward in response to the line-on-green cue will elicit a P300. As this P300 shrinks on successive reward trials, I suggest that the line-on-green cue will elicit a growing motivational CNV that reflects the progressive conditioning of positive net incentive motivation (Cant and Bickford, 1967; Irwin, Rebert, McAdam, and Knott, 1966). By contrast, I suggest that the unexpected nonoccurrence of a reward in response to green alone will elicit a P300. As this P300 shrinks on successive unrewarded trials, the green cue should elicit a shrinking motivational CNV as the net incentive motivation of the irrelevant green cue is extinguished. In the former case a conditioned response is learned, whereas in the latter case a conditioned response is extinguished. If these predictions are verified, then we can conclude that P300 size does not differentiate opposite outcomes in LTM because a monotonic decrease in P300 can predict either CNV increase (learning) or CNV decrease (extinction) within the same experiment.

50. Some Comparisons With the Formal Models

Pearce and Hall (1980) ascribe extinction to competition between CS-US and $CS - \overline{US}$ ($\overline{US}$ = no US) associations due to an "inhibitory link between the US and US memories" (p.546). They suggest this concept to replace Rescorla and Wagner's (1972) notion that extinction is due to weakening of previously established associations. My own concept of how a conditioned reinforcing cue's input to a gated dipole is extinguished is superficially similar to Pearce and Hall's (Grossberg, 1972a, 1972b). I also suggest, however, that the competitive extinction process is mediated by the drive representations and is due to gated dipole rebounds. Neither these concepts nor their mechanistic substrates appear in the formal models.

Instead, the formal models restrict themselves to links between CS and US memories, which in turn read out the CR. In my theory, readout of the CR does not require activation of a US memory, but only of the LTM-encoded patterns that were sampled by the CS from STM when the US was active, as in Sections 15 and 18. These LTM-encoded patterns can be a fractional component or other transformation of the US, due to nonisotropy of CS and US sampling pathways across the network, or due to STM transformations of the US pattern before it is encoded in LTM at the CS-activated synaptic knobs. I do not see how direct links from CS to US can account for the sometimes significant differences between UR and CR, whereas an STM-mediated theory can easily do so (Seligman and Hager, 1972).

Pearce and Hall (1980) suggest "that a US representation is activated only by the omission of an *expected* US" (p.543) and suggest a formula for the intensity λ of the reinforcer US, namely,

$$\bar{\lambda} = V_\Sigma - \bar{V}_\Sigma - \lambda. \tag{14}$$

I agree that an off-cell rebound can be activated by the nonoccurrence of an expected event, mediated by a mismatch-contingent arousal burst. However, this is not the only way to activate a US in my theory. Just as sudden offset of shock can trigger relief (Denny, 1971), a rebound can also be caused by the mere offset of a reinforcer. Furthermore, the equation (14) for rebound size is inadequate for many reasons: It does not explain the inverted U in reinforcement (Berlyne, 1969). It does not explain the analgesic effect whereby cutting J units of shock in half is less rewarding than shutting $J/2$ units of shock off (Campbell and Kraeling, 1953). It does not explain why the reinforcing effect of shock offset should depend on the prior duration of shock (Boe, 1966; Borozci, Storms, and Broen, 1964; Church, Raymond, and Beauchamp, 1967; Keehn, 1963; Strouthes, 1965). All of these properties obtain in gated dipoles (Grossberg, 1972b). Moreover, equation (14) lumps together LTM expectancy, STM matching, nonspecific arousal, and STM rebound properties in a way that obscures their mechanistic substrates, notably their influence on STM and LTM patterns rather than parameters.

At bottom, the formal models are led to these difficulties because they do not adequately distinguish the STM and LTM mechanisms that are used in the processing of expected and unexpected events. Consequently, the formal models cannot easily make the distinction that a surprising CS can reset STM in a manner that favors its own subsequent STM storage, whereas a fully predictable US can also be stored (or, as Pearce and Hall would say, "processed") in STM by resonating with an active feedback expectancy. The recent theorizing of Wagner (1978) on STM priming perhaps comes closest to making these distinctions within the stream of formal models.

51. Schedule Interactions and Behavioral Contrast

Similar difficulties occur in recent models of instrumental conditioning. Instead of overemphasizing LTM properties at the expense of STM properties, the Hinson and Staddon (1978) theory of schedule interactions and behavioral contrast completely forsakes the LTM effects to focus on STM competitive properties. In Grossberg (1981b) I show that the same theoretical ideas that I sketched herein can overcome some difficulties that Hinson and Staddon face in explaining their data, and I make some predictions to test these ideas.

Pavlovian and instrumental experiments that have heretofore been analysed in a fragmentary fashion by formal models, at the cost of implying internal paradoxes and restricting their predictive power, can be understood in a unified fashion in terms of a few psychophysiological mechanisms whose existence can be more directly validated by interdisciplinary experimental paradigms.

REFERENCE NOTE

1. Rusinov, V.S., An electrophysiological analysis of the connecting function in the cerebral cortex in the presence of a dominant area. Paper presented at the XIX International Physiology Congress, Montreal, 1953.

REFERENCES

Anand, B.K. and Pillai, R.V., Activation of single neurones in the hypothalamic feeding centres: Effect of gastric distension. *Journal of Physiology*, 1967, **192**, 63–77.

Beach, F.A., Characteristics of masculine "sex drive." In M.R. Jones (Ed.), **Nebraska symposium on motivation** (Vol. 4). Lincoln: University of Nebraska Press, 1956.

Berlyne, D.E., The reward-value of indifferent stimulation. In J.T. Tapp (Ed.), **Reinforcement and behavior**. New York: Academic Press, 1969.

Boe, E.E., Effect of punishment duration and intensity on the extinction of an instrumental response. *Journal of Experimental Psychology*, 1966, **72**, 125–131.

Bolles, R.C., **Theory of motivation**. New York: Harper and Row, 1967.

Borozci, G., Storms, L.H., and Broen, W.E., Response suppression and recovery of responding at different deprivation levels as functions of intensity and duration of punishment. *Journal of Comparative and Physiological Psychology*, 1964, **58**, 456–459.

Brown, J.L., Afterimages. In C.H. Graham (Ed.), **Vision and visual perception**. New York: Wiley, 1965.

Butcher, L.L. (Ed.), **Cholinergic-monoaminergic interactions in the brain**. New York: Academic Press, 1978.

Campbell, B.A. and Kraeling, D., Response strength as a function of drive level and amount of drive reduction. *Journal of Experimental Psychology*, 1953, **45**, 97–101.

Cant, B.R. and Bickford, R.G., The effect of motivation on the contingent negative variation (CNV). *Electroencephalography and Clinical Neurophysiology*, 1967, **23**, 594.

Carpenter, G.A. and Grossberg, S., Adaptation and transmitter gating in vertebrate photoreceptors. *Journal of Theoretical Neurobiology*, 1981, **1**, 1–42.

Church, R.M., Response suppression. In B.A. Campbell and R.M. Church (Eds.), **Punishment and aversive behavior**. New York: Appleton-Century-Crofts, 1969.

Church, R.M., Raymond, G.A., and Beauchamp, R.D., Response suppression as a function of intensity and duration of punishment. *Journal of Comparative and Physiological Psychology*, 1967, **63**, 39–44.

Denny, M.R., Relaxation theory and experiments. In F.R. Brush (Ed.), **Aversive conditioning and learning**. New York: Academic Press, 1971.

Dexter, W.R. and Merrill, H.K., Role of contextual discrimination in fear conditioning. *Journal of Comparative and Physiological Psychology*, 1969, **69**, 677–681.

Dickinson, A., Hall, G., and Mackintosh, N.J., Surprise and the attenuation of blocking. *Journal of Experimental Psychology: Animal Behavior Processes*, 1976, **2**, 213–222.

Dickinson, A. and Mackintosh, N.J., Reinforcer specificity in the enhancement of conditioning by posttrial surprise. *Journal of Experimental Psychology: Animal Behavior Processes*, 1979, **5**, 162–177.

Dunham, P.J., Punishment: Method and theory. *Psychological Review*, 1971, **78**, 58–70.

Dunham, P.J., Mariner, A., and Adams, H., Enhancement of off-key pecking by on-key punishment. *Journal of Experimental Analysis and Behavior*, 1969, **1**, 156–166.

Ellias, S.A. and Grossberg, S., Pattern formation, contrast control, and oscillations in the short term memory of shunting on-center off-surround networks. *Biological Cybernetics*, 1975, **20**, 69–98.

Epstein, A.N., Kissileff, H.R., and Stellar, E. (Eds.), **The neuropsychology of thirst: New findings and advances in concepts**. Washington, DC: V.H. Winston, 1973.

Estes, W.K., Outline of a theory of punishment. In B.A. Campbell and R.M. Church (Eds.), **Punishment and aversive behavior**. New York: Appleton-Century-Crofts, 1969.

Estes, W.K. and Skinner, B.F., Some quantitative properties of anxiety. *Journal of Experimental Psychology*, 1941, **29**, 390–400.

Freeman, W.J., **Mass action in the nervous system**. New York: Academic Press, 1975.

Freeman, W.J., EEG analysis gives model of neuronal template-matching mechanism for sensory search with olfactory bulb. *Biological Cybernetics*, 1980, **35**, 221–234.

Freeman, W.J., A neural mechanism for generalization over equivalent stimuli in the olfactory system. In S. Grossberg (Ed.), **Mathematical psychology and psychophysiology**. Providence, RI: American Mathematical Society, 1981.

Frey, P.W. and Sears, R.J., Model of conditioning incorporating the Rescorla-Wagner associative axiom, a dynamic attention rule, and a catastrophe rule. *Psychological Review*, 1978, **85**, 321–340.

Friedhoff, A.J. (Ed.), **Catecholamines and behavior: Vol. 1. Basic neurobiology**. New York: Plenum Press, 1975 (a).

Friedhoff, A.J. (Ed.), **Catecholamines and behavior, Vol. 2. Neuropsychopharmacology**. New York: Plenum Press, 1975 (b).

Gabriel, M., Foster, K., Orona, E., Saltwick, S.E., and Stanton, M., Neuronal activity of cingulate cortex, anteroventral thalamus and hippocampal formation in discriminative conditioning: Encoding and extraction of the significance of conditional stimuli. *Progress in Psychobiological and Physiological Psychology*, 1980, **9**, 125–231.

Gibson, J.J., **The ecological approach to visual perception**. Boston: Houghton Mifflin, 1979.

Grossberg, S., **The theory of embedding fields with applications to psychology and neurophysiology**. New York: Rockefeller Institute for Medical Research, 1964.

Grossberg, S., Nonlinear difference-differential equations in prediction and learning theory. *Proceedings of the National Academy of Sciences*, 1967, **58**, 1329–1334.

Grossberg, S., Some physiological and biochemical consequences of psychological postulates. *Proceedings of the National Academy of Sciences*, 1968, **60**, 758–765.

Grossberg, S., Embedding fields: A theory of learning with physiological implications. *Journal of Mathematical Psychology*, 1969, **6**, 209–239 (a).

Grossberg, S., On the serial learning of lists. *Mathematical Biosciences*, 1969, **4**, 201–253 (b).

Grossberg, S., Some networks that can learn, remember, and reproduce any number of complicated space-time patterns, I. *Journal of Mathematics and Mechanics*, 1969, **19**, 53–91 (c).

Grossberg, S., On the dynamics of operant conditioning. *Journal of Theoretical Biology*, 1971, **33**, 225–255.

Grossberg, S., A neural theory of punishment and avoidance, I: Qualitative theory. *Mathematical Biosciences*, 1972, **15**, 39–67 (a).

Grossberg, S., A neural theory of punishment and avoidance, II: Quantitative theory. *Mathematical Biosciences*, 1972, **15**, 253–285 (b).

Grossberg, S., Pattern learning by functional-differential neural networks with arbitrary path weights. In K. Schmitt (Ed.), **Delay and functional-differential equations and their applications**. New York: Academic Press, 1972 (c).

Grossberg, S., Contour enhancement, short-term memory, and constancies in reverberating neural networks. *Studies in Applied Mathematics*, 1973, **52**, 217–257.

Grossberg, S., Classical and instrumental learning by neural networks. In R. Rosen and F. Snell (Eds.), **Progress in theoretical biology** (Vol. 3). New York: Academic Press, 1974.

Grossberg, S., A neural model of attention, reinforcement, and discrimination learning. *International Review of Neurobiology*, 1975, **18**, 263–327.

Grossberg, S., Adaptive pattern classification and universal recoding, I: Parallel development and coding of neural feature detectors. *Biological Cybernetics*, 1976, **23**, 121–134 (a).

Grossberg, S., Adaptive pattern classification and universal recoding, II: Feedback, expectation, olfaction, and illusions. *Biological Cybernetics*, 1976, **23**, 187–202 (b).

Grossberg, S., Behavioral contrast in short-term memory: Serial binary memory models or parallel continuous memory models? *Journal of Mathematical Psychology*, 1978, **17**, 199–219 (a).

Grossberg, S., A theory of human memory: Self-organization and performance of sensory-motor codes, maps, and plans. In R. Rosen and F. Snell (Eds.), **Progress in theoretical biology** (Vol. 5). New York: Academic Press, 1978 (b).

Grossberg, S., How does a brain build a cognitive code? *Psychological Review*, 1980, **87**, 1–51.

Grossberg, S., Adaptive resonance in development, perception, and cognition. In S. Grossberg (Ed.), **Mathematical psychology and psychophysiology**. Providence, RI: American Mathematical Society, 1981 (a).

Grossberg, S., Psychophysiological substrates of schedule interactions and behavioral contrast. In S. Grossberg (Ed.), **Mathematical psychology and psychophysiology**. Providence, RI: American Mathematical Society, 1981 (b).

Grossberg, S., **Studies of mind and brain: Neural principles of learning, perception, development, cognition, and motor control**. Boston: Reidel Press, 1982.

Grossberg, S., Some psychophysiological and pharmacological correlates of a developmental, cognitive, and motivational theory. In R. Karrer, J. Cohen, and P. Tueting (Eds.), **Brain and information: Event related potentials**. New York: New York Academy of Sciences, 1984.

Grossberg, S. and Levine, D.S., Some developmental and attentional biases in contrast enhancement and short-term memory of recurrent neural networks. *Journal of Theoretical Biology*, 1975, **53**, 341–380.

Grossberg, S. and Pepe, J., Spiking threshold and overarousal effects in serial learning. *Journal of Statistical Physics*, 1971, **3**, 95–125.

Groves, P.M., Young, S.J., and Wilson, C.J., Nigrostriatal relations and the mechanisms of action of amphetamine. In L.L. Butcher (Ed.), **Cholinergic-monoaminergic interactions in the brain**. New York: Academic Press, 1978.

Hall, G. and Pearce, J.M., Latent inhibition of a CS during CS-US pairings. *Journal of Experimental Psychology: Animal Behavior Processes*, 1979, **5**, 31–42.

Hammond, L.J., Retardation of fear acquisition by a previously inhibitory CS. *Journal of Comparative and Physiological Psychology*, 1968, **66**, 756–758.

Hebb, D.O., **The organization of behavior**. New York: Wiley, 1949.

Hebb, D.O., Drives and the CNS (conceptual nervous system). *Psychological Review*, 1955, **62**, 243–254.

Held, R., Exposure-history as a factor in maintaining stability of perception and coordination. *Journal of Nervous Mental Diseases*, 1961, **132**, 26–32.

Held, R., Dissociation of visual functions by deprivation and rearrangement. *Psychologische Forschung*, 1967, **31**, 338–348.

Held, R. and Hein, A., Movement-produced stimulation in the development of visually guided behavior. *Journal of Comparative and Physiological Psychology*, 1963, **56**, 872–876.

Helmholtz, H. von, **Handbuch der physiologischen optik** (1st ed.). Leipzig, German Democratic Republic: Voss, 1866.

Helmholtz, H. von, **Physiological optics** (Vol. 2) (J.P. Southall, Ed.). New York: Dover, 1962 (originally published 1866).

Hinson, J.M. and Staddon, J.E.R., Behavioral competition: A mechanism for schedule interactions. *Science*, 1978, **202**, 432–434.

Honig, W.K., Attention and the modulation of stimulus control. In D.I. Mostofsky (Ed.), **Attention: Contemporary theory and analysis**. New York: Appleton-Century-Crofts, 1970.

Irwin, D.A., Rebert, C.S., McAdam, D.W., and Knott, J.R., Slow potential change (CNV) in the human EEG as a function of motivational variables. *Electroencephalography and Clinical Neurophysiology*, 1966, **21**, 412–413.

Janowitz, H.D., Hanson, M.E., and Grossman, M.I., Effect of intravenously administered glucose on food intake in the dog. *American Journal of Physiology*, 1949, **156**, 87–91.

John, E.R., Neural processes during learning. In R.W. Russell (Ed.), **Frontiers in physiological psychology**. New York: Academic Press, 1966.

John, E.R., **Mechanisms of memory**. New York: Academic Press, 1967.

Kaczmarek, L.K. and Babloyantz, A., Spatiotemporal patterns in epileptic seizures. *Biological Cybernetics*, 1977, **26**, 199–208.

Kamin, L.J., "Attention-like" processes in classical conditioning. In M.R. Jones (Ed.), **Miami symposium on the prediction of behavior: Aversive stimulation**. Miami: University of Miami Press, 1968.

Kamin, L.J., Predictability, surprise, attention, and conditioning. In B.A. Campbell and R.M.. Church (Eds.), **Punishment and aversive behavior**. New York: Appleton-Century-Crofts, 1969.

Keehn, J.D., Effect of shock duration on Sidman avoidance response rates. *Psychological Reports*, 1963, **13**, 852.

Kremer, E.F., Effect of posttrial episodes on conditioning in compound conditioned stimuli. *Journal of Experimental Psychology: Animal Behavior Processes*, 1979, **5**, 130–141.

Lantz, A.E., Effects of number of trials, interstimulus interval and dishabituation during CS habituation on subsequent conditioning in a CER paradigm. *Animal Learning and Behavior*, 1973, **1**, 273–277.

LeMagnen, J., Regulation of food intake. In F. Reichsman (Ed.), **Hunger and satiety in health and disease**. Basel, Switzerland: S. Karger, 1972.

Levine, D.S. and Grossberg, S., Visual illusions in neural networks: Line neutralization, tilt aftereffect, and angle expansion. *Journal of Theoretical Biology*, 1976, **61**, 477–504.

Lubow, R.E., Rifkin, B., and Alek, M., The context effect: The relationship between stimulus preexposure and environmental preexposure determines subsequent learning. *Journal of Experimental Psychology: Animal Behavior Processes*, 1976, **2**, 38–47.

Macchi, G. and Rinvik, E., Thalamo-telencephalic circuits: A neuroanatomical survey. In A. Remond (Ed.), **Handbook of electroencephalography and clinical neurophysiology** (Vol. 2, Pt. A). Amsterdam: Elsevier, 1976.

Mackintosh, N.J., An analysis of overshadowing and blocking. *Quarterly Journal of Experimental Psychology*, 1971, **23**, 118–125.

Mackintosh, N.J., A theory of attention: Variations in the associability of stimuli with reinforcement. *Psychological Review*, 1975, **82**, 276–298.

Mackintosh, N.J., Overshadowing and stimulus intensity. *Animal Learning and Behavior*, 1976, **4**, 186–192.

Mackintosh, N.J., Bygrave, D.J., and Picton, B.M.B., Locus of the effect of a surprising reinforcer in the attenuation of blocking. *Quarterly Journal of Experimental Psychology*, 1977, **29**, 327–336.

Mackintosh, N.J. and Reese, B., One-trial overshadowing. *Quarterly Journal of Experimental Psychology*, 1979, **31**, 519–526.

Maier, S.F., Seligman, M.E.P., and Solomon, R.L., Pavlovian fear conditioning and learned helplessness effects on escape and avoidance behavior of (a) the CS-US contingency and (b) the independence of the US and voluntary responding. In B.A. Campbell and R.M. Church (Eds.), **Punishment and aversive behavior**. New York: Appleton-Century-Crofts, 1969.

Masterson, F.A., Is termination of a warning signal an effective reward for the rat? *Journal of Comparative and Physiological Psychology*, 1970, **72**, 471–475.

McAllister, W.R. and McAllister, D.E., Behavioral measurement of conditioned fear. In F.R. Brush (Ed.), **Aversive conditioning and learning**. New York: Academic Press, 1971.

Miller, N.E., Learning resistance to pain and fear: Effects of overlearning, exposure, and rewarded exposure in context. *Journal of Experimental Psychology*, 1960, **60**, 137–145.

Morrell, F., Electrophysiological contributions to the neural basis of learning. *Physiological Review*, 1961, **41**, 443–494.

Näätänen, R., Hukkanen, S., and Järvilechto, T., Magnitude of stimulus deviance and brain potentials. In H.H. Kornhuber and L. Deecke (Eds.), **Progress in brain research, Vol. 54: Motivation, motor and sensory processes of the brain**. New York: Elsevier, 1980.

Newman, F.L. and Baron, M.R., Stimulus generalization along the dimension of angularity: A comparison of training procedures. *Journal of Comparative and Physiological Psychology*, 1965, **60**, 59–63.

O'Keefe, J.O. and Nadel, L., **The hippocampus as a cognitive map**. Oxford: Clarendon Press, 1978.

Pearce, J.M. and Hall, G., A model for Pavlovian learning: Variations in the effectiveness of conditioned but not of unconditioned stimuli. *Psychological Review*, 1980, **87**, 532–552.

Rescorla, R.A., Establishment of a positive reinforcer through contrast with shock. *Journal of Comparative and Physiological Psychology*, 1969, **67**, 260–263.

Rescorla, R.A. and LoLordo, V.M., Inhibition of avoidance behavior. *Journal of Comparative and Physiological Psychology*, 1965, **59**, 406–412.

Rescorla, R.A. and Wagner, A.R., A theory of Pavlovian conditioning: Variations in the effectiveness of reinforcement and nonreinforcement. In A.H. Black and W.F. Prokasy (Eds.), **Classical conditioning II: Current research and theory**. New York: Appleton-Century-Crofts, 1972.

Routtenberg, A., The two-arousal hypothesis: Reticular formation and limbic system. *Psychological Review*, 1968, **75**, 51–80.

Schwartz, E.L., Computational anatomy and functional architecture of striate cortex: A spatial mapping approach to perceptual coding. *Vision Research*, 1980, **20**, 645–669.

Seligman, M.E.P. and Hager, J.L. (Eds.), **Biological boundaries of learning**. New York: Appleton-Century-Crofts, 1972.

Seligman, M.E.P. and Johnston, J.C., A cognitive theory of avoidance learning. In F.J. McGuigan and D.B. Lumsden (Eds.), **Contemporary approaches to conditioning and learning**. Washington, DC: V.H. Winston, 1973.

Seward, J.P. and Proctor, D.M., Performance as a function of drive, reward, and habit strength. *American Journal of Psychology*, 1960, **73**, 448–453.

Seward, J.P., Shea, R.A., and Davenport, R.H., Further evidence for the interaction of drive and reward. *American Journal of Psychology*, 1960, **73**, 370–379.

Seward, J.P., Shea, R.A., and Elkind, D., Evidence for the interaction of drive and reward. *American Journal of Psychology*, 1958, **71**, 404–407.

Sharma, K.N., Anand, B.K., Dua, S., and Singh, B., Role of stomach in regulation of activities of hypothalamic feeding centers. *American Journal of Physiology*, 1961, **201**, 593–598.

Singer, W., Control of thalamic transmission by corticofugal and ascending reticular pathways in the visual system. *Physiological Review*, 1977, **57**, 386–420.

Singer, W., Central-core control of visual-cortex functions. In F.O. Schmitt *et al.* (Eds.), **Neurosciences fourth study program**. Cambridge, MA: MIT Press, 1979.

Solomon, R.L., Kamin, L.J., and Wynne, L.C., Traumatic avoidance learning: The outcomes of several extinction procedures with dogs. *Journal of Abnormal and Social Psychology*, 1953, **48**, 291–302.

Strouthes, A., Effects of CS-onset, UCS-termination delay, UCS duration, CS-onset interval, and number of CS-UCS pairings on conditioned fear response. *Journal of Experimental Psychology*, 1965, **69**, 287–291.

Sutton, R.S. and Barto, A.G., Toward a modern theory of adaptive networks: Expectation prediction. *Psychological Review*, 1981, **88**, 135–170.

Tsumoto, T., Creutzfeldt, O.D., and Legéndy, C.R., Functional organization of the corticofugal system from visual cortex to lateral geniculate body of the cat. *Experimental Brain Research*, 1976, **25**, 291–306.

Ullman, S., Against direction perception. *Behavioral and Brain Sciences*, 1980, **3**, 373–381.

Wagner, A.R., Frustrative nonreward: A variety of punishment. In B.A. Campbell and R.M. Church (Eds.), **Punishment and aversive behavior**. New York: Appleton-Century-Crofts, 1969.

Wagner, A.R., Priming in STM: An information processing mechanism for self-generated or retrieval-generated depression in performance. In T.J. Tighe and R.N. Leaton (Eds.), **Habituation: Perspectives from child development, animal behavior, and neurophysiology**. Hillsdale, NJ: Erlbaum, 1976.

Wagner, A.R., Expectancies and the priming of STM. In S.H. Hulse, H. Fowler, and W.K. Honig (Eds.), **Cognitive processes in animal behavior**. Hillsdale, NJ: Erlbaum, 1978.

Wagner, A.R. and Rescorla, R.A., Inhibition in Pavlovian conditioning: Application of a theory. In R.A. Boakes and M.S. Halliday (Eds.), **Inhibition and learning**. New York: Academic Press, 1972.

Wagner, A.R., Rudy, J.W., and Whitlow, J.W., Rehearsal in animal conditioning. *Journal of Experimental Psychology*, 1973, **97**, 407–426.

Wallach, H. and Karsh, E.B., The modification of stereoscopic depth-perception and the kinetic depth-effect. *American Journal of Psychology*, 1963, **76**, 429–435 (a).

Wallach, H. and Karsh, E.B., Why the modification of stereoscopic depth-perception is so rapid. *American Journal of Psychology*, 1963, **76**, 413–420 (b).

Wallach, H., Moore, M.E., and Davidson, L., Modification of stereoscopic depth-perception. *American Journal of Psychology*, 1963, **76**, 191–204.

Weisman, R.G. and Litner, J.S., The course of Pavlovian extinction and inhibition of fear in rats. *Journal of Comparative and Physiological Psychology*, 1969, **69**, 667–672.

Chapter 4

NEURAL DYNAMICS OF CATEGORY LEARNING
AND RECOGNITION: ATTENTION,
MEMORY CONSOLIDATION, AND AMNESIA

Preface

This Chapter completely characterizes the simplest example of an ART circuit. In so doing, it also achieves a number of new mechanistic insights which were not noticed when the ART theory was first introduced in 1976. Two new attentional mechanisms, called attentional gain control and attentional vigilance, are identified. The attentional gain control mechanism enables the theory to show how a processing level can be automatically activated by a bottom-up input, yet be subliminally primed by a top-down input. Once this is understood, a matching rule, called the 2/3 Rule, is implied and is shown to be necessary to achieve stable code self-organization even in certain simple input environments.

A new nonlinear associative rule, called the Weber Law Rule, is also identified. This rule enables the network to learn recognition codes in response to arbitrary lists of input patterns. We find this application of a Weber Law Rule to be particularly exciting, because it reveals an intimate connection between the psychophysical properties and the learning properties of neural systems.

The claim of adaptive resonance theory that it can handle arbitrary input environments is no longer merely a claim. Gail Carpenter and I have recently proved mathematically that the ART circuit described in this Chapter self-organizes and *self-stabilizes* its learning of cognitive recognition codes in response to arbitrarily many arbitrarily chosen binary input patterns. A proof for arbitrary graded patterns is also almost ready. Thus the ART circuit described in this Chapter totally overcomes the noise, saturation, capacity, orthogonality, and linear predictability constraints that have limited the codes which can be stably learned by other adaptive pattern recognition models.

We have also mathematically proved that this ART circuit automatically disengages the orienting subsystem, along with its adaptive memory search capabilities, as the code learning process self-stabilizes. Thereafter each familiar exemplar can directly access that cognitive representation whose critical feature pattern, or prototype, most closely matches the exemplar.

The article ends by showing that a lesion of the orienting subsystem of this ART architecture leads to a formal syndrome which exhibits many properties of medial temporal amnesia. We compare this syndrome with alternative models of amnesia and show how it begins to overcome some problems which these alternative models have not yet addressed. Although we do not for a moment believe that this formal syndrome provides a sufficient explanation of medial temporal amnesia, it has provided us with an opening which has enabled us to mount a frontal attack on this problem—an attack, moreover, that could never have been envisaged using a model in which interactions between an attentional subsystem and an orienting subsystem were not specified.

Brain Structure, Learning, and Memory, AAAS Symposium Series, 1986
J. Davis, R. Newburgh, and E. Wegman (Eds.)
©1986 Office of Naval Research
Reprinted by permission

NEURAL DYNAMICS OF CATEGORY LEARNING
AND RECOGNITION: ATTENTION,
MEMORY CONSOLIDATION, AND AMNESIA

Gail A. Carpenter† and Stephen Grossberg‡

Abstract

A theory is developed of how recognition categories can be learned in response to a temporal stream of input patterns. Interactions between an attentional subsystem and an orienting subsystem enable the network to self-stabilize its learning, without an external teacher, as the code becomes globally self-consistent. Category learning is thus determined by global contextual information in this system. The attentional subsystem learns bottom-up codes and top-down templates, or expectancies. The internal representations formed in this way stabilize themselves against recoding by matching the learned top-down templates against input patterns. This matching process detects structural pattern properties in addition to local feature matches. The top-down templates can also suppress noise in the input patterns, and can subliminally prime the network to anticipate a set of input patterns. Mismatches activate an orienting subsystem, which resets incorrect codes and drives a rapid search for new or more appropriate codes. As the learned code becomes globally self-consistent, the orienting subsystem is automatically disengaged and the memory consolidates. After the recognition categories for a set of input patterns self-stabilize, those patterns directly access their categories without any search or recoding on future recognition trials. A novel pattern exemplar can directly access an established category if it shares invariant properties with the set of familiar exemplars of that category. Several attentional and nonspecific arousal mechanisms modulate the course of search and learning. Three types of attentional mechanism—priming, gain control, and vigilance—are distinguished. Three types of nonspecific arousal are also mechanistically characterized. The nonspecific vigilance process determines how fine the learned categories will be. If vigilance increases due, for example, to a negative reinforcement, then the system automatically searches for and learns finer recognition categories. The learned top-down expectancies become more abstract as the recognition categories become broader. The learned code is a property of network interactions and the entire history of input pattern presentations. The interactions generate emergent rules such as a Weber Law Rule, a 2/3 Rule, and

---

† Supported in part by the National Science Foundation (DMS-84-13119) and the Office of Naval Research (ONR N00014-83-K0337)

‡ Supported in part by the Air Force Office of Scientific Research (AFOSR 85-0149) and the Office of Naval Research (ONR N00014-83-K0337).

an Associative Decay Rule. No serial programs or algorithmic rule structures are used. The interactions explain and predict properties of evoked potentials (processing negativity, mismatch negativity, P300). Malfunction of the orienting system causes a formal amnesic syndrome analogous to that caused by malfunction of medial temporal brain structures: limited retrograde amnesia, long-range anterograde amnesia, failure of memory consolidation, effective priming, and defective reactions to novel cues. Comparisons with alternative theories of amnesia are made.

1. Introduction: Self-Organization of Recognition Categories

A fundamental problem of perception and learning concerns the characterization of how recognition categories emerge as a function of experience. When such categories spontaneously emerge through an individual's interaction with an environment, the processes are said to undergo *self-organization* (Basar, Flohr, Haken, and Mandell, 1983). This article develops a theory of how recognition categories can self-organize, and relates these results to recent data about evoked potentials and about amnesias due to malfunction of medial temporal brain structures. Results of evoked potential and clinical studies suggest which macroscopic brain structures could carry out the theoretical dynamics (Section 19). The theory also specifies microscopic neural dynamics, with local processes obeying membrane equations (Appendix).

We focus herein upon principles and mechanisms that are capable of self-organizing stable recognition codes in response to arbitrary temporal sequences of input patterns. These principles and mechanisms lead to the design of a neural network whose parameters can be specialized for applications to particular problem domains, such as speech and vision. In these domains, preprocessing stages prepare environmental inputs for the self-organizing category formation and recognition system. Work on speech and language preprocessing has characterized those stages after which such a self-organizing recognition system can build up codes for phonemes, syllables, and words (Grossberg, 1978, 1985a; Grossberg and Stone, 1985). Work on form and color preprocessing has characterized those stages after which such a self-organizing recognition system can build up codes for visual object recognition (Grossberg and Mingolla, 1985a, 1985b).

Code Stabilization by Top-Down Expectancies

Mathematical analysis and computer simulations of the neural network described in the present article show how the network can learn bottom-up codes and top-down expectancies in response to a temporal stream of input patterns. The internal representations formed in this way stabilize themselves against recoding in response to irrelevant input patterns by using the matching properties of the learned top-down expectancies. This code-stabilizing mechanism also suppresses noise in the input patterns, and can attentionally prime a network to anticipate an input pattern or category of input patterns. Moreover, the network automatically rescales its noise criterion to each pattern context: A particular mismatched feature which is processed as noise in a complex pattern with many features may, in the context of a simple pattern with few features, signal a pattern mismatch. Thus the theory shows that a definition of signal vs. noise which is sensitive to the global structure of input patterns is an intrinsic property of the mechanisms whereby recognition codes for these patterns are learned in a self-stabilizing fashion.

Attentional and Orienting Subsystems

The class of networks that we consider develops the *adaptive resonance theory*. The theory's relationships to a wide variety of interdisciplinary data and other models is described in Grossberg (1976b, 1980, 1982, 1984a) and Grossberg and Stone (1985). In this theory, an interaction between two functionally complementary subsystems is needed to process familiar and unfamiliar events. Familiar events are processed within a consummatory, or attentional, subsystem. This subsystem establishes ever more precise internal representations of and responses to familiar events. It also builds up the

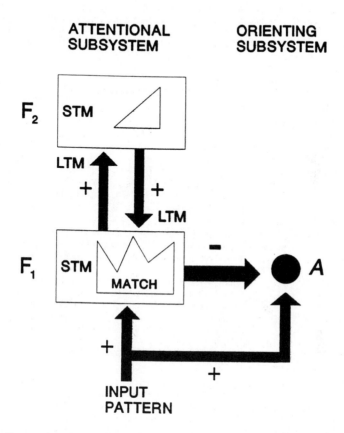

ATTENTIONAL SUBSYSTEM   **ORIENTING SUBSYSTEM**

Figure 1. Interactions between the attentional subsystem and the orienting subsystem: Adaptive bottom-up signals and top-down signals between levels F_1 and F_2 determine whether the input pattern will be matched or mismatched at F_1. A match inhibits the orienting subsystem A.

learned top-down expectations that help to stabilize the learned bottom-up codes of familiar events. By itself, however, the attentional subsystem is unable simultaneously to maintain stable representations of familiar categories and to create new categories for unfamiliar patterns. An isolated attentional subsystem is either rigid and incapable of creating new categories for unfamiliar patterns, or unstable and capable of ceaselessly recoding the categories for familiar patterns (Section 12).

The second subsystem is an orienting subsystem that overcomes the rigidity of the attentional subsystem when unfamiliar events occur and enables the attentional subsystem to learn from these novel experiences. The orienting subsystem is essential for expressing whether a novel pattern is "familiar" and well represented by an existing category, or "unfamiliar" and in need of a new category.

All input events start to be processed by the attentional subsystem. A familiar

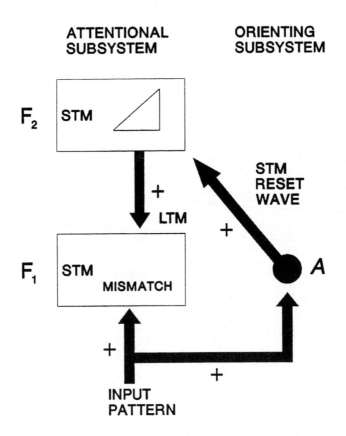

Figure 2. A mismatch at F_1 between the bottom-up input pattern and the top-down template, or expectancy, reduces inhibition from F_1 to the orienting subsystem A. The orienting subsystem can then release a burst of nonspecific arousal capable of resetting short term memory (STM) at F_2.

event can activate a top-down template, or expectancy, which it tries to match within the attentional subsystem (Figure 1). A successful approximate match can deform, amplify, and sustain in short-term memory (STM) the activity pattern that was initially activated by the input within the attentional subsystem. Amplified, or resonant, STM activities constitute the fully elaborated recognition event. They inhibit the orienting subsystem and engage the learning, or long-term memory (LTM), process. A familiar event can maintain or modify its prior learning as its recognition takes place.

An unfamiliar event also starts to be processed by the attentional subsystem. Such an event may also activate a category which thereupon reads-out a top-down template. If the unfamiliar event can approximately match this template, then it can be recognized as an exemplar of the category on its first presentation. If the unfamiliar event is too different from familiar exemplars of the sampled category, then it cannot approximately match this template (Figure 2). A mismatch within the attentional subsystem activates the orienting subsystem. Activation of the orienting subsystem functionally expresses the novelty, or unexpectedness, of the unfamiliar event. The orienting subsystem, in turn, rapidly resets the active representation within the attentional subsystem as it simultaneously energizes an orienting response.

The reset of the attentional subsystem by the orienting subsystem leads to the selection of a new representation within the attentional subsystem. This new representation may cause yet another mismatch, hence another STM reset event and the selection of yet another representation. In this way, the orienting subsystem mediates a rapid search which continues until a representation is found that does not cause a large mismatch. Then the search ends, an STM resonance develops, and the learning process can encode the active representation to which the search led. The system's recognition categories are hereby altered in either of two ways. If the search leads to an established category, then learning may change the criteria for accessing that category. If the search leads to uncommitted cells, then learning can add a new category to the recognition code.

This search process, although unfolding serially in time, is not controlled by a serial mechanism. Rather, it is driven by the successive release of nonspecific orienting bursts that are triggered by automatic processing of mismatch events. The entire history of learning determines the order of search in the network and, in turn, the new learning which can occur at the end of a search. Thus the search process adaptively modifies itself as the knowledge encoded by the network evolves. By contrast, a prewired search tree could not, in principle, maintain its efficiency after unpredictable changes in knowledge occurred. Instead, the novelty-sensitive orienting subsystem, through its interactions with the evolving knowledge of the attentional subsystem, defines an efficient, self-adjusting search routine.

Tuning of Categories by Attention

The criterion of mismatch is also determined by a parallel mechanism. In particular, a nonspecific vigilance, or attentional, parameter determines how fine the learned categories will be. If, for example, vigilance increases due to negative reinforcement or other attention-focusing agents, then the system will automatically search for and learn finer recognition categories.

Direct Access to Familiar Categories and Memory Consolidation

Although an unfamiliar event may initially drive a search for an internal representation, after this representation is learned, future presentation of the input pattern need not engage the search process. Instead, the memory consolidates and a familiar input pattern can directly access its recognition category. That is, the familiar pattern can directly activate its code with neither search nor recoding.

Top-Down Subliminal Priming

A familiar event may, however, also engage the search process (Figure 3). This can occur when the system is primed to expect a different familiar event, so that a top-down expectancy is already active when the familiar event occurs. The familiar input event may mismatch this expectancy. A search will then be elicited leading to activation of the familiar event's bottom-up code and top-down expectancy. Such a search resets the erroneous code so that the correct code can be activated, but does not lead to learning of a new category. By contrast, if the system is primed to expect a familiar event that then occurs, a resonance can develop more rapidly than in an unprimed network. Consequently, anticipation of a familiar event can enhance recognition of that event by the network.

The model's flexible and dynamic relationship between matching, orienting, attention, and learning proves its worth by enabling efficient learning and self-stabilization of recognition categories with any prescribed refinement. The coarseness of the categories is not prewired. Nor is an identity match performed. In fact, the learned top-down expectancies become more abstract as the categories become broader. Moreover, the

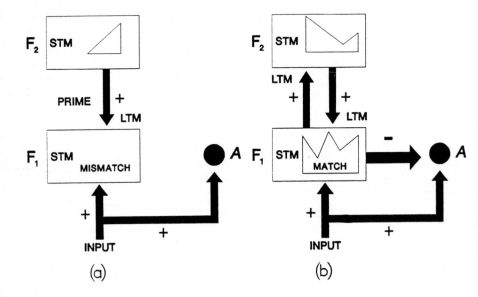

Figure 3. Reset of a subliminal prime: (a) The top-down expectancy, or prime, subliminally activates F_1 before the input pattern arrives. If the input pattern mismatches the prime, then an arousal burst from A can reset STM at F_2 and thereby deactivate the prime. (b) Then F_1 can access its correct F_2 code. The subsequent match at F_1 between the input pattern and a compatible top-down template prevents the input pattern from activating A and thereby erroneously resetting the correct F_2 code.

network automatically rescales its matching criterion so that even with a fixed level of attentional vigilance, the network can both differentiate finer details of simple input patterns and tolerate larger mismatches of complex input patterns. This same rescaling property defines the difference between irrelevant noise and significant pattern mismatches. As with many other network properties, the rescaling property also emerges from interactions between the attentional subsystem and the orienting subsystem. If a mismatch within the attentional subsystem does not generate a search, then the mismatched features are treated as noise in the sense that they are eliminated from the critical feature pattern learned by the template. If the mismatch does generate a search, then the mismatched features may be included in the template of the category to which the search leads. Since the orienting subsystem is sensitive to the *relative* degree of match between an input pattern and a template, finer template mismatches with simple input patterns may drive a search, whereas larger mismatches with complex input patterns may not. Thus whole activity *patterns* across a field of feature-selective cells, rather than activations of single cells or feature detectors, are the computational units of the network.

Short Term Memory and Long Term Memory

   Although the top-down expectancies, or templates, that are learned by the network are computed using deterministic laws, they support the recognition of categories whose degree of fuzziness can be tuned by altering the level of vigilance. The coexistence of deterministic computations with fuzzy, or seemingly probabilistic, recognitions is made possible in the network through interactions between short term memory (STM) and long term memory (LTM) mechanisms. Using its fuzzy recognition criteria, the network can transform a continuum of possible input patterns into a discrete set of recognition categories.

Interaction of STM and LTM processes also enables the entire past learning experience of the network to influence each of its future recognition and learning events. Thus the apparently evanescent moment of recognition, or resonance, embodies all the knowledge that the network has accumulated to that time. Recognition in such a network is intrinsically context-sensitive.

Reconciling Local Features and Context-Sensitive Interactions

Using its context-sensitive interactions the network is able both to maintain stable internal representations against erosion by irrelevant environmental fluctuations and to learn rapidly in a new environment. Although local properties of feature detection are necessary for building up such internal representations, local properties alone are insufficient to distinguish between relevant and irrelevant environmental inputs. The network's ability to stabilize its learned codes against adventitious recoding is due to the same context-sensitive mechanisms that make every recognition event reflect the network's global history of learning.

Thus we are led to consider how a single network can reconcile local features with global context-sensitivity, serial search with parallel processing, discrete categories with continuously varying events, deterministic computations with fuzzy sets, and stable memory with rapid learning.

2. Bottom-Up Adaptive Filtering and Contrast-Enhancement in Short Term Memory

We now introduce in a qualitative way the main mechanisms of the theory. We do so by considering the typical network reactions to a single input pattern I within a temporal stream of input patterns. Each input pattern may be the output pattern of a preprocessing stage. The input pattern I is received at the stage F_1 of the attentional subsystem. Pattern I is transformed into a pattern X of activation across the nodes of F_1 (Figure 4). The transformed pattern X represents a pattern in short term memory (STM). In F_1 each node whose activity is sufficiently large generates excitatory signals along pathways to target nodes at the next processing stage F_2. A pattern X of STM activities across F_1 hereby elicits a pattern S of output signals from F_1. When a signal from a node in F_1 is carried along a pathway to F_2, the signal is multiplied, or *gated*, by the pathway's long term memory (LTM) trace. The LTM gated signal (i.e., signal times LTM trace), not the signal alone, reaches the target node. Each target node sums up all of its LTM gated signals. In this way, pattern S generates a pattern T of LTM-gated and summed input signals to F_2 (Figure 5a). The transformation from S to T is called an *adaptive filter*.

The input pattern T to F_2 is quickly transformed by interactions among the nodes of F_2. These interactions contrast-enhance the input pattern T. The resulting pattern of activation across F_2 is a new pattern Y. The contrast-enhanced pattern Y, rather than the input pattern T, is stored in STM by F_2.

A special case of this contrast-enhancement process, in which F_2 chooses the node which receives the largest input, is here considered in detail. The chosen node is the only one that can store activity in STM. In more general versions of the theory, the contrast enhancing transformation from T to Y enables more than one node at a time to be active in STM. Such transformations are designed to simultaneously represent in STM many subsets, or groupings, of an input pattern (Cohen and Grossberg, 1985; Grossberg, 1985a). When F_2 is designed to make a choice in STM, it selects that global

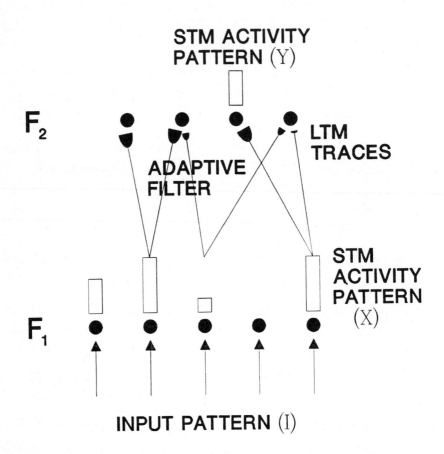

STM ACTIVITY
PATTERN (Y)

F_2

ADAPTIVE
FILTER

LTM
TRACES

STM
ACTIVITY
PATTERN
(X)

F_1

INPUT PATTERN (I)

Figure 4. Stages of bottom-up activation: The input pattern I generates a pattern of STM activation X across F_1. Sufficiently active F_1 nodes emit bottom-up signals to F_2. This signal pattern S is gated by long term memory (LTM) traces within the $F_1 \rightarrow F_2$ pathways. The LTM-gated signals are summed before activating their target nodes in F_2. This LTM-gated and summed signal pattern T generates a pattern of activation Y across F_2.

grouping of the input pattern which is preferred by the adaptive filter. This process automatically enables the network to partition all the input patterns which are received by F_1 into disjoint sets of recognition categories, each corresponding to a particular node in F_2. The present article analyses in detail the design of such a categorical mechanism. This special case is both interesting in itself and a necessary prelude to the analysis of recognition codes in which multiple groupings of X are simultaneously represented by Y.

Only those nodes of F_2 which maintain stored activity in STM can elicit new learning

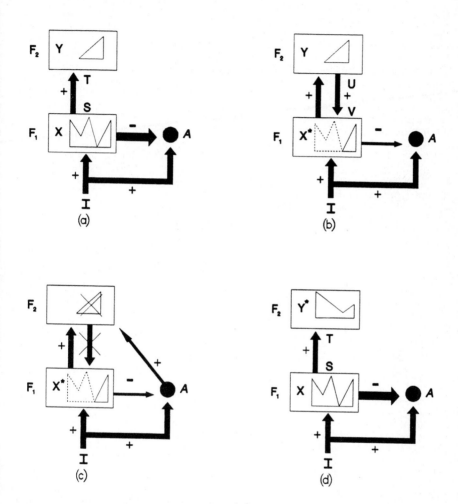

Figure 5. Search for a correct F_2 code: (a) The input pattern I generates the specific STM activity pattern X at F_1 as it nonspecifically activates A. Pattern X both inhibits A and generates the output signal pattern S. Signal pattern S is transformed into the input pattern T, which activates the STM pattern Y across F_2. (b) Pattern Y generates the top-down signal pattern U which is transformed into the template pattern V. If V mismatches I at F_1, then a new STM activity pattern X^* is generated at F_1. The reduction in total STM activity which occurs when X is transformed into X^* causes a decrease in the total inhibition from F_1 to A. (c) Then the input-driven activation of A can release a nonspecific arousal wave to F_2, which resets the STM pattern Y at F_2. (d) After Y is inhibited, its top-down template is eliminated, and X can be reinstated at F_1. Now X once again generates input pattern T to F_2, but since Y remains inhibited T can activate a different STM pattern Y^* at F_2. If the top-down template due to Y^* also mismatches I at F_1, then the rapid search for an appropriate F_2 code continues.

at contiguous LTM traces. Whereas all the LTM traces in the adaptive filter, and thus all learned past experiences of the network, are used to determine recognition via the transformation $I \to X \to S \to T \to Y$, only those LTM traces whose STM activities in F_2 survive the contrast-enhancement process can learn in response to the activity pattern X.

The bottom-up STM transformation $I \to X \to S \to T \to Y$ is not the only process that regulates network learning. In the absence of top-down processing, the LTM traces within the adaptive filter $S \to T$ (Figure 5a) can respond to certain sequences of input patterns by being ceaselessly recoded in such a way that individual events are never eventually encoded by a single category no matter how many times they are presented. An infinite class of examples in which temporally unstable codes evolve is described in Section 12. It was the instability of bottom-up adaptive coding that led Grossberg (1976a, 1976b) to introduce the adaptive resonance theory.

In the adaptive resonance theory, a matching process at F_1 exists whereby learned top-down expectancies, or templates, from F_2 to F_1 are compared with the bottom-up input pattern to F_1. This matching process stabilizes the learning that emerges in response to an arbitrary input environment. The constraints that follow from the need to stabilize learning enable us to choose among the many possible versions of top-down template matching and STM processes. These learning constraints upon the adaptive resonance top-down design have enabled the theory to explain data from visual and auditory information processing experiments in which learning has not been a manipulated variable (Grossberg, 1980, 1985a; Grossberg and Stone, 1985). The present article develops these mechanisms into a rigorously characterized learning system whose properties have been quantitatively analysed (Carpenter and Grossberg, 1985a, 1985b). This analysis has revealed new design constraints within the adaptive resonance theory. The system that we will describe for learned categorical recognition is one outcome of this analysis.

3. Top-Down Template Matching and Stabilization of Code Learning

We now begin to consider how top-down template matching can stabilize code learning. In order to do so, top-down template matching at F_1 must be able to prevent learning at bottom-up LTM traces whose contiguous F_2 nodes are only momentarily activated in STM. This ability depends upon the different rates at which STM activities and LTM traces can change. The STM transformation $I \to X \to S \to T \to Y$ takes place very quickly. By "very quickly" we mean much more quickly than the rate at which the LTM traces in the adaptive filter $S \to T$ can change. As soon as the bottom-up STM transformation $X \to Y$ takes place, the STM activities Y in F_2 elicit a top-down excitatory signal pattern U back to F_1. Only sufficiently large STM activities in Y elicit signals in U along the feedback pathways $F_2 \to F_1$.

As in the bottom-up adaptive filter, the top-down signals U are also gated by LTM traces before the LTM-gated signals are summed at F_1 nodes. The pattern U of output signals from F_2 hereby generates a pattern V of LTM-gated and summed input signals to F_1. The transformation from U to V is thus also an adaptive filter. The pattern V is called a *top-down template*, or *learned expectation*.

Two sources of input now perturb F_1: the bottom-up input pattern I which gave rise to the original activity pattern X, and the top-down template pattern V that resulted from activating X. The activity pattern X^* across F_1 that is induced by I and V taken together is typically different from the activity pattern X that was previously induced by I alone. In particular, F_1 acts to match V against I. The result of this matching process determines the future course of learning and recognition by the network.

The entire activation sequence

$$I \to X \to S \to T \to Y \to U \to V \to X^* \tag{1}$$

takes place very quickly relative to the rate with which the LTM traces in either the bottom-up adaptive filter S→T or the top-down adaptive filter U→V can change. Even though none of the LTM traces changes during such a short time, their prior learning strongly influences the STM patterns Y and X* that evolve within the network. We now discuss how a match or mismatch of I and V at F_1 regulates the course of learning in response to the pattern I.

4. Interactions Between Attentional and Orienting Subsystems: STM Reset and Search

This section outlines how a mismatch at F_1 regulates the learning process. With this general scheme in mind, we will be able to consider details of how bottom-up filters and top-down templates are learned and how matching takes place.

Level F_1 can compute a match or mismatch between a bottom-up input pattern I and a top-down template pattern V, but it cannot compute which STM pattern Y across F_2 generated the template pattern V. Thus the outcome of matching at F_1 must have a nonspecific effect upon F_2 that can potentially influence all of the F_2 nodes, any one of which may have read-out V. The internal organization of F_2 must be the agent whereby this nonspecific event, which we call a *reset wave*, selectively alters the stored STM activity pattern Y. The reset wave is one of the three types of nonspecific arousal that exist within the network. In particular, we suggest that a mismatch of I and V within F_1 generates a nonspecific arousal burst that inhibits the active population in F_2 which read-out V. In this way, an erroneous STM representation at F_2 is quickly eliminated before any LTM traces can encode this error.

The attentional subsystem and the orienting subsystem work together to carry out these interactions. All learning takes place within the attentional subsystem. All matches and mismatches are computed within the attentional subsystem. The orienting subsystem is the source of the nonspecific arousal bursts that reset STM within level F_2 of the attentional subsystem. The outcome of matching within F_1 determines whether or not such an arousal burst will be generated by the orienting subsystem. Thus the orienting system mediates reset of F_2 due to mismatches within F_1.

Figure 5 depicts a typical interaction between the attentional subsystem and the orienting subsystem.In Figure 5a, an input pattern I instates an STM activity pattern X across F_1. The input pattern I also excites the orienting population A, but pattern X at F_1 inhibits A before it can generate an output signal.

Activity pattern X also generates an output pattern S which, via the bottom-up adaptive filter, instates an STM activity pattern Y across F_2. In Figure 5b, pattern Y reads a top-down template pattern V into F_1. Template V mismatches input I, thereby significantly inhibiting STM activity across F_1. The amount by which activity in X is attenuated to generate X* depends upon how much of the input pattern I is encoded within the template pattern V.

When a mismatch attenuates STM activity across F_1, this activity no longer prevents the arousal source A from firing. Figure 5c depicts how disinhibition of A releases a nonspecific arousal burst to F_2. This arousal burst, in turn, selectively inhibits the active population in F_2. This inhibition is long-lasting. One physiological design for F_2 processing which has these necessary properties is a *dipole field* (Grossberg, 1980, 1984a). A dipole field consists of opponent processing channels which are gated by habituating chemical transmitters. A nonspecific arousal burst induces selective and enduring inhibition within a dipole field. In Figure 5c, inhibition of Y leads to inhibition of the top-down template V, and thereby terminates the mismatch between I and V. Input pattern I can thus reinstate the activity pattern X across F_1, which again generates the output pattern S from F_1 and the input pattern T to F_2. Due to the enduring inhibition at F_2, the input pattern T can no longer activate the same pattern Y at F_2. A new pattern Y* is thus generated at F_2 by I (Figure 5d). Despite the fact that some F_2 nodes may remain inhibited by the STM reset property, the new pattern Y^* may encode large STM activities. This is because level F_2 is designed so that its total suprathreshold activity remains approximately constant, or normalized, despite the fact that some of its nodes may remain inhibited by the STM reset mechanism. This property is related to the limited capacity of STM. A physiological process capable of achieving the STM normalization property, based upon on-center off-surround interactions among cells obeying membrane equations, is described in Grossberg (1980, 1983).

The new activity pattern Y^* reads-out a new top-down template pattern V^*. If a mismatch again occurs at F_1, the orienting subsystem is again engaged, thereby leading to another arousal-mediated reset of STM at F_2. In this way, a rapid series of STM matching and reset events may occur. Such an STM matching and reset series controls the system's search of LTM by sequentially engaging the novelty-sensitive orienting subsystem. Although STM is reset sequentially in time, the mechanisms which control the LTM search are all parallel network interactions, rather than serial algorithms. Such a parallel search scheme is necessary in a system whose LTM codes do not exist *a priori*. In general, the spatial configuration of codes in such a system depends upon both the system's initial configuration and its unique learning history. Consequently, no prewired serial algorithm could possibly anticipate an efficient order of search.

The mismatch-mediated search of LTM ends when an STM pattern across F_2 reads-out a top-down template which either matches I, to the degree of accuracy required by the level of attentional vigilance, or has not yet undergone any prior learning. In the latter case, a new recognition category is established as a bottom-up code and top-down template are learned.

We now begin to consider details of the bottom-up/top-down matching process across F_1. The nature of this matching process is clarified by a consideration of how F_1 distinguishes between activation by bottom-up inputs and top-down templates.

5. Attentional Gain Control and Attentional Priming

The importance of the distinction between bottom-up and top-down processing becomes evident when one observes that the same top-down template matching process which stabilizes learning is also a mechanism of attentional priming. Consider, for example, a situation in which F_2 is activated by a level other than F_1 before F_1 is itself activated. In such a situation, F_2 can generate a top-down template V to F_1. The level F_1 is then primed, or ready, to receive a bottom-up input that may or may not match the active expectancy. Level F_1 can be primed to receive a bottom-up input without necessarily eliciting suprathreshold output signals in response to the priming expectancy. If this were not possible, then every priming event would lead to suprathreshold consequences. Such a property would prevent subliminal anticipation of a future event.

On the other hand, an input pattern I must be able to generate a suprathreshold activity pattern X even if no top-down expectancy is active across F_1 (Figure 5). How does F_1 know that it should generate a suprathreshold reaction to a bottom-up input pattern but not to a top-down input pattern? In both cases, an input pattern stimulates F_1 cells. Some auxiliary mechanism must exist to distinguish between bottom-up and top-down inputs. We call this auxiliary mechanism *attentional gain control* to distinguish it from *attentional priming* by the top-down template itself. The attentional priming mechanism delivers *specific* template patterns to F_1. The attentional gain control mechanism has a *nonspecific* effect on the sensitivity with which F_1 responds to the template pattern, as well as to other patterns received by F_1. Attentional gain control is one of the three types of nonspecific arousal that exist within the network. With the addition of attentional gain control, we can explain qualitatively how F_1 can tell the difference between bottom-up and top-down signal patterns.

The need to dissociate attentional priming from attentional gain control can also be seen from the fact that top-down priming events do not lead necessarily to subliminal reactions at F_1. Under certain circumstances, top-down expectancies can lead to suprathreshold consequences. We can, for example, experience internal conversations or images at will. Thus there exists a difference between the read-out of a top-down template, which is a mechanism of attentional priming, and the translation of this operation into suprathreshold signals due to attentional gain control. An "act of will" can amplify attentional gain control signals to elicit a suprathreshold reaction at F_1 in response to an attentional priming pattern from F_2.

Figures 6 and 7 depict two schemes whereby supraliminal reactions to bottom-up signals, subliminal reactions to top-down signals, and supraliminal reactions to matched bottom-up and top-down signals can be achieved. Figures 6d and 7d show, in addition, how competitive interactions across modalities can prevent F_1 from generating a supraliminal reaction to bottom-up signals, as when attention shifts from one modality to another.

Both of the attentional gain control schemes in Figures 6 and 7 satisfy the same functional requirements. Both schemes are formally equivalent; that is, they obey the same system of differential equations. Both schemes can also explain the same body of psychological data. Each scheme can, for example, be used to clarify and modify the distinction between "automatic activation" and "conscious attention" that has arisen from psychological experiments on word recognition and related phenomena concerning human information processing (Grossberg and Stone, 1985). Physiological data are needed to choose one scheme over the other. In particular, within Figure 7, but not Figure 6, the bottom-up input pattern activates an attentional gain control channel. Thus in the scheme of Figure 6, bottom-up inputs activate two nonspecific processing channels, the attentional gain control channel within the attentional subsystem and the nonspecific arousal channel within the orienting subsystem. Herein, we will often motivate our formal constructions by considering the scheme in Figure 6, but its should not be forgotten that both schemes are formally, if not physiologically, equivalent.

6. Matching: The 2/3 Rule

We can now outline the matching and coding properties that are used to generate learning of self-stabilizing recognition categories. Two different types of properties need to be articulated: the bottom-up coding properties which determine the order of search, and the top-down matching properties which determine whether an STM reset event will be elicited. Order of search is determined entirely by properties of the attentional subsystem. The choice between STM reset and STM resonance is dependent upon whether or not the orienting subsystem will generate a reset wave. This computation is based on inputs received by the orienting subsystem from both the bottom-up input pattern I and the STM pattern which F_1 computes within the attentional subsystem (Figure 5). Both the order of search and the choice between reset and resonance are sensitive to the matched patterns *as a whole*. This global sensitivity is key to the design of a single system capable of matching patterns in which the number of coded features, or details, may vary greatly. Such global context-sensitivity is needed to determine whether a fixed amount of mismatch should be treated as functional noise, or as an event capable of eliciting search for a different category. For example, one or two details may be sufficient to differentiate two small but functionally distinct patterns, whereas the same details, embedded in a large, complex pattern may be quite irrelevant.

We first discuss the properties which determine the order of search. Network interactions which control search order can be described in terms of three rules: the 2/3 Rule, the Weber Law Rule, and the Associative Decay Rule.

The 2/3 Rule follows naturally from the distinction between attentional gain control and attentional priming. It says that two out of three signal sources must activate an F_1 node in order for that node to generate suprathreshold output signals. In Figure 6a,

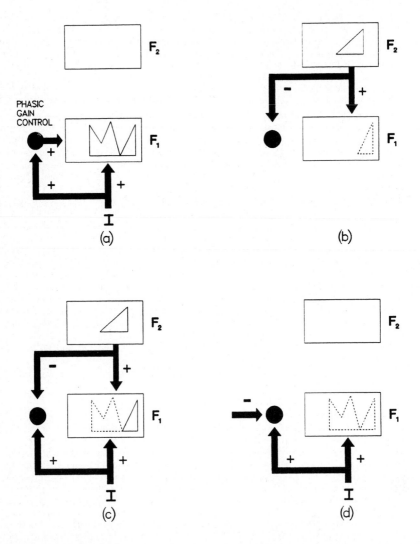

Figure 6. Matching by 2/3 Rule: (a) In this example, nonspecific attentional gain control signals are phasically activated by the bottom-up input. In this network, the bottom-up input arouses two different nonspecific channels: the attentional gain control channel and the orienting subsystem. Only F_1 cells that receive bottom-up inputs and gain control signals can become supraliminally active. (b) A top-down template from F_2 inhibits the attentional gain control source as it subliminally primes target F_1 cells. (c) When a bottom-up input pattern and a top-down template are simultaneously active, only those F_1 cells that receive inputs from both sources can become supraliminally active, since the gain control source is inhibited. (d) Intermodality inhibition can shut off the gain control source and thereby prevent a bottom-up input from supraliminally activating F_1.

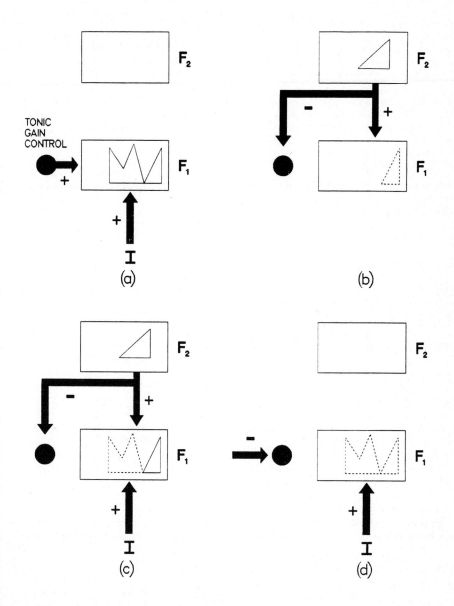

Figure 7. This figure differs from Figure 6 only in that the attentional gain control source is tonically active.

for example, during bottom-up processing, a suprathreshold node in F_1 is one which receives a specific input from the input pattern I and a nonspecific attentional gain control signal. All other nodes in F_1 receive only the nonspecific gain control signal. Since these cells receive inputs from only one pathway they do not fire.

In Figure 6b, during top-down processing, or priming, some nodes in F_1 receive a template signal from F_2, whereas other nodes receive no signal whatsoever. All the nodes of F_1 receive inputs from at most one of their three possible input sources. Hence no cells in F_1 are supraliminally activated by a top-down template.

During simultaneous bottom-up and top-down signaling, the attentional gain control signal is inhibited by the top-down channel (Figure 6c). Despite this fact, some nodes of F_1 may receive sufficiently large inputs from both the bottom-up and the top-down signal patterns to generate suprathreshold outputs. Other nodes may receive inputs from the top-down template pattern or the bottom-up input pattern, but not both. These nodes receive signals from only one of their possible sources, hence do not fire. Cells which receive no inputs do not fire either. Thus only cells that are conjointly activated by the bottom-up input and the top-down template can fire when a top-down template is active. The 2/3 Rule clarifies the apparently paradoxical process whereby the addition of top-down excitatory inputs to F_1 can lead to an overall decrease in F_1's STM activity (Figures 5a and 5b).

7. Direct Access To Subsets and Supersets

The Weber Law Rule can be motivated by considering the following situation. Suppose that a bottom-up input pattern $I^{(1)}$ activates a network in which pattern $I^{(1)}$ has already been perfectly coded by the adaptive filter from F_1 to F_2. Suppose, moreover, that another pattern $I^{(2)}$ has also been perfectly coded and that $I^{(2)}$ contains $I^{(1)}$ as a subset; that is, $I^{(2)}$ equals $I^{(1)}$ at all the nodes where $I^{(1)}$ is positive. If $I^{(1)}$ and $I^{(2)}$ are sufficiently different, they should have access to distinct categories at F_2. However, since $I^{(2)}$ equals $I^{(1)}$ at their intersection, and since all the F_1 nodes where $I^{(2)}$ does not equal $I^{(1)}$ are inactive when $I^{(1)}$ is presented, how does the network decide between the two categories when $I^{(1)}$ is presented? This question suggests that, in response to an input pattern $I^{(1)}$ that is perfectly coded, the node v_1 in F_2 which codes $I^{(1)}$ should receive a bigger signal from the adaptive filter than the node v_2 in F_2 which codes a superset $I^{(2)}$ of $I^{(1)}$ (Figure 8a). In order to realize this constraint, the LTM traces at v_2 which filter $I^{(1)}$ should be smaller than the LTM traces at v_1 which filter $I^{(1)}$. Since the LTM traces at v_2 were coded by the superset pattern $I^{(2)}$, this constraint suggests that larger input patterns are encoded by smaller LTM traces. Thus the absolute sizes of the LTM traces projecting to the different nodes v_1 and v_2 reflect the overall sizes of the input patterns $I^{(1)}$ and $I^{(2)}$ coded by these nodes.

The relative sizes of the LTM traces projecting to a single node reflect the internal structuring of the input patterns coded by that node. Consider, for example, the LTM traces in pathways between F_1 cells where $I^{(1)}$ equals zero and the F_2 node v_1 (Figure 8b). During learning of $I^{(1)}$, these LTM traces decay toward zero. By contrast, consider the LTM traces to v_2 in pathways from F_1 cells that are activated by $I^{(2)}$ but not $I^{(1)}$. These LTM traces become large as learning of $I^{(2)}$ proceeds.

The preceding discussion suggests a constraint that enables a subset $I^{(1)}$ to selectively activate its node v_1 rather than the node corresponding to a superset $I^{(2)}$. On the other hand, the superset $I^{(2)}$ should be able to directly activate its node v_2 rather than the node v_1 of a subset $I^{(1)}$. However, the positive LTM traces of v_1 are larger than the corresponding LTM traces of v_2, and presentation of $I^{(2)}$ activates the entire

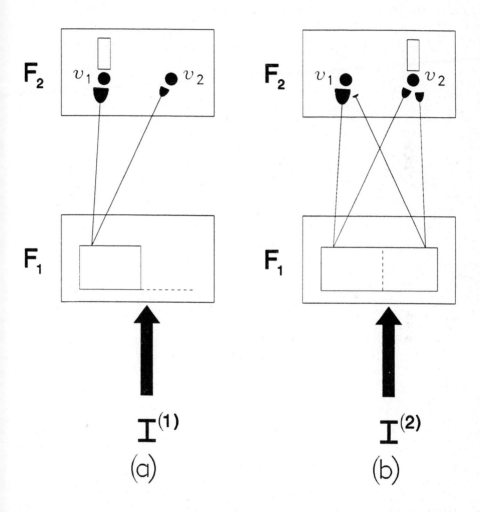

Figure 8. Weber law and associative decay rules for long term memory: When input $I^{(1)}$ activates F_1, node v_1 at F_2 is chosen. When input $I^{(2)}$ activates F_1, node v_2 at F_2 is chosen. (a) Because $I^{(2)}$ is a superset of $I^{(1)}$, the LTM traces in pathways to v_1 from F_1 nodes that are activated by $I^{(1)}$ are larger than the LTM traces to v_2 in pathways from these same F_1 nodes. (b) Consider F_1 nodes that are activated by $I^{(2)}$ but not $I^{(1)}$. The LTM traces in their pathways to v_1 are small. In contrast, the LTM traces in their pathways to v_2 are large, as are all the other LTM traces to v_2 whose pathways are activated by $I^{(2)}$.

subset pattern $I^{(1)}$. The fact that $I^{(2)}$ is filtered by more positive LTM traces at v_2 than it is at v_1 must be able to compensate for the larger size of the LTM traces at v_1. By establishing a proper balance between the size and the number of positive LTM traces, the Weber Law Rule allows both $I^{(1)}$ and $I^{(2)}$ to have direct access to their respective nodes v_1 and v_2.

8. Weber Law Rule and Associative Decay Rule for Long Term Memory

We now describe more precisely the two learning rules whereby the LTM traces allow direct access to both subset and superset F_2 codes. The conjoint action of a Weber Law Rule and an Associative Decay Rule for the learned sizes of LTM traces has the desired properties. To fix ideas, suppose that each input pattern I to F_1 is a pattern of 0's and 1's. Let $|\,I\,|$ denote the number of 1's in the input pattern I. The two rules can be summarized as follows.

Associative Decay Rule

After learning of I has taken place, LTM traces in the bottom-up coding pathways and the top-down template pathways between an inactive F_1 node and an active F_2 node equal 0, or at least are very small. Associative learning within the LTM traces can thus cause decreases as well as increases in the sizes of the traces. This is a non-Hebbian form of associative learning.

Weber Law Rule

After learning input pattern I, LTM traces in bottom-up coding pathways corresponding to active F_1 and F_2 nodes equal

$$\frac{\alpha}{\beta+|\,I\,|}. \tag{2}$$

By (2), the size of each positive LTM trace which codes I decreases as $|\,I\,|$ increases.

Consider again the subset $I^{(1)}$ and the superset $I^{(2)}$. By (2), the positive LTM traces which code $I^{(1)}$ have size

$$\frac{\alpha}{\beta+|\,I^{(1)}\,|} \tag{3}$$

and the positive LTM traces which code $I^{(2)}$ have size

$$\frac{\alpha}{\beta+|\,I^{(2)}\,|}, \tag{4}$$

where $|\,I^{(1)}\,|<|\,I^{(2)}\,|$. When $I^{(1)}$ is presented at F_1, $|\,I^{(1)}\,|$ nodes in F_1 are suprathreshold. Thus the *total* input to v_1 has size

$$J_{11} = \frac{\alpha\,|\,I^{(1)}\,|}{\beta+|\,I^{(1)}\,|} \tag{5}$$

and the *total* input to v_2 has size

$$J_{12} = \frac{\alpha\,|\,I^{(1)}\,|}{\beta+|\,I^{(2)}\,|}. \tag{6}$$

Because $|\,I^{(1)}\,|<|\,I^{(2)}\,|$, it follows that $J_{11} > J_{12}$. Thus $I^{(1)}$ activates v_1 instead of v_2.

When $I^{(2)}$ is presented at F_1, $|I^{(2)}|$ nodes in F_1 are suprathreshold. Thus the *total* input to v_2 is

$$J_{22} = \frac{\alpha \mid I^{(2)} \mid}{\beta + \mid I^{(2)} \mid}. \tag{7}$$

We now invoke the Associative Decay Rule. Because $I^{(2)}$ is a superset of $I^{(1)}$, only those F_1 nodes in $I^{(2)}$ that are also activated by $I^{(1)}$ project to positive LTM traces at v_1. Thus the *total* input to v_1 is

$$J_{21} = \frac{\alpha \mid I^{(1)} \mid}{\beta + \mid I^{(1)} \mid}. \tag{8}$$

Both J_{22} and J_{21} are expressed in terms of the function

$$W(\xi) = \frac{\alpha \xi}{\beta + \xi}, \tag{9}$$

which is an increasing function of ξ. Since $|I^{(1)}| < |I^{(2)}|$, $J_{22} > J_{21}$. Thus the superset $I^{(2)}$ activates its node v_2 more than the subset node v_1.

Thus the conjoint action of a Weber Law Rule and an Associative Decay Rule for bottom-up learning permits direct access to the F_2 nodes of both subset and superset input patterns. The Weber Law Rule is the outcome of mass action competitive interactions, as we will illustrate in the Appendix. These competitive interactions may occur among the nodes of F_1 or among the LTM traces abutting each F_2 node. We hereby suggest how the functional problem of direct access to subset and superset codes may be mechanistically solved by nonlinear neural interactions.

9. Fast Learning and Slow Learning: The Direct Access Rule

In order to characterize the course of learning, the rate of change of the LTM traces on each learning trial must be specified. In this article, we consider cases in which, on every learning trial, the LTM traces can reach the new equilibrium values imposed by the input pattern on that trial. We call these *fast learning* cases. We have also considered cases in which the LTM traces change too slowly to reach the new equilibrium values imposed by the input pattern on a single trial. We call these the *slow learning* cases.

During both fast learning and slow learning, the STM traces change more quickly than the LTM traces, and the learning process eventually self-stabilizes. However, the system is more sensitive to the ordering of the input patterns during fast learning than during slow learning. During slow learning, each LTM trace averages across time intervals that are much longer than a single trial, and thereby becomes less sensitive to the ordering of the inputs. In the next section, we will show how the input order can influence the choice of coding categories in the fast learning case. Slow learning is considered in Carpenter and Grossberg (1985b).

We note, finally, that the 2/3 Rule and the Weber Law Rule suggest how the initial values of STM traces and LTM traces should be chosen. The choice of initial STM traces is simple: the system starts out at equilibrium, or with zero STM traces, and the STM traces quickly return to equilibrium after each input pattern shuts off.

Initial LTM traces need to be chosen differently in the bottom-up adaptive filter than in the top-down adaptive filter. Due to the Weber Law Rule, the individual bottom-up LTM traces that are learned in response to large input patterns will be relatively small. In order for presentation of a perfectly coded large pattern to directly access its coded node, rather than an uncoded node, the initial values of the bottom-up LTM traces must be smaller than the learned LTM values corresponding to large input patterns. In addition, although some bottom-up LTM traces may initially equal zero, other LTM traces abutting each F_2 node must initially be positive in order for F_1 to excite that node at all.

Due to the 2/3 Rule, the initial top-down LTM traces cannot be too small. When an input pattern first chooses an F_2 node, the LTM traces that gate the top-down template of that node must satisfy the 2/3 Rule even before any template learning occurs. If the top-down LTM traces started out too small, no F_1 node would receive enough top-down input to satisfy the 2/3 Rule. Consequently, the whole system would shut down. Top-down learning is thus a type of learning-by-selection.

In summary, bottom-up LTM traces start out small, whereas top-down LTM traces start out large. Bottom-up learning and top-down learning sculpt the spatial distribution of their LTM traces, as well as their overall sizes, through time. The constraint that the initial sizes of the top-down LTM traces be large is a consequence of the 2/3 Rule. The constraint that the initial sizes of the bottom-up LTM traces be small is needed to guarantee direct access to perfectly coded F_2 nodes. We therefore call this latter constraint the Direct Access Rule.

10. Stable Choices in Short Term Memory

We can now begin to characterize the order of search in a network that obeys the following constraints: (1) Fast learning occurs (Section 9); (2) Input patterns are composed of 0's and 1's; (3) The 2/3 Rule holds (Section 6); (4) The Weber Law Rule holds (Section 8); (5) The Direct Access Rule holds (Section 9).

This discussion of search order does not analyse whether or not an STM reset event will stop the search at any given step. The criteria for STM reset are provided in Section 15. Other things being equal, a network with a higher level of vigilance will require better F_1 matches, and hence will search more deeply, in response to each input pattern. Thus when an input pattern is presented, the set of learned filters and templates depends upon the prior levels of vigilance. The same ordering of input patterns may thus generate different LTM encodings due to the prior settings of the nonspecific vigilance parameter. The present discussion considers the order in which search will occur in response to a single input pattern which is presented after an arbitrary set of filters and templates has been learned.

A simple function determines the order in which encoded F_2 nodes v_j are searched in response to an input pattern I. This function, which we call the Order Function, is defined as follows.

Order Function

$$T_j = \frac{\alpha \mid V^{(j)} \cap I \mid}{\beta + \mid V^{(j)} \mid}. \tag{10}$$

In equation (10), $V^{(j)}$ denotes the top-down template pattern that is read-out by node v_j of F_2. Since only one node at a time is active in F_2, the total template read-out by F_2 is the template corresponding to the node which is active at that time.

After I has been presented to F_1, but before F_2 becomes active, function T_j in (10) is the total bottom-up input to node v_j. As in Section 8, term $\alpha(\beta + \mid V^{(j)} \mid)^{-1}$ in (10) is a consequence of the Weber Law Rule. This term describes the size of the positive learned LTM traces which abut v_j. Term $\mid V^{(j)} \cap I \mid$ describes the number of pathways abutting node v_j which have positive learned LTM traces and which carry positive signals when input I is presented. The total number of pathways abutting v_j which have positive learned LTM traces is $\mid V^{(j)} \mid$. This is true because a bottom-up LTM trace from node v_i in F_1 to node v_j in F_2 grows due to learning if and only if the corresponding top-down LTM trace from v_j to v_i grows due to learning. There are as many positive learned LTM traces in pathways leading to v_j as there are in pathways leading from v_j. At times when input I is registered by F_1, only $| V^{(j)} \cap I |$ of these $| V^{(j)} |$ pathways are activated. The total input to node v_j in F_2 is thus given by T_j in (10).

Level F_2 chooses that node v_j which receives the largest input T_j. If we order the inputs in terms of decreasing size, as in

$$T_{j_1} > T_{j_2} > T_{j_3} > \ldots, \tag{11}$$

then node v_{j_1} is initially chosen by F_2. After v_{j_1} is chosen, it reads-out template $V^{(j_1)}$ to F_1. When $V^{(j_1)}$ and I both perturb F_1, a new activity pattern X^* is registered at F_1, as in (1) and Figure 5b. A new bottom-up signal pattern from F_1 to F_2 may then be registered at F_2. How can we be sure that v_{j_1} will continue to receive the largest input from F_1 after its template $V^{(j_1)}$ is processed by F_1? The 2/3 Rule provides this guarantee as follows.

The 2/3 Rule shuts off those active F_1 nodes whose top-down LTM traces from v_{j_1} are zero due to prior learning of $V^{(j_1)}$. A top-down LTM trace becomes zero if and only if the corresponding bottom-up LTM trace becomes zero. Thus F_1 nodes which are deactivated by the 2/3 Rule connect to bottom-up pathways whose LTM traces abutting v_{j_1} are zero. Hence, these pathways make no contribution to the total input T_{j_1} to node v_{j_1}. Thus the total input T_{j_1} is not altered due to read-out of the template $V^{(j_1)}$.

All other inputs T_j are either unchanged or decrease due to deactivation of some F_1 nodes by the 2/3 Rule. In general, after the template $V^{(j_1)}$ acts at F_1, the total input to node v_j at F_2 is

$$\frac{\alpha \mid V^{(j)} \cap V^{(j_1)} \cap I \mid}{\beta + \mid V^{(j)} \mid}. \tag{12}$$

By (11), T_{j_1} was the maximal input to F_2 before template $V^{(j_1)}$ was read-out. By (10) and (12) T_{j_1} remains the maximal input to F_2 after $V^{(j_1)}$ is read-out. In summary, the 2/3 Rule stabilizes the STM choice at F_2 before and after read-out of a top-down template.

Were the 2/3 Rule not operative, read-out of the template $V^{(j_1)}$ might supraliminally activate many F_1 nodes that had not previously been activated by the input I alone. These new F_1 activations could cause a different F_2 node to be chosen, and its template could cause yet another F_2 node to be chosen. A rapid and non-terminating series of F_2 choices could hereby be generated by an input I. Later F_2 choices in this series could be activated by F_1 nodes which receive no inputs whatsoever from I. The 2/3 Rule prevents this type of chaotic result from occurring. In other words, it instates a type of pattern matching within F_1 which ensures that the choice of F_2 nodes remains linked to the input pattern I.

11. Order of Search and the Subset Recoding Property

Because F_2 can make choices which are not changed by read-out of the chosen node's template, the ordering of the bottom-up signals

$$T_j = \frac{\alpha \mid V^{(j)} \cap I \mid}{\beta + \mid V^{(j)} \mid} \tag{10}$$

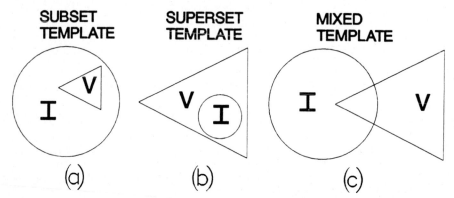

Figure 9. Three types of relationships between input pattern I and template pattern V: (a) Subset template. (b) Superset template. (c) Mixed template.

by size, namely

$$T_{j_1} > T_{j_2} > T_{j_3} > \ldots, \tag{11}$$

determines the order

$$v_{j_1}, v_{j_2}, v_{j_3}, \ldots \tag{13}$$

of search. Thus simple algebraic computations enable one to predict the order of search in this network.

To discuss the order of search in response to the input pattern I, we define three types of learned templates: subset templates, superset templates, and mixed templates. The LTM traces of a subset template V are large only at a subset of the F_1 nodes which are activated by the input pattern I (Figure 9a). The LTM traces of a superset template V are large at all the F_1 nodes which are activated by the input pattern I, as well as at some F_1 nodes which are not activated by I (Figure 9b). The LTM traces of a mixed template V are large at some. but not all, the F_1 nodes which are activated by the input pattern I, as well as at some F_1 nodes which are not activated by I (Figure 9c).

If a search ends when a prescribed template $V^{(j)} = V$ is being read-out by the F_2 node v_j, then this template's LTM traces recode to the new template $V^{(j)} = V \cap I$. This conclusion follows from the conjoint action of the 2/3 Rule and the Associative Decay Rule. Only F_1 nodes in the set $V \cap I$ can remain supraliminal due to the 2/3 Rule, and the LTM traces of pathways between v_j and inactive F_1 nodes converge to zero due to the Associative Decay Rule. Thus, after learning occurs, the active template $V^{(j)} = V$, whether it began as a subset template, a superset template, or a mixed template, is recoded into the subset template $V^{(j)} = V \cap I$ by the input pattern I. This subset recoding property is a key requirement for code stability.

12. Example of Code Instability

We now illustrate the importance of the subset recoding property by describing how its absence can lead to a temporally unstable code. In the simplest type of code instability example, the code becomes unstable because neither top-down template nor reset mechanisms exist (Grossberg, 1976a). Then, in response to certain input sequences that are repeated through time, a given input pattern can be ceaselessly recoded into more than one category. In the example that we will now describe, the top-down template signals are active and the reset mechanism is functional. However, the inhibitory top-down attentional gain control signals (Figures 6c and 7c) are chosen too small for the 2/3 Rule to hold at F_1. We show also that a larger choice of attentional gain control signals restores code stability by reinstating the 2/3 Rule. These simulations also illustrate three other points: how a novel exemplar can directly access a previously established category; how the category in which a given exemplar is coded can be influenced by the categories which form to encode very different exemplars; and how the network responds to exemplars as coherent groupings of features, rather than to isolated feature matches or mismatches.

Figure 10a summarizes a computer simulation of unstable code learning. Figure 10b summarizes a computer simulation that illustrates how reinstatement of the 2/3 Rule can stabilize code learning. The format used in this figure will also be used in displaying our other computer simulations. We therefore describe this figure in detail.

The first column of Figure 10a describes the four input patterns that were used in the simulation. These input patterns are labeled A, B, C, and D. Patterns B, C, and D are all subsets of A. The relationships among the inputs that make the simulation work are as follows:

Code Instability Example

$$D \subset C \subset A, \tag{14}$$

$$B \subset A, \tag{15}$$

$$B \bigcap C = \phi, \tag{16}$$

$$|\,D\,|<|\,B\,|<|\,C\,|\,. \tag{17}$$

These results thus provide infinitely many examples in which an alphabet of just four input patterns cannot be stably coded without the 2/3 Rule. The numbers 1, 2, 3, ... listed in the second column itemize the presentation order. The third column, labeled BU for Bottom-Up, describes the input pattern that was presented on each trial. In both Figures 10a and 10b, the input patterns were periodically presented in the order ABCAD.

Each of the Top-Down Template columns in Figure 10 corresponds to a different node in F_2, with column 1 corresponding to node v_1, column 2 corresponding to node v_2, and so on. Each row summarizes the network response to its input pattern. The symbol RES, which stands for *resonance*, designates the node in F_2 which codes the input pattern on that trial. For example, v_2 codes pattern C on trial 3, and v_1 codes pattern B on trial 7. The patterns in a given row describe the templates after learning has occurred on that trial.

In Figure 10a, input pattern A is periodically recoded: On trial 1, it is coded by v_1; on trial 4, it is coded by v_2; on trial 6, it is coded by v_1; on trial 9, it is coded by v_2. This alternation in the nodes v_1 and v_2 which code pattern A repeats indefinitely.

Violation of the 2/3 Rule occurs on trials 4, 6, 8, 9, and so on. This violation is illustrated by comparing the template of v_2 on trials 3 and 4. On trial 3, the template of v_2 is coded by pattern C, which is a subset of pattern A. On trial 4, pattern A is presented and directly activates node v_2. Because the 2/3 Rule does not hold, pattern A remains supraliminal in F_1 even after the subset template C is read-out from v_2. Thus no search is elicited by the mismatch of pattern A and its subset template C. Consequently the template of v_2 is recoded from pattern C to its superset pattern A.

In Figure 10b, by contrast, the 2/3 Rule does hold due to a larger choice of the attentional gain control parameter. Thus the network experiences a sequence of recodings that ultimately stabilizes. In particular, on trial 4, node v_2 reads-out the subset template C, which mismatches the input pattern A. The numbers beneath the template

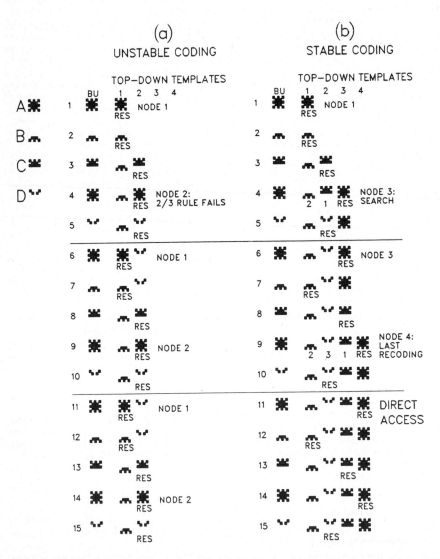

Figure 10. Stabilization of categorical learning by the 2/3 Rule: In both (a) and (b), four input patterns A, B, C, and D are presented repeatedly in the list order ABCAD. In (a), the 2/3 Rule is violated because the top-down inhibitory gain control mechanism be weak (Figures 6c and 7c). Pattern A is periodically coded by v_1 and v_2. It is never coded by a single stable category. In (b), the 2/3 Rule is restored by strengthening the top-down inhibitory gain control mechanism. After some initial recoding during the first two presentations of ABCAD, all patterns directly access distinct stable categories.

symbols in row 4 describe the order of search. First, v_2's template C mismatches **A**. Then v_1's template B mismatches **A**. Finally **A** activates the uncommitted node v_3, which resonates with F_1 as it learns the template **A**.

Scanning the rows of Figure 10b, we see that pattern **A** is coded by v_1 on trial 1; by v_3 on trials 4 and 6; and by v_4 on trial 9. On all future trials, input pattern **A** is coded by v_4. Moreover, all the input patterns **A**, **B**, **C**, and **D** have learned a stable code by trial 9. Thus the code self-stabilizes by the second run through the input list ABCAD. On trials 11 through 15, and on all future trials, each input pattern chooses a different node $(A \rightarrow v_4; B \rightarrow v_1; C \rightarrow v_3; D \rightarrow v_2)$. Each pattern belongs to a separate category because the vigilance parameter was chosen to be large in this example. Moreover, as explained in Section 7, after code learning stabilizes, each input pattern directly activates its node in F_2 without undergoing any additional search. Thus after trial 9, only the "RES" symbol appears under the top-down templates. The patterns shown in any row between 9 and 15 provide a complete description of the learned code. Examples of how a novel exemplar can activate a previously learned category are found on trials 2 and 5 in Figures 10a and 10b. On trial 2, for example, pattern **B** is presented for the first time and directly accesses the category coded by v_1, which was previously learned by pattern **A** on trial 1. In terminology from artificial intelligence, **B** activates the same categorical "pointer," or "marker," or "index" as in **A**. In so doing, **B** does not change the categorical "index," but it may change the categorical template, which determines which input patterns will also be coded by this index on future trials. The category does not change, but its invariants may change.

An example of how presentation of very different input patterns can influence the category of a fixed input pattern is found through consideration of trials 1, 4, and 9 in Figure 10b. These are the trials on which pattern **A** is recoded due to the intervening occurrence of other input patterns. On trial 1, pattern **A** is coded by v_1. On trial 4, **A** is recoded by v_3 because pattern **B** has also been coded by v_1 and pattern **C** has been coded by v_2 in the interim. On trial 9, pattern **A** is recoded by v_4 both because pattern **C** has been recoded by v_3 and pattern **D** has been coded by v_2 in the interim.

In all of these transitions, the global structure of the input pattern determines which F_2 nodes will be activated, and global measures of pattern match at F_1 determine whether these nodes will be reset or allowed to resonate in STM.

13. Search of Subsets, Supersets, and Mixed Sets

Before the code in Figure 10b finally stabilizes, it searches the network in the order characterized by (13). We now describe implications of this search order in a case of special interest, which includes the example described in Figure 10b. This is the case wherein parameter β in (10) is "small." By small, we mean that parameter β satisfies the inequality

$$\beta < \frac{1}{|I|_{\max} - 1},$$
(18)

where $|I|_{\max}$ is the largest number of F_1 nodes that are activated by any input pattern I. The following assertions are proved in Carpenter and Grossberg (1985b).

A. Subset Templates

Suppose that there exist learned templates which are subsets of the input pattern I (Figure 9a). Then, if inequality (18) holds, the first node in F_2 to be chosen corresponds to the largest subset template V. Whether or not template V can match the input I well enough to prevent STM reset of F_2 depends upon the choice of the vigilance parameter, as well as upon how much smaller V is than I. If V = I, then reset never occurs. In this case, the Direct Access Rule (Section 9) implies that the node corresponding to V is chosen first. This node's template V covers I at F_1. Consequently, no reduction in F_1 activity is caused by the 2/3 Rule, and STM reset does not occur.

If the first chosen node does not cover I, then reset may occur. If reset does occur, then the network continues to search F_2 nodes which possess subset templates. Search order proceeds from larger to smaller subset templates. This search order follows from (10), (11), and (13), because, whenever $V^{(j)} \subset I$, then $V^{(j)} \cap I = V^{(j)}$, so that the order function T_j satisfies

$$T_j = \frac{\alpha \mid V^{(j)} \mid}{\beta + \mid V^{(j)} \mid}. \tag{19}$$

Thus the order in which subset templates are searched is determined by the relative sizes of $\mid V^{(j)} \mid$ across all subset templates. Figure 10b illustrates these subset search properties. On trial 9, for example, in response to the input pattern A, the nodes corresponding to the subset templates C, B, and D are searched in order of decreasing template size, as in (17).

B. *Superset Templates and No Mixed Templates*

Suppose that the network has searched all learned subset templates corresponding to the input pattern I. We now consider the subsequent search order by breaking up the possibilities into several cases. In this section, we suppose that no mixed templates have been learned, but that at least one superset template has been learned.

Our main conclusion is that, if all subset templates have already been reset, then the system will code input I using the F_2 node v_j with the smallest superset template $V^{(j)} = V$. Due to this coding event, $V^{(j)}$ will be recoded to

$$V^{(j)} = V \cap I = I. \tag{20}$$

The network chooses the smallest superset template first because

$$T_j = \frac{\alpha \mid I \mid}{\beta + \mid V \mid} \tag{21}$$

whenever $V \supset I$. Thus the smallest of the superset templates generates the largest bottom-up input T_j. The network does not reset this choice because the superset template V completely covers the input pattern I at F_1. By the 2/3 Rule, the F_1 activity pattern caused by I alone persists after the superset template takes effect. No reduction of F_1 activity is caused by the superset template. Hence its F_2 code is not reset by the orienting subsystem. Thus the same property which guarantees stable choices in STM (Section 10) also implies that search ends if it can reach the smallest superset template.

It remains to explain why subsets are searched before supersets, and why supersets are searched before uncommitted nodes.

Given a subset template $V^{(i)}$ and a superset template $V^{(j)}$ of the input pattern I,

$$\mid V^{(i)} \mid \le \mid I \mid < \mid V^{(j)} \mid, \tag{22}$$

$$T_i = \frac{\alpha \mid V^{(i)} \mid}{\beta + \mid V^{(i)} \mid}, \tag{23}$$

and

$$T_j = \frac{\alpha \mid I \mid}{\beta + \mid V^{(j)} \mid}. \tag{24}$$

It follows from (18), (22), (23), and (24) that

$$T_i > T_j, \tag{25}$$

and hence that subset templates are searched before superset templates. This property depends critically on the small choice of β in (18).

Nodes with superset templates are searched before uncommitted nodes due to the same property that guarantees direct access to perfectly coded nodes. In Section 9 we noted that initial bottom-up LTM values must be chosen small enough to permit direct access to nodes which perfectly code any input pattern. In particular,

$$z_0 < \frac{\alpha}{\beta + |V^{(j)}|}, \tag{26}$$

where z_0 is the maximal size of any initial bottom-up LTM trace, and $\alpha(\beta + |V^{(j)}|)^{-1}$ is the learned LTM value corresponding to the superset template $V^{(j)}$. The total bottom-up input to an uncommitted node in response to input I is thus at most $z_0 |I|$, which is less than the total bottom-up input $\alpha |I| (\beta + |V^{(j)}|)^{-1}$ to a superset node v_j.

C. Superset Templates and Mixed Templates

Suppose that the network has already searched its subset templates. Suppose also that both superset templates and mixed templates have previously been learned. Section 13B showed that, if a node with a superset template is activated, then the input pattern will be coded by that node. In particular, the node's template will be recoded to match the input pattern perfectly. We now characterize the circumstances under which the network will search mixed templates before it searches superset templates.

Consider nodes v_i which code mixed templates $V^{(i)}$ with respect to the input pattern I. Also let $V^{(J)}$ be the smallest superset template corresponding to I. Then

$$T_i = \frac{\alpha |V^{(i)} \cap I|}{\beta + |V^{(i)}|} \tag{27}$$

and

$$T_J = \frac{\alpha |I|}{\beta + |V^{(J)}|}. \tag{28}$$

A mixed template $V^{(i)}$ will be searched before the superset template $V^{(J)}$ if and only if

$$T_i > T_J. \tag{29}$$

When parameter B satisfies (18), inequality (29) holds if and only if

$$\frac{|V^{(i)} \cap I|}{|V^{(i)}|} > \frac{|I|}{|V^{(J)}|}. \tag{30}$$

This fact is proved in Carpenter and Grossberg (1985b).

Since a search always ends when a superset node is chosen, only nodes v_i whose mixed templates satisfy (30) can possibly be searched. These nodes are searched in order of decreasing $|V^{(i)} \cap I| |V^{(i)}|^{-1}$. If two nodes have the same ratio, then the one with the larger mixed template is searched first. If the search reaches the node v_J with the smallest superset template, then it terminates at v_J.

D. Mixed Templates But No Superset Templates

Suppose that the network has already searched its subset templates. Suppose that mixed templates, but no superset templates, have previously been learned. In this situation, the search can end by choosing either a node v_i with a mixed template $V^{(i)}$

or a node which has not previously been chosen. For example, a node v_i with mixed template will be chosen before a new node if

$$\frac{\alpha \mid V^{(i)} \cap I \mid}{\beta + \mid V^{(i)} \mid} > z_0 \mid I \mid, \tag{31}$$

where z_0 is the maximal initial size of the bottom-up LTM traces. Recall that

$$\frac{\alpha}{\beta + \mid V^{(i)} \mid} > z_0 \tag{26}$$

for all templates $V^{(i)}$ in order to enable perfectly coded nodes to be directly accessed. Inequality (31) can thus hold when $\mid V^{(i)} \cap I \mid$ is not too much smaller than $\mid I \mid$.

E. *Neither Mixed Templates Nor Superset Templates*

In this case, after all subset nodes are searched, the previously uncommitted nodes are searched. Their initial bottom-up input sizes to F_2 depend upon the choice of initial LTM traces. Thus the order of search among the uncommitted nodes is determined by a random factor. The first uncommitted node that is activated ends the search and codes the input pattern I. This is true because all initial top-down LTM traces are chosen large enough to satisfy the 2/3 Rule (Section 9).

In case there are no uncommitted nodes to be searched after all committed nodes are rejected, then the input pattern cannot be coded by the network. This property is a consequence of the network's ability to buffer, or protect, its codes against persistent recoding by unappropriate events.

Figures 11 and 12 depict two coding sequences that illustrate the main points in the preceding discussion. In Figure 11, each of nine input patterns was presented once. We consider the order of search that occurred in response to the final input pattern I that was presented on trial 9. By trial 8, nodes v_1 and v_2 had already encoded subset templates of this input pattern. On trial 9, these nodes were therefore searched in order of decreasing template size. Nodes v_3, v_4, v_5, and v_6 had encoded mixed templates of the input pattern. These nodes were searched in the order $v_3 \rightarrow v_5 \rightarrow v_4$. This search order was not determined by template size *per se*, but was rather governed by the ratio $\mid V^{(i)} \cap I \mid \mid V^{(i)} \mid^{-1}$ in (30). These ratios for nodes v_3, v_5, and v_4 were 9/10, 14/16, and 7/8, respectively. Since $14/16 = 7/8$, node v_5 was searched before node v_4 because $\mid V^{(5)} \mid = 16 > 8 = \mid V^{(4)} \mid$. The mixed template node v_6 was not searched. After searching v_5, the network activated the node v_7 which possessed the smallest superset template. A comparison of rows 8 and 9 in column 7 shows how the superset template of v_7 was recoded to match the input pattern. Node v_7 was searched before node v_6 because the ratio $\mid I \mid \mid V^{(7)} \mid^{-1} = 17/21$ was larger than $\mid V^{(6)} \cap I \mid \mid V^{(6)} \mid^{-1} = 14/18$.

The eight input patterns of Figure 12 were chosen to illustrate a search followed by coding of an uncommitted node. The last input pattern I in Figure 12 was the same as the last input pattern in Figure 11. In Figure 12, however, there were no superset templates corresponding to input pattern I. Consequently I was coded by a previously uncommitted node v_8 on trial 8. In particular, on trial 8, the network first searched the nodes with subset templates in the order $v_2 \rightarrow v_1$. Then the mixed template nodes were searched in the order $v_4 \rightarrow v_6 \rightarrow v_5 \rightarrow v_7$. The mixed template node v_3 was not searched because its template badly mismatched the input pattern I. Instead, the uncommitted node v_8 was activated and learned a template that matched the input pattern.

If parameter β is not small enough to satisfy inequality (18), then mixed templates or superset templates may be searched before subset templates. The order of search when β violates (18) is characterized in Carpenter and Grossberg (1985b). In all cases, direct access of a perfectly coded pattern is achieved.

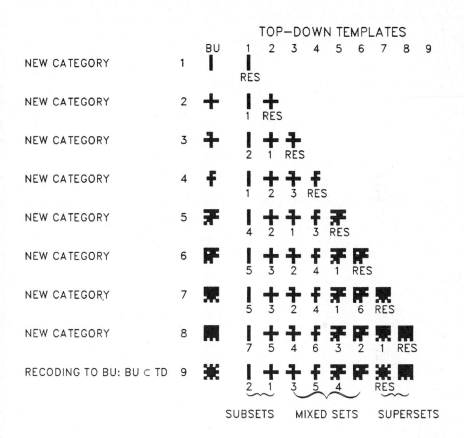

Figure 11. Computer simulation to illustrate order of search: On trial 9, the input pattern first searches subset templates, next searched some, but not all, mixed templates, and finally recodes the smallest superset template. A smaller choice of vigilance parameter could have terminated the search at a subset template or mixed set template node.

14. The Nature of Categorical Invariance During Learning

The preceding discussion casts new light on the issue of how invariant properties of a category can persist even while new learning takes place. Two main cases need to be differentiated. In the first case, a novel input pattern is coded by a node whose bottom-up filter and top-down template have previously undergone learning. In the second case, a novel input pattern is coded by a previously unchosen node. Our remarks herein will focus on the first case.

In this case, presentation of the novel input pattern does not immediately change the number of categories that are coded by the network, nor the set of nodes which code these categories in STM at F_2. Output signals from F_2 generate the network's observable responses. Hence, in this case, the novel pattern is assimilated into the

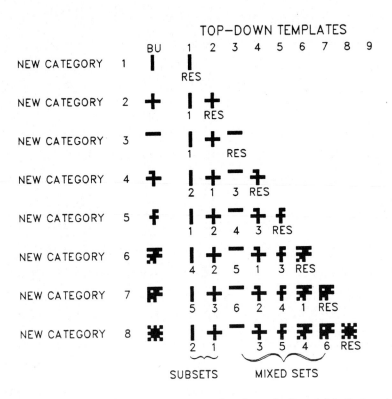

Figure 12. Computer simulation to illustrate order of search: On trial 8, the input pattern first searches subset templates and then searches some, but no all, mixed templates before choosing an uncommitted node, whose template learns the input pattern.

previously established set of categorical alternatives and observable responses. At least two different types of learning can accompany such an assimilation process: learning that is external to the categorical recognition process and learning that is internal to this process.

As an example of external learning, suppose that the novel input is associated with a different reinforcement schedule than previous inputs in the same category. New learning between the category in F_2 and reinforcement mechanisms may alter the network's response to *all* the inputs in the category. Thus the very fact of membership in the same category may force forgetting of old external contingencies as new category exemplars are associated with new external contingencies.

As an example of internal learning, we consider the following facts. Even if a novel input pattern is coded by an "old" F_2 node, this input pattern may alter the bottom-up filter and top-down template corresponding to that node. In so doing, the novel input pattern may alter the categorical boundaries of the network as a whole. Input patterns which were coded by prescribed nodes on previous trials may no longer be coded by the same nodes when they are presented later on. Thus, even if the number of categories and their pathways to overt responses do not change, the categorical invariants may change.

The 2/3 Rule implies, however, that the filters and templates of a category are subsets of all the input patterns that are coded by that category. Adding a new input pattern to a category through learning can only refine further the filters and templates of the category. Thus, after a template becomes a subset of an input pattern by coding that pattern, the template remains a subset of the input pattern for all future time, no matter how many times the template is refined as other input patterns join the same category. As a template becomes progressively finer, the mismatch between the template and the largest input patterns coded by its category becomes progressively greater. If this mismatch becomes too great, then some of these large input patterns may eventually be recoded. For example, in Figure 10b, pattern B is coded by node v_1 on trial 2, and no new categories are established. Later, however, when pattern A is next presented on trial 4, it can no longer adequately match the template from node v_1, as it did after trial 1. Hence pattern A establishes a new category.

Two main conclusions follow from these considerations. First, the code learning process is one of progressive refinement of distinctions. The distinctions that emerge are the resultant of all the input patterns which the network ever experiences, rather than of some preassigned features. Second, the matching process compares whole patterns, not just separate features. For example, two different templates may overlap an input pattern to F_1 at the same set of feature detectors, yet the network could reset the F_2 node of one template yet not reset the F_2 node of the other template. The degree of mismatch of template and input *as a whole* determines whether recoding will occur. Thus the learning of categorical invariants resolves two opposing tendencies. As categories grow larger, and hence code increasingly global invariants, the templates which define them become smaller, and hence base the code on sets of critical feature groupings. This article shows how these two opposing tendencies can be resolved, leading to dynamic equilibration, or self-stabilization, of recognition categories in response to a prescribed input environment.

The next section describes how a sufficiently large mismatch between an input pattern and a template can lead to STM reset, while a sufficiently good match can terminate the search and enable learning to occur.

15. Vigilance, Orienting, and Reset

We now show how matching within the attentional subsystem at F_1 determines whether or not the orienting subsystem will be activated, thereby leading to reset of the attentional subsystem at F_2. The discussion can be broken into three parts:

A. *Distinguishing Active Mismatch from Passive Inactivity*

A severe mismatch at F_1 activates the orienting subsystem A. In the worst possible case of mismatch, none of the F_1 nodes can satisfy the 2/3 Rule, and thus no supraliminal activation of F_1 can occur. Thus in the worst case of mismatch, wherein F_1 becomes totally inactive, the orienting subsystem must surely be engaged.

On the other hand, F_1 may be inactive simply because no inputs whatsoever are being processed. In this case, activation of the orienting subsystem is not desired. How does the network compute the difference between active mismatch and passive inactivity at F_1?

This question led Grossberg (1980) to assume that the bottom-up input source activates two parallel channels (Figure 5a). The attentional subsystem receives a specific input pattern at F_1. The orienting subsystem receives convergent inputs at A from all the active input pathways. Thus the orienting subsystem can be activated only when F_1 is actively processing bottom-up inputs.

B. *Competition between the Attentional and Orienting Subsystems*

How, then, is a bottom-up input prevented from resetting its own F_2 code? What mechanism prevents the activation of A by the bottom-up input from *always* resetting the STM representation at F_2? Clearly inhibitory pathways must exist from F_1 to A (Figure 5a). When F_1 is sufficiently active, it prevents the bottom-up input to A from generating a reset signal to F_2. When activity at F_1 is attenuated due to mismatch, the orienting subsystem A is able to reset F_2 (Figure 5b,c,d). In this way, the orienting subsystem can distinguish between active mismatch and passive inactivity at F_1.

Within this general framework, we now show how a finer analysis of network dynamics, with particular emphasis on the 2/3 Rule, leads to a vigilance mechanism capable of regulating how coarse the learned categories will be.

C. *Collapse of Bottom-Up Activation due to Template Mismatch*

Suppose that a bottom-up input pattern has activated F_1 and blocked activation of A (Figure 5a). Suppose, moreover, that F_1 activates an F_2 node which reads-out a template that badly mismatches the bottom-up input at F_1 (Figure 5b). Due to the 2/3 Rule, many of the F_1 nodes which were activated by the bottom-up input alone are suppressed by the top-down template. Suppose that this mismatch event causes a large collapse in the total activity across F_1, and thus a large reduction in the total inhibition which F_1 delivers to A. If this reduction is sufficiently large, then the excitatory bottom-up input to A may succeed in generating a nonspecific reset signal from A to F_2 (Figure 5c).

In order to characterize when a reset signal will occur, we make the following natural assumptions. Suppose that an input pattern I sends positive signals to $| I |$ nodes of F_1. Since every active input pathway projects to A, I generates a total input to A that is proportional to $| I |$. We suppose that A reacts linearly to the total input $\gamma | I |$. We also assume that each active F_1 node generates an inhibitory signal of fixed size to A. Since every active F_1 node projects to A, the total inhibitory input $\delta | X |$ from F_1 to A is proportional to the number $| X |$ of active F_1 nodes. When $\gamma | I | > \delta | X |$, A receives a net excitatory signal and generates a nonspecific reset signal to F_2 (Figure 5c).

In response to a bottom-up input pattern I of size $| I |$, as in Figure 5a, the total inhibitory input from F_1 to A equals $\delta | I |$, so the net input to A equals $(\gamma - \delta) | I |$. In order to prevent A from firing in this case (Figure 5a), we assume that $\delta \geq \gamma$. We call

$$\rho = \frac{\gamma}{\delta} \tag{32}$$

the *vigilance parameter* of the orienting subsystem. The constraints $\delta \geq \gamma \geq 0$ are equivalent to $0 \leq \rho \leq 1$. The size of ρ determines the proportion of the input pattern which must be matched in order to prevent reset.

When both a bottom-up input I and a top-down template $V^{(j)}$ are simultaneously active (Figure 5b), the 2/3 Rule implies that the total inhibitory signal from F_1 to A equals $\delta | V^{(j)} \cap I |$. In this case, the orienting subsystem is activated only if

$$\gamma | I | > \delta | V^{(j)} \cap I |; \tag{33}$$

that is, if

$$\frac{| V^{(j)} \cap I |}{| I |} < \rho. \tag{34}$$

The function which determines whether or not F_2 will be reset in response to an input pattern I is called the Reset Function. Inequality (34) shows that the Reset Function should be defined as follows.

Reset Function

$$R_j = \frac{|\,V^{(j)} \cap I\,|}{|\,I\,|}. \tag{35}$$

The Reset Function R_j and the Order Function

$$T_j = \frac{\alpha\,|\,V^{(j)} \cap I\,|}{\beta + |\,V^{(j)}\,|} \tag{10}$$

determine how the search will proceed.

This line of argument can be intuitively recapitulated as follows. Due to the 2/3 Rule, a bad mismatch at F_1 causes a large collapse of total F_1 activity, which leads to activation of A. In order for this to happen, the system must maintain a measure of the prior level of total F_1 activity and compare this criterion level with the collapsed level of total F_1 activity. The criterion level is computed by summing bottom-up inputs at A. This sum can provide a criterion because it is proportional to the initial activation of F_1 by the bottom-up input, and yet it remains unchanged as the matching process unfolds in real-time.

Figure 13 summarizes the total network architecture. It includes the modulatory processes, such as attentional gain control, which regulate matching within F_1, as well as the modulatory processes, such as orienting arousal, which regulate reset within F_2. Figure 13 also includes an attentional gain control process at F_2. Such a process enables offset of the input pattern to terminate all STM activity within the attentional subsystem in preparation for the next input pattern. In this example, STM storage can persist after the input pattern terminates only if an internally generated or intermodality input source maintains the activity of the attentional gain control system.

16. Distinguishing Signal from Noise in Patterns of Variable Complexity: Weighing the Evidence

A variety of important properties follow from the conception outlined in Section 15 of how the orienting system is engaged by mismatch within the attentional subsystem. These properties all address the fundamental issue of how a system can distinguish between signal and noise as it processes inputs of variable complexity.

We now indicate how the network automatically rescales its noise criterion as the complexity of the input pattern varies. In particular, even with fixed parameters, the network can tolerate larger mismatches in response to larger input patterns. Suppose, for example, that the network processes two input patterns at different times. One input pattern $I^{(1)}$ activates just a few F_1 feature detectors, whereas the other input pattern $I^{(2)}$ activates many F_1 feature detectors; that is,

$$|\,I^{(1)}\,| < |\,I^{(2)}\,|\,. \tag{36}$$

Suppose, moreover, that $I^{(1)}$ activates the F_2 node v_1, $I^{(2)}$ activates the F_2 node v_2, and that

$$|\,V^{(1)} \cap I^{(1)}\,| = |\,V^{(2)} \cap I^{(2)}\,|\,. \tag{37}$$

In other words, both input patterns overlap their templates by the same amount. Due to (36), however,

$$R_1 = \frac{|\,V^{(1)} \cap I^{(1)}\,|}{|\,I^{(1)}\,|} > \frac{|\,V^{(2)} \cap I^{(2)}\,|}{|\,I^{(2)}\,|} = R_2. \tag{38}$$

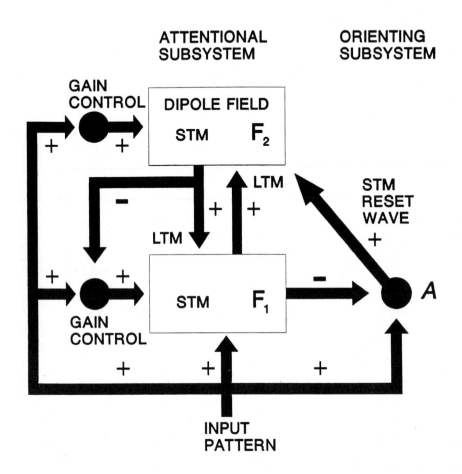

Figure 13. Anatomy of the attentional-orienting system: This figure describes all the interactions of the model without regard to which components are active at any given time.

By inequalities (34) and (38), the network is more likely to reset v_2 in response to $I^{(2)}$ than it is to reset v_1 in response to $I^{(1)}$. Thus a fixed amount of match with a large input pattern provides less evidence for coding than the same amount of match with a small input pattern. If (37) holds, then the larger pattern $I^{(2)}$ disagrees with the template at more features than does the smaller pattern $I^{(1)}$. Hence, by (38), v_2 may be reset whereas v_1 may not be reset; this will, in fact, be the case when ρ lies between R_1 and R_2.

The rescaling property shows that the network processes input patterns as a whole. The functional units of the network are activation patterns across a field of feature detectors, rather than individual activations of feature detectors.

If the network does not reset v_1 in response to $I^{(1)}$, then the template of v_1 is refined to equal the intersection $V^{(1)} \cap I^{(1)}$. In other words, given that the network accepts the evidence that $I^{(1)}$ should be coded by v_1, it then suppresses as noise the features at which $I^{(1)}$ disagrees with $V^{(1)}$, both in STM and in LTM.

Using this property, the network can also distinguish finer differences between small input patterns than between large input patterns. Suppose that the amount of mismatch between a small input pattern $I^{(1)}$ and its template $V^{(1)}$ equals the amount of mismatch between a large input pattern $I^{(2)}$ and its template $V^{(2)}$; that is,

$$I^{(1)} - | V^{(1)} \cap I^{(1)} | = I^{(2)} - | V^{(2)} \cap I^{(2)} | . \tag{39}$$

By (36) and (39),

$$R_1 = \frac{| V^{(1)} \cap I^{(1)} |}{| I^{(1)} |} < \frac{| V^{(2)} \cap I^{(2)} |}{| I^{(2)} |} = R_2. \tag{40}$$

Thus v_1 is more likely to be reset by $I^{(1)}$ than is v_2 to be reset by $I^{(2)}$. This shows that a fixed amount of mismatch offers more evidence for reset when the input pattern is simple than when it is complex. Otherwise expressed, since the network is reset by smaller mismatches when processing smaller input patterns, it automatically makes finer distinctions between smaller input patterns than between larger input patterns.

The simulation in Figure 14 illustrates how the network automatically rescales its matching criterion. On the first four presentations, the patterns are presented in the order ABAB. By trial 2, coding is complete. Pattern A directly accesses node v_1 on trial 3, and pattern B directly accesses node v_2 on trial 4. Thus patterns A and B are coded within different categories. On trials 5–8, patterns C and D are presented in the order CDCD. Patterns C and D are constructed from patterns A and B, respectively, by adding identical upper halfs to A and B. Thus, pattern C differs from pattern D at the same locations where pattern A differs from pattern B. However, because patterns C and D represent many more active features than patterns A and B, the difference between C and D is treated as noise, whereas the difference between A and B is considered significant. In particular, both patterns C and D are coded within the same category on trials 7 and 8.

The network's different categorization of patterns A and B vs. patterns C and D can be understood as follows. The core issue is: why on trial 2 does B reject the node v_1 which has coded A, whereas D on trial 6 accepts the node v_3 which has coded C? This occurs despite the fact that the mismatch between B and $V^{(1)}$ equals the mismatch between D and $V^{(3)}$:

$$| B | - | V^{(1)} \cap B | = 3 = | D | - | V^{(3)} \cap D |, \tag{41}$$

as in equation (39). The reason can be seen by comparing the relevant reset functions:

$$R_{1B} = \frac{| V^{(1)} \cap B |}{| B |} = \frac{8}{11} \tag{42}$$

and

$$R_{3D} = \frac{| V^{(3)} \cap D |}{| D |} = \frac{14}{17}. \tag{43}$$

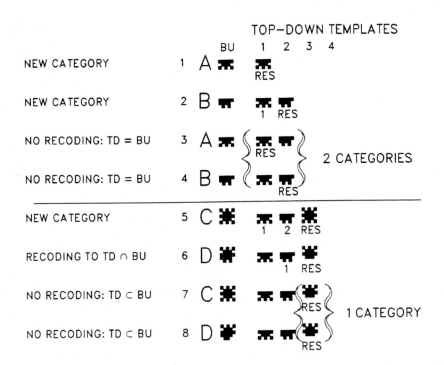

Figure 14. Distinguishing noise from patterns of inputs of variable complexity: Input patterns A and B are coded by the distinct category nodes v_1 and v_2, respectively. Input patterns C and D include A and B as subsets, but also possess idential subpatterns of additional features. Due to this additional pattern complexity, C and D are coded by the same category node v_3. At this vigilance level ($\rho = .8$), the network treats the difference between C and D as noise, and suppresses the discordant elements in the v_3 template. By contrast, it treats the difference between A and B as informative, and codes the difference in the v_1 and v_2 templates, respectively.

In this simulation, the vigilance parameter $\rho = .8$. Thus

$$R_{1B} < \rho < R_{3D}. \tag{44}$$

By (34), pattern B resets v_1 but D does not reset v_3. Consequently, B is coded by a different category than A, whereas D is coded by the same category as C.

17. Vigilance Level Tunes Categorical Coarseness: Environmental Feedback

The previous section showed how, given each fixed vigilance level, the network automatically rescales its sensitivity to patterns of variable complexity. The present section shows that changes in the vigilance level can regulate the coarseness of the categories that are learned in response to a fixed sequence of input patterns.

A low vigilance level leads to learning of coarse categories, whereas a high vigilance level leads to learning of fine categories. Suppose, for example, that a low vigilance level has led to a learned grouping of inputs which need to be distinguished for successful adaptation to a prescribed input environment. Suppose, moreover, that a punishing event occurs as a consequence of this erroneous grouping. Such a punishing event may have multiple effects on the organism. In addition to its negative reinforcing effects, we suppose that it also has a direct cognitive effect; namely, it increases attentive sensitivity to the environment. Such an increase in sensitivity is modeled within the network by an increase in the vigilance parameter, ρ. Increasing this single parameter enables the network to discriminate patterns which previously were lumped together. Once these patterns are coded by different categories in F_2, the different categories can be associated with different behavioral responses.

In this way, environmental feedback such as a punishing event can act as a "teacher" for a self-organizing recognition system. This teaching function does not take the form of an algorithm or any other type of pattern-specific information. Rather, it sets a single nonspecific parameter whose interaction with the internal organization of the network enables the network to parse more finely whatever input patterns happen to occur. The vigilance parameter will be increased, for example, if all the signals from the input pattern to A are nonspecifically amplified, so that parameter γ increases. A nonspecific decrease in the size of signals δ from F_1 to A will also increase ρ. Alternatively, reinforcement-activated nonspecific excitatory input to A can also facilitate mismatch-mediated activation of A. The process whereby the level of vigilance is monitored is one of the three types of nonspecific arousal that exist within the network.

Figure 15 describes a series of simulations in which four input patterns—A, B, C, D—are coded by a network with 4 nodes in F_2. In this simulation, $A \subset B \subset C \subset D$. The different parts of the figure show how categorical learning changes with changes of ρ. The simulation shows that any consecutive pair of patterns—(A, B), (B, C), (C, D)— can be coded in the same category at different vigilance levels. When $\rho = .8$ (Figure 15a), 4 categories are learned: (A)(B)(C)(D). When $\rho = .7$ (Figure 15b), 3 categories are learned: (A)(B)(C,D). When $\rho = .6$ (Figure 15c), 3 different categories are learned: (A)(B,C)(D). When $\rho = .5$ (Figure 15d), 2 categories are learned: (A,B)(C,D). When $\rho = .3$ (Figure 15e), 2 different categories are learned: (A,B,C,)(D). When $\rho = .2$ (Figure 15f), all the patterns are lumped together into a single category.

18. Universal Recognition Design Across Modalities

The properties that we have demonstrated using illustrative simulations generalize to the coding of arbitrary sequences of input patterns. The ability to group arbitrary inputs is needed, we suggest, because the same mechanisms of grouping are used across modalities. Each modality, such as speech and vision, undergoes multiple stages of preprocessing through which different invariant properties of its environmental inputs are abstracted. These abstract representations then feed, as input patterns, into an attentional-orienting system. We suggest that the attentional-orienting system obeys the same processing rules across modalities. In this sense, the attentional-orienting system realizes a universal processing design.

In order to illustrate how such a network codifies a more complex series of patterns, we show in Figure 16 the first 20 trials of a simulation using alphabet letters as input patterns. In Figure 16a, the vigilance parameter $\rho = .5$. In Figure 16b, $\rho = .8$. Three properties are notable in these simulations. First, choosing a different vigilance parameter can determine different coding histories, such that higher vigilance induces coding into finer categories. Second, the network modifies its search order on each trial to reflect the cumulative effects of prior learning, and bypasses the orienting system to directly access categories after learning has taken place. Third, the templates of coarser categories tend to be more abstract because they must approximately match a larger number of input pattern exemplars.

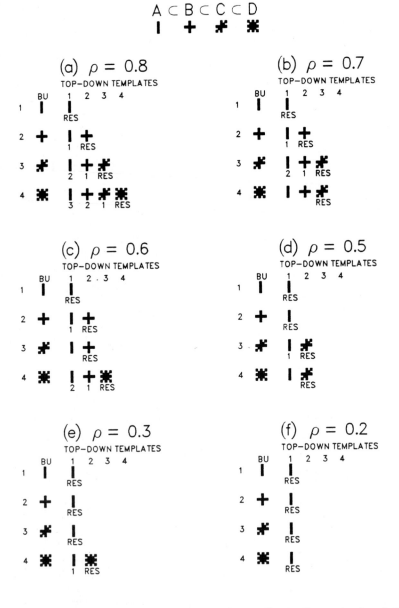

Figure 15. Influence of vigilance level on categorical groupings: As the vigilance parameter ρ decreases, the number of categories progressively decreases.

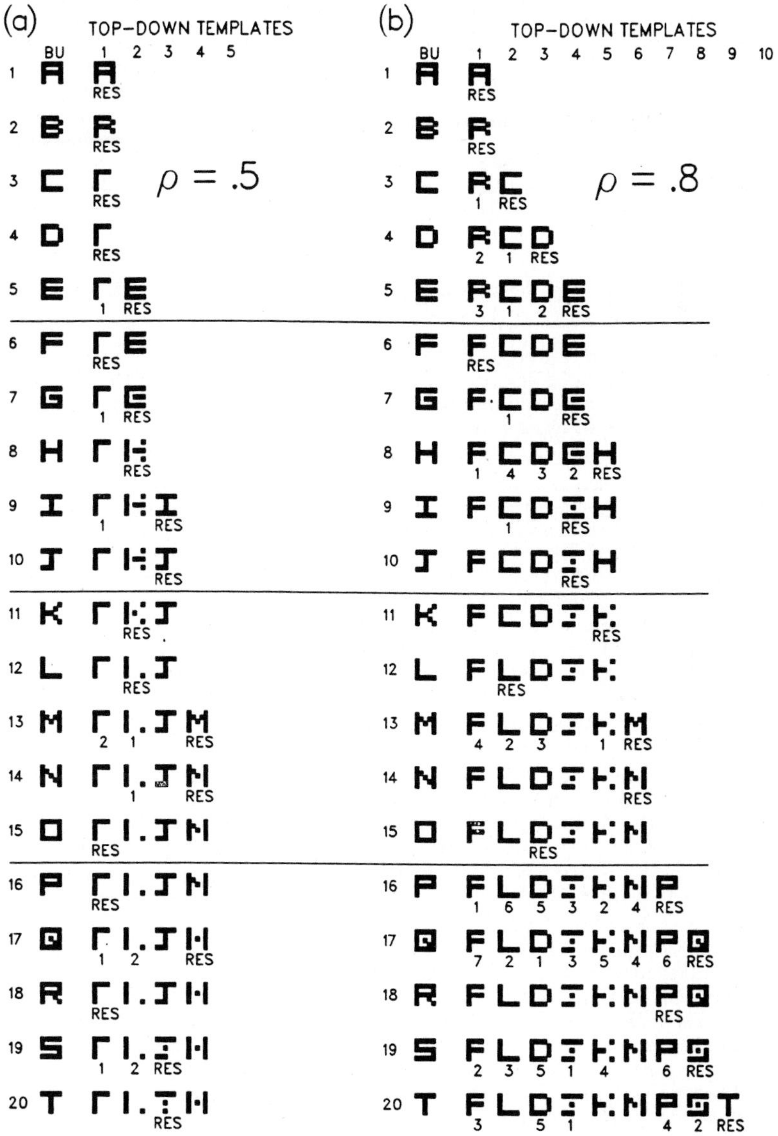

Figure 16. Alphabet learning: Different vigilance levels cause different numbers of letter categories to form.

Given $\rho = .5$, the network groups the 26 letter patterns into 8 stable categories within 3 presentations. In this simulation, F_2 contains 15 nodes. Thus 7 nodes remain uncoded because the network self-stabilizes its learning after satisfying criteria of vigilance and global code self-consistency. Given $\rho = .8$ and 15 F_2 nodes, the network groups 25 of the 26 letters into 15 stable categories within 3 presentations. The 26th letter is rejected by the network in order to self-stabilize its learning while satisfying its criteria of vigilance and global code self-consistency. These simulations show that the network's use of processing resources depends upon an evolving dynamical organization with globally context-sensitive properties. This class of networks is capable of organizing arbitrary sequences of arbitrarily complex input patterns into stable categories subject to the constraints of vigilance, global code self-consistency, and number of nodes in F_1 and F_2. If slow learning rather than fast learning rates are used (Section 9), then the categorical code may be learned more slowly but it still enjoys the critical properties just listed.

19. Interdisciplinary Relationships: Word Recognition, Evoked Potentials, and Medial Temporal Amnesia

In this article, we have described the formal properties of a neural network which is capable of self-stabilizing its learning of recognition categories. The theory which this network develops arose from an analysis of several types of data, and is currently being refined through its use in explaining other types of data.

For example, the adaptive resonance theory acticipated the discovery of the processing negativity evoked potential and has successfully predicted several important properties of the processing negativity, mismatch negativity, and P300 evoked potentials. A review of these applications is found in Grossberg (1984a). This article is contained in a book (Karrer, Cohen, and Tueting, 1984) which includes detailed descriptions of relevant evoked potential data. The attentional-orienting network enhibits properties that are homologous to those of evoked potentials. In particular, the process whereby a top-down attentional prime is matched against a bottom-up input pattern at F_1 may be compared with data about the *processing negativity* evoked potential. The process whereby the orienting subsystem is activated at A when a mismatch occurs may be compared with data about the *mismatch negativity* evoked potential. The process whereby STM is reset at F_2 in response to an unexpected event may be compared with data about the *P300* evoked potential.

The bottom-up and top-down interactions within the attentional subsystem have also been used to explain and predict data about word recognition and recall in normal subjects (Grossberg, 1984b, 1985a; Grossberg and Stone, 1985). In these data analyses, concepts such as attentional gain control and attentional primimg, which we have here related to code stabilization via the 2/3 Rule (Section 12), have enabled us to clarify and modify empirical models of "automatic activation" and "conscious attention" (Neely, 1977; Posner and Snyder, 1975a, 1975b).

Certain abnormal learning and recognition phenomena are strikingly similar to properties of a damaged attentional-orienting system. In considering this comparison, it is necessary to keep in mind that the attentional-orienting system is only one component in a larger neural theory of learning and memory. In particular, we do not herein extend this comparison to consider theoretical circuits for learned cognitive-motivational interactions, for serially ordered language utterances, or for sensory-motor coordination. Despite these limitations, it is of interest that injury to the orienting subsystem generates a type of amnesia that is reminiscent of amnesia in human patients, such as H.M., who have suffered injury to their medial temporal brain structures (Lynch, McGaugh, and Weinberger, 1984; Squire and Butters, 1984). In making this comparison, we will focus on issues relating to retrograde and anterograde amnesia, memory consolidation, impaired reactions to novel events, and differences between priming and recognition capabilities.

Suppose that the orienting subsystem ceases to function. Then the network cannot generate a search for new recognition categories. Consequently it cannot build up new recognition codes that would require a depthful search. On the other hand, well-established recognition categories can be directly accessed. Since they do not require intervention of the orienting subsystem, recognition codes which were established before the orienting subsystem failed are still accessible. Codes which were partially learned when the orienting subsystem failed may suffer variable degrees of impairment. Thus, failure of the orienting subsystem generates an amnesic syndrome with temporally limited retrograde amnesia and a temporally prolonged anterograde amnesia.

This amnesic syndrome is, in some respects, consistent with the following statement of Squire and Cohen (1984). "The medial temporal region establishes a relationship with distributed memory storage sites in neocortex and perhaps elsewhere; it then maintains the coherence of these ensembles until, as a result of consolidation, they can be maintained and can support retrieval on their own ... the amnesic deficit is due to impaired consolidation" (p.45). In a normal attentional-orienting system, memory consolidation occurs as the system progresses from searching the attentional subsystem via the orienting subsystem to directly accessing its learned codes without engaging the orienting subsystem. During this consolidation process, the orienting subsystem is disengaged as unfamiliar environmental events gain familiarity by building learned recognition categories. The amnesic syndrome of the attentional-orienting subsystem is thus due to "impaired consolidation," in agreement with Squire and Cohen (1984). However, the orienting subsystem does not "maintain the coherence of these ensembles." Rather, when these ensembles become coherent and globally self-consistent, they disengage the orienting subsystem.

The role played by the orienting subsystem in driving a search for a globally self-consistent code coexists with its equally important role in enabling the network to react to the mismatches generated by unexpected and/or unfamiliar events. This latter role is the basis for calling this system the orienting subsystem (Grossberg, 1982, 1984a). The theory thus shows how memory consolidation and novelty detection can be mediated by the same structure, which is suggested to be a medial temporal brain structure such as hippocampus. This interpretation is consistent with data concerning the inability of hippocampectomized rats to orient to novel cues (O'Keefe and Nadel, 1978) and with the progressive reduction in novelty-related hippocampal potentials as learning proceeds (Deadwyler, West, and Lynch, 1979; Deadwyler, West, and Robinson, 1981). In summary, ablation of the orienting subsystem, and by interpretation medial temporal brain regions such as hippocampus, can interfere both with reactions to novel cues and with memory consolidation.

The attentional-orienting subsystem clarifies how normal priming and abnormal recognition can coexist in amnesia. In brief, the attentional priming mechanism may be intact even if the orienting subsystem is not working. An attentional prime can improve recognition by facilitating direct access to the correct learned category. These properties are consistent with data showing effective priming in amnesic patients (Cohen, 1984; Graf, Squire, and Mandler, 1984; Mattis and Kovner, 1984; Warrington and Weiskrantz, 1970, 1974).

The dynamics of the attentional-orienting system also shed new light on concepts about the properties of multiple memory systems (Lynch, McGaugh, and Weinberger, 1984; Squire and Butters, 1984). These memory systems have been given different names by different authors. Ryle (1949) distinguished "knowing that" from "knowing how"; Bruner (1969) discussed "memory with record" and "memory without record"; Mishkin (1982) analysed "memories" and "habits"; Squire and Cohen (1984) contrasted "declarative memory" and "procedural memory." The attentional-orienting system may be classified, at least qualitatively, as a "declarative memory" system because it governs "the storage of or access to memory ordinarily acquired during the learning experience" (Squire and Cohen, 1984, p.39). Recent theoretical progress has enabled such a learned recognition system to be clearly distinguished, on the level of neural mechanism, from the learning systems which govern the acquisition of sensory-motor coordinations and plans (Grossberg, 1985a, 1985b; Grossberg and Kuperstein, 1985). These sensory-motor learning circuits provide examples of "procedural memory" systems.

When analysed on the level of mechanism, however, different types of memory systems cannot be neatly separated. For example, Squire and Cohen (1984) assume that attentional priming mechanisms form part of a procedural memory system *because* they are effective in amnesics whose recognition memory is impaired. In an attentional-orienting system, priming mechanisms form part of the attentional subsystem. The attentional subsystem, however, governs "the storage of or access to memory ordinarily acquired during the learning experience" (Squire and Cohen, 1984, p.39). Hence, by this criterion, attentional priming mechanisms should be included in a declarative memory system, not a procedural memory system. This difficulty reflects the general proposition that "procedures" cannot be separated from the contents, or "facts," that they manipulate, either in recognition systems or sensory-motor systems. This proposition in necessitated by the fact that the contents are learned, and thus the procedures must be defined interactively with respect to the evolving contents in order to be effective. In a sensory-motor system, the contents may not be "facts" that represent recognition events. They may represent different types of information, such as terminal motor maps, or short term memory patterns of temporal order information over item representations (Cohen and Grossberg, 1985; Grossberg and Kuperstein, 1985). These contents define the "procedures" which govern how the sensory-motor systems will operate.

Another example of this interdependence can be seen in the attentional-orienting system. This system, on the level of mechanism, exhibits both "procedural" and "declarative" elements. Moreover, it is a defect of its procedures that leads to amnesia for its facts. The "procedures" of the attentional-orienting system are the search routines that are mediated by the orienting subsystem. The orienting subsystem cannot search except through its interactions with the attentional subsystem, in keeping with the goal of the search to preserve old "facts" while learning new "facts" within the attentional subsystem. Thus there can be no search programs—no independently definable procedures—within the orienting subsystem because the global organization of the codes being searched changes during learning.

In summary, the processing terms which have been chosen to emphasize the separateness of multiple memory systems—such as procedures and facts—become less clear-cut on the mechanistic level. Both types of process seem to exist in each memory system. This observation does not deny the basic fact that different memory systems react to environmental inputs in different ways, so that a patient may be able to learn a sensory-motor skill without being able to recognize a person's face. However, it does clarify how an amnesic can use familiar visual recognition codes as the inputs which trigger new learning within a sensory-motor system, without also generating new visual recognition codes within the very object recognition system which processes the visual signals. In other words, these results suggest how H.M. may use familiar "facts" to generate novel "procedures" without also learning to recognize the unfamiliar "facts" that are perceptually grouped in new ways during the "procedures."

We conclude with a prediction. If the data about evoked potentials and medial temporal amnesics both reflect a common level of neural processing, then the mismatch negativity and P300 evoked potential of medial temporal amnesic patients should be much more impaired than their processing negativity evoked potentials during attentional priming experiments, with the processing negativity tested in a match situation and the mismatch negativity and P300 tested in a mismatch situation.

APPENDIX
NETWORK EQUATIONS

STM Equations

The STM activity of any node v_k in F_1 or F_2 obeys a membrane equation of the form

$$\frac{d}{dt}x_k = -Ax_k + (B - Cx_k)J_k^+ - Dx_kJ_k^-, \qquad (A1)$$

where J_k^+ and J_k^- are the total excitatory input and total inhibitory input, respectively, to v_k and A, B, C, D are nonnegative parameters. If $C > 0$, then the STM activity $x_k(t)$ remains within the finite interval $[0, BC^{-1}]$ no matter how large the inputs J_k^+ and J_k^- are chosen.

We denote nodes in F_1 by v_i, where $i = 1, 2, \ldots, M$. We denote nodes in F_2 by v_j, where $j = M + 1, M + 2, \ldots, N$. Thus by (A1),

$$\frac{d}{dt}x_i = -A_1x_i + (B_1 - C_1x_i)J_i^+ - D_1x_iJ_i^- \qquad (A2)$$

and

$$\frac{d}{dt}x_j = -A_2x_j + (B_2 - C_2x_j)J_j^+ - D_2x_jJ_j^-. \qquad (A3)$$

The input J_i^+ is a sum of the bottom-up input I_i and the top-down template

$$V_i = \sum_j f(x_j)z_{ji}, \qquad (A4)$$

that is,

$$J_i^+ = I_i + V_i, \qquad (A5)$$

where $f(x_j)$ is the signal generated by activity x_j of v_j, and z_{ji} is the LTM trace in the pathway from v_j to v_i.

The inhibitory input J_i^- controls the attentional gain:

$$J_i^- = F\sum_j f(x_j). \qquad (A6)$$

Thus $J_i^- = 0$ if and only if F_2 is inactive (Figures 6 and 7).

The inputs and parameters of STM activities in F_2 were chosen so that the F_2 node which received the largest input from F_1 wins the competition for STM activity. Theorems in Ellias and Grossberg (1975), Grossberg (1973), and Grossberg and Levine (1975) show how these parameters can be chosen. The inputs J_j^+ and J_j^- have the following form.

Input J_j^+ adds a positive feedback signal $g(x_j)$ from v_j to itself to the bottom-up adaptive filter input

$$T_j = \sum_i h(x_i)z_{ij}, \qquad (A7)$$

that is,

$$J_j^+ = g(x_j) + T_j, \qquad (A8)$$

where $h(x_i)$ is the signal emitted by v_i and z_{ij} is the LTM trace in the pathway from v_i to v_j. Input J_j^- adds up negative feedback signals $g(x_k)$ from all the other nodes in F_2:

$$J_j^- = \sum_{k \neq j} g(x_k). \tag{A9}$$

Such a network behaves approximately like a binary switching circuit:

$$x_j = \begin{cases} G & \text{if } T_j > \max(T_k : k \neq j) \\ 0 & \text{otherwise.} \end{cases} \tag{A10}$$

LTM Equations

The LTM trace of the bottom-up pathway from v_i to v_j obeys a learning equation of the form

$$\frac{d}{dt} z_{ij} = f(x_j)[-H_{ij} z_{ij} + K h(x_i)]. \tag{A11}$$

In (A11), term $f(x_j)$ is a postsynaptic sampling, or learning, signal because $f(x_j) = 0$ implies $\frac{d}{dt} z_{ij} = 0$. Term $f(x_j)$ is also the output signal of v_j to pathways from v_j to F_1, as in (A4).

The LTM trace of the top-down pathway from v_j to v_i also obeys a learning equation of the form

$$\frac{d}{dt} z_{ji} = f(x_j)[-H_{ji} z_{ji} + K h(x_i)]. \tag{A12}$$

In the present simulations, the simplest choice of H_{ji} was made for the top-down LTM traces:

$$H_{ji} = H = \text{constant.} \tag{A13}$$

A more complex choice of H_{ji} was made for the bottom-up LTM traces. This was done to directly generate the Weber Law Rule of Section 8 via the bottom-up LTM process itself. The Weber Law Rule can also be generated indirectly by exploiting a Weber Law property of competitive STM interactions across F_1. Such an indirect instantiation of the Weber Law Rule enjoys several advantages and will be developed elsewhere. In particular, it would enable us to also choose $H_{ij} = H = \text{constant}$. Instead, we allowed the bottom-up LTM traces at each node v_j to compete among themselves for synaptic sites. Malsburg and Willshaw (1981) have used a related idea in their model of retinotectal development. In the present usage, it was essential to choose a shunting competition to generate the Weber Law Rule, unlike the Malsburg and Willshaw usage. Thus we let

$$H_{ij} = L h(x_i) + \sum_{k \neq i} h(x_k). \tag{A14}$$

A physical interpretation of this choice can be seen by rewriting (A11) in the form

$$\frac{d}{dt} z_{ij} = f(x_j)[(K - L z_{ij}) h(x_i) - z_{ij} \sum_{k \neq i} h(x_k)]. \tag{A15}$$

By (A15), when the postsynaptic signal $f(x_j)$ is positive, a positive presynaptic signal $h(x_i)$ commits receptor sites to the LTM process z_{ij} at a rate $(K - L z_{ij}) h(x_i) f(x_j)$. Simultaneously, signals $h(x_k)$, $k \neq i$, which reach v_j at different regions of the v_j

membrane compete for sites which are already committed to z_{ij} via the mass action competitive terms $-z_{ij}f(x_j)h(x_k)$. When z_{ij} equilibrates to these competing signals,

$$z_{ij} = \frac{Kh(x_i)}{(L-1)h(x_i) + \sum_k h(x_k)}. \tag{A16}$$

The signal function $h(w)$ was chosen to rise quickly from 0 to 1 at a threshold activity level w_0. Thus if v_i is a suprathreshold node in F_1, (A16) approximates

$$z_{ij} \cong \frac{K}{(L-1) + |X|} \tag{A17}$$

where $|X|$ is the number of active nodes in F_1. Thus z_{ij} obeys a Weber Law Rule if $L > 1$. By comparison with (2), $\alpha = K$ and $\beta = L - 1$.

STM Reset System

The simplest possible mismatch-mediated activation of A and STM reset of F_2 by A were implemented in the simulations. As outlined in Section 15, each active input pathway sends an excitatory signal of size γ to A. Potentials x_i of F_1 which exceed a signal threshold T generate an inhibitory signal of size $-\delta$ to A. Population A, in turn, generates a nonspecific reset wave to F_2 whenever

$$\gamma\,|\,I\,| - \delta\,|\,X\,| > 0, \tag{A18}$$

where I is the current input pattern and $|X|$ is the number of nodes across F_1 such that $x_i > T$. The nonspecific reset wave shuts off the active F_2 node until the input pattern I shuts off. Thus (A10) must be modified to shut off all F_2 nodes which have been reset by A during the presentation of I.

REFERENCES

Basar, E., Flohr, H., Haken, H., and Mandell, A.J. (Eds.), **Synergetics of the brain.** New York: Springer-Verlag, 1983.

Bruner, J.S., Modalities of memory. In G.A. Talland and N.C. Waugh (Eds.), **The pathology of memory.** New York: Academic Press, 1969.

Carpenter, G.A. and Grossberg, S., Neural dynamics of adaptive pattern recognition: Priming, search, attention, and category formation. *Society for Neuroscience Abstracts,* **11,** 1985 (a).

Carpenter, G.A. and Grossberg, S., Self-organization of neural recognition categories. In preparation, 1985 (b).

Cohen, M.A. and Grossberg, S., Neural dynamics of speech and language coding: Developmental programs, perceptual grouping, and competition for short term memory. *Human Neurobiology,* in press, 1985.

Cohen, N.J., Preserved learning capacity in amnesia: Evidence for multiple memory systems. In L. Squire and N. Butters (Eds.), **The neuropsychology of memory.** New York: Guilford Press, 1984, pp.83–103.

Deadwyler, S.A., West, M.O., and Lynch, G., Activity of dentate granule cells during learning: Differentiation of perforant path inputs. *Brain Research,* 1979, **169,** 29–43.

Deadwyler, S.A., West, M.O., and Robinson, J.H., Entorhinal and septal inputs differentially control sensory-evoked responses in the rat dentate gyrus. *Science,* 1981, **211,** 1181–1183.

Ellias, S.A. and Grossberg, S., Pattern formation, contrast control, and oscillations in the short term memory of shunting on-center off-surround networks. *Biological Cybernetics,* 1975, **20,** 69–98.

Graf, P., Squire, L.R., and Mandler, G., The information that amnesic patients do not forget. *Journal of Experimental Psychology: Learning, Memory, and Cognition,* 1984, **10,** 164–178.

Grossberg, S., Contour enhancement, short-term memory, and constancies in reverberating neural networks. *Studies in Applied Mathematics,* 1973, **52,** 217–257.

Grossberg, S., Adaptive pattern classification and universal recoding, I: Parallel development and coding of neural feature detectors. *Biological Cybernetics,* 1976, **23,** 121–134 (a).

Grossberg, S., Adaptive pattern classification and universal recoding, II: Feedback, expectation, olfaction, and illusions. *Biological Cybernetics,* 1976, **23,** 187–202 (b).

Grossberg, S., A theory of human memory: Self-organization and performance of sensory-motor codes, maps, and plans. In R. Rosen and F. Snell (Eds.), **Progress in theoretical biology, Vol. 5.** New York: Academic Press, 1978, pp.233–374.

Grossberg, S., How does a brain build a cognitive code? *Psychological Review,* 1980, **87,** 1–51.

Grossberg, S., Processing of expected and unexpected events during conditioning and attention: A psychophysiological theory. *Psychological Review,* 1982, **89,** 529–572.

Grossberg, S., The quantized geometry of visual space: The coherent computation of depth, form, and lightness. *Behavioral and Brain Sciences,* 1983, **6,** 625–692.

Grossberg, S., Some psychophysiological and pharmacological correlates of a developmental, cognitive, and motivational theory. In R. Karrer, J. Cohen, and P. Tueting (Eds.), **Brain and information: Event related potentials.** New York: New York Academy of Sciences, 1984 (a).

Grossberg, S., Unitization, automaticity, temporal order, and word recognition. *Cognition and Brain Theory*, 1984, **7**, 263–283 (b).

Grossberg, S., The adaptive self-organization of serial order in behavior: Speech, language, and motor control. In E.C. Schwab and H.C. Nusbaum (Eds.), **Pattern recognition by humans and machines**, Vol. 1. New York: Academic Press, 1985 (a).

Grossberg, S., The role of learning in sensory-motor control. *Behavioral and Brain Sciences*, in press, 1985 (b).

Grossberg, S. and Kuperstein, M., **Adaptive neural dynamics of sensory-motor control: Ballistic eye movements**. Amsterdam: North-Holland, 1985.

Grossberg, S. and Levine, D.S., Some developmental and attentional biases in the contrast enhancement and short term memory of recurrent neural networks. *Journal of Theoretical Biology*, 1975, **53**, 341–380.

Grossberg, S. and Mingolla, E., Neural dynamics of form perception: Boundary completion, illusory figures, and neon color spreading. *Psychological Review*, 1985, **92**, 173–211 (a).

Grossberg, S. and Mingolla, E., Neural dynamics of perceptual grouping: Textures, boundaries, and emergent segmentations. Submitted for publication, 1985 (b).

Grossberg, S. and Stone, G.O., Neural dynamics of word recognition and recall: Attentional priming, learning, and resonance. *Psychological Review*, in press, 1985.

Karrer, R., Cohen, J., and Tueting, P. (Eds.), **Brain and information: Event related potentials**. New York: New York Academy of Sciences, 1984.

Lynch, G., McGaugh, J.L., and Weinberger, N.M. (Eds.), **Neurobiology of learning and memory**. New York: Guilford Press, 1984.

Malsburg, C. von der and Willshaw, D.J., Differential equations for the development of topological nerve fibre projections. In S.Grossberg (Ed.), **Mathematical psychology and psychophysiology**. Providence, RI: American Mathematical Society, 1981.

Mattis, S. and Kovner, R., Amnesia is as amnesia does: Toward another definition of the anterograde amnesias. In L. Squire and N. Butters (Eds.), **Neuropsychology of memory**. New York: Guilford Press, 1984.

Mishkin, M., A memory system in the monkey. *Philosophical Transactions of the Royal Society of London*, 1982, **B298**, 85–95.

Neely, T.H., Semantic priming and retrieval from lexical memory: The roles of inhibitionless spreading activation and limited capacity attention. *Journal of Experimental Psychology: General*, 1977, **106**, 226–254.

O'Keefe, J. and Nadel, L., **The hippocampus as a cognitive map**. Oxford: Oxford University Press, 1978.

Posner, M.I. and Snyder, C.R.R., Attention and cognitive control. In R.L. Solso (Ed.), **Information processing and cognition: The Loyola symposium**. Hillsdale, NJ: Erlbaum, 1975 (a).

Posner, M.I. and Snyder, C.R.R., Facilitation and inhibition in the processing of signals. In P.M.A. Rabbitt and S. Dornic (Eds.), **Attention and performance V**. New York: Academic Press, 1975 (b).

Ryle, G., **The concept of mind**. San Francisco: Hutchinson, 1949.

Squire, L.R. and Butters, N. (Eds.), **Neuropsychology of memory**. New York: Guilford Press, 1984.

Squire, L.R. and Cohen, N.J., Human memory and amnesia. In G. Lynch, J. McGaugh, and N.M. Weinberger (Eds.), **Neurobiology of learning and memory**. New York: Guilford Press, 1984, pp.3–64.

Warrington, E.K. and Weiskrantz, L., The amnesic syndrome: Consolidation or re-trieval? *Nature*, 1970, **228**, 628-630.

Warrington, E.K. and Weiskrantz, L., The effect of prior learning on subsequent reten-tion in amnesic patients. *Neuropsychologia*, 1974, **12**, 419-428.

Chapter 5

ABSOLUTE STABILITY OF GLOBAL PATTERN FORMATION AND PARALLEL MEMORY STORAGE BY COMPETITIVE NEURAL NETWORKS

Preface

Competitive interactions have played an important role in all of the previous chapters, whether in preventing a network's response from saturating in response to an intense input pattern, or choosing the population which receives the largest input, or normalizing a network's total activation capacity, or storing an activation pattern in short term memory. Stephen Smale has proved, however, that the set of all competitive dynamical systems contains systems which are capable of exhibiting essentially arbitrary dynamical behavior. It is therefore essential that we rigorously identify those competitive systems which are capable of the types of desirable biological behavior that we desire.

This Chapter describes some of the types of competitive dynamical systems that can generate complex oscillations in response to their inputs. A theorem is then proved which identifies a large class of competitive dynamical systems whose members are capable of storing an activation pattern in short term memory in response to any sustained input pattern, no matter how the system's numerical parameters are chosen. This class of competitive dynamical systems includes all the recurrent on-center off-surround networks whose inhibitory interaction strengths are a function of the distance between the populations in the network.

The mathematical insights derived from this analysis have been used to guide the computer simulations of speech, visual, and cognitive grouping processes that are reported in Volume II. These results also contrast sharply with the computer simulations in Chapters 6–8 of mammalian circadian rhythms. Our model of circadian rhythms is also built up from a competitive network, but one whose feedback pathways are multiplicatively gated by slowly accumulating chemical transmitters. When such a competitive network's feedback pathways are gated by very rapidly accumulating chemical transmitters, it obeys the hypotheses of the theorem in this Chapter, and hence cannot generate any sustained oscillations. Together these results illustrate how parameter selection by the evolutionary process can choose networks with qualitatively different emergent properties from a basic network design, or template.

IEEE Transactions on Systems, Man, and Cybernetics
SMC-13, 815–826 (1983)
©1983 IEEE
Reprinted by permission of the publisher

ABSOLUTE STABILITY OF GLOBAL PATTERN FORMATION AND PARALLEL MEMORY STORAGE BY COMPETITIVE NEURAL NETWORKS

Michael A. Cohen† and Stephen Grossberg†

Abstract

The process whereby input patterns are transformed and stored by competitive cellular networks is considered. This process arises in such diverse subjects as the short-term storage of visual or language patterns by neural networks, pattern formation due to the firing of morphogenetic gradients in developmental biology, control of choice behavior during macromolecular evolution, and the design of stable context-sensitive parallel processors. In addition to systems capable of approaching one of perhaps infinitely many equilibrium points in response to arbitrary input patterns and initial data, one finds in these subjects a wide variety of other behaviors, notably traveling waves, standing waves, resonance, and chaos. The question of what general dynamical constraints cause global approach to equilibria rather than large amplitude waves is therefore of considerable interest. In another terminology, this is the question of whether global pattern formation occurs. A related question is whether the global pattern formation property persists when system parameters slowly change in an unpredictable fashion due to self-organization (development, learning). This is the question of absolute stability of global pattern formation. It is shown that many model systems which exhibit the absolute stability property can be written in the form

$$\frac{d}{dt}x_i = a_i(x_i)\left[b_i(x_i) - \sum_{k=1}^{n} c_{ik}d_k(x_k)\right] \qquad (1)$$

$i = 1, 2, \ldots, n$, where the matrix $C = \| c_{ik} \|$ is symmetric and the system as a whole is competitive. Under these circumstances, this system defines a global Liapunov function. The absolute stability of systems with infinite but totally disconnected sets of equilibrium points can then be studied using the LaSalle invariance principle, the theory of several complex variables, and Sard's theorem. The symmetry of matrix C is important since competitive systems of the form (1) exist wherein C is arbitrarily close to a symmetric matrix but almost all trajectories persistently oscillate, as in the voting paradox. Slowing down the competitive feedback without violating symmetry, as in the systems

$$\frac{d}{dt}x_i = a_i(x_i)\left[b_i(x_i) - \sum_{k=1}^{n} c_{ik}d_k(y_k)\right]$$

† Supported in part by the Air Force Office of Scientific Research (AFOSR 82-0148) and the National Science Foundation (NSF IST-80-00257).

$$\frac{d}{dt} y_i = e_i(x_i)[f_i(x_i) - y_i],$$

also enables sustained oscillations to occur. Our results thus show that the use of fast symmetric competitive feedback is a robust design constraint for guaranteeing absolute stability of global pattern formation.

I. Introduction: Absolute Stability of Global Pattern Formation in Self-Organizing Networks

This article proves a global limit theorem for a class of n-dimensional competitive dynamical systems that can be written in the form

$$\dot{x}_i = a_i(x_i)[b_i(x_i) - \sum_{k=1}^{n} c_{ik} d_k(x_k)], \tag{1}$$

$i = 1, 2, \ldots, n$, where the coefficients $\| c_{ij} \|$ form a symmetric matrix. The systems (1) are more general in some respects but less general in other respects than the *adaptation level* competitive dynamical systems

$$\dot{x}_i = a_i(x)[b_i(x_i) - c(x)] \tag{2}$$

where $x = (x_1, x_2, \ldots, x_n)$ and $i = 1, 2, \ldots, n$, that have previously been globally analysed (Grossberg, [14], [18], [21]). To clarify the significance of the present theorem, some of the varied physical examples that can be written in the form (1) are summarized in this section. Section II indicates how these examples physically differ from related examples wherein sustained oscillations of various types can occur. Section III begins the mathematical development of the article.

System (1) includes the nonlinear neural networks

$$\dot{x}_i = -A_i x_i + (B_i - C_i x_i)[I_i + f_i(x_i)] - (D_i x_i + E_i)[J_i + \sum_{k=1}^{n} F_{ik} g_k(x_k)], \tag{3}$$

$i = 1, 2, \ldots, n$. In (3), x_i is the potential, or short-term memory activity, of the ith cell (population) v_i in the network. Term $-A_i x_i$ describes the passive decay of activity at rate $-A_i$. Term

$$(B_i - C_i x_i)[I_i + f_i(x_i)] \tag{4}$$

describes how an excitatory input I_i and an excitatory feedback signal $f_i(x_i)$ increase the activity x_i. If $C_i = 0$, then term (4) describes an additive effect of input and feedback signal activity (Grossberg [10]). If $C_i > 0$, then the input and feedback signal become ineffective when $x_i = B_i C_i^{-1}$ since then $B_i - C_i x_i = 0$. In this case, term (4) describes a shunting or multiplicative effect of input and feedback signals on activity. In a shunting network, the initial value inequality $x_i(0) \leq B_i C_i^{-1}$ implies that $x_i(t) \leq B_i C_i^{-1}$ for all $t \geq 0$, as occurs in nerve cells which obey the membrane equation (Hodgkin [24], Katz [26], Kuffler and Nicholls [28]). Term

$$-(D_i x_i + E_i)[J_i + \sum_{k=1}^{n} F_{ik} g_k(x_k)] \tag{5}$$

in (3) describes how an inhibitory input J_i and inhibitory feedback signals $F_{ik} g_k(x_k)$ from cell v_k to v_i decrease the activity x_i of v_i. If $D_i = 0$, then (5) describes an additive effect of input and feedback signals on activity. If $D_i > 0$, then the input and feedback signals become ineffective when $x_i = -D_i^{-1}E_i$, since then $D_i x_i + E_i = 0$. In this case, (5) describes a shunting effect of input and feedback signals on activity. An initial value choice $x_i(0) \geq -D_i^{-1}E_i$ implies that $x_i(t) \geq -D_i^{-1}E_i$ for all $t \geq 0$. Thus in a shunting network, but not an additive network, each activity $x_i(t)$ is restricted to a finite interval for all time $t \geq 0$. Suitably designed shunting networks can automatically retune their sensitivity to maintain a sensitive response within these finite intervals even if their inputs fluctuate in size over a much broader dynamic range (Grossberg [12], [21]).

The networks (1) are part of a mathematical classification theory, reviewed in [21], which characterizes how prescribed changes in system parameters alter the transformation from input patterns $(I_1, I_2, \ldots, I_n, J_1, J_2, \ldots, J_n)$ into activity patterns $(x_1, x_2, \ldots, x_n)$. In addition to the study of prescribed transformations, the mathematical classification theory seeks the most general classes of networks wherein important general processing requirements are guaranteed. In the present article, we study a class of networks which transform arbitrary input patterns into activity patterns that are then stored in short-term memory until a future perturbation resets the stored pattern. This property, also called *global pattern formation*, means that given any physically admissible input pattern $(I_1, I_2, \ldots, I_n, J_1, J_2, \ldots, J_n)$ and initial activity pattern $x(0) = (x_1(0), x_2(0), \ldots, x_n(0))$, the limit $x(\infty) = \lim_{t \to \infty}(x_1(t), x_2(t), \ldots, x_n(t))$ exists. The networks (1) include examples wherein nondenumerably many equilibrium points $x(\infty)$ exist (Grossberg [12], [21]).

A related property is the *absolute stability* of global pattern formation, which means that global pattern formation occurs given *any* choice of parameters in (1). The absolute stability property is of fundamental importance when (1) is part of a self-organizing (e.g., developing, learning) system, as in Grossberg ([15], [19]). Then network parameters can slowly change due to self-organization in an unpredictable way. Each new parameter choice may determine a different transformation from input pattern to activity pattern. An absolute stability theorem guarantees that, whatever transformation occurs, the network's ability to store the activity pattern is left invariant by self-organization. Thus the identification of an absolutely stable class of systems constrains the mechanisms of self-organization with which a system can interact without becoming destabilized in certain input environments.

The neural networks (3) include a number of models from population biology, neurobiology, and evolutionary theory. The Volterra-Lotka equations

$$\dot{x}_i = G_i x_i \left(1 - \sum_{k=1}^{n} H_{ik} x_k\right) \tag{6}$$

of population biology are obtained when $A_i = C_i = I_i = E_i = J_i = 0$ and $f_i(w) = g_i(w) = w$ for all $i = 1, 2, \ldots, n$. The related Gilpin and Ayala system [6]

$$\dot{x}_i = G_i x_i \left[1 - \left(\frac{x_i}{K_i}\right)^{\theta_i} - \sum_{k=1}^{n} H_{ik}\left(\frac{x_k}{K_k}\right)\right] \tag{7}$$

is obtained when $A_i = C_i = I_i = E_i = J_i = 0$, $f_i(w) = 1 - w^{\theta_i} K_i^{-\theta_i}$ and $g_i(w) = wK_i^{-1}$ for all $i = 1, 2, \ldots, n$.

The Hartline-Ratliff equation [34]

$$r_i = e_i - \sum_{k=1}^{n} K_{ik} \max(r_k - r_{ik}^{(0)}, 0) \tag{8}$$

for the steady-state outputs r_i of the Limulus retina arises as the equation of equilibrium of an additive network $(C_i = D_i = 0)$ if, in addition, $f_i(w) = 0$ and $g_i(w) = \max(w - L_i, 0)$ for all $i = 1, 2, \ldots, n$ (Grossberg [8], [9]).

The Eigen and Schuster equation [4]

$$\dot{x}_i = x_i \left(m_i x_i^{p-1} - q \sum_{k=1}^{n} m_k x_k^p \right) \qquad (9)$$

for the evolutionary selection of macromolecular quasi-species is a special case of (3) such that $A_i = C_i = I_i = E_i = J_i = 0$, $B_i = F_{ik} = 1$, $D_i = q$, and $f_i(w) = g_i(w) = m_i x_i^p$ for all $i, k = 1, 2, \ldots, n$. Feedback interactions among excitatory and inhibitory morphogenetic substances leading to "firing," or contrast enhancement, of a morphogenetic gradient can also be modeled by shunting networks (Grossberg [13], [16], [20]).

II. Some Sources of Sustained Oscillations

The tendency of the trajectories (1) to approach equilibrium points is dependent on the symmetry of the matrix $\| c_{ij} \|$ of interaction coefficients. Examples exist wherein the coefficient matrix may be chosen as close to a symmetric matrix as one pleases, yet almost all trajectories persistently oscillate even if all the functions $a_i(x_i)$, $b_i(x_i)$, and $d_k(x_k)$ are linear functions of their arguments. The May and Leonard model [33] of the voting paradox is illustrative. This model is defined by the three-dimensional system

$$
\begin{aligned}
\dot{x}_1 &= x_1(1 - x_1 - \alpha x_2 - \beta x_3) \\
\dot{x}_2 &= x_2(1 - \beta x_1 - x_2 - \alpha x_3) . \\
\dot{x}_3 &= x_3(1 - \alpha x_1 - \beta x_2 - x_3)
\end{aligned}
\qquad (10)
$$

Grossberg [17] and Schuster *et al.* [36] proved that if $\beta > 1 > \alpha$ and $\alpha + \beta > 2$, then all positive trajectories except the uniform trajectories $x_1(0) = x_2(0) = x_3(0)$ persistently oscillate as $t \to \infty$. The matrix

$$
\begin{pmatrix}
1 & \alpha & \beta \\
\beta & 1 & \alpha \\
\alpha & \beta & 1
\end{pmatrix}
\qquad (11)
$$

can be chosen arbitrarily close to a symmetric matrix by letting α and β approach one without violating the hypotheses of Grossberg's theorem.

In a neural network such as (3), the hypothesis that the coefficient matrix $\| F_{ij} \|$ is symmetric is justified when the inhibitory interaction strengths F_{ij} and F_{ji} between cell v_i and cell v_j depend on the intercellular distance. Thus the tendency of the trajectories of (1) to approach equilibrium is interpreted in physical examples as a consequence of intercellular geometry.

The tendency to approach equilibrium also depends upon the rapidity with which feedback signals are registered. In (3), for example, the excitatory and inhibitory feedback signals $f_i(x_i)$ and $F_{ik}g_k(x_k)$, respectively, both depend explicitly on the excitatory activities x_i. *In vivo* these feedback signals are often emitted by interneuronal cells that are activated by the activities x_i before they return signals to v_i. Then (3) is replaced by the more general system

$$
\begin{aligned}
\dot{x}_i = &- A_i x_i + (B_i - C_i x_i)[I_i + f_i(w_i)] \\
&- (D_i x_i + E_i)[J_i + \sum_{k=1}^{n} F_{ik}g_k(y_k)]
\end{aligned}
\qquad (12)
$$

$$\dot{w}_i = U_i(x_i)[W_i(x_i) - w_i] \tag{13}$$

$$\dot{y}_i = V_i(x_i)[Y_i(x_i) - y_i] \tag{14}$$

where w_i is the potential of an excitatory interneuron and y_i is the potential of an inhibitory interneuron that is activated by x_i. Large amplitude standing and traveling periodic waves have been found in continuum analogs of (12)–(14) (Ellias and Grossberg [5]). System (12)–(14) is more general than (3) because (12)–(14) reduce to a system of the form (3) when both w_i and y_i equilibrate very rapidly to fluctuations in x_i. Thus the tendency to approach equilibrium in (1) is due to both the symmetry and the speed of its feedback signals. Often as one perturbs off system (3) to a system of the form (12)–(14), one finds limiting patterns followed by standing waves followed by traveling waves [5]. In the neural network theory of short-term memory storage, both limiting patterns and standing waves are acceptable storage mechanisms; see [15] and [19] for physical background. One approach to achieving these properties is to prove directly the global existence of limiting patterns for fast feedback systems such as (1), as we do in this article, and then to perturb off (1) by slowing down the feedback to characterize the parameter region wherein large amplitude standing waves are found before they bifurcate into large amplitude traveling waves.

Much more complex oscillations can also be inferred to exist in neural networks due to a mathematical relationship that exists between neural networks and models of individual nerve cells wherein complex oscillations have been proved to exist (Carpenter [1], [2]). This relationship allows the inference that traveling bursts and chaotic waveforms can be generated by suitably designed networks. To see why this is so, consider the following generalization of system (12)–(14):

$$\dot{x}_i = -A_i x_i + (B - C_i x_i)[I_i + \sum_{k=1}^{n} f_{ik}(w_k) z_{ik}]$$
$$- (D_i x_i + E_i)[J_i + \sum_{k=1}^{n} g_{ik}(y_k)] \tag{15}$$

$$\dot{w}_i = U_i(x_i)[W_i(x_i) - w_i] \tag{13}$$

$$\dot{y}_i = V_i(x_i)[Y_i(x_i) - y_i] \tag{14}$$

and

$$\dot{z}_{ik} = M_{ik} - N_{ik} z_{ik} - P_{ik} f_{ik}(w_k) z_{ik}. \tag{16}$$

Equation (15) permits excitatory feedback signaling from a cell v_k to v_i via the term $f_{ik}(w_k) z_{ik}$, as well as inhibitory feedback signaling via the term $g_{ik}(y_k)$. The new terms z_{ik} *gate* the excitatory feedback signal $f_{ik}(w_k)$ before it reaches v_i. *In vivo* such a gating action often corresponds to the release of a chemical transmitter at a rate proportional to $f_{ik}(w_k) z_{ik}$. Correspondingly, term $M_{ik} - N_{ik} z_{ik}$ in (16) describes the transmitter's slow accumulation to an asymptote $M_{ik} N_{ik}^{-1}$, whereas term $P_{ik} f_{ik}(w_k) z_{ik}$ describes the removal of transmitter at a rate proportional to $f_{ik}(w_k) z_{ik}$ (Grossberg [8], [11]). Equation (16) can be rewritten, analogous to (13) and (14), in the form

$$\dot{z}_{ik} = Q_{ik}(w_k)[Z_{ik}(w_k) - z_{ik}]. \tag{17}$$

However, whereas $W_i(x_i)$ and $Y_i(x_i)$ in (13) and (14) are increasing functions of x_i,

$$Z_{ik}(w_k) = M_{ik}[N_{ik} + P_{ik} f_{ik}(w_k)]^{-1} \tag{18}$$

is a decreasing function of w_k. Often *in vivo* the excitatory interneuronal potential w_i equilibrates rapidly to x_i in (13). Then $Z_{ik}(w_k)$ may be approximated by a decreasing function of x_i. When this is true, the variables w_i, y_i, and z_{ik} play a role in the network that is formally analogous to the role played by the variables m, n, and h of the Hodgkin-Huxley equations for nerve impulse transmissions ([1], [2]). By relabeling cells appropriately, letting w_i rapidly equilibrate to x_i, and making a special choice of parameters and signals, then sum $-A_i x_i + (B - C_i x_i) \sum_{k=1}^{n} f_{ik}(w_k) z_{ik}$ in (15) can be rewritten in the form

$$D(x_{i-1} + x_{i+1} - 2x_i) + (B - x_i)h_i(x_i)z_i. \tag{19}$$

Term $D(x_{i-1} = x_{i+1} - 2x_i)$ plays the role of the diffusion term in the Hodgkin-Huxley equations. Carpenter's results on bursts and chaotic waves therefore hold in neural networks just so long as a spatially discrete version of the Hodgkin-Huxley equations can also support these waves.

Our concern in this article is not, however, to generate complex traveling waves but rather to rule them out. To accomplish this in a robust fashion, we turn to (1) because it eliminates both the waves due to fast feedback in an asymmetric geometry and the waves due to slow feedback in a symmetric geometry.

III. A Global Liapunov Function

The adaptation level competitive systems

$$\dot{x}_i = a_i(x)\big(b_i(x_i) - c(x)\big) \tag{2}$$

were globally analysed by associating a suitable Liapunov functional $M^+(x_t)$ to every such system. This functional, which is an integral of a maximum function

$$M^+(x_t) = \int_0^t \max_i [b_i(x_i(v)) - c(x(v))]dv, \tag{20}$$

permitted a concept of *jump*, or *decision*, to be associated with (2). Using this concept, the idea could be explicated that the decision schemes of adaptation level systems are globally consistent and thereby cause every trajectory to approach an equilibrium point ([14], [18]). By contrast, when the same method was applied to the voting paradox system (10), it was found that the decision scheme of this system is globally inconsistent, and thus almost all trajectories persistently oscillate ([17], [18]). Although every competitive system defines such a Liapunov functional and a decision scheme, this method has not yet succeeded in proving that the decision scheme of (1) is globally consistent. Such a theorem is greatly to be desired.

In its absence, we have found that the systems (1) admit a global Liapunov function which can be analysed. A considerable amount of work has already been done on finding Liapunov functions for special cases of (1). For example, a Liapunov function which proves local asymptotic stability of isolated equilibrium points of Volterra-Lotka systems was described in a classical paper of MacArthur [32]. Global Liapunov functions for Volterra-Lotka and Gilpin-Ayala systems have been found in cases where only one equilibrium point exists (Goh and Agnew [7]). This constraint is much too strong in systems that are designed to transform and store a large variety of patterns. Our analysis includes systems which possess infinitely many equilibrium points. Liapunov functions have also been described for Volterra-Lotka systems whose off-diagonal interaction terms are relatively small (Kilmer [27], Takeuchi *et al.* [37]). We do not need this type of constraint to derive our results.

The function

$$V(x) = -\sum_{i=1}^{n} \int_0^{x_i} b_i(\xi_i)d_i'(\xi_i)d\xi_i$$
$$+ \frac{1}{2} \sum_{j,k=1}^{n} c_{jk}d_j(x_j)d_k(x_k) \tag{21}$$

is a global Liapunov function for (1) because

$$\dot{V}(x) = -\sum_{i=1}^{n} a_i(x_i) d_i'(x_i) \left[b_i(x_i) - \sum_{k=1}^{n} c_{ik} d_k(x_k) \right]^2. \tag{22}$$

Function $\dot{V}(x) \leq 0$ along trajectories just so long as every function $d_i(x_i)$ is monotone nondecreasing. This condition implies that (1) is competitive. In (3), where $d_i \equiv g_i$, the condition means that inhibitory feedback $g_i(x_i)$ cannot decrease as activity x_i increases. Systems (1) can, in fact, be written in the gradient form

$$\dot{x} = A(x) \nabla B(x) \tag{23}$$

if each function $d_i(x_i)$ is strictly increasing by choosing the matrix $A(x) = \| A_{ij}(x) \|$ to satisfy

$$A_{ij}(x) = \frac{a_i(x_i)\delta_{ij}}{d_i'(x_i)} \tag{24}$$

and $B(x) = -V(x)$.

The standard theorems about Liapunov functions and gradient representations imply that each trajectory converges to the largest invariant set M contained in the set E where [22]

$$\frac{d}{dt}V = 0. \tag{25}$$

Given definition (21) of $V(x)$, it is easy to see that points in E are equilibrium points if each function $d_i(x_i)$ is strictly increasing. It still remains to show in this case that each trajectory approaches a unique equilibrium point, although for all practical purposes every trajectory that approaches M becomes approximately constant in any bounded interval of sufficiently large times.

Further argument is required when each function $d_i(x_i)$ is not strictly increasing, which is the typical situation in a neural network. There each inhibitory feedback signal function $d_i(x_i)$ can possess an *inhibitory signal threshold* Γ_i^- such that $d_i(x_i) = 0$ if $x_i \leq \Gamma_i^-$ and $d_i'(x_i) > 0$ if $x_i > \Gamma_i^-$. Since each $d_i(x_i)$ is still monotone nondecreasing, although not strictly increasing, function $V(x)$ in (21) continues to define a Liapunov function. Consequently, every trajectory still converges to the invariant set M. However, further analysis is now required to guarantee that M consists of equilibrium points, let alone isolated equilibrium points. Even in the cases wherein no such degeneracy occurs, it has not previously been noticed that so many physically important examples can be written in the form (1) and that (1) admits a global Liapunov function.

IV. Application of the LaSalle Invariance Principle

We will study the general system

$$\dot{x}_i = a_i(x_i) \left[b_i(x_i) - \sum_{k=1}^{n} c_{ik} d_k(x_k) \right] \tag{1}$$

under hypotheses that include the shunting competitive neural networks

$$\dot{y}_i = -A_i y_i + (B_i - C_i y_i)[I_i + f_i(y_i)]$$
$$- (D_i y_i + E_i)[J_i + \sum_{k=1}^{n} F_{ik} g_k(y_k)]. \tag{26}$$

In the shunting case, $C_i \neq 0 \neq D_i$. The simpler additive neural networks wherein $C_i = 0 = D_i$ are also included in our analysis but will not be explicitly discussed. In the shunting case, (26) can be rewritten without loss of generality in the form

$$\dot{y}_i = - A_i y_i + (B_i - y_i)[I_i + f_i(y_i)]$$
$$- (y_i + C_i)[J_i + \sum_{k=1}^{n} F_{ik} g_k(y_k)] \qquad (27)$$

by a suitable redefinition of terms.

We distinguish x_i in (1) from y_i in (27) because our hypotheses hold when

$$x_i = y_i + C_i. \qquad (28)$$

Then (27) reduces to (1) via the definitions

$$a_i(x_i) = x_i, \qquad (29)$$

$$b_i(x_i) = x_i^{-1}\{A_i C_i - (A_i + J_i)x_i + (B_i + C_i - x_i)[I_i + f_i(x_i - C_i)]\}, \qquad (30)$$

$$c_{ik} = F_{ik}, \qquad (31)$$

and

$$d_k(x_k) = g_k(x_k - C_k). \qquad (32)$$

Our first task is to prove that $V(x)$ is a Liapunov function of x in the positive orthant $\Re_n^+$. To do this, we study (1) under the following hypotheses:

a) *symmetry*: matrix $\| c_{ij} \|$ is a symmetric matrix of nonnegative constants;

b) *continuity*: function $a_i(\xi)$ is continuous for $\xi \geq 0$; function $b_i(\xi)$ is continuous for $\xi > 0$;

c) *positivity*: function $a_i(\xi) > 0$ for $\xi > 0$; function $d_i(\xi) \geq 0$ for $\xi \in (-\infty, \infty)$;

d) *smoothness and monotonicity*: function $d_i(\xi)$ is differentiable and monotone nondecreasing for $\xi \geq 0$.

To prove that $V(x)$ is a Liapunov function, we first show that positive initial data generate positive bounded trajectories of (1), henceforth called *admissible* trajectories. This can be shown if two more hypotheses are assumed. The choice of hypotheses (34)–(36) below is influenced by the fact that function b_i in (30) may become unbounded as $x_i \to 0+$.

Lemma 1 (Boundedness and Positivity):

Boundedness: For each $i = 1, 2, \ldots, n$, suppose that

$$\limsup_{\xi \to \infty}[b_i(\xi) - c_{ii} d_i(\xi)] < 0. \qquad (33)$$

Positivity: For each $i = 1, 2, \ldots, n$, suppose either that

$$\lim_{\xi \to 0+} b_i(\xi) = \infty \qquad (34)$$

or that

$$\lim_{\xi \to 0+} b_i(\xi) < \infty \qquad (35)$$

and

$$\int_0^\epsilon \frac{d\xi}{a_i(\xi)} = \infty \quad \text{for some } \epsilon > 0. \tag{36}$$

Then any positive initial data generate an admissible trajectory.

Proof: Boundedness is proved using (33) as follows. Inequality

$$b_i(x_i) - \sum_{k=1}^n c_{ik}d_k(x_k) \leq b_i(x_i) - c_{ii}d_i(x_i) \tag{37}$$

is true because all c_{ik} and d_k are nonnegative. Since also $a_i(x_i)$ is positive at large x_i values, (37) shows that $(d/dt)x_i < 0$ at large x_i values. Indeed, given any positive initial data, an $L_i < \infty$ exists such that $x_i(t) \leq L_i$ at sufficiently large times t, $i = 1, 2, \ldots, n$.

Condition (34) implies positivity because each term $\sum_{k=1}^n c_{ik}d_k(x_k)$ is bounded if all $x_k \leq L_k$, $k = 1, 2, \ldots, n$; hence term $b_i(x_i) - \sum_{k=1}^n c_{ik}d_k(x_k)$ becomes positive if all $x_k \leq L_k$, $k = 1, 2, \ldots, n$ as $x_i \to 0+$. Since also $a_i(x_i) > 0$ for $x_i > 0$, $(d/dt)x_i > 0$ before x_i reaches 0, hence x_i can never reach zero.

If (35) and (36) hold, then at the first time $t = T$ such that $x_i(T) = 0$,

$$-\infty = \int_{x_i(0)}^0 \frac{d\xi}{a_i(\xi)} = \int_0^T \left[b_i(x_i(t)) - \sum_{k=1}^n c_{ik}d_k(x_k(t)) \right] dt > -\infty, \tag{38}$$

which is a contradiction. Hence $x_i(t)$ remains positive for all $t \geq 0$.

Using the fact that positive initial data generate admissible trajectories, we can easily verify that the function

$$V(x) = -\sum_{k=1}^n \int_0^{x_i} b_i(\xi_i)d_i'(\xi_i)d\xi_i + \frac{1}{2} \sum_{j,k=1}^n c_{jk}d_j(x_j)d_k(x_k) \tag{21}$$

is a Liapunov function.

Proposition I (Liapunov Function): The function $V(x)$ satisfies

$$\frac{d}{dt}V(x(t)) \leq 0 \tag{39}$$

on admissible trajectories.

Proof: By direct computation,

$$\frac{d}{dt}V(x(t)) = -\sum_{i=1}^n a_i(x_i(t))d_i'(x_i(t)) \cdot \left[b_i(x_i(t)) - \sum_{k=1}^n c_{ik}d_k(x_k(t)) \right]^2. \tag{22}$$

Since $a_i \geq 0$ on admissible trajectories and $d_i' \geq 0$ by hypothesis, (39) follows.

In some cases where d_i admits a threshold, d_i' is only piecewise differentiable. In these cases, the trajectory derivative $(d/dt)V$ can be replaced by

$$D^+V(x) = \lim_{h \to 0+} \inf \frac{1}{h}[V(x + h\dot{x}) - V(x)] \tag{40}$$

and the Riemann integral $\int_0^{x_i} b_i(\xi_i)d_i'(\xi_i)d\xi_i$ in the definition of $V(x)$ can be replaced by a Radon integral.

To apply the LaSalle invariance principle ([22], [29], [30]) to $V(x)$, we also need to guarantee that $V(x)$ is bounded and continuous on admissible trajectories.

Proposition 2: If the hypotheses of Lemma 1 hold, then $V(x)$ (or a simple redefinition thereof) is bounded and continuous on admissible trajectories.

Proof: If (35) holds, then the integrals

$$\int_0^{x_i} b_i(\xi_i) d_i'(\xi_i) d\xi_i \tag{41}$$

in (21) are bounded because admissible trajectories are bounded. The remaining terms

$$\sum_{j,k=1}^n c_{jk} d_j(x_j) d_k(x_k) \tag{42}$$

of (21) are bounded because the functions $d_j(x_j)$ are continuous functions of bounded variables.

If (34) holds but

$$\lim_{\xi \to 0+} | b_i(\xi) d_i'(\xi) | < \infty, \tag{43}$$

then the same argument as above is valid. If (43) does not hold, then the integral $\int_0^{x_i}$ in (21) can be replaced by an integral $\int_{\lambda_i}^{x_i}$, where λ_i is a positive constant that is chosen below. Such a choice is possible due to several facts working together. Each d_k is a nonnegative and monotone nondecreasing function of the variable x_k, where $0 \leq x_k \leq L_k$ at sufficiently large time, $k = 1, 2, \ldots, n$. Consequently, a positive finite L exists such that

$$\sum_{k=1}^n c_{ik} d_k(x_k) \leq L \tag{44}$$

on all admissible trajectories at sufficiently large times. Since (34) holds, an interval $[0, 2\lambda_i]$ exists such that

$$b_i(x_i) - \sum_{k=1}^n c_{ik} d_k(x_k) \geq L \tag{45}$$

and thus

$$\dot{x}_i \geq L a_i(x_i) \tag{46}$$

whenever $0 < x_i \leq 2\lambda_i$ on any admissible trajectory at sufficiently large times. Since function a_i is positive on any interval $[x_i(T), 2\lambda_i]$ where $x_i(T) > 0$, a_i has a positive lower bound on this interval. Thus by (46), if T is chosen so large that (44) holds for $t \geq T$, then $x_i(t)$ increases at least at a linear rate until it exceeds λ_i and remains larger than λ_i thereafter. Since this argument holds for any admissible trajectory. the choice of λ_i in the integral $\int_{\lambda_i}^{x_i}$ is justified.

Continuity follows by inspection of each term in (21), replacing the integral $\int_0^{x_i}$ by $\int_{\lambda_i}^{x_i}$ where necessary.

The LaSalle invariance principle therefore implies the following theorem.

Theorem 1 (Convergence of Trajectories): In any system

$$\dot{x}_i = a_i(x_i) \Big[b_i(x_i) - \sum_{k=1}^n c_{ik} d_k(x_k) \Big] \tag{1}$$

such that

a) matrix $\| c_{ij} \|$ is symmetric and all $c_{ij} \geq 0$;

b) function a_i is continuous for $\xi \geq 0$; function b_i is continous for $\xi > 0$;

c) function $a_i > 0$ for $\xi > 0$; function $d_i \geq 0$ for all ξ;

d) function d_i is differentiable and monotone nondecreasing for $\xi \geq 0$;

e)$\limsup_{\xi \to \infty}[b_i(\xi) - c_{ii}d_i(\xi)] < 0$ (33)

for all $i = 1, 2, \ldots, n$;

f) and either

$$\lim_{\xi \to 0+} b_i(\xi) = \infty \qquad (34)$$

or

$$\lim_{\xi \to 0+} b_i(\xi) < \infty \qquad (35)$$

and

$$\int_0^\epsilon \frac{d\xi}{a_i(\xi)} = \infty \quad \text{for some } \epsilon > 0; \qquad (36)$$

all admissible trajectories approach the largest invariant set M contained in the set

$$E = \{y \in \Re^n : \frac{d}{dt}V(y) = 0, y \geq 0\}, \qquad (47)$$

where

$$\frac{d}{dt}V = -\sum_{i=1}^n a_i d_i' \Big[b_i - \sum_{k=1}^n c_{ik}d_k\Big]^2. \qquad (22)$$

Corollary 1: If each function d_i is strictly increasing, then the set E consists of equilibrium points of (1).

Proof: Because each function a_i and d_i' is nonnegative on admissible trajectories, each summand in (22) is nonnegative. Hence the result follows by inspection of (47) and (22).

V. Decomposition of Equilibria into Suprathreshold and Subthreshold Variables

Our strategy for analysing M when the functions d_i can have thresholds is to decompose the variables x_i into suprathreshold and subthreshold variables, and then to show how sets of suprathreshold equilibria can be used to characterize the ω-limit set of the full system (1). To say this more precisely, we now define some concepts.

The *inhibitory threshold* of d_i is a constant $\Gamma_i^- \geq 0$ such that

$$\begin{cases} d_i(\xi) = 0 & \text{if } \xi \leq \Gamma_i^- \\ d_i'(\xi) > 0 & \text{if } \xi > \Gamma_i^-. \end{cases} \qquad (48)$$

The function $x_i(t)$ is *suprathreshold* at t if $x_i(t) > \Gamma_i^-$ and *subthreshold* at t if $x_i(t) \leq \Gamma_i^-$. At any time t, suprathreshold variables receive signals only from other suprathreshold variables.

Because only suprathreshold variables signal other suprathreshold variables, we can first restrict attention to all possible subsets of suprathreshold values that occur in the ω-limit points $\omega(\gamma)$ of each admissible trajectory γ. Using the fact that each function d_i is strictly increasing in the suprathreshold range, we will show that the suprathreshold subset corresponding to each ω-limit point defines an equilibrium point of the subsystem of (1) that is constructed by eliminating all the subthreshold variables of the ω-limit point. We will show that the set of all such subsystem suprathreshold equilibrium points is countable. We can then show that under a weak additional hypothesis, the ω-limit set of each trajectory is an equilibrium point, and that the set of equilibrium points is totally disconnected. First we make a generic statement about almost all systems (1), and then we study particular classes of neural networks (3) whose global pattern formation properties can be directly verified.

VI. Almost All Suprathreshold Equilibrium Sets Are Countable

In this section, we observe that, for almost all choices of the parameters c_{ik} in (1), Sard's theorem routinely implies that the set of suprathreshold equilibrium points is countable ([23], [25]). A generic statement can also be made by varying functions a_i, b_i, and d_i within the class C^1 by combining the Sard theorem with Fubini's theorem. The Sard theorem is stated as Theorem 2 for completeness.

Let X be an open set in $\Re^m$, P an open set in $\Re^k$, and Z an open set in $\Re^n$. Let $S : X \times P \to Z$ be a C^1 map. A point $z \in \Re^n$ is said to be a *regular value* of S if rank $dS(\cdot, \cdot) = n$ whenever $S(x, p) = z$, where dS denotes the $n \times (m + k)$ Jacobian matrix of S.

Theorem 2 (Sard): Let z be a regular value of S. Then z is a regular value of $S(\cdot, p)$ for almost all $p \in P$ in the sense of Lebesgue measure.

Corollary 2: Let each a_i, b_i, and d_i be in $C^1(0, \infty)$. Let P denote the matrix of parameters $|| c_{ik} ||$. Then a measure zero subset $Q \subset P$ exists such that the suprathreshold equilibria of (1) corresponding to parameters $p \in P \backslash Q$ are countable.

Proof: To consider the equilibrium points of (1), we let $z = 0$ and define the vector function $S = (S_1, S_2, \ldots, S_n)$ by

$$S_i(x) = a_i(x_i)\Big[b_i(x_i) - \sum_{k=1}^{n} c_{ik}d_k(x_k)\Big], \qquad (49)$$

$i = 1, 2, \ldots, n$. Then the points for which $S = 0$ are the equilibrium points of (1).

To prove that $dS(\cdot, \cdot)$ has rank n at the suprathreshold equilibria $S = 0$, we prove the stronger statement that $dS(\cdot, \cdot)$ has rank n at all suprathreshold vectors x; that is, at all $x_i > \Gamma_i^- \geq 0$, $i = 1, 2, \ldots, n$. By (49)

$$\frac{\partial S_i}{\partial c_{ii}} = -a_i(x_i)d_i(x_i) \qquad (50)$$

where, by the positivity of a_i when $x_i > 0$ and the inhibitory threshold condition (48), $a_i(x_i)d_i(x_i) > 0$ at any suprathreshold value of x_i. The corresponding n rows and columns of dS form a diagonal submatrix whose ith entry is given by (50). Matrix dS therefore has rank n at all suprathreshold vectors x.

The main condition of Sard's theorem is hereby satisfied by this matrix S. Thus a set Q of measure zero exists such that $dS(\cdot, p)$ has rank n for all $p \in P \backslash Q$. Now the inverse function theorem can be used at each $p \in P \backslash Q$ to show that the suprathreshold equilibrium points x of $S(x, p) = 0$ are isolated, hence countable.

VII. All ω-Limit Points Are Equilibria

Theorem 3 (Global Pattern Formation): Let all the hypotheses of Theorem 1 hold. Also suppose that no level sets of the functions b_i contain an open interval and that the subsystem suprathreshold equilibrium vectors are countable. Then each admissible trajectory converges to an equilibrium point.

Proof: Consider the ω-limit set $\omega(\gamma)$ of a given admissible trajectory γ. Since Theorem 1 holds, each component x_i of $x \in \omega(\gamma)$ satisfies either

$$a_i(x_i)\Big[b_i(x_i) - \sum_{k=1}^{n} c_{ik}d_k(x_k)\Big] = 0 \tag{51}$$

or

$$d_i'(x_i) = 0. \tag{52}$$

In the former case, x_i is suprathreshold; in the latter case, subthreshold.

Using this decomposition, we can show that a unique vector of subsystem suprathreshold values exist corresponding to each $\omega(\gamma)$ in the following way. The set $\omega(\gamma)$ is connected. If two or more vectors of subsystem suprathreshold values existed, an uncountable set of subsystem suprathreshold vectors would exist in $\omega(\gamma)$. This basic fact can be seen by projecting $\omega(\gamma)$ onto a coordinate where the two hypothesized vectors differ. The image of $\omega(\gamma)$ on this coordinate is a connected set. This fact, together with the definition of a suprathreshold value, implies that a nontrivial interval of suprathreshold values exists in this image. The inverse image of this interval therefore contains a nondenumerable set of subsystem suprathreshold vectors, a conclusion that contradicts the hypothesis that the set of subsystem suprathreshold vectors is countable. Hence no more than one subsystem suprathreshold vector exists in each $\omega(\gamma)$.

Using this fact, we now show that the subthreshold values of each $\omega(\gamma)$ are uniquely determined. Let $U(\gamma)$ be the indices of the unique subsystem suprathreshold vector $(x_i^* : i \in U(\gamma))$ of $\omega(\gamma)$. For every $i \notin U(\gamma)$, (1) can be rewritten as

$$\dot{x}_i = a_i(x_i)[b_i(x_i) - e_i] + \epsilon(t) \tag{53}$$

where the constant e_i satisfies

$$e_i = \sum_{k \in U(\gamma)} c_{ik}d_k(x_k^*) \tag{54}$$

and

$$\lim_{t \to \infty} \epsilon(t) = 0 \tag{55}$$

because a_i is bounded on admissible trajectories. To complete the proof, we use the fact that the level sets of b_i do not contain an open interval to conclude that each x_i, $i \notin U(\gamma)$, has a limit. Since also each x_i, $i \in U(\gamma)$, has a limit, it will follow that each $\omega(\gamma)$ is an equilibrium point.

The proof shows that the ω-limit set of the one-dimensional equation (53) is a point. Suppose not. Since (53) defines a one-dimensional system, the ω-limit set, being connected, is then a nontrivial closed interval V_i. By hypothesis, the function $b_i - e_i$ in (53) cannot vanish identically on any nontrivial subinterval of V_i. Since function $b_i - e_i$ is continuous, a subinterval $W_i \subset V_i$ and an $\epsilon > 0$ exist such that either $b_i(\xi) - e_i \geq \epsilon$ if $\xi \in W_i$ or $b_i(\xi) - e_i \leq -\epsilon$ if $\xi \in W_i$. In either case, x_i will be forced off interval W_i at all sufficiently large times by (55) and the fact that $a_i > 0$ except when $x_i = 0$. Hence no nontrivial interval W_i can be contained in the ω-limit set of (53). This ω-limit set is thus a point, and the proof is complete.

Corollary 3 (Almost Absolute Stability): Consider the class of systems (1) such that

1) hypotheses (a)–(f) of Theorem 1 hold;

2) each function a_i, b_i, and d_i is in $C^1(0, \infty)$;

3) none of the level sets of b_i contains an open interval.

Then for almost all choices of the parameters c_{ik}, global pattern formation occurs.

Proof: The proof follows directly from Corollary 2 and Theorem 3.

The hypotheses of Theorem 3 allow us to conclude that the set of all equilibrium points of (1) is a totally disconnected set. A *totally disconnected* set is a set whose largest connected subset is a point.

Instead of considering the solutions of $b_i(\xi) = e_i$ corresponding to the ω-limit set $\omega(\gamma)$ of individual trajectories, as we did to prove Theorem 3, in this proof we consider the set of solutions of $b_i(\xi) = e_i$ generated by arbitrary admissible trajectories.

Theorem 4 (Totally Disconnected Equilibrium Set): Suppose that each b_i is continuous, that no level set of b_i contains an open interval, and that the system suprathreshold equilibrium vectors are countable. Then the set of all equilibrium points of (1) is totally disconnected.

Proof: Each choice of subsystem suprathreshold vectors defines a constant value of e_i in (54). For fixed e_i, the level set

$$\{\xi : b_i(\xi) - e_i = 0\} \tag{56}$$

is nowhere dense, since if (56) were dense on some interval, the continuity of b_i would imply that the level set (56) contains an open interval, which is impossible.

By hypothesis, only countably many choices of e_i exist for each $i = 1, 2, \ldots, n$. Since each set (56) is nowhere dense, the set of all subthreshold equilibrium solutions of (53) is a countable union of nowhere dense sets and is therefore nowhere dense by the Baire category theorem. By hypothesis, the set of all subsystem suprathreshold equilibrium solutions of (1) is countable. The set of all x_i solutions corresponding to the subsystem suprathreshold equilibrium solutions of (1) is therefore also countable. The union P_i of the nowhere dense subthreshold set and the countable suprathreshold set is totally disconnected. The product set $X_{i=1}^n P_i$ is also totally disconnected. Since the set of all equilibria of (1) is contained in $X_{i=1}^n P_i$, it is totally disconnected.

VIII. Neural Networks with Finitely Many Suprathreshold Equilibrium Points

To remove the "almost all" from results such as Corollary 3, we consider various special cases that are of physical interest, notably the shunting competitive networks (27) with polynomial or sigmoid feedback signal functions. We write the networks (27) using the change of variables

$$x_i = y_i + C_i \tag{28}$$

to make the results comparable to previous results about (1). Then (27) can be written as

$$\dot{x}_i = S_i(x), \qquad i = 1, 2, \ldots, n \tag{57}$$

such that

$$S_i(x) = \alpha_i + (\beta_i - x_i) F_i(x_i) - x_i \left(\gamma_i + \sum_{k=1}^n c_{ik} G_k(x_k)\right) \tag{58}$$

where

$$\alpha_i = a_i c_i + (b_i + c_i) I_i, \tag{59}$$

$$\beta_i = b_i + c_i, \tag{60}$$

$$\gamma_i = a_i + I_i + J_i, \tag{61}$$

$$F_i(x_i) = f_i(x_i - c_i), \tag{62}$$

and

$$G_i(x_i) = g_i(x_i - c_i). \tag{63}$$

One natural approach to proving that only finitely many suprathreshold equilibrium points exist is to apply a basic theorem from the theory of several complex variables [35]. The following results illustrate rather than exhaust the applications of this theorem to our systems.

The theorem in question concerns analytic subvarieties of a connected open set Ω of $C^n = \{n-\text{tuplets of complex variables}\}$. A set $V \subset \Omega$ is an *analytic subvariety* of Ω if every point $p \in \Omega$ has a neighborhood $N(p)$ such that

$$V \cap N(p) = \bigcap_{i=1}^{r} Z(h_i) \tag{64}$$

where $Z(h_i)$ is the set of zeros of the function h_i holomorphic in $N(p)$. Our applications derive from the following theorem.

Theorem 5: Every compact analytic subvariety of a connected open set Ω is a finite set of points.

A general strategy for applying Theorem 5 to neural networks can be stated as five steps.

1) Choose the signal functions F_i and G_i in (62) and (63), respectively, to be real analytic on their suprathreshold intervals.

2) Extend the definitions of F_i and G_i to make them complex analytic inside a sufficiently large open disk. (It does not matter that the analytic extension of the signal function to the subthreshold interval no longer agrees with the original definition of the function.)

3) Extend S_i in (58) to be an analytic function $\Phi(z)$ in an open connected set $\Omega_i \subset C^n$.

4) Show that the solutions to the system of equations

$$\phi(z) = 0, \qquad i = 1, 2, \ldots, n \tag{65}$$

are contained in a bounded open set P whose closure is contained in $\Omega = \cap_{i=1}^{n}\Omega_i$. Since the set sof zeros is closed, the set of zeros is a compact analytic subvariety of Ω, hence finite.

5) Set all imaginary parts of these zeros equal to zero to prove that finitely many suprathreshold equilibria exist.

The method is illustrated by the following three theorems.

Theorem 6 (Polynomial Signals): Let each function $F_i(\xi)$ and $G_i(\xi)$ be a polynomial in the suprathreshold domain $\xi \geq \Gamma_i^-$ and suppose that deg $F_i >$ deg G_j whenever $c_{ij} > 0, i, j = 1, 2, \ldots, n$. Then only finitely many suprathreshold equilibrium points of (1) exist.

Proof: Analytically continue the functions $S_i(x), x_i \geq \Gamma_i^-, i = 1, 2, \ldots, n$ to be polynomial functions $\tilde{S}_i(z)$ of n complex variables z. The zeros of system $\tilde{S}_i(z) = 0, i = 1, 2, \ldots, n$ are thus an analytic subvariety W of C^n. We show that W is bounded, hence compact. Then using Theorem 5 and the fact that $S_i(x) = \tilde{S}_i(z)$ when z is real and

$x_i \geq \Gamma_i^-, i = 1, 2, \ldots, n$, it follows that at most finitely many suprathreshold equilibria of (57) exist.

Boundedness is easily proved as follows. Choose any $z = (z_1, z_2, \ldots, z_n) \in \mathbf{C}^n$. Let z_i be the component of maximal modulus in z; that is, $|z_i| \geq |z_j|, j \neq i$. Consider the highest degree term of $\tilde{S}_i(z)$. This term corresponds to the highest degree term of the analytic continuation of term $x_i F_i(x_i)$ in $S_i(x)$. If $|z|$ is chosen sufficiently large, the degree condition on the signal functions along with the inequalities $|z_i| \geq |z_j|, j \neq i$, imply that the modulus of this highest degree term exceeds the sum of moduli of all other terms in $\tilde{S}_i(z)$. Consequently, $\tilde{S}_i(z) \neq 0$ if $|z| \gg 0$. In other words, no zero exists of the full system $\tilde{S}_i(z) = 0, i = 1, 2, \ldots, n$, outside some bounded ball in $\mathbf{C}^n$, and the proof is complete.

Corollary 4 (Polynomial Absolute Stability): Let system (57) be given with a symmetric matrix $\| c_{ij} \|$ of nonnegative interaction coefficients and signal functions that are polynomial in their suprathreshold region such that $\deg F_i > \deg G_j$ for all $c_{ij} > 0$ and each G_j has nonnegative coefficients. Then global pattern formation is absolutely stable within this class of networks.

The proof consists in verifying that the hypotheses of Theorems 1, 3, and 6 are satisfied.

Theorem 6 demonstrates that suprathreshold polynomial signal functions for which the norm of excitatory feedback grows more quickly than the norm of inhibitory feedback lead to global pattern formation. Any smooth signal functions can be uniformly approximated within this class of polynomials, but that does not imply that (58) has countably many zeros using these signal functions. The next result considers sigmoid signal functions to illustrate how Theorem 5 can be applied to a nonpolynomial case of great physical interest (Grossberg [12], [21]). Sigmoid signal functions, unlike polynomials, approach finite asymptotes at large activity values. Absolute stability holds within a class of sigmoid functions wherein a trade-off exists between the rate of signal growth, the asymptote of signal growth, and the spatial breadth and size of inhibitory interaction strengths.

To illustrate the factors that control sigmoid signal behavior, we consider sigmoid signal functions such that if $x_i \geq \Gamma_i^-$,

$$F_i(x_i) = \frac{p_i(x_i - \Gamma_i^-)^{N_i}}{q^{N_i} + (x_i - \Gamma_i^-)^{N_i}} \tag{66}$$

and

$$G_i(x_i) = \frac{(x_i - \Gamma_i^-)^{M_i}}{r^{M_i} + (x_i - \Gamma_i^-)^{M_i}} \tag{67}$$

where M_i and N_i are positive integers, $i = 1, 2, \ldots, n$. The asymptote of G_i is set equal to one without loss of generality because G_i multiplies a coefficient c_{ij} in all its appearances in (55), and the symmetry $c_{ij} = c_{ji}$ is not needed in the following estimate.

Theorem 7 (Sigmoid Signals): Suppose that the parameters in (66) and (67) are chosen to satisfy the following three conditions:

1) $\epsilon > 0$ and $\delta > 1$ exist such that

$$\max(b_i + c_i - \Gamma_i^-, q_i) < \epsilon < \delta\epsilon < r_i, \quad i = 1, 2, \ldots, n. \tag{68}$$

2) The constants

$$s_i = \sum_{k=1}^n c_{ik}(\delta^{M_k} - 1)^{-1} \tag{69}$$

satisfy the inequalities

$$2s_i < p_i, \qquad i = 1, 2, \ldots, n. \tag{70}$$

3) The inequality

$$(p_i - 2s_i)q_i > 2 \mid \alpha_i - \gamma_i \Gamma_i^- \mid + p_i \mid \beta_i - \Gamma_i^- \mid + 2s_i \Gamma_i^- \tag{71}$$

holds, $i = 1, 2, \ldots, n$. Then at most finitely many suprathreshold equilibrium points of (57) exist.

Remark: Inequality (68) says that the excitatory signal functions change faster-than-linearly at smaller activities than the inhibitory signal functions, and that the turning points q_i and r_i are uniformly separated across signal functions. Inequality (70) says that the excitatory feedback elicited by large activities dominates the total inhibitory feedback elicited by these activities. These two inequalities are thus analogous to the conditions on polynomial degrees in the previous theorem. The left-hand side of inequality (71) refines these constraints by requiring the faster-than-linear range of the excitatory signal function to occur at large activities if the strength of feedback inhibition is close to the strength of feedback excitation at these activities.

Proof: To simplify notation, let $w_i = x_i - \Gamma_i^-$ and define $S_i^*(w) = S_i(x)$. Now multiply $S_i^*(w)$ by the denominator of F_i to find

$$U_i(w) = (q_i^{N_i} + z_i^{N_i})S_i^*(w). \tag{72}$$

Function $U_i(w) = 0$ at some $w \in \Re_+^n$ iff $S_i(x) = 0$ at a suprathreshold value of x, $i = 1, 2, \ldots, n$. Use inequality (68) to analytically continue $U_i(w)$ to a function $\tilde{U}_i(z)$ analytic on the polydisk $\Omega = \{z : \mid z_i \mid < \epsilon\}$. (In fact, we could define $\tilde{U}_i(z)$ analytic for $\mid z_i \mid < r_i$.) Inequality (68) guarantees that all real suprathreshold zeros are included in Ω. We will show the subvariety W of zeros $\tilde{U}_i(z) = 0$, $i = 1, 2, \ldots, n$, is contained in the polydisk $\Omega' = \{z : \mid z_i \mid < q_i\}$. By (68), $q_i < \epsilon, i = 1, 2, \ldots, n$. Hence the subvariety W is compact, and the theorem will follow.

To complete the proof, we write $\tilde{U}_i(z)$ in the following form using the notation $R_i(z)$ for the sum of inhibitory feedback terms that analytically continue $\sum_{k=1}^{n} c_{ik} G_k(w_k + \Gamma_k^-)$:

$$
\begin{aligned}
\tilde{U}_i(z) = &-z_i^{N_i+1}[\gamma_i + p_i + R_i(z)] \\
&+ z_i^{N_i}[\alpha_i - \gamma_i \Gamma_i^- + p_i(\beta_i - \Gamma_i^-) - \Gamma_i^- R_i(z)] \\
&- z_i q_i^{N_i}[\gamma_i + \Gamma_i^- R_i(z)] \\
&+ q_i^{N_i}[\alpha_i - \gamma_i \Gamma_i^- - \Gamma_i^- R_i(z)]
\end{aligned}
\tag{73}
$$

The analytic continuation $\tilde{G}_k(z_k)$ of $G_k(w_k + \Gamma_i^-)$ can be rewritten as

$$\tilde{G}_k(z_k) = \frac{1}{r_k^{M_k} z_k^{-M_k} + 1}. \tag{74}$$

Because $\mid z_k \mid \leq \epsilon$, (68) implies

$$\mid \tilde{G}_k(z_k) \mid \leq (\delta^{M_k} - 1)^{-1}. \tag{75}$$

Since (75) is true for every z_k when $z \in \Omega$, it follows for every $i = 1, 2, \ldots, n$ that

$$\mid R_i(z) \mid \leq s_i \quad \text{if } z \in \Omega. \tag{76}$$

By (73) and (75), if $z \in \Omega$,

$$| \hat{U}_i(z) | \geq L_i(| z_i |) \tag{77}$$

where

$$L_i(\xi) = \xi^{N_i+1}(\gamma_i + p_i - s_i)$$
$$- \xi^{N_i}[| \alpha_i - \gamma_i \Gamma_i^- | + p_i | \beta_i - \Gamma_i^- | + \Gamma_i^- s_i] \tag{78}$$
$$- \xi q_i^{N_i}[\gamma_i + s_i] - q_i^{N_i}[| \alpha_i - \gamma_i \Gamma_i^- | + \Gamma_i^{-1} s_i].$$

To show that $L_i(| z_i |) > 0$ if $\epsilon <| z_i | \geq q_i$, we verify that $L_i(q_i) > 0$ and $(dL_i/d\xi)(\xi) \geq 0$ for $\epsilon > \xi \geq q_i$ using (71). This fact along with (76) completes the proof.

Inequality (68) requires that $q_i < r_i$. Analogous results hold even if $q_i \geq r_i$ when both q_i and r_i are chosen sufficiently large. We state without proof such a theorem.

Theorem 8 (Sigmoid Signals): Suppose that $\epsilon > 0$ and $\delta > 1$ exist such that

$$\max_i(b_i + c_i - \gamma_i, v_i) < \epsilon < \delta\epsilon < \min_{j,k}(q_k, r_k) \tag{79}$$

where

$$v_i = \frac{| \alpha_i - \gamma_i \Gamma_i^- | + \beta_i t_i + \Gamma_i^- (s_i + t_i)}{\gamma_i - (s_i + t_i)}, \tag{80}$$

s_i is defined as in (69),

$$t_i = (\delta^{N_i} - 1)^{-1}, \tag{81}$$

and

$$\gamma_i > s_i + t_i, \tag{82}$$

$i = 1, 2, \ldots, n$. Then there are at most finitely many suprathreshold equilibrium points of (57).

Because not all parameter choices of the sigmoid signal functions of (66) and (67) have been shown to imply global pattern formation, it is inappropriate to summarize Theorems 7 and 8 as absolute stability results. Instead we summarize the constraints which have been shown to yield global pattern formation when these sigmoid signal functions are used.

Corollary 5 (Sigmoid Global Pattern Formation): Let system (57) possess a nonnegative symmetric interaction matrix $\| c_{ij} \|$, positive decay rates A_i, and suprathreshold sigmoid signal functions (66) and (67) that satisfy the constraints of Theorems 7 or 8 and the inequalities $M_i > 1$ in (67), $i = 1, 2, \ldots, n$. Then global pattern formation occurs.

Proof: The new constraint $M_i > 1$ implies that d_i is differentiable even when $x_i = \Gamma_i^-$, as is required by Theorem 1. The constraint of Theorem 3 that b_i possesses no nontrivial level intervals can be violated in (30) only if

$$A_i C_i + (B_i + C_i)I_i = 0. \tag{83}$$

Since $A_i > 0$, this case can occur if $C_i = 0 = I_i$, which implies that x_i remains between 0 and B_i. Suppose $\Gamma_i^- = 0$. Then all $x_i > 0$ are suprathreshold values, and x_i can attain only one subthreshold equilibrium value, namely zero. Suppose $\Gamma_i^- > 0$. If $x_i(T) \leq \Gamma_i^-$ for some $t = T$, then $x_i(t) \leq \Gamma_i^-$ for all $t = T$. This is true because the excitatory threshold of F_i in (66) equals the inhibitory threshold Γ_i^- of G_i in (67), no input I_i can excite x_i due to (83), and all other v_k, $k \neq i$, can only inhibit x_i. Thus for $t \geq T, \dot{x}_i \leq -A_i x_i$, so that x_i approaches the unique subthreshold value zero. In all cases, only one subthreshold equilibrium value of each x_i can exist, which completes the proof.

IX. Concluding Remarks

The present article notes that systems (1) that are competitive and possess symmetric interactions admit a global Liapunov function. Given this observation, it remains to characterize the set E and its relationship to the equilibrium points of (1). Despite useful partial results, this approach has not yet handled all of the physically interesting neural networks wherein absolute stability may be conjectured to occur. For example, extensive numerical analysis of neural networks of the form

$$
\begin{aligned}
\dot{x}_i = &- A_i x_i + (B_i - C_i x_i)\Big[I_i + \sum_{k=1}^{n} D_{ik} f_k(x_k)\Big] \\
&- (E_i x_i + F_i)\Big[J_i + \sum_{k=1}^{n} G_{ik} g_k(x_k)\Big]
\end{aligned}
\tag{84}
$$

where both matrices $D = \| D_{ik} \|$ and $G = \| G_{ik} \|$ are symmetric suggests that an absolute stability result should exist for these networks, which generalize (3) ([3], [5], [31]). In these networks, cooperative interactions $\sum_{k=1}^{n} D_{ik} f_k(x_k)$ as well as competitive interactions $\sum_{k=1}^{n} G_{ik} g_k(x_k)$ are permissible. A global Liapunov function whose equilibrium set can be effectively analysed has not yet been discovered for the networks (84).

It remains an open question whether the Liapunov function approach, which requires a study of equilibrium points, or an alternative global approach, such as the Liapunov functional approach which sidesteps a direct study of equilibrium points ([14], [18], [21]), will ultimately handle all of the physically important cases.

REFERENCES

[1] Carpenter, G.A., Bursting phenomena in excitable membranes. *SIAM Journal of Applied Mathematics*, 1979, **36**, 334–372.

[2] Carpenter, G.A., Normal and abnormal signal patterns in nerve cells. In S. Grossberg (Ed.), **Mathematical psychology and psychophysiology**. Providence, RI: American Mathematical Society, 1981, pp.48–90.

[3] Cohen, M.A. and Grossberg, S., Some global properties of binocular resonances: Disparity matching, filling-in, and figure-ground synthesis. In P. Dodwell and T. Caelli (Eds.), **Figural synthesis**. Hillsdale, NJ: Erlbaum, 1984.

[4] Eigen, M. and Schuster, P., The hypercycle: A principle of natural self-organization, B: The abstract hypercycle. *Naturwissenschaften*, 1978, **65**, 7–41.

[5] Ellias, S.A. and Grossberg, S., Pattern formation, contrast control, and oscillations in the short term memory of shunting on-center off-surround networks. *Biological Cybernetics*, 1975, **20**, 69–98.

[6] Gilpin, M.E. and Ayala, F.J., Global models of growth and competition. *Proceedings of the National Academy of Sciences*, 1973, **70**, 3590–3593.

[7] Goh, B.S. and Agnew, T.T., Stability in Gilpin and Ayala's models of competition. *Journal of Mathematical Biology*, 1977, **4**, 275–279.

[8] Grossberg, S., Some physiological and biochemical consequences of psychological postulates. *Proceedings of the National Academy of Sciences*, 1968, **60**, 758–765.

[9] Grossberg, S., On learning information, lateral inhibition, and transmitters. *Mathematical Biosciences*, 1969, **4**, 225–310.

[10] Grossberg, S., Neural pattern discrimination. *Journal of Theoretical Biology*, 1970, **27**, 291–337.

[11] Grossberg, S., A neural theory of punishment and avoidance, II: Quantitative theory. *Mathematical Biosciences*, 1972, **15**, 39–67.

[12] Grossberg, S., Contour enhancement, short term memory, and constancies in reverberating neural networks. *Studies in Applied Mathematics*, 1973, **52**, 217–257.

[13] Grossberg, S., On the development of feature detectors in the visual cortex with applications to learning and reaction diffusion systems. *Biological Cybernetics*, 1976, **21**, 145–159.

[14] Grossberg, S., Competition, decision, and consensus. *Journal of Mathematical Analysis and Applications*, 1978, **66**, 470–493.

[15] Grossberg, S., A theory of human memory: Self-organization and performance of sensory-motor codes, maps, and plans. In R. Rosen and F. Snell (Eds.), **Progress in theoretical biology**, Vol. 5. New York: Academic Press, 1978.

[16] Grossberg, S., Communication, memory, and development. In R. Rosen and F. Snell (Eds.), **Progress in theoretical biology**, Vol. 5. New York: Academic Press, 1978.

[17] Grossberg, S., Decisions, patterns, and oscillations in the dynamics of competitive systems with applications to Volterra-Lotka systems. *Journal of Theoretical Biology*, 1978, **73**, 101–130.

[18] Grossberg, S., Biological competition: Decision rules, pattern formation, and oscillations. *Proceedings of the National Academy of Sciences*, 1980, **77**, 2338–2342.

[19] Grossberg, S., How does a brain build a cognitive code? *Psychological Review*, 1980, **87**, 1–51.

[20] Grossberg, S., Intracellular mechanisms of adaptation and self-regulation in self-organizing networks: The role of chemical transducers. *Bulletin of Mathematical Biology*, 1980, **42**.

[21] Grossberg, S., Adaptive resonance in development, perception, and cognition. In S. Grossberg (Ed.), **Mathematical psychology and psychophysiology.** Providence, RI: American Mathematical Society, 1981.

[22] Hale, J., **Ordinary differential equations.** New York: Wiley Interscience, 1969.

[23] Hirsch, M.W., **Differential topology.** New York: Springer-Verlag, 1976.

[24] Hodgkin, A.L., **The conduction of the nervous impulse.** Liverpool: Liverpool University Press, 1964.

[25] Kaplan, J. and Yorke, J., Competitive exclusion and nonequilibrium co-existence. *American Naturalist*, 1977, **111**, 1031–1036.

[26] Katz, B., **Nerve, muscle, and synapse.** New York: McGraw-Hill, 1966.

[27] Kilmer, W.L., On some realistic constraints in prey-predator mathematics. *Journal of Theoretical Biology*, 1972, **36**, 9–22.

[28] Kuffler, S.W. and Nicholls, J.G., **From neuron to brain.** Sunderland, MA: Sinauer Associates, 1976.

[29] LaSalle, J.P., An invariance principle in the theory of stability. In J.K. Hale and J.P. LaSalle (Eds.), **Differential equations and dynamical systems.** New York: Academic Press, 1967.

[30] LaSalle, J.P., Stability theory for ordinary differential equations. *Journal of Differential Equations*, 1968, 4, 57–65.

[31] Levine, D. and Grossberg, S., On visual illusions in neural networks: Line neutralization, tilt aftereffect, and angle expansion. *Journal of Theoretical Biology*, 1976, **61**, 477–504.

[32] MacArthur, R.H., Species packing and competitive equilibrium for many species. *Theoretical Population Biology*, 1970, **1**, 1–11.

[33] May, R.M. and Leonard, W.J., Nonlinear aspects of competition between three species. *SIAM Journal of Applied Mathematics*, 1975, **29**, 243–253.

[34] Ratliff, F., **Mach bands: Quantitative studies of neural networks in the retina.** San Francisco: Holden-Day, 1965.

[35] Rudin, W., **Function theory on the unit ball of C^n.** New York: Springer-Verlag, 1980.

[36] Schuster, P., Sigmund, K., and Wolff, R., On ω-limits for competition between three species. *SIAM Journal of Applied Mathematics*, 1979, **37**, 49–54.

[37] Takeuchi, Y., Adachi, N., and Tokumaru, H., The stability of generalized Volterra equations. *Journal of Mathematical Analysis and Applications*, 1978, **62**, 453–473.

Chapter 6

A NEURAL THEORY OF CIRCADIAN RHYTHMS:
THE GATED PACEMAKER

Preface

Chapters 6–8 illustrate how the theory of gated dipole opponent processes provides mechanistic bridges capable of joining together apparently unrelated data domains. Using these mechanistic bridges, incomplete data from one experimental paradigm can be significantly clarified in the light of mechanistically related data from several other experimental paradigms. No single experimental paradigm can completely characterize a neural system, but convergent experimental evidence from a number of mechanistically related paradigms can provide many more constraints on system design.

Gated dipoles were originally discovered through studies of the neural mechanisms which process reinforcing and homeostatic signals and convert them into incentive motivational feedback signals (Chapters 1–3). In this application, the gated dipoles were interpreted as simple models of hypothalamic circuits.and the gating chemicals were assumed to include norepinephrine. From the start, however, it was clear that the rebound properties of gated dipoles are useful in thalamocortical circuits to explain how the offset of cues can be conditioned to responses, and how negative afterimages in perception can be explained.

Opponent processes are known to be ubiquitous in behavior. The mounting evidence that gated dipole opponent processes may be widely used by the brain suggested to us that we classify the dynamical behaviors of which gated dipoles are capable. Although scientists cannot replay evolution, a classification of the possibilities latent within a basic neural module can uncover some of the parametric discoveries that evolution may have made about that module.

By thinking in this way, Gail Carpenter and I realized that a specialized gated dipole circuit has circadian clocklike properties. We also knew about the circadian pacemaker that exists within the suprachiasmatic nuclei of the mammalian hypothalamus. Since the appetitive gated dipole opponent processes were also interpreted as hypothalamic circuits, we wondered if many specialized hypothalamic circuits, including both the appetitive and the circadian circuits, might not be built up from gated dipole components connected in different ways to input and output pathways and to each other.

The behavioral data base about mammalian circadian rhythms is large and highly constraining. We therefore studied this problem both to better understand these complex circadian data and to provide further formal constraints upon the design of gated dipole circuits. This study has led us to a circadian model *each* of whose processes is homologous to a process in the eating circuit that was described in Chapter 2. We take these facts as convergent evidence that gated dipole circuits indeed play a major role in hypothalamic design.

In much the same way that Chapter 5 analysed how oscillations are prevented in one class of networks, this Chapter analyses how oscillations are created in a different class of networks. We simulate basic properties like the phase response curves in diurnal and nocturnal models, including the "dead zone" during the subjective day of the nocturnal model; the dependence of oscillation period on system parameters; and the structure of oscillations in different parameter ranges.

Three themes underlying this Chapter are particularly noteworthy. The first theme concerns what we mean by saying that these circuits behave like a tunable clock. We do not mean simply that the circuits can generate oscillations. Were this their only property, then every parameter change could change the period of the oscillation. In a neural circuit that is built up from a number of components, this would mean that a modest change in any component could ruin the clock. We demonstrate that the clock period in the dark is insensitive to all but one of the parameters. The controlling parameter is the transmitter accumulation rate. Slower accumulation rates generate longer periods. Thus any mechanism perhaps a genetic or a prenatal developmental mechanism—which sets the transmitter accumulation rate could set, once and for all, the period of the clock in the dark.

The second theme of special interest is the following. There exists a robust parameter range wherein clocklike oscillations occur. Outside this range, however, very complex oscillations can occur, including chaotic oscillations. This gated dipole model therefore provides a new example of a simple biological system which can generate complex dynamical behavior. The oscillations that are generated by a gated pacemaker are, moreover, of a qualitatively new type. In much the same way as a gated dipole circuit can generate a single antagonistic rebound in response to offset of its input (Chapter 2), the oscillations of a gated pacemaker circuit are due to a succession of endogenously generated antagonistic rebounds.

The third theme concerns the curious fact that the literature on circadian rhythms and the literature on operant behavior have developed essentially independently, despite the fact that most data about circadian rhythms are collected by observing operant behavior. As a result, most discussions of circadian data analyse properties of formal clocks rather than ethological properties of behavior.

Our circadian model bridges this gap by using mechanisms that were discovered to analyse operant behavior to suggest explanations of circadian data. In particular, Chapter 8 explicitly discusses our conception of how the gated pacemaker circuit interacts with the drive representations which were used to explain conditioning data in Chapters 1–3. The gated pacemaker model may thus be viewed as a further development of our theory of cognitive-emotional interactions.

Biological Cybernetics **48**, 35 59 (1983)
© 1983 Springer-Verlag, Inc.
Reprinted by permission of the publisher

A NEURAL THEORY OF CIRCADIAN RHYTHMS:
THE GATED PACEMAKER

Gail A. Carpenter† and Stephen Grossberg‡

Abstract

This article describes a behaviorally, physiologically, and anatomically predictive model of how circadian rhythms are generated by each suprachiasmatic nucleus (SCN) of the mammalian hypothalamus. This gated pacemaker model is defined in terms of competing on-cell off-cell populations whose positive feedback signals are gated by slowly accumulating chemical transmitter substances. These components have also been used to model other hypothalamic circuits, notably the eating circuit. A parametric analysis of the types of oscillations supported by the model is presented. The complementary reactions to light of diurnal and nocturnal mammals as well as their similar phase response curves are obtained. The "dead zone" of the phase response curve during the subjective day of a nocturnal rodent is also explained. Oscillations are suppressed by high intensities of steady light. Operations that alter the parameters of the model transmitters can phase shift or otherwise change its circadian oscillation. Effects of ablation and hormones on model oscillations are summarized. Observed oscillations include regular periodic solutions, periodic plateau solutions, rippled plateau solutions, period doubling solutions, slow modulation of oscillations over a period of months, and repeating sequences of oscillation clusters. The model period increases inversely with the transmitter accumulation rate but is insensitive to other parameter choices except near the breakdown of oscillations. The model's clocklike nature is thus a mathematical property rather than a formal postulate. A singular perturbation approach to the model's analysis is described.

† Supported in part by the Air Force Office of Scientific Research (AFOSR 82-0148), the National Science Foundation (NSF MCS-82-07778), the Northeastern University Research and Scholarship Development Fund, and the Office of Naval Research (ONR N00014-83-K0337).

‡ Supported in part by the Air Force Office of Scientific Research (AFOSR 82-0148), the National Science Foundation (NSF IST-80-00257), and the Office of Naval Research (ONR N00014-83-K0337).

1. Introduction

A. A Physiological Model of a Circadian Pacemaker

Circadian rhythms occur in a wide variety of mammalian physiological systems. Moore-Ede, Sulzman, and Fuller (1982) have, for example, written that "as the documentation of rhythms in various human physiological systems proceeded apace, it became apparent that it was often more significant to find no circadian rhythm in a physiological variable than to find one" (p.16). Despite the widespread occurrence of circadian properties, the physiological mechanisms that generate circadian rhythms have yet to be characterized. In every mammal studied so far, a pacemaker for the control of the wake-sleep and activity-rest cycles has been located in the pair of suprachiasmatic nuclei (SCN) of the hypothalamus (Moore, 1973, 1974). This article defines and analyses a behaviorally, physiologically, and anatomically predictive model of the SCN circadian pacemaker. We call this model the *gated pacemaker* model due to the central role played by transmitter gating actions in generating the model's circadian rhythms (Carpenter and Grossberg, 1983).

Some of the gated pacemaker's behavioral properties are the following. Although both nocturnal mammals and diurnal mammals possess a pacemaker within their SCN, these animals react to the daily light-dark cycle in a complementary fashion (Moore-Ede, Sulzman, and Fuller, 1982). We show that the same model mechanisms can be used to produce these complementary reactions, as well as the similar phase response curves of nocturnal and diurnal mammals in response to pulses of light. The diurnal gated pacemaker can generate approximately 48-hour days (period doubling) when it is placed into dim steady light, as occasionally happens to humans who live in caves for long periods of time (Jouvet, Mouret, Chouvet, and Siffre, 1974). The circadian rhythm of the diurnal model can be suppressed by intense steady light. Aschoff (1979, p.238) writes about this property that "at high intensities of illumination circadian systems often seem to break down, as primarily exemplified by arhythmicity in records of locomotor activity." Biorhythms on a time scale of months have been observed superimposed on the model's circadian rhythm. Very complex breakdowns of the model's circadian rhythmicity, suggestive of chaos, have also been observed. Some of these oscillatory waveforms are of independent mathematical interest due to their novel properties.

Since each of the model's mechanisms has a physiological interpretation, the parameter ranges in which the above behaviors occur suggest tests of the model by predicting how prescribed physiological manipulations may alter circadian properties of behavior. The model's physiological interpretation suggests a set of predictions that are of particular importance. Chemical transmitters form a part of the gated pacemaker. Many neural transmitters are known to oscillate with a circadian rhythm (Naber, Wirz-Justice, and Kafka, 1981; Kafka, Wirz-Justice, and Naber, 1981; Kafka, Wirz-Justice, Naber, and Wehr, 1981). The model's transmitters oscillate because their gating action forms part of the pacemaker mechanism, not merely because they are driven by a separate pacemaker. If chemical transmitters play a role in the SCN pacemaker, then a potent antagonist of these transmitters should abolish the SCN rhythm. The role of chemical transmitters in the gated pacemaker is also compatible with the fact that antidepressant drugs can alter the mood of manic-depressive patients by modifying their wake-sleep circadian cycle (Wehr, Wirz-Justice, Goodwin, Duncan, and Gillin, 1979; Kafka, Wirz-Justice, Naber, Marangos, O'Donohue, and Wehr, 1982; Wehr and Wirz-Justice, 1982).

The model's anatomical interpretation suggests another set of predictions. These predictions describe effects on gated pacemaker activity of cutting out one of the two SCN or part of each SCN, or of severing the neural pathways that join the SCN through the optic chiasm (Carpenter and Grossberg, 1984; Sisk and Turek, 1982).

B. Multiple Oscillators from Similar Mechanisms

The model oscillators are built up from mechanisms that have been used to analyse other phenomena, such as eating and drinking (Grossberg, 1982a, 1984), that are known to be mediated by the hypothalamus (Olds, 1977). We therefore suggest that the hypothalamic circuits that control different types of emotion-related behaviors may all be built up from similar physiological components. This hypothesis may prove helpful in characterizing the hypothalamic circuit that controls the human temperature rhythm (Wever, 1979) as well as hypothalamically mediated rhythmic properties of the eating cycle (Rosenwasser, Boulos, and Terman, 1981; Moore-Ede, Sulzman, and Fuller, 1982).

C. Metabolic Feedback and Slow Gain Control

In this article, we focus on the model's circadian pacemaker. The full circadian model augments the gated pacemaker with two auxiliary processes. Each of these auxiliary processes is driven by the pacemaker and modulates the pacemaker activity via feedback signaling (Carpenter and Grossberg, 1983, 1984).

One of these processes regulates a metabolic feedback signal: the gated pacemaker generates behavioral activity which, in turn, produces a feedback signal to the pacemaker that serves as a metabolic index of fatigue. We use this metabolic feedback signal to explain how the circadian activity rhythm can split into two components either due to appropriate lighting conditions (Pittendrigh, 1960; Hoffman, 1971; Earnest and Turek, 1982; Pickard and Turek, 1982) or to hormones in the bloodstream (Gwinner, 1974). In the homologous model circuit that is used to analyse eating behavior, the metabolic feedback signal is replaced by a satiety signal that also acts through the bloodstream (Grossberg, 1982a, 1984). Aschoff's rule (Aschoff, 1979) is observed in the model due to two factors operating together. The activation of nocturnal model off-cells by light plus the action of metabolic feedback on the off-cells leads to examples (Carpenter and Grossberg, 1984) wherein the duration of behavioral activity decreases and the total period increases as the steady light level is parametrically increased. The activation of diurnal model on-cells by light plus the action of metabolic feedback on the off-cells leads to examples wherein the duration of behavioral activity increases and the total period decreases as the steady light level is parametrically increased. Exceptions to Aschoff's rule are more common in the diurnal model than in the nocturnal model, as also occurs *in vivo*, due to the asymmetric role of metabolic feedback relative to the site of action of the light input within the diurnal and nocturnal models (Carpenter and Grossberg, 1984).

The second auxiliary process is a slowly varying gain control process that buffers the model's reaction to adventitious lighting changes, such as cloudy weather, and alters the model's properties in response to statistically reliable lighting changes, such as seasonal fluctuations. We use this slow gain control process to explain the slow onset of split rhythms and the several types of long-term after-effects that prior lighting conditions can have on subsequent activity cycles (Pittendrigh, 1974). In the homologous model circuit that is used to analyse eating behavior, the slow gain control process is replaced by conditionable signals that are activated by food-related cues.

The correspondences between the model SCN circuit and eating circuit support the hypothesis that similar mechanisms are adapted to specialized functions within the hypothalamus.

D. Comparison with other Pacemaker Models

Previous models of circadian rhythms have been defined in terms of oscillators that were originally developed to explain non-circadian phenomena. A pair of coupled van der Pol oscillators has been used to model interactions between the activity-rest pacemaker and the temperature pacemaker of humans (Kronauer, Czeisler, Pilato, Moore-Ede, and Weitzman, 1982). Our results complement this study by suggesting a physiological model for each pacemaker.

A pair of coupled FitzHugh-Nagumo oscillators (FitzHugh, 1960; Nagumo, Arimoto, and Yoshizawa, 1961) has been used to analyse the splitting of the circadian rhythm (Kawato and Suzuki, 1980). This model faces several difficulties. The FitzHugh-Nagumo model is a simplified version of the Hodgkin-Huxley model of nerve impulse propagation. As such, its physical time scale is in the millisecond range rather than the circadian range. As Kawato and Suzuki have noted, "the BVP [van der Pol] equation and Nagumo's equation were derived for neural rhythms with much shorter periods than 24h. However, in the absence of information regarding the state variables relevant to circadian pacemakers, we use the abstract model" (p.557).

A second difficulty of the FitzHugh-Nagumo coupled oscillator model concerns its explanation of split rhythms. Split rhythms are caused in the Kawato-Suzuki model when its two oscillators become out-of-phase with each other. This happens because light is assumed to strengthen the inhibitory coupling between the oscillators. In order to explain splitting in both nocturnal and diurnal animals using this approach, one would need to suppose that light strengthens the inhibitory coupling between the oscillators of a nocturnal model and weakens the inhibitory coupling between the oscillators of a diurnal model. Moreover, the inhibitory coupling between the oscillators would have to be weak when the nocturnal model is in the dark and when the diurnal model is in the light, so that splitting does not routinely occur under these conditions. These formal hypotheses do not seem to play any role in the model except to cause split rhythms.

The gated pacemaker model avoids these interpretive difficulties as follows. The time scale difficulties are avoided due to the role of slowly accumulating transmitter substances in generating the gated pacemaker rhythm. Our split rhythm explanation does not hypothesize a light-sensitive coupling strength between SCN oscillators. Instead, we show how the metabolic feedback process, which plays a physically important role, can cause splits under certain circumstances.

2. The Gated Pacemaker

The gated pacemaker model describes the dynamics of on-cell/off-cell pairs, called *gated dipoles*, in which the on-cells and the off-cells mutually inhibit one another. Populations of these gated dipoles are assumed to exist in each SCN. The following processes define a gated pacemaker (Figure 1):

1) slowly accumulating transmitter substances are depleted by gating the release of feedback signals;

2) the feedback signals are organized as an on-center off-surround, or competitive, anatomy;

3) both on-cells and off-cells are tonically aroused;

4) light excites the on-cells of a diurnal model and the off-cells of a nocturnal model;

5) the on-cells drive observable activity, such as wheel-turning, in both the diurnal model and the nocturnal model.

The model equations for a nocturnal gated pacemaker are:

$$\frac{dX_1}{dT} = -AX_1 + (B - X_1)[I + F(X_1)Z_1] - (X_1 + C)G(X_2), \qquad (1)$$

$$\frac{dX_2}{dT} = -AX_2 + (B - X_2)[I + F(X_2)Z_2] + J(T)] - (X_2 + C)G(X_1), \qquad (2)$$

$$\frac{dZ_1}{dT} = D(E - Z_1) - KF(X_1)Z_1, \qquad (3)$$

$$\frac{dZ_2}{dT} = D(E - Z_2) - KF(X_2)Z_2. \qquad (4)$$

Variable X_1 in equation (1) is the potential of an on-cell (population) V_1. Variable X_2 in equation (2) is the potential of an off-cell (population) V_2. Both X_1 and X_2 obey membrane equations (Hodgkin, 1964; Katz, 1966; Kuffler and Nicholls, 1976; Plonsey, 1969). In (1) and (2), the parameter $-A$ in the terms $-AX_1$ and $-AX_2$ determines the fast decay rate of the potentials X_1 and X_2. Also in (1) and (2), term I represents the arousal level that equally excites V_1 and V_2. In (1), the transmitter substance Z_1 gates the nonnegative feedback signal $F(X_1)$ from V_1 to itself. Term $F(X_1)Z_1$ is proportional to the rate at which transmitter is released from the feedback pathway from V_1 to itself, thereby re-exciting X_1. The off-cells V_2 inhibit the on-cells V_1 via the nonnegative signal $G(X_2)$ in term $-(X_1 + C)G(X_2)$ of (1). Equation (2) is the same as equation (1), except that the indices 1 and 2 are interchanged, and the light input $J(T)$ excites V_2, but not V_1, because system (1)-(4) represents a nocturnal model.

Equations (3) and (4) define the transmitter processes Z_1 and Z_2. In (3), the transmitter Z_1 accumulates to its maximal level E at a slow rate D via the term $D(E - Z_1)$. This slow accumulation process is balanced by the release of Z_1 at rate $KF(X_1)Z_1$, leading to the excitation of X_1 in equation (1). A similar combination of slow accumulation and gated release defines the dynamics of transmitter Z_2 in (4).

In all, system (1)-(4) describes a four-dimensional fast-slow process in which two fast potentials interact with two slow auxiliary processes. By comparison, the Hodgkin-Huxley model of nerve impulse transmission (Hodgkin and Huxley, 1952) is also a four-dimensional fast-slow process, but one in which just one potential interacts with three auxiliary processes (Carpenter and Grossberg, 1984). Also the accumulation rate of the two slow transmitter processes in the gated pacemaker model is assumed to be substantially slower than the reaction rates of the ionic processes that couple to the Hodgkin-Huxley potential.

The dimensionless model equations corresponding to equations (1)-(4) are:

$$\frac{dx_1}{dt} = -x_1 + (1 - x_1)[C_1 + C_2 f(x_1)z_1] - (x_1 + C_3)C_4 g(x_2), \tag{5}$$

$$\frac{dx_2}{dt} = -x_2 + (1 - x_2)[C_1 + C_2 f(x_2)z_2 + L(t)] - (x_2 + C_3)C_4 g(x_1), \tag{6}$$

$$\frac{dz_1}{dt} = C_5[1 - z_1 - C_6 f(x_1)z_1], \tag{7}$$

and

$$\frac{dz_2}{dt} = C_5[1 - z_2 - C_6 f(x_2)z_2]. \tag{8}$$

The symbols in the dimensionless system (5)-(8) are related to the symbols in the defining system (1)-(4) by the following identities:

Variables

$$x_1 = \frac{X_1}{B} \tag{9}$$

$$x_2 = \frac{X_2}{B} \tag{10}$$

$$z_1 = \frac{Z_1}{E} \tag{11}$$

$$z_2 = \frac{Z_2}{E} \tag{12}$$

$$t = AT \tag{13}$$

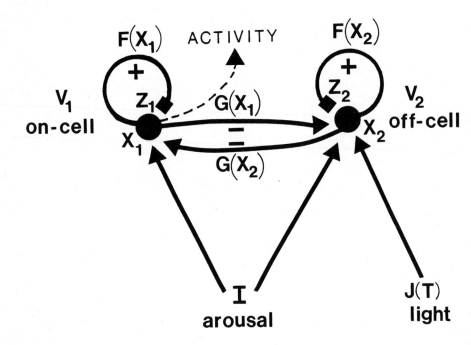

Figure 1. Anatomy and physiology of a gated pacemaker. The potential X_1 of an on-cell (population) and the potential X_2 of an off-cell (population) obey membrane equations (1) and (2), respectively. Transmitter substance Z_1 gates the positive feedback signal $F(X_1)$ from the on-cell (population) to itself, and transmitter substance Z_2 gates the positive feedback signal $F(X_2)$ from the off-cell (population) to itself. Term I is the nonspecific arousal level, which is held constant during the simulations reported herein. The off-cells inhibit the on-cells via signal $G(X_2)$ in (1), and the on-cells inhibit the off-cells via signal $G(X_1)$ in (2). The light input $J(T)$ excites the off-cells (nocturnal model). The transmitter Z_1 in (3) accumulates via term $D(E - Z_1)$ and is released at rate $-KF(X_1)Z_1$ by gating the signal $F(X_1)$. A similar law governs Z_2 in (4). Many basic model properties persist in modified versions of equations (1)–(4). Species-specific variations and future data may support particular versions without altering the qualitative explanations of model properties.

Constants

$$C_1 = \frac{I}{A} \tag{14}$$

$$C_2 = \frac{E F_{\max}}{A}, \tag{15}$$

where

$$F_{\max} = \max(F), \tag{16}$$

$$C_3 = \frac{C}{B} \tag{17}$$

$$C_4 = \frac{G_{\max}}{A}, \tag{18}$$

where

$$G_{\max} = \max(G), \tag{19}$$

$$C_5 = \frac{D}{A} \tag{20}$$

$$C_6 = \frac{K F_{\max}}{D}. \tag{21}$$

Functions

$$f(w) = \frac{F(Bw)}{F_{\max}} \tag{22}$$

$$g(w) = \frac{G(Bw)}{G_{\max}} \tag{23}$$

and

$$L(t) = \frac{J(t/A)}{A}. \tag{24}$$

Note that the feedback signals $f(w)$ and $g(w)$ in (22) and (23) are scaled so that $0 \leq f \leq 1$ and $0 \leq g \leq 1$. These signals are chosen to be either a sigmoid (S-shaped) function of activity, such as

$$f(w) = \begin{cases} \frac{w^2}{C_7^2 + w^2} & \text{if } w \geq 0 \\ 0 & \text{if } w < 0, \end{cases} \tag{25}$$

or a threshold-linear function (linear above a threshold cut-off), such as

$$g(w) = \begin{cases} w & \text{if } 0 \leq w \leq 1 \\ 0 & \text{if } w < 0. \end{cases} \tag{26}$$

3. Qualitative Basis of Oscillations

An intuitive understanding of why a gated pacemaker oscillates, and of how to choose system parameters, may be derived from the following qualitative remarks. Suppose that the system starts out with x_1 large and x_2 small, but with both transmitters fully accumulated, so that $z_1 \cong 1$ and $z_2 \cong 1$. At first, x_1 maintains its advantage over x_2 as follows. Because x_1 is large and $z_1 \cong 1$, the feedback signal $f(x_1)z_1$ from V_1 to itself

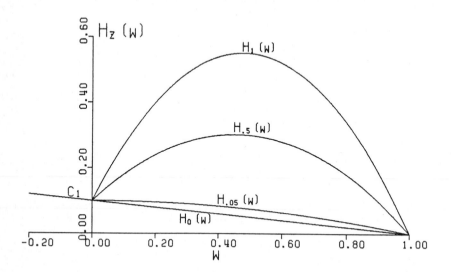

Figure 2. The family of positive feedback functions $H_z(w)$. At intermediate values of x_1, $H_{z_1}(x_1) > C_1$ if z_1 is sufficiently close to 1, whereas $C_1 > H_{z_1}(x_1)$ if z_1 is sufficiently close to 0. At small values of x_2, $H_{z_2}(x_2) \cong C_1$ for all z_2, $0 \le z_2 \le 1$. Consequently, as z_1 decreases from large to small values, the function $H_{z_1}(x_1) - H_{z_2}(x_2)$ decreases until a switch in the relative sizes of x_1 and x_2 is initiated.

is large, as is the negative feedback signal $g(x_1)$ from V_1 to V_2. Because $f(x_1)$ is large, however, z_1 is slowly depleted at the rate $-C_5 C_6 f(x_1) z_1$, by (7). Consequently, the gated signal $f(x_1) z_1$ gradually becomes small despite the fact that x_1 remains large.

As this is going on, x_2 and its feedback signal $f(x_2)$ remain small, so that the transmitter release rate $-C_5 C_6 f(x_2) z_2$ in (8) also remains small. Consequently, z_2 remains large as z_1 is gradually depleted. As a result of these changes, the positive feedback term

$$(1 - x_1)[C_1 + C_2 f(x_1) z_1] \tag{27}$$

in (5) diminishes relative to the positive feedback term

$$(1 - x_2)[C_1 + C_2 f(x_2) z_2] \tag{28}$$

in (6), even though x_1 remains larger than x_2.

This relative change can be understood more precisely by graphing the function

$$H_z(w) = (1 - w)[C_1 + C_2 f(w) z] \tag{29}$$

at extreme values $z = 0$ and $z = 1$ of the parameter z (Figure 2). The function $H_0(w)$ decreases linearly from C_1 to 0 as w increases from 0 to 1, no matter how $f(w)$ is chosen.

TABLE 1

Typical Parameter Values for a Threshold-Linear Nocturnal Pacemaker

$$C_1 = 0.10$$

$$C_2 = 2.00$$

$$C_3 = 0.10$$

$$C_4 = 5.00$$

$$C_5 = 0.01$$

$$C_6 = 10.00$$

The function $f(w)$ is chosen so that the graph of $H_1(w)$ increases from $H_1(0) = C_1$ to a maximum before decreasing to $H_1(1) = 0$. For example, if

$$f(w) = \begin{cases} w & \text{if } w \geq 0 \\ 0 & \text{if } w < 0, \end{cases} \tag{30}$$

then these properties of $H_1(w)$ hold if and only if

$$C_1 < C_2. \tag{31}$$

By Figure 2, if x_2 is sufficiently small, then $H_z(x_2) \cong C_1$ no matter how $z \in [0, 1]$ is chosen. In particular, if $z = z_2 \cong 1$, then $H_{z2}(x_2) \cong C_1$. By contrast, if x_1 is fairly large, then the inequalities

$$H_1(x_1) > C_1 \tag{32}$$

and

$$H_0(x_1) < C_1 \tag{33}$$

hold. In other words, if x_1 and x_2 remain approximately constant while $x_1 > x_2$ and $x_2 \cong 0$, then the relative sizes of (27) and (28) can reverse as z is depleted.

Due to the relatively large decrease in the positive feedback term (27) in (5), x_1 itself begins to decrease, as does $g(x_1)$ in (6). The positive feedback term

$$(1 - x_2)[C_1 + C_2 f(x_2)z_2] \tag{28}$$

from V_2 to itself in (6) can therefore begin to overcome the negative feedback term

$$-(x_2 + C_3)C_4 g(x_1) \tag{34}$$

in (6), and x_2 begins to grow. At first, the growth of x_2 does not depend upon the size of z_2, because if x_2 is small then $H_z(x_2) \cong C_1$ no matter how z is chosen. As x_2 begins to increase, however, the *continued* increase of x_2 depends crucially upon the fact that z_2 is large, due to the different graphs of $H_1(w)$ and $H_0(w)$ at middle values of w. Since z_2 is large when x_2 begins to grow, a switch in the relative sizes of x_1 and x_2 occurs. As x_2 becomes large, it suppresses x_1 via the large negative feedback signal $g(x_2)$. Now x_2 has the advantage, and the competitive cycle starts to repeat itself as z_2 is progressively depleted and z_1 is replenished.

4. Parameter Estimation

The parameters C_1, C_2, ..., C_6 are chosen to guarantee that the qualitative properties described in Section 3 occur. The parameters need to be chosen so that no one term in system (5)-(8) dominates any of the others. It turns out that a broad range of parameters can accomplish this goal. We first show that some simple balancing rules lead to a successful choice of parameters. Then we illustrate the robustness of this parameter choice by varying each parameter separately while the others are held fixed.

The parameters in Table I are arrived at as follows. Consider the positive feedback term

$$(1 - x_1)[C_1 + C_2 f(x_1)z_1] \tag{27}$$

of (5). We want to balance the terms C_1 and $C_2 f(x_1)z_1$ to prevent either term from totally dominating the other in all system states. To fix ideas, let $f(x_1) = \max(x_1, 0)$. Since by (5), $0 \le x_1 \le 1$, it follows that $0 \le f(x_1) \le 1$. Also by (7), $0 \le z_1 \le 1$. In all, C_2 is multiplied by a variable term that is always less than 1. As a first approximation, we therefore need to choose $C_1 < C_2$, as in (31).

A more precise restriction upon C_1 and C_2 is needed, because we want $C_2 f(x_1)z_1$ to exceed C_1 some of the time but not all of the time. To achieve this property, suppose on the average that $x_1 \cong .2$, $x_2 \cong .2$, $z_1 \cong .7$, and $z_2 \cong .7$. These scale-setting estimates are suggested by the facts that x_1 and x_2 in (5) and (6), respectively, are each affected by two negative terms that tend to drive them towards zero, whereas z_1 and z_2 in (7) and (8), respectively, tend to accumulate towards 1 when they are not being depleted by a gating action. These average estimates imply that

$$C_2 f(x_1)z_1 \cong (.14)C_2 \tag{35}$$

on the average. In order to keep term $C_2 f(x_1)z_1$ bigger than C_1 some of the time, we choose

$$C_2 = 20C_1, \tag{36}$$

since then

$$C_2 f(x_1)z_1 \cong 2.8C_1 \tag{37}$$

on the average.

In order to choose C_1, we consider term

$$-x_1 + (1 - x_1)[C_1 + C_2 f(x_1)z_1] \tag{38}$$

of (5). We want the positive feedback term (27) to exceed the decay term $-x_1$ some of the time. If we choose

$$C_1 = .1, \tag{39}$$

and thus by (36)

$$C_2 = 2, \tag{40}$$

then using the average estimates $x_1 \cong .2$ and $z_1 \cong .7$, (38) is approximately equal to

$$-.2 + .3 > 0, \tag{41}$$

which achieves a satisfactory balance of terms. (In (39), C_1 could be chosen significantly larger, provided subsequent terms are balanced properly. For example, oscillations can also occur when $C_1 = .5$ and $C_2 = 10$.)

The parameters C_3 and C_4 in the negative feedback term

$$-(x_1 + C_3)C_4 g(x_2) \tag{42}$$

are chosen as follows. By (17), parameter $C_3 = C/B$. In a membrane equation such as (1) or (2), parameter B equals the sodium saturation point and C equals the potassium saturation point. *In vivo*, B is often ten times larger than C (Hodgkin and Huxley, 1952). Hence we choose

$$C_3 = .1. \tag{43}$$

We choose C_4 so that the positive feedback term (27) and the negative feedback term (42) can alternately be smaller or larger than one another. Letting $g(x_2) = \max(x_2, 0)$ for definiteness, (42) is approximately $(.06)C_4$. If we let

$$C_4 = 5 \tag{44}$$

then (42) approximately equals .3, which balances the estimate of (27) that appears in (41).

To choose C_5, we observe by (20) that C_5 is the ratio of D to A. Since the transmitter accumulation rate (D) is much slower than the decay rate (A) of the potentials, $C_5 \gg 1$. For definiteness, we choose

$$C_5 = .01. \tag{45}$$

Parameter C_6 is chosen as follows. First, we want the rate $-C_5 C_6$ of transmitter depletion in (7) and (8) to be slower than the unit decay rate of the potential; that is

$$C_5 C_6 = (.01)C_6 < 1. \tag{46}$$

Second, we want the gated signal $C_2 f(x_1) z_1$ in (5) to decrease significantly as z_1 is maximally depleted and x_1 remains large. By (7), if z_1 equilibrates to $f(x_1)$, then

$$z_1 \cong \frac{1}{1 + C_6 f(x_1)}. \tag{47}$$

If x_1 is estimated by its maximum value of 1, then

$$z_1 \cong \frac{1}{1 + C_6}. \tag{48}$$

If we choose

$$C_6 = 10, \tag{49}$$

then (46) is valid because $.1 < 1$. Also a significant decrease in $C_2 f(x_1) z_1$ can be achieved since, by (48), the minimal value of z_1 is approximately .09.

5. A Typical Oscillation in the Dark

This section describes the oscillations that occur with parameters chosen as in Table I and no light inputs (free-run in the dark). Due to the fact that system (5)-(8) is four-dimensional, we plot its solutions in three different ways. In Figure 3a, each of the variables x_1 and z_1 is plotted through time. In Figure 3b, both pairs (x_1, z_1) and (x_2, z_2) are plotted in the (x, z) coordinate plane through time. In Figure 3c, each of the variables x_1 and x_2 is plotted through time.

Figure 3a illustrates how z_1 accumulates while x_1 is small. This figure also shows that the graph of x_1 exhibits an overshoot shortly after x_1 reaches its maximum. This overshoot is due to the multiplicative form of the feedback signal $f(x_1) z_1$ (Carpenter and Grossberg, 1981; Grossberg, 1968, 1981, 1984). Term $f(x_1) z_1$ reaches its maximum value when x_1 and z_1 are large. Then z_1 starts to deplete so the product $f(x_1) z_1$ also decreases. As a result, x_1 decreases to a plateau value until the balance of terms that

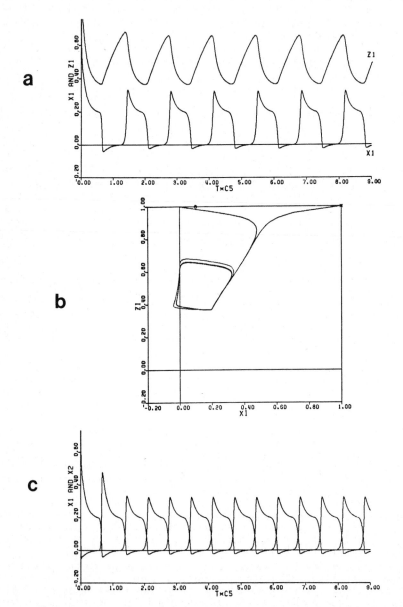

Figure 3. Three ways to plot gated pacemaker trajectories. (a) Functions $x_1(t)$ and $z_1(t)$ are plotted through time. (b) The phase portraits of $(x_1(t), z_1(t))$ and $(x_2(t), z_2(t))$ are plotted through time in (x, z) coordinates. (c) Functions $x_1(t)$ and $x_2(t)$ are plotted through time. Parameters are chosen as in Table 1.

was described in Section 3 causes a rapid switch to occur in the relative sizes of x_1 and x_2.

Figure 3b shows that the two pairs (x_1, z_1) and (x_2, z_2) approach the same limit cycle from their distinct initial values in (x, z) space. Figure 3c shows that the x_1 and x_2 potentials are out-of-phase with each other near this limit cycle. In particular, the rapid decay of x_1 occurs during the rapid rise of x_2, and conversely.

6. Phase Response Curves in Diurnal and Nocturnal Gated Pacemakers

In the gated pacemaker model, the assumption that light inputs excite the on-cells of diurnal animals and the off-cells of nocturnal animals is compatible with the familiar day activity of diurnal animals and night activity of nocturnal animals. Although these hypotheses generate complementary activity cycles in response to a daily cycle of light-dark episodes, they also imply that isolated light pulses delivered to an animal living in the dark reset the phases of both diurnal and nocturnal models in a similar way, as the data demand (Daan and Pittendrigh, 1976; DeCoursey, 1960; Kramm, 1971; Pittendrigh, 1960; Pohl, 1982). This property of gated pacemakers contrasts with the explanation of phase resetting that is suggested when van der Pol oscillators are used to model the pacemaker. The latter approach suggests that complementary reactions to light of diurnal and nocturnal animals are controlled by interactions that occur beyond the SCN pacemaker stage. As Moore-Ede, Sulzman, and Fuller (1982, pp.81–82) have noted: "The circadian systems of diurnal and nocturnal species must be organized differently to account for the dramatic differences in the phase relationships of their rhythms to the light-dark cycle [i.e., day-active vs. night-active]. It is possible that the differences lie in the coupling between zeitgeber and pacemaker. However, ... the similarities between nocturnal and diurnal species in the way that light resets circadian pacemakers [i.e., the phase response curves] makes it more likely that the difference in the phase relationships of the rhythms of nocturnal and diurnal animals actually depends on differences in the coupling mechanisms between the circadian pacemaker and the rhythms it drives."

Figure 4 depicts the phase response curves of diurnal and nocturnal gated pacemakers in response to light pulses. These curves indicate that complementary light-dark cycles and similar phase response curves can coexist at the SCN level if these structures are built up from gated pacemakers. The similar phase response curves of diurnal and nocturnal models are intuitively explained as follows.

During the "early subjective night" of a model diurnal animal, a light pulse that excites the on-cell prolongs its active phase, delays the rest cycle, and thereby causes a phase delay. During the "early subjective night" of a model nocturnal animal, a light pulse that excites the off-cell prolongs its active phase, delays the ensuing activity cycle, and again creates a phase delay. During the "late subjective night" of a diurnal animal, a light pulse that excites the on-cell induces a premature onset of on-cell activity, thereby causing a phase advance in the onset of activity. During the "late subjective night" of a nocturnal model animal, a light pulse that excites the off-cell induces a premature onset of off-cell activity, thereby causing a phase advance in the onset of the next activity cycle. A light pulse during the "subjective day" of either a diurnal or a nocturnal model has relatively little effect.

One way to test whether a gated pacemaker controls phase resetting *in vivo* is to parametrically excite or inhibit the pacemaker transmitter while the phase resetting light pulse is active. A combination of drugs and light pulses may accomplish this joint manipulation. Then predictable changes in the phase response curves beyond those obtainable with a light pulse alone should occur. Such an experimental result could not be explained by a formal oscillator model.

Some details about how the phase response curves are generated are worthy of note. During a diurnal animal's subjective night, for example, both phase advances and phase

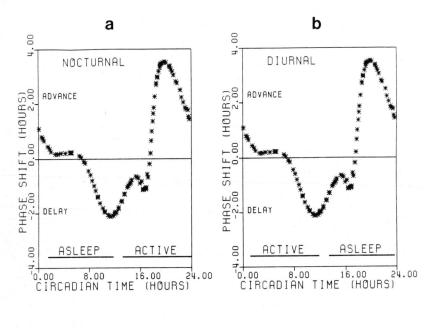

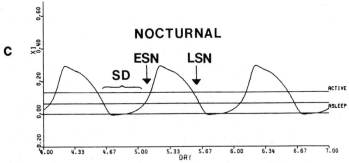

Figure 4. Phase response curves of nocturnal and diurnal gated pacemakers. (a) A typical phase response curve for a nocturnal pacemaker. Parameters are chosen as in Table 1, except that $C_1 = 0.13$. Light pulses of dimensionless intensity 0.1 were flashed for 30 minutes. (b) A typical phase response curve for a diurnal pacemaker. Parameters are chosen as in (a). (c) The on-cell potential $x_1(t)$ of a nocturnal pacemaker is plotted as a function of time. Small values correspond to sleep $(x_1(t) \leq C_8)$ and large values correspond to the waking state. The model is asleep during the day and awake at night. The "subjective day" (SD), "early subjective night" (ESN), and "late subjective night" (LSN) of the model are defined accordingly.

delays can be caused by light pulses (Kramm, 1971; Pohl, 1982). Thus light pulses that occur while the animal is asleep can alter its circadian rhythm, so that light can affect the animal's pacemaker even when its eyes are closed.

The gated pacemaker model incorporates this property in terms of the following hypothesis. If $L^*(t)$ is the light signal that reaches the SCN when the eyes are open, we define the light input $L(t)$ in equation (6) at all times by

$$L(t) = \begin{cases} L^*(t) & \text{if model is awake} \\ \theta L^*(t) & \text{if model is asleep} \end{cases} \tag{50}$$

where $0 < \theta \leq 1$. In Figure 4, $\theta = 1$. The form of the phase response curve is quite insensitive to the absolute size of θ just so long as $0 < \theta \leq 1$. The definition of $L(t)$ in (50) is made more precise by characterizing whether or not the animal is awake in terms of the on-cell activity $x_1(t)$. We assume that the animal wakes up whenever $x_1(t)$ exceeds a constant threshold C_8. Then (50) becomes

$$L(t) = \begin{cases} L^*(t) & \text{if } x_1(t) > C_8 \\ \theta L^*(t) & \text{if } x_1(t) \leq C_8 \end{cases}. \tag{51}$$

Figure 4 depicts the case in which $\theta = 1$. The case $\theta = 1$, however, corresponds to the unphysical assumption that light is equally effective whether or not the animal's eyes are closed. When θ is chosen less than 1, some subtle but important differences in the phase response curves of nocturnal and diurnal models occur. Figure 5 depicts these phase response curves when $\theta = .1$. Analogous differences have been reported in data about nocturnal and diurnal rodents (Pohl, 1982, pp.341–342). Pohl suggests that these differences have an "important adaptive value" (p.342). This may indeed be the case, but in our model the differences are due simply to the attenuation of a light pulse when the model animal is asleep.

Pohl describes differences in the phase response curves of nocturnal and diurnal rodents as follows. "In contrast to nocturnal rodents, which are mostly irresponsive to light pulses during rest time (subjective day), the day-active rodents do not show a particular 'dead zone' of the PRC" (1982, p.342). This difference between nocturnal and diurnal animals is explained by our model as follows.

Consider the subjective day of a nocturnal model; that is, the time when the model is asleep (Figure 5a, left half). When $\theta = 1$ (Figure 4a), the nocturnal animal is relatively insensitive to a light pulse during the early subjective day because the light pulse excites the off-cells while they are already excited. A small phase advance is nonetheless visible in response to such a pulse. When $\theta = .1$ (Figure 5a), by contrast, hardly any phase shift is evident because the large attenuation of the light pulse occurs at a time when the off-cells are already insensitive to light. When $\theta = 1$ (Figure 4a), the nocturnal animal is more sensitive to a light pulse during the late subjective day because such a light pulse excites the off-cells while the pacemaker on-cells are becoming active. A significant phase delay therefore occurs. When $\theta = .1$ (Figure 5a), by contrast, the phase delay during the late subjective night is significantly attenuated. The flattening of the phase response curve during the subjective day of a nocturnal model is analogous to the "dead zone" of which Pohl speaks. When the nocturnal model is awake (its subjective night), its phase response curves are the same when $\theta = 1$ (Figure 4a, right half) and when $\theta = .1$ (Figure 5a, right half).

Similar reasoning explains why the phase response curves of an awake diurnal model are the same whether $\theta = 1$ (Figure 4b, left half) or $\theta = .1$ (Figure 5b, left half). During the subjective night of a diurnal model, its phase response curve when $\theta = .1$ (Figure 5b, right half) is compressed relative to its phase response curve when $\theta = 1$ (Figure 4b, right half). Because a diurnal model is asleep while its on-cells are very sensitive to light pulses, the residual phase shift during the subjective night of a diurnal

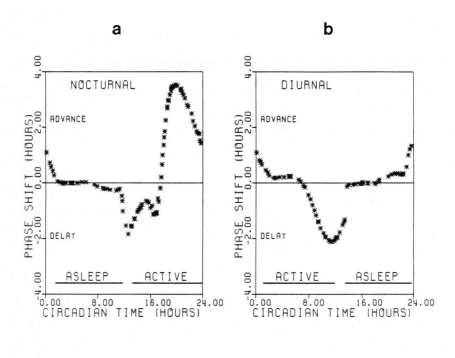

Figure 5. Phase response curves of nocturnal and diurnal gated pacemakers with light attenuation during sleep. (a) A typical phase response curve for a nocturnal pacemaker with $\theta = 0.1$. All other parameters are chosen as in Figure 4. (b) A typical phase response curve for a diurnal pacemaker with all parameters chosen as in (a).

model is greater than the residual phase shift during the subjective day of a nocturnal model. Thus the "adaptive value" of these differences between nocturnal and diurnal animals arise in our model from the simple facts that nocturnal animals go to sleep in response to daylight. These differences can be more quantitatively assessed when more data are collected about how phase response curves of nocturnal and diurnal animals parametrically depend upon the intensity of light pulses.

7. Parametric Structure of Oscillations: Threshold-Linear Signal Function

In this section and the next, we describe how system oscillations depend on choices of the numerical parameters C_1, C_2, ..., C_6 in equations (5)-(8). We choose both the positive feedback function $f(w)$ and the negative feedback function $g(w)$ to be linear above a zero threshold; i.e., $f(w) = g(w) = \max(w, 0)$. In Section 9 we show how our conclusions are altered when $f(w)$ is an S-shaped function. To emphasize properties of endogenous oscillations, we shut the light off $(L(t) \equiv 0)$ and observe the model's free-running behavior in the dark. For all choices of the parameters, the symmetry of equations (5)-(8) during free-run implies that solutions that start out "on the diagonal" remain on the diagonal for all future time. That is, if $x_1(0) = x_2(0)$ and $z_1(0) = z_2(0)$, then $x_1(t) = x_2(t)$ and $z_1(t) = z_2(t)$ for all $t \geq 0$. The parametric studies reported below illustrate the fact that the diagonal $(x_1 = x_2$ and $z_1 = z_2)$ is unstable for some, but not all, choices of parameters. In the ensuing discussion, all conclusions are stated for solutions that start off the diagonal:

$$|x_1(0) - x_2(0)| + |z_1(0) - z_2(0)| \neq 0. \tag{52}$$

In this section, we vary each of the parameters C_1, C_2, C_3, C_4, and C_6 separately while holding all the other parameters fixed at the values given in Table I. The effects of varying C_5 will be discussed in Section 8 because they are qualitatively different from the effects of varying the other five parameters.

Figure 6 and Table II depict the effects of varying parameters C_1, C_2, C_3, C_4, and C_6. Figure 6 depicts the effects of decreasing the arousal parameter C_1. In Figure 6a, a large C_1 value causes the system to approach a "diagonal limit" such that $x_1(\infty) = x_2(\infty)$ and $z_1(\infty) = z_2(\infty)$. This is because the large and equal arousal signals to V_1 and V_2 overcome the influence that the feedback signals $f(x_1)z_1$ and $f(x_2)z_2$ can have on system dynamics. As C_1 is parametrically decreased, the system undergoes a bifurcation leading to small amplitude oscillations near the diagonal (Figure 6b). As C_1 is further decreased, the small amplitude oscillations become large amplitude oscillations (Figure 6c) that eventually develop a long plateau phase followed by sudden switching between x_1 and x_2 (Figure 6d). At still smaller C_1 values, all oscillations are quenched, and the system approaches an "off-diagonal limit" (Figure 6e). That is, one of the potentials wins out over the other potential, in such a way that

$$[x_1(\infty) - x_2(\infty)][z_1(\infty) - z_2(\infty)] < 0. \tag{53}$$

The choice of initial data determines which potential will win. Oscillations are quenched at small C_1 values for the following reason. Suppose that C_1 is small and that the pair (x_1, z_1) has the initial advantage over the pair (x_2, z_2); e.g., $x_1 > x_2$ and $z_1 > z_2$. Then the initially large term $C_2 f(x_1)z_1$, which gives positive feedback to V_1, is never offset by the small arousal C_1 to V_2 as z_1 depletes. That is, although z_1 is eventually depleted by the large signal $f(x_1)$, thereby reducing positive feedback from V_1 to itself, x_2 can never recover because its only sources of excitatory input come from its own positive feedback signal, which is small due to x_1's initial advantage, and from the small arousal level C_1. Thus x_1 remains larger than x_2 for all time.

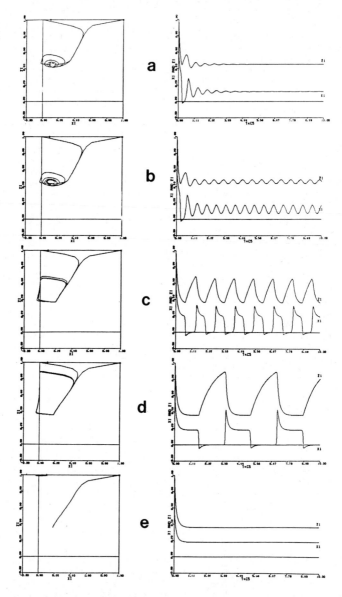

Figure 6. Oscillation sequence in response to a decrease in dimensionless arousal C_1 (threshold-linear case). (a) Diagonal limits ($C_1 = 0.18$). (b) Small amplitude oscillation ($C_1 = 0.17$). (c) Large amplitude oscillation ($C_1 = 0.1$; Table 1). (d) Plateau oscillation ($C_1 = 0.0895$). (e) Off-diagonal limit ($C_1 = 0.0893$). The same time scale is used on all the graphs.

TABLE 2

Oscillation Sequences due to Individual Parametric Variations
($C_5 = 0.01$; threshold-linear case)

a	b	c	d	e
Limit on the diagonal: $x_1 = x_2$ and $z_1 = z_2$	Small amplitude oscillations near the diagonal	Large amplitude oscillations, with $C_1 \ldots C_6$ as in Table 1	Large amplitude oscillations with long plateau	Limit off the diagonal: x_1 wins or x_2 wins
Large C_1: $C_1 > 0.177$	← decreasing C_1	$C_1 = 0.1$	→	Small C_1: $0.0895 > C_1$
Small C_2: $C_2 < 1.28$	→ increasing C_2	$C_2 = 2$	→	Large C_2: $2.24 < C_2$
Small C_3: $C_3 < 0.062$	→ increasing C_3	$C_3 = 0.1$	→	Large C_3: $0.106 < C_3$
Small C_4: $C_4 < 3.46$	→ increasing C_4	$C_4 = 5$	→	Large C_4: $5.34 < C_4$
Large C_6: $C_6 > 23.0$	← decreasing C_6	$C_6 = 10$	→	Small C_6: $8.34 > C_6$

Varying each of the other parameters C_2, C_3, C_4, and C_6 causes a similar bifurcation series to occur with diagonal and off-diagonal limits flanking out-of-phase oscillations. Table II depicts whether an increase or a decrease of a given parameter moves the system from diagonal to off-diagonal limits. An increase in C_2 causes such a transition because it magnifies the positive feedback signals that help V_1 and V_2 to dominate each other. An increase in C_2 thus has an effect similar to a decrease in C_1. An increase in C_3 or C_4 causes similar transitions because it enables a negative feedback signal of fixed size to have a larger inhibitory effect on its target population. The case wherein $C_4 = 0$ deserves special mention. Then, by equations (5) and (6), no inhibition couples the two-dimensional systems (x_1, z_1) and (x_2, z_2). Then, each system (x_1, z_1) and (x_2, z_2) approaches a unique limit. Consequently, due to the symmetry of equations (5)-(6) and (7)-(8), the 4-dimensional system (5)-(8) approaches a limit on the diagonal. We emphasize this fact because of its physical importance: inhibitory coupling between on-cells and off-cells is necessary in order for any oscillations to occur. Thus the present model does not take the existence of oscillators for granted and then go on to study how coupling between such oscillators alters their properties, as many contributions based on classical oscillators have done. Instead, we study in detail the mechanisms that generate the oscillatory properties of each pacemaker.

A decrease in C_6 causes a similar oscillation series for a more subtle reason. Large values of C_6 cause both of the positive feedback signals $f(x_1)z_1$ and $f(x_2)z_2$ to decay so much that the arousal term C_1 can drive the system to a diagonal limit. Small values of C_6 prevent transmitters from being depleted. Consequently, the transmitters can only accumulate towards their maximal value of 1. Then an initial advantage of (say) x_1 over x_2 tends to be preserved by the large positive feedback signal function $f(x_1)$, since z_1 never depletes enough to cause a significant reduction in $f(x_1)z_1$.

8. Circadian Period and the Transmitter Decay Rate

Parameter C_5 essentially determines the dimensionless period of the free-running gated oscillator. Figure 7a shows that for sufficiently small C_5, the period of the oscillation varies linearly with C_5^{-1}. Thus the slow rate of transmitter accumulation determines a long period of the oscillation.

By contrast with the linear dependence of period on C_5^{-1}, the model period is insensitive to the choice of the other parameters within a wide range. This important property of our model, which is the basis of its claim to being a "clock," is often assumed as a postulate in other circadian models. Figure 7b illustrates the insensitivity of the period by plotting the period as a function of parameter C_1. Over most of the parameter range of C_1 values that cause oscillations, the period is approximately constant. At the small C_1 values that border the parameter range giving rise to off-diagonal limits, the period increases rapidly. At the large C_1 values that approach the range of diagonal limits, the period remains approximately constant until C_1 attains a value where the solution bifurcates to diagonal limits.

In summary, given any fixed choice of C_5, the period of the oscillator is essentially determined no matter how the other parameters are chosen, except near the limiting parametric values where the oscillation is quenched.

An increase of C_5 from zero causes the following sequence of solutions to occur. When $C_5 = 0$, z_1 and z_2 are constant by (7) and (8). The system approaches off-diagonal limits except possibly when $z_1 = z_2$. As soon as $C_5 > 0$, large amplitude oscillations occur. At sufficiently large C_5 values, diagonal limits occur.

9. Dependence of Solution Types on Signal Function: The Sigmoid Case

All of the above properties hold when the positive feedback signal $f(w)$ and the negative feedback signal $g(w)$ equal a threshold-linear signal function $\max(w, 0)$. When

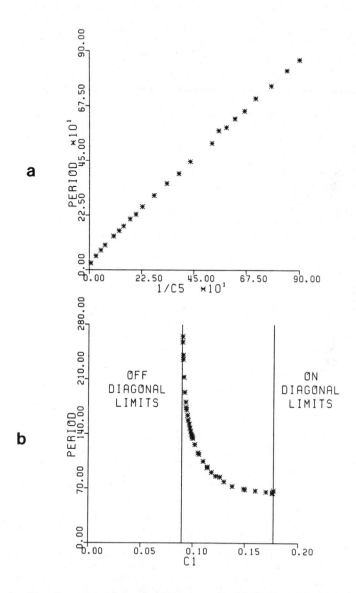

Figure 7. Circadian period (threshold-linear case). (a) For small values of the dimensionless transmitter accumulation rate C_5, the period varies linearly with C_5^{-1}. When $C_5 > 0.143$, the system goes to diagonal limits. (b) The period is relatively insensitive to the dimensionless arousal level C_1 except near its extreme values where oscillations break down.

$f(w)$ is chosen instead to be the sigmoid function

$$f(w) = \begin{cases} \frac{w^2}{C_7^2+w^2} & \text{if } w \geq 0 \\ 0 & \text{if } w < 0 \end{cases}, \tag{25}$$

then a much richer family of solution types can occur.

Sigmoid signal functions play an important role in competitive feedback networks whose feedback signals are not modulated by slow gates. In such networks, the sigmoid signal function attenuates small activities (noise suppression) and amplifies large activities (contrast enhancement) before storing the contrast enhanced activity pattern in short term memory via feedback signaling (Grossberg, 1982b). When slow gates can modulate sigmoid feedback signals, as in a gated pacemaker, then the storage process is replaced by a wide variety of oscillatory possibilities.

Sigmoid signal functions also have a simple physical interpretation that is of independent interest. Suppose that $f(w)$ is the total output of a large population of cells. Let each cell fire a signal of unit intensity when its activity exceeds a threshold Γ; otherwise let the cell output equal zero. Suppose that the number $p(\Gamma)$ of cells having a fixed threshold Γ is a bell-shaped function of Γ. Then

$$f(w) = \int_0^w p(\Gamma)d\Gamma \tag{54}$$

is a sigmoid function of w. Thus if the signal thresholds of a cell population are randomly distributed about a mean threshold value, then the total population signal is a sigmoid function of its mean activity.

In the following examples, the nonlinear curvature of $f(w)$ causes the new oscillatory types, rather than a rescaling of numerical parameters. This claim is illustrated in Figure 8, which graphs the previous choice of threshold-linear signal function and the present choice of sigmoid signal function. In the threshold-linear case, we chose $C_2 = 2$ so that $C_2f(w) = 2w$ when $w \geq 0$. In the sigmoid case,

$$C_2f(w) = \frac{w^2}{.04 + w^2} \tag{55}$$

if $w \geq 0$, which remains very close to $2w$ throughout the interval $[0, .4]$ wherein the graphs of $x_1(t)$ and $x_2(t)$ are concentrated. Note that at very small values of $w \in [0, .4]$, the sigmoid signal is smaller than $2w$, whereas at larger values of $w \in [0, .4]$, the sigmoid signal exceeds $2w$. Thus $2w$ closely interpolates the sigmoid signal throughout the interval of interest. In particular, we choose $C_7 = .2$ so that $w^2/(C_7^2 + w^2) = 1/2$ when $w = .2$. Thus the sigmoid signal function attains half its maximum value at the estimated average value .2 of x_1 and x_2. Table III summarizes the choice of parameters off which we will perturb to study the sigmoid case. Parameters C_1, C_3, C_4, C_5, and C_6 have the same values as in Table I, and parameters C_2 and C_7 are chosen so that the sigmoid function interpolates the threshold-linear function.

10. Parametric Structure of Oscillations: Sigmoid Signal Function

In this section, we will summarize the oscillation sequences that can occur when the parameters C_1, C_2, C_3, C_4, and C_6 are separately varied. The next section will consider the remarkable oscillation sequences that can occur when C_7 is varied. These new sequences can also occur when any one of the other parameters is varied, albeit in a region of parameter space other than that summarized in Table III.

A decrease in the arousal parameter C_1 generates an oscillation sequence much like that described in Section 7 and illustrated in Figure 6, with one notable exception.

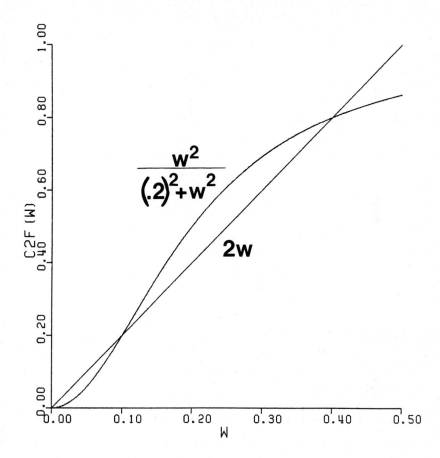

Figure 8. Interpolated sigmoid and threshold-linear signal functions. The parameters $C_2 = 1$ and $C_7 = 0.2$ are chosen so that the sigmoid signal function closely interpolates the threshold-linear signal function ($C_2 = 2$) throughout the range of oscillations.

In Section 7, a decrease in C_1 transformed large amplitude oscillations into plateau oscillations in which x_1 and x_2 overshot and then decreased to a plateau level before being inhibited (Figure 6d). As C_1 decreased in this parameter range, the period of the oscillation increased continuously (Figure 7b). By contrast, in the sigmoid case, a decrease of C_1 transforms a large amplitude oscillation (Figure 9a) into an oscillation in which a second bump occurs in the graphs of x_1 and x_2 instead of a smooth plateau (Figure 9b). As this bump appears, a discontinuous increase of the period also occurs. A further decrease of C_1 eventually causes a second, then a third, etc., bump to occur in the graphs of x_1 and x_2 (Figure 9c). Each new bump is accompanied by a discontinuous increase of the period. At sufficiently small values of C_1, these oscillations are replaced by off-diagonal limits, as in the threshold-linear case. These *rippled plateau* solutions have never been observed during our numerical studies of the threshold-linear case and are thus presumably due to the nonlinear form of the sigmoid signal function.

TABLE 3

Typical Parameter Values for a Sigmoid Nocturnal Pacemaker

$$C_1 = 0.10$$
$$C_2 = 1.00$$
$$C_3 = 0.10$$
$$C_4 = 5.00$$
$$C_5 = 0.01$$
$$C_6 = 10.00$$
$$C_7 = 0.20$$

Changing each of the parameters C_2, C_3, C_4, and C_6 in the direction described in Table II, while holding the other parameters at their values in Table III, also generates the sequence of diagonal limits, small amplitude oscillations, large amplitude oscillations, rippled plateau solutions, and off-diagonal limits.

11. Mittens, Oyster Shells, Sequence Clusters, and Chaos

When C_7 is increased with the parameters $C_1, \ldots, C_6$ fixed at their values in Table III, then the following type of oscillation sequence is observed:

a) diagonal limits;

b) large amplitude, small period oscillations;

c) larger amplitude oscillations, monotone increase in period;

d) smaller amplitude oscillations, levelling off of period;

e) mittens (period doubling);

f) oyster shells (slowly modulated mittens);

g) sequence clusters (periodic sequences of oscillation clusters);

h) complex transitions, chaos?;

i) unstable small amplitude oyster shells;

j) diagonal limits.

Figure 10 illustrates these solution types.

The diagonal limits (Figure 10a) that are found when C_7 is very small are due to the fact that the positive feedback signals $f(x_1)$ and $f(x_2)$ are approximately equal and constant in this range. The large amplitude oscillations (Figure 10b) that occur at slightly larger C_7 values are due to the fact that $f(w)$ approximates a step function with a transition from approximately 0 to 1 as w exceeds C_7 (Figure 11a). The longer periods of large amplitude oscillations (Figure 10c) that are found at larger C_7 values (Figure 11b) can be explained as follows. The reversal of the relative sizes of x_1 and x_2 occurs relatively quickly. This reversal is called a *jump* in the terminology of singular

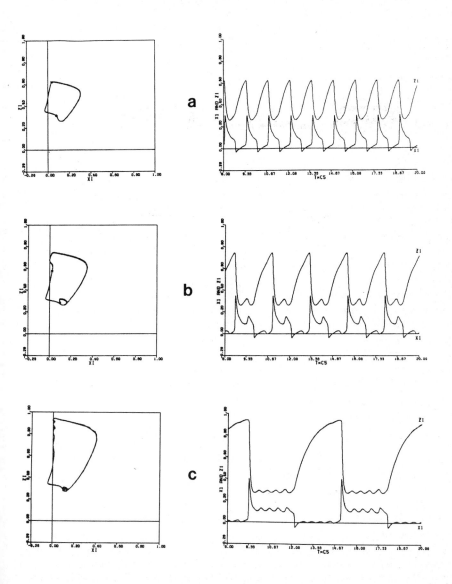

Figure 9. Rippled plateau solutions in response to a decrease in dimensionless arousal C_1 (sigmoid case). (a) At $C_1 = 0.076048$, a large amplitude oscillation occurs. (b) At $C_1 = 0.076047$, a second bump occurs during each cycle. (c) At $C_1 = 0.066$, the plateau contains four ripples. At slightly smaller C_1 values, off-diagonal limits occur.

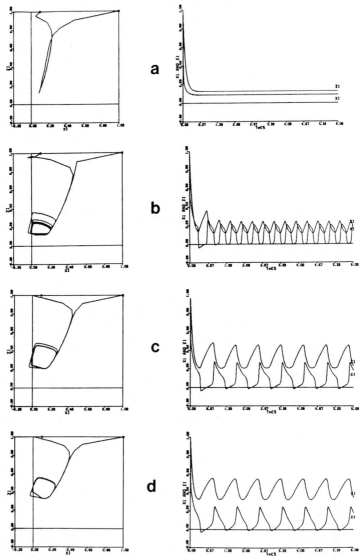

Figure 10. Oscillation sequence in response to an increase in the half-maximum argument $w = C_7$ of the sigmoid signal $f(w)$. (a) Diagonal limit ($C_7 = 0.0577$). (b) Fast large amplitude oscillation ($C_7 = 0.0578$). In this case, the values of z_1 are so small that the graphs of $x_1(t)$ and $z_1(t)$ intersect. (c) Longer period and larger amplitude oscillation ($C_7 = 0.17$). (d) Smaller amplitude oscillation and same period as in (c) ($C_7 = 0.25$). (e) Mittens ($C_7 = 0.348$). (f) Oyster shells ($C_7 = 0.35$). (g) 8,5,5 sequence cluster ($C_7 = 0.36$). (h) Triplets ($C_7 = 0.363$). (i) Unstable small amplitude oyster shells become regular periodic ($C_7 = 0.368$). (j) Diagonal limit ($C_7 = 0.375$). The phase portraits have been enlarged in (f) and (g).

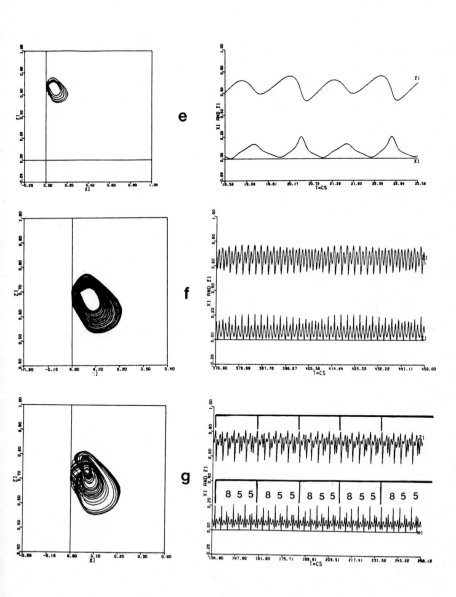

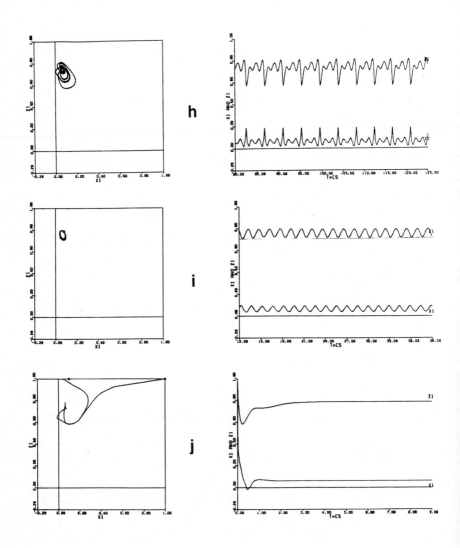

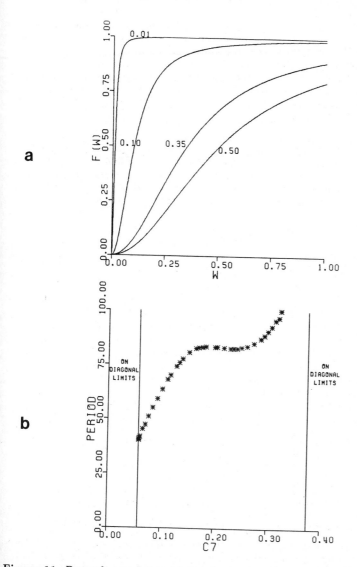

Figure 11. Dependence of sigmoid signal function and oscillation period on C_7. (a) A family of sigmoid signal functions parameterized by C_7. (b) Period as a function of C_7. Note the constancy of the period except where the sigmoid approximates a 0–1 switch (small C_7) or near where complex oscillations occur (large C_7).

perturbation theory (Section 12). At larger values of C_7, the maximal difference between x_1 and x_2 is also larger. Hence z_1 and z_2, which change slowly (Section 8) take longer to equilibrate to the x_1 and x_2 values. In the terminology of singular perturbation theory, this slow process is said to take place on the *slow manifold* (Section 12). The longer duration of the slow manifold process is the major factor determining how the period can increase with C_7.

As C_7 increases further, one might expect, as in Section 7, that small amplitude oscillations will be generated, because an increase in C_7 acts in much the same way as an increase in C_1 or a decrease in C_2 (Figure 11a). However, this is not all that happens. The amplitude of oscillations does not begin to decrease as the period levels off (Figures 10d and 11b). As C_7 increases further, however, period doubling occurs (Figure 10e) due to the attenuation of alternate peaks in the graphs of each x_i and z_i, $i = 1, 2$ ("mittens"). When this occurs, the largest peaks and troughs of $x_1(t)$ are aligned with the largest troughs and peaks of $x_2(t)$, respectively. Consequently, the graphs of $x_1(t)$ and $x_2(t)$ are out of phase, but no longer 180° out of phase.

At larger C_7 values, the envelopes of the mittens are modulated on a slow time scale (Figure 10f). We call this oscillation type an *oyster shell* due to the appearance of its (x_1, z_1) phase portrait. A striking feature of the oyster shell is that a periodic modulation of the envelope of oscillation peaks coexists with a periodic modulation of the envelope of oscillation troughs. This type of envelope modulation differs, say, from the modulation that occurs during the beats of a harmonic oscillator, where the peaks and troughs share a common envelope.

At larger C_7 values, periodic sequences of oscillation clusters appear. Figure 10g depicts an oscillation in which a cluster of eight peaks is followed by two repetitions of a different cluster of five peaks, after which the (8,5,5) sequence repeats itself. Interspersed among the modulated solutions are relatively simple patterns, such as the unmodulated triplets depicted in Figure 10h. This complex sequence of patterns suggests that chaotic solutions may be present for some C_7 values.

Only after these complex waveforms are generated does the system experience a progressive decrease in the amplitude of oyster shells (Figure 10i). Figure 10i indicates that the small amplitude oyster shell is unstable, since the solution eventually approaches a small amplitude regular periodic solution. At still larger C_7 values, diagonal limits are obtained. The diagonal limits occur because a sufficient attenuation of $f(w)$ acts much like a large C_1 or small C_2 value (Section 7).

Why does a series of complex oscillation types occur instead of just a steady reduction in the amplitude of a regular periodic solution, as when $f(w)$ is a threshold-linear signal function (Section 7)? A mathematical explanation of this phenomenon is not yet available, but the following facts indicate that the quadratic nonlinearity in $f(w)$ at small w values causes the phenomenon.

In all of our numerical studies of these oscillations, $x_1(t)$ and $x_2(t)$ remain smaller than C_7 at all times $t \geq 0$. Within this range of values, $f(w)$ is well approximated by w^2/C_7^2. To test whether a quadratically nonlinear signal function can generate Figures 10a–10j, we replaced the sigmoid $f(w)$ by w^2/C_7^2 and verified that a complex oscillation sequence was in fact generated using this quadratic signal function.

An indication of how mittens (Figure 10e) and the modulated mittens, or oyster shells (Figure 10f), may be generated is contained in the following intuitive argument. Mittens consist of small amplitude peaks that alternate with large amplitude peaks. The large amplitude peaks are analogous to the large amplitude peaks of a regular periodic solution (Figure 10d). Our problem is to understand why the smaller peaks are not full size. Consider the time $t = \alpha$ in Figure 12a at which $x_1(t)$ attains a minimum. At this time, x_1 and x_2 begin to switch because z_2 is sufficiently depleted to make

$$(1 - x_1)(C_1 + C_2 f(x_1)z_1) > (1 - x_2)(C_1 + C_2 f(x_2)z_2) \tag{56}$$

despite the fact that $f(x_1) \cong 0$ (Section 3). Consequently x_1 begins to grow. A complete switch from x_2 to x_1 is caused when, as x_1 grows, also $f(x_1)z_1$ grows sufficiently quickly to support this regenerative reaction. Figure 12b indicates, however, that when x_1 is in this range of values, and numerically approximates .1, the value of x_1^2/C_7^2 is very small. By "very small" we mean small compared to a linear signal function $1.3x_1$ at which small amplitude, regular periodic oscillations are found (Table II). The insufficient positive feedback from x_1^2/C_7^2 prevents x_1 from completing a full switch with x_2.

Due to x_1's partial growth, z_1 continues to deplete, thereby causing a decrease in $f(x_1)z_1$ that accompanies a decrease in x_1 between times $t = \beta$ and $t = \gamma$. During these times, z_1 attains an intermediate set of values, neither maximal nor minimal, because x_1 itself has not reached its extrema. As x_1 continues to decrease, z_1 begins to accumulate again, this time starting from a larger initial value than is attained at time $t = \alpha$. Thus when the next opportunity for switching between x_1 and x_2 occurs at time $t = \delta$, $f(x_1)z_1$ is bolstered by a large z_1 value. This boost enables x_1 to move towards a value of approximately .2. By Figure 12b, x_1^2/C_7^2 is much larger when $x_1 = .2$ than is the comparison linear signal function $1.3x_1$. Thus a better switch between x_1 and x_2 is assured than in the threshold-linear case, where small amplitude oscillations occurred.

12. Singular Perturbation Analysis

This section outlines a singular perturbation analysis of how a gated pacemaker oscillates. The analysis can be expanded into a formal proof using known techniques for building isolated blocks in four-dimensonal fast-slow dynamical systems (Carpenter, 1977a, 1977b). The discussion will focus on system (5)-(8) when $f(w) = g(w) = \max(w,0)$ and $L(t) \equiv 0$ (free-run). We consider this system in the singular limit where C_5 is very small. Then z_1 and z_2 change very slowly compared to x_1 and x_2 except near the set S where both $\dot{x}_1 = 0$ and $\dot{x}_2 = 0$. The set

$$S = \{(x_1, x_2, z_1, z_2) : \dot{x}_1 = 0 \text{ and } \dot{x}_2 = 0\} \tag{57}$$

is called the *slow manifold* of the system. Off the set S, z_1 and z_2 can be approximated by constants along system trajectories. Then the four-dimensional system (5)-(8) is approximately described by the two-dimensional *fast system* F

$$\dot{x}_1 = -x_1 + (1 - x_1)[C_1 + C_2 f(x_1)z_1] - (x_1 + C_3)C_4 g(x_2) \tag{58}$$

and

$$\dot{x}_2 = -x_2 + (1 - x_2)[C_1 + C_2 f(x_2)z_2] - (x_2 + C_3)C_4 g(x_1) \tag{59}$$

in which z_1 and z_2 are constant. The fast system (58)-(59) can be rewritten in the form

$$\dot{y}_1 = a_1(y_1)[b_1(y_1) - c(y_1, y_2)] \tag{60}$$

and

$$\dot{y}_2 = a_2(y_2)[b_2(y_2) - c(y_1, y_2)] \tag{61}$$

in terms of the variables $y_i = x_i + C_3, i = 1, 2$. When a competitive system has this form, it is called an *adaptation level* system. Adaptation level systems have the property that all their trajectories are attracted to equilibrium points (Grossberg, 1978, 1982b). Consequently, the trajectory approaches the slow manifold S. When this occurs, $\dot{x}_1 \cong 0$ and $\dot{x}_2 \cong 0$ so that even if C_5 is small, the rates of change of z_1 and z_2 become significant. Then the motions of z_1 and z_2 are studied while the trajectory remains on S. In other words, we consider equations

$$\dot{z}_1 = C_5[1 - z_1 - C_6 f(x_1)z_1] \tag{7}$$

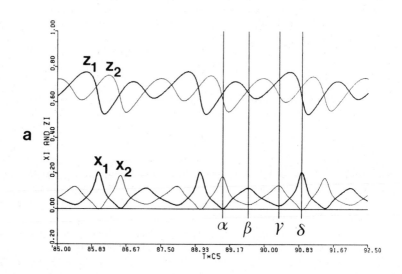

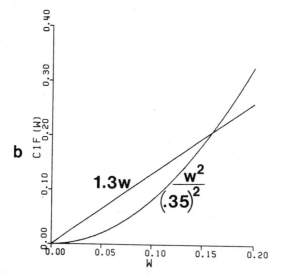

Figure 12. Dependence of mittens on quadratic growth of the sigmoid signal. (a) Graphs of $x_1(t)$ and $z_1(t)$ (dark curves) and $x_2(t)$ and $z_2(t)$ (light curves). Text describes how lower peaks in x_1's graph are caused by insufficient quadratic feedback. Here, $C_7 = 0.35$, as in Figure 10f. (b) When $w = 0.1$, $w^2/(0.35)^2 < 1.3w$. By contrast, when $w = 0.2$, $w^2/(0.35)^2 > 1.3w$. The different relative sizes of quadratic vs. linear feedback signals control whether mittens or a small amplitude, regular periodic solution occurs.

and

$$\dot{z}_2 = C_5[1 - z_2 - C_6 f(x_2) z_2] \tag{8}$$

given the hypothesis that x_1 and x_2 satisfy the simultaneous equations

$$0 = -x_1 + (1 - x_1)[C_1 + C_2 f(x_1) z_1] - (x_1 + C_3) C_4 g(x_2) \tag{62}$$

and

$$0 = -x_2 + (1 - x_2)[C_1 + C_2 f(x_2) z_2] - (x_2 + C_3) C_4 g(x_1). \tag{63}$$

In this case, x_1 and x_2 satisfy equations of the form

$$x_1 = h_1(z_1, z_2) \tag{64}$$

and

$$x_2 = h_2(z_1, z_2) \tag{65}$$

which represent a single-valued branch of the solution of (62)-(63). Then (7) and (8) become

$$\dot{z}_1 = C_5[1 - z_1 - C_6 f(h_1(z_1, z_2)) z_1] \tag{66}$$

and

$$\dot{z}_2 = C_5[1 - z_2 - C_6 f(h_2(z_1, z_2)) z_2]. \tag{67}$$

This two-dimensional system determines the motion of (z_1, z_2) unless a phase point is reached at which a solution (x_1, x_2) of (66)-(67) no longer exists on S. At such a time, the trajectory *jumps* off S. Then F controls system dynamics until x_1 and x_2 approach S once again.

A *singular solution* of the system is constructed from alternating solution segments on $F, S, F, S, \ldots$. Singular perturbation techniques can be used to show that solutions of the full system exist close to a singular solution when C_5 is very small. The following description indicates how the phase portraits of F and S can generate a singular periodic solution.

Suppose for definiteness that the trajectory is not in S at time $t = 0$. Figure 13 indicates how the trajectory moves in F. Figure 13 is an (x_1, x_2) phase portrait in which two curves intersect. One curve describes the set

$$S_1(z_1) = \{(x_1, x_2) : \dot{x}_1 = 0\}. \tag{68}$$

This set is the solution curve of (62) under the hypothesis that z_1 remains constant. The other curve describes the set

$$S_2(z_2) = \{(x_1, x_2) : \dot{x}_2 = 0\}. \tag{69}$$

This set is the solution curve of (63) under the hypothesis that z_2 remains constant. The values of z_1 and z_2 can be held fixed because the trajectory is not near S at the outset.

The set

$$S(z_1, z_2) = S_1(z_1) \bigcup S_2(z_2) \tag{70}$$

describes the subset of S that is reachable from F given the initial values z_1 and z_2. The set $S(z_1, z_2)$ consists of three points P_1, P_2, P_3 in Figure 13. These points are equilibrium points of (x_1, x_2) in the two-dimensional fast system F. To determine how $S(z_1, z_2)$ is approached, we need to know the stability of these equilibrium points.

To analyse stability, note that set $S_1(z_1)$ is a set of points (x_1, x_2) which satisfy an equation of the form

$$x_1 = H(x_2, z_1). \tag{71}$$

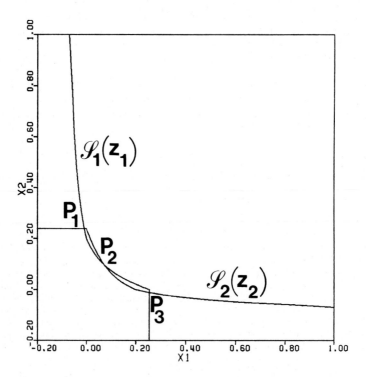

Figure 13. Fast manifold and its equilibrium points P_1, P_2, and P_3 (threshold-linear case). Parameters C_1, C_2, C_3, and C_4 are chosen as in Table 1. Parameter $z_1 = 0.473$ and $z_2 = 0.448$. Sets $S_1(z_1)$ and $S_2(z_2)$ are defined in the text.

Similarly, the set $S_2(z_2)$ satisfies an equation of the form

$$x_2 = H(x_1, z_2). \tag{72}$$

The same function $H(x, z)$ appears in both equations due to the symmetry of (62) and (63). $H(x, z)$ is single-valued if and only if

$$C_2 \leq 1 + C_1 + C_1/C_3. \tag{73}$$

The parameter values in Table I satisfy (73). If (73) is satisfied, then

$$\frac{\partial H}{\partial x} \leq 0. \tag{74}$$

An equilibrium point is stable if

$$\frac{\partial H}{\partial x}(x_1, z_2)\frac{\partial H}{\partial x}(x_2, z_1) < 1 \tag{75}$$

and is a saddle point if

$$\frac{\partial H}{\partial x}(x_1, z_2)\frac{\partial H}{\partial x}(x_2, z_1) > 1. \tag{76}$$

Using inequalities (75) and (76), we verify below that P_2 is a saddle point, whereas P_1 and P_3 are stable equilibrium points. Thus all trajectories that start off the one-dimensional stable manifold of P_2 will be attracted to one of the stable equilibrium points P_1 or P_3.

Equilibrium point P_1 is stable because the graph of $S_2(z_2)$ is flat near P_1; hence its slope $\frac{\partial H}{\partial x}(x_1, z_2) = 0$ at P_1. Equilibrium point P_2 is a saddle point because the graph of $S_2(z_2)$ has a slope $\frac{\partial H}{\partial x}(x_1, z_2)$ with respect to x_1, whereas the graph of $S_1(z_1)$ has a slope

$$\frac{1}{\frac{\partial H}{\partial x}(x_2, z_1)} \tag{77}$$

when it is considered as a function of x_1. Figure 12 shows that

$$\frac{\partial H}{\partial x}(x_1, z_2) < \frac{1}{\frac{\partial H}{\partial x}(x_2, z_1)} \tag{78}$$

at P_2. Since both slopes in (78) are negative, (78) implies (76). The stability of P_3 can be similarly determined.

Consider a trajectory that starts away from the set $\{P_1, P_2, P_3\}$ and quickly jumps towards P_3. In the singular solution, the trajectory then lies in $S(z_1, z_2)$. Once the trajectory is in $S(z_1, z_2)$, the equations (66)-(67) governing the slow manifold S take over and z_1 and z_2 slowly change. These changes cause the trajectory to move within S. By Figure 13, P_3 lies at an (x_1, x_2) position where x_1 is large and x_2 is small. If z_1 and z_2 start at moderate values, then (66) causes a decrease in z_1 while (67) causes an increase in z_2. These changes tend to cause an upward shift in the set $S_2(z_2)$ and a downward shift in the set $S_1(z_1)$. As this shift in the sets takes place, the singular trajectory (x_1, x_2, z_1, z_2) continues to satisfy the constraint that $(x_1, x_2) \in S(z_1, z_2)$.

The motion in S can continue until the sets $S_1(z_1)$ and $S_2(z_2)$ become tangent (Figure 14a) and then separate (Figure 14b). When this occurs, the trajectory suddenly leaves S. Its motion is then controlled by F. By Figure 14b, there is only one equilibrium point P in F that can attract the trajectory at this time. By (75), P is a stable equilibrium point. A rapid jump of (x_1, x_2) to P thus occurs. Then the system is in S again, but now x_1 is small and x_2 is large. Hence z_1 tends to increase, thereby tending to drag $S_1(z_1)$ upward, and z_2 tends to decrease, thereby tending to drag $S_2(z_2)$ downward until the trajectory is forced off S onto F, and the cycle repeats itself.

Two other outcomes are easily interpreted using this type of geometric description. It is possible for a motion in S that starts at P_3 to continue for all time. This will happen if $S_1(z_1)$ and $S_2(z_2)$ never become tangent, as in Figure 14a. Then instead of jumping off S onto F, the sets $S_1(z_1)$ and $S_2(z_2)$ can continue to shift slowly as the system approaches an off-diagonal limit.

By contrast, an intersection of $S_1(z_1)$ and $S_2(z_2)$ such as that depicted in Figure 15 may also arise. Then $S(z_1, z_2)$ contains a single stable equilibrium point of F. If this portrait persists, then an equilibrium point on the diagonal is approaches. Only a finite number of equilibrium points exist when the signal functions are threshold-linear.

The above geometrical description indicates the issues that need to be resolved to prove rigorous theorems about this system. For example, a complete understanding of how the sets $S_1(z_1)$ and $S_2(z_2)$ change as functions of z_1 and z_2, given all possible choices of parameters, is needed. One also needs to know the location of the stable equilibrium points in $S(z_1, z_2)$ when $S_1(z_1)$ and $S_2(z_2)$ are tangent, and whether a jump

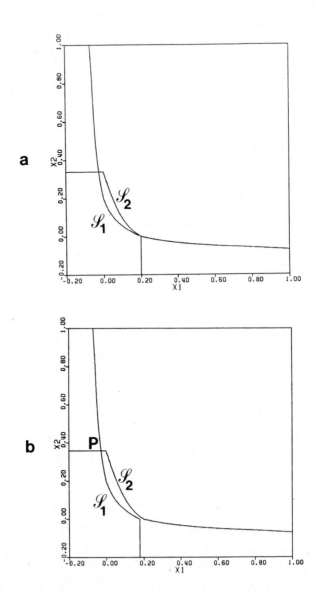

Figure 14. A jump off the slow manifold. In (a), $S_1(0.3723)$ and $S_2(0.6074)$ are tangent. In (b), slightly different z_1 and z_2 values cause the curves $S_1(z_1)$ and $S_2(z_2)$ to separate at their rightmost intersection, thereby forcing a jump within the fast manifold to P. $S_1(0.33)$ and $S_2(0.64)$ are graphed.

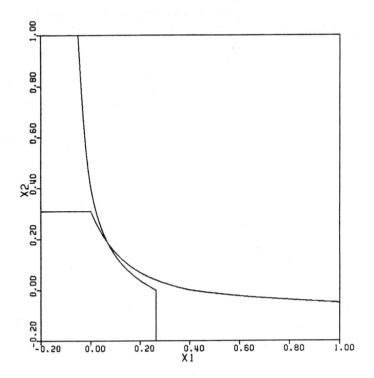

Figure 15. A switch from F to S is followed by approach to a diagonal equilibrium point on S. Parameters C_2, C_3, and C_4 are chosen as in Table 1. Parameter $C_1 = 0.2$.

in F between a pair of these equilibrium points will cause z_1 and z_2 to increase or to decrease during the next motion within S.

13. Concluding Remarks: Interdisciplinary Applications

This article analyses the parametric structure of oscillations that can be generated by a gated pacemaker. Other articles in this series augment the gated pacemaker model with metabolic feedback and slow gain control processes that together help to explain difficult data such as split rhythms, several types of after-effects, Aschoff's rule and its exceptions, results of ablation studies and hormonal manipulations, and relationships between antidepressants and circadian rhythms (Carpenter and Grossberg, 1983, 1984). The augmented circadian model is homologous to a model of the hypothalamic eating circuit (Grossberg, 1982a, 1983). We believe that this homology illustrates how different hypothalamic circuits may be constructed from similar mechanistic components (Olds, 1977). Thus the results herein about the circadian wake-sleep and activity-rest cycle may find application in studies of motivational rhythms (Rosenwasser, Boulos, and Terman, 1981). Gated dipole circuits have also been used to help analyse certain perceptual and cognitive phenomena (Grossberg, 1980, 1982b, 1983, 1984). Although the rhythms that occur in these contexts are much faster than circadian rhythms, the same gated pacemaker circuit can be made to generate rhythms of essentially any period just by altering the dimensionless gain C_5 of its transmitter gating process (Section 8). Thus the parametric studies reported herein may find their way into discussions of fast perceptual and cognitive rhythmic phenomena that seem to be unrelated to circadian rhythms, but on a mechanistic level may be properties of gated pacemaker circuitry.

REFERENCES

Aschoff, J., Influences of internal and external factors on the period measured in constant conditions. *Z. Tierpsychol.*, 1979, **49**, 225–249.

Carpenter, G.A., A geometric approach to singular perturbation problems with applications to nerve impulse equations. *Journal of Differential Equations*, 1977, **23**, 335–367 (a).

Carpenter, G.A., Periodic solutions of nerve impulse equations. *Journal of Mathematical Analysis and Applications*, 1977, **58**, 152–173 (b).

Carpenter, G.A. and Grossberg, S., Adaptation and transmitter gating in vertebrate photoreceptors. *Journal of Theoretical Neurobiology*, 1981, **1**, 1–42.

Carpenter, G.A. and Grossberg, S., Dynamic models of neural systems: Propagated signals, photoreceptor transduction, and circadian rhythms. In J.P.E. Hodgson (Ed.), **Oscillations in mathematical biology**. New York: Springer-Verlag, 1983.

Carpenter, G.A. and Grossberg, S., A neural theory of circadian rhythms: Aschoff's rule in diurnal and nocturnal mammals. *American Journal of Physiology*, 1984, **247**, R1067–R1082.

Daan, S. and Pittendrigh, C.S., A functional analysis of circadian pacemakers in nocturnal rodents, II: The variability of phase response curves. *Journal of Comparative Physiology*, 1976, **106**, 253–266.

DeCoursey, P.J., Phase control of activity in a rodent. *Cold Spring Harbor Symposium on Quantitative Biology*, 1960, **25**, 49–55.

Earnest, D. and Turek, F.W., Splitting of the circadian rhythm of activity in hamsters: Effects of exposure to constant darkness and subsequent re-exposure to constant light. *Journal of Comparative Physiology*, 1982, **145**, 405–411.

FitzHugh, R., Impulses and physiological states in theoretical models of nerve membrane. *Biophysical Journal*, 1961, **1**, 445–466.

Grossberg, S., Some physiological and biochemical consequences of psychological postulates. *Proceedings of the National Academy of Sciences*, 1968, **60**, 758–765.

Grossberg, S., Competition, decision, and consensus. *Journal of Mathematical Analysis and Applications*, 1978, **66**, 470–493.

Grossberg, S., How does a brain build a cognitive code? *Psychological Review*, 1980, **87**, 1–51.

Grossberg, S., Psychophysiological substrates of schedule interactions and behavioral contrast. In S. Grossberg (Ed.), **Mathematical psychology and psychophysiology**. Providence, RI: American Mathematical Society, 1981.

Grossberg, S., The processing of expected and unexpected events during conditioning and attention: A psychophysiological theory. *Psychological Review*, 1982, **89**, 529–572 (a).

Grossberg, S., **Studies of mind and brain: Neural principles of learning, perception, development, cognition, and motor control**. Boston: Reidel Press, 1982 (b).

Grossberg, S., The quantized geometry of visual space: The coherent computation of depth, form, and lightness. *Behavioral and Brain Sciences*, 1983, **6**, 625–692.

Grossberg, S., Some psychophysiological and pharmacological correlates of a developmental, cognitive, and motivational theory. In R. Karrer, J. Cohen, and P. Tueting (Eds.), **Brain and information: Event related potentials**. New York: New York Academy of Sciences, 1984.

Gwinner, E., Testosterone induces "splitting" of circadian locomotor activity rhythm in birds. *Science*, 1974, **185**, 72–74.

Hodgkin, A.L., **The conduction of the nervous impulse**. Liverpool: Liverpool University Press, 1964.

Hodgkin, A.L. and Huxley, A.F., A quantitative description of membrane current and its application to conduction and excitation in nerve. *Journal of Physiology*, 1952, **117**, 500–544.

Hoffman, K., Splitting of the circadian rhythm as a function of light intensity. In M. Menaker (Ed.), **Biochronometry**. Washington, DC: National Academy of Sciences, 1971.

Jouvet, M., Mouret, J., Chouvet, G., and Siffre, M., Toward a 48-hour day: Experimental bicircadian rhythm in man. In C.S. Pittendrigh (Ed.), **Circadian oscillations and organization in nervous systems**. Cambridge, MA: MIT Press, 1974.

Kafka, M.S., Wirz-Justice, A., Naber, D., Marangos, P.J., O'Donohue, T.L., and Wehr, T.A., Effect of lithium on circadian neurotransmitter receptor rhythms. *Neuropsychobiology*, 1982, **8**, 41–50.

Kafka, M.S., Wirz-Justice, A., and Naber, D., Circadian and seasonal rhythms in α- and β-adrenergic receptors in the rat brain. *Brain Research*, 1981, **207**, 409–419.

Kafka, M.S., Wirz-Justice, A., Naber, D., and Wehr, T.A., Circadian acetylcholine receptor rhythm in rat brain and its modification by imipramine. *Neuropharmacology*, 1981, **20**, 421–425.

Katz, B., **Nerve, muscle, and synapse**. New York: McGraw-Hill, 1966.

Kawato, M. and Suzuki, R., Two coupled neural oscillators as a model of the circadian pacemaker. *Journal of Theoretical Biology*, 1980, **86**, 547–575.

Kramm, K.R., Circadian activity in the antelope ground squirrel *Ammospermophilus leucurus*. Ph.D. Thesis, University of California at Irvine, 1971.

Kronauer, R.E., Czeisler, C.A., Pilato, S.F., Moore-Ede, M.C., and Weitzman, E.D., Mathematical model of the human circadian system with two interacting oscillators. *American Journal of Physiology*, 1982, **242**, R3–R17.

Kuffler, S.W. and Nicholls, J.G., **From neuron to brain**. Sunderland, MA: Sinauer Press, 1976.

Moore, R.Y., Retinohypothalamic projection in mammals: A comparative study. *Brain Research*, 1973, **49**, 403–409.

Moore, R.Y., Visual pathways and the central control of diurnal rhythms. In C.S. Pittendrigh (Ed.), **Circadian oscillations and organization in nervous systems**. Cambridge, MA: MIT Press, 1974.

Moore-Ede, M.C., Sulzman, F.M., and Fuller, C.A., **The clocks that time us**. Cambridge, MA: Harvard University Press, 1982.

Naber, D., Wirz-Justice, A., and Kafka, M.S., Circadian rhythm in brain opiate receptor. *Neuroscience Letters*, 1981, **21**, 45–50.

Nagumo, J., Arimoto, S., and Yoshizawa, S., An active pulse transmission line simulating nerve axon. *Proceedings I.E.E.E.*, 1962, **50**, 2061–2070.

Olds, J., **Drives and reinforcements: Behavioral studies of hypothalamic functions**. New York: Raven Press, 1977.

Pickard, G.E. and Turek, F.W., Splitting of the circadian rhythm of activity is abolished by unilateral lesions of the suprachiasmatic nuclei. *Science*, 1982, **215**, 1119–1121.

Pittendrigh, C.S., Circadian rhythms and the circadian organization of living systems. *Cold Spring Harbor Symposium Quantitative Biology*, 1960, **25**, 159–185.

Pittendrigh, C.S., Circadian oscillations in cells and the circadian organization of multicellular systems. In C.S. Pittendrigh (Ed.), **Circadian oscillations and organization in nervous systems**. Cambridge, MA: MIT Press, 1974.

Plonsey, R., **Bioelectric phenomena**. New York: McGraw Hill, 1969.

Pohl, H., Characteristics and variability in entrainment of circadian rhythms in light in diurnal rodents. In J. Aschoff, S. Daan, and G.A. Groos (Eds.), **Vertebrate circadian systems**. Berlin: Springer-Verlag, 1982.

Rosenwasser, A.M., Boulos, Z., and Terman, M., Circadian organization of food intake and meal patterns in the rat. *Physiology and Behavior*, 1981, **27**, 33–39.

Sisk, C.L. and Turek, F.W., Role of the inter-connections of the suprachiasmatic nuclei in the hamster circadian system. *Society of Neuroscience Abstracts*, 1982, **8**, 35.

Wehr, T.A. and Wirz-Justice, A., Circadian rhythm mechanisms in affective illness and in antidepressant drug action. *Pharmacopsychiatry*, 1982, **15**, 30–38.

Wehr, T.A., Wirz-Justice, A., Goodwin, F.K., Duncan, W., and Gillin, J.C., Phase advance of the circadian sleep-wake cycle as an antidepressant. *Science*, 1979, **206**, 710–713.

Wever, R.A., **The circadian system of man: Results of experiments under temporal isolation**. New York: Springer-Verlag, 1979.

Chapter 7

A NEURAL THEORY OF CIRCADIAN RHYTHMS:
ASCHOFF'S RULE IN DIURNAL AND NOCTURNAL MAMMALS

Preface

This Chapter simulates and mathematically analyses deeper properties of circadian data using the gated pacemaker model, notably Aschoff's rule, the circadian rule, and the tendency of nocturnal mammals to lose circadian rhythmicity at lower light levels than diurnal mammals.

Aschoff's rule and the circadian rule describe how the activity interval and the circadian period of nocturnal and diurnal mammals depend upon light intensity. Both nocturnal and diurnal mammals tend to obey the circadian rule: in nocturnal mammals, activity is an increasing function of light intensity, whereas in diurnal mammals, activity is a decreasing function of light intensity. In contrast, although nocturnal mammals tend to consistently obey Aschoff's rule, there are many exceptions to Aschoff's rule among diurnal mammals: In nocturnal mammals, circadian period tends to increase with light intensity. In diurnal mammals, circadian period can either decrease or increase with light intensity. How can this "broken symmetry" between the activity and period responses of nocturnal and diurnal models be explained?

We explain these data by considering the actions of light—an external zeitgeber—and fatigue—an internal zeitgeber—on the nocturnal and diurnal gated pacemaker models. The fatigue signal is a functional homolog of the satiety signal in the gated dipole eating circuit (Chapter 2). From an ethological perspective, the fatigue signal prevents the circadian circuit from driving an animal to destructive extremes of activity, much as a satiety signal protects against dangerous levels of eating. We hereby suggest an operant analysis of Aschoff's rule and the circadian rule in which the gated pacemaker adapts its outputs to the internal homeostatic state of the organism.

American Journal of Physiology **247**, R1067 R1082 (1984)   353
©1984 American Physiological Society
Reprinted by permission of the publisher

A NEURAL THEORY OF CIRCADIAN RHYTHMS:
ASCHOFF'S RULE IN DIURNAL AND NOCTURNAL MAMMALS

Gail A. Carpenter† and Stephen Grossberg‡

Abstract

A neural model of the circadian pacemaker within the suprachiasmatic nuclei (SCN) explains how behavioral activity, rest, and circadian period depend on light intensity in diurnal and nocturnal mammals. These properties are traced to the action of light input (external Zeitgeber) and an activity-mediated fatigue signal (internal Zeitgeber) upon the circadian pacemaker. Light enhances activity of the diurnal model and suppresses activity of the nocturnal model. Fatigue suppresses activity in both diurnal and nocturnal models. The asymmetric action of light and fatigue in diurnal vs. nocturnal models explains the more consistent adherence of nocturnal mammals to Aschoff's rule; the consistent adherence of both diurnal and nocturnal mammals to the circadian rule; and the tendency of nocturnal mammals to lose circadian rhythmicity at lower light levels than diurnal mammals. The fatigue signal is related to the sleep Process S of Borbély, and contributes to the stability of circadian period. Predictions include: diurnal mammals obey Aschoff's rule less consistently during a self-selected light-dark cycle than in constant light; if light level is increased enough during sleep in diurnal mammals to compensate for eye closure, then Aschoff's rule will tend to hold more consistently; nocturnal mammals which obey Aschoff's rule will either be arhythmic or violate Aschoff's rule if their fatigue signal is blocked before it can modulate their SCN pacemaker; in nocturnal mammals, there are SCN pacemaker cells where the effects of a light pulse and the fatigue signal summate; in diurnal mammals, a light pulse and the fatigue signal are mutually inhibitory at all SCN pacemaker cells; in both diurnal and nocturnal mammals, a light pulse excites some SCN cells and inhibits other SCN cells. The results are compared with those of Enright's model.

† Supported in part by the Air Force Office of Scientific Research (AFOSR 82-0148) and the National Science Foundation (NSF MCS-82-07778).

‡ Supported in part by the Air Force Office of Scientific Research (AFOSR 82-0148).

1. Introduction: A Neural Model of the Circadian System in the Mammalian Suprachiasmatic Nuclei

A circadian pacemaker that helps to control the wake-sleep and activity-rest cycles of mammals has been identified in the suprachiasmatic nuclei (SCN) of the hypothalamus (Inouye and Kawamura, 1979; Moore and Eichler, 1972; Stephan and Zucker, 1972). A neural model of the SCN circadian system has recently been developed (Carpenter and Grossberg, 1983a, 1983b, 1985). This model was constructed from neural components that have also been used to model motivated behaviors, such as eating and drinking, that are controlled by other hypothalamic circuits (Grossberg, 1982, 1984a; Olds, 1977). Thus our SCN model forms part of a larger theory of how hypothalamic circuits are specialized to control different types of motivated behaviors.

Perhaps for this reason, our model has been able to quantitatively simulate a large body of circadian data. These data include split rhythms (Hoffmann, 1971; Pittendrigh, 1960, 1976); several types of long-term after-effects (Aschoff, 1979; Pittendrigh, 1960, 1976); phase response curves to pulses of light in diurnal and nocturnal mammals, including the "dead zone" of phase resetting insensitivity during the subjective day of a nocturnal mammal (Daan and Pittendrigh, 1976; DeCoursey, 1960; Kramm, 1971; Pohl, 1982); SCN ablation studies (Pickard and Turek, 1982); and suppression of the pacemaker by high light intensities (Aschoff, 1979; Enright, 1980). Due to the fact that every process in the model has a physical interpretation, the model also suggests a number of anatomical, physiological, and pharmacological predictions to test its validity. Notable among these are predictions that test whether slowly varying transmitter gating actions form part of the SCN pacemaker. In model circuits controlling motivated behaviors such as eating and drinking, such slow gating processes have already been used to analyse a variety of abnormal behaviors, such as juvenile hyperactivity, Parkinsonism, hyperphagia, and simple schizophrenia (Grossberg, 1984a, 1984b). If a slow gating action is verified in the SCN, it would provide a new basis for analysing certain abnormalities of circadian rhythms and their effects on the motivational circuits that they modulate.

The present article analyses Aschoff's rule and its exceptions and the circadian rule in diurnal and nocturnal mammals (Aschoff, 1958, 1960, 1979). This analysis is based upon the same processes that have been used to explain all the phenomena mentioned above. Each of these processes can, in principle, be experimentally manipulated to test the analysis by causing determinate changes in Aschoff's rule. For example, we predict in Section 10 that a diurnal mammal which obeys Aschoff's rule in a constant light environment will obey the rule less consistently at high light levels when given dark shelter or lights out during sleep. In Section 15, we compare our analysis of Aschoff's rule with that of other models in the literature.

2. Aschoff's Rule, The Circadian Rule, and Exceptions

Enright (1980) describes Aschoff's rule and the circadian rule as follows:

1. "Aschoff's rule": For diurnal animals, the free-running period of a circadian activity rhythm usually decreases with increasing light intensity; the brighter the constant light, the faster the animal's "clock" runs. For nocturnal animals, the converse is usually observed: the free-running period of the rhythm increases with increasing light intensity.

2. The "circadian rule": For diurnal animals, brighter constant light prolongs daily wakefulness under free-running conditions, and also increases the level of arousal, as indicated by the intensity of locomotor activity. For nocturnal animals, the converse is true: light usually shortens the duration of wakefulness and decreases the intensity of activity.

These rules hold when an animal is exposed to a constant light level at all times. The changes in period and activity levels are functions of this light level as it is parametrically varied. Enright says that the described changes "usually" occur in diurnal and nocturnal animals. Actually there are pronounced differences in how universally these rules hold in diurnal and nocturnal mammals. For example, Aschoff (1979) writes

> For night-active species of mammals ... there is again an unambiguous picture: with the exception of the fruit bat, *Rousettus aegyptiacus*, all species lengthen τ [period] as I_{LL} [light intensity] increases ... [but] a bimodal [decreasing-then-increasing] dependence of τ on I_{LL} could be characteristic for at least some species of night-active mammals. Other than the quite uniform τ-characteristics obtained from night-active mammals and day-active birds, the daytime species of mammals ... show large differences in the dependence of τ on I_{LL}. A lengthening of τ with increasing I_{LL} prevails, but four species shorten τ, at least within certain ranges of intensities....

Figure 1 describes characteristic data that illustrate Aschoff's rule.

Thus diurnal and nocturnal mammals are asymmetrical with respect to how frequently they violate Aschoff's rule. Nocturnal mammals obey the rule more consistently than diurnal mammals. When nocturnal mammals do not obey Aschoff's rule, a shortening of period usually occurs followed by a lengthening of period. Remarkably a similar shortening followed by a lengthening of period occurs in many diurnal mammals that do not obey Aschoff's rule (1979), thereby sharpening the sense in which diurnal and nocturnal animals asymmetrically follow the rule.

3. Asymmetry of Fatigue and Light in Diurnal and Nocturnal Models

Our SCN model consists of a circadian pacemaker with a rhythm modulated by several types of signals. One signal is an external zeitgeber due to the action of light. Light input is defined to have opposite effects on the diurnal and nocturnal pacemaker. A second type of signal is a feedback signal to the pacemaker. This signal F is interpreted to be an index of the animal's metabolic activity as delivered to the pacemaker through the bloodstream. We call this F signal a fatigue signal because it tends to inhibit the activity-generating output signal in both the diurnal and nocturnal models. Sources of the F signal are not necessarily restricted to metabolic consequences of overt motor activity. In its present form the model assumes that the signal builds up progressively as a function of its activity-generating output signal and exponentially decays during inactive intervals. The F signal is thus a type of activity-mediated internal zeitgeber. A third type of signal is also a feedback signal to the pacemaker. This signal buffers the pacemaker against adventitious light fluctuations, such as cloudy weather, yet enables it to react to pervasive lighting changes, such as seasonal changes. This feedback signal, which causes long-term aftereffects and the slow onset of split rhythms in the model (Carpenter and Grossberg, 1983b, 1985), will not be considered here.

We explain Aschoff's rule and its exceptions by analyzing the interactions between steady light inputs, the F signal, and the pacemaker. In particular, the predicted differences in the way diurnal and nocturnal activity durations and periods react to different levels of steady light will be traced to asymmetries in the action of light input and F signal on the diurnal and nocturnal pacemakers. Whereas both light and fatigue tend to inhibit activity-generating output of a nocturnal pacemaker, light excites and fatigue inhibits activity-generating output of a diurnal pacemaker. The more regular adherence of nocturnal mammals to Aschoff's rule will also be traced to this asymmetry.

In contrast, the circadian rule is robustly obeyed in the model except in situations where long-term aftereffects predominate. The circadian rule states that an increase of steady light intensity stimulates activity in the diurnal animal and depresses activity in the nocturnal animal. We will explain why action of the light input tends to cause

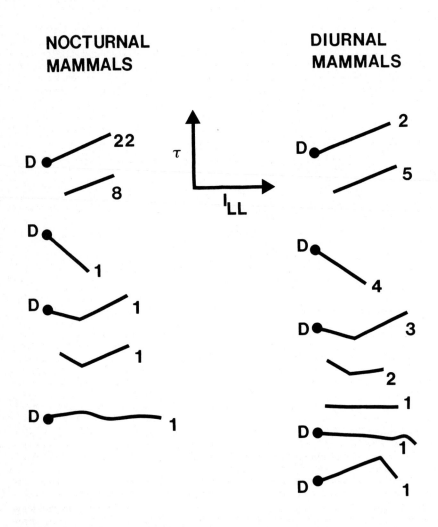

Figure 1. Schematic graphs of τ vs. I_{LL} summarized by Aschoff (1979). Aschoff's review includes 34 experiments on 20 species of nocturnal mammals and 19 experiments on 16 species of diurnal mammals. *Numbers*, no. of Aschoff's graphs with similar shapes. *D* indicates that furthest left data point was computed from a free run in the dark. Most nocturnal τ functions are monotone increasing. Diurnal τ functions are more varied. See Aschoff (1979) for references.

the circadian rule, despite action of the F signal, even in parameter ranges where the F signal plays a role in causing exceptions to Aschoff's rule.

4. A Connection Between Fatigue Signal and Sleep-Dependent Process S

Due to the importance of the F signal process in our explanation of Aschoff's rule, it is interesting to compare properties of this process with related concepts in the circadian literature. The sleep-dependent process S (Borbély, 1982) is formally similar to our F process. If these two processes turn out to be the same, then manipulations of process S should affect period and activity levels in the manner predicted by our model.

Borbély (1982) introduces process S to explain his data about sleep regulation in humans. Process S is hypothesized to summate with the output of a circadian oscillator C that, in Borbély's measurements, covaries with the human temperature rhythm. The hypothesis that the sum of S and C signals regulates sleep is used to explain variations of sleep duration as a function of sleep deprivation and onset time.

Process S is assumed to progressively build up during an activity period and to exponentially decay within a few hours during sleep. These properties are also properties of our F signal. Our model can be combined with the sleep model of Borbély (1982) in humans in two different ways. In one realization 1) the F signal accumulates during the waking state and exponentially decays on an ultradian time scale during sleep; 2) the F signal feeds back to the SCN pacemaker and depresses its activity-generating output; and 3) output from the SCN summates with a signal that covaries with the temperature rhythm. This sum controls onset and duration of sleep.

In the other realization 1) and 2) still hold. The large F signal shifts the base line, but not rhythmicity, of the SCN pacemaker. Output from the SCN controls the onset and duration of sleep and entrains the temperature rhythm.

5. Testing Existence of Fatigue Signal

The F signal plays a role in our SCN circadian model that is homologous to the role played by a satiety signal in our model of the hypothalamic eating circuit (Grossberg, 1982, 1984a). As in the case of the satiety signal is it far more difficult to characterize the biochemistry of a physiological signal than its existence and its behavioral properties. Our theory argues for the existence and properties of an F signal by demonstrating behavioral consequences of its presence or absence. Without this predictive linkage between behavior and physiology, it would be impossible to discover the chemical signals mediating fatigue feedback and its SCN receptors.

The present theory enables such biochemical tests to be made. For example, if a putative receptor is found, its elimination should cause either arhythmicity or violation of Aschoff's rule in the manner predicted by the theory. Likewise if F signal receptors are found using this method, then putative chemical signals to the receptors can be tested by directly applying them to the receptor sites. Different courses of controlled chemical release lead to predictions about the dependence of circadian period or dosage.

The F signal also figures prominently in our explanation of split rhythms and long-term aftereffects (Carpenter and Grossberg, 1985). Destroying putative receptors or applying putative chemical signals leads to behavioral predictions about how split rhythms or long-term aftereffects will be altered. Finally the formal linkage between the F signal and Borbély's process S (Borbély, 1982) enables electroencephalographic (EEG) measures to be used to test whether process S varies concurrently with the F signal in all experiments where Borbély's procedure can be used.

The net effect of our theory is thus to suggest many interdisciplinary experiments using biochemical, physiological, behavioral, and EEG methods to test for the existence and properties of the F signal.

6. Gated Pacemaker Model

The gated pacemaker model describes the dynamics of on-cell/off-cell pairs, called gated dipoles, in which on-cells and off-cells mutually inhibit one another. Populations of these gated dipoles are assumed to exist in each SCN. The following processes define the gated pacemaker dynamics that will be used in this article (Figure 2): 1) slowly accumulating transmitter substances are depleted by gating the release of feedback signals; 2) feedback signals are organized as an on-center off-surround, or competitive, anatomy; 3) both on-cells and off-cells are tonically aroused; 4) light excites on-cells of a diurnal model and off-cells of a nocturnal model; 5) on-cells drive observable activity, such as wheel turning, in both diurnal and nocturnal models; 6) on-cell activity gives rise to an F signal that is fed back to the off-cells in both diurnal and nocturnal models. The F signal is a time average of the on-cell output signal. The model equations for a nocturnal gated pacemaker are defined as follows.

$$\frac{dx_1}{dt} = -Ax_1 + (B - x_1)[I + f(x_1)z_1] - (x_1 + C)g(x_2) \tag{1n}$$

$$\frac{dx_2}{dt} = -Ax_2 + (B - x_2)[I + f(x_2)z_2 + F + J(t)] - (x_2 + C)g(x_1) \tag{2n}$$

$$\frac{dz_1}{dt} = D(E - z_1) - Hf(x_1)z_1 \tag{3}$$

$$\frac{dz_2}{dt} = D(E - z_2) - Hf(x_2)z_2 \tag{4}$$

$$\frac{dF}{dt} = -KF = h(x_1) \tag{5}$$

Variable x_1 in $(1n)$ is the potential of an on-cell (population) v_1. Variable x_2 in $(2n)$ is the potential of an off-cell (population) v_2. Both x_1 and x_2 obey membrane equations (Hodgkin, 1964). In equations $(1n)$ and $(2n)$ the parameter $-A$ in terms $-Ax_1$ and $-Ax_2$ determines the fast decay rate of potentials x_1 and x_2. Also in equations $(1n)$ and $(2n)$ term I represents the arousal level that equally excites v_1 and v_2. In equation $(1n)$ the transmitter substance z_1 gates the nonnegative feedback signal $f(x_1)$ from v_1 to itself. Term $f(x_1)z_1$ is proportional to the rate at which transmitter is released from the feedback pathway from v_1 to itself, thereby reexciting x_1. Off-cells inhibit the on-cells via the nonnegative signal $g(x_2)$ in term $-(x_1 + C)g(x_2)$. Equation $(2n)$ is the same as equation $(1n)$, except that indices 1 and 2 are interchanged and the light input $J(t)$ excites v_2, not v_1, because equations (1)–(5) represent a nocturnal model. Also the F signal excites v_2 in both nocturnal and diurnal models.

Equations (3) and (4) define the transmitter processes z_1 and z_2. In equation (3), the transmitter z_1 accumulates to its maximal level E at a slow rate D via the term $D(E - z_1)$. This slow accumulation process is balanced by the release of z_1 at rate $Hf(x_1)z_1$, leading to the excitation of x_1 in $(1n)$. A similar combination of slow accumulation and gated release defines the dynamics of transmitter z_2 in equation (4).

The F signal in equation (5) is a time average of the on-cell output signal $h(x_1)$. The decay rate K of F is chosen to be slower than A in equations $(1n)$ and $(2n)$ but faster than D in equations (3) and (4). Whereas parameter D contributes to the model's circadian time scale, parameter K contributes to the model's ultradian time scale.

The diurnal gated pacemaker differs from the nocturnal pacemaker only in equations $(1d)$ and $(2d)$, which define its on-cell and off-cell potentials.

$$\frac{dx_1}{dt} = -Ax_1 + (B - x_1)[I + f(x_1)z_1 + J(t)] - (x_1 + C)g(x_2) \tag{1d}$$

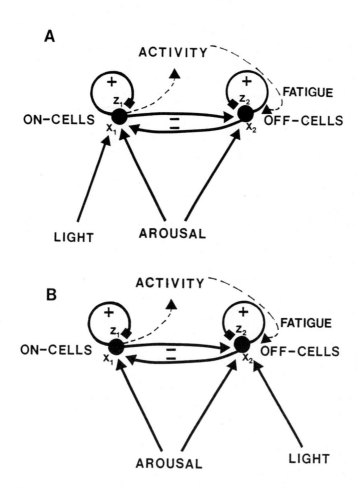

Figure 2. Anatomy and physiology of diurnal (A) and nocturnal (B) gated pacemakers. Potential x_1 of an on-cell (population) and potential x_2 of an off-cell (population) obey equations (1) and (2), respectively. Transmitter substance z_1 gates the positive feedback signal $f(x_1)$ from on-cell (population) to itself, and transmitter substance z_2 gates positive feedback signal $f(x_2)$ from off-cell (population) to itself. I, nonspecific arousal level, which excites on-cells and off-cells equally. F excites off-cells. Light input $J(t)$ excites on-cells of diurnal model (A) and off-cells of nocturnal model (B). Transmitter z_1 in equation (3) accumulates via term $D(E - z_1)$ and is released at rate $-Hf(x_1)z_1$. A similar law governs z_2 in equation (4). F signal in equation (5) builds up with behavioral activity via term $h(x_1)$ and decays at a constant rate via term $-KF$. Many basic model properties persist in modified versions of equations (1)–(5). Species-specific variations and future data may support particular versions without altering qualitative explanations of model properties.

$$\frac{dx_2}{dt} = -Ax_2 + (B - x_2)[I + f(x_2)z_2 + F] - (x_2 + C)g(x_1) \qquad (2d)$$

$$\frac{dz_1}{dt} = D(E - z_1) - Hf(x_1)z_1 \qquad (3)$$

$$\frac{dz_2}{dt} = D(E - z_2) - Hf(x_2)z_2 \qquad (4)$$

$$\frac{dF}{dt} = -KF + h(x_1) \qquad (5)$$

Interpretation of the diurnal equations is similar to that of the nocturnal equations.

A comparison of the nocturnal pacemaker with the diurnal pacemaker leads to the following physiological predictions. In nocturnal mammals there are SCN pacemaker cells at which the effects of a light pulse J and the fatigue signal F summate. These are the off-cells of equation $(2n)$. In diurnal mammals a light pulse and the F signal are mutually inhibitory at all SCN pacemaker cells. Thus a light pulse J excites on-cells in equation $(1d)$, the F signal excites off-cells in equation $(2d)$, and on-cells and off-cells are mutually inhibitory. In both diurnal and nocturnal mammals a light pulse excites some SCN cells and inhibits other SCN cells. This is because light J excites either on-cells or off-cells, and these cell populations are mutually inhibitory. Also see section 16, which notes that light pulses may differentially excite both types of cells in some mammals.

7. Signal Functions, Activity Thresholds, and Attenuation of Light Input During Sleep

Models in equations (1)–(5) are completely defined by a choice of the signal functions (f, g, h), light input $J(t)$, and parameters. In all simulations the signal functions $f(w)$ and $g(w)$ in equations (1)–(4) are chosen to be threshold-linear functions of activity w:

$$f(w) = \max(w, 0) \qquad (6)$$

$$g(w) = \max(w, 0). \qquad (7)$$

The signal function $h(w)$ is defined in two steps. First, the on-cell output signal function $h^*(w)$ is defined. Then we choose

$$h(w) = M \max[h^*(w) - h^*(N), 0]. \qquad (8)$$

Function $h^*(w)$ is a sigmoid, or S-shaped, function of activity w:

$$h^*(w) = \frac{w^2}{(P^2 + w^2)}. \qquad (9)$$

In our numerical runs, only values of w where $h(w)$ is approximately threshold-linear were used. Carpenter and Grossberg (1983b) analyse how pacemaker dynamics are altered by choosing different types of signal functions.

Physical interpretations of f and g have already been given. The definitions of h and h^* require further explanation. Function $h^*[x_1(t)]$ is interpreted to be the on-cell output signal of the pacemaker. Behavioral activity is triggered when $x_1(t)$ exceeds threshold N. The function $h[x_1(t)]$ defined by equation (8) provides an index of behavioral activity. By equation (5), fatigue builds up at a rate proportional to behavioral activity. Activity ceases when $x_1(t) \leq N$. During such a time interval, fatigue decays at exponential rate K.

By so defining fatigue we provide a relatively simple description of the model. In more complex versions of the model, pacemaker output modulates the arousal level of motivational circuits (e.g., for eating, drinking, sex, exploratory activity). This arousal level helps to determine the sensitivity of these circuits to external and internal cues. The resultant behaviors have metabolic consequences that contribute to the fatigue signal (Carpenter and Grossberg, 1985; Grossberg, 1984a). This additional complexity has not been needed to qualitatively explain Aschoff's rule or the circadian rule.

Another factor that we consider herein concerns the distinction between overt activity (e.g., wheel turning), wakeful rest, and sleep. In the circadian literature the total period (τ) is divided into time (α) during which the animal engages in overt activity and the remaining rest time (ρ) (Aschoff, 1960). No distinction is made between wakeful rest and sleep despite a transitional time of wakeful rest before, after, and possibly during the overt activity cycle. This time of wakeful rest, during which the eyes are open but fatigue is decaying, plays a role in our analysis of Aschoff's rule because different light intensities can have differential effects on the durations of wakeful rest and sleep in the model.

To mathematically distinguish these three states, we assume as in equation (8) that overt activity takes place when

$$x_1(t) > N. \tag{10}$$

A sleep threshold Q is also assumed to exist such that $N > Q$. When

$$Q < x_1(t) \leq N \tag{11}$$

the model is in a state of wakeful rest. When

$$x_1(t) \leq Q \tag{12}$$

the model is in a state of sleep. We define sleep in terms of its effects on the pacemaker. The main effect is that eye closure (or entering a dark nest) can attenuate the light input to the pacemaker. Letting $L(t)$ be the light input that reaches the pacemaker when its "eyes" are open, we define the net light input in equations $(1d)$ and $(2n)$ to be

$$J(t) = \begin{cases} L(t) & \text{if } x_1(t) > Q \\ \theta L(t) & \text{if } x_1(t) \leq Q. \end{cases} \tag{13}$$

Parameter θ is a light attenuation factor due to eye closure. Hence $0 \leq \theta \leq 1$. We systematically vary the size of θ in our analysis. The fact that θ is not always zero is implied by the ability of light pulses to phase shift a mammal's circadian rhythm while the mammal is asleep (Carpenter and Grossberg, 1983b; Pohl, 1982).

Our definitions of wakeful rest and sleep are chosen for simplicity. In species for whom a separate temperature pacemaker helps control sleep onset, a more complex definition is needed to discuss situations wherein the SCN and temperature pacemakers become desynchronized (Czeisler, Weitzman, Moore-Ede, Zimmerman, and Kronauer, 1980; Wever, 1979). Also, our definition of the feedback F signal assumes that no fatigue accumulates during wakeful rest The simulations thus make the approximations that the F signal builds up much faster during overt activity than during wakeful rest, and that all oscillators controlling sleep onset are approximately synchronized. In species that spend most waking hours actively exploring or consummating, the lack of fatigue buildup during wakeful rest causes no loss of generality. In other species, an obvious extension of the model would postulate a smaller rate of fatigue buildup during wakeful rest than during overt activity. In any case, the present hypotheses have proved sufficient to qualitatively explain Aschoff's rule and the circadian rule.

8. Aschoff's Rule and its Exceptions: Numerical Studies

This section describes parametric numerical studies that indicate the dynamic factors subserving Aschoff's rule and its exceptions in our model. The next section describes numerical studies of the circadian rule, and section 10 continues the analysis of how these numerical properties are generated. This analysis provide a dynamic explanation of how Aschoff's rule and the circadian rule depend on the physiological processes of our model. We pay particular attention to how the F signal and the amount of light attenuation that occurs during eye closure or lights out influences these rules. Analysis of the effects of light attenuation led, for example, to the prediction that diurnal mammals obey Aschoff's rule less consistently during a self-selected light-dark cycle than in constant light. As greater experimental control is achieved over the F signal, the analysis can be used to suggest behaviorally testable predictions about that process too. For example, we predict that nocturnal mammals which obey Aschoff's rule will either by arhythmic (section 15) or violate Aschoff's rule if their F signal is blocked before it can modulate their SCN pacemaker. Given the formal similarity of the F signal to Borbély's sleep-dependent process S (section 15), these predictions may provide a way to experimentally probe process S using properties of Aschoff's rule and the circadian rule.

The numerical studies consider eight cases that arise from combining the following three alternatives in all possible ways: 1) nocturnal vs. diurnal, 2) no fatigue signal vs. large fatigue signal, and 3) no light attenuation by eye closure ($\theta = 1$) vs. maximal light attenuation by eye closure ($\theta = 0$).

Our main mechanistic insight about Aschoff's rule is that fatigue causes the rule to hold. The asymmetrical frequency with which the rule holds in diurnal vs. nocturnal mammals is traced to the asymmetrical manner in which light perturbs diurnal and nocturnal models with respect to site of action of fatigue (Figure 2).

To start, consider the nocturnal and diurnal models with no fatigue ($F \equiv 0$) and no light attenuation ($\theta = 1$). By equations (1)–(5), the nocturnal and diurnal pacemaker models are symmetrical: off-cells in the nocturnal model play the role of on-cells in the diurnal model and conversely. Thus τ of both models is the same. Consequently Aschoff's rule cannot occur in this case. It must depend on either fatigue, light attenuation, or both. In nocturnal and diurnal models on-cell output causes behavioral activity. The α of the nocturnal model consequently varies in a complementary manner with respect to the α of the diurnal model. This property exemplifies the fact that the circadian rule holds in our model in all eight cases.

Figure 3 summarizes how τ varies with increasing steady light levels in the eight cases. In every case all parameters are held constant, other than the parameters controlling light attenuation (θ) and the amount of fatigue (M in equation (8)). The fixed parameters are listed in Table 1. These parameters were chosen so that no single term in equations (1)–(4) dominates any other term. A method for balancing terms in this way is described in Carpenter and Grossberg (1983b), where it is shown that clock-like oscillations are generated within a wide numerical range of balanced parameters.

The parameters θ and M were chosen to maximize the differences between small and large light attenuation and fatigue effects. In particular we chose $\theta = 0$ in Figures 3B and 3D to illustrate maximal light attenuation during sleep. We chose $\theta = 1$ in Figures 3A and 3C to illustrate no light attenuation during sleep. We chose $M = 0$ and $F(0) = 0$ in Figures 3C and 3D to illustrate the case of zero fatigue. In Figures 3A and 3B, M was chosen to maximize the effects of fatigue. Very large M values cause such a large F signal that behavioral activity is suppressed almost as soon as it begins. In Figure 3, comparing A with C and B with D shows the choice $M = 0.1$ causes a significant effect of fatigue without preventing sustained bouts of behavioral activity from occurring.

We now consider Figure 3 in detail. Each graph depicts period of the nocturnal

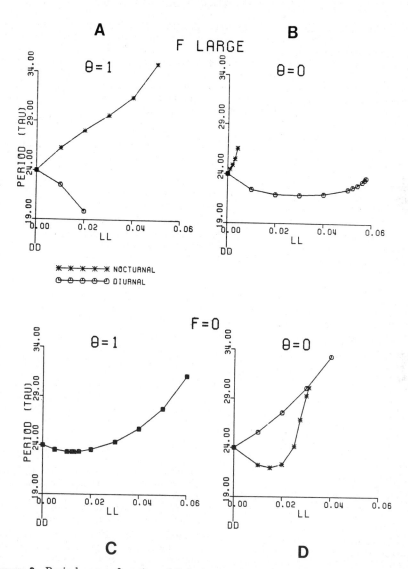

Figure 3. Period τ as a function of light intensity LL: 8 curves correspond to 8 combinations of nocturnal vs. diurnal, $\theta = 1$ vs. $\theta = 0$, and F large vs. $F \equiv 0$. All model parameters are chosen as in Table 1. LL, linear function of logarithm of ambient light intensity. This transformation is assumed to occur in pathway from retinal receptors to suprachiasmatic nuclei. Choice $A = 1$ in Table 1 fixes dimensionless time scale. For comparison we have transformed time scale so that in each case $\tau = 24$ hours in the dark. This is accomplished by multiplying dimensionless τ of equations (1)–(5) by 0.552 hours (A, B) or by 0.305 hours (C, D).

TABLE 1

Parameter Values

Parameter	Value	Interpretation
A	1	x_i decay rate
B	5	maximal x_i
C	0.5	minimal x_i
D	0.01	z_i accumulation rate (slow)
E	0.4	maximal z_i
H	0.02	z_i release rate
I	0.13	arousal
K	0.17	F decay rate
N	0.72	activity threshold
Q	0.67	sleep threshold
P	1	x_1 value where on-cell output is half-maximal
M	0	$F \equiv 0$
	0.1	F large
θ	1	no light attenuation during sleep
	0	complete light attenuation during sleep

model and the diurnal model as a function of parametric increases in steady light level (LL). Figure 3C describes the case of no light attenuation ($\theta = 1$) and no fatigue ($F \equiv 0$). Because both nocturnal and diurnal models have the same period in this case, only one curve is shown. As a function of increasing LL, this curve decreases before it increases. Thus the curve does not obey Aschoff's rule for either nocturnal or diurnal mammals. However, as shown in Figure 1, there exist both nocturnal and diurnal mammals whose period changes in the manner of Figure 3C as a function of LL.

In Figure 3A no light attenuation during eye closure occurs, but there exists a significant F signal. The F signal causes distinct τ values to occur in the nocturnal and diurnal models. Moreover, each graph of τ vs. LL exhibits Aschoff's rule. In Figure 3, the comparisons of A and C with B and D are the basis for our claim that fatigue is a primary factor in generating Aschoff's rule. This comparison also leads to the prediction that nocturnal mammals obeying Aschoff's rule with either be arhythmic (section 15) or will violate Aschoff's rule if their F signal is blocked before it can modulate their SCN pacemaker.

Deviations from Aschoff's rule are explained by the joint action of fatigue and light attenuation due to eye closure. A comparison between Figures 3A and 3B illustrates one of these deviations. In both figures, fatigue feedback is effective. The figures differ only in how much light attenuation occurs during sleep. In Figure 3B, the nocturnal model continues to obey Aschoff's rule, whereas the diurnal model does not. This fact is a basis for our explanation of the greater tendency of nocturnal mammals to obey Aschoff's rule. Despite violation of Aschoff's rule by the diurnal model, the diurnal model's period curve is similar to curves generated by certain diurnal mammals (Figure 1). The differential reactions of nocturnal and diurnal models to the interaction between light attenuation and fatigue reflects the asymmetrical sites of action of these factors in the nocturnal and diurnal pacemakers.

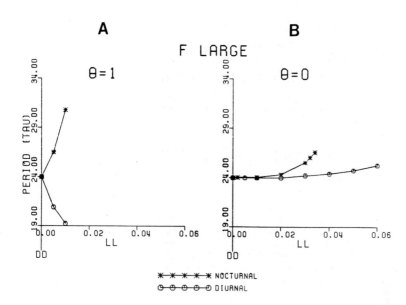

Figure 4. Period τ as function of light intensity LL. The 4 curves correspond to 4 combinations of nocturnal vs. diurnal and $\theta = 1$ vs. $\theta = 0$ when F is large. Arousal level $I = 0.1$. All other parameters are chosen as in Table 1. By multiplying dimensionless τ values of equations (1)–(5) by scaling factor 0.472 hours, τ in the dark is fixed at 24 hours.

The rate-limiting role of fatigue in generating Aschoff's rule is again shown by comparing Figures 3B and 3D. In both cases light is significantly attenuated during eye closure. In Figure 3D, however, no fatigue is registered at either pacemaker. At low light levels, curves generated by the nocturnal and diurnal models are opposite those one would expect from Aschoff's rule. Thus our model predicts that if a technique could be found to prevent registration of the hypothesized F signal by SCN off-cells, then the experimental animal should violate Aschoff's rule. The period τ of the nocturnal model in Figure 3D increases with LL at large values of LL. Thus in all the graphs of Figure 3, the nocturnal model obeys Aschoff's rule, at least for large values of LL. This property also supports the idea that nocturnal mammals obey Aschoff's rule more consistently than diurnal mammals.

Due to the importance of the comparison between Figures 3A and 3B, we compare these curves with curves generated in response to a different choice of pacemaker parameters. Figure 4 shows the curves obtained when all parameters except the arousal level (I in equations (1) and (2)) are the same as in Table 1. To obtain Figure 4, a lower arousal level $(I = 0.1)$ was used. All qualitative properties of Figures 3A and 3B are preserved in Figures 4A and 4B, respectively. Aschoff's rule again holds in Figure 4A. The curves in Figure 4B look as if their abscissas have been stretched at small values of LL. The effect causes, for example, the period curve of the nocturnal model in Figure 4B to increase more slowly as a function of LL than in Figure 3B. In Figures 3B and 4B, the nocturnal model loses circadian rhythmicity at a lower light level than the diurnal model. Thus the model reflects Aschoff's observation (Aschoff, 1979): "Among the mammals, an intensity of 100 lx. is surpassed by 37% of nightactive species, and by 71% of the dayactive species."

9. Circadian Rule: Numerical Studies

In contrast to Aschoff's rule, the circadian rule holds for both nocturnal and diurnal models in all eight cases. Figure 5 summarizes illustrative numerical results by plotting α (duration of behavioral activity) as a function of LL. We define α in the model as the total amount of time during each cycle when

$$x_1(t) > N \tag{10}$$

as in section 7. In all cases, α increases with LL in the diurnal model and decreases with LL in the nocturnal model, as essentially always occurs in the mammalian data. The circadian rule is primarily due to the fact that light excites on-cells in the diurnal model and off-cells in the nocturnal model, whereas in both cases on-cell output supports behavioral activity.

Why do light attenuation and fatigue not cause frequent exceptions to the circadian rule as they do to Aschoff's rule? This issue will be more extensively discussed in sections 12 and 13, but some intuitive comments can immediately be made. Fatigue is a feedback signal that is contingent upon on-cell activity. Whenever fatigue becomes strong enough to attenuate on-cell activity while the animal is active, it also undermines its own source of activation. An analysis of wakeful rest and sleep shows how fatigue causes its different effects on α and τ. Light attenuation occurs only when the animal is asleep. Hence is has little effect on α and the circadian rule, as can be seen by comparing Figure 5A with 5B and Figure 5C with 5D.

By comparing Figures 3 and 5, numerical plots of ρ (duration of wakeful rest plus sleep) as a function of LL are obtained. Figure 6 shows that ρ is not always a monotonic function of LL despite the fact that α is always a monotonic function of LL. The comparison between Figures 5 and 6 provides one of many examples showing that the relationship between activity and subsequent rest-sleep is far from simple.

10. Light Attenuation and Self-Selected Light-Dark Cycles in Diurnal Mammals: A Prediction

The importance of the light attenuation factor θ is shown by experiments on diurnal mammals which contrast the τ that is found under steady light conditions with the τ that occurs when the mammal can eliminate light before going to sleep. Our analysis leads to some predictions within this paradigm.

As reported by Aschoff (Aschoff, 1979) "... lengthenings of τ due to self-selected light-dark cycles have been observed in the Rhesus monkey, *Macaca mulatta* (Yellin and Hauty, 1971), in the squirrel monkey, *Saimiri sciureus* (Tokura and Aschoff, unpubl.), and in man (Wever, 1969)." Wever (1979) reports numerous experiments on man in which τ is longer during self-selected light-dark cycles than during constant illumination.

We predict that a diurnal mammal which self-selects light-dark cycles will, at sufficiently high illuminations, tend to violate Aschoff's rule more than the same mammal kept in continuous light at these illumination levels. We also predict that if light level is

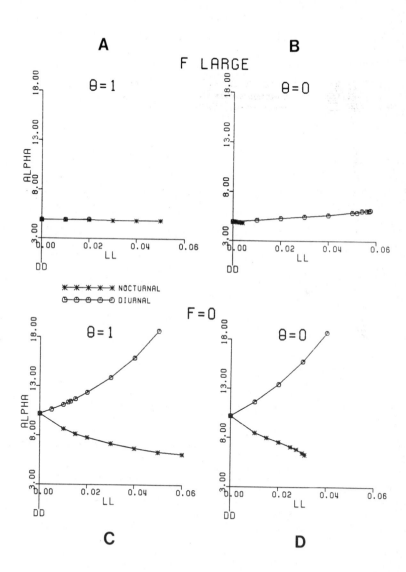

Figure 5. Length α of activity interval as a function of light intensity LL. Systems in A–D correspond to systems in Figures 3A–D, respectively.

increased enough during sleep in diurnal mammals to compensate for eye closure, then Aschoff's rule will tend to hold more consistently.

As pointed out by Wever (1979), a self-selected light-dark cycle is experienced, to some extent, by any animal that shuts its eyes during sleep. In the model, normal eye closure in a lighted room corresponds to a value of θ between 0 and 1. A self-selected light-dark cycle is identified with the case $\theta = 0$. The case $\theta = 1$, in contrast, corresponds to an animal which is sensitive to light even when its eyes are closed and has no dark hiding place.

Figures 3 and 4 indicate that a lengthening of τ occurs in the diurnal gated pace-maker with complete light attenuation during sleep. In all cases and at all light levels, τ is lengthened when $\theta = 0$ (right columns) compared with when $\theta = 1$ (left columns). This is because a model animal asleep in the dark ($\theta = 0$) must wait for the internal pacemaker dynamics to cause awakening. However, a model animal asleep in the light ($\theta > 0$) has the joint action of both arousal (I) and light input ($J = \theta L$) in equations (1d) and (13) working to hasten the onset of the next activity cycle. Thus ρ is shorter when θ is positive than when $\theta = 0$, as in Figure 6 (diurnal). Consequently, τ is also shorter when θ is positive than when $\theta = 0$, as in Figures 3 and 4 (diurnal).

Finally, comparisons between A and B in both Figures 3 and 4 suggest the following prediction. When F is large and $\theta = 1$ (Figures 3A and 4A), Aschoff's rule holds: diurnal τ decreases as LL increases. In contrast, when $\theta = 0$, the graph of diurnal τ values first decreases and then increases. The model thus predicts that a diurnal mammal which obeys Aschoff's rule in a constant light environment will obey the rule less consistently at high light levels when given dark shelter or lights out during sleep, and will obey Aschoff's rule more consistently if light level is increased during sleep.

11. Stability of τ: Clock-like Properties of Gated Pacemaker

Almost by definition a circadian pacemaker must keep approximately accurate time despite the intrusion of a fluctuating chemical or electrical environment. The basic gated pacemaker, without fatigue, is clock-like in the dark (Carpenter and Grossberg, 1983b). In particular, the transmitter accumulation rate (D) in equations (3) and (4) determines the approximate period of the pacemaker in the dark, except near the limits where circadian rhythmicity breaks down. Once D is fixed, the other parameters such as arousal level (I) have comparatively little effect on τ.

Except at extreme parameter values, this stability of τ is maintained by the joint action of fatigue and light attenuation (Figure 4B). Section 13 will analyse the following properties in detail. If the diurnal pacemaker receives a light input at the on-cells, the subsequent increased on-cell activity causes a larger F signal to the off-cells, and the new balance between light and fatigue keeps α close to its dark value. If the nocturnal pacemaker receives a light input at the off-cells, the subsequent decreased on-cell activity causes a smaller F signal to the off-cells: the sum of light input plus fatigue at the off-cells is balanced, and α is again preserved. During sleep, in both diurnal and nocturnal models, light attenuation implies that ρ is relatively unaffected by the ambient light level. Thus the sum $\tau = \alpha + \rho$ is kept approximately constant and independent of the light levels.

12. Analysis of Aschoff's Rule

We will now analyse the factors that generate curves of the form shown in Figures 3–6. Of the eight cases (nocturnal vs. diurnal, $F \equiv 0$ vs. F large, and $\theta = 0$ vs. $\theta = 1$), some can be easily explained by using qualitative arguments. These cases will be treated in the present section. The more difficult cases are discussed in sections 13 and 14.

A. *Basic pacemaker:* $F \equiv 0$ *and* $\theta = 1$. Consider Figure 3C. In this case, neither fatigue feedback nor light attenuation due to eye closure occurs, so both diurnal and

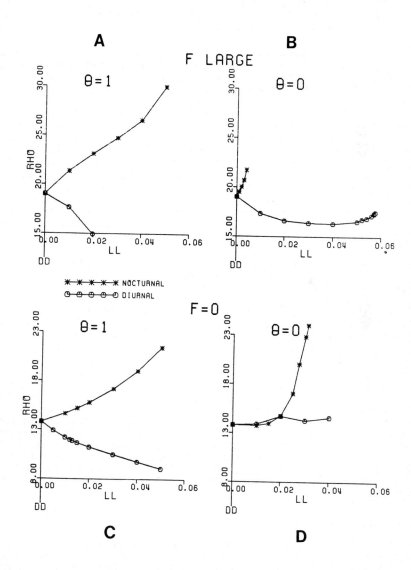

Figure 6. Length ρ of rest interval as a function of light intensity LL. Systems A–D correspond to systems in Figures 3A–D, respectively.

nocturnal models generate the same τ as a function of LL. Consider a diurnal model for definiteness. How can we explain the effect of a parametric increase in steady light level on such a model?

By equation $(1d)$, the light input $J(t)$ directly excites on-cells. As a first approximation, an increase in J tends to shift the graph of $x_1(t)$ upward. Figure 7A depicts an upward shift of the graph $x_1(t)$ generated by the model in the dark. This upward shift idealizes the effect of a parametric increase in LL. Figure 7B compares the graph of $x_1(t)$ generated in the dark with the graph of $x_1(t)$ generated by a positive level of LL.

In Figure 7A, the graph of $x_1(t)$ is compared with the threshold N at which the model becomes active. The activity period α is the total time when

$$x_1(t) > N \qquad (10)$$

during one cycle. In Figure 7A, the increment $\Delta\alpha$ in α caused by an upward shift in the graph of $x_1(t)$ is compensated by an equal decrement $\Delta\rho$ in ρ. Consequently, τ does not change as LL increases if the only effect of LL is to cause an upward shift in the graph of $x_1(t)$. Figure 7B shows that the upward shift described by Figure 7A is approximately valid. At the light level chosen for Figure 7B, $\Delta\alpha$ exactly balances $\Delta\rho$ so that τ in LL equals τ in DD. The shift approximation is valid at low and moderate light levels (Figure 3C), but begins to break down at high light levels. Section 14 explains why this happens.

B. *Aschoff's rule is due to fatigue: F large and* $\theta = 1$. Our explanation of Aschoff's rule depends on the fact that fatigue can cause a relatively large change in the approximate balance between $\Delta\alpha$ and $\Delta\rho$. A comparison between Figures 5A and 5C (α) and between Figures 6A and 6C (ρ) illustrates this property of the model. In Figure 5A, the graphs of α as a function of LL are relatively flat; in Figure 5C, the graph of the diurnal α rises sharply, and the graph of the nocturnal α falls sharply as LL increases. In contrast, the graph of nocturnal ρ in Figure 6A is similar to that of the nocturnal ρ in Figure 6C, and the diurnal ρ graphs are also similar. The effect of fatigue on the balance between α and ρ gives Aschoff's rule in Figure 3A and 4A. We now consider how fatigue causes large deviations in this approximate balance of $\Delta\alpha$ and $\Delta\rho$.

Consider the diurnal model depicted in Figure 3A. In this model the F signal becomes large during activity, but no light attenuation occurs during sleep. We assume that fatigue decays with a time scale that is shorter than the duration of ρ in the no-fatigue case (Figure 3C). Under these circumstances, light activates on-cell activity that in turn causes a build up of fatigue. Fatigue excites the off-cells that inhibit the on-cells, thereby tending to shut down the on-cell activity. Fatigue then tends to shorten, or clip, the time intervals when $x_1(t)$ is large. Parameter α is hereby significantly decreased by the action of fatigue. In contrast, after on-cell activity is reduced and rest or sleep begins, the F signal is no longer activated by the on-cells. Fatigue exponentially decays with a time scale that is shorter than the duration of ρ in the no-fatigue case. Thus the F signal has significantly decayed before off-cell activity would otherwise spontaneously decay. Fatigue consequently has little effect on ρ.

The net effect of fatigue in this case is to cause a significant decrease of α relative to the no-fatigue case, and a small change in ρ relative to the no-fatigue case. In all, a decrease in τ is caused. As LL is parametrically increased, these effects of fatigue also increase. Thus a decrease of τ as a function of LL is predicted in the diurnal model of Figure 3A. A comparison of α values for the diurnal models, as described in Figures 5A and 5C, shows that a large F signal can almost eliminate the increase in α that would otherwise be caused by light. A similar comparison of Figures 6A and 6C shows that a large F signal has little effect on ρ as a function of LL.

A similar argument applies to the nocturnal model in Figure 3A. The main difference with the diurnal model is that light and fatigue both activate off-cells. In the absence of

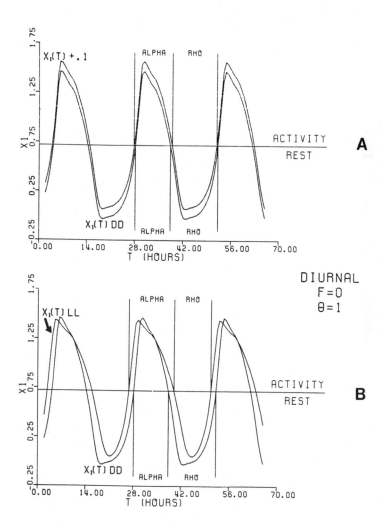

Figure 7. Comparison of on-cell potential in light with an upward shift of on-cell potential in the dark. Diurnal on-cell potentials $x_1(t)$ are plotted for case $F \equiv 0$ and $\theta = 1$, as in Figures 3C, 5C, and 6C. All parameters are chosen as in Table 1. (A) plots $x_1(t)$ in the dark, and same curve shifted upward by 0.1. (B) plots $x_1(t)$ in the dark and $x_1(t)$ when LL = 0.026. In all 4 curves $\tau = 24$ hours.

fatigue, LL increases ρ and decreases α (Figures 5C and 6C). In the nocturnal model with fatigue, a parametric increase in LL causes a parametric decrease in on-cell activity that in turn causes a parametric decrease in fatigue. This parametric decrease in fatigue tends to disinhibit parametrically on-cell activity. Consequently, fatigue tends to compensate for the direct effect of LL on the decrease in α. Thus α decreases more slowly with fatigue than without fatigue as LL increases. The increase of ρ with LL accompanied by the attenuated decrease in α with LL predicts that τ increases with LL in this nocturnal model. A comparison of the nocturnal models described in Figures 5A and 5C shows that a large F signal can almost eliminate the decrease in α that would otherwise be caused by light. A similar comparison of Figures 6A and 6C shows that a large F signal has little effect upon ρ as a function of LL.

C. *Light attenuation during sleep:* $\theta = 0$. We now consider some of the main effects that are due to light attenuation during sleep. Two general properties guide this discussion: 1) because light is not attenuated when the model is active, light attenuation has little effect on α in Figures 5B and 5D, compared with Figures 5A and 5C, respectively, in which no light attenuation occurs; 2) the effects of light attenuation on ρ are more subtle. Parameter ρ is the sum of the durations of wakeful rest and sleep within one cycle. Light attenuation occurs only during the sleep component of ρ. Figure 8 describes the effects of a shift in the curve of $x_1(t)$ on the duration of wakeful rest. The shift in Figure 8 causes approximately no change in this duration. This is not always true, and section 13 will investigate those cases in which the duration of wakeful rest changes significantly as LL increases. Where this approximation holds, we can conclude that the duration of wakeful rest changes relatively little as a function of LL. The main differential effects of $\theta = 0$ vs. $\theta = 1$ on ρ occur during the sleep interval.

If $\theta = 0$, then no light is registered during sleep. Let us assume that the model is in approximately the same state whenever $x_1(t)$ reaches the sleep threshold Q, as in equation (12). Because no light is registered during sleep, the duration of sleep will then be approximately constant as LL increases.

Because ρ is the sum of wakeful rest and sleep duration, ρ is approximately constant as LL increases, if the approximations we have made are valid for diurnal models. A comparison of Figures 6B and 6D with Figures 6A and 6C illustrates the extent to which this property holds, especially for diurnal models.

D. *Exceptions to Aschoff's rule:* $F \equiv 0$ and $\theta = 0$. Let us apply these approximations to the diurnal model in Figure 3D. This diurnal model differs from the diurnal model in Figure 3C only because it attenuates light during sleep. In the diurnal model of Figure 3C, an increase of LL causes an increase of α and a decrease of ρ. By the above argument, the increase of α is little affected by light attenuation, but the decrease of ρ (Figure 6C) is eliminated in the diurnal model with $\theta = 0$ (Figure 6D). The net effect is an increase of τ as a function of LL, which is observed (Figure 3D).

Similarly, to understand the nocturnal model of Figure 3D, we compare it with the nocturnal model of Figure 3C. In this latter model ($F \equiv 0$ and $\theta = 1$), an increase of LL causes a decrease of α and an increase of ρ. This decrease of α is little affected by switching from case $\theta = 1$ to $\theta = 0$ because light attenuation during sleep has little effect on wakeful activity (Figure 5D). In contrast, switching from case $\theta = 1$ to $\theta = 0$ has a large effect on ρ. If $\theta = 0$, changes in light intensity tend not to influence ρ. Figure 6D shows that this tendency is valid at low and moderate light levels. Section 14 explains why ρ increases with LL at large light levels.

E. *Difficult cases.* The preceding analysis does not answer the following questions: 1) When F is large and $\theta = 0$, why does the nocturnal model obey Aschoff's rule while the diurnal model generates a non-monotonic τ (Figure 3B)? 2) In the absence of fatigue, why does the nocturnal τ always increase at high light levels (Figures 3C and 3D)? Answers to these questions require a more detailed analysis of the dynamics of equations (1)–(5) than that which was used to explain the other cases. This finer analysis is described in sections 13 and 14.

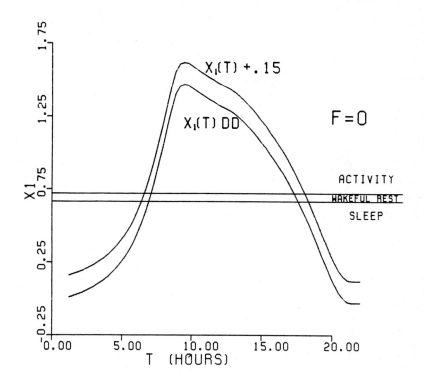

Figure 8. Graph $x_1(t)$ in the dark is compared with same curve shifted up by 0.15. Durations of 2 brief wakeful rest periods are little affected by such a shift. All parameters are chosen as in Table 1.

13. Analysis of Joint Action of Fatigue and Light Attenuation on Circadian Period

To answer the first question, we need to consider more closely the asymmetrical action of fatigue and light attenuation of the diurnal and nocturnal models. No argument has yet studied how these factors alter dynamics of the transmitter gates z_1 and z_2 through time. Now we do so.

First we will discuss the diurnal model of Figure 3B. This model differs from the diurnal model of Figure 3A only because it attenuates light during sleep. We can therefore use the same reasoning as in Figure 3A to conclude that α in Figures 3B and 5B is relatively insensitive to LL. All our analysis will be devoted to showing why ρ (Figure 6B), and hence τ, first decreases and then increases as a function of LL. We consider the decreasing and the increasing portions of the ρ curve separately.

A. *Basic pacemaker in the dark.* To begin this analysis, we need to study how x_1 and x_2 are switched on and off. For simplicity, we first consider the pacemaker when the light input is zero ($J \equiv 0$) and fatigue is zero ($F \equiv 0$). This basic pacemaker is analysed in detail in Carpenter and Grossberg (1983b). The pacemaker equations for the gated pacemaker in the dark with no fatigue are

$$\frac{d}{dt}x_1 = -Ax_1 + (B - x_1)[I + f(x_1)z_1] - (x_1 + C)g(x_2) \tag{14}$$

$$\frac{d}{dt}x_2 = -Ax_2 + (B - x_2)[I + f(x_2)z_2] - (x_2 + C)g(x_1) \tag{15}$$

$$\frac{d}{dt}z_1 = D(E - z_1) - Hf(x_1)z_1 \tag{3}$$

$$\frac{d}{dt}z_2 = D(E - z_2) - Hf(x_2)z_2. \tag{4}$$

Suppose that this system begins with x_1 large and x_2 small, but with both transmitters fully accumulated, so that by equations (3) and (4) $z_1 \cong E$ and $z_2 \cong E$. At first, x_1 maintains its advantage over x_2 as follows. Because x_1 is large and $z_1 \cong E$, the feedback signal from the on-cell (population) v_1 to itself is large, as is the negative feedback signal $g(x_1)$ from v_1 to the off-cell (population) v_2. Because $f(x_1)$ is large, however, z_1 is slowly depleted at the rate $-Hf(x_1)z_1$ by equation (3). As a result, the gated signal $f(x_1)z_1$ gradually becomes small despite the fact that x_1 remains large.

During this time x_2 and its feedback signal $f(x_2)$ remain small. Thus the transmitter release rate $-Hf(x_2)z_2$ in equation (4) also remains small, and z_2 remains large as z_1 is gradually depleted. As a result of these changes, the positive feedback term

$$(B - x_1)[I + f(x_1)z_1] \tag{16}$$

in equation (14) diminishes relative to the positive feedback term

$$(B - x_2)[I + f(x_2)z_2] \tag{17}$$

in equation (15). Because $f(w) = \max(w, 0)$ by equation (6), the feedback functions

$$H_z(w) = (B - w)[I + f(w)z] \tag{18}$$

have the form depicted in Figure 9 at different values of z. If x_2 is near zero, then $H_{z_2}(x_2) \cong BI$ given any value of z_2, $0 \le z_2 \le E$. In contrast, if x_1 is large, $H_{z_1}(x_1) > BI$ for $z_1 \cong E$, whereas $H_{z_1}(x_1) < BI$ for $z_1 \cong 0$. Thus as z_1 is depleted, the relative sizes of equations (16) and (18) can reverse, even while x_1 is still large.

Due to the relatively large decrease in equation (16), x_1 itself begins to decrease, as does $g(x_1)$ in equation (15). The positive term (17) in equation (15) can therefore begin to overcome the negative feedback term

$$-(x_2 + C)g(x_1) \tag{19}$$

in equation (15), and x_2 begins to grow. At first the growth of x_2 does not depend on the size of z_2, because if x_2 is small then $H_z(x_2) \cong BI$ no matter how z is chosen. As x_2 begins to increase, however, the continued increase of x_2 depends critically on the fact that z_2 is large, since $H_E(x_2)$ is an increasing function of x_2, whereas $H_0(x_2)$ is a decreasing function of x_2 (Figure 9). Because z_2 is large when x_2 begins to grow, a switch in the relative sizes of x_1 and x_2 occurs. As x_2 becomes large, it suppresses x_1 via the large negative feedback signal $g(x_2)$ in equation (14). Now x_2 has the advantage, and the competitive cycle starts to repeat itself as z_2 is depleted and z_1 is replenished.

B. *Diurnal model with F large and $\theta = 0$.* To understand the diurnal model of Figures 3B and 4B, the influences of fatigue **and** light attenuation on the pacemaker

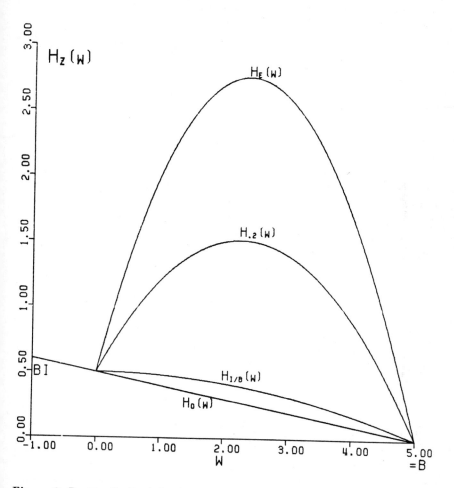

Figure 9. Positive feedback function $H_z(\omega)$ in equation (18) plotted as a function of ω at several values of parameter z. When $z < I/B$, $H_z(\omega)$ is a decreasing function of ω. When $z > I/B$, $H_z(\omega)$ has a local maximum between $\omega = 0$ and $\omega = B$. In the plots, $B = 5$, $E = 0.4$, $I = 0.1$, and $f(\omega) = \max(\omega, 0)$.

must be considered. To study the influence of these factors on ρ, we consider the phase of the circadian cycle when x_2 has just won the competition with x_1. Due to the earlier large values of x_1, the F signal is large at this transition by equation (5). As x_1 decreases below the sleep threshold Q in equation (12), the light input $J(t)$ shuts off, because $\theta = 0$ in equation (13). Consequently, throughout the sleep interval, only the arousal input I occurs in equation (1d) to help x_1 compete with x_2, and x_1 obeys equation (14) of a basic pacemaker in the dark.

In contrast, at the beginning of wakeful rest and sleep, x_2 receives a large F signal. This signal acts like an excitatory input that increases the asymptote of x_2 relative to the values attained by the pacemaker in equation (15) without fatigue. Furthermore,

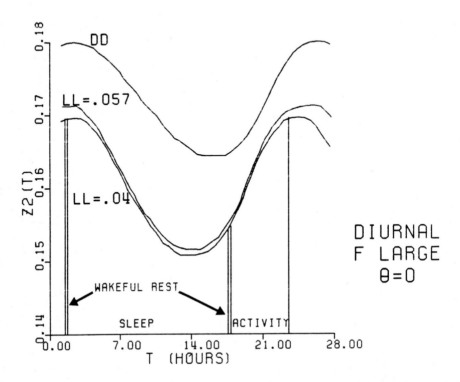

Figure 10. Graphs of $z_2(t)$ at 3 light levels (LL): LL = 0, 0.04, and 0.057. All parameters are chosen as in Table 1 for diurnal model with F large and $\theta = 0$. Graph of $z_2(t)$ when LL = 0.04 lies below graphs of $z_2(t)$ when LL = 0 and 0.057. Similarly, in Figure 3B, τ is smaller when LL = 0.04 than when LL = 0 and 0.057. See text for explanation of covariance of z_2 and τ. Intervals of sleep, wakeful rest, and activity for case LL = 0.04 are bound by vertical lines.

increased LL causes increased levels of fatigue, and hence larger x_2 values, early in sleep. A larger x_2 function causes a smaller z_2 function by equation (4). Figure 10 shows how the graph of z_2 is depressed by the action of light, via the F signal in equation (2d).

During wakeful rest and sleep, $h(x_1) = 0$ by equation (8). Thus F decays at the exponential rate K during this interval, as in equation (5). Because F decays on an ultradian time scale, it becomes approximately zero significantly before the end of the sleep interval. The transmitter gate z_2 fluctuates on a slower time scale, however, so the depression of z_2 caused by F persists for a longer time.

The transition between increasing values of x_1 and decreasing values of x_2 begins while the model is asleep. During this time, potential x_1 is activated only by arousal I. Potential x_2 is no longer directly influenced by F, although z_2 is still smaller than it would have been in the dark. The transition toward wakeful rest is controlled by the pacemaker equations without fatigue in the dark, namely equations (3), (4), (14), and (15). For wakeful rest to begin, z_2 must first decay to a value such that the arousal I of

x_1 can begin the switch between x_2 and x_1. In other words, the value to which z_2 must decay is relatively insensitive to the prior light intensity J and the prior size of the F signal. Because z_2 was already driven to smaller values by F, however, the remaining decrement in z_2 needed for the transition to begin takes less time to occur than in the absence of F. This property explains the decrease of ρ with increasing LL in Figure 5B.

The increase of ρ at large values of LL is due to an increase in the durations of both wakeful rest (following activity) and sleep. The increased duration of wakeful rest is explained as follows. As light input J is parametrically increased, the potential x_1 remains within a fixed interval $-C \leq x_1 \leq B$. By equation (5), the F signal averages $h(x_1)$ at a constant rate K. Thus at relatively large values of J, the maximal size of F does not grow linearly with J. In particular, at the threshold N between activity and wakeful rest, the value $F_N(J)$ of F does not grow linearly with J. As soon as wakeful rest begins, $h(x_1) = 0$, and F decays exponentially at the constant rate K from its initial value $F_N(J)$. Thus the size of the decaying signal F that excites x_2 does not keep up with the size of J that excites x_1. It therefore takes longer for x_1 to decay from the activity threshold N to the sleep threshold Q.

The duration of sleep increases at large J values for the following reason. Due to the longer duration of wakeful rest at large values of J, the value $F_Q(J)$ of fatigue at the onset of sleep is a decreasing function of J at these J values. As in the explanation of why sleep duration decreases at small values of J, a smaller value of $F_Q(J)$ implies a large value of z_2 at the onset of sleep (Figure 10). Consequently, it takes longer for z_2 to decay to the point where a switch from large x_2 values to large x_1 values can begin. The duration of sleep thus increases with J at large values of J.

C. *Nocturnal model with F large and $\theta = 0$.* We now explain why τ increases with LL in the nocturnal model of Figures 3B and 4B wherein both large F signals and light attenuation occur. This increase in τ is due to the increase of ρ with LL (Figure 6B), because α is fairly constant as a function of LL (Figure 5B). Most of this increase in ρ is due to an increase in the duration of sleep. The duration of wakeful rest is relatively constant and brief.

The reasons for these properties follow. In the nocturnal model, light input J excites the off-cell potential x_2. In the absence of fatigue, increasing LL would imply decreasing α, as in Figure 5D. The decrease in x_1 that would otherwise cause a decrease in α also causes a decrease in F. Consequently, α is approximately constant as LL increases in Figure 5B (section 9). Despite the relative insensitivity of α to LL in this case, the size of x_1 during the active period depends on LL. Early in the active period, a larger light input J (equation (2n)) causes a larger x_2, hence a smaller x_1 (Figure 11). The smaller x_1 graph gradually gives rise to a smaller F. By the end of the activity period, a larger J is compensated by a smaller F. Thus the sum $J + F$ in equation (2n) is relatively independent of J by the end of the activity period.

At the onset of sleep, J shuts off because $\theta = 0$. Because at sleep onset $J + F$ in LL is about the same size as F alone in DD, F in LL is smaller than F in DD. The smaller F input to x_2 causes x_2 to increase more slowly and hence causes x_1 to decrease more slowly in the light than in the dark. In LL, then, x_1 takes longer to reach its minimum (Figure 11). The increase in ρ caused by this lengthening of the early sleep interval accounts for the increase of τ with increasing light levels in the nocturnal model with large F and $\theta = 0$.

We have now answered the first question of section 12E.

14. Analysis of Pacemaker Without Fatigue

The second question of section 12E addresses the problem of why nocturnal models without fatigue have increasing τ values at high light intensities, as do all the nocturnal mammals in Aschoff's survey (Aschoff, 1979). Sections 12 and 13 have already shown why, with a large F signal, nocturnal τ values increase monotonically as light increases.

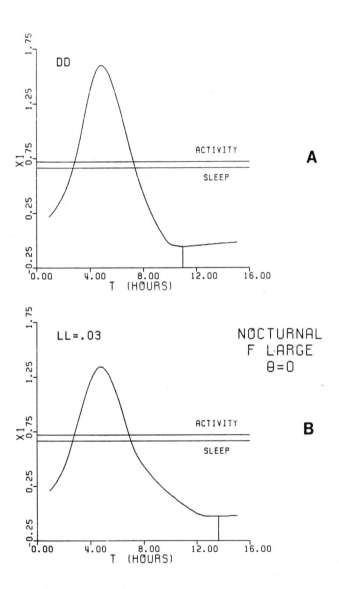

Figure 11. Increase in initial segment of sleep interval when light level (LL) is increased. This increase occurs in nocturnal model with **F** large and $\theta = 0$. In (**A**), LL = 0. On-cell potential $x_1(t)$ has a maximum value of 1.6 and a minimum value that occurs 3.5 hours after sleep onset. In (**B**), LL = 0.03. Then $x_1(t)$ has a maximum value of 1.35 and a minimum value that occurs 6 hours after sleep onset. In both (**A**) and (**B**), arousal level $I = 0.1$, as in Figure 4.

To answer the question about nocturnal models without fatigue, we again need to investigate the dynamics of transmitters z_1 and z_2.

A. *Nocturnal pacemaker with* $F \equiv 0$ *and* $\theta = 0$. We first consider why ρ, and hence τ, increases with LL at large light intensities in the nocturnal model with $F \equiv 0$ and $\theta = 0$ (Figures 3D and 6D). We will explain how bright light forces the nocturnal model to terminate its activity cycle before the pacemaker, in the absence of light, would have induced sleep. A period of restless oscillation between waking and sleeping follows the active phase until sleep is finally induced. This restless time below the threshold of overt activity accounts for the increase in ρ and τ at high light intensities.

Explanation of these properties follow. During the active phase when $x_1 > N$, the on-cell potential x_1 is larger than the off-cell potential x_2. A large light input J to the off-cell v_2 boosts x_2 to larger values than x_2 would have reached in the dark. The inhibitory term

$$-(x_1 + C)g(x_2) \tag{20}$$

in equation $(1n)$ is also boosted when x_2 is boosted and thereby hastens termination of the active phase.

In the absence of the large light input J, the active phase would have terminated only after the transmitter z_1 had been depleted (section 13A). In the presence of this light input, termination occurs without the full depletion of z_1. Due to its slow rate of change, z_1 is still larger at the onset of sleep than it would have been in the absence of light input. Also at the onset of sleep the large light input J suddenly shuts off. At this time the "restless oscillation" between sleep and wakeful rest is triggered for the following reasons.

When J shuts off, x_2 loses its major source of excitatory input. The still large z_1 then enables x_1 to increase. As soon as x_1 recrosses the sleep threshold Q, however, the light input J turns on, and x_2 begins to grow again. Consequently, x_1 is forced below Q, and J shuts off. This oscillation of x_1 around Q continues while z_1 slowly depletes. Finally, z_1 depletes to a value that prevents x_1 from recovering in the dark, and a sustained sleep epoch ensues. The time during which $x_1(t)$ oscillates about the sleep threshold Q is the main factor causing the sharp increase in ρ at high LL values that is seen in Figure 6D.

The diurnal pacemaker exhibits no large change in ρ at high light levels (Figure 6D). This difference between the diurnal and nocturnal models is explained as follows. In the diurnal model, bright light enhances and prolongs behavioral activity by its direct input to the on-cell (equation $(1d)$). The increased x_1 values in bright light lead to additional depletion of z_1 by the onset of sleep. This extra depletion of z_1 accelerates the rise of x_2 after the light input shuts off and thus shortens ρ somewhat (Figure 6D).

The restless oscillation that causes a large change in ρ in the nocturnal model does not occur because the light cooperates with x_1 to cause z_1 depletion. In particular, at the onset of sleep z_1 is smaller due to prior light than it would have been in the dark. The offset of light and the smaller z_1 value at sleep onset cause a sustained sleep epoch to ensue. The duration of this sleep epoch is not prolonged by the smaller z_1 value because the depletion of z_2 triggers the onset of activity. Only after x_2 decreases and x_1 increases due to z_2 depletion does the accumulated z_1 value maintain large x_1 values (section 13).

B. *Diurnal and nocturnal pacemakers with* $F \equiv 0$ *and* $\theta = 1$. As noted in section 12A, the nocturnal and diurnal pacemakers are symmetrical if $F \equiv 0$ and $\theta = 1$. They therefore have identical τ graphs (Figure 3C). We also remarked that small constant light inputs tend to cause upward (diurnal) or downward (nocturnal) shifts in the graph of x_1 (Figure 7). Because such shifts leave τ unchanged, the graph of τ is relatively flat at low light levels (Figure 3C).

We will now consider the diurnal model at the high constant light levels where α grows rapidly with LL (Figure 5C). We will show that an increase in LL elongates the plateau of x_1 values during the active phase, thereby increasing α.

In the dark, a switch from large x_1 to small x_1 occurs when the on-cell positive feedback term

$$(B - x_1)[I + f(x_1)z_1] \tag{16}$$

diminishes relative to the off-cell positive feedback term

$$(B - x_2)[I + f(x_2)z_2]. \tag{17}$$

Recall that equation (17) approximately equals BI before the switch. A constant light input of intensity J changes the on-cell positive feedback term (equation (16)) to

$$(B - x_1)[I + f(x_1)z_1 + J]. \tag{21}$$

The off-cell positive feedback term (17) is unchanged.

To see why the switch from large x_1 to small x_1 is progressively delayed by larger values of J, consider times shortly after x_1 becomes large. During these times, the gradual decay of z_1 causes equation (21) to diminish relative to equation (17), which approximately equals BI. For a switch to small x_1 values to occur, z_1 must decay to values in the presence of a large J smaller than in the dark. Other parameters being equal, an increase in J prolongs the time necessary for z_1 to decay the requisite amount to cause a switch. While z_1 is decaying, x_1 remains at a large value. The graph of x_1 thus develops a progressively larger plateau as J is parametrically increased (Figure 7B).

15. Comparison With Other Models

Most other models of circadian rhythms do not explain exceptions to Aschoff's rule. The model of Enright (Enright, 1980) is a notable exception. This section compares our results with those of Enright so as to clarify the implications of both models.

Enright's model is a quasi-neural model in the following sense. The model's intuitive basis derives from a formal description of pacemaker neurons with activation thresholds that decay during each recovery phase. These pacemakers are not dynamically defined. Enright defines his model in terms of stochastic variables such as the average duration of the discharge phase, the average duration of the recovery phase, and the amount by which internal feedback shortens the average recovery phase. This stochastic description enables Enright to analyse consequences of his main hypothesis. This hypothesis states that circadian properties are due to entrainment of many individual circadian pacemakers with individual circadian properties only roughly specified.

The main elements of the Enright model are depicted in Figure 12. A large population of endogenously active pacers P_1, P_2, ..., P_n are assumed to have approximately circadian periods. The output of each pacer is a binary function that equals one when the pacer is "active" and zero when the pacer is "inactive." Each pacer excites the discriminator D. The total input to the discriminator at any time equals the number of active pacers.

The discriminator fires an output signal only if the total input exceeds a threshold θ. The output of D is also a binary function. When D fires, it generates a feedback signal that equally excites every pacer. The model does not describe how this feedback signal alters the individual pacers. Instead, Enright (1980) makes the statistical hypothesis that the feedback signal decreases the average duration of recovery of the pacer population. The net effect of the feedback signal is to synchronize the pacer population. It does this by speeding up the recovery phase of inactive pacers so that all pacers become active more synchronously during the next activity cycle.

The only effect of light in the model is to change the discriminator threshold θ. In a diurnal model, θ decreases as LL increases. In a nocturnal model, θ increases as LL

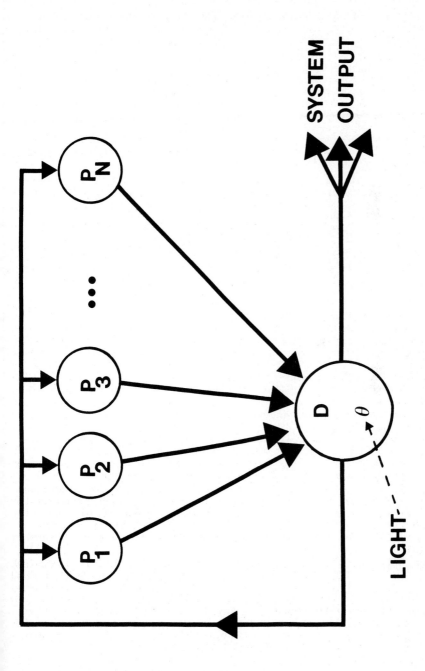

Figure 12. Schematic representation of Enright's coupled stochastic system.

increases. Thus a diurnal model with increasing LL is indistinguishable from a nocturnal model with decreasing LL. If the family of all nocturnal models and the family of all diurnal models are chosen to exhaust the same parameter space, then nocturnal and diurnal properties are completely symmetrical.

Using these hypotheses, Enright (1980) simulates Aschoff's rule and the circadian rule in his nocturnal and diurnal models. Once these rules are simulated for the diurnal model, they automatically follow for the nocturnal model by symmetry. The decrease of τ with increasing LL in Enright's model follows from the assumption that as light level increases, fewer pacers need to be active for D to fire. The feedback signal from D to the pacer thus acts earlier during the aggregate buildup of pacer activity and thereby shortens the mean duration of the pacers' recovery phases. Because duration of each pacer's active phase is assumed to be directly proportional to the previous recovery phase, τ is shortened as LL increases.

At extreme parameter values, Enright's model can violate Aschoff's rule (Enright, 1980). These exceptions occur when 1) each pacer's active phase is a large fraction of the previous recovery phase and 2) discriminator firing causes a large reduction (ϵ) in mean recovery time of all the pacers. "In this circumstance, the accelerating influence of ϵ, during the latter portion of the activity time, extends through the entire inactive phase of the cycle, and therefore affects many of those pacers which would ordinarily be involved in the subsequent onset of feedback." In other words, when θ is small, several pacers are able to fire twice during a single discriminator cycle, and this brings about both a lengthening of τ and a lengthening of α. In this case Aschoff's rule is violated while the circadian rule still holds.

The circadian rule holds in Enright's model because, first, each pacer is assumed to be active a fixed proportion of the time. This proportion is assumed not to change due to discriminator feedback or light input. Thus when a decrease of θ causes a decrease in the average recovery duration of all pacers, the average active duration also decreases. Each individual pacer therefore tends to violate the circadian rule. By a second assumption, however, the fixed ratio of active time to recovery time in each pacer maintains the time average of the total input to D, integrated over at least one period, at a constant level. Thus at smaller values of θ, D is active for a larger fraction of the cycle, so α tends to be larger.

The formal nature of the hypotheses leading to these explanations of Aschoff's rule and the circadian rule is not problematic. These formal hypotheses could, in principle, later be instated by neural mechanisms. More serious difficulties in explaining mammalian data concern the symmetry between nocturnal and diurnal models in Enright's explanation of Aschoff's rule and the consistency with which Enright's model obeys Aschoff's rule in diurnal models. These formal properties are compatible with Enright's goal of considering all vertebrates, not only mammals. In particular, as Aschoff (1979) points out, "The data on birds ... show an unambiguous picture for the day active species ... with increasing I_{LL}, τ shortens above a certain threshold-intensity, whereas towards low values of I_{LL}, τ seems to level off." Thus diurnal birds tend to obey Aschoff's rule, following Enright's interpretation of his discriminator D as a model of the pineal organ in birds. However, Aschoff (1979) then goes on to say "other than the quite uniform τ-characteristics obtained from nightactive mammals and dayactive birds, the dayactive species of mammals ... show large differences in the dependence of τ on I_{LL}." Thus, diurnal mammals do not consistently obey Aschoff's rule, following the absence of any mention of the mammalian SCN in Enright's discussion.

Enright formally explains a nonmonotonic τ by assuming that the model acts like a diurnal model at small values of LL and like a nocturnal model at large values of LL. Other difficulties of the Enright model concern its inability to explain phase response curves to brief light pulses, long-term aftereffects, and split rhythms (Enright, 1980) without making additional hypotheses for each phenomenon.

Points of comparison exist between the gated pacemaker model and the Enright model. The most important comparison concerns the possible role of asynchronous pacers and of synchronizing feedback in Enright's explanation of Aschoff's rule and the circadian rule. Our model also possesses individual pacers and a synchronizing feedback signal. The individual pacers are gated pacemakers, located in the SCN or, by extension, in other parts of the brain. The feedback signal is the F signal that, like the Enright discriminator, is activated by output from all pacers and acts as a internal zeitgeber, keeping the pacemakers in phase. In contrast to the Enright model, we have shown that Aschoff's rule and the circadian rule can be explained even if the dispersions of individual pacer periods and phases are small relative to the time scales of the F signal and slow gating processes. An extension of our argument to the case in which individual pacers have significantly different periods and phases during free run can be given. These gated pacemakers would still be synchronized by the feedback F signal. At present, however, our argument suggests that these properties are unnecessary to explain Aschoff's rule. Direct measurement of individual periods and phases of SCN pacemakers cells during free run would clarify this issue.

16. Switching Between Diurnal and Nocturnal Properties

Other analogs also exist between the two models. In Enright (1980), a switch between diurnal and nocturnal properties in a single model can be effected by changing the rule whereby discriminator threshold θ is modified by light. In our model, diurnal vs. nocturnal properties are due to the excitation of on-cells vs. off-cells by light. Both nocturnal and diurnal properties can be generated by specifying the light intensity ranges where on-cells or off-cells will be excited. For example, Enright (1980) reviews the Martinez (1972) data about the rhesus monkey that may be compatible with such a possibility. Whatever the interpretation of these data, a mechanism for switching between diurnal and nocturnal properties at different intensity levels is easily imagined in our model: let the light-activated off-cell input pathway have a higher threshold than the light-activated on-cell pathway, and let the off-cell pathway vigorously inhibit the on-cell pathway when it is activated.

Some mammals, such as the vole, switch from nocturnal to diurnal properties as the seasons change (Rowsemitt, Petterborg, Claypool, Hoppensteadt, Negus, and Berger, 1982). This change can be conceptualized in our model by a switch from activation of the on-cell input pathway to activation of the off-cell input pathway due to a seasonally modulated gating action on these pathways. The slow gain control process we use to explain the slow onset of split rhythms and of long-term aftereffects is sensitive to seasonal variations in lighting level (Carpenter and Grossberg, 1983a, 1985). Either this process or a formally analogous process could, in principle, be the source of the gating signals that control seasonal switches between nocturnal and diurnal properties in a gated pacemaker model.

REFERENCES

Aschoff, J., Tierische Periodik unter dem Einfluss von Zeitgebern. *Z. Tierpsychologie*, 1958, **15**, 1–30.

Aschoff, J., Exogenous and endogenous components in circadian rhythms. *Cold Spring Harbor Symposium on Quantitative Biology*, 1960, **25**, 11–28.

Aschoff, J., Influences of internal and external factors on the period measured in constant conditions. *Z. Tierpsychologie*, 1979, **49**, 225–249.

Borbély, A.A., A two process model of sleep regulation. *Human Neurobiology*, 1982, **1**, 195–204.

Carpenter, G.A. and Grossberg, S., Dynamic models of neural systems: Propagated signals, photoreceptor transduction, and circadian rhythms. In J.P.E. Hodgson (Ed.), **Oscillations in mathematical biology**. New York: Springer-Verlag, 1983(a), pp.102–196.

Carpenter, G.A. and Grossberg, S., A neural theory of circadian rhythms: The gated pacemaker. *Biological Cybernetics*, 1983, **48**, 35–59 (b).

Carpenter, G.A. and Grossberg, S., A neural theory of circadian rhythms: Split rhythms, after-effects, and motivational interactions. *Journal of Theoretical Biology*, 1985, **113**, 163–223.

Czeisler, C.A., Weitzman, E.D., Moore-Ede, M.C., Zimmerman, J.C., and Kronauer, R.S., Human sleep: Its duration and organization depend on its circadian phase. *Science*, 1980, **210**, 1264–1267.

Daan, S. and Pittendrigh, C.S., A functional analysis of circadian pacemakers in nocturnal rodents, II: The variability of phase response curves. *Journal of Comparative Physiology*, 1976, **106**, 253–266.

DeCoursey, P.J., Phase control of activity in a rodent. *Cold Spring Harbor Symposium on Quantitative Biology*, 1960, **25**, 49–55.

Enright, J.T., **The timing of sleep and wakefulness**. New York: Springer-Verlag, 1980.

Grossberg, S., The processing of expected and unexpected events during conditioning and attention: A psychophysiological theory. *Psychological Review*, 1982, **89**, 529–572.

Grossberg, S., Some psychophysiological and pharmacological correlates of a developmental, cognitive, and motivational theory. In R. Karrer, J. Cohen, and P. Tueting (Eds.), **Brain and information: Event related potentials**. New York: New York Academy of Sciences, 1984 (a).

Grossberg, S., Some normal and abnormal behavioral syndromes due to transmitter gating of opponent processes. *Biological Psychiatry*, 1984, **19**, 1075–1118 (b).

Hodgkin, A.L., **The conduction of the nervous impulse**. Liverpool: Liverpool University Press, 1964.

Hoffman, K., Splitting of the circadian rhythm as a function of light intensity. In M. Menaker (Ed.), **Biochronometry**. Washington, DC: National Academy of Sciences, 1971, pp.134–150.

Inouye, S.T. and Kawamura, H., Persistence of circadian rhythmicity in a mammalian hypothalamic "island" containing the suprachiasmatic nucleus. *Proceedings of the National Academy of Sciences*, 1979, **76**, 5962–5966.

Kramm, K.R., Circadian activity in the antelope ground squirrel *Ammospermophilus leucurus*. Ph.D. Thesis, University of California at Irvine, 1971.

Martinez, J.L., Effects of selected illumination levels on circadian periodicity in the rhesus monkey (*Macaca mulatta*). *Journal of Interdisciplinary Cycle Research*, 1972, **1**, 47–59.

Moore, R.Y. and Eichler, V.B., Loss of a circadian adrenal corticosterone rhythm following suprachiasmatic lesions in the rat. *Brain Research*, 1972, **42**, 201-206.

Olds, J., **Drives and reinforcements: Behavioral studies of hypothalamic functions**. New York: Raven Press, 1977.

Pickard, G.E. and Turek, F.W., Splitting of the circadian rhythm of activity is abolished by unilateral lesions of the suprachiasmatic nuclei. *Science*, 1982, **215**, 1119-1121.

Pittendrigh, C.S., Circadian rhythms and the circadian organization of living systems. *Cold Spring Harbor Symposium on Quantitative Biology*, 1960, **25**, 159-185.

Pittendrigh, C.S. and Daan, S., A functional analysis of circadian pacemakers in nocturnal rodents, I: The stability and lability of spontaneous frequency. *Journal of Comparative Physiology*, 1976, **106**, 223-252 (a).

Pittendrigh, C.S. and Daan, S., A functional analysis of circadian pacemakers in nocturnal rodents, V: Pacemaker structure: A clock for all seasons. *Journal of Comparative Physiology*, 1976, **106**, 333-355 (b).

Pohl, H., Characteristics and variability in entrainment of circadian rhythms in light in diurnal rodents. In J. Aschoff, S. Daan, and G.A. Groos (Eds.), **Vertebrate circadian systems**. Berlin: Springer-Verlag, 1982, pp.339-346.

Rowsemitt, C.N., Petterborg, N.J., Claypool, L.E., Hoppensteadt, F.C., Negus, N.C., and Berger, P.J., Photoperiodic induction of diurnal locomotor activity in *Microtus montanus*, the montane vole. *Canadian Journal of Zoology*, 1982, **60**, 2798-2803.

Stephan, F.Y. and Zucker, I., Circadian rhythm in drinking behavior and locomotor activity of rats are eliminated by hypothalamic lesions. *Proceedings of the National Academy of Sciences*, 1972, **69**, 1583-1586.

Wever, R.A., Autonome circadiane Periodik des Menschen unter dem Einfluss verschiedner Beleuchtungs-Bedingungen. *Pfluegers Arch.*, 1969, **306**, 71-91.

Wever, R.A., **The circadian system of man: Results of experiments under temporal isolation**. New York: Springer-Verlag, 1979.

Yellin, A.M. and Hauty, G.T., Activity cycles of the rhesus monkey (*Macaca mulatta*) under several experimental conditions, both in isolation and in a group situation. *Journal of Interdisciplinary Cycle Research*, 1971, **2**, 475-490.

Chapter 8

A NEURAL THEORY OF CIRCADIAN RHYTHMS: SPLIT RHYTHMS, AFTER-EFFECTS, AND MOTIVATIONAL INTERACTIONS

Preface

This Chapter uses the complete gated pacemaker model to simulate difficult circadian data about split rhythms and long-term after-effects. The Chapter also suggests how the output of the gated pacemaker model generates inputs to the appetitive-emotional drive representations that were described in Chapters 1–3.

In addition to the homeostatic fatigue signal, which varies on an ultradian time scale, this Chapter posits the existence of a slowly varying gain control process. Just as the fatigue signal is functionally homologous to a satiety signal in the eating model, the slow gain control signal is homologous to a conditioned reinforcer signal in the eating model. This slow gain control process buffers the circadian clock against adventitious lighting changes, such as a cloudy day, yet enables the clock to adapt to pervasive lighting changes, such as seasonal changes in the number of hours of sunshine per day.

The slow gain control process copes with a danger that is inherent in having a circadian clock at all. A perfectly clock-like circadian oscillator would be of limited value if it could not be modulated by seasonal changes in the duration of day and night. A nocturnal mammal on a summer night has less time available to carry out vital consummatory activities than it does on a winter night. "Speeding up" the clock to cope with statistical fluctuations in light can also be dangerous if it drives the animal to exhaustion. This problem is partially overcome by the homeostatic fatigue signal.

Thus the complete gated pacemaker model assumes simple homeostatic (fatigue) and nonhomeostatic (gain control) processes to enable the circadian clock to cope with unpredictable changes in the animal's internal and external environments. Remarkably, such simple ethological mechanisms can reproduce difficult and paradoxical data about split rhythms and long-term after-effects. Using the model as a conceptual bridge, these data have, in turn, provided us with important quantitative constraints about how to design the microscopic mechanisms of homeostatic and nonhomeostatic regulation.

Journal of Theoretical Biology **113**, 163–223 (1985)
©1985 Academic Press, Inc. (London) Ltd.
Reprinted by permission of the publisher

A NEURAL THEORY OF CIRCADIAN RHYTHMS:
SPLIT RHYTHMS, AFTER-EFFECTS,
AND MOTIVATIONAL INTERACTIONS

Gail A. Carpenter† and Stephen Grossberg‡

Abstract

A neural theory of the circadian pacemaker within the hypothalamic suprachias-matic nuclei (SCN) is used to explain parametric data about mammalian operant be-havior. The intensity, duration, and patterning of ultradian activity-rest cycles and the duration of circadian periods due to parametric (LL) and nonparametric (LD) light-ing regimes are simulated. Paradoxical data about split rhythms and after-effects are explained using homeostatic and nonhomeostatic neural mechanisms that modulate pacemaker activity. These modulatory mechanisms enable the pacemaker to adjust to pervasive changes in its lighting regime, as during the passage of seasons, and to ultradian changes in internal metabolic conditions. The model circadian mechanisms are homologous to mechanisms that model hypothalamically mediated appetitive be-haviors, such as eating. The theory thus suggests that both circadian and appetitive hypothalamic circuits are constructed from similar neural components. Mechanisms of transmitter habituation, opponent feedback interactions between on-cells and off-cells, homeostatic negative feedback, and conditioning are used in both the circadian and the appetitive circuits. Output from the SCN circadian pacemaker is assumed to modulate the sensitivity of the appetitive circuits to external and internal signals by controlling their level of arousal. Both underarousal and overarousal can cause abnormal behav-ioral syndromes whose properties have been found in clinical data. A model pacemaker can also be realized as an intracellular system.

† Supported in part by the National Science Foundation (NSF MCS-82-07778) and the Office of Naval Research (ONR N00014-83-K0337).
‡ Supported in part by the Office of Naval Research (ONR N00014-83-K0337).

1. Introduction: A Neural Model of the Circadian System in the Mammalian Suprachiasmatic Nuclei

A circadian pacemaker that helps to control the wake-sleep and activity-rest cycles of mammals has been identified in the suprachiasmatic nuclei (SCN) of the hypothalamus (Hedberg and Moore-Ede, 1983; Inouye and Kawamura, 1979; Moore, 1973, 1974; Moore and Eichler, 1972; Stephan and Zucker, 1972). A neural model of this SCN circadian system has recently been developed (Carpenter and Grossberg, 1982, 1983a, 1983b, 1984). This model, called the gated pacemaker, was constructed from neural components that have also been used to model motivated behaviors, such as eating and drinking, that are controlled by other hypothalamic circuits (Grossberg, 1972a, 1972b, 1975, 1982a, 1982b, 1984a; Olds, 1977). Thus our SCN model forms part of a larger theory of how hypothalamic circuits may be specialized to control different types of motivated behaviors.

The gated pacemaker model of the SCN has been used to quantitatively simulate a large body of circadian data. These data include Aschoff's rule in nocturnal and diurnal mammals (Aschoff, 1960) and exceptions to Aschoff's rule in diurnal mammals (Aschoff, 1979); the circadian rule in nocturnal and diurnal mammals (Aschoff, 1960); the tendency of nocturnal mammals to lose circadian rhythmicity at lower light levels than diurnal mammals (Aschoff, 1979); the suppression of circadian rhythmicity by bright light (Aschoff, 1979; Enright, 1980); the increase of circadian period during a self-selected light-dark cycle in diurnal mammals (Aschoff, 1979; Wever, 1979); and the phase response curves to pulses of light in diurnal and nocturnal mammals, including the "dead zone" of phase resetting insensitivity during the subjective day of a nocturnal mammal (Daan and Pittendrigh, 1976; DeCoursey, 1960; Kramm, 1971; Pohl, 1982). Due to the fact that every process in the model has a physical interpretation, the model suggests a number of anatomical, physiological, and pharmacological predictions to test its validity. Notable among these are predictions that test whether slowly varying transmitter gating actions form part of the SCN pacemaker. In model circuits controlling motivated behaviors such as eating and drinking, such slow gating processes have been used to analyse a variety of abnormal behaviors, such as juvenile hyperactivity, Parkinsonism, hyperphagia, and simple schizophrenia (Grossberg, 1972a, 1984a, 1984b). If a slow gating action is verified in the SCN, it would provide a new basis for analysing certain abnormalities of circadian rhythms and their effects on the motivational circuits that they modulate.

This article suggests an explanation of several types of long-term after-effects (Aschoff, 1979; Pittendrigh, 1960, 1974; Pittendrigh and Daan, 1976a), split rhythms (Earnest and Turek, 1982; Hoffmann, 1971; Pittendrigh, 1960; Pittendrigh and Daan, 1976b), and SCN ablation studies (Pickard and Turek, 1982). We also note a functional similarity that exists between the SCN pacemaker model and a model of the transduction of light by vertebrate photoreceptors (Carpenter and Grossberg, 1981). This comparison suggests how photoreceptor mechanisms may be modified to form retinal circadian pacemakers, as in the isolated eye of *Aplysia* (Jacklet, 1969) and the frog *Xenopus laevis* (Iuvone, Besharse, and Dunis, 1983). The models of vertebrate photoreceptor, SCN circadian pacemaker, and hypothalamic motivational circuits are all variations of a neural network design called a *gated dipole* (Grossberg, 1972b, 1975). Gated dipoles model opponent processes wherein slowly accumulating chemical transmitters are depleted, or habituated, by gating signals which are energized by tonic arousal and phasic inputs.

The gated pacemaker model has a neurophysiological interpretation as the neural pacemaker within the mammalian SCN. Most models of circadian rhythms have assumed a classical oscillator, such as a van der Pol or FitzHugh-Nagumo oscillator (Kawato and Suzuki, 1980; Kronauer *et al.*, 1982) as their starting point. Other approaches replace an analysis of pacemaker dynamics by formal algebraic or stochastic rules that govern phase relationships (Daan and Berde, 1978; Enright, 1980). Such models focus upon how couplings between two oscillators, or populations of oscillators, can stimulate circadian properties.

Our theory focuses instead upon the physiological characterization of each oscillator and upon the circadian properties of a single population of these oscillators.

In other approaches, circadian properties are explained in terms of the phase differences between oscillators. Our analysis suggests that circadian properties, such as long-term after-effects (Section 3) and aspects of split rhythms (Section 10), which were thought to be necessarily due to two or more out-of-phase oscillators, can be generated by a single population of in-phase oscillators. Our analysis also suggests that the two-oscillator explanation of split rhythm and after-effect data are in need of revision (Sections 3 and 23). The gated pacemaker model is not, however, incompatible with the idea that certain split rhythms may occur when individual pacemakers drift out-of-phase. In fact, the gated pacemaker model postulates the existence of modulatory processes which, among other roles, may better entrain pacemaker cells under certain experimental conditions than others. We now describe these modulatory processes.

2. Homeostatic and Nonhomeostatic Modulators of the Circadian Pacemaker

In order to simulate split rhythm and after-effect data using a single in-phase pacemaker population, we introduce processes which homeostatically and nonhomeostatically modulate the circadian pacemaker. These modulatory processes are distinct from the pacemaker mechanism *per se*. Analogous modulatory processes are known to regulate hypothalamically controlled appetitive behaviors such as eating (Grossberg, 1984a, 1985b).

For example, eating behavior is modulated by internal homeostatic influences, such as satiety signals, that build up on an ultradian time scale. These homeostatic influences prevent undue gastric distention and metabolic overload from occurring due to unrestricted eating behavior. We assume that a homeostatic feedback signal also modulates the circadian pacemaker on an ultradian time scale. This negative feedback signal serves as a metabolic index of fatigue (Carpenter and Grossberg, 1982, 1983a, 1984) which is suggested to reach the pacemaker via the bloodstream. The fatigue signal acts on all the oscillators in the pacemaker circuit. It can thus act as an internal Zeitgeber that synchronizes these pacemakers as it also modulates their activity level through time. This internal Zeitgeber has the same formal properties as the sleep-dependent Process S that was discovered by Borbély (1982) using EEG methods. The EEG techniques of Borbély provide an independent experimental procedure for testing properties of the fatigue signal. A variety of substances in the bloodstream may contribute to the total fatigue signal. This observation suggests that many types of receptors may exist in SCN cells to sense the total fatigue signal. Alternatively, a single chemical signal may reach the SCN after being released due to the action of many bloodstream substances, or other processes, upon a different brain region. Our theory suggests that the chemical receptors which sense the fatigue signal are not part of the pacemaker mechanism *per se*. The formal homolog between the ultradian satiety and fatigue signals also suggests the possibility that some chemical components of both signals may be the same. More generally, this homolog may be related to clinical correlations between eating and sleeping disorders.

A perfect internal homeostatic control of eating would badly serve an animal's survival if it could not be modulated by external signals of food availability and quality. Consequently the eating behavior of many mammals is also influenced by nonhomeostatic constraints. These nonhomeostatic constraints include oropharyngeal factors, such as taste, which endow food-predictive cues with their gustatory appeal. They also include reinforcing events which enable indifferent cues, such as the sight of food, to act as effective predictors of food. Both types of nonhomeostatic factors can override homeostatic constraints to enable a mammal to eat when food becomes available.

Oropharyngeal factors, such as taste, act on a fast time scale. By contrast, reinforcement can have effects that persist on a much slower time scale.

We suggest that fast and slow nonhomeostatic factors also modulate activity within the SCN circadian pacemaker. The fast nonhomeostatic factor describes the influence of the momentary patterning of light within the experimental chamber upon the SCN pacemaker. We distinguish between the light intensity within the experimental chamber and the actual effects of light upon the pacemaker. In particular, the attenuation of light input to the pacemaker during sleep due, for example, to eye closure, retreat to a dark nest, or self-selected light-dark cycles, plays an important role in our explanation of violations of Aschoff's rule in diurnal mammals (Aschoff, 1979; Carpenter and Grossberg, 1984) and of the "dead zone" during the subjective day of a nocturnal mammal (Carpenter and Grossberg, 1983b; Pohl, 1982). Our explanations of split rhythms and long-term after-effects in this article also use a real-time light input to the pacemaker. Previous explanations of these data have postulated distinct mechanisms for processing constant and non-constant experimental light sources (Daan and Berde, 1978; Pittendrigh and Daan, 1976a). These mechanisms are incompatible with light attenutation factors (Sections 3 and 23).

The slow nonhomeostatic factor modulates pacemaker activity in response to statistically reliable lighting changes, such as seasonal fluctuations, and buffers the pacemaker against adventitious lighting changes, such as cloudy weather. This slowly varying gain control process thus acts like a third type of Zeitgeber to the pacemaker. The gain control signal is physically interpreted in terms of factors that control the production and release of a chemical transmitter substance. In the model eating circuit, homologous gain control signals control the conditioned reinforcing properties of food-related cues.

Four distinct chemically mediated processes are thus used to define the SCN model. Each of these processes normally functions on a different time scale: the rapid light signal; the ultradian fatigue signal; the circadian pacemaker gating signal; and the slow gain control signal. The time scales on which these signals normally oscillate within the model do not necessarily equal the time scales of the model's reaction to experimental application of chemical agonists. A rapid phase shift in the circadian rhythm could, for example, be caused by applying an agonist of the transmitter which controls the slow gain control process.

A possible chemical interpretation of these transmitter systems is suggested by comparing the gated pacemaker model with the homologous model circuit that is used to analyse hypothalamically controlled eating behavior. In the eating circuit, for example, the transmitter system that is homologous to the slow gain control transmitter is interpreted as a cholinergic transmitter. Earnest and Turek (1983) have reported that carbachol, a cholinergic agonist, can rapidly phase shift the SCN pacemaker. In order to determine whether carbachol is activating the slow nonhomeostatic gain control pathway, or a fast nonhomeostatic pathway that is directly activated by light (Earnest and Turek, 1983), or both, locally applied cholinergic inhibitors might be useful. Suppose, for example, that the circadian rhythm is phase shifted by light, but no longer by carbachol, after a suitable local application of a cholinergic inhibitor. Then a long-term after-effect experiment could test whether or not the slow gain control process is cholinergic. If no long-term after-effects are generated (Section 3), then the cholinergic system in question may be part of the slow gain control pathway. This experimental strategy can be used to characterize the slow gain control transmitter even if it turns out not to be cholinergic.

A gated pacemaker model can also be realized as an intracellular system in which opponent membrane interactions play the role of on-cells and off-cells (Section 22).

3. Long-Term After-Effects: Parametric and Nonparametric Experiments

Concerning long-term after-effects, Pittendrigh (1974) has written: "They are more widespread than the current literature suggests; they are not accounted for by any of

TABLE 1

Light Regime	After-Effect
LD 1:23	larger τ_{DD}
LD 18:6	smaller τ_{DD}
LD 12:12	smaller τ_{DD}
LL	larger τ_{DD}

(After Pittendrigh and Daan, 1976a)

the several mathematical models so far published; and they must be reckoned with in the mechanisms of entrainment" (p.441). Again in 1976, Pittendrigh and Daan (1976a, p.234) wrote: "The literature has paid little attention to after-effects in the 15 years since they were first reported."

Long-term after-effects are changes in activity and/or period that persist in the dark after their inducing light regimes are terminated (Pittendrigh, 1960). These changes can persist for months. Long-term after-effects with ostensibly contradictory properties are caused by parametric and nonparametric light regimes. A parametric light regime is one in which a steady light is maintained for a number of days before the animal free-runs in the dark. A nonparametric light regime is one in which light and dark intervals alternate for a number of days before the animal free-runs in the dark.

The main paradox that is raised by parametric and nonparametric light regimes is summarized in Table 1. After stating the paradox, we will describe related data and our simulations of long-term after-effect data.

In Table 1 the notation LD $M : N$ means that a nocturnal mammal is placed in M hours of light followed by N hours of darkness for a number of days before being allowed to free-run in the dark (DD). The notation LL means that the animal is run in steady light for a number of days before being allowed to free-run in the dark. The notation τ_{DD} stands for the circadian period during free-run in the dark.

A comparison between the nonparametric cases LD 1:23 and LD 18:6 shows that more light (case LD 18:6) causes a smaller τ_{DD} in most cases. The main parametric result is derived from comparing the parametric case LL with the nonparametric case LD 12:12. Although case LL exposes the animal to more light, the subsequent period τ_{DD} is larger than after LD 12:12. Why does the total amount of light have opposite effects on τ_{DD} after parametric versus nonparametric light regimes?

Pittendrigh and Daan (1976a) claim that the differences between parametric and nonparametric after-effects are due to the onsets and offsets of light in the nonparametric (LD), but not the parametric (LL), paradigms. They write (pp.242-243): "By definition we must conclude that the lengthening of τ in constant illumination is due to a parametric effect on the pacemaker: no change in external conditions occurs throughout its cycle. The after-effect of photoperiod is surprising only if we assume that the parametric action of a long light pulse (photoperiod) is its dominant effect. In *Drosophila pseudoobscura* the characteristically different effect of each photoperiod on the circadian pacemaker can be accounted for by the interaction of the two nonparametric effects due to the transitions at the beginning and end of each photoperiod (Pittendrigh and Minis, 1964)....[T]he after-effect of photoperiod on our rodent pacemakers is similarly attributed to the interaction of nonparametric effects at the beginning and end of the photoperiod."

Although LL is "by definition" parametric at the light source, LL does not necessarily have a "parametric effect on the pacemaker." During LL, an animal periodically
goes to sleep and wakes up as part of its circadian cycle. When the animal goes to sleep,
eye closure or a retreat to a dark nest can cause a decrease in the light input that is
registered. Similarly, when the animal wakes up, eye opening can cause an increase in
the effective light input. In this sense, even the parametric LL paradigm may be experienced as a nonparametric paradigm by the nervous system. Moreover, Terman and
Terman (1983) have demonstrated that sensitivity to light oscillates with a circadian
rhythm in the rat. This rhythm persists after the SCN is ablated. Thus even if external
light intensity remains constant, the animal's internal sensitivity to light does not. The
fact that both parametric and nonparametric light regimes may be experienced non-
parametrically at central pacemakers suggests that the explanation of Pittendrigh and
Daan (1976a) is incomplete.

Our explanation recognizes the fact that both LD and LL light regimes may be
functionally nonparametric at central pacemakers. But then how can the differences
between LD and LL light regimes on subsequent τ_{DD} be explained? We will focus on
the fact that during an LD 18:6 regime the animal is active in the dark, whereas during
an LL regime the animal is active in the light.

Figure 1 describes two simulations showing long-term after-effects of photoperiod in
two versions of the nocturnal model. Just as individual animals exhibit distinct activity
cycles, these different versions of the model exhibit individual differences in circadian
period and the patterning of activity (dark lines) while displaying the shared qualitative
properties of Table 1. The simulations in Figure 1 illustrate the nonparametric after-
effect experiments that Pittendrigh (1974, p.438) and Pittendrigh and Daan (1976a,
pp.240–243) carried out using the white-footed deermouse (*Peromyscus leucopus*). In
Figure 1a, 1 hour of light alternated with 23 hours of darkness (LD 1:23) for 60 days.
The bracketed white regions define the time intervals during which light was on. A
free-run in the dark (DD) for 30 days followed. Then 18 hours of light alternated with 6
hours of darkness (LD 18:6) for 60 days. Thereafter the model free-ran in the dark for
30 days. Figure 1b models a similar experiment, except that LD 18:6 occurs for 50 days
before the model free-runs in DD for 30 days, as in the Pittendrigh (1974) experiment.

In both simulations, the free-running period in the dark (τ_{DD}) is shorter after LD
18:6 than after LD 1:23. In Figure 1a, the two periods are 24.04 hours and 23.96 hours.
In Figure 1b, the two periods are 23.7 hours and 22.7 hours. In both simulations, the
duration of the active phase (dark lines) after LD 18:6 is less than the duration of the
active phase after LD 1:23, as also occurs in the data.

Figure 2 describes a simulated after-effect of constant light (LL). In this parametric
setting, the main effect of steady light on the white-footed deermouse is to significantly
increase the period both in the light and in the dark (Pittendrigh and Daan, 1976a,
p.239). In both the deermouse and the model, the after-effect due to an LD 12:12
nonparametric light regime was compared with the after-effect due to an LL parametric
light regime. In both the animals and the simulation, the free-running period after LL
exceeds the free-running period after LD 12:12.

Thus, although an increase in light duration (as in LD 1:23 versus LD 18:6) decreases
circadian period in a nonparametric paradigm, an increase in light duration (as in LD
12:12 versus LL) increases circadian period in a parametric paradigm. The simulations
in Figures 1 and 2 hereby reproduce the main data features described in Table 1.
In Figures 1a and 2, the identical model and light intensity are used to simulate the
nonparametric and parametric properties.

The simulated properties of Figures 1 and 2 depend upon the action of the slow gain
control process $y(t)$ (Section 2). The process $y(t)$ slowly averages pacemaker activity
through time. Then $y(t)$ modulates the activity of the pacemaker by acting as a gain
control signal. Thus process $y(t)$ is part of a feedback loop whereby past levels of
pacemaker activity modulate future levels of pacemaker activity.

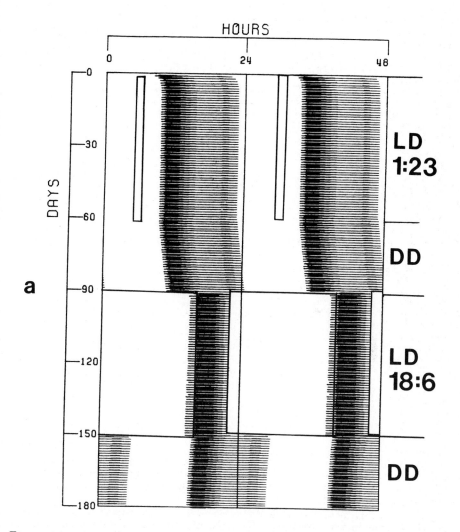

Figure 1. Two simulations of photoperiod after-effects: In both simulations, the model is exposed to an LD 1:23 lighting regime (1 hour of light every 24 hours) before free-running in the dark. Then the model experiences an LD 18:6 lighting regime before free-running in the dark. The free-running activity levels and periods depend upon the prior lighting regimes and persist throughout the 30-day free-run intervals. Each figure is a double-plot. Two successive days are plotted in each row and each successive day is plotted in the left-hand column. Thus the day plotted in the right-hand column of the ith row is also plotted in the left-hand column of the (i+1)st row. Parameter values are given in the Appendix.

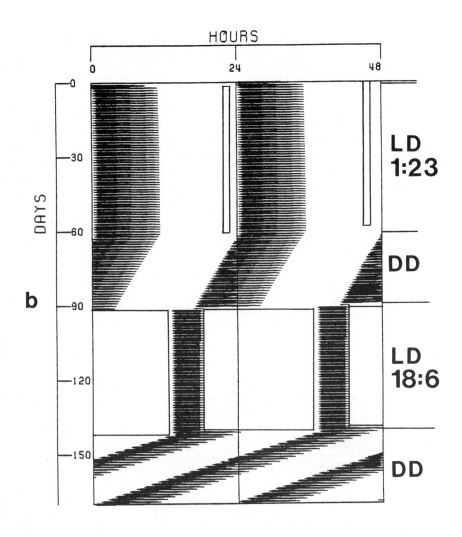

b

Figure 1 (continued).

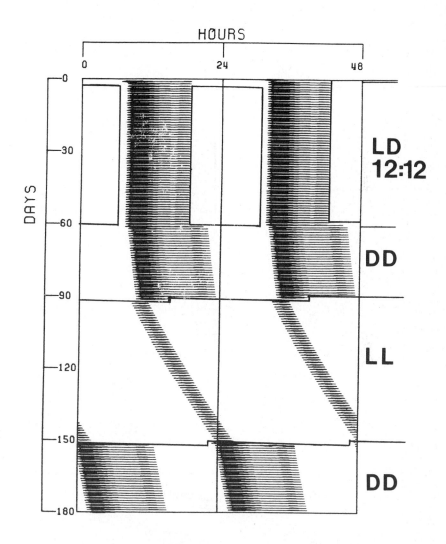

Figure 2. Simulation of an after-effect of constant light: An LD 12:12 lighting regime followed by a free-run in the dark (DD) establishes a baseline free-run circadian period τ_{DD}. Then the model experiences constant light (LL) before again free-running in the dark. After the transition from DD to LL, the circadian period increases, as expected by Aschoff's rule for nocturnal mammals (Aschoff, 1960, 1979; Carpenter and Grossberg, 1984). The free-running period after LL is greater than after LD 12:12. Model parameters and light intensities are the same as in Figure 1a.

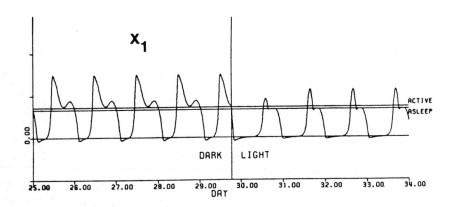

Figure 3. Real-time plot of the pacemaker on-cell activity $x_1(t)$, defined in Section 4, at the transition from DD to LL, as in Figures 2 and 10b. The bimodal waveform during DD is compressed into a unimodal waveform during LL. This compression is due to the action of a single nonlinear oscillator, not due to the rephasing of two separate oscillators. In LL, the second, smaller portion of the bimodal wave remains near the sleep threshold.

Different lighting regimes help to set up different patterns of pacemaker activity which, in turn, cause differential effects on the slow gain control process. For example, during the LD 18:6 regime in Figure 1a, the model is active in the dark, whereas during the LL regime in Figure 2, the same model is active in the light. Note that the model is much more active in the dark during LD 18:6 than it is in the light during LL. Such a difference also occurs in the data (Pittendrigh and Daan, 1976a). The differences between these activity patterns induce differences in the gain control process, which lead to different after-effects.

Another aspect of the LD 12:12 versus LL experiments of Pittendrigh and Daan (1976a, 1976b) is explained by our model. They write: "What these records show convincingly is that the bimodal pattern of activity in LD 12:12 is indeed produced by the same two components diverging during the DD-interval from their prior compressed state in LL" (p.341). In Figure 2, one can see the bimodal nature of the simulated activity pattern during LD 12:12 and DD as well as its unimodal form during LL. Figure 3 shows the time evolution of gated pacemaker activity from its bimodal form in DD to its unimodal form in LL. These simulations suggest that the unimodal form is not necessarily the compression of two separate oscillators. In the simulations, the apparent compression is due to a change in waveform of a single nonlinear oscillator.

The slow gain control process that is used to explain these parametric and non-parametric after-effects does not directly trace the pattern of light through time. The skeleton photoperiod experiments of Pittendrigh and Daan (1976a) show that the pattern of light alone cannot be responsible for after-effects. These experiments were run on the mouse *Mus musculus*. In such an experiment, two 1-hour light pulses are presented every 24 hours. The intervening daily dark intervals are 7 hours and 15 hours long. During this 1:7:1:15 light-dark regime, the animal is active either during the 7-hour dark interval or during the 15-hour dark interval. The initial phase of the animal's activity determines whether it will be active during the 7-hour or the 15-hour dark interval. During subsequent free-runs in the dark, the after-effect on period depends upon the phase of the animal's activity with respect to the prior lighting regime. In most cases, τ_{DD} is shorter after activity has taken place in the 7-hour dark interval than it is after activity has taken place in the 15-hour dark interval.

This result may be explained using the hypothesis that the animal's pattern of activity during a light regime, rather than the light regime itself, is a primary factor in determining properties of subsequent after-effects. For example, an animal that is active only during the 7-hour dark interval under the 1:7:1:15 regime will be active only during the 7-hour dark interval of an LD 17:7 regime. An animal that is active only during the 15-hour dark interval under the 1:7:1:15 regime will be active only during the 15-hour dark interval of an LD 9:15 regime. The size of τ_{DD} after the regimes LD 17:7 and LD 9:15 can be inferred from Table 1, where LD 18:6 and LD 1:23 are compared. From this Table, one would predict that τ_{DD} is shorter after an animal has been active during a 7-hour dark interval than after it has been active during a 15-hour dark interval, as also occurs in the skeleton photoperiod data.

Section 7 describes in greater detail how the gain control process averages activity rather than light while it modulates pacemaker dynamics. After-effects of LD 10:10 versus LD 14:14 light regimes, which both receive 50% light during days of different duration, and of a single pulse of light will also be considered.

In contrast to the species considered above, the hamster (*Mesocricetus auratus*) does not exhibit consistent after-effect on circadian period (Pittendrigh and Daan, 1976a). This species does, however, exhibit split rhythms. Our explanation of split rhythms indicates why a species that exhibits split rhythms may not exhibit consistent after-effects on τ_{DD} (Section 16).

4. Split Rhythms: Influences of Light, Hormones, and SCN Ablation

Pittendrigh (1960) first noted and recognized the importance of the phenomenon of *split rhythms*. Split rhythm experiments have shown that about half of all golden hamsters with a single daily activity cycle in the dark (DD) may generate an activity cycle which splits into two components in constant light (LL). Remarkably, the split does not occur until about 2 months after the hamster begins to free-run in constant light (Pittendrigh, 1974). In recent years, several examples of split rhythms have been discovered. Hoffmann (1971) described a diurnal mammal (*Tupaia belangeri*) whose rhythm splits when the level of illumination is reduced. Gwinner (1974) noted that the hormone testosterone induces split rhythms in starlings. Aschoff (1954) and Pittendrigh (1974, p.450) also noted that "Many animals tend to be bimodal in their activity pattern" even when the activity pattern does not split.

Since Pittendrigh's original observations, many circadian models have adopted Pittendrigh's assumption that split rhythms are due to a pacemaker consisting of two or more coupled oscillators which drift out-of-phase when the split occurs (Daan and Berde, 1978; Gwinner, 1974; Hoffmann, 1971; Kawato and Suzuki, 1980; Moore-Ede, Sulzman, and Fuller, 1982; Pittendrigh, 1974; Winfree, 1967). Wever (1962) was the first of several authors to use coupled oscillators of van der Pol type to model circadian rhythms. Our own SCN model is also built up from many oscillating components, and is compatible with results concerning desynchronization between the SCN pacemaker and a temperature pacemaker in humans (Kronauer *et al.*, 1982; Wever, 1979). We demonstrate, however, that split rhythm experiments can be simulated by our model even if its oscillating components remain in-phase. Our explanation shows how split rhythms may arise months after a change in light level, how changes in both light and hormone levels can induce splits, and how ultradian rhythms may occur even if the circadian rhythm does not split. We do not deny that certain splits may be due to out-of-phase oscillations. However, our simulations show that complex circadian waveforms are not necessarily the sum of outputs from distinct oscillators with simple (e.g., sinusoidal or van der Pol) waveforms. In a similar vein, the existence of ultradian rhythms and multimodal activity patterns does not imply the existence of an independent ultradian oscillator.

We suggest that certain split rhythms and ultradian rhythms are caused by the negative feedback signal due to fatigue, and that a slow onset of split rhythms can be traced to the slow time scale of the gain control process (Section 2). Our model thus claims that certain split rhythms may be due to the joint action of two biologically useful processes. Due to the critical role of the fatigue signal in generating this type of split rhythm, we now consider the fatigue signal in greater detail.

The fatigue signal is assumed to act on the SCN pacemaker by means of substances in the bloodstream. This suggestion is consistent with electron miscroscopic evidence that some SCN cells are clustered in direct apposition to the walls of blood capillaries (Moore, Card, and Riley, 1980; Card, Riley, and Moore, 1980). Moore-Ede *et al.* (1982, p.172) note that these cells "may act as receptors, sensing hormonal signals from elsewhere." Attributing splits to a metabolic signal through the bloodstream also suggests how injection of hormones can induce split rhythms (Gwinner, 1974). This mechanism for generating split rhythms also explains and predicts properties that are difficult for models of out-of-phase oscillators to rationalize. To understand this issue, we briefly describe the gated pacemaker model to show how the fatigue signal can, under certain circumstances, generate split rhythms.

The gated pacemaker includes populations of two types of cells, called on-cells and off-cells (Figure 4). On-cells inhibit off-cells, and off-cells inhibit on-cells. This property of mutual inhibition leads to the prediction that each suprachiasmatic nucleus contains populations of pacemaker opponent processes. In a model pacemaker that represents a diurnal mammal, light is assumed to excite on-cells. In a model pacemaker that represents a nocturnal mammal, light is assumed to excite off-cells. These hypotheses enable the model to explain both the complementary reactions to light of nocturnal and diurnal mammals and their similar phase response curves (PRCs) to pulses of light, as well as the PRC "dead zone" during the subjective day of a nocturnal mammal (Carpenter and Grossberg, 1983b; Pohl, 1982).

The hypothesis that both on-cells and off-cells form part of the SCN pacemaker is consistent with neurophysiological data showing that electrical stimulation of the optic nerve, or stimulation of the retina by light, excites some SCN cells while inhibiting other SCN cells (Groos, 1982; Groos and Hendricks, 1979; Groos and Mason, 1978; Lincoln, Church, and Mason, 1975; Nishino, Koizumi, and Brooks, 1976). These experiments unequivocally show that both on-cells and off-cells exist in the SCN by demonstrating that increments in light intensity cause increasing activity in some SCN cells and decreasing activity in other SCN cells. Complementing these studies of single cells, there are studies of multiple units of activity and of overall SCN metabolism using 2-deoxyglucose (Green and Gillette, 1982; Groos and Hendricks, 1982; Inouye and Kawamura, 1979; Sato and Kawamura, 1984; Schwartz and Gainer, 1977; Schwartz, Davidsen, and Smith, 1980; Schwartz *et al.*, 1983; Shibata *et al.*, 1982). These studies show that a daytime peak in SCN activity can occur in both nocturnal and diurnal animals. There is little discussion in the literature concerning how the on-cell and off-cell SCN populations contribute to the overall level of SCN metabolism. In fact, Groos and Mason (1980, p.355) write: "It remains unclear why the SCN is equipped with two oppositely reacting visual subsystems, the light activated and the light suppressed cell types." Some 2-deoxyglucose results do point to an involvement of opponent responses in the SCN pacemaker. For example, Schwartz *et al.* (1980) show that 2-deoxyglucose utilization can be decreased by light input during certain phases of the SCN rhythm. They conclude that "measured levels of SCN glucose utilization do not translate simply into firing rates of SCN output cells; rather, they represent complex, weighted summations of myriad excitatory and

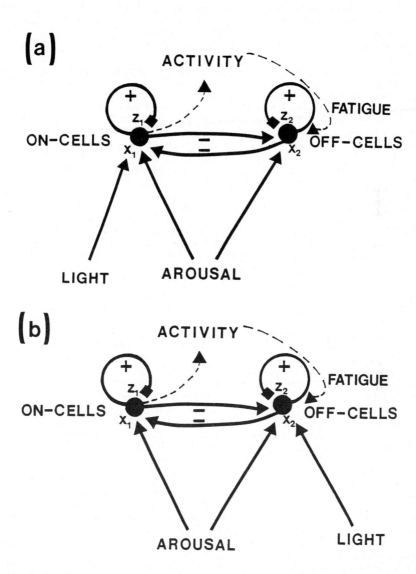

Figure 4. Gated pacemaker circuits of diurnal (a) and nocturnal (b) models. In both circuits, on-cells and off-cells excite themselves via positive feedback, inhibit each other via negative feedback, and are tonically aroused. Light excites on-cells in the diurnal circuit and off-cells in the nocturnal circuit. Activation of on-cells or suppression of off-cells energizes wakefulness and activity. Fatigue builds up during the wakeful state and excites off-cells in both diurnal and nocturnal circuits. A conditionable slow gain control process activates on-cells in both diurnal and nocturnal circuits. Versions of the slow gain control process are shown in Figures 13, 16, and 18.

inhibitory events within the nucleus" (p.166).

Our model is consistent with both the data about SCN on-cells and off-cells and the data about daytime peaks in overall SCN activity if the following hypothesis is made: The population of SCN pacemaker cells which receives light inputs is larger, or has stronger output signals, than the population of pacemaker cells which does not receive light inputs, in both the diurnal and nocturnal mammals. This hypothesis is consistent with the data on on-cell and off-cell responses in the rat and the cat that Groos and Mason (1980) and Nishino et al. (1976) have reported. In both of these studies, light-activated cells were encountered approximately twice as often as light-suppressed cells. The hypothesis of more light-activated than light-suppressed cells reconciles single cell, multiple unit, and metabolic data as follows. In a diurnal gated pacemaker model, increased on-cell activity would dominate decreased off-cell activity during the subjective day, thereby causing a peak in overall SCN activity. In a nocturnal gated pacemaker model, increased off-cell activity would dominate decreased on-cell activity during the subjective day, thereby again causing a peak in overall SCN activity. Because the data have not yet fully determined how on-cells and off-cells contribute to SCN pacemaker dynamics, we have analysed the simplest *symmetric* gated pacemaker model in which the on-cell and off-cell populations have the same parameters. All of our arguments can be translated into the asymmetric case.

To clarify the relationship of on-cells and off-cells to multiple unit and metabolic indices of SCN activity, the following experiments would be very helpful:

(1) Continuously measure single unit SCN activity in DD. Observe whether each cell is day-active or night-active. Then use light inputs to test whether each cell is an on-cell or an off-cell. Count the number of cells encountered of each type.

(2) In LD, test whether the activity of some cells is in-phase with light whereas the activity of other cells is out-of-phase with light. The similarity of SCN multiple unit activity in DD and LD (Sato and Kawamura, 1984) leads to the expectation that cells which are mutually out-of-phase in LD will also be out-of-phase in DD.

In a gated pacemaker model, until on-cells and off-cells are caused to differentially interact with processes external to the SCN, there is no distinction between a nocturnal and a diurnal pacemaker. Two feedback interactions with the SCN pacemaker are posited in the model: the output interaction whereby the pacemaker energized observable behavior, and the input interaction whereby the fatigue signal homeostatically modulates pacemaker activity.

In both the nocturnal pacemaker and the diurnal pacemaker, behavior is energized when on-cells are active and off-cells are inactive. When the difference between on-cell activity and off-cell activity becomes sufficiently great, an output signal is generated from the pacemaker. A time-average of this output signal, taken on an ultradian time scale, determines the size of the fatigue signal. The fatigue signal is partly due to metabolic consequences of overt behavioral activities that are energized by the pacemaker output signal. Over activity is not, however, the only metabolic source of fatigue. In particular, physical restraints imposed upon an awake experimental subject do not prevent a fatigue signal from feeding back to the pacemaker.

In both the nocturnal pacemaker and the diurnal pacemaker, the fatigue signal is assumed to excite off-cells, thereby indirectly inhibiting on-cells (Figure 4). Thus both light and fatigue signals act at the off-cells of a nocturnal pacemaker, whereas light acts at the on-cells and fatigue acts at the off-cells of a diurnal pacemaker. This asymmetric action of light and fatigue across diurnal and nocturnal models has been used to explain violation of Aschoff's rule (circadian period as a function of LL) by diurnal mammals but not nocturnal mammals, the consistent adherence to the circadian rule (behavioral activity as a function of LL) of both diurnal and nocturnal mammals, and the tendency of nocturnal mammals to lose circadian rhythmicity at lower light levels than diurnal mammals (Aschoff, 1979; Carpenter and Grossberg, 1984). The posited interaction between light and fatigue also leads to several predictions. For example, nocturnal mammals which obey Aschoff's rule will either be arrhythmic or violate Aschoff's rule if their fatigue signal is blocked before it can affect the SCN pacemaker; in nocturnal mammals, there are SCN pacemaker cells where the effects of a light pulse and the fatigue signal summate (Figure 4b); in diurnal mammals, a light pulse and the fatigue signal are mutually inhibitory at all SCN pacemaker cells (Figure 4a); in both diurnal and nocturnal mammals, a light pulse excites some SCN cells and inhibits other SCN cells.

The relationship between Aschoff's rule and split rhythms that our model posits can be used to suggest other predictions. For example, Pittendrigh and Dann (1976b, p.336) review data which show that certain diurnal mammals split their rhythm when light intensity (LL) is increased whereas other diurnal mammals split their rhythm when light intensity is decreased. Our concept of the fatigue process relates this variability in the split rhythm data of diurnal mammals to the violations of Aschoff's rule in diurnal mammals (Section 17). Nocturnal mammals, by contrast, tend to split their rhythm in response to light increases and also tend to consistently obey Aschoff's rule. In order to test more precise details about the relationship between split rhythm variability and Aschoff's rule violations, parametric data are needed that control for processes which are theoretically important. For example, self-selected light-dark cycles, dark nests, and lighting regimes that compensate for eye closure during sleep are all factors which influence predictions about Aschoff's rule (Carpenter and Grossberg, 1984).

Using this theoretical background, some of the factors that cause split rhythms in a nocturnal model can now be summarized. The presence of constant light (LL), when combined with a large fatigue signal, can prematurely induce sleep by causing abnormally rapid activation of the off-cells. In the model the total on-cell output determines the size of the fatigue signal that will be registered at the off-cells. Consequently, any procedure that reduces the total on-cell output can eliminate a split rhythm because the total on-cell output determines the size of the fatigue signal, and thus the total input to the off-cells. This explanation of how reducing total on-cell output an eliminate a split rhythm tacitly assumes that the fatigue signal is registered at all the off-cells in a nonspecific fashion (Carpenter and Grossberg, 1983a, 1984).

If one model SCN is removed, then the total on-cell output is greatly reduced. A split rhythm in the model can be abolished by such an ablation (Carpenter and Grossberg, 1982). Pickard and Turek (1982) have shown that surgical ablation of one SCN in the golden hamster does eliminate its split rhythm. They also recognized that this result may not be due to out-of-phase oscillators: "...the two SCN oscillators...might normally be coupled, but this coupling might be altered under...the split condition....Another possibility is that a set of interacting pacemakers may reside in each SCN, and the loss of the split rhythm may be a consequence of the total number of these oscillators destroyed; whether or not the destruction is unilateral may not be important" (Pickard and Turek, 1982, p.1121).

Our model also predicts that partial extirpation of both SCN can abolish splits by reducing total on-cell output. This prediction assumes that the remaining SCN oscillating circuits and signal pathways are not damaged by the lesion.

Other investigators have suggested that split rhythms are caused when two populations of oscillators become out-of-phase (Daan and Berde, 1978; Gwinner, 1974; Hoffmann, 1971; Moore-Ede et al., 1982; Pittendrigh, 1974). Many of these contributions use phenomenological or algebraic statements to describe how this occurs. Kawato and Suzuki (1980) have furthered this analysis by studying the parameters that control rhythm splitting in a dynamical model of coupled FitzHugh-Nagumo oscillators. The same qualitative conclusions can, however, be drawn using other classical oscillators, such as van der Pol oscillators. In such a model, the strength of the inhibitory coupling between the oscillators determines whether they will be driven out-of-phase. To explain split rhythms in both nocturnal and diurnal animals using light-sensitive inhibitory coupling strengths, one needs to suppose that light strengthens the inhibitory coupling between the oscillators of models that split in the light, and weakens the inhibitory coupling between the oscillators of models that split in the dark. The inhibitory coupling between oscillators also has to be weak to prevent splits in the dark, and strong to prevent splits in the light. In our model, by contrast, split rhythms can occur when the homeostatic fatigue signal and the nonhomeostatic slow gain control process react to certain lighting regimes.

Figures 5 and 6 depict the model simulations of a split rhythm experiment and SCN ablation experiment of Pickard and Turek (1982) in which they study golden hamsters. The dark bars indicate the times at which the model animal is active. In Figure 5, the model is kept in the dark (DD) for 20 days and then is placed in constant light (LL). Initially, the free-running period (τ) increases, as predicted by Aschoff's rule (Aschoff, 1960, 1979). On day 72, the rhythm starts to split. The split rhythm stabilizes after 5 days of transitional activity. The split period is shorter than the period prior to the split, as in the data. One model SCN is ablated on day 140, after which the split rhythm is abolished. The subsequent τ is shorter than any previous τ, as in the data.

Figure 6 shows that fine details of the split and its abolition can depend on model parameters. Carpenter (1983) describes yet another parametric choice in which, for example, the transitional period leading to the split is 15 days long, rather than 5 days long as in Figure 5. Figure 7 shows that the wave form of on-cell activity through time is qualitatively different during different phases of the simulation. Figure 7 thus illustrates how a single oscillator circuit can generate very different wave forms. Figure 7a depicts the on-cell activity several days before and after the split occurs. Note the multimodal activity profile that exists before the split. Figure 7b depicts the on-cell activity before and after the ablation of one model SCN. Again the activity profile undergoes a qualitative change in form, amplitude, and period due to the transition. Throughout the time intervals depicted in Figure 7, the light regime is constant (LL).

Earnest and Turek (1982) also perform split rhythm experiments in which hamsters are returned to DD for 10 to 30 days after having split their rhythm in LL. The return to DD eliminates the split rhythm. If animals are returned to LL 4–5 hours after their activity cycle begins, then the split rhythm is often promptly re-established. If animals are returned to LL at other phases of their circadian cycle, their split rhythm can reappear weeks later.

Earnest and Turek suggest that the rapid onset of splitting may be "due to the abrupt onset of light phase delaying one oscillator, while the other is phase advanced, which rapidly leads to the oscillators being 180° out-of-phase with each other" (p.411). This hypothesis assumes that some oscillators only phase delay in response to light, other oscillators only phase advance in response to light, and the two types of oscillators are mutually inhibitory. The hypothesis is compatible with the experiment in question, but conceptual and mechanistic questions remain. For example, the splitting property reported by Earnest and Turek is clearly sensitive to both the onset of light and to its maintenance after onset. Were the property dependent only on light onsets, splits should occur whenever light pulses cause phase delays or advances 4–5 hours after the onset of activity. Were the property dependent only on light maintenance, animals should split independent of the activity phase during which a light is turned on and thereafter maintained. The suggested explanation of Earnest and Turek focuses upon the initiation of the split by a properly timed light onset. The further development of the split could then be discussed in terms of a light-sensitive, history-dependent inhibitory coupling strength between the two types of oscillators.

An alternative explanation of these data can be offered. Within our theoretical framework, transmitter gating actions have been hypothesized to occur in visual pathways (Carpenter and Grossberg, 1981) as well as in the pathways whereby other sensory cues, such as food and water cues, activate motivational hypothalamic circuits (Grossberg, 1975, 1982a, 1984a). These gating actions recalibrate the sensitivity, or adapt, input pathways in response to sustained cues, much as they recalibrate the sensitivity of

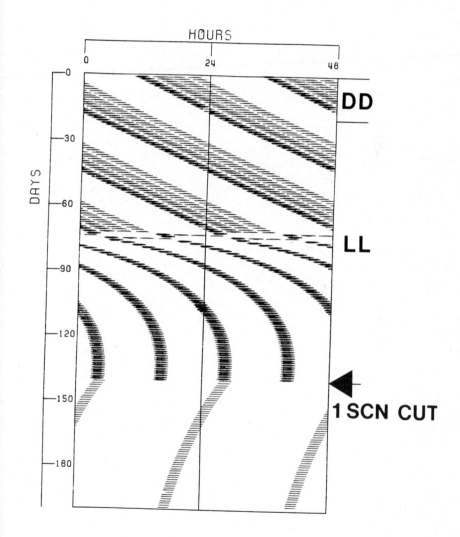

Figure 5. A split rhythm and SCN ablation simulation: The text describes how the activity rhythm starts to split 52 days after being placed in steady light (LL) and how the split rhythm is abolished by ablation of one model SCN.

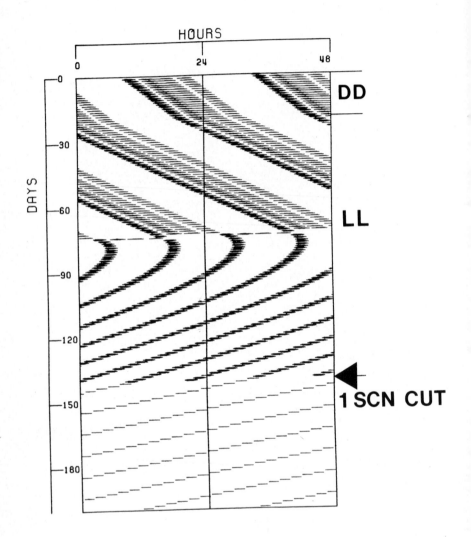

Figure 6. A split rhythm and SCN ablation simulation: Simulation of the same experiment as in Figure 5 using a related version of the model, to be described in Section 10. Behavioral properties such as the duration of the transition from the non-split rhythm to the split rhythm can vary with model parameters. Gradual or abrupt transitions can occur both in the model and in behavioral data.

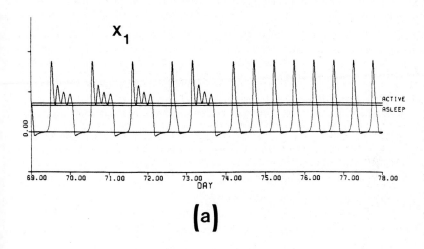

(a)

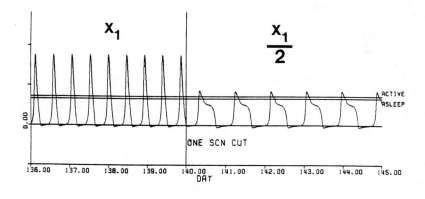

(b)

Figure 7. Real-time plot of the pacemaker on-cell activity $x_1(t)$, defined in Section 5. In (a), the multimodal activity waveform becomes unimodal after the split rhythm emerges. In (b), the split rhythm changes waveform when the split is abolished by ablation of one model SCN. Section 14 describes why $x_1(t)$ is plotted before the ablation and $\frac{1}{2}x_1(t)$ is plotted after the ablation.

a gated pacemaker's positive feedback loops, albeit on a different time scale. Let such a transmitter gating action modulate the light-activated input pathway to the pacemaker. Then an overshoot in input intensity occurs in response to light onset, followed by habituation of the input intenstiy to a lower level in response to sustained light. Suppose that this input overshoot occurs at a time when the fatigue feedback signal is large due to several hours of prior activity. Then the sum of the large light input plus the large fatigue signal may initiate a split if the slow gain process has not totally recovered from the prior split. By contrast, if the light input overshoot and the large fatigue feedback signal do not coincide, then a split will not occur until the slow gain control process can equilibrate to the input level due to the sustained light. Further experiments are needed to settle the issue.

The hypothesis that an input overshoot occurs at light onset does not imply that the mechanisms needed to explain parametric and nonparametric after-effects are different (Section 3). Indeed, both LL and LD lighting conditions are still functionally nonparametric at the pacemaker. In both cases, the input overshoot that may occur when an animal awakens or emerges from a dark nest does not coincide with a large fatigue signal.

5. The Gated Pacemaker Model

The gated pacemaker model describes the dynamics of on-cell/off-cell pairs, called *gated dipoles*, in which the on-cells and the off-cells mutually inhibit one another. Populations of these gated dipoles are assumed to exist in each SCN. The following processes define the gated pacemaker dynamics that are used in this article (Figure 4).

(1) Slowly accumulating transmitter substances are depleted, or habituated, by gating the release of feedback signals.

(2) The feedback signals are organized as an on-center off-surround, or competitive, anatomy.

(3) Both on-cells and off-cells are tonically aroused.

(4) Light excites the on-cells of a diurnal model and the off-cells of a nocturnal model.

(5) The on-cells drive observable activity, such as wheel-turning, in both the diurnal model and the nocturnal model.

(6) On-cell activity gives rise to a fatigue signal that excites the off-cells in both the diurnal model and the nocturnal model. The fatigue signal is a time-average of the on-cell output signal on an ultradian time scale.

(7) On-cell activity gives rise to a slowly varying gain control signal that excites the on-cells in both the diurnal model and the nocturnal model. The gain control signal is a time-average of the output signal on a time scale of months.

The general model equations for a nocturnal gated pacemaker are defined as follows.

NOCTURNAL MODEL

On-potential

$$\frac{d}{dt}x_1 = -Ax_1 + (B - x_1)[I + f(x_1)z_1 + Sy] - (x_1 + C)g(x_2), \qquad (1n)$$

Off-potential

$$\frac{d}{dt}x_2 = -Ax_2 + (B - x_2)[I + f(x_2)z_2 + F + J(t)] - (x_2 + C)g(x_1), \qquad (2n)$$

On-gate

$$\frac{d}{dt}z_1 = D(E - z_1) - Hf(x_1)z_1, \tag{3}$$

Off-gate

$$\frac{d}{dt}z_2 = D(E - z_2) - Hf(x_2)z_2, \tag{4}$$

Fatigue

$$\frac{d}{dt}F = -KF + h(x_1), \tag{5}$$

Gain control

$$\frac{d}{dt}y = -Uy + Vf(x_1). \tag{6}$$

Variable x_1 in equation $(1n)$ is the potential of an on-cell (population) v_1. Variable x_2 in equation $(2n)$ is the potential of an off-cell (population) v_2. Both x_1 and x_2 obey membrane equations (Hodgkin, 1964; Katz, 1966; Kuffler and Nicholls, 1976; Plonsey, 1969). In $(1n)$ and $(2n)$, the parameter $-A$ in the terms $-Ax_1$ and $-Ax_2$ determines the fast decay rate of the potentials x_1 and x_2. Also in $(1n)$ and $(2n)$, term I represents the constant arousal level that equally excites v_1 and v_2. In $(1n)$, the transmitter substance z_1 gates the non-negative feedback signal $f(x_1)$ from v_1 to itself. Term $f(x_1)z_1$ is proportional to the rate at which transmitter is released from the feedback pathway from v_1 to itself, thereby re-exciting x_1. Term Sy describes the effect of the gain control process y on v_1 (Figure 8). Term S is a signal that is gated by y, thereby generating a net excitatory input Sy at the on-cells v_1. The choice of signal S is described below, as well as its possible cellular realizations. The off-cells v_2 inhibit the on-cells v_1 via the non-negative signal $g(x_2)$ in term $-(x_1 + C)g(x_2)$. Equation $(2n)$ is the same as equation $(1n)$, except that the indices 1 and 2 are interchanged; both the light input $J(t)$ and the fatigue signal F excite v_2 but not v_1; and the slow gain control process excites v_1 but not v_2.

Equations (3) and (4) define the transmitter processes z_1 and z_2. In equation (3), the transmitter z_1 accumulates to its maximal level E at a slow constant rate D via the term $D(E - z_1)$. This slow accumulation process provides a lumped description of a temperature compensated system of biochemical reactions. This slow accumulation process is balanced by the release of z_1 at rate $Hf(x_1)z_1$, leading to the excitation of x_1 in equation $(1n)$. A similar combination of slow accumulation and gated release defines the dynamics of transmitter z_2 in equation (4).

The endogenous interactions between potentials x_1 and x_2 and transmitters z_1 and z_2 define a clock-like pacemaker (Carpenter and Grossberg, 1983b). This pacemaker has a stable period in the dark that varies inversely with the transmitter accumulation rate. Any genetic or prenatal factor capable of fixing this accumulation parameter can specify the period of the clock in the dark. The remaining processes F and y modulate the behavioral patterns that are generated by the pacemaker, as during split rhythms and long-term after-effects, but are not the source of the pacemaker's clock-like properties. Both F and y average indices of pacemaker activity, but are not independent oscillators.

The fatigue signal F in equation (5) is a time-average of $h(x_1)$, which increases with on-cell activity x_1. Speaking intuitively, an increase in x_1 and a decrease in x_2 arouse neural circuits that support the awake state. Fatigue builds up as a function of increased metabolic activity during the awake state, including but not restricted to overt action. Fatigue, in this sense, can thus build up in an alert but physically restrained animal. Since F excites the off-cells v_2 in equation $(2n)$, it tends to inhibit the arousal generated by the pacemaker. The decay rate K of the fatigue signal F is assumed to be ultradian. In particular, $A > K > D$ so that the potentials x_1 and x_2 react faster than the fatigue signal F, which in turn reacts faster than the pacemaker gates z_1 and z_2.

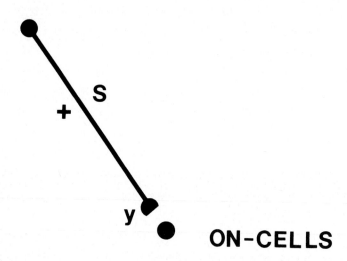

Figure 8. The slow gain control process y gates the performance signal S. The gated signal Sy activates the on-cell potential x_1 and alters the rate of change. Choices of S and laws for the temporal evolution of y are described in Sections 7, 9, and 11.

The slow gain control process y in equation (6) is also a time-average, but on a time scale that is much slower than the circadian time scale. Process y averages term $Vf(x_1)$ at an averaging rate U. Then Sy in (1n) acts as an excitatory input to the on-cells v_1. Term Sy in equation (1n) combined with equation (6) formally define a long-term memory trace y (Grossberg, 1968, 1969, 1982a). In all the simulations, terms S, U, and V are chosen to be constant, or to vary as a function of light or on-cell activity. A single choice of these terms can be used, for example, to simulate all of the long-term after-effects. These choices are described in Sections 7, 9, and 11.

The diurnal model differs from the nocturnal model only in the equations (1d) and (2d) that define its on-cell and off-cell potentials. In particular, light input $J(t)$ excites the on-cells but not the off-cells of the diurnal model. By contrast, the fatigue input F excites off-cells in both the diurnal and the nocturnal models, and the slow gain input y excites on-cells in both the diurnal and the nocturnal models. The diurnal model equations are listed below.

DIURNAL MODEL

On-potential

$$\frac{d}{dt}x_1 = -Ax_1 + (B - x_1)[I + f(x_1)z_1 + J(t) + Sy] - (x_1 + C)g(x_2), \qquad (1d)$$

Off-potential

$$\frac{d}{dt}x_2 = -Ax_2 + (B - x_2)[I + f(x_2)z_2 + F] - (x_2 + C)g(x_1), \qquad (2d)$$

On-gate

$$\frac{d}{dt}z_1 = D(E - z_1) - Hf(x_1)z_1, \qquad (3)$$

Off-gate

$$\frac{d}{dt}z_2 = D(E - z_2) - H f(x_2)z_2,$$ (4)

Fatigue

$$\frac{d}{dt}F = -KF + h(x_1),$$ (5)

Gain control

$$\frac{d}{dt}y = -Uy + V f(x_1).$$ (6)

6. Signal Functions, Activity Thresholds, and Attenuation of Light Input During Sleep

The models in equations (1)–(6) are completely defined by a choice of the signal functions f, g, and h; the light input $J(t)$; the signals S, U, and V; and the parameters. In all the simulations, the signal functions $f(w)$ and $g(w)$ in equations (1)–(6) are chosen to be threshold-linear functions of activity w:

$$f(w) = g(w) = \max(w, 0).$$ (7)

The signal function $h(w)$ in equation (5) is defined by

$$h(w) = M \, \max[f(w) - N, 0].$$ (8)

The definition of $h(w)$ can be interpreted as follows. We assume that $f(x_1(t))$ is the output signal of the pacemaker. Behavioral activity is triggered when $f(x_1(t))$ exceeds the positive threshold N. We assume that the function $h(x_1(t))$ defined by equation (8) provides an index of behavioral activity. Since, by equation (7), $f(w) = w$ when $w \geq 0$, we can simplify the definition of $h(w)$ in equation (8) to

$$h(w) = M \, \max(w - N, 0).$$ (9)

Equation (5) says that the fatigue signal F builds up at a rate proportional to behavioral activity $h(x_1(t))$. Activity ceases when $x_1(t) \leq N$. During such a time interval, fatigue decays at the ultradian rate K. Defining fatigue in this way enables us to provide a relatively simple description of the model. In more complex versions of the model (Section 18), the pacemaker output modulates the arousal level of motivational circuits (e.g., for eating, drinking, sex, exploratory activity). This arousal level helps to determine the sensitivity of these circuits to external and internal cues which trigger incentive motivational signals that energize observable behaviors. The resultant behaviors have metabolic consequences that contribute to the fatigue signal. Metabolic sources other than overt activity may also contribute to the fatigue signal, for example during a time interval when an alert animal is physically restrained or a human subject is confined to bed. This additional complexity has not been needed to qualitatively explain after-effects and split rhythms.

In the circadian literature (Aschoff, 1960), the total period (τ) is broken up into the time (α) during which the animal engages in overt activity and the remaining rest time (ρ). In our model, the time α corresponds to the time when

$$x_1(t) > N,$$ (10)

since equation (10) holds when $h(x_1(t)) > 0$. In our analysis, we further subdivide ρ into the sleep time and a transitional time of wakeful rest before, after, and possibly within the overt activity or sleep cycle. To mathematically distinguish these states, we assume that a sleep threshold P exists such that when

$$P < x_1(t) \leq N, \tag{11}$$

the model is in a state of wakeful rest. When

$$x_1(t) \leq P, \tag{12}$$

the model is in a state of sleep (Figures 3 and 7).

We operationally define sleep in terms of its effects on the pacemaker. The main effect is that eye closure (or entering a dark nest) can attenuate the light input to the pacemaker. Letting $L(t)$ be the light input that reaches the pacemaker when its "eyes" are open, we define the net light input in equations $(1d)$ and $(2n)$ to be

$$J(t) = \begin{cases} L(t) & \text{if } x_1(t) > P \\ \theta L(t) & \text{if } x_1(t) \leq P \end{cases}. \tag{13}$$

Parameter θ is a light attenuation factor. A value of $\theta = 1$ means that no light attenuation occurs during sleep. A value of $\theta = 0$ means that complete light attenuation occurs during sleep, either due to eye closure, access to a dark nest, or a self-selected light-dark cycle. The fact that θ is not always zero is implied by the ability of light pulses to phase shift a mammal's circadian rhythm while the mammal is asleep (Carpenter and Grossberg, 1983b; Pohl, 1982). In our analysis of Aschoff's rule, light attenuation during sleep contributes to violations of the rule by diurnal mammals but not by nocturnal mammals (Carpenter and Grossberg, 1984).

Our definitions of wakeful rest and sleep are chosen for simplicity. In species for which a separate temperature pacemaker helps to control sleep onset, a more complex definition is needed to discuss situations wherein the SCN and temperature pacemakers become desynchronized (Czeisler *et al.*, 1980; Wever, 1979). Also, our definition of the fatigue feedback signal assumes that no fatigue accumulates during wakeful rest. The simulations thus make the approximations that the fatigue signal builds up much faster during overt activity than during wakeful rest, and that all the oscillators controlling sleep onset are approximately synchronized. In species which spend most of their waking hours actively exploring or consummating, the lack of fatigue build-up during wakeful rest causes no loss of generality. In other species, an obvious extension of the model would postulate a smaller rate of fatigue build-up during wakeful rest than during overt activity.

7. Long-Term After-Effects: Slow Gain Control and Associative Conditioning

The long-term after-effects in Figures 1a and 2 are both generated by a single choice of the slow gain control process described in equations (1) and (6). The same choice of the gain control process can be used to simulate experimental after-effects of LD 1:23, LD 18:6, LD 12:12, LL, LD 10:10, and LD 14:14 (Pittendrigh and Daan, 1976a). In this section, we will describe this gain control process, explain how its works, and display after-effect simulations. We have also found that these after-effects can be simulated by certain variations of this gain control process but not others. Thus the simulations identify a small number of possible physiological mechanisms. These variations and their after-effects will also be described (Section 9).

In Figures 9–11, the model starts out with identical initial data and free-runs in the dark (DD) for 30 days before being exposed to different lighting regimes for 90 days. Then the model free-runs in the dark (DD) for 30 days. Using this procedure, we can

TABLE 2

Light Regime	τ_{DD} After-Effect (hours)	Figure
LD 1:23	24.15	9(a)
LD 18:6	23.97	9(b)
LD 12:12	24.01	10(a)
LL	24.15	10(b)
LD 10:10	23.99	11(a)
LD 14:14	24.04	11(b)

systematically compare after-effects. Table 2 describes the free-running periods τ_{DD} in the dark after the lighting regime terminates. A comparison of LD 1:23 and LD 18:6 in Figure 9 confirms the conclusion drawn from Figure 1 that an increase of light in this situation causes a decrease in τ_{DD}. A comparison of LD 12:12 and LL in Figure 10 confirms the conclusion drawn from Figure 2 that an increase of light in this situation causes an increase of τ_{DD}. In the comparison of LD 10:10 and LD 14:14 in Figure 11, the model is in the light one-half of the time in both simulations. As in the data of Pittendrigh and Daan (1976a), τ_{DD} is larger after LD 14:14 than after LD 10:10.

It cannot be overemphasized that the slow gain control process does not cause the circadian rhythmicity of the model pacemaker. The underlying period of the pacemaker in the dark is controlled by the accumulation rate of the transmitter gates within the pacemaker's positive feedback loops (Figure 4). It is precisely because of this endogenous rhythmicity that the fatigue signal and the slow gain control process are needed. The slow gain control process enables the pacemaker to adapt its activity cycles to long-term trends in the light-dark cycle. The fatigue signal exercises a homeostatic role that prevents the pacemaker from generating metabolically excessive bouts of activity. For example, the slow gain control process can enable a nocturnal model animal to become very active during the short nights of summer, while the fatigue feedback process prevents this heightened activity level from exhausting the model animal.

The slow gain control process is formally equivalent to a process of associative conditioning, and $y(t)$ in equations (1) and (6) obeys the law of a long-term memory (LTM) trace. In gated dipole models of appetitive hypothalamic circuits, a similar LTM process enables cues of various types to become conditioned reinforcers (Grossberg, 1972a, 1982b, 1982c, 1984a). For example, cues that become conditioned reinforcers by being associated with food enable the eating circuit to adapt to temporally irregular presentations of food. Cues that become conditioned reinforcers by being associated with shock enable the fear circuit to anticipate expected occurrences of shock. A large data base about instrumental and classical conditioning of motivated behaviors leads to the conclusion that four conditionable pathways converge on an appetitive gated dipole circuit in response to each sensory cue capable of becoming a conditioned reinforcer for that circuit.

Our study of circadian after-effect data has guided us to choose versions of this LTM process specialized to deal with cues that are related to lighting conditions or activity levels. In every case treated so far, we have needed to invoke only one conditionable pathway, rather than four. Adding the other three pathways would not constitute a violation of principle, and future data may require this generalization.

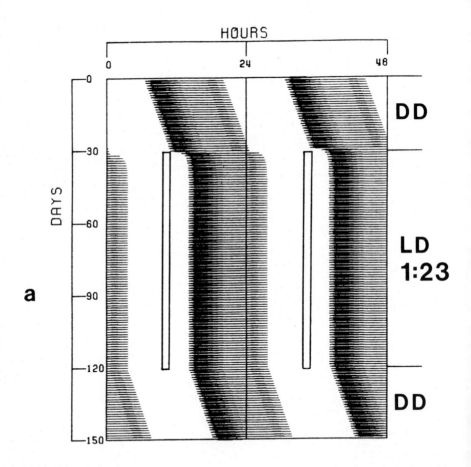

Figure 9a. Photoperiod after-effect simulations: Both simulations start with 30 days in the dark (DD), followed by a 90-day periodic light-dark (LD) lighting regime, followed by a 30-day free-run in the dark to test for after-effects. In (a), LD 1:23 is the lighting regime.

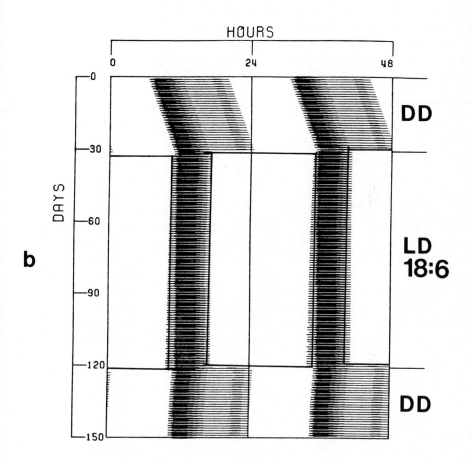

Figure 9b. In (b), LD 18:6 is the lighting regime.

A typical circuit in which four conditionable pathways modulate a gated dipole is depicted in Figure 12. In Figure 12, a cell population that is activated by an on-event sends sampling signals along a pair of conditionable pathways that abut the on-cells and the off-cells of the gated dipole. An LTM trace is computed at the end of each conditionable pathway. Each LTM trace gates the signals in its pathway before the gated signal can influence its target cells, as in Figure 8. In Figure 12, a cell population activated by an off-event can also send signals along a pair of conditionable pathways that abut the on-cells and the off-cells of the gated dipole. For example, an on-event population might be active whenever light is on, whereas an off-event population might be active whenever light is off. Increasing light intensity increases the activity of the on-event population and decreases the activity of the off-event population. Every event can hereby influence the activity of four conditionable pathways.

The after-effect experiments described in Section 3 can be explained using an LTM

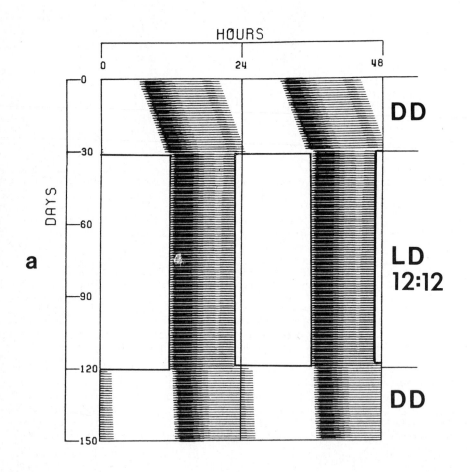

Figure 10. After-effect of constant light: After-effects of an LD 12:12 lighting regime in (a) are compared with after-effects of an LL lighting regime in (b).

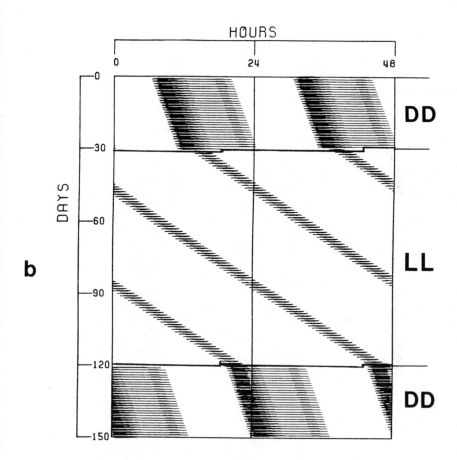

Figure 10 (continued).

trace which temporally averages an index of on-cell activity while the model is awake. One version of this type of LTM trace is illustrated in Figure 13. Each version is characterized by a special choice of S in equation (1) and of U and V in equation (6).

The LTM trace in Figure 13 is the one that was used to generate Figures 1a, 2, 3, 9, 10, and 11. This LTM trace gates a tonically active pathway. Hence the performance signal

$$S(t) \equiv S_{tonic}(t) = Q \tag{14}$$

in equation (1), where Q is a positive constant. The terms U and V in equation (6) are both switched on when the model wakes up, and are switched off when the model goes to sleep. Thus

$$U(t) = R S_{awake}(t), \tag{15}$$

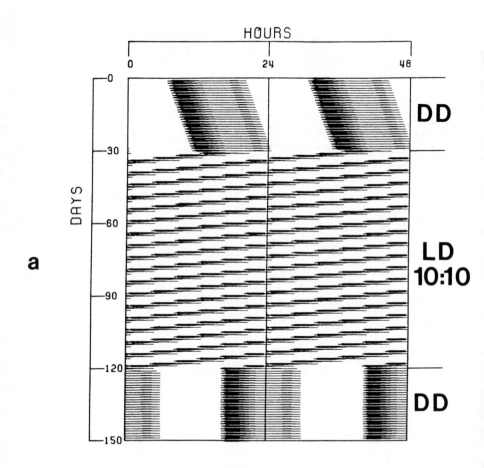

Figure 11. After-effects of period: After-effects of an LD 10:10 lighting regime in (a) are compared with after-effects of an LD 14:14 lighting regime in (b). In both lighting regimes, light is on 50% of the time.

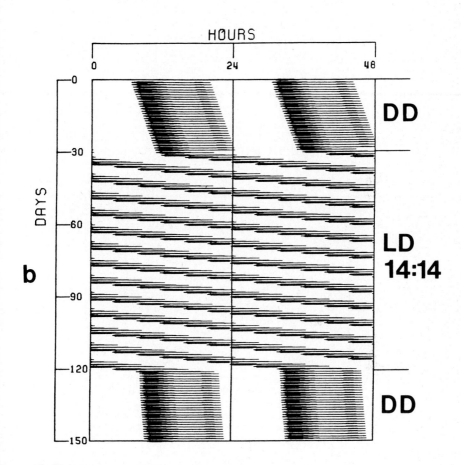

Figure 11 (continued).

where R is a positive constant, and

$$V(t) = S_{awake}(t),\qquad(16)$$

where

$$S_{awake}(t) = \begin{cases} 1 & \text{if } x_1(t) > P \\ 0 & \text{if } x_1(t) \le P \end{cases}.\qquad(17)$$

Parameter P in equation (17) is the sleep threshold that was defined in equation (12). By equations (6), (15), and (16), equation (6) for the LTM trace is

$$\frac{d}{dt}y = S_{awake}[-Ry + f(x_1)].\qquad(18)$$

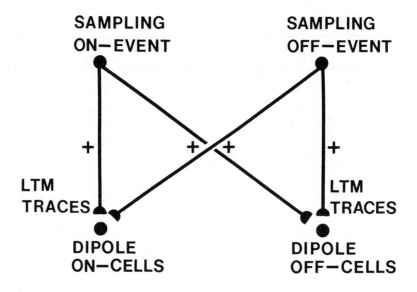

Figure 12. In general, four conditionable pathways to the pacemaker may be influenced by a single sensory cue. Onset of the cue is an on-event that can cause performance signals to both the on-cells and the off-cells of the gated dipole circuit. Offset of the cue is an off-event that can also cause performance signals to both on-cells and off-cells. Each of these signal pathways can be gated by its own conditionable long-term memory (LTM) trace. All versions of our model that have been used in simulations employ only one of these four possible conditionable pathways.

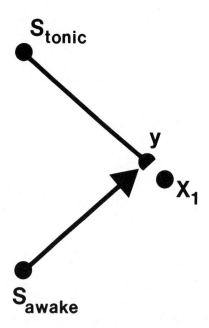

Figure 13. A slow gain control process used in after-effect simulations: The LTM trace y time-averages x_1 when the model is awake and gates a tonically active performance signal, as in equations (14)–(19).

By equation (17), S_{awake} is positive only when x_1 is positive. Since $f(x_1) = \max(x_1, 0)$ by equation (7), equation (18) can be written in the simpler form

$$\frac{d}{dt} y = S_{awake} [-Ry + x_1]. \tag{19}$$

By equation (19), the LTM trace $y(t)$ does not change when the model is asleep. When the model is awake, $y(t)$ averages the on-cell activity $x_1(t)$ at the rate R.

By equation (18), the sampling signal S_{awake} gates the sensitivity of y to the postsynaptic potential x_1. Process y is therefore located in Figure 13 abutting synapses where it can both sample the postsynaptic potential x_1 and receive the presynaptic sampling signal S_{awake}.

8. Analysis of After-Effects

In this section, we explain how the LTM trace $y(t)$, whose action is defined by equations (14) and (19), determines the experimentally correct periods in Figures 1a, 2, 3, 9, 10, and 11. Figure 14 describes the critical property of this LTM trace. Figure 14 plots the model's period τ_{DD} during a free-run in the dark against the initial value of y at the onset of the free-run. The period τ_{DD} is a decreasing function of y. Thus if a previous lighting regime causes an increase in y, then the subsequent τ_{DD} will decrease,

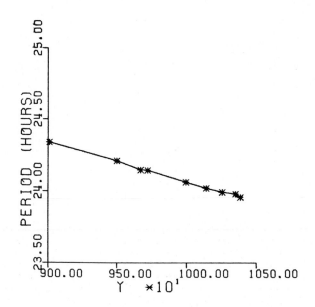

Figure 14. Consistent after-effects on τ_{DD} depend upon a monotone decreasing relationship between the free-running period in the dark (τ_{DD}) and the size of the slow gain control variable (y).

whereas if a previous lighting regime causes a decrease in y, then the subsequent τ_{DD} will increase.

Table 3 describes the effects of several lighting regimes on the size of y. Table 3 lists the value that y attains just before each lighting regime terminates. Using Figure 14, these y values predict the τ_{DD} values during the subsequent free-run in the dark. This computation produces the τ_{DD} values that are listed in Table 2 and that are in accord with experimental data.

To understand these results, we need to explain how the lighting regimes in Table 3 cause their respective changes in y, and why τ_{DD} decreases as y increases. The first explanation requires an analysis of how the LTM equation (19) reacts to the lighting regimes. The second explanation requires an analysis of how different levels of y alter pacemaker dynamics via equation (1) for the on-cell potential x_1, in the case that the performance signal $S(t)$ is constant.

The main effect of different lighting regimes on y can be understood by comparing Figures 9a and 9b, which describe after-effects of LD 1:23 and LD 18:6. During LD 1:23, on-cell activity is suppressed by light for only 1 hour every day. During LD 18:6, by contrast, on-cell activity is suppressed by light for 18 hours every day. Consequently, in the case of LD 18:6, on-cell activity is intense while the model is awake during the 6 hours of darkness. By contrast, in the case of LD 1:23, the model's activity, which is distributed over a larger period of time, is lower on the average.

The influence of lighting regimes LD 12:12 and LL on y can be similarly understood. In particular, during LL the animal can only be active while light is suppressing its on-

TABLE 3

Light Regime	y After-Effect	Figure
LD 1:23	9.7×10^3	9(a)
LD 18:6	1.0375×10^4	9(b)
LD 12:12	1.021×10^4	10(a)
LL	9.675×10^3	10(b)
LD 10:10	1.0285×10^4	11(a)
LD 14:14	1.01×10^4	11(b)

$$S = Q, \quad U = RS_{awake}, \quad V = S_{awake}$$

cells. Consequently the average on-cell activity while the animal is awake during LL is less than the average on-cell activity while the animal is awake during LD 12:12. Figure 10b illustrates the suppressive effect of LL on on-cell activity. The comparison of LD 10:10 with LD 14:14 makes a similar point. As in the comparison of LD 18:6 with LD 1:23, the on-cell activity cycle is compressed and intensified during LD 10:10 relative to LD 14:14. In summary, the single hypothesis that the LTM trace y averages on-cell potential while the model is awake suffices to explain the effects listed in Table 3 of both parametric and nonparametric lighting regimes on y.

It remains to explain how a parametric increase in y causes a decrease in τ_{DD}, as in Figure 14. This property is due to the combined effects of the slow gain control and fatigue processes in our model. The model, in fact, predicts that systematic deviations from the observed after-effects will occur *in vivo* if the fatigue feedback signal is blocked. Predicted effects of blocking fatigue on Aschoff's rule are described in Carpenter and Grossberg (1984).

In the dark, equation (1) becomes

$$\frac{d}{dt}x_1 = -Ax_1 + (B - x_1)[I + f(x_1)z_1 + Qy] - (x_1 + C)g(x_2) \tag{20}$$

due to the assumption in equation (14) that $S(t)$ equals the constant Q. On any given day, term Qy in equation (20) is approximately constant, since y is assumed to change very slowly. An increased value of y thus acts to enhance x_1 by a constant amount throughout the day. The primary effect of an increase in y is to approximately shift the graph of $x_1(t)$ upwards, as in Figure 15. Such an approximate upward shift would cause a significant increase in the duration of activity (α) and a significant decrease in the duration of rest (ρ) without significantly changing the period (τ). This primary effect of an increase in y is, however, modified by the action of the fatigue signal. The enhancement of activity due to an increase in y quickly generates a larger fatigue signal. This increased fatigue signal feeds back to the pacemaker. There it more actively excites the off-cells and thereby partially offsets the increased on-cell activity caused by the increased y. During sleep, on the other hand, fatigue decays to zero on an ultradian time scale. Fatigue is small long before the internal dynamics of the pacemaker wake the model up. The fatigue signal has a comparatively small effect on ρ. Thus an increase in y causes a relatively small increase in α, a relatively large decrease in ρ, and a net decrease in $\tau_{DD} = \alpha + \rho$, as in Figure 14.

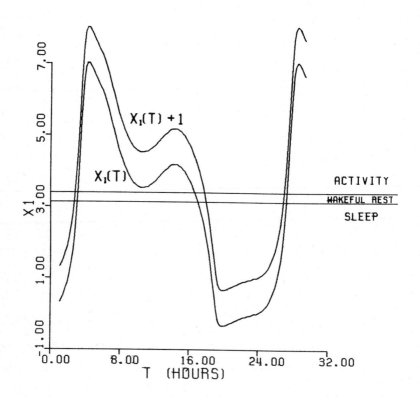

Figure 15. An increase in the gain y tends to shift the graph of the on-cell potential x_1 upward. Such an upward shift tends to increase activity duration (α) and to decrease rest duration (ρ) without changing period (τ). In this figure, an upward shift of x_1 by 1 unit changes α from 13.51 hours to 14.85 hours and ρ from 10.64 hours to 9.30 hours. The period of both graphs is 24.15 hours.

9. Alternative Slow Gain Control Processes

The discussion in Section 8 explains the functional properties that enable an LTM process $y(t)$ to generate long-term after-effect data. The question therefore arises whether other LTM processes also possess these functional properties. Two such LTM processes are described in this section. In these processes, light levels rather than activity levels determine the choice of S, U, and V, and light acts as an off-event rather than as an on-event. These three examples of the LTM process, as a group, suggest the types of design variations that may be sought in physiological and biochemical data.

Figure 16 describes two light-sensitive LTM processes. In Figure 16a, the LTM trace gates a tonically active pathway. Hence the performance signal is

$$S(t) \equiv S_{tonic}(t) = Q \tag{14}$$

in equation (1), where Q is a positive constant. This is the same performance signal that was used in the previous LTM process. In the present case, however, the terms U and V in equation (6) are both inhibited when the light turns on, and are disinhibited when the light turns off. Thus

$$U(t) = RS_{light}(t) \tag{21}$$

and

$$V(t) = S_{light}(t), \tag{22}$$

where

$$S_{light}(t) = \frac{1}{1 + WJ(t)} \tag{23}$$

and $J(t)$ is the light intensity defined by equation (13). By equations (6), (21), and (22), the equation for the LTM trace is

$$\frac{d}{dt}y = S_{light}[-Ry + f(x_1)]. \tag{24}$$

As in Figure 13, the LTM trace gates a tonically active pathway. Unlike Figure 13, the plasticity of the LTM trace is presynaptically gated by a pathway that is tonically on when light is off, but is inhibited when light turns on.

This LTM process has the requisite functional properties for the following reasons. The performance pathway that is gated by the LTM trace is tonically active, just as in the previous example. The presynaptic sampling signal S_{light} equals 1 in the dark and is approximately 0 in bright light. Since a nocturnal mammal tends to be active in the dark, S_{light} tends to be large when the animal is awake. Both sampling signals S_{light} and S_{awake} thus tend to be large during the same time intervals. The sampling signal S_{light} can also be large in the dark at times when the animal goes to sleep. This difference between S_{light} and S_{awake} can be used to devise lighting regimes capable of distinguishing which presynaptic sampling signal is operative in different animals. Table 4 lists the y values and τ_{DD} values that are generated by this version of the LTM process. All the τ_{DD} values are in the same direction as after-effect data.

The third version of the LTM process also uses S_{light} to presynaptically gate the LTM sampling process. Consequently, equation (24) again holds. The performance signal is, however, no longer constant, as in equation (14). Instead, let

$$S(t) = QS_{light}(t). \tag{25}$$

Thus $S_{light}(t)$ is both the performance signal and the sampling signal is this process. Figure 16b shows that a separate presynaptic pathway is no longer needed to gate LTM sampling. A single pathway can accomplish both functions.

This LTM process has the necessary functional properties for the following reasons. Equation (24) for the LTM trace $y(t)$ is the same as in the previous model. The performance signal $S(t)$ in equation (25) equals the constant Q in the dark. Except in the LL case, the performance signal tends to be constant when the animal is awake, as in the previous model. The performance signal decreases only at times when light excites the off-cells. The decrease in the performance signal $S(t)$ at the on-cells thus acts like an increase in light intensity $J(t)$ at the off-cells. Such a shift in the scale of light intensity does not damage the model's ability to simulate after-effects. Table 5 lists the y values and τ_{DD} values that are generated by this version of the LTM process. All the τ_{DD} values are in the same direction as after-effect data.

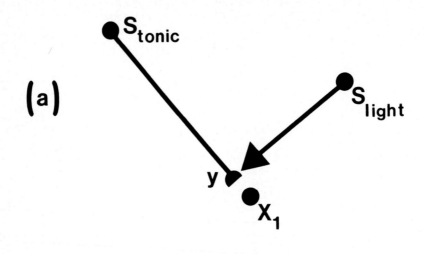

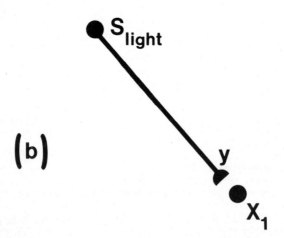

Figure 16. Slow gain control processes used in after-effect simulations: In (a), the gain y averages on-cell output faster when light is off and slower when light is on, as in equations (23)–(24). The resultant gain y gates a tonically active performance signal, as in equation (14). In (b), both the rate of averaging by y and the size of the performance signal decrease when light is turned on, as in equations (23)–(25). Both (a) and (b) use the same conditioning rule for y.

TABLE 4

Light Regime	τ_{DD} After-Effect (hours)	y After-Effect
LD 1:23	23.47	6.55×10^3
LD 18:6	23.32	7.295×10^3
LD 12:12	23.28	7.67×10^3
LL	23.64	5.935×10^3
LD 10:10	23.28	7.65×10^3
LD 14:14	23.28	7.66×10^3

$$S = Q, \quad U = RS_{light}, \quad V = S_{light}$$

TABLE 5

Light Regime	τ_{DD} After-Effect (hours)	y After-Effect
LD 1:23	23.5	6.52×10^3
LD 18:6	23.4	6.835×10^3
LD 12:12	23.3	7.315×10^3
LL	23.9	5.4×10^3
LD 10:10	23.3	7.295×10^3
LD 14:14	23.3	7.29×10^3

$$S = QS_{light}, \quad U = RS_{light}, \quad V = S_{light}$$

10. Split Rhythms and Inconsistent After-Effects on Period

The split rhythm simulations in Figures 5–7 are of data collected from the nocturnal hamster. The hamster does not, however, generate consistent after-effects on τ_{DD} (Pittendrigh and Daan, 1976a), despite the fact that it does exhibit after-effects and a slow onset of split rhythms. Thus one would not expect a model of hamster split rhythms to possess the same slow gain control process as a model which exhibits consistent after-effects on τ_{DD}.

The slow gain control processes which succeed in modeling split rhythm data do not, in fact, generate consistent after-effects on τ_{DD}. This is because, as a function of y, τ_{DD} is not monotone decreasing, as in Figure 14. Instead, τ_{DD} varies non-monotonically as a function of y, as in Figure 17. Consequently, in one y range, τ_{DD} increases with y, whereas in a different y range, τ_{DD} decreases with y, thereby generating inconsistent after-effects on τ_{DD} across model animals.

It is also of importance, however, that the slow gain control processes which succeed in modeling split rhythms data are closely related to the processes that model consistent after-effects on τ_{DD}. Then one can envisage that a relatively simple evolutionary

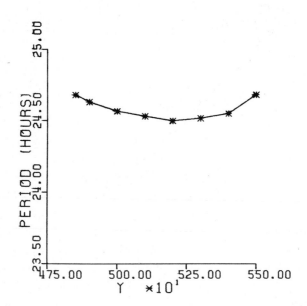

Figure 17. Inconsistent after-effects on τ_{DD} occur when τ_{DD} depends in a non-monotonic way upon the size of y.

modification converts a model with consistent after-effects on τ_{DD} to a model with split rhythms but inconsistent after-effects on τ_{DD}.

11. Split Rhythms: Slow Gain Control Processes

As in our discussion of after-effects, we will describe three variations of the slow gain control process that all possess the functional properties needed to generate split rhythm simulations. Then we will describe how these processes give rise to split rhythms, how they differ from processes that produce consistent after-effects on τ_{DD}, and how the graphs of τ_{DD} versus y in Figures 14 and 17 are related to data about Aschoff's rule (Aschoff, 1960, 1979).

Figure 18 depicts the anatomies of slow gain control processes that can give rise to split rhythms. In every case, the performance signal is the same; namely,

$$S(t) = Q S_{awake}(t), \tag{26}$$

where

$$S_{awake}(t) = \begin{cases} 1 & \text{if } x_1(t) > P \\ 0 & \text{if } x_1(t) \le P \end{cases}. \tag{17}$$

In none of the models producing consistent after-effects on τ_{DD} was this performance signal used. The three split rhythm models use different U and V terms within the LTM trace equation (6). The functional property that all of these LTM traces guarantee is the following: y becomes smaller in LL than in DD.

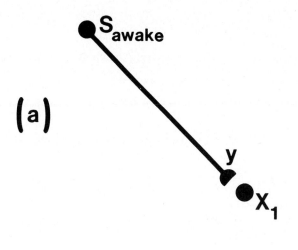

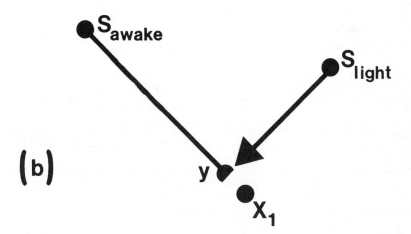

Figure 18. Slow gain control processes used in split rhythm simulations: In the processes, the performance signal is on only when the model is awake. The anatomy in (a) can support two closely related conditioning rules capable of causing split rhythms. In one rule, the gain y samples the on-cell output at a constant rate, as in equation (28). In the other rule, y samples the on-cell output only when the model is awake. In (b), the gain y samples on-cell output at a faster rate when light is off than when light is on.

The anatomy in Figure 18a is the same for the first two models. In the first model,

$$\frac{d}{dt}y = -Ry + S_{awake}f(x_1);$$ (27)

that is, $U = R$ and $V = S_{awake}$. This LTM trace averages the product of S_{awake} and $f(x_1)$ at the constant rate R. The signal S_{awake} thus acts as a performance signal and a sampling signal. This model was used to generate Figures 6 and 7.

In the second model,

$$\frac{d}{dt}y = -Ry + f(x_1);$$ (28)

that is, $U = R$ and $V = 1$. This LTM trace averages $f(x_1)$ at the constant rate R.

The third model uses the anatomy in Figure 18b. Its LTM trace is

$$\frac{d}{dt}y = S_{light}[-Ry + f(x_1)],$$ (29)

where

$$S_{light}(t) = \frac{1}{1 + WJ(t)},$$ (23)

and the light input $J(t)$ is defined by equation (13). Thus in equation (29), $U(t) = RS_{light}(t)$ and $V(t) = S_{light}(t)$. In this model, S_{awake} is the performance signal and S_{light} is the presynaptic sampling signal.

The split rhythm model in Figure 18b differs from the after-effect model in Figure 16a only in the choice of performance signal $S(t)$. Changing $S(t)$ from $S_{tonic}(t)$ to $S_{awake}(t)$ transforms the model from one capable of consistent after-effects on τ_{DD} to one capable of split rhythms and inconsistent after-effects on τ_{DD}.

12. Analysis of Split Rhythms: Depression of Gain by LL

All of the LTM traces in equations (27)–(29) have the property that y becomes smaller in LL than in DD for the following reasons.

By equation $(2n)$, the light input $J(t)$ excites the off-cells during LL but not during DD. The off-cells, in turn, inhibit the on-cells due to equation $(1n)$. Consequently, on the average, the on-cells are less active during LL than during DD. In equation (28), the LTM trace averages $f(x_1)$ at a constant rate R. Since x_1 is smaller, on the average, during LL than during DD, y becomes smaller during LL than during DD, as desired. Equation (27) differs from equation (28) only in that $f(x_1)$ is replaced by $S_{awake}f(x_1)$. Since S_{awake} equals 1 when the model is awake and equals 0 when the model is asleep, y averages $f(x_1)$ while the model is awake and averages 0 while the model is asleep. Since LL caused x_1 to be smaller on the average when the model is awake, y becomes smaller during LL than during DD, as desired.

In equation (29), $S_{light} \equiv 1$ during DD. Hence the LTM trace averages $f(x_1)$ at the constant rate R. During LL,

$$S_{light}(t) = \begin{cases} \frac{1}{1+WL(t)} & \text{if } x_1(t) > P \\ \frac{1}{1+W\theta L(t)} & \text{if } x_1(t) \le P \end{cases}$$ (30)

by equations (13) and (23). In equation (30), the light intensity $L(t)$ is a positive constant during LL. Since $\theta < 1$, $S_{light}(t)$ is larger when the model is asleep than when the model is awake. Consequently, the LTM trace averages the small x_1 values that occur during sleep faster than the larger x_1 values that occur during wakefulness. Moreover, during LL, all x_1 values are depressed on the average as compared to DD. Consequently, y becomes smaller during LL than during DD.

It remains to explain how the decrease of y during LL and the choice of performance signal $S = QS_{awake}$ in equation (26) generate split rhythms.

13. Analysis of Split Rhythms: Interaction of Slow Gain, Pacemaker Gate, and Fatigue

Our explanation of the slow onset of split rhythms is based upon properties of the interaction between the LTM trace, the fatigue signal, and the pacemaker. This explanation depends, moreover, on the fact that the pacemaker rhythm derives from an interaction between fast potentials and slow transmitter gates, as in equations (1)–(4) and Figure 4. Thus the type of explanation that we offer lies outside the scope of classical oscillator models, such as models based upon van der Pol oscillators.

The fatigue signal acts on an ultradian time scale in our model. Since an increase in model activity causes an increased build-up of fatigue, multimodal bouts of activity can be generated by the negative feedback that fatigue exerts upon the on-cells (Figure 4). Such multimodal bouts of activity are visible on days 1–72 in Figure 6, prior to the onset of the split rhythm.

The fatigue feedback acts on an ultradian time scale, whereas the transmitter gates act on a circadian time scale. Thus fatigue can build up before the on-cell transmitter gate in equation (3) becomes depleted. Model activity can thus be depressed by fatigue at times when the on-cell transmitter gates are still quite large.

When the model is placed from DD into LL, its on-cell activity is depressed, on the average. Consequently, due to the form of the LTM trace equations (27), (28), or (29), y gradually decreases. As y gradually decreases, so too does its excitatory effect on the on-cell activity x_1 in equation (1n). The net effect of this feedback exchange between x_1 and y is a slow, progressive decrease in the average activity of x_1 while the LL lighting regime is maintained. Eventually a level of x_1 activity is approached at which an interaction between the performance signal $S(t) = QS_{awake}(t)$, the fatigue signal $F(t)$, and the transmitter gate $z_1(t)$ can initiate a split rhythm. How this happens can be understood by considering Figure 7a.

Figure 7a describes the on-cell activity $x_1(t)$ at times just before and just after the split rhythm is initiated. Note the multimodal activity bouts on days 70–72. On day 73, the first peak in activity is not followed by three subsequent peaks. This is because the LTM trace $y(t)$ has decreased to such a level that $x_1(t)$ falls below the sleep threshold P after the first peak. As soon as the model falls asleep, the performance signal $S(t) = QS_{awake}(t)$ in equation (26) suddenly becomes zero. Consequently the gain term $S(t)y$ in equation (1n) suddenly becomes zero. In effect, the on-cell activity loses a source of excitatory input at that moment. Due to this event, $x_1(t)$ continues to decrease after the model falls asleep, thereby preventing a multimodal activity bout from occurring.

At the time when this first bout of activity terminates, the on-cell transmitter gate $z_1(t)$ is relatively large. The fatigue signal, not the endogenous pacemaker rhythm, caused the onset of sleep. After sleep begins, the transmitter $z_1(t)$ grows to even larger values, while the fatigue signal $F(t)$ decays on an ultradian time scale. The combination of the decay of $F(t)$ and the large values of $z_1(t)$ wakes up the model after a relatively short sleep interval. As in Figure 7a, the multimodal activity bout may temporarily recover after the first unimodal peak is over. This transitional time may last for a number of cycles that varies with the choice of model parameters. However, once $y(t)$ decreases a little more, a split rhythm is maintained by the interaction between fatigue $F(t)$, the on-cell transmitter gate $z_1(t)$, and the performance signal $S(t)$.

14. Analysis of Split Rhythms: SCN Ablation Experiments

In Figure 6, on day 140, one model SCN is removed and the split rhythm is abolished. This effect was discovered by Pickard and Turek (1982) using hamsters. As we indicated in Section 4, our model generates this effect due to the sudden decrease in fatigue feedback that is sensed by each surviving off-cell. This decrease is caused as follows.

Cutting out half of the model cells causes a sudden decrease in total on-cell output. The total fatigue signal is correspondingly reduced. Every surviving off-cell is influenced by the total fatigue signal. In other words, the output signals from all the on-cells combine to generate behavioral activity and fatigue. The fatigue level, in turn, is communicated nonspecifically to every off-cell. This non-specific property of the fatigue signal is compatible with the hypothesis that fatigue feedback is delivered *in vivo* to SCN off-cells via the bloodstream.

Figure 7b plots the total on-cell potential of the model just before and after the ablation. Cutting out half of the on-cells reduces the size of the fatigue signal and thereby unmasks the basic unsplit pacemaker period. This basic pacemaker prior is shorter than the pre-split pacemaker priod, where fatigue prolongs the period by causing intermittent rest intervals during which $z_1(t)$ can recover.

Simulation of an SCN ablation is achieved by reducing the size of the on-cell output signal feedback to the pacemaker in equation (5). When half of the model SCN is removed, the feedback signal is reduced to half its previous size. Equation (5) then becomes

$$\frac{d}{dt}F = -KF + h(x_1/2). \tag{31}$$

This change is interpreted as follows. Equation (1) described the dynamics of a single on-cell potential x_1. Previously our model has considered situations in which all the on-cell potentials of the pacemaker are synchronized. Then x_1 is proportional to the sum of all the on-cell potentials in the pacemaker. By suitably interpreting the parameters that define $h(w)$ in equation (9), $h(x_1)$ in equation (5) can be defined as the total effect of all pacemaker cells on the fatigue signal. Cutting out half of the pacemaker cells reduces this total effect to $h(x_1/2)$, as in equation (31).

The graph in Figure 7b describes $x_1(t)$ before the ablation and $\frac{1}{2}x_1(t)$ after the ablation. These functions are proportional to the sum of all pacemaker on-cell outputs before and after the ablation, respectively.

The significant reduction in total pacemaker activity after the ablation is also found in the Pickard and Turek (1982) data.

15. Fatigue as an Internal Zeitgeber

Another important effect of SCN ablation occurs in the Pickard and Turek (1982) data. After ablation, behavioral activity is reduced in both overall intensity and synchrony. The low levels of activity gradually become more diffusely distributed throughout each day.

In our model, both light and fatigue can act to synchronize the many on-cell off-cell dipoles that constitute the total pacemaker. In steady light (LL) or dark (DD), light loses its capacity to act as an effective external Zeitgeber. This is not, however, true of the fatigue signal, which can act as an internal Zeitgeber which is nonspecifically sensed by all the off-cells.

After ablating half of the pacemaker cells, however, the fatigue signal is markedly reduced. Its ability to entrain the individual dipoles of the pacemaker is correspondingly reduced, so that these dipoles can gradually drift out-of-phase with one another.

16. Analysis of Inconsistent After-Effects on Period

It remains to analyse how a parametric increase in y causes a non-monotonic change in τ_{DD}, as in Figure 17. This property is due to the combined effects of the slow gain control and fatigue processes in our model. The non-monotonic graph in Figure 17 differs from the monotone decreasing graph in Figure 14 due to a different choice of performance signal $S(t)$ in the corresponding models. The monotone decreasing graph of Figure 14 was explained in Section 8 using the tonically active performance signal

$$S(t) \equiv S_{tonic}(t) = Q. \tag{14}$$

The non-monotonic graph in Figure 17 is due to the performance signal

$$S(t) = QS_{awake}(t) \tag{26}$$

where $S_{awake}(t)$ is defined by equation (17).

On any given day, the gain term y is approximately constant due to its slow rate of change. Thus the gated performance signal Sy in equation (1) changes significantly on any given day only if S changes. In Section 8, we noted that Sy does not change significantly on any given day if $S(t) = S_{tonic}$, as in equation (14). This is no longer true if $S(t) = QS_{awake}(t)$. Then by equations (17) and (26),

$$Sy = \begin{cases} Qy & \text{if } x_1 > P \\ 0 & \text{if } x_1 \leq P \end{cases}. \tag{32}$$

By equation (32), Sy is the same for both the choices $S = S_{tonic} = Q$ and $S = QS_{awake}$ when the model is awake. Hence a parametric increase in y causes only a slight increase in α, by the same argument as in Section 8. By contrast with the case treated in Section 8, equation (32) implies that different values of y have no direct effect on the pacemaker during sleep. Thus, other things being equal, increasing the value of y should have little effect on ρ. Since both α and ρ tend to change by only small amounts as y is increased, the net effect of these changes upon $\tau = \alpha + \rho$ can be an increase or a decrease in period, as illustrated by Figure 17. A precise understanding of this situation requires a lengthy analysis. Such an analysis is provided for a formally identical problem concerning Aschoff's rule in Carpenter and Grossberg (1984). The formal relationship between this problem and Aschoff's rule is described in Section 17.

Although an increase in LL causes a decrease in y (Section 12), a decrease in y can cause a decrease or an increase in τ_{DD}. Thus an increase in LL does not cause consistent after-effects on τ_{DD} in a model animal capable of split rhythms.

We now describe a remarkable formal relationship between after-effects and Aschoff's rule. Parametric properties of Aschoff's rule have been extensively analysed in Carpenter and Grossberg (1984). This formal connection enables the Aschoff's rule analysis to be used to explain parametric properties of after-effects.

17. A Formal Connection Between After-Effects and Aschoff's Rule

In its classical form (Aschoff, 1960), Aschoff's rule states that circadian period (τ) is an increasing function of LL in nocturnal animals and a decreasing function of LL in diurnal animals. The related circadian rule states that circadian activity (α) is a decreasing function of LL in nocturnal animals and an increasing function of LL in diurnal animals. The circadian rule has been upheld by many experiments on nocturnal mammals and diurnal mammals. By contrast, although Aschoff's rule consistently holds in nocturnal mammals, many exceptions to the rule have been observed in diurnal mammals (Aschoff, 1979).

TABLE 6

After-Effects on τ_{DD}	Performance Signal	Degree of Light Attenuation	Aschoff's rule in diurnal pacemaker
consistent	$S = Q$	$\theta = 1$	consistent
inconsistent	$S = QS_{awake}$	$\theta = 0$	inconsistent

These experimental properties also arise in gated pacemaker models of diurnal and nocturnal circadian rhythms (Carpenter and Grossberg, 1984). The properties are due to the fact that light excites on-cells of a diurnal pacemaker and off-cells of a nocturnal pacemaker, whereas the fatigue signal excites off-cells in both diurnal and nocturnal pacemakers. The action of fatigue feedback is, in fact, necessary to explain Aschoff's rule in both diurnal and nocturnal pacemakers. An analysis of the interaction between fatigue feedback and the attenuation of light that occurs at the pacemaker during sleep explains both the Aschoff's rule and the circadian rule data. Several behavioral and physiological predictions aimed at testing this explanation are provided in Carpenter and Grossberg (1984), along with analyses of related data.

The formal connection between after-effects and Aschoff's rule can be seen by considering equation $(1d)$ for the on-cell potential x_1 of a diurnal model. Consider term

$$Sy + J \tag{33}$$

in that equation. By equation (13), (33) can be written as

$$Sy + \Theta L, \tag{34}$$

where $L(t)$ is the external light intensity at time t, and

$$\Theta(t) = \begin{cases} 1 & \text{if model is awake} \\ \theta & \text{if model is asleep.} \end{cases} \tag{35}$$

Recall that θ $(0 \leq \theta \leq 1)$ measures the amount of light attenuation at the pacemaker during sleep.

In a constant light condition (LL) and over a time span of a day, both y and L in equation (34) are approximately constant. This fact draws attention to a formal relationship between S and Θ (Table 6). If $\theta = 1$ in equation (35), then $\Theta \equiv$ constant. Similarly, the choice $S = S_{tonic}$ implies $S \equiv$ constant. If $\theta = 0$ in equation (35), then $\Theta = 1$ or 0 depending upon whether the model is awake or asleep. The same is true of S_{awake} in equation (17). Thus Sy influences after-effects on period in a nocturnal model in a manner formally identical to the effect of ΘL on period in a diurnal model exposed to LL.

Due to this correspondence, one expects that the choice $\Theta \equiv 1$ will generate a monotone decreasing dependence of τ on LL in an Aschoff's rule simulation. This graph is shown in Figure 19a. One also expects that choosing $\Theta = 1$ if the model is awake, and 0 if the model is asleep will generate a non-monotonic dependence of τ on LL in an Aschoff's rule simulation. This graph is shown in Figure 19b. This formal correspondence permits the quantitative analysis of Aschoff's rule and its exceptions in Carpenter and Grossberg (1984) to be used to explain consistent and inconsistent after-effects on τ_{DD}.

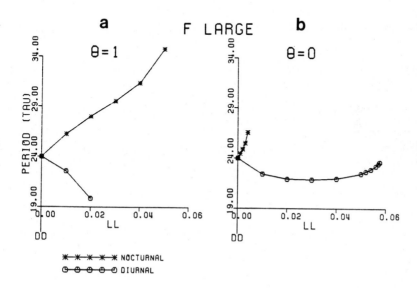

Figure 19. Dependence of Aschoff's rule on light attenuation during sleep: In (a), no light attenuation occurs $(\theta = 1)$. Period (τ) decreases as steady light intensity (LL) increases in the diurnal model; that is, Aschoff's rule holds. In (b), total light attenuation occurs $(\theta = 0)$. Period (τ) is a non-monotonic function of steady light intensity (LL) in the diurnal model (o); that is, Aschoff's rule is violated. In the nocturnal model (×), Aschoff's rule holds whether or not light attenuation occurs.

18. Regulation of Motivated Behavior by Hierarchical Networks: The Homology Between Pacemaker Circuits and Motivational Circuits

Our conception of how pacemaker output modulates motivated behavior is outlined below. This conception joins together properties of the gated pacemaker with properties of neural network models that have been used to explain behavioral, evoked potential, physiological, and pharmacological data concerning reinforcement, drive, motivation, and attention (Grossberg, 1982b, 1982c, 1984a). It also clarifies the sense in which gated pacemaker circuits are formally homologous to motivational gated dipole circuits. We hypothesize that both types of hypothalamic circuits *in vivo* are fashioned out of similar components, albeit in evolutionarily specialized designs.

Figure 20 describes a neural network that has been used to analyse data about motivated behavior. In Figure 20, pathways such as 1 and 2 carry specific, but complementary, drive inputs (e.g., hunger versus satiety) to a single gated dipole circuit.

Pathways labeled 3 carry nonspecific arousal to this, and every, motivational dipole in the network. We hypothesize that the gated pacemaker output modulates the size of the nonspecific arousal input carried by pathway 3. This modulatory action will be described in detail below. In order to clarify how such an action can influence motivated behavior, it is first necessary to describe some of the basic properties of the network in Figure 20.

Cells such as 4 and 5 add up their drive input (pathway 1 or 2) and arousal input (pathway 3) and thereupon inhibit the tonically active cells 6 and 7. (Tonic cells have open symbols; phasic cells have closed symbols.) Pathways $4 \to 6$ and $5 \to 7$ contain slowly accumulating transmitter gates (square synapses) that are assumed to be catecholaminergic. If drive input 1 exceeds drive input 2, then the transmitter in pathway $4 \to 6$ is depleted, or habituated, more than the transmitter in pathway $5 \to 7$. This differential habituation across the competing dipole channels calibrates the dipole for a possible rapid reset, or rebound event, later on.

Before input 1 exceeds input 2, the tonic cells 6 and 7 equally inhibit each other. As soon as input 1 exceeds input 2, cell 6 is inhibited more than cell 7. This imbalance disinhibits tonic cell 8 and further inhibits tonic cell 9. Both cells 8 and 9 are polyvalent, meaning that all their excitatory inputs must be active for these cells to vigorously fire. (Triangles denote polyvalence.) The polyvalent cells are assumed to be pyramidal cells. Because cells 8 and 9 are polyvalent, a larger input to cell 1 than cell 2 is insufficient to fire these cells. However, such an imbalance can prevent cell 9 from firing.

To see how cell 8 can fire, we consider the polyvalent cells, 8 and 10, of two different motivational channels (e.g., hunger versus sex). Cells 8 and 10 compete via the inhibitory pathways 13. The polyvalent cells 8 and 10 also receive inputs from external cue representations via the conditionable pathways 11 and 12, respectively. The long-term memory (LTM) traces of these pathways are computed within the filled hemicircles abutting cells 8 and 10. These LTM traces encode the conditioned reinforcing properties of their respective external cues. For example, a sensory cue that effectively predicts the occurrence of food will have large LTM traces abutting the hunger dipole's polyvalent on-cell population. The LTM traces are assumed to be cholinergic *in vivo* (Grossberg, 1972b).

The conditioned reinforcer inputs combine with drive and arousal inputs at their respective polyvalent cells, which begin to fire if their thresholds are exceeded. The polyvalent cells thereupon compete among themselves via the inter-dipole inhibitory interneurons 13, as they simultaneously try to excite themselves via positive feedback pathways such as $8 \to 4 \to 6 \to 8$.

If, say, cell 8 wins this competition, then its dipole generates incentive motivational output signals that can energize motivationally compatible action patterns. Simultaneously, the transmitter gate in pathway $4 \to 6$ is depleted, or habituated, due to the suprathreshold reverberation bursting through cell 8 via pathway $8 \to 4 \to 6 \to 8$. This reverberation simultaneously causes LTM changes in pathway 11. The reverberation hereby induces conditioned reinforcer changes in its abutting LTM traces even as it prepares the network, via the depleting transmitters, for motivational reset due to subsequent offset of the sensory cues controlling pathway 11.

The conditioned reinforcer pathways 11 and 12 in Figure 20 are formally homologous to the slow gain control pathways in Figures 8 and 12. The satiety input pathway 2 in Figure 20 is homologous to the fatigue feedback pathway in Figure 4. Unconditional reinforcing inputs, such as taste or shock inputs (not pictured in Figure 20), are homologous to the light input in Figure 4. The on-cell and off-cell transmitter gates in pathways $4 \to 6$ and $5 \to 7$ of Figure 20 are homologous to the on-cell and off-cell transmitter gates in Figure 4. In Figure 20, these transmitter gates occur within positive feedback pathways $4 \to 6 \to 8 \to 4$ and $5 \to 7 \to 9 \to 5$. In Figure 4, the gates occur within positive feedback pathways $v_1 \to v_1$ and $v_2 \to v_2$. In Figure 20, dipole competition occurs between cell populations 6 and 7. In Figure 4, dipole competition occurs

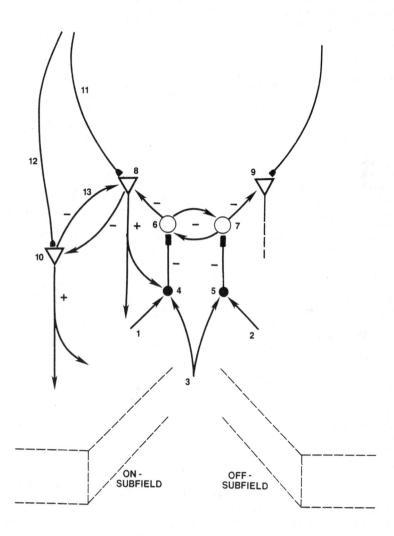

Figure 20. A motivational dipole field: The text describes how individual motivational dipoles are joined together by competitive feedback networks to decide which dipole(s) will reverberate in short-term memory (STM) and thereby release positive or negative incentive motivation in response to the changing balance of reinforcing cue and internal drive signals. The gated pacemaker modulates the sensitivity of this motivational circuit by altering its arousal level (pathway 3).

between v_1 and v_2. Thus, although the gated dipoles in Figures 4 and 20 have been specialized to generate different functional properties, the formal homology that exists between the gated dipoles enables them to be recognized as variations on a common evolutionary design.

19. Circadian Modulation of Sensitivity: Inverted U in Motivational Dipoles

The circuitry in Figure 20 determines which behavioral commands will receive incentive motivational signals through time. The pacemaker modulates how sensitively this circuit responds to its external reinforcer and internal drive inputs, and thus the circuit's ability to energize motivated behavior. The ability of pacemaker output to modulate motivational processing follows from a basic property of gated dipole circuits (Grossberg, 1972b, 1981a, 1984a, 1984b). When a gated dipole's arousal level (pathway 3) is parametrically increased, the outputs of the dipole are altered according to an inverted U law: dipole outputs are depressed in response to input signals if the arousal level is chosen either too low or too high. The dipole optimally responds to phasic inputs at intermediate arousal levels.

We hypothesize that the pacemaker causes a circadian oscillation to occur in the arousal level of motivational circuits. The inverted U property of the gated dipoles in motivational circuits prevents these dipoles from reacting when their arousal level is too high or too low. Behaviors that require motivational signals for their execution will thus not be emitted if the circadian output is too high or too low (Grossberg, 1972b, 1981a, 1982c, 1984a). We hypothesize that, under normal conditions, the arousal level during the wakeful state brings motivational dipoles into the middle range of their inverted U.

It remains to discuss whether the arousal level becomes smaller ("underarousal") or larger ("overarousal") during sleep than it is during the wakeful state. We hypothesize that underarousal occurs during sleep. This hypothesis is based upon the following property of gated dipoles in the underaroused state. During underarousal, the threshold intensity that an input must exceed to generate an output signal is significantly raised. The network will not react to many inputs that would cause a reaction during the wakeful state. If, however, an input is sufficiently intense to exceed this elevated threshold, then the dipole output is hypersensitive to the input; that is, suprathreshold increments in the input cause larger than normal increments in dipole output. Thus a dipole that is underaroused during sleep can react to intense inputs. An overaroused dipole, by contrast, does not react to inputs of any intensity.

Gated dipoles have been hypothesized to occur in circuits that carry out perceptual and cognitive processing (Grossberg, 1978, 1980, 1984a, 1985a). Circadian oscillation of the nonspecific arousal signal to these circuits can also modulate their sensitivity during the wake-sleep cycle.

20. The Underaroused and Overaroused Depressive Syndromes

From the perspective of the circadian wake-sleep cycle, the inverted U property of a gated dipole is a valuable one. This property also creates the danger that the arousal level may be improperly chosen during the wakeful state. Symptoms of mental disorders have been interpreted, and indeed predicted, using the formal syndromes of functional properties that obtain in underaroused and overaroused gated dipoles. These disorders include juvenile hyperactivity, Parkinsonism, hypothalamic hyperphagia, and simple schizophrenia (Grossberg, 1972b, 1984a, 1984b). An unsolved problem of fundamental importance is to determine how the circadian pacemaker is calibrated to select an arousal level in the normal range during the wakeful state.

The hypothesis that motivational circuits are underaroused during sleep can be experimentally tested. For example, gated dipole dynamics predict the existence of a transitional period just before and/or after sleep when behavioral thresholds and suprathreshold sensitivities, suitably defined, are both elevated.

It remains to discuss how the arousal level in pathway 3 of Figure 20 is modulated by the pacemaker. Is this modulatory action excitatory, inhibitory, or disinhibitory? Total ablation of the SCN does not put an animal to sleep (Stephan and Zucker, 1972). Correspondingly, in Figure 20 the pacemaker cannot be the sole agent of a direct excitatory effect on pathway 3. Two alternative hypotheses are compatible with the data:

(1) Pacemaker output disinhibits a population of tonically active arousal cells which, in turn, excite pathway 3. To model this property, suppose that pacemaker on-cell output inhibits cells which inhibit the tonically active arousal cells, or that pacemaker off-cell output inhibits the tonically active arousal cells.

(2) Pacemaker output both excites and inhibits the population of tonic cells which activate pathway 3. To model this property, let pacemaker on-cell output add to the tonically active level, and pacemaker off-cell output subtract from the tonic level. The tonic level defines a baseline that can be calibrated to ensure that the motivational dipoles are neither underaroused nor overaroused during the wakeful state.

21. Anticipatory Wheel Turning, Ultradian Feeding Cycles, and After-Effects of a Single Pulse of Light

When a gated pacemaker circuit, as in Figure 4, is joined to a motivational circuit, as in Figure 20, then light can influence the total circuit along several distinct pathways. As an input to the pacemaker, light can act as an external Zeitgeber, as in equations $(1d)$ or $(2n)$, and as a presynaptic gate of slow gain control sensitivity, as in equations (24) or (25). As an input to the motivational circuit, light can act as a reinforcing cue via pathways such as 11 and 12 in Figure 20.

In much of the circadian literature, reinforcing actions of external cues such as light are not explicitly analysed. In situations where light is left on for long periods of time, one can argue that reinforcing factors are less important than circadian factors due to the long time scale of the light-mediated events. Even in cases where light does act like a negative conditioned reinforcer within a nocturnal model, its suppressive effects as a conditioned reinforcer (Grossberg, 1972a, 1972b, 1982c) can often parallel its suppressive effects as a Zeitgeber. These two actions of light may be difficult to dissociate.

It is less easy to ignore the reinforcing action of light in the explanation of behaviors that can be induced on a single trial, or behaviors that are anticipatory in nature. Under these circumstances, reinforcement mechanisms may interact with circadian mechanisms in a complex fashion. For example, in the generation of after-effects by a single intense pulse of light (Pittendrigh, 1960), light may act as a punishing stimulus in addition to acting like a Zeitgeber. Such a punishing event may influence the conditioned reinforcing properties of situational cues in a manner that is difficult to determine without experimental controls. A change in the conditioned reinforcing properties of situational cues could, in turn, phase shift or otherwise change the animal's behavioral repertoire.

In a similar fashion, the eating cycle can be phase shifted by presenting food-related conditioned reinforcing cues. The direct phase-shifting action of these cues can phase shift the onset of the satiety signal. The phase-shifted satiety signal can, in turn, help to phase shift the subsequent eating cycle. This is because the satiety signal can maintain an ultradian eating cycle, even in the absence of a circadian pacemaker, just so long as food and other reinforcers are constantly available.

These remarks indicate the need to join together concepts about circadian rhythms with concepts about reinforcement and motivated behavior. The properties of gated dipole circuits provide a formal language with which to expedite this synthesis.

22. Intracellular Gated Dipoles: Photoreceptors and Pacemakers

The discussion in Sections 19 and 20 shows that the formal properties of gated dipole circuits may be specialized to generate different behavioral properties. This section points out that the same formal gated dipole circuit can, in principle, be realized biologically in many different ways. To build the basic pacemaker of Figure 4, all one needs are opponent processes, habituating transmitter gates, a tonic metabolic source, and appropriately wired feedback pathways. All of these requirements can be met at an early phylogenetic stage. Moreover, all of these requirements can, in principle, be realized within a single cell. The opponent processes can be realized by opponent membrane channels in a single cell, in the same way that an Na^+ channel and a K^+ channel are opponent channels in a membrane equation (Carpenter, 1981; Grossberg, 1981b). Transmitter gating actions can modulate the sensitivity of these membrane channels on a slow time scale.

Carpenter and Grossberg (1981, 1983a) have, in fact, quantitatively simulated parametric data taken from isolated vertebrate photoreceptors using a gated dipole model of the internal transmitter that exists within a single photoreceptor cell. This intracellular transmitter process mediates the transduction of photons into electrical potential (Baylor and Hodgkin, 1974; Baylor, Hodgkin, and Lamb, 1974a, 1974b). The entire gated dipole circuit is hypothesized to occur within a single photoreceptor cell. Spontaneous oscillations do not occur within this model because its circuit is designed to sensitively react to phasic fluctuations in light intensity. A comparison of this gated photoreceptor circuit with a gated pacemaker circuit suggests several ways that a single photoreceptor circuit can be transformed into a pacemaker circuit, or how two or more photoreceptor circuits can be coupled to form a pacemaker circuit.

These formal connections between photoreceptor and circadian models suggest a potentially important new tool for comparative neurological and biochemical studies in this area, since circadian pacemakers exist within certain retinas, such as the *Aplysia* retina (Jacklet, 1969), and the pineal organ, which may be the circadian pacemaker site in birds, is also photoreceptive (Menaker, 1974). In the vertebrate photoreceptor, a Ca^{++} current plays the role of the gating transmitter. It remains to be seen whether a Ca^{++} current plays a gating role in certain primitive circadian pacemakers.

23. Comparison With Other Models

Many circadian models have focused on the coupling and phasing of two or more oscillators. In these models, the individual pacemakers are chosen for convenience and simplicity, but do not admit a detailed physiological interpretation. For example, the Kronauer *et al.* (1982) and Wever (1962, 1975) models consist of a pair of equations of van der Pol type. The model of Kawato and Suzuki (1980) consists of a pair of coupled FitzHugh-Nagumo equations. As Kawato and Suzuki have noted: "the BVP [van der Pol] equations and Nagumo's equation were derived for neural rhythms with much shorter periods than 24h. However, in the absence of information regarding the state variables relevant to circadian pacemakers, we use the abstract model" (p.557). The model of Daan and Berde (1978) describes a pacemaker entirely in terms of its period, phase, and phase shifts. Enright (1980) develops a quasi-neural model in terms of stochastic variables such as the average durations of the discharge phase and the recovery phase, and the amount by which an internal Zeitgeber shortens the average recovery phase. The relationship of the Enright (1980) model to the gated pacemaker model is discussed in detail by Carpenter and Grossberg (1984).

Our analysis complements these contributions concerning the coupling of formal oscillators by explicating the dynamics of a single pacemaker. Figures 4a and 4b, in particular, do not describe coupled oscillators, but a single oscillator which is hypothesized to occur in many copies within each SCN. Those results about coupled oscillators which are insensitive to the detailed properties of the individual oscillators will carry over to the case where gated pacemakers are the oscillators to be coupled.

Our results indicate, however, that many properties, such as split rhythms and after-effects, which have heretofore been assumed to require coupling between oscillators can be explained by internal properties of a single oscillator. We also suggest a new explanation of the effects of parametric and nonparametric lighting regimes. These claims do not deny the existence of coupling between distinct sleep and temperature systems (Kronauer et al., 1982; Wever, 1979). Nor do they deny the existence of distinct pacemakers in each SCN that may, under certain circumstances, drift out-of-phase. Rather we show how data properties which cannot be explained by classical oscillators unless they are allowed to drift out-of-phase can be explained by a population of gated pacemaker oscillators that remain in-phase. At the very least, our results point out those areas where further argument is needed to conclude that a coupling between out-of-phase oscillators generates a data property.

Previous circadian models explain split rhythms by describing how two oscillators, or two populations of oscillators, can drift out-of-phase under certain conditions (Daan and Berde, 1978; Enright, 1980; Kawato and Suzuki, 1980; Pavlidis, 1973; Pittendrigh, 1960; Pittendrigh and Daan, 1976b; Wever, 1984; Winfree, 1967). Models of this type simulate after-effects as long-term transients that persist subsequent to initial phasing differences between constituent oscillators (Daan and Berde, 1978; Enright, 1980). The long-term nature of these transients is due to the weakness of the coupling whereby constituent oscillators mutually influence each other. None of these approaches provides a unified explanation of the data base that the gated pacemaker model has simulated in this and previous articles.

A notable difficulty arises in simulating both parametric (LL) and nonparametric (LD) after-effects (Section 3). For example, the sequence of models developed by Pittendrigh (1974), Pittendrigh and Daan (1976b), and Daan and Berde (1978) assumes that separate mechanisms process parametric and nonparametric lighting regimes. A parametric lighting regime induces a change in model parameters, such as oscillator periods or coupling strengths. In a nonparametric lighting regime, light onset or offset phase-resets both of the model oscillators, but has no effect on model parameters. In Section 2, we noted that all lighting regimes are nonparametric at the pacemaker. In the Daan and Berde (1978) model, by contrast, internal light onset and offset due to waking and sleeping in LL have no phase-resetting properties (p.305), and the 18 hours of light experienced during LD 18:6 have no effects on model parameters (p.309). By extension, LD 23:9:0.1 would have no effects on model parameters, but LL≡LD 24:0 would.

Many of the difficulties that arise when classical oscillators are used to model circadian data are eliminated by using the physiologically motivated gated pacemaker design. Future work may show that a synthesis of recent concepts concerning physiologically characterized individual oscillators with classical concepts concerning the phasing of oscillators may explain an even larger data base. For example, in our explanation of split rhythms, a reduction in the level of fatigue feedback occurs in LL. This reduction could allow individual gated pacemakers to drift out-of-phase, in a manner more in tune with other explanations. Simulations of gated pacemaker populations may shed further light on the transitional activity patterns which occur prior to a fully split rhythm.

Independent of such considerations, the gated pacemaker model introduces several types of processes into the circadian literature which may prove to be important in future theories: a possible role for chemical gating actions and on-cell off-cell interactions in a circadian pacemaker, homeostatic ultradian feedback signals, slowly gating nonhomeostatic feedback signals, and rapidly acting nonhomeostatic signals, such as light, whose mode of action upon the pacemaker is distinguished from their strength at the environmental source.

APPENDIX

Choice of Parameters

This section describes the parameter choices that were used in the nocturnal model equations $(1n)$, $(2n)$, (3)–(6). These equations are already almost in dimensionless form (Lin and Segel, 1974). In general, converting a full system of equations to dimensionless form eliminates as many parameters as there are dependent and independent variables. The nocturnal model contains six dependent variables $(x_1, x_2, z_1, z_2, F, y)$ and one independent variable (t). The nocturnal model equations already contain six fewer parameters than could have been used to describe this system. Coefficients have been eliminated in front of the terms $f(x_1)z_1$ and $g(x_2)$ in equation $(1n)$, the terms $f(x_2)z_2$, F, and $g(x_1)$ in equation $(2n)$, and term V in equation (6). Recall that the functions f, g, and V are all scaled to vary between 0 and 1. It remains to eliminate one more parameter. Dimensional analysis of the nocturnal model shows that the parameter A can be used to fix the time scale of the model. Thus some model parameters are expressed below as multiples of A. These multiples contain physical information about relative sizes and speeds. A fixed choice of A determines the time scale without altering these relative relationships.

Alternate versions of the model were used for illustrative purposes in Figures 1b and 5. In all other simulations described in the article, the following parameters were always constant ratios of A:

$$B = 5A, \tag{A1}$$

$$C = 0.5A, \tag{A2}$$

$$D = 0.01A, \tag{A3}$$

$$E = 0.4, \tag{A4}$$

$$H = 0.02, \tag{A5}$$

$$I = 0.1A, \tag{A6}$$

$$K = 0.17A, \tag{A7}$$

$$N = 0.72A, \tag{A8}$$

$$P = 0.665A, \tag{A9}$$

$$R = 0.0001A, \tag{A10}$$

$$W = 100A^{-1}, \tag{A11}$$

$$\theta = 0.5. \tag{A12}$$

Carpenter and Grossberg (1983b) provide a detailed analysis of how parameters can be chosen within a wide parameter range to generate physically plausible oscillations in the absence of fatigue and slow gain control. This 4-dimensional system is called the basic gated pacemaker. Our focus in the present article has been to understand how the fatigue and slow gain control processes modulate the properties of the basic gated pacemaker. We therefore chose the relative sizes of the equations $(A1)$–$(A12)$ once and for all based on the Carpenter and Grossberg (1983b) analysis and focused our attention upon how to choose fatigue and slow gain control parameters. Other parametric ranges in Carpenter and Grossberg (1983b) could also have been used to generate similar results.

The following relative sizes are physically important in the model. By equations $(A1)$ and $(A2)$,

$$C/B = 0.1. \tag{A13}$$

In equations $(1n)$ and $(2n)$, parameters B and C are the excitatory saturation point (V_{Na}) and inhibitory saturation point (V_K) of their respective potentials. The ratio $V_K/V_{Na} \cong 0.1$ in many cells (Hodgkin and Huxley, 1952). The ratio

$$K/A = 0.17 \cong \frac{1}{6} \qquad (A14)$$

in equation $(A7)$ is also physically interesting. By equation (5), equation $(A7)$ says that fatigue decays on an ultradian time scale of approximately $1/6$ of a day. By equations $(A8)$ and $(A9)$, the activity threshold N is always chosen larger than the sleep threshold P.

Carpenter and Grossberg (1983b) show that the order of magnitude of the circadian period in the basic gated pacemaker is $1/D$. By equations $(A3)$ and $(A10)$,

$$R/D = 0.01. \qquad (A15)$$

Parameter R is the decay rate of the slow gain control process y in equations (18), (24), and (27)–(29). By equation $(A15)$, y decays on a time scale of months $(\cong 100$ days$)$.

Parameter W in equation $(A11)$ was chosen large so that light significantly attenuates S_{light} in equation (23). Choosing parameter $\theta = 0.5$ in equation $(A12)$ says that a 50% attenuation of light intensity occurs during sleep, due to equation (13).

All the parameters in equations $(A1)$–$(A12)$ are specified by a choice of the single parameter A. In all the after-effect simulations, we chose

$$A = \frac{113}{24} \cong 4.7083. \qquad (A16)$$

In all the split rhythm simulations, we chose

$$A = \frac{144}{24} = 6. \qquad (A17)$$

These choices of A determine the time scale in hours. This conclusion follows from the fact, demonstrated in Carpenter and Grossberg (1983b), that the order of magnitude of the *dimensionless* circadian period in the basic gated pacemaker is A/D. By equation $(A3)$,

$$A/D = 100. \qquad (A18)$$

Since the order of magnitude of the circadian period in equations (1)–(6) is $1/D$, to get $1/D \cong 24$ hours, it follows by equation $(A18)$ that choices of $A \cong 100/24$, as in equations $(A16)$ and $(A17)$, determine the unit of time to be hours.

Only parameters M and Q remain to be specified. The choice of M in equation (8) determines the magnitude of the fatigue signal in equations (2) and (5). In all after-effect simulations, we chose

$$M = 0.01A. \qquad (A19)$$

In all split rhythm simulations, we chose

$$M = 0.028A. \qquad (A20)$$

Parameter Q determines the magnitude of the performance signal S in equation (1). In all split rhythm simulations, $S = QS_{awake}$, and we chose

$$Q = 6.4 \times 10^{-6}A. \qquad (A21)$$

In the after-effect simulations, we showed that more than one choice of S could simulate the data. For the gain control process defined by equations (14)–(16) and shown in Figure 13, we chose

$$Q = 1.4 \times 10^{-6}A. \qquad (A22)$$

For both of the other gain control processes used to simulate after-effects (Figure 16), we chose

$$Q = 2.8 \times 10^{-6}A. \qquad (A23)$$

In equation (13), the light $L(t)$ is either on or off. "Bright light" is experimentally defined to be an intensity somewhat less than the intensity at which wheel turning ceases in constant light (LL). We chose light intensity in a similar way by using intensities somewhat smaller than those intensities at which $x_1(t)$ remains less than the activity threshold of N in LL.

It remains only to say how the initial data of x_1, x_2, z_2, F, and y were chosen at time $t = 0$. The simulations were insensitive to the initial values of x_1, x_2, z_1, z_2, and F. Due to its slow time scale, $y(0)$ was chosen in each case at its equilibrium value in the dark (DD).

REFERENCES

Aschoff, J., Zeitgeber der tierischen Jahresperiodik. *Naturwissenschaften*, 1954, **41**, 49 -56.

Aschoff, J., Exogenous and endogenous components in circadian rhythms. *Cold Spring Harbor Symposium on Quantitative Biology*, 1960, **25**, 11–28.

Aschoff, J., Influences of internal and external factors on the period measured in constant conditions. *Z. Tierpsychologie*, 1979, **49**, 225–249.

Baylor, D.A. and Hodgkin, A.L., Changes in time scale and sensitivity in turtle photoreceptors. *Journal of Physiology*, 1974, **242**, 729–758.

Baylor, D.A., Hodgkin, A.L., and Lamb, T.D., The electrical response of turtle cones to flashes and steps of light. *Journal of Physiology*, 1974, **242**, 685–727 (a).

Baylor, D.A., Hodgkin, A.L., and Lamb, T.D., Reconstruction of the electrical responses of turtle cones to flashes and steps of light. *Journal of Physiology*, 1974, **242**, 759–791 (b).

Borbély, A.A., A two process model of sleep regulation. *Human Neurobiology*, 1982, **1**, 195–204.

Card, J.P., Riley, J.N., and Moore, R.Y., The suprachiasmatic hypothalamic nucleus: Ultrastructure of relations to optic chiasm. *Neuroscience Abstracts*, 1980, **6**, 758.

Carpenter, G.A., Normal and abnormal signal patterns in nerve cells. In S. Grossberg (Ed.), **Mathematical psychology and psychophysiology**. Providence, RI: American Mathematical Society, 1981, 49–90.

Carpenter, G.A., A comparative analysis of structure and chaos in models of single nerve cells and circadian rhythms. In E. Basar, H. Flohr, H. Haken, and A.J. Mandell (Eds.), **Synergetics of the brain**. New York: Springer-Verlag, 1983, 311–329.

Carpenter, G.A. and Grossberg, S., Adaptation and transmitter gating in vertebrate photoreceptors. *Journal of Theoretical Neurobiology*, 1981, **1**, 1–42.

Carpenter, G.A. and Grossberg, S., A chemical gating theory of circadian rhythms. *Neuroscience Abstracts*, 1982, **8**, 546.

Carpenter, G.A. and Grossberg, S., Dynamic models of neural systems: Propagated signals, photoreceptor transduction, and circadian rhythms. In J.P.E. Hodgson (Ed.), **Oscillations in mathematical biology**. New York: Springer-Verlag, 1983, 102–196 (a).

Carpenter, G.A. and Grossberg, S., A neural theory of circadian rhythms: The gated pacemaker. *Biological Cybernetics*, 1983, **48**, 35–59 (b).

Carpenter, G.A. and Grossberg, S., A neural theory of circadian rhythms: Aschoff's rule in diurnal and nocturnal mammals. *American Journal of Physiology*, 1984, **247**, R1067–R1082.

Czeisler, C.A., Weitzman, E.D., Moore-Ede, M.C., Zimmerman, J.C., and Kronauer, R.S., Human sleep: Its duration and organization depend on its circadian phase. *Science*, 1980, **210**, 1264–1267.

Daan, S. and Berde, C., Two coupled oscillators: Simulations of the circadian pacemaker in mammalian activity rhythms. *Journal of Theoretical Biology*, 1978, **70**, 297–313.

Daan, S. and Pittendrigh, C.S., A functional analysis of circadian pacemakers in nocturnal rodents, II: The variability of phase response curves. *Journal of Comparative Physiology*, 1976, **106**, 253–266.

DeCoursey, P.J., Phase control of activity in a rodent. *Cold Spring Harbor Symposium on Quantitative Biology*, 1960, **25**, 49–55.

Earnest, D. and Turek, F.W., Splitting of the circadian rhythm of activity in hamsters: Effects of exposure to constant darkness and subsequent re-exposure to constant light. *Journal of Comparative Physiology*, 1982, **145**, 405–411.

Earnest, D. and Turek, F.W., Phase shifting and entrainment of the hamster circadian system: Role for acetylcholine in mediating the effects of light. *Neuroscience Abstracts*, 1983, **9**, 626.

Enright, J.T., **The timing of sleep and wakefulness**. New York: Springer-Verlag, 1980.

Green, D.J. and Gillette, R., Circadian rhythm of firing rate recorded from single cells in the rat suprachiasmatic brain slice. *Brain Research*, 1982, **245**, 198–200.

Groos, G.A., The neurophysiology of the mammalian suprachiasmatic nucleus and its visual afferents. In J. Aschoff, S. Daan, and G.A. Groos (Eds.), **Vertebrate circadian systems**. New York: Springer-Verlag, 1982, 96–105.

Groos, G.A. and Hendricks, J., Regularly firing neurons in the rat suprachiasmatic nucleus. *Experientia*, 1979, **35**, 1597–1598.

Groos, G.A. and Hendricks, J., Circadian rhythms in electrical discharge of rat suprachiasmatic neurons recorded *in vitro*. *Neuroscience Letters*, 1982, **34**, 283–288.

Groos, G.A. and Mason, R., Maintained discharge of rat suprachiasmatic neurons at different adaptation levels. *Neuroscience Letters*, 1978, **8**, 59–64.

Groos, G.A. and Mason, R., The visual properties of rat and cat suprachiasmatic neurons. *Journal of Comparative Physiology*, 1980, **135**, 349–356.

Grossberg, S., Some physiological and biochemical consequences of psychological postulates. *Proceedings of the National Academy of Sciences*, 1968, **60**, 758–765.

Grossberg, S., On the production and release of chemical transmitters and related topics in cellular control. *Journal of Theoretical Biology*, 1969, **22**, 325–364.

Grossberg, S., A neural theory of punishment and avoidance, I: Qualitative theory. *Mathematical Biosciences*, 1972, **15**, 39–67 (a).

Grossberg, S., A neural theory of punishment and avoidance, II: Quantitative theory. *Mathematical Biosicences*, 1972, **15**, 253–285 (b).

Grossberg, S., A neural model of attention, reinforcement, and discrimination learning. *International Review of Neurobiology*, 1975, **18**, 263–327.

Grossberg, S., A theory of human memory: Self-organization and performance of sensory-motor codes, maps, and plans. In R. Rosen and F. Snell (Eds.), **Progress in theoretical biology**, Vol. 5. New York: Academic Press, 1978, 233–374.

Grossberg, S., How does a brain build a cognitive code? *Psychological Review*, 1980, **87**, 1–51.

Grossberg, S., Psychophysiological substrates of schedule interactions and behavioral contrast. In S. Grossberg (Ed.), **Mathematical psychology and psychophysiology**. Providence, RI: American Mathematical Society, 1981, 157–186 (a).

Grossberg, S., Adaptive resonance in development, perception, and cognition. In S. Grossberg (Ed.), **Mathematical psychology and psychophysiology**. Providence, RI: American Mathematical Society, 1981, 107–156 (b).

Grossberg, S., **Studies of mind and brain: Neural principles of learning, perception, development, cognition, and motor control**. Boston: Reidel Press, 1982 (a).

Grossberg, S., The processing of expected and unexpected events during conditioning and attention: A psychophysiological theory. *Psychological Review*, 1982, **89**, 529–572 (b).

Grossberg, S., A psychophysiological theory of reinforcement, drive, motivation, and attention. *Journal of Theoretical Neurobiology*, 1982, **1**, 286–369 (c).

Grossberg, S., Some psychophysiological and pharmacological correlates of a developmental, cognitive, and motivational theory. In R. Karrer, J. Cohen, and P. Tueting (Eds.), **Brain and information: Event related potentials.** New York: New York Academy of Sciences, 1984, 58–151 (a).

Grossberg, S., Some normal and abnormal behavioral syndromes due to transmitter gating of opponent processes. *Biological Psychiatry*, 1984, **19**, 1075–1118 (b).

Grossberg, S., The adaptive self-organization of serial order in behavior: Speech, language, and motor control. In E.C. Schwab and H.C. Nusbaum (Eds.), **Pattern recognition by humans and machines**, Vol. 1. New York: Academic Press, 1985 (a).

Grossberg, S., The hypothalamic control of eating and circadian rhythms: Opponent processes and their chemical modulators. In L. Rensing (Ed.), **Temporal order.** New York: Springer-Verlag, 1985 (b).

Gwinner, E., Testosterone induces "splitting" of circadian locomotor activity rhythm in birds. *Science*, 1974, **185**, 72–74.

Hedberg, T.G. and Moore-Ede, M.C., Circadian rhythmicity in multiple-unit activity of rat hypothalamic slice. *Neuroscience Abstracts*, 1983, **9**, 1068.

Hodgkin, A.L., **The conduction of the nervous impulse.** Liverpool: Liverpool University Press, 1964.

Hodgkin, A.L. and Huxley, A.F., A quantitative description of membrane current and its application to conduction and excitation in nerve. *Journal of Physiology*, 1952, **117**, 500–544.

Hoffman, K., Splitting of the circadian rhythm as a function of light intensity. In M. Menaker (Ed.), **Biochronometry**, pp.134–150. Washington, DC: National Academy of Sciences, 1971.

Inouye, S.T. and Kawamura, H., Persistence of circadian rhythmicity in a mammalian hypothalamic "island" containing the suprachiasmatic nucleus. *Proceedings of the National Academy of Sciences*, 1979, **76**, 5962–5966.

Iuvone, P.M., Besharse, J.C., and Dunis, D.A., Evidence for a circadian clock in the eye controlling retinal serotonin n-acetyltransferase and photoreceptor disc shedding. . *Neuroscience Abstracts*, 1983, **9**, 624.

Jacklet, J.W., Circadian rhythm of optic nerve impulses recorded in darkness from isolated eye of *Aplysia*. *Science*, 1969, **164**, 562–563.

Katz, B., **Nerve, muscle, and synapse.** New York: McGraw-Hill, 1966.

Kawato, M. and Suzuki, R., Two coupled neural oscillators as a model of the circadian pacemaker. *Journal of Theoretical Biology*, 1980, **86**, 547–575.

Kramm, K.R., Circadian activity in the antelope ground squirrel *Ammospermophilus leucurus*. Ph.D. Thesis, University of California at Irvine, 1971.

Kronauer, R.E., Czeisler, C.A., Pilato, S.F., Moore-Ede, M.C., and Weitzman, E.D., Mathematical model of the human circadian system with two interacting oscillators. *American Journal of Physiology*, 1982, **242**, R3–R17.

Kuffler, S.W. and Nicholls, J.G., **From neuron to brain.** Sunderland, MA: Sinauer Press, 1976.

Lin, C.C. and Segel, L.A., **Mathematics applied to deterministic problems in the natural sciences.** New York: Macmillan, 1974.

Lincoln, D.W., Church, J., and Mason, C.A., Electrophysiological activation of suprachiasmatic neurones by changes in retinal illumination. *Acta Endocrinologica*, 1975, **199**, 184.

Menaker, M., Aspects of the physiology of circadian rhythmicity in the vertebrate central nervous system. In C.S. Pittendrigh (Ed.), **Circadian oscillations and** organization in the nervous system. Cambridge, MA: MIT Press, 1974, pp.479–489.

Moore, R.Y., Retinohypothalamic projection in mammals: A comparative study. *Brain Research*, 1973, **49**, 403–409.

Moore, R.Y., Visual pathways and the central control of diurnal rhythms. In C.S. Pittendrigh (Ed.), **Circadian oscillations and organization in nervous systems.** Cambridge, MA: MIT Press, 1974, pp.537–542.

Moore, R.Y., Card, J.P., and Riley, J.N., The suprachiasmatic hypothalamic nucleus: Neuronal ultrastructure. *Neuroscience Abstracts*, 1980, **6**, 758.

Moore, R.Y. and Eichler, V.B., Loss of a circadian adrenal corticosterone rhythm following suprachiasmatic lesions in the rat. *Brain Research*, 1972, **42**, 201–206.

Moore-Ede, M.C., Sulzman, F.M., and Fuller, C.A., **The clocks that time us.** Cambridge, MA: Harvard University Press, 1982.

Nishino, H., Koizumi, K., and Brooks, C.M., The role of suprachiasmatic nuclei of the hypothalamus in the production of circadian rhythm. *Brain Research*, 1976, **112**, 45–59.

Olds, J., **Drives and reinforcements: Behavioral studies of hypothalamic functions.** New York: Raven Press, 1977.

Pavlidis, T., **Biological oscillators: Their mathematical analysis.** New York: Academic Press, 1973.

Pickard, G.E. and Turek, F.W., Splitting of the circadian rhythm of activity is abolished by unilateral lesions of the suprachiasmatic nuclei. *Science*, 1982, **215**, 1119–1121.

Pittendrigh, C.S., Circadian rhythms and the circadian organization of living systems. *Cold Spring Harbor Symposium Quantitative Biology*, 1960, **25**, 159–185.

Pittendrigh, C.S., Circadian oscillations in cells and the circadian organization of multicellular systems. In C.S. Pittendrigh (Ed.), **Circadian oscillations and organization in nervous systems.** Cambridge, MA: MIT Press, 1974.

Pittendrigh, C.S. and Daan, S., A functional analysis of circadian pacemakers in nocturnal rodents, I: The stability and lability of spontaneous frequency. *Journal of Comparative Physiology*, 1976, **106**, 223–252 (a).

Pittendrigh, C.S. and Daan, S., A functional analysis of circadian pacemakers in nocturnal rodents, V: Pacemaker structure: A clock for all seasons. *Journal of Comparative Physiology*, 1976, **106**, 333–355 (b).

Pittendrigh, C.S. and Minis, D.H., The entrainment of circadian oscillations by light and their role as photoperiodic clocks. *American Naturalist*, 1964, **98**, 261–294.

Plonsey, R., **Bioelectric phenomena.** New York: McGraw Hill, 1969.

Pohl, H., Characteristics and variability in entrainment of circadian rhythms in light in diurnal rodents. In J. Aschoff, S. Daan, and G.A. Groos (Eds.), **Vertebrate circadian systems.** Berlin: Springer-Verlag, 1982, pp.339–346.

Sato, T. and Kawamura, H., Circadian rhythms in multiple unit activity inside and outside the suprachiasmatic nucleus in the diurnal chipmunk (*Eutamias sibiricus*). *Neuroscience Research*, 1984, **1**, 45–52.

Schwartz, W.J., Davidsen, L.C., and Smith, C.B., *In vivo* metabolic activity of a putative circadian oscillator, the rat suprachiasmatic nucleus. *Journal of Comparative Neurology*, 1980, **189**, 157–167.

Schwartz, W.J. and Gainer, H., Suprachiasmatic nucleus: Use of ^{14}C-labeled deoxyglucose uptake as a functional marker. *Science*, 1977, **197**, 1089–1091.

Schwartz, W.J., Reppert, S.M., Eagan, S.M., and Moore-Ede, M.C., *In vivo* metabolic activity of the suprachiasmatic nuclei: A comparative study. *Brain Research*, 1983, **274**, 184–187.

Shibata, S., Oomura, Y., Kita, H., and Hattori, K., Circadian rhythmic changes of neuronal activity in the suprachiasmatic nucleus of the rat hypothalamic slice. *Brain Research*, 1982, **247**, 154–158.

Stephan, F.Y. and Zucker, I., Circadian rhythms in drinking behavior and locomotor activity of rats are eliminated by hypothalamic lesions. *Proceedings of the National Academy of Sciences*, 1972, **69**, 1583–1586.

Terman, M. and Terman, J., Circadian rhythm of luminance detectability in the rat: Independence from SCN pacemaker. *Neuroscience Abstracts*, 1983, **9**, 1071.

Wever, R.A., Zum Mechanismus der biologischen 24-Stunden-Periodik. *Kybernetik*, 1962, **1**, 139–154.

Wever, R.A., The circadian multi-oscillator system of man. *International Journal of Chronobiology*, 1975, **3**, 19–55.

Wever, R.A., **The circadian system of man: Results of experiments under temporal isolation.** New York: Springer-Verlag, 1979.

Wever, R.A., Toward a mathematical model of circadian rhythmicity. In M.C. Moore-Ede and C.A. Czeisler (Eds.), **Mathematical models of the circadian sleep-wake cycle.** New York: Raven Press, 1984, pp.17–77.

Winfree, A.T., Biological rhythms and the behavior of populations of coupled oscillators. *Journal of Theoretical Biology*, 1967, **16**, 15–42.

Chapter 9

ASSOCIATIVE AND COMPETITIVE PRINCIPLES OF LEARNING
AND DEVELOPMENT: THE TEMPORAL UNFOLDING
AND STABILITY OF STM AND LTM PATTERNS

Preface

This Chapter reviews some of the mathematical systems and theorems that arose through analyses of data in a variety of behavioral and neural experimental paradigms. Included are systems and theorems about associative list learning; associative spatial pattern learning; absolutely stable cooperative-competitive decision making and memory storage; and feature discovery, category learning, and pattern recognition by competitive learning networks. A historical mode of exposition has been adopted in order to help bridge the years of specialized investigations in which these theorems were embedded.

Such theorems provide a secure foundation for using in specialized circuits the general learning, recognition, and decision-making mechanisms that they characterize. At the time that the theorems were proved, few workers in the mind and brain sciences appreciated the important role which a mathematical analysis plays in the identification of good physical laws. No one who has succeeded in proving a global limit or oscillation theorem about a nonlinear feedback system with arbitrarily many variables takes the system whose nice properties have admitted such an analysis for granted. By now, mathematical studies of mind and brain have led to the discovery of one of the larger sets of global theorems about nonlinear feedback systems in any number of variables of any scientific discipline. This fact argues against the oft-made claim that neural network theory is still in its infancy.

Armed with such a mathematical understanding, a theorist is much better equipped to successfully carry out quantitative computer simulations of difficult behavioral and neural data. A mathematical understanding also quickly enables one to spot points of weakness in models which seem to work well in a limited domain of applications. Finally, a mathematical understanding enables one to distinguish those model properties which are essentially model-independent or well-understood from properties which add key new elements to the modeling literature.

A study of this mathematical literature reveals that a surprising number of neural models, concepts, and methods which are introduced today as major new contributions are recapitulating results which have been well-known in the neural modeling literature for some time. Since many more people are introducing neural network models today than in the past, this may be an unpopular conclusion, but it is true nonetheless and must be reckoned with to properly appreciate the proven richness of this field, and to enable truly new discoveries to be easily identified and developed.

Competition and Cooperation in Neural Nets
S. Amari and M. Arbib (Eds.)
Lecture Notes in Biomathematics **45**: 295 341 (1982)
©1982 Springer-Verlag, Inc.
Reprinted by permission of the publisher

ASSOCIATIVE AND COMPETITIVE PRINCIPLES OF LEARNING

AND DEVELOPMENT: THE TEMPORAL UNFOLDING

AND STABILITY OF STM AND LTM PATTERNS

Stephen Grossberg†

1. Introduction: Brain, Behavior, and Babel

This article reviews some principles, mechanisms, and theorems from my work over the past twenty-five years. I review these results here to illustrate their interconnectedness from a recent perspective, to indicate directions for future work, and to reaffirm an approach to theorizing on problems of mind and brain that is still not fashionable despite growing signs that it needs to become so soon.

I say this because, despite the explosive growth of results on the fundamental issues of mind and brain, our science remains organized as a patchwork of experimental and theoretical fiefdoms which rarely interact despite the underlying unity of the scientific problems that they address. The territorial lines that bound these fiefdoms often seem to be as sacrosanct as national boundaries, and for similar cultural and economic reasons. A theorist who succeeds in explaining results from distinct experimental preparations by discovering their unifying mechanistic substrates may, through repeated crossings of these territorial boundaries, start to feel like a traveler without a country, and will often be treated accordingly. My own intellectual travels have repeatedly left me with such a feeling, despite the reassuring belief that theory had provided me with an international passport. To quickly review how some of these territorial passages were imposed by the internal structure of my theory, I will use a personal historical format of exposition, since the familiar territories do not themselves provide a natural descriptive framework.

2. From List Learning to Neural Networks: The Self-Organization of Individual Behavior

My scientific work began unexpectedly in 1957–58 while I was an undergraduate psychology major at Dartmouth College. A great deal of structured data and classical theory about topics like verbal learning, classical and instrumental conditioning,

---

† Supported in part by the Air Force Office of Scientific Research (AFOSR 82-0148) and the National Science Foundation (NSF IST-80-00257).

perceptual dynamics, and attitude change were then available. It struck me that the revolutionary meaning of these data centered in issues concerning the self-organization of individual behavior in response to environmental pressures. I was exhilarated by the dual problems of how one could represent the emergence of behavioral units that did not exist before, and how one could represent the environmental interaction that stimulated this emergence even before the units emerged that would ultimately stabilize this interaction. I soon realized that various data which seemed paradoxical when viewed in terms of traditional concepts seemed inevitable when viewed in a network framework wherein certain laws hold. In fact, the same laws seemed to hold, in one version or another, in all the learning data that I studied. This universality suggested an important role for mathematics to quantitatively classify these various cases, which is why I sit in a mathematics department today. Although the laws were derived from psychological ideas, once derived they readily suggested a neurophysiological interpretation. In fact, that is how I learned my first neurophysiology, and crossed my first major experimental boundaries. To a nineteen-year-old, these heady experiences were motivationally imprinting, and they supplied enough energy to face the sociological difficulties that my blend of psychology, physiology, and mathematics tends to cause. I might add that this interdisciplinary penetration of boundaries by my laws has prevented them from being widely studied by psychologists to the present time, despite the fact that their manifestations have appeared in a vast array of data and specialized models during the past decade.

3. Unitized Nodes, Short Term Memory, and Automatic Activation

The network framework and the laws themselves can be derived in several ways (Grossberg, 1969a, 1974). My first derivation was based on classical list learning data (Grossberg, 1961, 1964) from the serial verbal learning and paired associate paradigms (Dixon and Horton, 1968; Jung, 1968; McGeogh and Irion, 1952; Osgood, 1953; Underwood, 1966). List learning data force one to confront the fact that new verbal units are continually being synthesized as a result of practice, and need not be the obvious units which the experimentalist is directly manipulating (Young, 1968). All essentially stationary concepts, such as the concept of information itself (Khinchin, 1957) hereby become theoretically useless. I therefore find the recent trend to discuss results about human memory in terms of "information processing" misleading (Klatsky, 1980; Loftus and Loftus, 1976; Norman, 1969). Such approaches either implicitly or explicitly adopt a framework wherein the self-organization of new behavioral units cannot be intrinsically characterized. Because these approaches miss processing constraints that control self-organization, they often construct special-purpose models to explain experiments in which the formation of new units is not too important, or deal indirectly with the self-organization problem by using computer models that would require a homunculus to carry out their operations in a physical setting. I will clarify these assertions as I go along.

By putting the self-organization of individual behavior in center stage, I realized that the phenomenal simplicity of familiar behavioral units, and the evolutionary aggregation of these units into new representations which themselves achieve phenomenal simplicity through experience, should be made a fundamental property of my theory. To express the phenomenal simplicity of familiar behavioral units, I represented them by indecomposable internal representations, or unitized nodes, rather than as composites of phonemes or as individual muscle movements. The problem of how phonemic, syllabic, and word-like representations might all coexist with different importance in different learning contexts was hereby vividly raised.

Once unitized nodes were conceived, it became clear that experimental inputs can activate these nodes via conditionable pathways. A distinction between sensory activation (the input source) and short term memory (the node's reaction) hereby became natural, as well as a concept of "automatic" activation of a node by its input. These network concepts have become popular in psychology during the past decade under the pressure of recent data (e.g., Schneider and Shiffrin, 1976), but they were already needed to analyze classical list learning data that are currently out of fashion.

The following properties of list learning helped to constrain the form of my associative laws. To simplify the discussion, I will only consider associative interactions within a given level in a coding hierarchy, rather than the problem of how coding hierarchies develop and interact between several levels. All of my conclusions can be, and have been, generalized to a hierarchical setting (Grossberg, 1974, 1978a, 1980a).

4. Backward Learning and Serial Bowing

Backward learning effects and, more generally, error gradients between nonadjacent, or remote, list items (Jung, 1968; McGeogh and Irion, 1952; Murdock, 1974; Osgood, 1953; Underwood, 1966) suggest that pairs of nodes v_i and v_j can interact via distinct directed pathways e_{ij} and e_{ji} over which conditionable signals can travel. Indeed, an analysis of how any node v_i can know where to send its signals reveals that no local information exists at the node itself whereby such a decision can be made. By the principle of sufficient reason, the node must therefore send signals towards all possible nodes v_j with which it is connected by directed paths e_{ij}. Some other variables must exist which can discriminate which combination of signals should reach their target nodes based on past experience. These auxiliary variables turn out to be the long term memory traces. The concept that each node sends out signals to all possible nodes has recently appeared in models of *spreading activation* (Collins and Loftus, 1975; Klatsky, 1980) to explain semantic recognition and reaction time data.

The form that the signaling and conditioning laws should take is forced by data about serial verbal learning. A main paradox about serial learning concerns the form of the bowed serial position curve which relates cumulative errors to list positions (Figure 1a). This curve is paradoxical for the following reason. If all that happens during serial learning is a build-up of various types of interference at each list position due to the occurrence of prior list items, then the error curve should be monotone increasing (Figure 1b). Because the error curve is bowed, and the degree of bowing depends on the length of the intertrial interval between successive list presentations, the *nonoccurrence* of list items after the last item occurs somehow improves learning across several prior list items.

5. The Inadequacy of Rehearsal as an Explanatory Concept

Just saying that rehearsal during the intertrial interval causes this effect does not explain it, because it does not explain why the middle of the list is less rehearsed. Indeed the middle of the list has more time to be rehearsed than does the end of the list before the next learning trial occurs. In the classical literature, one reads that the middle of the list experiences maximal proactive interference (from prior items) and retroactive interference (from future items), but this just labels what we have to explain (Jung, 1953; Osgood, 1953; Underwood, 1966). In the more recent literature, rehearsal is given a primary role in determining the learning rate (Rundus, 1971) although it is believed that only certain types of rehearsal, called *elaborative* rehearsal, can accomplish this (Bjork, 1975; Craik and Watkins, 1973; Klatsky, 1980). Notwithstanding the type of rehearsal used, one still has to explain why the list middle is rehearsed less than the list end in the serial learning paradigm.

The severity of such difficulties led the serial learning expert Young (1968) to write: "If an investigator is interested in studying verbal learning processes ... he would do well to choose some method other than serial learning" (p.146). Another leading verbal learning expert Underwood (1966) realized the magnitude of the difficulties, but also that they would not go away by ignoring them, when he wrote: "The person who

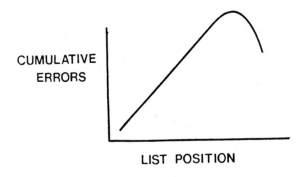

CUMULATIVE
ERRORS

LIST POSITION

(a)

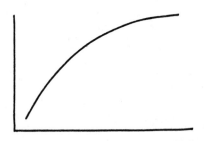

(b)

Figure 1. (a) The cumulative error curve in serial verbal learning is a skewed bowed curve. Items between the middle and end of the list are hardest to learn. Items at the beginning of the list are easiest to learn. (b) If position-dependent difficulty of learning were all due to interference from previously presented items, the error curve would be monotone increasing.

originates a theory that works out to almost everyone's satisfaction will be in line for an award in psychology equivalent to the Nobel prize" (p.491).

Most recent investigators have followed Young's advice. They have turned to paradigms like free recall (Bower, 1977; Murdock, 1974) wherein single trial presentations minimize self-organizing effects and subject-determined recall strategies simplify the interactions between item recall and retrieval probes. However, analysis of the free recall paradigm has not proved deep enough to explain the serial bowed curve. In particular, one cannot resort to the type of free recall explanations which are used to explain the bowed effects in that paradigm (Atkinson and Shiffrin, 1968), since the improvement in recall at the end of a serially learned list is due to long term memory rather than to short term memory. Indeed, I have elsewhere argued that popular free recall theories contain internal problems of a homuncular nature, cannot explain some critical free recall data concerning primacy effects in STM which are not supposed to exist, and cannot even explain how a telephone number can be accurately repeated out of STM, because they do not address various issues which are also raised by serial learning data (Grossberg, 1978b).

6. The Inadequacy of Programmatic Time

The massive backward effect that causes the bowed serial curve forces the use of a real-time theory that can parameterize the temporal unfolding of both the occurrences and the nonoccurrences of events. The bowed curve hereby weakens the foundations of all theories whose time variable is counted in terms of computer program operations, no matter how successful these theories might be in simulating data via homuncular constructions (Anderson and Bower, 1973). The existence of facilitative effects due to nonoccurring items also shows that traces of prior list occurrences must endure beyond the last item's presentation time, so they can be influenced by the future nonoccurrences of items. This fact leads to the concept of stimulus traces, or short term memory (STM) traces, $x_i(t)$ at the nodes v_i, $i = 1, 2, \ldots, n$, which are activated by inputs $I_i(t)$, but which decay at a rate slower than the input presentation rate.

Thus in response to serial inputs, *patterns* of STM activity are set up across the network's nodes. By sufficient reason, each supraliminally activated node also sends signals along all its directed pathways. The combination of serial inputs, distributed internodal signals, and spontaneous STM changes at each node changes the STM pattern as the experiment proceeds. A major task of learning theory is to characterize the rules whereby these STM patterns evolve through time. Indeed, a major mathematical task is to learn how to think in terms of pattern transformations, rather than just in terms of feature detectors or other local entities.

7. Network versus Computer Parsing: Distinct Error Gradients at Different List Positions

The general philosophical interest of the bowed curve can be better appreciated by asking: What is the first time a learning subject can possibly know that item r_n is the last list item in a newly presented list $r_1 r_2 \ldots r_n$, given that a new item is presented every w time units until r_n occurs? The answer obviously is: not until at least w time units *after* r_n has been presented. Only after this time passes and no item r_{n+1} is presented can r_n be correctly reclassified from the list's "middle" to the list's "end". Since parameter w is under experimental control and is not a property of the list ordering *per se*, spatiotemporal network interactions parse a list in a way that is fundamentally different from the parsing rules that are natural to apply to a list of symbols in a computer. Indeed, increasing the intratrial interval w during serial learning can flatten the entire bowed error curve and minimize the effects of the intertrial interval (Jung, 1968; Osgood, 1953).

To illustrate the difference between computer models and my network approach, suppose that after a node v_i is excited by an input I_i, its STM trace gets smaller through time due to either internodal competition or to passive trace decay. Then in response to a serially presented list, the last item to occur always has the largest STM trace—in other words, at every time a *recency* gradient obtains in STM (Figure 2). Given this natural assumption—which, however, is not always true (Grossberg, 1978a, 1978b)—how do the generalization gradients of errors at each list position get learned (Figure 3)? In particular, how does a gradient of anticipatory errors occur at the beginning of the list, a two-sided gradient of anticipatory and perseverative errors occur near the middle of the list, and a gradient of perseverative errors occur at the end of the list (Osgood, 1953)? Otherwise expressed, how does a temporal succession of STM recency gradients generate an LTM *primacy* gradient at the list beginning but an LTM *recency* gradient at the list end? These properties immediately rule out any linear theory, as well as any theory which restricts itself to nearest neighbor associative links, unless the theory makes the homuncular assumption that the system has absolute knowledge of how to compute the list's beginning, end, and direction towards its middle (Feigenbaum and Simon, 1962).

8. Graded STM and LTM Patterns: Multiplicative Sampling and Slow Decay by LTM Traces

Figures 2 and 3 can be reconciled by positing the existence of STM traces and LTM traces that evolve according to different time scales and rules. Indeed, this reconciliation is one of the strongest arguments that I know for these rules.

Suppose, as above, that each node v_j can send out a sampling signal S_j along each directed path e_{jk} towards the node v_k, $j \neq k$. Suppose that each path e_{jk} contains a long term memory (LTM) trace z_{jk} at its terminal point, where z_{jk} can compute, using only local operations, the product of signal S_j and STM trace x_k. Also suppose that the LTM trace decays slowly, if at all, during a single learning trial. The simplest law for z_{jk} that satisfies these constraints is

$$\frac{d}{dt} z_{jk} = -c z_{jk} + d S_j x_k, \quad j \neq k. \tag{1}$$

To see how this rule generates an LTM primacy gradient at the list beginning, we need to study the LTM pattern $(z_{12}, z_{13}, \ldots, z_{1n})$ and to show that $z_{12} > z_{13} > \ldots > z_{1n}$. To see how the same rule generates an LTM recency gradient at the list end, we need to study the LTM pattern $(z_{n1}, z_{n2}, \ldots, z_{n,n-1})$ and to show that $z_{n1} < z_{n2} < \ldots < z_{n,n-1}$. The two-sided gradient at the list middle can then be understood as a combination of these effects.

By (1), node v_1 sends out a sampling signal S_1 shortly after item r_1 is presented. After rapidly reaching peak size, signal S_1 gradually decays as future list items $r_2, r_3, \ldots$ are presented. Thus S_1 is largest when trace x_2 is maximal, S_1 is smaller when both traces x_2 and x_3 are active, S_1 is smaller still when traces x_2, x_3, and x_4 are active, and so on. Consequently, the product $S_1 x_2$ in row 2 of Figure 2 exceeds the product $S_1 x_3$ in row 3 of Figure 2, which in turn exceeds the product $S_1 x_4$ in row 4 of Figure 2, and so on. Due to the slow decay of each LTM trace z_{1k} on each learning trial, z_{12} adds up to the products $S_1 x_2$ in successive rows of column 1, z_{13} adds up to the products $S_1 x_3$ in successive rows of column 2, and so on. An LTM primacy gradient $z_{12} > z_{13} > \ldots > z_{1n}$ is hereby generated. This gradient is due to the way signal S_1 multiplicatively *samples* the successive STM recency gradients and the LTM traces z_{1k} sum up the sampled STM gradients.

By contrast, the signal S_n of a node v_n at the end of the list samples a different set of STM gradients. This is because v_n starts to sample (viz., $S_n > 0$) only after

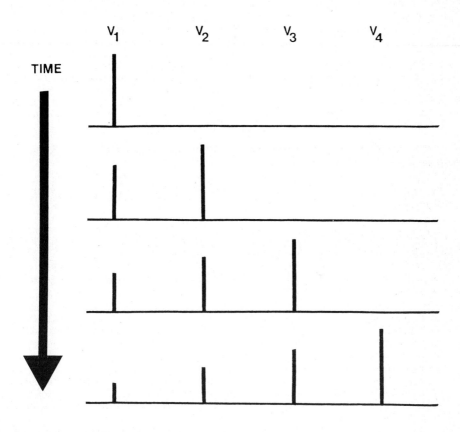

Figure 2. Suppose that items $r_1, r_2, r_3, r_4, \ldots$ are presented serially to nodes $v_1, v_2, v_3, v_4, \ldots$, respectively. Let the activity of node v_i at time t be described by the height of the histogram beneath v_i at time t. If each node is initially excited by an equal amount and its excitation decays at a fixed rate, then at every time (each row) the pattern of STM activity across nodes is described by a recency gradient.

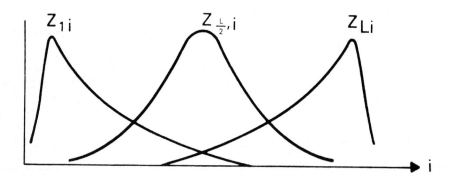

Figure 3. At each node v_j, the LTM pattern $z_j = (z_{j1}, z_{j2}, \ldots, z_{jn})$ that evolves through time is different. In a list of length $n = L$ whose intertrial interval is sufficiently long, the LTM pattern at the list beginning $(j \cong 1)$ is a primacy gradient. At the list end $(j \cong L)$, a recency gradient evolves. Near the list middle $(j \cong \frac{L}{2})$, a two-sided gradient is learned. These gradients are reflected in the distribution of anticipatory and perseverative errors in response to item probes at different list positions.

all past nodes $v_1, v_2, \ldots, v_{n-1}$ have already been activated on that trial. Consequently, the LTM traces $(z_{n1}, z_{n2}, \ldots, z_{n,n-1})$ of node v_n encode a recency gradient $x_1 < x_2 < x_3 < \ldots < x_{n-1}$ at *each* time. When all the recency gradients are added up through time, the total effect is a recency gradient in v_n's LTM pattern. In summary, nodes at the beginning, middle, and end of the list encode different LTM gradients because they multiplicatively sample and store STM patterns at different times.

Lest the reader who is sensitized to the functional unit issue object to these internodal feedback effects, let me reiterate that similar LTM gradients obtain if the sequences of nodes which are active at any time selectively excite higher-order nodes (chunks) which in turn sample the field of excited nodes via feedback signals (Grossberg, 1974, 1978a).

9. Binary versus Continuous Associative Laws

The LTM gradient problem illustrates why I have always avoided binary laws for STM and LTM traces. Binary laws have often attracted workers who began with the all-or-none character of individual axon spikes. However, the continuously fluctuating potentials that receive these spikes often average them in time, thereby yielding graded intercellular signaling effects. For similar reasons, population interactions often obey continuous laws. Workers like Amari (1974, 1977) and Geman (1981) have formally studied how to justify the averaging procedures that can convert binary microscopic rules into continuous macroscopic rules. Because of the psychological derivation of my networks, I have always worked with preaveraged equations from the start.

The example of continuous LTM error gradients is not the only one wherein binary and continuous models yield distinct outcomes. In fact, they usually do. For example, just changing sigmoid feedback signals to binary feedback signals in a competitive network can significantly change network dynamics (Grossberg, 1973, 1978c), notably because sigmoid signals can support infinitely many equilibrium points in competitive geometries wherein binary signals cannot.

10. Retrieval Probes and LTM Gating of STM Mediated Signals

Having shown how STM patterns may be read into LTM patterns, we now need to describe how a retrieval probe r_m can read v_m's LTM pattern back into STM on recall trials, whereupon the STM traces can be transformed into observable behavior. In particular, how can LTM be read into STM without distorting the learned LTM gradients?

The simplest rule generates an STM pattern which is proportional to the LTM pattern that is being read out, and allows distinct probes to each read their LTM patterns into STM in an independent fashion.

To achieve faithful read-out of the LTM pattern $(z_{m1}, z_{m2}, \ldots, z_{mn})$ by a probe r_m that turns on signal S_m, I let the product $S_m z_{mi}$ determine the growth rate of x_i. In other words, LTM trace z_{mi} *gates* the signal S_m along e_{mi} before the gated signal reaches v_i. The independent action of several probes implies that the gated signals $S_m z_{mi}$ are added, so that the total effect of all gated signals on v_i is $\sum_{m=1}^{n} S_m z_{mi}$. The simplest equation for the STM trace x_i that abides by this rule is

$$\frac{d}{dt} x_i = -a x_i + b \sum_{m=1}^{n} S_m z_{mi} + I_i, \tag{2}$$

where $-a$ is the STM decay rate that produces Figure 2, S_m is the mth sampling signal, z_{mi} is the LTM trace of pathway e_{mi}, and I_i is the ith experimental input.

The reaction of equations (1) and (2) to serial inputs I_i is much more complex than is their response to an isolated retrieval probe r_m. Due to the fact that STM traces may decay slower than the input presentation rate, several sampling signals S_m can be simultaneously active, albeit in different phases of their growth and decay.

11. Behavioral Choices and Competitive Feedback

Once one accepts that patterns of STM traces are evolving through time, one also needs a mechanism for choosing those activated nodes which will influence observable behavior. Lateral inhibitory feedback signals are readily implicated as a choice mechanism (Grossberg, 1968, 1969b, 1970). The simplest extension of (2) which includes competitive interactions is

$$\frac{d}{dt} x_i = -a x_i + \sum_{m=1}^{n} S_m^+ b_{mi}^+ z_{mi} - \sum_{m=1}^{n} S_m^- b_{mi}^- + I_i \tag{3}$$

where $S_m^+ b_{mi}^+$ $(S_m^- b_{mi}^-)$ is the excitatory (inhibitory) signal emitted from node v_m along the excitatory (inhibitory) pathway e_{mi}^+ (e_{mi}^-). Correspondingly, equation (1) is generalized to

$$\frac{d}{dt} z_{jk} = -c z_{jk} + d_{jk} S_j^+ x_k. \tag{4}$$

The asymmetry between terms $\sum_{m=1}^{n} S_m^+ b_{mi}^+ z_{mi}$ and $\sum_{m=1}^{n} S_m^- b_{mi}^-$ in (3) readily suggests a modification of (3) and a definition of inhibitory LTM traces analogous to (4), where such traces exist (Grossberg, 1969d).

Because lateral inhibition can change the sign of each x_i from positive to negative in (3), and thus change the sign of each z_{jk} from positive to negative in (4), some refinements of (3) and (4) are needed to prevent absurdities like the following: $S_m^+ < 0$ and

$x_i < 0$ implies $z_{mi} > 0$; and $S_m^+ < 0$ and $z_{mi} < 0$ implies $x_i > 0$. Threshold constraints accomplish this in the simplest way. Letting $[\xi]^+ = \max(\xi, 0)$, these absurdities are prevented if threshold cut-offs are imposed on signals, such as in

$$S_j^+ = [x_j(t - \tau_j^+) - \Gamma_j^+]^+ \tag{5}$$

and

$$S_j^- = [x_j(t - \tau_j^-) - \Gamma_j^-]^+, \tag{6}$$

as well as on sampled STM traces, such as in

$$\frac{d}{dt}z_{jk} = -cz_{jk} + d_{jk}S_j^+[x_k]^+. \tag{7}$$

The equations (3), (5), (6), and (7) have been used by modelers for a variety of purposes. For example, in his seminal article on code development, Malsburg (1973) used these equations, supplemented by his synaptic conservation rule.

12. Skewing of the Bow: Symmetry-Breaking Between the Future and the Past

To explain the bowed error curve, we now need to compare the LTM patterns $z_i = (z_{i1}, z_{i2}, \ldots, z_{in})$ which evolve at all list nodes v_i. In particular, we need to explain why the bowed curve is *skewed*; that is, why the list position where learning takes longest occurs nearer to the end of the list than to its beginning (Figure 1a). This skewing effect has routinely demolished learning theories which assume that forward and backward effects are equally strong, or symmetric (Asch and Ebenholtz, 1962; Murdock, 1974). I have elsewhere argued that the symmetry-breaking between the future and the past, by favoring forward over backward associations, makes possible the emergence of a global "arrow in time," or the ultimate learning of long event sequences in their correct order (Grossberg, 1969c, 1974).

Theorem 1 below asserts that a skewed bowed curve does occur in the network, and predicts that the degree of skewing will decrease and the relative learning rate at the beginning and end of the list will reverse as the network's arousal level increases or its excitatory signal thresholds Γ_j^+ decrease to abnormal levels (Grossberg and Pepe, 1970, 1971). The arousal and threshold predictions have not yet been tested to the best of my knowledge. They are of some conceptual importance because abnormally high arousal or low thresholds can hereby generate a formal network syndrome characterized by contextual collapse, reduced attention span, and fuzzy response categories that resembles some symptoms of simple schizophrenia (Grossberg and Pepe, 1970; Maher, 1977).

To understand what is involved in my explanation of bowing, note that by equation (7), each correct LTM trace $z_{12}, z_{23}, z_{34}, \ldots, z_{n-1,n}$ may grow at a comparable rate, albeit w time units later than the previous correct LTM trace. However, the LTM patterns $z_1, z_2, \ldots, z_n$ will differ no matter when you look at them, as in Figure 3. Thus when a retrieval probe r_j reads its LTM pattern z_j into STM, the entire pattern must influence overt behavior to explain why bowing occurs. The relative size of the correct LTM trace $z_{j,j+1}$ compared to all other LTM traces in z_j will influence its success in eliciting r_{j+1} after competitive STM interactions occur. A larger $z_{j,j+1}$ relative to the sum of all other z_{jk}, $k \neq j, j+1$, should yield better performance of r_{j+1} given r_j, other things being equal. To measure the distinctiveness of a trace z_{jk} relative to all traces in z_j, I therefore define the relative LTM traces, or stimulus sampling probabilities

$$Z_{jk} = z_{jk}\Big(\sum_{m \neq j} z_{jm}\Big)^{-1}. \tag{8}$$

The appropriateness of definition (8) is strengthened by the following observation. The ordering within the LTM gradients of Figure 3 is unchanged by the relative LTM traces; for example, if $z_{12} > z_{13} > \ldots > z_{1n}$, then $Z_{12} > Z_{13} > \ldots > Z_{1n}$ because all the Z_{1k}'s have the same denominator. Thus all conclusions about LTM gradients are valid for relative LTM gradients.

In terms of the relative LTM traces, the issue of bowing can be mathematically formulated as follows. Define the *bowing function* $B_i(t) = Z_{i,i+1}(t)$. Function $B_i(t)$ measures how distinctive the ith correct association is at time t. After a list of n items is presented with an intratrial interval w and a sufficiently long intertrial interval W elapses, does the function $B_i((n-1)w + W)$ decrease and then increase as i increases from 1 to n? Does the minimum of the function occur in the latter half of the list? The answer to both of these questions is "yes."

To appreciate the subtlety of the bowing issue, it is necessary to understand how the bow depends upon the ability of a node v_i to sample incorrect future associations, such as $r_i r_{i+2}, r_i r_{i+3}, \ldots$ in addition to incorrect past associations, such as $r_i r_{i-1}, r_i r_{i-2}, \ldots$. As soon as S_i becomes positive, v_i can sample the entire past field of STM traces at $v_1, v_2, \ldots, v_{i-1}$. However, if the sampling threshold is chosen high enough, S_i might shut off before r_{i+2} occurs. Thus the sampling duration has different effects on the sampling of past than future incorrect associations. For example, if the sampling thresholds of all v_i are chosen so high that S_i shuts off before r_{i+2} is presented, then the function $B_i(\infty)$ decreases as i increases from 1 to n. In other words, the monotonic error curve of Figure 1b obtains because no node v_i can encode incorrect future associations.

Even if the thresholds are chosen so that incorrect future associations can be formed, the function $B_i((i + 1)w)$ which measures the distinctiveness of $z_{i,i+1}$ just before r_{i+2} occurs is again a decreasing function of i. The bowing effect thus depends on threshold choices which permit sampling durations that are at least $2w$ in length.

The shape of the bow also depends on the duration of the intertrial interval, because before the intertrial interval occurs, all nodes build up increasing amounts of associative interference as more list items are presented. The first effect of the nonoccurrence of items after r_n is presented is the growth through time of $B_{n-1}(t)$ as t increases beyond the time nw when item r_{n+1} would have occurred in a larger list (Grossberg, 1969c). The last correct association is hereby facilitated by the absence of interfering future items during the intertrial interval. This facilitation effect is a nonlinear property of the network. Indeed, bowing itself is a nonlinear phenomenon in my theory, because it depends on a comparison of ratios of integrals of sums of products as they evolve through time.

In my review of a bowing theorem below, I will emphasize the effect of the signal threshold Γ on the degree of skewing. One can, however, also compute the effect of the intertrial interval W on skewing, as well as the role of other network parameters, such as STM decay rate and LTM growth rate.

The position of the bow has not yet been quantitatively computed although it has been qualitatively demonstrated within the full system (3), (5), (6), (7). Complete computations have been made in a related system, the *bare field*, wherein the primary effects of serial inputs on associative formation and competition are preserved (Grossberg, 1969c; Grossberg and Pepe, 1971) on a single learning trial. In the bare field, serial inputs occur with intratrial interval w:

$$I_1(t) = I_2(t + w) = \ldots = I_n(t + (n-1)w); \tag{9}$$

the STM traces decay after they are excited by their inputs: .

$$\frac{d}{dt} x_i = -a x_i + I_i; \tag{10}$$

the LTM traces add up products of signals and STM traces:

$$\frac{d}{dt}z_{jk} = d[x_j(t-\tau) - \Gamma]^+ x_k, \quad j \neq k; \tag{11}$$

and the relative LTM traces, or stimulus sampling probabilities, estimate how well as given LTM trace fares after it is read into STM and STM competition takes place:

$$Z_{jk} = z_{jk}\left(\sum_{m \neq j} z_{jm}\right)^{-1}. \tag{12}$$

Theorem 1 (Skewing of the Bowed Curve):
(I) If the bare field is initially at rest and associatively unbiased; that is, all

$$x_i(t) = 0, \quad -\tau \leq t \leq 0, \quad \text{and} \quad z_{jk}(0) = \alpha > 0, \quad j \neq k; \tag{13}$$

(II) the signals S_i and inputs r_{i+1} are well-correlated; that is

$$W = \tau \tag{14}$$

(this condition is convenient but not essential);

(III) successive inputs do not overlap in time; that is, $I_1(t)$ is positive only in an interval $(0, \lambda)$ with $\lambda < \tau$ and is zero elsewhere;

(IV) the inputs are not too irregular; that is, $I_1(t)$ is continuous and grows monotonically until it reaches a maximum at time $t = T_{\max}$, after which it monotonically decreases to zero at time $t = \lambda$;

(V) at high threshold, the sampling signals don't last too long; that is, if Γ is chosen so large that v_1 first emits a signal S_1 at the time $T_{\max}$, then S_1 shuts off before r_3 occurs: if $\Gamma_0 = \int_0^{T_{\max}} e^{-a(T_{\max}-v)} I_1(v)dv$, then

$$\int_0^{\lambda} e^{-a(\lambda-v)} I_1(v)dv > \Gamma_0 \geq \int_0^{2\tau} e^{-a(2\tau-v)} I_1(v)dv. \tag{15}$$

Under hypotheses (I)–(V), if the intertrial interval is infinite, then the bow occurs ($B_i(\infty)$ is minimized) at the list position closest to $M(\Gamma)$, where
A. (Overaroused Bowing)

$$M(0) = \frac{1}{2}(n-1), \tag{16}$$

B. (Skewing)

$$\frac{dM}{d\Gamma} > 0, \tag{17}$$

C. (No Incorrect Future Associations)

$$M(\Gamma) = n \text{ if } \Gamma \geq \Gamma_0. \tag{18}$$

If the intertrial interval is $W < \infty$, then the bow occurs ($B_i((n-1)w + W)$ is minimized) at a list position strictly greater than $M(\Gamma)$.

The function $M(\Gamma)$ can, moreover, be explicitly computed. It satisfies the equation

$$M(\Gamma) = \frac{1}{a\tau} \log\left[\frac{E + \sqrt{E^2 + 4CD}}{2D}\right] \tag{19}$$

where

$$C = \tau E^{-1}(-\tau, 0)[AB(\lambda - T_1, T_1) + A\Gamma E(T_2, T_1) + \frac{A^2}{2}E(2\lambda, 2T_2) - \frac{\Gamma^2}{2a}E(-L)], \tag{20}$$

$$D = A\tau E(L)E^{-1}(0, \tau)[B(\lambda, 0) + \frac{A}{2a}e^{-2a\lambda}], \tag{21}$$

$$E = \Gamma[C(\lambda, 0) + \frac{A}{a}e^{-a\lambda}], \tag{22}$$

with

$$A = \int_0^\lambda e^{av}I_1(v)\,dv, \tag{23}$$

$$B(t, p) = \int_0^t e^{-2a(v+p)} \int_0^{v+p} e^{aw}I_1(w)\,dw\,dv, \tag{24}$$

$$C(t, p) = \int_0^t e^{-a(v+p)} \int_0^{v+p} e^{aw}I_1(w)\,dw\,dv, \tag{25}$$

$$E(x) = e^{-a\tau x}, \tag{26}$$

and

$$E(x, y) = \frac{1}{a}(e^{-ax} - e^{-ay}). \tag{27}$$

13. Evolutionary Invariants of Associative Learning: Absolute Stability of Parallel Pattern Learning

Many features of system (3), (5), (6), (7) are special; for example, the exponential decay of STM and LTM and the signal threshold rule. Because associative processing is ubiquitous throughout phylogeny and within functionally distinct subsystems of each individual, a more general mathematical framework is needed. This framework should distinguish universally occurring associative principles which guarantee essential learning properties from evolutionary variations that adapt these principles to specialized environmental demands. Before we can speak with confidence about variations on an evolutionary theme, we first need to identify the theme.

I approached this problem during the years 1967 to 1972 in a series of articles wherein I gradually realized that the mathematical properties that I used to globally analyze specific learning examples were much more general than the examples themselves. This work culminated in my universal theorems on associative learning (Grossberg, 1969d, 1971a, 1972a).

The theorems are universal in the following sense. They say that if certain associative laws were invented at a prescribed time during evolution, then they could achieve unbiased associative pattern learning in essentially any later evolutionary specialization. To the question: Is it necessary to re-invent a new learning rule to match every perceptual or cognitive refinement, the theorems say "no". More specifically, the universal associative laws enable arbitrary spatial patterns to be learned by arbitrarily many, simultaneously active sampling channels that are activated by arbitrary continuous data preprocessing in an essentially arbitrary anatomy. Arbitrary space-time patterns can also be learned given modest constraints on the temporal regularity of stimulus sampling. The universal theorems thus describe a type of parallel processing whereby unbiased pattern learning can occur despite mutual crosstalk between very complex feedback signals.

Such results cannot be taken for granted. They obtain only if crucial network operations, such as spatial averaging, temporal averaging, preprocessing, gating, and cross-correlation are computed in a canonical ordering. This canonical ordering constitutes a general purpose design for unbiased parallel pattern learning, as well as a criterion for whether particular networks are acceptable models for this task. The universality of the design mathematically takes the form of a classification of oscillatory and limiting possibilities that is invariant under evolutionary specializations.

The theorems can also be interpreted in another way that is appropriate in discussions of self-organizing systems. The theorems are *absolute stability* theorems. They show that evolutionary invariants obtain no matter how system parameters are changed within this class of systems. Absolute stability is an important property in a self-organizing system because parameters may change in ways that cannot be predicted in advance, notably before specialized environments act on the system. Absolute stability guarantees that the onset of self-organization does not subvert the very properties which make self-organization possible.

The systems which I considered have the form

$$\frac{d}{dt}x_i = A_i x_i + \sum_{k \in J} B_{ki} z_{ki} + C_i(t) \tag{28}$$

$$\frac{d}{dt}z_{ji} = D_{ji} z_{ji} + E_{ji} x_i \tag{29}$$

where $i \in I$, $j \in J$, and I and J parameterize arbitrarily large, not necessarily disjoint, sets of sampled and sampling cells, respectively. As in my equations for list learning, A_i is an STM decay rate, B_{ki} is a nonnegative performance signal, $C_i(t)$ is an input function, D_{ji} is an LTM decay rate, and E_{ji} is a nonnegative learning signal. Unlike the list learning equations, A_i, B_{ki}, D_{ji}, and E_{ji} are continuous functionals of the entire history of the system. Equations (28) and (29) are therefore very general, and include many of the specialized models in the literature.

For example, although (28) does not seem to include inhibitory interactions, such interactions may be lumped into the STM decay functional A_i. The choice

$$A_i = -a_i + (b_i - c_i x_i)G_i(x_i) - \sum_{k=1}^{n} H_k(x_k)d_{ki} \tag{30}$$

describes the case wherein system nodes compete via shunting, or membrane equation, interactions (Cole, 1968; Grossberg, 1973; Kuffler and Nicholls, 1976; Plonsey, 1969). The performance, LTM decay, and learning functionals may include slow threshold changes, nonspecific Now Print signals, signal velocity changes, presynaptic modulating effects, arbitrary continuous rules of dendritic preprocessing and axonal signaling, as well as many other possibilities (Grossberg, 1972a, 1974). Of special importance are the variety of LTM decay choices that satisfy the theorems. For example, an LTM law like

$$\frac{d}{dt}z_{ji} = [x_j(t - \tau_j) - \Gamma_j(y_t)]^+ (-d_j z_{ji} + e_j x_i) \tag{31}$$

achieves an interference theory of forgetting, rather than exponential forgetting, since $\frac{d}{dt}z_{ji} = 0$ except when v_j is sampling (Adams, 1967). Equation (31) also allows the vigor of sampling to depend on changes in the threshold $\Gamma_j(y_t)$ that are sensitive to the prior history $y_t = (x_i, z_{ji} : i \in I, j \in J)_t$ of the system before time t.

In this generality, too many possibilities exist to as yet prove absolute stability theorems. One further constraint on system processing paves the way towards such results. This constraint still admits the above processing possibilities, but it imposes some spatiotemporal regularity on the sampling process. Indeed, if the performance signals B_{ji} from a fixed sampling node v_j to all the sampled nodes v_i, $i \in I$, were arbitrary nonnegative and continuous functionals, then the irregularities in each B_{ji} could override any regularities in z_{ji} within the gated performance signal $B_{ji}z_{ji}$ from v_j to v_i.

14. Local Symmetry and Self-Similarity in Pattern Learning and Developmental Invariance

Absolute stability does obtain even if different functionals B_j, D_j, and E_j are assigned to each node v_j, $j \in J$, just so long as the same functional is assigned to all pathways e_{ji}, $i \in I$. Where this is not globally true, one can often partition the network into maximal subsets where it is true, and then prove unbiased pattern learning in each subset. This restriction is called the property of *local symmetry axes* since each sampling cell v_j can act as a source of coherent history-dependent waves of STM and LTM processing. Local symmetry axes still permit (say) each B_j to obey different history-dependent preprocessing, threshold, time lag, and path strength laws among arbitrarily many mutually interacting nodes v_j.

When local symmetry axes are imposed on (28) and (29), the resulting class of systems takes the form

$$\frac{d}{dt}x_i = Ax_i + \sum_{k \in J} B_k z_{ki} + C_i(t) \tag{32}$$

and

$$\frac{d}{dt}z_{ji} = D_j z_{ji} + E_j x_i. \tag{33}$$

A simple change of variables shows that constant interaction coefficients b_{ji} between pairs v_j and v_i of nodes can depend on $i \in I$ without destroying unbiased pattern learning in the systems

$$\frac{d}{dt}x_i = Ax_i + \sum_{k \in J} B_k b_{ki} z_{ki} + C_i(t) \tag{34}$$

and

$$\frac{d}{dt}z_{ji} = D_j z_{ji} + E_j b_{ji}^{-1} x_i. \tag{35}$$

By contrast, the systems (34) and

$$\frac{d}{dt}z_{ji} = D_j z_{ji} + E_j b_{ji} x_i \tag{36}$$

are not capable of unbiased parallel pattern learning (Grossberg, 1972a). A dimensional analysis shows that (34) and (35) hold if action potentials transmit the network's intercellular signals, whereas (34) and (36) hold if electrotonic propagation is used.

The dimensional analysis hereby suggests that spatial biases in the b_{ji} which are due to differences in axonal diameters can be overcome by an interaction between action potentials and mass action properties of the LTM traces. Temporal biases in time lags that are due to differences in intercellular distances are overcome by the proportionality of action potential velocity to axon diameter (Katz, 1966; Ruch, Patton, Woodbury, and Towe, 1961) in cells whose axon lengths and diameters covary. Such cells are said to be *self-similar* (Grossberg, 1969f). Self-similar cell populations can preserve the learned meaning of patterns under significant developmental deformations of their mutual distances and sizes. Self-similar rules of network design also permit individual nodes to arrive at globally correct decisions from locally ambiguous data (Grossberg, 1978a). In the developmental biology literature, self-similarity is called self-regulation (Wolpert, 1969).

15. The Unit of LTM is a Spatial Pattern: Global Constraints on Local Network Design

To illustrate the global theorems that have been proved, I consider first the simplest case, wherein only one sampling node exists (Figure 4a). Then the network is called an *outstar* because it can be drawn with the sampling node at the center of outward-facing conditionable pathways (Figure 4b) such that the LTM trace z_i in the ith pathway samples the STM trace x_i of the ith sampled cell, $i \in I$. An *outstar* is thus a functional-differential system of the form

$$\frac{d}{dt}x_i = Ax_i + Bz_i + C_i(t) \tag{37}$$

$$\frac{d}{dt}z_i = Dz_i + Ex_i \tag{38}$$

where A, B, D, and E are continuous functionals such that B and E are nonnegative.

Despite the fact that the functionals A, B, D, and E can fluctuate in extremely complex system-dependent ways, and the inputs $C_i(t)$ can also fluctuate wildly through time, an outstar can learn an arbitrary spatial pattern $C_i(t) = \theta_i C(t)$ ($\theta_i \geq 0, \sum_{k \in I} \theta_k = 1$) with a minimum of oscillations in its pattern variables $X_i = x_i(\sum_{k \in I} x_k)^{-1}$ and $Z_i = z_i(\sum_{k \in I} z_k)^{-1}$. Recall that the Z_i's are the stimulus sampling probabilities that played such a central role in my explanation of serial bowing. Because the limits and oscillations of the pattern variables have a classification that is independent of particular choices of A, B, C, D, and E, these properties are the evolutionary invariants of outstar learning.

The following theorem summarizes, albeit not in the most general known form, some properties of outstar learning. One of the constraints in this theorem is called a *local flow* condition. This constraint says that a performance signal B can be large only if its associated learning signal E is large. Local flow prevents the read-out of old LTM memories from a sampling pathway which has lost its plasticity. Such a read-out would prevent accurate registration of the UCS in STM and thus accurate LTM encoding of the UCS via STM sampling.

I should immediately remark that a plastic synapse can be dynamically buffered against recoding by global network interactions (Grossberg, 1976c, 1980a). Such a synapse can still obey the local flow condition. I should also say that the local flow condition is needed only if all sampling sources are trying to encode the same pattern without bias, as in the parallel learning of sensory expectancies (Grossberg, 1980a) or of motor synergies (Grossberg, 1978a).

If the threshold of B is no smaller than the threshold of E, then local flow is assured. Such a threshold inequality occurs automatically if the LTM trace z_{ji} is physically interpolated between the axonal signal $S_j b_{ji}$ and the postsynaptic target cell v_i. That is why I call the condition a local flow condition. Such a geometric interpretation of

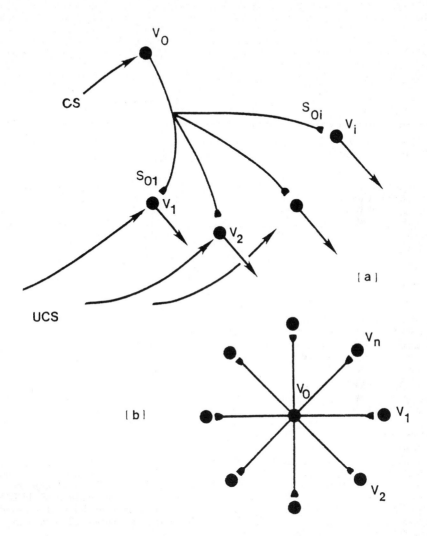

Figure 4. (a) In the minimal anatomy capable of associative learning in a classical conditioning paradigm, a conditioned stimulus (CS) excites a single node, or cell population, v_0 which thereupon sends sampling signals to a set of nodes $v_1, v_2, \ldots, v_n$. An input pattern representing the unconditioned stimulus (UCS) excites the nodes $v_1, v_2, \ldots, v_n$, which thereupon elicit output signals that contribute to the unconditioned response (UCR). The sampling signals from v_0 activate the LTM traces z_{0i} (which I denote by z_i in the text for brevity) that are computed at the synaptic knobs S_{0i}, $i = 1, 2, \ldots, n$. The activated LTM traces can learn the activity pattern across $v_1, v_2, \ldots, v_n$ that represents the UCS. (b) When the sampling structure in (a) is redrawn to emphasize its symmetry, the result is an *outstar*, whose sampling source is v_0 and whose sampled border is the set $\{v_1, v_2, \ldots, v_n\}$.

the location of the LTM trace is not forced by the psychological derivation of the associative equations, although it is the minimal anatomical realization of this derivation. Local flow gives unexpected support to the minimal realization by showing that pattern learning depends upon a mathematical constraint which automatically obtains in the minimal realization, but is at best *ad hoc* and difficult to guarantee in other anatomical interpretations of the associative equations.

Theorem 2 (Outstar Pattern Learning)

Suppose that

(I) the functionals are chosen to keep system trajectories bounded;

(II) a local flow condition holds:

$$\int_0^\infty B(t)dt = \infty \quad \text{only if} \quad \int_0^\infty E(t)dt = \infty; \tag{39}$$

(III) the UCS is practiced sufficiently often, and there exist positive constants K_1 and K_2 such that for all $T \geq 0$,

$$f(T, T + t) \geq K_1 \quad \text{if} \quad t \geq K_2 \tag{40}$$

where

$$f(U, V) = \int_U^V C(\xi) \exp\left[\int_\xi^V A(\eta)d\eta\right]d\xi. \tag{41}$$

Then, given arbitrary continuous and nonnegative initial data in $t \leq 0$ such that $\sum_{k \in I} z_k(0) > 0$,

(A) practice makes perfect:

The stimulus sampling probabilities $Z_i(t)$ are monotonically attracted to the UCS weights θ_i if

$$[Z_i(0) - X_i(0)][X_i(0) - \theta_i] \geq 0, \tag{42}$$

or may oscillate at most once due to prior learning if (42) does not hold, no matter how wildly A, B, C, D, and E oscillate;

(B) the UCS is registered in STM and partial learning occurs:

The limits $Q_i = \lim_{t \to \infty} X_i(t)$ and $P_i = \lim_{t \to \infty} Z_i(t)$ exist with

$$Q_i = \theta_i, \quad i \in I. \tag{43}$$

(C) If, moreover, the CS is practiced sufficiently often, then perfect learning occurs: if

$$\int_0^\infty E(t)dt = \infty, \quad \text{then} \quad P_i = \theta_i, \quad i \in I. \tag{44}$$

Remarkably, similar global theorems hold for systems (32)–(33) wherein arbitrarily many sampling cells can be simultaneously active and mutually signal each other by very complex feedback rules (Geman, 1981; Grossberg, 1969d, 1971a, 1972a, 1980b). This is because all systems of the form (32)–(33) can *factorize* information about STM and LTM pattern variables from information about how fast energy is being pumped into the system. Pattern variable oscillations can therefore be classified even if wild fluctuations in input and feedback signal energies occur through time. In the best theorems now available, only one hypothesis is not known to be necessary and sufficient (Grossberg, 1972a). It would be most satisfying if this imperfection in the theorems could be overcome.

When many sampling cells v_j, $j \in J$, can send sampling signals to each v_i, $i \in I$, the outstar property that each stimulus sampling probability $Z_{ji} = z_{ji}(\sum_{k \in I} z_{jk})^{-1}$

oscillates at most once fails to hold. This is so because the Z_{ji} of all active nodes v_j track $X_i = x_i(\sum_{k \in I} x_k)^{-1}$, while X_i tracks θ_i and the Z_{ji} of all active nodes v_j. The oscillations of the functions $Y_i = \max\{Z_{ji} : j \in J\}$ and $y_i = \min\{Z_{ji} : j \in J\}$ can, however, be classified much as the oscillations of each Z_i can be classified in the outstar case. Since each Z_{ji} depends on all z_{jk}, $k \in I$, each Y_i and y_i depends on all z_{jk}, $j \in J$, $k \in I$, and each X_i depends on all x_k, $k \in I$, the learning at each v_i is influenced by *all* x_k and z_{jk}, $j \in J$, $k \in I$. No local analysis can provide an adequate insight into the learning dynamics of these networks.

Because the oscillations of all X_i, Y_i, and y_i relative to θ_i can be classified, the following generalization of the outstar learning theorem holds.

Theorem 3 (Parallel Pattern Learning)

Suppose that

(I) the functionals are chosen to keep system trajectories bounded;

(II) every sampling cell obeys a local flow condition: for every $j \in J$,

$$\int_0^\infty B_j dt = \infty \quad \text{only if} \quad \int_0^\infty E_j dt = \infty; \tag{45}$$

(III) the UCS is presented sufficiently often: there exist positive constants K_1 and K_2 such that (40) holds.

Then given arbitrary nonnegative and continuous initial data in $t \leq 0$ such that $\sum_{k \in I} x_k(0) > 0$ and all $\sum_{k \in I} z_{jk}(0) > 0$,

(A) the UCS is registered in STM and partial learning occurs: the limits $Q_i = \lim_{t \to \infty} X_i(t)$ and $P_{ji} = \lim_{t \to \infty} Z_{ji}(t)$ exist with

$$Q_i = \theta_i, \quad i \in I. \tag{46}$$

(B) If the jth CS is practiced sufficiently often, then it learns the UCS pattern perfectly: if

$$\int_0^\infty E_j dt = \infty \quad \text{then} \quad P_{ji} = \theta_i, \quad i \in I. \tag{47}$$

Because LTM traces z_{ji} gate the performance signals B_j which are activated by a retrieval probe r_j, the theorem enables any and all nodes v_j which sampled the pattern $\theta = (\theta_i, i \in I)$ during learning trials to read it out with perfect accuracy on recall trials. The theorem does not deny that oscillations in overall network activity can occur during learning and recall, but shows that these oscillations merely influence the rates and intensities of learning and recall. Despite the apparent simplicity of these statements, the details of learning, memory, and recall can be dramatically altered by different choices of functionals. As one of many examples, phase transitions in memory can occur, and the nature of the phases can depend on a complex interaction between network rates and geometry (Grossberg, 1974).

Neither Theorem 2 nor Theorem 3 needs to assume that the CS and UCS are presented at correlated times. This is because the UCS condition keeps the baseline STM activity of sampled cells from ever decaying below the positive value K_1 in (40). For purposes of space-time pattern learning, this UCS uniformity condition is too strong. In Grossberg (1972a) I show how to replace the UCS uniformity condition by a weaker condition which guarantees that CS–UCS presentations are well enough correlated to guarantee perfect pattern learning of a given spatial pattern by certain cells v_j, even if other spatial patterns are presented at irregular times when they are sampled by distinct cells v_j.

16. The Teleology of the Pattern Calculus: Retina, Command Cell, Reward, Attention, Motor Synergy, Sensory Expectancy, Cerebellum

Three simple but fundamental facts emerge from the mathematical analysis of pattern learning: the unit of LTM is a spatial pattern $\theta = (\theta_i : i \in I)$; suitably designed neural networks can factorize invariant pattern θ from fluctuating energy; the size of a node's sampling signal can render it adaptively sensitive or blind to a pattern θ. These concepts helped me to think in terms of pattern transformations, rather than in terms of feature detectors, computer programs, linear systems, or other types of analysis. When I confronted equally simple environmental constraints with these simple pattern learning properties, the teleological pressure that was generated drove me into a wide-ranging series of specialized investigations.

What is the minimal network that can discriminate θ from background input fluctuations? It looks like a retina, and the θ's became reflectances. What is the minimal network that can encode and/or perform a space-time pattern or ordered series of spatial patterns? It looks like an invertebrate command cell. How can one synchronize CS–UCS sampling if the time intervals between CS and UCS presentations are unsynchronized? The result leads to psychophysiological mechanisms of reward, punishment, and attention. What are the associative invariants of motor learning? Spatial patterns become motor synergies wherein fixed relative contraction rates across muscles occur, and temporally synchronized performance signals read-out the synergy as a unit. What are the associative invariants of sensory learning? The potential ease of learning and reading-out complex sensory expectancies and spatial representations shows that even eidetic memory is more remarkable as a memory retrieval property than as a learning property. What is the minimal network that can bias the performance of motor acts with learned motor expectancies? It looks like a cerebellum.

An historical review of these investigations is found in the prefaces to a selection of my articles reprinted in Grossberg (1982a). Individually and collectively, these results add force to the idea that patterns rather than features are the functional units which regulate the neural designs subserving behavioral adaptation.

17. The Primacy of Shunting Competitive Networks Over Additive Networks

These specialized investigations repeatedly drove me to consider competitive systems. As just one of many instances, the same competitive normalization property which arose during my modeling of receptor-bipolar-horizontal cell interactions in retina (Grossberg, 1970a, 1972b) also arose in studies of the decision rules needed to release the right amount of incentive motivation in response to interacting drive inputs and conditioned reinforcer inputs within midbrain reinforcement centers (Grossberg, 1972c, 1972d). Because I approached these problems from a behavioral perspective, I knew what interactive properties the competition had to have. I have repeatedly found that shunting competition has all the properties that I need, whereas additive competition often does not.

As solutions to specialized problems involving competition piled up, networks capable of normalization, sensitivity changes via automatic gain control, attentional biases, developmental biases, pattern matching, shift properties, contrast enhancement, edge and curvature detection, tunable filtering, multistable choice behavior, normative drifts, traveling and standing waves, hysteresis, and resonance began to be classified within the framework of shunting competitive feedforward and feedback networks. See Grossberg (1981) for a recent review. As in the case of associative learning, the abundance of special cases made it seem more and more imperative to find an intuitive and mathematical framework within which these results could be unified and generalized. I also began to wonder whether many of the pattern transformations and STM storage properties of specialized examples were not instances of an absolute stability property of a general class of networks.

18. The Noise-Saturation Dilemma and Absolute Stability of Competitive Decision-Making

A unifying intuitive theme of particular simplicity can be recognized by considering the processing of continuously fluctuating patterns by cellular tissues. This theme is invisible to theories based on binary codes, feature detectors, or additive models. All cellular systems need to solve the *noise-saturation dilemma* which might cause sensitivity loss in their responses to both low and high input intensities. Mass action, or shunting, competition enables cells to elegantly solve this problem using automatic gain control by lateral inhibitory signals (Grossberg, 1973, 1980a). Additive competition fails in this task because it does not, by definition, possess an automatic gain control property.

A unifying mathematical theme is that every competitive system induces a decision scheme that can be used to prove global limit and oscillation theorems, notably absolute stability theorems (Grossberg, 1978c, 1978d, 1980c). This decision scheme interpretation is just a vivid way to think about a Liapunov functional that is naturally associated with each competitive system.

A class of competitive systems with absolutely stable decision schemes is the class of *adaptation level systems*

$$\frac{d}{dt} x_i = a_i(x)[b_i(x_i) - c(x)], \tag{48}$$

$i = 1, 2, \ldots n$, where $x = (x_1, x_2, \ldots, x_n)$. These systems include all shunting competitive feedback networks of the form

$$\frac{d}{dt} x_i = -A_i x_i + (B_i - x_i)[I_i + f_i(x_i)] - (x_i + C_i)[J_i + \sum_{k \neq i} f_k(x_k)] \tag{49}$$

which, in turn, are capable of many of the special properties listed above, given suitable choices of parameters and feedback signal functions. A special case of my theorem concerning these systems is the following.

Theorem 4 (Absolute Stability of Adaptation Level Systems)

Suppose that

(I) *Smoothness:* the functions $a_i(x)$, $b_i(x_i)$, and $c(x)$ are continuously differentiable;

(II) *Positivity:*

$$a_i(x) > 0 \quad \text{if} \quad x_i > 0, \quad x_j \geq 0, \quad j \neq i; \tag{50}$$

$$a_i(x) = 0 \quad \text{if} \quad x_i = 0, \quad x_j \geq 0, \quad j \neq i; \tag{51}$$

for sufficiently small $\lambda > 0$, there exists a continuous function $\bar{a}_i(x_i)$ such that

$$\bar{a}_i(x_i) \geq a_i(x) \quad \text{if} \quad x \in [0, \lambda]^n \tag{52}$$

and

$$\int_0^\lambda \frac{dw}{\bar{a}_i(w)} = \infty; \tag{53}$$

(III) *Boundedness:* for each $i = 1, 2, \ldots, n$,

$$\limsup_{x_i \to \infty} b_i(x_i) < c(0, 0, \ldots, \infty, 0, \ldots, 0) \tag{54}$$

where ∞ is in the ith entry of $(0, 0, \ldots, \infty, 0, \ldots, 0)$;

(IV) *Competition*:

$$\frac{\partial c(x)}{\partial x_i} > 0, \quad x \in \mathbf{R}_+^n, \quad i = 1, 2, \ldots, n; \tag{55}$$

(V) *Decision Hills*: The graph of each $b_i(x_i)$ possesses at most finitely many maxima in every compact interval.

Then the pattern transformation is stored in STM because all trajectories converge to equilibrium points: given any $x(0) > 0$, the limit $x(\infty) = \lim_{t \to \infty} x(t)$ exists.

This theorem intuitively means that the decision schemes of adaptation level systems are globally consistent. Globally inconsistent decision schemes can, by contrast, force almost all trajectories to persistently oscillate. This can occur even if $n = 3$ and all feedback signals are linear, as the voting paradox vividly illustrates (Grossberg, 1978c, 1980c; May and Leonard, 1975).

Adaptation level systems exclude distance-dependent interactions. To overcome this gap, Michael Cohen and I (Cohen and Grossberg, 1982) recently studied the absolute stability of the distance-dependent networks

$$\frac{d}{dt} x_i = -A_i x_i + (B_i - C_i x_i)[I_i + f_i(x_i)] - (D_i x_i + E_i)[J_i + \sum_{k=1} g_k(x_k) F_{ki}]. \tag{56}$$

Distance-dependence means that $F_{ki} = F_{ik}$. The networks (56) include examples of Volterra-Lotka systems, Hartline-Ratliff networks, Gilpin-Ayala systems, and shunting and additive networks.

In this setting, we constructed a global Liapunov function for these systems and used the LaSalle Invariance Principle, Sard's lemma, and some results about several complex variables to analyze the limiting behavior of (56). Modulo some technical hypotheses, we have proved that almost all systems of the form (56) are absolutely stable, and that systems with polynomial and sigmoid feedback signals can be directly analyzed.

These results show that adaptation level and distance-dependent competitive networks represent stable neural designs for competitive decision-making. The fact that adaptation level systems have been analyzed using Liapunov functionals whereas distance-dependent networks have been analyzed using Liapunov functions shows that the absolute stability theory of competitive systems is still incomplete. Absolute stability theorems for cooperative systems have also been recently discovered (Hirsch, 1982a, 1982b). This is an exciting area for intensive mathematical investigation.

The final sections of the article discuss code development issues wherein interactions between associative and competitive rules play a central role.

19. The Babel of Code Development Models

The experimental interest in geniculo-cortical and retino-tectal development (Gottlieb, 1976; Hubel and Wiesel, 1977; Hunt and Jacobson, 1974) has been paralleled by a vigorous theoretical interest in these basic phenomena. Perhaps in no other area of brain theory is the issue of what constitutes a new model, a new idea, or real progress so badly discussed. A literal reading of this literature might lead one to conclude that a one-to-one correspondence between articles and models exists, or at least between authors and models. A world of theoretical nomads is an anarchy, which is the antithesis of what a theoretical community should be. If we are to achieve the coherence that theory must have to be effective, then the endless numerical and experimental variations on our laws must not be confused with the invariant structure of these laws. A new model is not a change of notation, a use of a discrete instead of a continuous time variable, a different setting of numerical parameters, or a presentation of the same equations with a different input series.

When Malsburg (1973) adapted the equations which he found in Grossberg (1972b) for computer simulation and subjected them to a series of input patterns, I was delighted but not surprised by his findings. I was delighted because here was an interesting new twist in the use of the equations. I was not surprised because the results are a variant of pattern learning properties which had already been studied. Now I will review some of the relationships between code development and pattern learning, state some mathematical results on code development which computer studies missed, and make some comparative remarks about recent articles in the literature.

20. The Duality Between Code Development and Pattern Learning

In both pattern learning and code development situations, one often finds two sets, or fields, $F^{(1)}$ and $F^{(2)}$ of cells, which are not necessarily disjoint. The set of sampled cells v_i, $i \in J$, and sampling cells v_j, $j \in J$, are illustrative. Conditionable pathways e_{ji} are assumed to exist from one set to the other set of cells, and LTM traces z_{ji} are assigned to the pathways e_{ji}. Competitive interactions are assumed to occur within $F^{(1)}$ and $F^{(2)}$, if only to solve the noise-saturation dilemma at each level of pattern processing. In what, then, does the difference between a pattern learning and a code development model consist?

In a word, the answer is arrow-reversal, or duality. Whereas the conditionable pathways in a pattern learning example point from sampling cell to sampled cells, the conditionable pathways in a code development example point from sampled cells to sampling cell. Because of arrow-reversal, each sampling cell receives a sum of LTM-gated signals from sampled cells, which in turn influence the activity of the sampling cell and thus whether the sampled cells will be sampled.

If we apply the principle of sufficient reason to the arrow-reversal distinction, it becomes more ambiguous. How, after all, does an individual LTM trace z_{ji} from v_j to v_i know whether v_j is a sampling cell and v_i a sampled cell, or conversely? The answer is that it doesn't. Consequently, similar principles of pattern learning hold in both cases. Only when we ask more global questions about network design do distinctions between the two problems emerge.

For example, how do the fields $F^{(1)}$ and $F^{(2)}$ determine whether their cells will be sampling cells, sampled cells, or both? A major part of the answer lies in how sharply $F^{(1)}$ and $F^{(2)}$ contrast enhance their input patterns. To fix ideas, suppose that conditionable pathways pass between $F^{(1)}$ and $F^{(2)}$ in both directions and that both $F^{(1)}$ and $F^{(2)}$ directly receive input patterns. If $F^{(1)}$ does not sharply contrast enhance the input patterns but $F^{(2)}$ does, then $F^{(2)}$ will encode patterns across $F^{(1)}$ within the $F^{(1)} \to F^{(2)}$ LTM traces, and $F^{(2)}$ will learn patterns across $F^{(1)}$ within the $F^{(2)} \to F^{(1)}$ LTM traces. The difference between code development and pattern learning in this example thus resides in an asymmetric choice of competitive parameters within $F^{(1)}$ and $F^{(2)}$, not in a choice of new associative or competitive laws.

21. Outstars and Instars

These facts become clearer if we start with the simplest examples of pattern learning and code development, and then build up towards more complex examples. As Section 15 noted, the simplest network capable of pattern learning is an outstar (Figure 5a). By duality, the simplest network capable of code development is an instar (Figure 5b). The main difference between an outstar and an instar is that the source of an outstar excites the outstar border, whereas the border of an instar excites the instar source.

The changing efficacy with which practiced border patterns can excite the instar source constitutes code development. Because of the outstar learning theorem, it is no surprise that the LTM traces of an instar can learn a spatial pattern that perturbs its border. In an outstar, if a space-time pattern or sequence of spatial patterns plays upon its border while the source cell is sampling, then the source learns a weighted average of the sampled patterns (Grossberg, 1970b). This fact also holds in an instar for the same mathematical reason.

It is instructive to write down equations for an instar and to compare them with illustrative examples in the literature. Because an instar reverses the arrows between sampling and sampled cells, an instar with a local symmetry axis with respect to its sampling cell v_1 ($J = \{1\}$) obeys equations such as

$$\frac{d}{dt}x_1 = A_1 x_1 + \sum_{k \in I} B_k z_{k1} + C_1, \tag{57}$$

$$\frac{d}{dt}x_i = A x_i + C_i, \quad i \in I, \tag{58}$$

and

$$\frac{d}{dt}z_{i1} = D_1 z_{i1} + E_1 x_i, \tag{59}$$

$i \in I$. In (57), the sampling cell v_1 receives LTM gated signals from the sampled cells v_i, $i \in I$, in addition to a possible input C_1. In (58), the sampled cells v_i share a common STM decay functional A due to the local symmetry axis, but receive distinct inputs C_i from the input patterns $(C_i : i \in I)$. In (59), the usual LTM trace law holds with a shared LTM decay functional D_1 and a shared learning functional E_1 due to the local symmetry axis.

The article by Bienenstock, Cooper, and Munro (1982) is devoted to the study of a locally symmetric instar. These authors consider the equation

$$\frac{d}{dt}m_j = -\epsilon m_j + \phi d_j \tag{60}$$

for the jth LTM trace m_j and the jth input d_j. They define ϕ to be a functional of the past and present values of the function

$$c = \sum_j d_j m_j. \tag{61}$$

In particular, they use an average of past values of c as a threshold against which a present value of c is compared. If the present value exceeds threshold, $\phi > 0$, otherwise not. The threshold is assumed to increase as a function of past values of c.

A simple change of notation shows that equations (60) and (61) are a lumped version of an instar. In (59), let $i = j$, $z_{i1} = m_j$, $D_1 = -\epsilon$, and $E_1 = \phi$ to see that (59) subsumes (60). In (58), let A average C_1 so fast that

$$x_i \cong C_i, \quad i \in I. \tag{62}$$

In (57), let $C_1 \simeq 0$ and let A_1 rapidly average $\sum_{k \in I} B_k z_{k1}$ so fast that

$$x_1 \cong \sum_{k \in I} B_k z_{k1}. \tag{63}$$

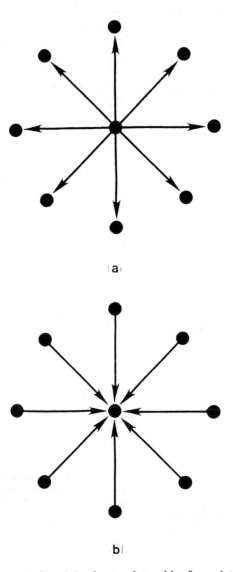

(a)

b)

Figure 5. (a) An *outstar* is the minimal network capable of associative pattern learning. (b) An *instar* is the minimal network capable of code development. The source of an outstar excites the outstar border, whereas the border of an instar excites the instar source. In both cases, source activation is necessary to drive an LTM sampling process. Since the instar border signals are gated by LTM traces before activating the instar source, code learning changes the efficacy of source activation and is changed by it.

Letting $B_k = x_k$ shows, by (62), that

$$x_1 \cong \sum_{k \in I} C_k z_{ki}, \tag{64}$$

which is the same as c in (61), but in different notation. Now plug x_1 into E_1 and use a threshold rule as in (31) to complete the reduction.

Despite the obvious nature of this reduction, the authors make a number of claims that illustrate the present fragmentation of the theoretical community. They say that they have introduced in the threshold rule "a new and essential feature" which they call "temporal competition between input patterns." They also write that Cooper, Lieberman, and Oja (1979) were the first to introduce "the idea of such a modification scheme." They note that their equations result "in a form of *competition between incoming patterns* rather than competition between synapses" which they allege to be the conclusion of alternative theories. They also suggest that "our theory is in agreement with classical experimental results obtained over the last generation." Finally, in 1981 they feel free to "conjecture that some form of correlation modification is a very general organizational principle."

The status of some of these claims is clear from the preceding discussion. I will, however, indicate below how the threshold rule in (60) and (61) generates a temporally unstable code when more than one sampling node exists, and why this threshold rule either cannot explain critical period termination or cannot explain the results of Pettigrew and Kasamatsu (1978). Thus although equations (60) and (61) are a special case of an instar, not all choices of instar functionals are equally good for purposes of stable code development.

22. Adaptive Filtering of Spatial Pattern Sequences

The comparison between pattern learning and code development becomes more interesting when a space-time pattern, or sequence of spatial patterns, is to be parsed by pattern learning or code development mechanisms. In either case, the fact that the LTM unit is a spatial pattern is fundamental, and the task is to show how individual spatial patterns, or subsequences of spatial patterns, can be differentially processed. To do this, one needs to show how distinguishable sampling sources, or subsets of sources, can be sequentially activated by the spatial patterns in the pattern sequence (Figure 6).

In the simplest pattern learning examples, pre-wired sequentially activated sampling nodes can learn an arbitrary space-time pattern (Grossberg, 1969e, 1970b). The price paid for such a ritualistic encoding is that the order of pattern performance, although not its velocity, is rigidly constrained. This *avalanche* type of anatomy is isomorphic to the anatomies of certain invertebrate command cells (Grossberg, 1974; Stein, 1971), and illustrates that complex acts can be encoded by small numbers of cells if ritualistic performance is acceptable. In examples wherein the order with which sampling nodes will be activated is not prewired into the network, serial learning mechanisms—notably associative and competitive interactions such as those utilized in Section 12—are needed to learn the correct ordering as practice of the ordering proceeds (Grossberg, 1969c, 1974, 1978a). In examples wherein the filtering rules whereby individual sampling nodes are selected are not prewired into the network, we are confronted with a problem in code development, notably the problem of how *sequences* of events adaptively select the nodes that will elicit the most accurate predictive commands within their sequential context (Grossberg, 1978a). Most code development models consider special cases of this general problem.

If we generalize the instar equations (57) and (59) to include the possibility that many sampling (encoding) cell indices occur in J, we find equations

$$\frac{d}{dt} x_j = A_j x_j + \sum_{k \in I} B_k z_{kj} + I_j \tag{65}$$

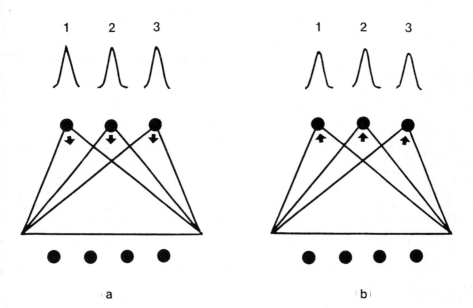

Figure 6. (a) In the simplest problem of space-time pattern learning, a mechanism is needed to excite discriminable sampling sources in a prescribed order $1, 2, 3, \ldots$ during learning trials, and to repeat the same order $1, 2, 3, \ldots$ of excitation during recall trials. (b) In the simplest problem of space-time code development, a space-time pattern at the sampled cells initially excites sampling sources in a prescribed order $1, 2, 3, \ldots$ due to the *a priori* biases in the filter from sampled cells to sampling cells. Whether this ordering approaches a stable configuration as development proceeds, or a temporally unstable sequence of coding representations is triggered, depends on details of network design.

and

$$\frac{d}{dt} z_{ij} = D_j z_{ij} + E_j x_i, \qquad (66)$$

$i \in I, j \in J$. Although all the terms in (65) and (66) work together to achieve code development, perhaps the terms $F_j \equiv \sum_{k \in I} B_k z_{kj}$ should be singled out as the principal ones. We all learn in calculus or linear algebra that the terms F_j are dot products, or inner products, of the vector $B = (B_k : k \in I)$ with the vectors $z_j = (z_{kj} : k \in I)$; viz.,

$$F_j = B \cdot z_j. \qquad (67)$$

If we define the vector $F = (F_j : j \in J)$ of dot products, then we can also recognize that the mapping $B \to F$ is a *linear filter*. By reversing arrows to go from pattern learning to code development, we hereby convert the property of independent read-out of probed pattern recall (Section 10) into the property of linear filtering—*without a change of model.*

An elementary formula about dot products underlies basic properties of code development. This formula is the law of cosines:

$$B \cdot z_j = \| B \| \| z_j \| \cos(B, z_j), \tag{68}$$

where $\| V \|$ is the Euclidean length of vector V. By (68), given a fixed signal pattern B, F_j is maximized among all z_j of fixed length by choosing z_j parallel to B. Thus in response to a fixed pattern B, the nodes v_j for which z_j is most parallel to B will be the ones most highly activated by B, other things being equal. If (66) causes the LTM vectors z_j of highly activated nodes v_j to become more parallel to B due to frequent past B presentations, then on future B presentations these nodes will respond ever more vigorously to B. Let us call alterations in F due to past experience with B *adaptive filtering.* Then we can say that an interaction between adaptive filtering from $\{v_i : i \in I\}$ to $\{v_j : j \in J\}$ and competition within $\{v_j : j \in J\}$ to select active nodes controls at least the most elementary features of code development.

23. Synaptic Conservation, Code Invariance, and Code Instability

These observations about adaptive filtering did not, perhaps surprisingly, appear in Malsburg's original paper. Other important properties also have not been sharply articulated by computer analysis. For example, presenting a given pattern several times can recode not only the nodes which respond most vigorously to this pattern but also the responses of inactive nodes to other patterns presented later on, because each node can encode infinite sets of patterns which it has never before experienced. This has the nice consequence that the code can learn to recognize certain invariant properties of pattern classes without having to experience all the patterns in each class (Fukushima, 1980; Grossberg, 1978a).

Another deeper consequence is not so pleasant. If there exist many more patterns than encoding nodes v_j, $j \in J$, there need not exist *any* temporally stable coding rule; that is, the nodes which respond most vigorously to a given pattern can continually change through time as the same list is repetitively practiced (Grossberg, 1976b). I was led to suspect that such a result might hold due to my prior theorems about absolute stability of parallel pattern learning, which suggested possible destabilizing effects of the STM decay terms A_j in (65). This important instability result has been missed by all the computer studies that I know because these studies typically present small numbers of patterns to small numbers of cells. Indeed, they usually present small numbers of patterns (e.g., 19) to much larger sets of cells (e.g., 169), as in the careful analysis of Amari and Takeuchi (1978).

An instability result forces one to ask which properties are essential to code development and which properties are adventitious. For example, Malsburg supplemented equations (3), (5), (6), and (7) with a synaptic conservation rule that requires the sum $\sum_{k \in I} z_{kj}$ of all the synaptic strengths which converge on a node v_j to be constant through time. Because I was aware of the duality between pattern learning and code development, I realized that the synaptic conservation rule is incompatible with the simplest example of associative learning, namely classical conditioning (Grossberg, 1976a). This is because the UCR pattern must be extinguished in memory as the CR pattern is learned if synaptic conservation holds. I was therefore reluctant to accept the synaptic conservation rule without an important physical or mathematical reason.

I could, however, see the need for a type of conservation, or normalization, that would regulate the temporal stability of the sampling process. By the time I read Malsburg's paper, I knew that long-range shunting competition, as opposed to the additive competition which Malsburg inherited from me, can automatically normalize the total suprathreshold STM activity of a network (Grossberg, 1973). The normalized STM activity can, in turn, normalize, or conserve, total synaptic strength across the network via feedback of E_j to z_{ij} in (66). This synaptic conservation mechanism is, moreover, compatible with classical conditioning. I therefore concluded that shunting competition, which can be absorbed into the STM decay terms A_j of (65), should formally replace synaptic conservation until more pressing reasons to the contrary are given. Some experimental tests of synaptic competition versus STM normalization are suggested in Grossberg (1981).

In their more recent contributions to retinotectal development, Malsburg and Willshaw have continued to use additive interactions, supplemented by the synaptic conservation rule and another rule for matching the similarity between retinal and tectal marker patterns (Malsburg and Willshaw, 1977, 1981; Willshaw and Malsburg, 1976). Since shunting networks automatically have matching properties as well as normalization properties, I take the need for these special assumptions as support for the idea that shunting operations subserve retinotectal development (Grossberg, 1976b, 1981). I have also argued that shunting interactions are operative in a variety of non-neural developmental examples, such as gastrulation in the sea urchin, slime mold aggregation, and regeneration in *Hydra* (Grossberg, 1978e). In all of these cases, I believe that alternative models have adapted analogies from chemical kinetics that do not incorporate mass action properties of cellular tissues. Notable differences between additive and shunting models occur in their explanations of the self-regulation mechanism that underlies the invariance of form when growth occurs (Gierer and Meinhardt, 1972; Grossberg, 1980b; Meinhardt and Gierer, 1974) and the contrast enhancement mechanism of categorical perception (Anderson, Silverstein, Ritz, and Jones, 1977; Grossberg, 1978f).

24. Critical Period Termination, the Stability-Plasticity Dilemma, and Adaptive Resonance

The fact that no temporally stable code need exist in response to a large family of input patterns, such as occurs in vision, made the problem of terminating those critical periods which are sensitive to behavioral experience seem more severe. This fact suggested that either the critical period is terminated by a chemical switch, but then there is a high likelihood that the code will incorporate adventitious statistical fluctuations of the most recent input sequences, or that the code is stabilized by a gradual process of dynamic buffering in response to network states that signify the behavioral relevance of the coded data. This dilemma led me to build my theory of *adaptive resonances* (Grossberg, 1976c, 1978a, 1980a, 1982b) which formalizes an answer to what I call the *stability-plasticity dilemma*.

The stability-plasticity dilemma asks how internal representations can maintain themselves in a stable fashion against the erosive effects of behaviorally irrelevant environmental fluctuations, yet can nonetheless adapt rapidly in response to environmental fluctuations that are crucial to survival. How does a network as a whole know the difference between behaviorally irrelevant and relevant events even though its individual cells do not possess this knowledge? How does a network transmute this knowledge into the difference between slow and fast rates of adaptation, respectively? Classical examples of the stability-plasticity balance are found in the work of Held and his colleagues on rapid visual adaptation in adults to discordant visuomotor data (Held, 1961, 1967; Held and Hein, 1963) and in the work of Wallach and his colleagues on rapid visual adaptation to discordant cues for the kinetic depth effect and cues for retinal disparity (Wallach and Karsh, 1963a, 1963b; Wallach, Moore, and Davidson, 1963). The stability-plasticity issue is raised on a pharmacological level by the experiments of Pettigrew and Kasamatsu (1978) which show that the visual plasticity of normal adult cats can be restored by selectively adding some noradrenaline to cortical tissues which already possess a functioning noradrenaline arousal system.

The adaptive resonance theory which I introduced in Grossberg (1976c) can explain the Pettigrew and Kasamatsu (1978) data; see Grossberg (1982b) for a review. Let me briefly indicate why the Bienenstock, Cooper, and Munro (1982) work cannot.

First note what happens when (60) is embedded in a system such as (65) wherein several sampling nodes can compete for activity. By the threshold rule of (60), a node v_j which has successfully won this competition in the past will acquire a progressively higher threshold due to persistent activation by its own input $\sum_k B_k z_{kj}$. By contrast, other nodes v_m which do not win the STM competition when $\sum_k B_k z_{kj}$ occurs, but which receive significant projections $\sum_k B_k z_{km}$, will maintain a low threshold. Thus, the tradeoff between input size and threshold can ultimately favor a new set of nodes. When this happens, the pattern will be recoded, and a temporally unstable coding cycle will be initiated. This instability does not require a large number of coding patterns to occur. It can occur only when one pattern is repeatedly presented to a network containing more than one encoding node. In fact, the last examples in Grossberg (1976b, p.132) consider history-dependent threshold changes, much like those in the Bienenstock *et al.* example. I note their instability in a competitive sampling milieu before introducing the adaptive resonance theory in Grossberg (1976c) as a possible way out.

One might object to the above criticism by claiming that the original winning node v_j acquries a high threshold so quickly that only the adaptively enhanced input $\sum_k B_k z_{kj}$ can exceed this threshold. In other words, the parameters may be carefully chosen to quickly shut off the critical period. But then one cannot understand how adding a little noradrenaline can turn it back on. In this example, either the critical period does not shut off, whence temporal instabilities in coding can occur, or its does shut off, whence critical period reversal by noradrenaline application cannot be explained. Of course, quickly raising the threshold might in any case trigger unstable coding by favoring new nodes.

25. Stable Coding of Pattern Sequences

I will end my remarks with two theorems about stable pattern coding (Grossberg, 1976b). These theorems do not even dent the surface of the mathematical challenges raised by the theory of adaptive resonances. The theorems consider the simplest case wherein:

(1) The patterns across nodes v_i, $i \in I$, are immediately and perfectly normalized. Thus input $C_i(t) = \theta_i C(t)$ generates activity $x_i(t) = \theta_i$.

(2) The signals B_k in (65) are linear functions of the activities x_k. Choose $B_k = \theta_k$ for definiteness.

(3) The competition among nodes v_j, $j \in J$, normalizes the total activity (to the value 1 for definiteness) and rapidly chooses the nodes v_j for STM storage which receive the largest input. In other words,

$$x_j = \begin{cases} 1 & \text{if } F_j > \max\{\epsilon, F_k : k \neq j\} \\ 0 & \text{if } F_j \leq \max\{\epsilon, F_k : k \neq j\} \end{cases} \tag{69}$$

where

$$F_j = \sum_{k \in I} \theta_k z_{kj} \tag{70}$$

and ϵ represents the quenching threshold of the competition (Grossberg, 1973).

(4) The LTM traces sample the pattern $\theta = (\theta_1, \theta_2, \ldots, \theta_n)$ only when their sampling cell is active. Thus

$$\frac{d}{dt} z_{ij} = (-z_{ij} + \theta_i) x_j. \tag{71}$$

Amari and Takeuchi (1978) study essentially identical equations and arrive at related results in the case of one encoding cell. They also study the response of the equations to inputs which simulate experiments on monocular and alternate-monocular deprivation of the kitten visual cortex.

The first result shows that if a single pattern is practiced, it maximizes the input (inner product) to its encoding cell population v_j by making z_j become parallel to θ. Simultaneously, the length of z_j becomes normalized.

Theorem 5 (Single Pattern Code)

Given a pattern θ, suppose that there exists a unique $j \in J$ such that

$$F_j(0) > \max\{\epsilon, F_k(0) : k \neq j\}. \tag{72}$$

Let θ be practiced during a sequence of non-overlapping intervals $[U_k, V_k]$, $k = 1, 2, \ldots$. Then the angle between $z_j(t)$ and θ monotonically decreases, the signal $F_j(t)$ is monotonically attracted towards $\| \theta \|^2$, and $\| z_j(t) \|^2$ oscillates at most once as it tracks $F_j(t)$. In particular, if $\| z_j(0) \| \leq \| \theta \|$, then $F_j(t)$ is monotone increasing. Except in the trivial case that $F_j(0) = \| \theta \|^2$, the limiting relations

$$\lim_{t \to \infty} \| z_j(t) \|^2 = \lim_{t \to \infty} F_j(t) = \| \theta \|^2 \tag{73}$$

hold if and only if

$$\sum_{k=1}^{\infty} (V_k - U_k) = \infty. \tag{74}$$

The second result characterizes those sets of input patterns which can generate a temporally stable code, and shows that the classifying vectors $z_j(t)$ approach the convex hull of the patterns which they encode. The latter property shows that the nodes v_j ultimately receive the maximal possible inputs from the pattern sets which they encode.

To state the theorem, the following notion is convenient. A *partition* $\oplus_{k=1}^{K} P_k$ of a finite set P is a subdivision of P into non-overlapping and exhaustive subsets P_j. The *convex hull* $H(P)$ of P is the set of all convex combinations of elements in P. Given a set $Q \subset P$, let $R = P \backslash Q$ denote the elements in P that are not in Q. If the classifying vector $z_j(t)$ codes the set of patterns $P_j(t)$, let $P_j^*(t) = P_j(t) \cup \{z_j(t)\}$. The distance between a vector p and a set of vectors Q, denoted by $\| p - Q \|$, is defined by $\| p - Q \| = \inf\{\| p - Q \| : q \in Q\}$.

Theorem 6 (Stability of Sparse Pattern Codes)

Let the network practice any finite set $P = \{\theta^{(i)} : i = 1, 2, \ldots M\}$ of patterns for which there exists a partition $P = \oplus_{k=1}^{N} P_k(T)$ at some time $t = T$ such that

$$\min\{u \cdot v : u \in P_j(T), v \in P_j^*(T)\} > \max\{u \cdot v : u \in P_j(T), v \in P^*(T) \backslash P_j^*(T)\} \tag{75}$$

for all $j = 1, 2, \ldots N$. Then

$$P_j(t) = P_j(T) \quad \text{for} \quad t \geq T, \quad j = 1, 2, \ldots, N, \tag{76}$$

and the functions

$$D_j(t) = \| z_j(t) - H(P_j(t)) \| \tag{77}$$

are monotone decreasing for $t \geq T$, $j = 1, 2, \ldots, N$. If, moreover, the patterns $P_j(T)$ are practiced in the time intervals $[U_{jk}, V_{jk}]$, $k = 1, 2, \ldots$ such that

$$\sum_{k=1}^{\infty} (V_{jk} - U_{jk}) = \infty, \tag{78}$$

then

$$\lim_{t \to \infty} D_J(t) = 0. \tag{79}$$

Despite the fact that the code of a sparse pattern class is stable, it is easy to construct examples of pattern sequences which are densely distributed in pattern space for which no temporally stable code exists. To stabilize a behaviorally sensitive developing code in an arbitrary input environment, I have constructed the adaptive resonance theory, which uses the same feedback laws to stabilize infant code development as are needed to analyze data on adult attention. I have therefore elsewhere suggested that adult attention is a continuation on a developmental continuum of the mechanisms needed to solve the stability-plasticity dilemma in infants.

REFERENCES

Adams, J.A., **Human memory**. New York: McGraw-Hill, 1967.

Amari, S.-I., A method of statistical neurodynamics. *Kybernetik*, 1974, **14**, 201–215.

Amari, S.-I., A mathematical approach to neural systems. In J. Metzler (Ed.), **Systems neuroscience**. New York: Academic Press, 1977.

Amari, S.-I. and Takeuchi, A., Mathematical theory on formation of category detecting nerve cells. *Biological Cybernetics*, 1978, **29**, 127–136.

Anderson, J.R. and Bower, G.H., **Human associative memory**. Washington, DC: V.H. Winston and Sons, 1973.

Anderson, J.A., Silverstein, J.W., Ritz, S.A., and Jones, R.S., Distinctive features, categorical perception, and probability learning: Some applications of a neural model. *Psychological Review*, 1977, **84**, 413–451.

Asch, S.E. and Ebenholtz, S.M., The principle of associative symmetry. *Proceedings of the American Philosophical Society*, 1962, **106**, 135–163.

Atkinson, R.C. and Shiffrin, R.M., Human memory: A proposed system and its control processes. In K.W. Spence and J.T. Spence (Eds.), **Advances in the psychology of learning and motivation research and theory** (Vol. 2). New York: Academic Press, 1968.

Bienenstock, E.L., Cooper, L.N., and Munro, P.W., Theory for the development of neuron selectivity: Orientation specificity and binocular interaction in visual cortex. Preprint, 1982.

Bower, G.H. (Ed.), **Human memory: Basic processes**. New York: Academic Press, 1977.

Cohen, M.A. and Grossberg, S., Absolute stability of global pattern formation and parallel memory storage by competitive neural networks. Submitted for publication, 1982.

Cole, K.S., **Membranes, ions, and impulses**. Berkeley, CA: University of California Press, 1968.

Collins, A.M. and Loftus, E.F., A spreading-activation theory of semantic memory. *Psychological Review*, 1975, **82**, 407–428.

Cooper, L.N., Lieberman, F., and Oja, E., A theory for the acquisition and loss of neuron specificity in visual cortex. *Biological Cybernetics*, 1979, **33**, 9.

Dixon, T.R. and Horton, D.L., **Verbal behavior and general behavior theory**. Englewood Cliffs, NJ: Prentice-Hall, 1968.

Feigenbaum, E.A. and Simon, H.A., A theory of the serial position effect. *British Journal of Psychology*, 1962, **53**, 307–320.

Fukushima, K., Neocognitron: A self-organizing neural network model for a mechanism of pattern recognition unaffected by shift in position. *Biological Cybernetics*, 1980, **36**, 193–202.

Geman, S., The law of large numbers in neural modelling. In S. Grossberg (Ed.), **Mathematical psychology and psychophysiology**. Providence, RI: American Mathematical Society, 1981.

Gierer, A. and Meinhardt, H., A theory of biological pattern formation. *Kybernetik*, 1972, **12**, 30–39.

Gottlieb, G. (Ed.), **Neural and behavioral specificity** (Vol. 3). New York: Academic Press, 1976.

Grossberg, S., Senior Fellowship thesis, Dartmouth College, 1961.

Grossberg, S., **The theory of embedding fields with applications to psychology and neurophysiology**. New York: Rockefeller Institute for Medical Research, 1964.

Grossberg, S., Some physiological and biochemical consequences of psychological postulates. *Proceedings of the National Academy of Sciences*, 1968, **60**, 758–765.

Grossberg, S., Embedding fields: A theory of learning with physiological implications. *Journal of Mathematical Psychology*, 1969, **6**, 209–239 (a).

Grossberg, S., On learning, information, lateral inhibition, and transmitters. *Mathematical Biosciences*, 1969, **4**, 255–310 (b).

Grossberg, S., On the serial learning of lists. *Mathematical Biosciences*, 1969, **4**, 201–253 (c).

Grossberg, S., On learning and energy-entropy dependence in recurrent and nonrecurrent signed networks. *Journal of Statistical Physics*, 1969, **1**, 319–350 (d).

Grossberg, S., Some networks that can learn, remember, and reproduce any number of complicated space-time patterns, I. *Journal of Mathematics and Mechanics*, 1969, **19**, 53–91 (e).

Grossberg, S., On the production and release of chemical transmitters and related topics in cellular control. *Journal of Theoretical Biology*, 1969, **22**, 325–364 (f).

Grossberg, S., Neural pattern discrimination. *Journal of Theoretical Biology*, 1970, **27**, 291–337 (a).

Grossberg, S., Some networks that can learn, remember, and reproduce any number of complicated space-time patterns, II. *Studies in Applied Mathematics*, 1970, **49**, 135–166 (b).

Grossberg, S., Pavlovian pattern learning by nonlinear neural networks. *Proceedings of the National Academy of Sciences*, 1971, **68**, 828–831 (a).

Grossberg, S., On the dynamics of operant conditioning. *Journal of Theoretical Biology*, 1971, **33**, 225–255 (b).

Grossberg, S., Pattern learning by functional-differential neural networks with arbitrary path weights. In K. Schmitt (Ed.), **Delay and functional-differential equations and their applications**. New York: Academic Press, 1972 (a).

Grossberg, S., Neural expectation: Cerebellar and retinal analogs of cells fired by learnable or unlearned pattern classes. *Kybernetik*, 1972, **10**, 49–57 (b).

Grossberg, S., A neural theory of punishment and avoidance, I: Qualitative theory. *Mathematical Biosciences*, 1972, **15**, 39–67 (c).

Grossberg, S., A neural theory of punishment and avoidance, II: Quantitative theory. *Mathematical Biosciences*, 1972, **15**, 253–285 (d).

Grossberg, S., Contour enhancement, short term memory, and constancies in reverberating neural networks. *Studies in Applied Mathematics*, 1973, **52**, 217–257.

Grossberg, S., Classical and instrumental learning by neural networks. In R. Rosen and F. Snell (Eds.), **Progress in theoretical biology**. New York: Academic Press, 1974.

Grossberg, S., On the development of feature detectors in the visual cortex with applications to learning and reaction-diffusion systems. *Biological Cybernetics*, 1976, **21**, 145–159 (a).

Grossberg, S., Adaptive pattern classification and universal recoding, I: Parallel development and coding of neural feature detectors. *Biological Cybernetics*, 1976, **23**, 121–134 (b).

Grossberg, S., Adaptive pattern classification and universal recoding, II: Feedback, expectation, olfaction, and illusions. *Biological Cybernetics*, 1976, **23**, 187–202 (c).

Grossberg, S., A theory of human memory: Self-organization and performance of sensory-motor codes, maps, and plans. In R. Rosen and F. Snell (Eds.), **Progress**

in theoretical biology, Vol. 5. New York: Academic Press, 1978 (a).

Grossberg, S., Behavioral contrast in short term memory: Serial binary memory models or parallel continuous memory models? *Journal of Mathematical Psychology*, 1978, **3**, 199–219 (b).

Grossberg, S., Decisions, patterns, and oscillations in nonlinear competitive systems with applications to Volterra-Lotka systems. *Journal of Theoretical Biology*, 1978, **73**, 101–130 (c).

Grossberg, S., Competition, decision, and consensus. *Journal of Mathematical Analysis and Applications*, 1978, **66**, 470–493 (d).

Grossberg, S., Communication, memory, and development. In R. Rosen and F. Snell (Eds.), **Progress in theoretical biology**, Vol. 5. New York: Academic Press, 1978 (e).

Grossberg, S., Do all neural models really look alike? A comment on Anderson, Silverstein, Ritz, and Jones. *Psychological Review*, 1978, **85**, 592–596 (f).

Grossberg, S., How does a brain build a cognitive code? *Psychological Review*, 1980, **1**, 1–51 (a).

Grossberg, S., Intracellular mechanisms of adaptation and self-regulation in self-organizing networks: The role of chemical transducers. *Bulletin of Mathematical Biology*, 1980, **42**, 365–396 (b).

Grossberg, S., Biological competition: Decision rules, pattern formation, and oscillations. *Proceedings of the National Academy of Sciences*, 1980, **77**, 2338–2342 (c).

Grossberg, S., (Ed.), Adaptive resonance in development, perception, and cognition. In **Mathematical psychology and psychophysiology**. Providence, RI: American Mathematical Society, 1981.

Grossberg, S., **Studies of mind and brain: Neural principles of learning, perception, development, cognition, and motor control**. Boston: Reidel Press, 1982 (a).

Grossberg, S., Some psychophysiological and pharmacological correlates of a developmental, cognitive, and motivational theory. In J. Cohen, R. Karrer, and P. Tueting (Eds.), **Proceedings of the 6th evoked potential international conference**, June 21–26, 1981, Lake Forest, Illinois. New York: New York Academy of Sciences, 1982 (b). (Published as **Brain and information: Event related potentials, 425**, 58–151, Annals of the New York Academy of Sciences, 1984.)

Grossberg, S. and Pepe, J., Schizophrenia: Possible dependence of associational span, bowing, and primacy versus recency on spiking threshold. *Behavioral Science*, 1970, **15**, 359–362.

Grossberg, S. and Pepe, J., Spiking threshold and overarousal effects in serial learning. *Journal of Statistical Physics*, 1971, **3**, 95–125.

Held, R., Exposure-history as a factor in maintaining stability of perception and coordination. *Journal of Nervous and Mental Diseases*, 1961, **132**, 26–32.

Held, R., Dissociation of visual functions by deprivation and rearrangement. *Psychologische Forschung*, 1967, **31**, 388–348.

Held, R. and Hein, A., Movement-produced stimulation in the development of visually guided behavior. *Journal of Comparative and Physiological Psychology*, 1963, **56**, 872–876.

Hirsch, M., Systems of differential equations which are competitive or cooperative, I: Limit sets. Preprint, 1982 (a).

Hirsch, M., Systems of differential equations which are competitive or cooperative, II: Convergence almost everywhere. Preprint, 1982 (b).

Hubel, D.H. and Wiesel, T.N., Functional architecture of macaque monkey visual cortex. *Proceedings of the Royal Society of London (B)*, 1977, **198**, 1–59.

Hunt, R.K. and Jacobson, M., Specification of positional information in retinal ganglion cells of *Xenopus laevis*: Intraocular control of the time of specification. *Proceedings of the National Academy of Sciences*, 1974, **71**, 3616–3620.

Jung, J., **Verbal learning**. New York: Holt, Rinehart, and Winston, 1968.

Katz, B., **Nerve, muscle, and synapse**. New York: McGraw-Hill, 1966.

Khinchin, A.I., **Mathematical foundations of information theory**. New York: Dover Press, 1967.

Klatsky, R.L., **Human memory: Structures and processes**. San Francisco: W.H. Freeman, 1980.

Kuffler, S.W. and Nicholls, J.G., **From neuron to brain**. Sunderland, MA: Sinauer Press, 1976.

Loftus, G.R. and Loftus, E.F., **Human memory: The processing of information**. Hillsdale, NJ: Erlbaum, 1976.

Maher, B.A., **Contributions to the psychopathology of schizophrenia**. New York: Academic Press, 1977.

Malsburg, C. von der, Self-organization of orientation sensitive cells in the striate cortex. *Kybernetik*, 1973, **14**, 85–100.

Malsburg, C. von der and Willshaw, D.J., How to label nerve cells so that they can interconnect in an ordered fashion. *Proceedings of the National Academy of Sciences*, 1977, **74**, 5176–5178.

Malsburg, C. von der and Willshaw, D.J., Differential equations for the development of topological nerve fibre projections. In S. Grossberg (Ed.), **Mathematical psychology and psychophysiology**. Providence, RI: American Mathematical Society, 1981.

May, R.M. and Leonard, W.J., Nonlinear aspects of competition between three species. *SIAM Journal on Applied Mathematics*, 1975, **29**, 243–253.

McGeogh, J.A. and Irion, A.L., **The psychology of human learning**, Second Edition. New York: Longmans and Green, 1952.

Meinhardt, H. and Gierer, A., Applications of a theory of biological pattern formation based on lateral inhibition. *Journal of Cell Science*, 1974, **15**, 321–346.

Murdock, B.B., **Human memory: Theory and data**. Potomac, MD: Erlbaum, 1974.

Norman, D.A., **Memory and attention: An introduction to human information processing**. New York: Wiley and Sons, 1969.

Osgood, C.E., **Method and theory in experimental psychology**. New York: Oxford, 1953.

Pettigrew, J.D. and Kasamatsu, T., Local perfusion of noradrenaline maintains visual cortical plasticity. *Nature*, 1978, **271**, 761–763.

Plonsey, R., **Bioelectric phenomena**. New York: McGraw-Hill, 1969.

Ruch, T.C., Patton, H.D., Woodbury, J.W., and Towe, A.L., **Neurophysiology**. Philadelphia: Saunders, 1961.

Schneider, W. and Shiffrin, R.M., Automatic and controlled information processing in vision. In D. LaBarge and S.J. Samuels (Eds.), **Basic processes in reading: Perception and comprehension**. Hillsdale, NJ: Erlbaum, 1976.

Stein, P.S.G., Intersegmental coordination of swimmeret and motoneuron activity in crayfish. *Journal of Neurophysiology*, 1971, **34**, 310–318.

Underwood, B.J., **Experimental psychology**, Second Edition. New York: Appleton-Century-Crofts, 1966.

Wallach, H. and Karsh, E.B., Why the modification of stereoscopic depth-perception is so rapid. *American Journal of Psychology*, 1963, **76**, 413–420 (a).

Wallach, H. and Karsh, E.B., The modification of stereoscopic depth-perception and the kinetic depth-effect. *American Journal of Psychology*, 1963, **76**, 429–435 (b).

Wallach, H., Moore, M.E., and Davidson, L., Modification of stereoscopic depth-perception. *American Journal of Psychology*, 1963, **76**, 191–204.

Willshaw, D.J. and Malsburg, C. von der, How patterned neural connections can be set up by self-organization. *Proceedings of the Royal Society of London (B)*, 1976, **194**, 431–445.

Wolpert, L., Positional information and the spatial pattern of cellular differentiation. *Journal of Theoretical Biology*, 1969, **25**, 1–47.

Young, R.K., Serial learning. In T.R. Dixon and D.L. Horton (Eds.), **Verbal behavior and general behavior theory**. Englewood Cliffs, NJ: Prentice-Hall, 1968.

AUTHOR INDEX

SUBJECT INDEX